THE ROYAL
ARMY SERVICE CORPS

THE ROYAL ARMY SERVICE CORPS

A HISTORY OF TRANSPORT AND SUPPLY IN THE BRITISH ARMY

BY

Colonel R. H. BEADON
C.B.E., p.s.c., *late* R.A.S.C.

With an Introduction
by
JOHN FORTESCUE
LL.D., D.Litt.

Vol. II

PRINTED AND BOUND BY ANTHONY ROWE LTD, EASTBOURNE

PREFACE

FOR good and sufficient reasons the length of this volume has been strictly limited. Accordingly, out of the various authorities consulted and the mass of papers, diaries, records and reminiscences from which material has been available it has only been possible to utilise a fraction. Without undue repetition a considerable work could have been compiled on the activities of the Royal Army Service Corps in every theatre of war. But it is not only the author's powers of compression which have been taxed, for two other factors intervene. The first of these lies in the proportion of space that can be devoted to each campaign. It was a healthy spirit that caused almost every writer to stress the importance on the outcome of the war of the theatre in which he happened to serve. Books dealing with the Egyptian Expeditionary Force inform their readers that Lord Allenby's victories were largely instrumental in bringing about the final collapse of Germany; those on Italy and the Balkans say the same about the battle of Vittorio Veneto and the offensive of September 1918 respectively. To adjudicate on the importance of each theatre and to allot space accordingly would be impracticable, and the fact that approximately equal attention has been given to the operations in, for example, Palestine and East Africa does not imply any attempt at comparison in the wider sense. In each case the aim has been to show the transport and supply

PREFACE

problems and their solution, and in so doing to bring out the different aspects of each rather than to traverse ground that was more or less common to all or several.

In the second place there is the complication which is inevitable from the existence of the three main branches of the Royal Army Service Corps. To those who served throughout in any one of these, either supply, horse or mechanical transport, the activities of their own side naturally loom greatest. That all three worked in harmonious co-operation goes without saying; there could have been no success otherwise. But one side or another stood out in the various theatres, and where such side has been therefore emphasised it is not intended to minimise the rôle of the others. In the supply sense for instance France was remarkable for the bulk to be handled; Mesopotamia for the paucity of local resources and the long "carry" by uncertain river communication; East Africa for the difficulties of distribution. In the transport sense France demands special attention on account of the extensive use of heavy mechanical transport; Macedonia for pack animals; Egypt and Palestine for camels; Mesopotamia for light mechanical transport; and North Russia for sleigh transport.

By stressing these various aspects it has been essayed to throw into relief the more important operations of the Corps and emphasise the principles which underlay its success in the field. There must necessarily be left unrecorded here by far the greater part of the technical and internal details of its work; but since the culminating aim of that work, and indeed the sole justification of the existence of the Corps, is the maintenance of the fighting troops in face of the enemy, it is the part that the Royal

PREFACE

Army Service Corps played in operations of war which is its real history.

In general, administrative troops are apt to overlook the importance of studying war in its wider aspects, and the fact that they have too often tended to become immersed in technicalities has been responsible for many failures in the past. The Royal Army Service Corps did not come into existence because it was necessary for a military body to administer the services of transport and supply in peace. The bulk of such duties could more cheaply be done by contract. But no extensive knowledge of military history is required to show how vital is a trained military body for carrying out those duties in war, and the higher the military spirit of that body the better it is for the troops which it serves. Regimental tradition so admirably fostered among the fighting troops is no less important to those concerned with administration. To the latter belong memories of great feats or triumphs of organisation which have been accomplished in the past.

It is no part of its claim that the Royal Army Service Corps carried any burden which could compare in effort and sacrifice with that of the fighting arms which it was privileged to serve. Yet in so far as was humanly possible it never failed those arms. Obviously most of its work was not in the limelight or such as could command the applause of the multitude, but under the best of conditions it was monotonous and incessant.

In the text no distinction is made between Regular, Territorial or New Army *personnel*, and individuals are referred to by the rank held during the period under consideration. The spelling of place names has followed

PREFACE

that of the *Official History of the War* in so far as that history is yet available.

Where assistance in the compilation has been derived from so many sources, it has seemed best to make acknowledgment through the medium of the bibliography at the end of the chapters; but the thanks of the author are specially due to the following for the trouble taken by them in supplying information and criticism: The Hon. Sir John Fortescue, K.C.V.O., Lieut.-General Sir Frederick Clayton, K.C.B., K.C.M.G., Major-General S. S. Long, C.B., Colonel Sir Harold Percival, K.C.M.G., C.B.E., D.S.O., Colonel H. G. Reid, C.M.G., C.B.E., D.S.O., Colonel W. Elliott, C.B., C.B.E., D.S.O., Colonel H. G. Burrard, C.B., C.S.I., D.S.O., Colonel W. M. Parker, C.B., C.M.G., D.S.O., Colonel O. Striedinger, C.B.E., D.S.O., Lieut.-Colonel F. G. Taylor, M.B.E., R.A.S.C., Major B. H. H. Barrett, R.A.S.C., and Captain H. J. Cooper, R.A.S.C.

R. H. BEADON

BRIDGWATER
SOMERSET
August 1930

CONTENTS

Preface . . . . *page* v

Introduction, by Sir John Fortescue xvii

Chap. I. "AFTER SOUTH AFRICA". . . . 1

H.R.H. The Duke of Connaught becomes Colonel of the Army Service Corps; Colonel F. T. Clayton appointed to the War Office; his previous career; steps taken by him to enhance status of the Army Service Corps; their results; the history of the remount companies; Army Service Corps responsibility for barrack duties; the clerks' section; formation of second line Army Service Corps in the Territorial Force; the Somaliland Campaign of 1909.

II. THE EARLY DEVELOPMENT OF THE MECHANICAL TRANSPORT . . . 24

Early uses of mechanical transport; War Office Committee set up in 1901; its terms of reference; preliminary experiments; the motor volunteers; creation of an Inspectorate Branch; formation of the first mechanical transport units; progress from 1904 onwards; measures taken to train *personnel* and provide vehicles; practical tests in operations; adoption of the internal combustion engine in 1911; workshop organisation; subsidy schemes; steps taken to provide *personnel* on mobilisation; various measures of preparation for war; higher control; progress in foreign armies.

III. THE EVE OF THE GREAT WAR . . . 46

Re-organisation of the transport and supply system for the field; former methods and their application; Brig.-General Paul's memorandum of December, 1910; new possibilities brought about by mechanical transport; tests on manœuvres in 1912 and 1913; the recasting of the supply system for the maintenance of the Army overseas and at home in war; various measures adopted as regards provision of commodities; projected establishment of Home Base Supply Depots; experiments made in 1913 as to composition of service ration; short history of the Supply Reserve Depot at Woolwich; the Army Service Corps of the Dominions —Canadian—Australian—New Zealand—South African; the strength, dispositions and general standard of training of the Army Service Corps on the outbreak of the Great War.

CONTENTS

Chap. IV. THE BRITISH EXPEDITIONARY
FORCE . . . . . . *page* 83
General conditions obtaining; the heads of the supply and transport directorates; summary of the task of supply; summary of the task of the transport; the Labour Corps; the working of the supply system; the transport directorate; base transport establishments; a Base Mechanical Transport Depot; an Advanced Mechanical Transport Depot; heavy repair shops; the Advanced Horse Transport Depot.

V. THE BRITISH EXPEDITIONARY FORCE
(*contd.*) 115
Preliminary observations; opening phase of the campaign; transfer of bases at Boulogne and Le Havre to St Nazaire; the army on the Aisne and the First Battle of Ypres; some supply difficulties; the work of the ambulance transport; events of 1915–16; the manpower situation and steps taken in the Army Service Corps to meet it; the work of the divisional trains; some transport considerations in the modern battle; mechanical transport at the Third Battle of Ypres; steps taken to re-organise during winter of 1917–18; French organisation; the Omnibus Companies; a great troop movement; events of 1917 and 1918; the advance to the Rhine; the Inter-Allied Supply Board; some statistics.

VI. THE OPERATIONS ON THE GALLIPOLI
PENINSULA 156
Inauguration of the campaign; misconception as to the conditions; the transport and supply situation following the original landing; the Zion Mule Corps; reinforcements; summary of the transport and supply situation at the end of April; communications; the August offensive; the months preceding evacuation; General Monro's appreciation; the army leaves the peninsula; Army Service Corps *personnel*; the Levant Base.

VII. THE BALKANS AND THE BLACK SEA . 179
Initiation of the campaign; the advanced party lands; steps taken to prepare for the army; the 10th Division moves to Doiran; transport and supply arrangements during the retreat; base organisation; arrival of further divisions; General Monro's despatch; some incidents with the mechanical transport; the military situation in January 1916; the transport and supply situation; recruitment of Greek muleteers; the allied troops advance to the Struma line; provision made for the

CONTENTS

Serbian army; shortage of transport; work on the Seres road; the great fire of August 1917; Army Service Corps motor boats; the offensive in 1918; the movement against Turkey; the Commander-in-Chief on the work of the Corps; mechanical transport units with the Serbian army; strengths; an outline of the operations on the Black Sea littoral following the Armistice.

Chap. VIII. THE CAMPAIGNS IN EGYPT AND
PALESTINE . . . . . *page* 221
Various operations of the Army in Egypt; defence of the Suez Canal; the Western Desert; the advance into the Sinai Desert; on the Beersheba–Gaza front; the advance into Palestine and capture of Beersheba and Jerusalem; the final offensive; various sources of supply; some special transport activities; the *personnel* of the Army Service Corps.

IX. THE CAMPAIGN IN MESOPOTAMIA . . 250
Conditions in the Mesopotamia theatre; inadequate equipment of the Expeditionary Force; the Indian Supply and Transport Corps; the War Office assumes control of the campaign; summary of the situation up to the fall of Kut-el-Amara; appearance of the Army Service Corps; re-organisation of the Army under General Maude; measures taken to bring order out of chaos; the administrative situation at the end of 1916; preparations for the future; General Maude resumes the offensive; the work of the mechanical transport during the advance to Baghdad; some supply activities; railway progress; various mechanical transport operations; organisation of mechanical transport columns; more operations; increase in mechanical transport formations; the affair at Hit; Transport and supply difficulties in the advance to Kirkuk; the Persian lines of communication; criticism on this project; the final operations in Mesopotamia and surrender of the Turkish forces at Sharquat; some aspects of the work of the Army Service Corps; casualties.

X. THE CAMPAIGN IN EAST AFRICA . . 292
Introductory; the East African theatre of war; German transport methods; the situation on the arrival of General Smuts and the commencement of Army Service Corps administration; the British take the offensive; occupation of the Moschi-Aruscha area; General Van Deventer at Kondoa-Irangi; his supply difficulties; the advance down the Pangani River and thence on to Handeni; hardships endured by the troops; the advance resumed to Makindu; and appre-

CONTENTS

ciation of the situation from the maintenance point of view; some minor operations; General Smuts reaches Morogoro; the mechanical transport situation; from Morogoro to the Ruwu River; coast landings; preparations for a further advance; the army south of the Rufiji River; General Smuts hands over command; General Hoskyns leaves and is succeeded by General Van Deventer; the advance on Kilwa; guerilla operations; transport and supply considerations during the campaign; the *personnel* of the mechanical transport; communications of General Northey's force; base mechanical transport establishments; concluding observations.

Chap. XI. THE BRITISH ARMY IN ITALY . *page* 328

Intervention in Italy foreseen by General Robertson and British mission despatched April 1917; the administrative arrangements made by the mission; defeat of the Italians at Caporetto and movement of British army to Italy; concentration on the Piave Front; return of General Plumer and Eleventh Army Corps to France; the British troops on the Asiago plateau and the transport and supply system thereon; the failure of the Austrian offensive in June; the Allied offensive in October; transport and supply services in the advance to Trent and the Tagliamento; the work of the mechanical transport during the campaign; the organisation of the Base Supply Depot at Arquata; concluding remarks.

XII. NORTH RUSSIA 352

The North Russian expedition; the Archangel force leaves Murmansk; its rôle in re-organising a Russian army; transport and supply conditions at Murmansk; relations with civilian population; introduction of sleigh transport; some supply difficulties; reindeer transport; the Army Service Corps shortage of *personnel*; operations in the spring of 1918; formation of schools of instruction; continuance of operations; some special activities of the Army Service Corps at Murmansk; initial movements on the Archangel Front; the maintenance problem and its solution; organisation of transport; the evacuation in September 1919; observations on types of transport animals used in North Russia.

XIII. THE WAR PERIOD IN THE UNITED KINGDOM 379

The Quartermaster-General to the Forces; the higher direction of the Army Service Corps; Brig.-General S. S. Long becomes Director of Supplies and Trans-

CONTENTS

port; some aspects of his administration; provision made for food inspection; problems of sugar, meat, and hay supply; *personnel* difficulties; effect of War Office financial control; the inauguration of the Expeditionary Force canteens; some transport activities; intervention by the Ministry of Munitions; General Long resigns, succeeded by Brig.-General Crofton Atkins; the expansion of the Army Service Corps during the course of the war; the quartering of the Army at home.

Chap. XIV. THE WAR PERIOD IN THE UNITED KINGDOM (*contd.*) . . . . . *page* 412

War Office mechanical transport organisation; provision of vehicles; of *personnel*; the development of Q.M.G. 3; the Home Mechanical Transport Depot; the reception and training area; sub-divisions of same; the Bulford mobilisation area; embarkation depots; the tractor depot; petrol supply; provision of supply *personnel*; of horse transport *personnel*; animals, vehicles and equipment; the Machine Gun Corps Transport Training School; amalgamation of the regular and territorial Army Service Corps; observations on the administration in the United Kingdom; some personalities.

XV. THE CORPS IN INDIA 457

The transport and supply organisation of the Indian Army prior to the Great War; early experiments with mechanical transport; the Army Service Corps makes its appearance; various activities; the Waziristan operations of 1919-20; the circular road; the Khyber ropeway; a convoy to Kabul; situation of mechanical transport in India by October 1923; proposed amalgamation of British and British-Indian transport and supply services and its outcome; the Royal Army Service Corps leaves India.

XVI. IN DIVERS FIELDS 487

The campaign in the Cameroons; outline of the operations during the first year; mechanical transport arrives in September 1915; the advance to Jaunde; the work of the Army Service Corps during operations; a comparison between mechanical transport and carriers; concluding remarks; the campaign in German South-West Africa; general outline of the operations; transport and supply difficulties; the insurrection of 1920 in Mesopotamia; general observations on the task of transport and supply during the operations; concluding remarks.

DIAGRAMS

Scheme of Supply from the Base to the Trenches,
British Expeditionary Forces   *facing page* 154

System of Supply to the various Expeditionary Forces
and the Troops in the United Kingdom, exclusive of
Fortresses and other Garrisons abroad   *facing page* 410

MAPS AT END

1. SOMALILAND, 1909
2. WESTERN EUROPE
3. YPRES SALIENT
4. GALLIPOLI PENINSULA
5. THE BALKANS
6. THE BALKANS, SALONIKA AREA
7. EGYPT
8. PALESTINE AND SYRIA
9. MESOPOTAMIA
10. EAST AFRICA
11. ITALY
12. NORTH RUSSIA
13. WAZIRISTAN
14. CAMEROONS
15. S.W. AFRICA

VOLUME I

CORRIGENDUM

page 269, line 6, *for* 1822 *read* 1818

NOTE ON THE UNIFORMS OF THE ROYAL WAGGON TRAIN OF 1799 (*v. page* 268)

In the Army Lists of 1800–1812 there is no mention of the uniforms of the Royal Waggon Train. In the Army Lists of 1813–1817 the uniform is given as "blue, facings red"; and from 1818 onwards as "red, facings blue". Colonel Astley Terry, however, who has been kind enough to write to me on the subject, tells me that he has a print in colour by Captain Hamilton Smith, D.A.A.G., published in 1812, which shows the uniform of the Royal Waggon Train as "red, facings blue." The question then arises whether the Waggon Train was always dressed in scarlet (which is quite possible, owing to the evil name of the "Newgate Blues") but that the compilers of the Army List did not take the trouble to ascertain the fact until the Waggon Train returned from the Army of Occupation in France in 1818; or whether their uniform, "blue, facings red" from 1799 to 1811, was changed in 1812. This latter view seems more likely to be correct, because, while the Waggon Train was at home, the compilers of the Army List should have had no difficulty in ascertaining the truth, and Wellington was known to be adverse to blue clothing for British troops since it rendered them liable to be mistaken for French. But the point is one on which readers may take their choice.

J. W. F.

INTRODUCTION

IN the first volume of this *History* some account was given of the arrangements for transport and supply in the British Army to the close of the nineteenth century; and it may be of service here to recapitulate very briefly the principal stages in its development.

First, we find fighting men fed by the sales of speculative tradesmen or sutlers, market prices being fixed by a military official called the Provost. The animals and vehicles were more or less under the control of another military official called the Wagon-Master. This signified that the force was attended by a rabble of men, women and children, who were grouped together under the name of followers, an obscene crowd who plundered everywhere, rifled the corpses of the dead and were an encumbrance and a curse, whether in India (where they were at their worst) or in Europe.

Next, contractors took the place of speculators in some measure. The contracts were made by officials of the Treasury called Commissaries and were limited to the provision of bread and bread wagons. The Commissaries further were required to furnish forage and fuel. Everything else was provided by sutlers, the number of their vehicles and animals being, however, subject to military regulation. There was no restraint on private baggage of officers, some of whom took with them enormous quantities. Soldiers' wives and children and the sutlers' assistants still formed a rabble of followers.

The next step was to limit the number of soldiers' wives that accompanied a regiment on foreign service to six per company, selected by lot.

INTRODUCTION

At the end of the eighteenth century an effort was made to place transport in some degree upon a military footing, so as to diminish the number of the irresponsible on the lines of communication and subject the selected few to military discipline.

A corps of gunner-drivers was formed in 1794, and a Royal Wagon Train in the same year. This latter came to a speedy end, but was replaced by a second Royal Wagon Train in 1799, which lasted until 1834.

In the Maratha campaign of 1803, Sir Arthur Wellesley introduced a new era in India by cutting down his *impedimenta* as low as possible, and taking special care that the drivers of vehicles should look after their beasts.

In the Peninsular campaigns of 1809–14 this same Sir Arthur Wellesley, Duke of Wellington, found himself compelled to strike out a new line. No contractors could be found to do the business of transport and supply, wherefore the Commissaries had to do the work themselves; the greater part of the transport being hired pack-mules with their own muleteers. Wellington was ruthless in cutting down private baggage to the lowest point. He had only one light carriage of his own, which he seldom used for his own purposes, and in Spain he allowed no one else to use private wheeled transport. In due time the Commissariat became most efficient.

The nation allowed the whole of the experience thus gained to go for naught. In 1854 the services of transport and supply broke down completely in the Crimea. A Land Transport Corps, presently re-christened the Military Train, was formed as a military organisation, but, since it placed transport on a different footing from supply, was a failure. After much wrangling it was forced upon the authorities that transport and supply were really inseparable services, and in 1868 the two were united under a single head.

Nothing effective, however, was done until Sir

INTRODUCTION

Redvers Buller in 1888 formed the present Army Service Corps as a combatant branch of the Army, on much the same footing as the Royal Engineers.

Meanwhile a new complication affecting transport arose from the improvement in firearms. Muzzle-loaders gave place to breech-loaders, breech-loaders to magazine rifles, machine-guns and quick-firing cannon. The consumption of ammunition was enormously augmented and the carriage of it seriously increased the strain upon the transport service.

The Army Service Corps was first tested by the South African War of 1899–1902. Lord Kitchener, who knew nothing of transport and supply, began by upsetting the whole of its system and reducing its order to chaos. Officers of the Army Service Corps restored it to order and thus enabled the war to be brought to a successful issue.

The principal reforms were as follows. The Army Service Corps took into its hands

(1) All repairs to vehicles,

(2) The checking and control of all requisitions submitted to the Ordnance Department for transport vehicles and equipment, and to the Remounts for animals.

(3) It also rigidly enforced the regulations limiting the transport of any given body of troops, allowing no latitude to any officers, no matter what their rank. Thus it kept the lines of communication free of an irresponsible rabble.

With this preamble I pass to the history of the Corps from 1902 to the present year; though I trust that I may be pardoned for expressing my admiration for the masterly fashion in which Colonel Beadon has handled a subject of vast scope and of enormous difficulty. To compress the survey of a body of over 300,000 officers and men, dispersed over eight different spheres of action, into a few hundred pages, calls for a width of grasp

INTRODUCTION

and a hold upon essentials not often found even among professional writers, much less among amateurs.

At the close of the South African War there was much searching of heart respecting the Army, and many spasmodic recommendations were made by various individuals, most of which were swallowed up by the report of what was known, from the name of its chairman, Lord Esher, as the Esher Committee. The competence of this body to deal with questions of transport and supply may be judged from its inclination once again to divorce the one from the other. Evidently the members were unaware that the union of these two services had only been accomplished after a battle of two centuries, when sheer unanswerable experience had proved that the division of them was fatal to sound work.

However, the Corps on the whole emerged from those trying years comparatively uninjured. It had an able and resolute champion at the War Office in the person of Colonel Clayton (now Lieut.-General Sir Frederick Clayton) who fought for it with skill, patience and tact, never wasting strength on minor points but concentrating his efforts upon main issues. Thanks to him the Corps attracted a body of singularly capable officers, who were moreover well trained for the work before them; and in fact, between 1909 and 1914 the Corps reached the highest degree of efficiency.

Meanwhile the momentous question of mechanical transport had forced itself into prominence. The Army Service Corps was foremost in making the necessary experiments, and became *the* mechanical transport service of the Army.

Reading Colonel Beadon's account of its progress one can see that at first officers were as loth to forsake steam for internal combustion as the Royal Navy had once

INTRODUCTION

been to abandon masts and sails for steam. But the victory of internal combustion was accepted in good time, and its influence on the mobility of armies was carefully studied. Officers began to realise that the new mechanical transport would be employed as much for the swift conveyance of men as of supplies and stores. There had been a few crude examples of the carriage of men by road-transport in the past. Luxemburg hastily reinforced his line at Steenkirk by making every dragoon take up a foot-soldier behind his saddle. Napoleon essayed to move a considerable body of troops from Germany to Spain in horse-drawn vehicles. But the experiment was not a success. The men were worn out by fatigue, and their arms and equipment suffered great damage. With the new automobiles the problem of swift mobility was solved, and the art of war entered upon a new era.

Mechanical transport, moreover, relieved the misgivings of many that animal-drawn transport, on the scale and under the system which prevailed at the opening of the South African War, would hopelessly encumber the roads in rear of a large force operating in any European country. The entire service, therefore, required re-organisation almost from top to bottom, in order to meet the new conditions. It was a heavy task, but it was done and well done in good time under the guiding hand of General Paul of the Army Service Corps. There was, indeed, one blot on the scheme, which was forced upon General Paul by the higher powers. In defiance of the teaching of the South African War the Ordnance Department was made responsible for the overhaul of motor vehicles and the Army Service Corps only for running repairs.

Concurrently, Colonel Long, after a term of service in educating all ranks at the Army Service Corps Training School, had passed to the command of the Supply Reserve Depot at Woolwich, and from thence to the post of Director of Supplies at the War Office. He perceived at once that the existing arrangements for the supply of meat and bread to the troops, in case of war, were hopelessly obsolete. In the teeth of some opposition he insisted that meat must be supplied from frozen-meat vessels at the base, and that bread must also be baked at the base and distributed from thence. Experiments at manœuvres proved him to be right in the matter of bread, and the financial arguments against his suggestions as to the supply of meat were easily overthrown. His ideas, therefore, prevailed; and he arranged further for the setting apart of a special Home Base Supply port which should be used exclusively for the despatch of supplies. Lastly, once again in the face of prolonged resistance, he worked out a new scheme for the feeding of all troops in England upon mobilisation; eliminating all minor contractors and throwing the duty wholly upon the War Office.

Thus before the War broke out every detail within the province of transport and supply had been thought out, and provision had been made that, on the order for mobilisation, every one concerned should know his duty and do it.

The nation little knows what is its debt to Colonel Clayton, General Paul and Colonel Long.

Not the least valuable work of the Army Service Corps was that done by this same Colonel Long when the War actually broke out. Since the 1st of January, 1913, he had been Director of Supplies at the War Office, and in September 1914 he took over the Directorate of Transport also. He had foreseen the thousand complications that would arise at home upon the declaration of hostilities, and thought out methods of meeting them. One of the foremost was the certainty that there would be hoarding of food and a rise in prices, with every probability of food riots and other disturbances to follow. At the first symptom of an effort to extort fancy prices for foodstuffs, General Long took a high tone and announced that he would requisition all that he wanted. He had recommended before the War that such powers should be granted to the Government upon mobilisation, but had been told that it was impossible. He was now told that his action was illegal. He answered that he was aware of the fact, and that the sooner it was legalised the better. And legalised it was by Act of Parliament within a few hours. All danger of food-hoarding and famine-prices therewith passed away.

The next question was the supply of meat, and here his first task was to persuade the Admiralty to restore all the frozen-meat ships which they had taken up as store vessels. With proper co-ordination of course these vessels should never have been hired by the Admiralty for odd purposes at all. This point gained, the next struggle was with the South American meat packers, who asked an extravagant price for frozen meat. General Long declined to pay it. The packers thereupon shipped loads of inferior meat to England, hoping that, when it was refused by the War Office, they would be able to sell it at high prices to the general public. General Long checkmated them by arranging that these inferior cargoes should on arrival be condemned for all purposes; and then the packers, smarting under the dead loss of their bad goods, submitted to General Long's terms.

Later, when Italy came into the War, the American packers tried to take their revenge. The agent of an American firm went to Italy and persuaded the Italian Government, contrary to its agreement with the Allied Powers, to sign a contract for a large quantity of meat at a price 25 per cent. higher than had hitherto been paid. The representatives of the packers then came to England and proposed a general increase in price, which General Long refused to pay. Thereupon they threatened that they would send no more meat to England, but would divert it to the United States or elsewhere. General Long quietly replied that all the frozen-meat ships were under the British flag, and that, unless meat were sent to England, the ships would be withdrawn, so that there would be no means of transporting it to any quarter. Further, he hinted that, if the packers thus brought the trade to a standstill, the British Government would advise the Argentine Government to carry it on themselves. This silenced the packers, and the price was for the present kept down.

These are a few of the ways in which General Long averted dangerous troubles and saved countless millions. And he was not less resourceful in matters of transport than of supply. When other departments were in despair over a shortage of military horsed vehicles, it was he who at once applied to the great railway companies and within a week obtained thousands of them. So again upon the mobilisation of the Territorial Forces, there were difficulties because, in spite of the teaching of the South African War, it had been laid down that units should draw wagons and equipment from the Ordnance Department and animals from the Remounts Department. General Long repeated in London in 1914 the system which he had established at Bloemfontein in 1901, and arranged that the Army Service Corps should issue wagons, horses, harness and so forth complete.

It must be observed that General Long in time of war resisted the control of the Financial Department of the War Office, though of course respecting it in time of peace. He simply ordered what he considered necessary and insisted upon having it. The Ordnance Department gave ample orders for munitions but submitted to have them cut down by the financial authorities, and hence arose a shortage at a very critical moment. Later it was seen that the Ordnance Department was in the right. The munitions which they had ordered began to pour in, and Mr Lloyd George took the credit for them, as though he had called guns and shells into existence by waving a wand. If the Ordnance had been as resolute

INTRODUCTION

as General Long, they would not have failed; but they were too deferential to the regulations of peace.

But General Long was never very patient of civilian control. When the Ministry of Munitions was first formed, Sir Eric Geddes was sent by Mr Lloyd George to the War Office with the proposal that the ministry should take over control of all motor factories and of the provision of motor vehicles for the Army. General Long flatly refused, seeing that his military subordinates were doing the work with perfect efficiency. But in March 1916 he resigned his post for reasons wholly creditable to him, and the politicians saw their chance. The Army Service Corps had managed this whole business of motor vehicles and the provision thereof with a staff of twenty-six officers and under one hundred clerks. The Ministry of Munitions found it necessary to take the whole of the Grand Hotel, where no fewer than five hundred officials and countless clerks were employed in doing what a military staff of fewer than one hundred and twenty-five souls had done perfectly well before. Such was the meaning of the invasion of the transport by the so-called "men of business," at the behest of Mr Lloyd George. Its effects in other departments may be judged by this example. "One day," says Colonel Beadon, "it may be believed that the truth will emerge." Here at any rate is one instalment of it which helps to account for the gigantic cost of the War. Whether more will come to light remains to be seen.

The resignation of General Long was a serious misfortune. But a masterful, irascible, independent man does not always commend himself either to superiors or to inferiors. Moreover, he was no respecter of persons. Very early in the War, casual individuals began to career about in motor cars behind the lines, choking the roads and making free with the Government's petrol and spare tyres. It was the nucleus of the rabble which always tends to infest the skirts of an army in the field.

INTRODUCTION

General Long put as peremptory a stop to this in France as he had in South Africa by positively forbidding any motor car to be landed in France without a permit signed by himself. Of course he had to listen to outcries and to go through stormy interviews with indignant nonentities who boasted themselves to be somebody; but his answer, whether to duke or dustman, was the same, a very resolute negative. At the same time it must not be thought that he discountenanced civilians merely because they were civilians. On the contrary he enlisted the service of tens of thousands, demanding only that that service should be good and efficient. Thus he appointed a Territorial officer of great ability to a high administrative post on the Western Front. A regular officer of the Army Service Corps thereupon complained of having to take orders from a Territorial. He was so effectually silenced that he did not venture upon such a protest again.

However, before he resigned, General Long had time to initiate upon the right lines the gigantic task of expanding a force of 500 officers and 6000 men into one which ultimately reached the strength of 12,000 officers and 320,000 men. Colonel Beadon gives us glimpses of the process, of the schools organised for the training of all ranks in all descriptions of the work of transport and supply, of the provision of motor vehicles, and of the furnishing of all that was needful for vast armies scattered all over the world. The supply of petrol alone constituted a gigantic problem. The feeding of a quarter of a million labourers of many nations, each nation requiring a special diet, was another. And officers and men needed training, not only in the management and driving of motor cars, but in the ways of horses, mules, camels, oxen and even dogs and reindeer, to say nothing of the care of wagons, harness and pack equipment.

And, as if its own duties were not sufficient, the Army Service Corps was called upon to be maid-of-all-work to

INTRODUCTION

the Army. It will be remembered that, by an unwise reversion to primitive times, the Ordnance Corps was entrusted with the general overhaul of motor vehicles, while the running repairs were committed to the Army Service Corps. In less than three months the Ordnance Department was found unequal to the work, and *all* repairs were transferred to the Army Service Corps. But apart from this the Army Service Corps was called upon to furnish traction for heavy artillery, the detachments becoming an integral part of the fighting units. Heavy drafts were made upon it for the formation of the Tank Corps, the first unit of which was made up almost exclusively from the Army Service Corps; and it was called upon to instruct thousands of recruits in riding and driving when the Machine Gun Corps was first established. These duties had in strictness nothing to do with supply allied with transport, and involved a great deal of hard work and hard thought. But they were cheerfully undertaken and successfully carried out. General Long was a glutton for work and responsibility, and understood his position to mean that the Army Service Corps must always give its best help and never raise difficulties. Any fool can complain or obstruct, but it needs a man to think, foresee, act, and overthrow obstacles as fast as they arise.

Governed by an admirable system, and with such a chief at its head, the Army Service Corps showed everywhere a readiness of initiative and resource which is one of the most remarkable features of the War. It was no light matter for 500 officers and 6000 men to leaven such a lump as 12,000 officers and over 300,000 men; but leavened the lump was. To the lasting credit of the regular *personnel* their spirit entered into their pupils as thoroughly as the spirit of the "Old Contemptibles" into the New Armies. It was not only at the War Office but all over the world that they emulated their chiefs in cheerful and successful wrestling with difficulties, bold

INTRODUCTION

improvisation and fearless assumption of responsibility. It is not two or three names only but many that deserve commemoration, as I shall very briefly show by glancing at the various spheres of action, of which Colonel Beadon has given, in a short space, so graphic an account. But I must first close this sketch of headquarters at the War Office.

General Long after his resignation was very quickly snapped up by one of the greatest trading firms in the country, and thus ended his military career. His very name is unknown to the public, except possibly to a few who remember that he called into being the Expeditionary Force Canteen, which has since developed into the Navy, Army and Air Force Institute. This was only one of his many "by-products" during the first months of the War, but not the least remarkable. He received no adequate reward. But when history takes cold account of the past it will record that he did much to save the campaign in South Africa and wrought as well, perhaps, as did any one man to ensure success in the Great War.

He was succeeded by Lieut.-Colonel Crofton Atkins, who had for some time acted as his deputy at the War Office. Coming after any predecessor other than General Long, General Crofton Atkins would have made his mark even more conspicuously than he did, being a man of outstanding ability, though lacking General Long's driving power and ruthless impatience of inefficiency. He held his post to the end of the War and was very deservedly rewarded with the rank of Major-General and the K.C.B. He died, however, not very long after, worn out, as were so many men, by the strain of excessive work.

Passing now first to the Western Front, I must content myself by accepting Colonel Beadon's dictum that the most remarkable point about the operations, so far as concerned the Army Service Corps, was their scale and scope. It may be noted, however, that General

INTRODUCTION

Paul's re-organisation stood the test of a difficult and rapid retreat at the outset; and that the shifting of the base from Le Havre to St Nazaire—60,000 tons of stores, 15,000 men and 1500 horses—in nine days was no ordinary feat. When the war became what is called "static", matters were so far simplified; but the conditions were often such that the Army Service Corps could only feed the troops in the trenches by coming within four hundred yards of the enemy's lines to positions swept by machine-gun fire. Naturally the Corps suffered casualties, being fired at without much chance of retaliation; but that was all in the day's work, and gave opportunity, which was not thrown away, not merely for acts of individual heroism but for a steady endurance indicative of very fine discipline. Nor should it be forgotten that the transport of the Royal Army Medical Corps is wholly found by the Army Service Corps, which shared in the devotion of the medical service to the sick and wounded. The peril of the Corps is proved by the fact that its casualties, in round numbers, totalled 16,000, of whom the dead numbered over 8000. The casualties among the 80,000 of its members who, first and last, were drafted into the infantry, are not included in this total.

Turning next to Italy, there is little extraordinary to notice except the swiftness and readiness with which the Army Service Corps adapted itself to new conditions of transport, the excellence of their arrangements and the regularity with which they supplied the troops with all that they needed. This is not to say that there were no difficulties, but that they were quickly overcome by the Director of Supplies and Transport, Brig.-General Swabey.

And so we pass to Eastern Europe, and first to the Dardanelles. To find a parallel to the blindness and ignorance with which this luckless expedition was undertaken we must go back to the eighteenth century and to

INTRODUCTION

he days of Henry Dundas. Lord Kitchener, by repute the greatest soldier in the British Empire, actually directed that the troops should sail without their first line transport, intimating that, as they were to be landed on the beach and would only have to walk across the Peninsula, they would need no transport. General Long was obliged to wait upon the great man and explain that even a battalion encamped in Hyde Park would require at least some transport, if only to fetch water from the Serpentine, adding further that on active service a reserve of ammunition was not out of place. Then arose a question whether there were roads on the Peninsula and whether mechanical transport could be used upon them. No one could give any information, though General Maxwell had some time before informed Lord Kitchener that there were no roads and that pack transport would be imperatively needed.

From the nature of the case it was impossible to form any depots of supplies until the troops had won a landing. This they did on the 25th of April, 1915; and by the evening of the 26th supply depots were beginning to appear on the beaches in spite of incessant artillery fire on the anchorages. But it had been impossible to land any transport animals, and the supply of the troops during the first three days was a very anxious matter. These little details had not been foreseen by those who despatched the expedition, nor had they considered the difficulty of carrying on operations from a main base nearly seven hundred miles by sea from the advanced bases, and from advanced bases—totally unequipped for the purpose—sixteen miles and sixty miles respectively from the scene of action.

However, the Army Service Corps adapted itself as usual to all adverse conditions, though the troops struggled in vain to move forward in order to gain some little space for the administrative services in rear. Everything, even the baking of bread, was carried on

INTRODUCTION

under artillery fire, but it was carried on. The failure at Suvla Bay, it is interesting to note, is ascribed by Colonel Beadon to lack of means of mobility. Every preparation which human forethought could suggest was made, but some of the landing craft took the ground at a distance from the beach, and hence the landing of transport mules was fatally delayed. The men had to come back to the beach for food, ammunition and even water; the fighting line was seriously depleted during their absence; and the men were naturally much fatigued. The operations were, therefore, delayed and crippled, with fatal results.

English ministers have a genius for thrusting their armies into positions from which they can neither advance nor retire. They did so in the Crimea and they did so in the Dardanelles, and, as their armies escaped upon both occasions, though cruelly wasted by sickness and battle casualties, they will very likely do so again. The opening of the Straits and the capture of Constantinople may be counted a fine strategic conception, but such enterprises need forethought and preparation, also at least some bowing acquaintance with the alphabet of transport and supply.

From the Dardanelles the troops were shifted to Salonika, a political move and conducted in a political fashion. In the first place the ground to be occupied was that of a neutral power, which made the occupation neither more nor less than an outrage. In the second place the troops arrived before their transport, so that there was no adequate administrative staff to supply them. Colonel Striedinger, A.S.C., however, by energy and resourcefulness contrived to keep matters going somehow, though with enormous difficulty. Then a division was moved up into Serbia, where it was only supplied with difficulty, and presently it had to retreat over lakes of mud. This signified conversion of wheeled transport into pack transport, and a series of extremely

INTRODUCTION

delicate operations until the troops were successfully extricated and brought back to Salonika. But meanwhile more troops were arriving and bringing no food with them, so that it was impossible to build up any reserve of supplies. The first ten weeks at Salonika were a period of continual apprehension to the officers of the Army Service Corps, through the fault not of themselves but of the authorities who sent them there; but they triumphed over all difficulties in a fashion which called down unstinted praise from the Commander-in-Chief, Sir Charles Monro.

By January 1916 the ration strength of the Salonika army numbered 90,000 men. At the end of the month fresh formations of the Army Service Corps were arriving and Brig.-General A. Long (not to be confounded with General S. S. Long of the War Office) landed and assumed the Directorate of Supplies and Transport. Troops were still pouring in, and the demands for men in other theatres of action were so heavy that none could be spared for the pack transport at Salonika. It was, therefore, necessary, despite of the Greek Government's prohibition, to enlist Greek muleteers and train them to the work. Hardly had this been done when the troops were moved forward forty miles, which involved the enlargement of pack trains and the enlistment of three thousand more muleteers in Cyprus. Meanwhile, both France and Serbia made demands for transport; fever and sickness made havoc of the *personnel* of the Army Service Corps, and in the autumn of 1916 matters were almost desperate for the Directorate of Supplies and Transport. Then in the nick of time the arrival of the divisional ammunition parks afforded relief.

Even so the situation was most harassing. The constant sinking of supply and store ships by submarines prevented the accumulation of large reserves; and the maintenance of some 45,000 men, fifty miles from railhead over a single bad road, was a difficult matter. By

INTRODUCTION

heroic measures the road was improved, but was only by incessant efforts kept in repair. Then a great fire broke out in Salonika. The Army Service Corps was in charge of the only fire-engines, and one of the drivers remained at his post without sleep for nearly sixty hours. Eighty thousand homeless people had to be got out of the way, and the greatest share of the work was done by the British mechanical transport. And meanwhile, as if they had not already jobs enough on hand, the Corps obtained motor boats and formed a motor-boat section to patrol the lakes.

At last in September 1918 the long period of waiting came to an end. The Allies advanced and the Serbians, with British transport to maintain them, "retook their country in their stride." One company of the Army Service Corps, which did its work daily under continual heavy fire, received as an unit the French *Croix de Guerre*—a rare distinction which had not previously been conferred on any British unit. The Commander-in-Chief, Sir George Milne, testified with unusual enthusiasm to the ability of the Army Service Corps which, in maintaining forces extending from the Black Sea to the Adriatic had, despite of endless difficulties, never failed for one day.

Finally, after the Armistice the Army of Occupation was spread over an area of 300,000 square miles; the British troops stretching from Varna, their old Crimean quarters, on the west to the western coast of the Caspian Sea. Then the British Army Service Corps provided maintenance not only for 90,000 British, but for 70,000 Serbs, 200,000 Greeks and a proportion of French and Italians, to say nothing of 100,000 animals, and endless starving refugees. The old Commissariat could never even have dreamed of undertaking a task requiring such powers of organisation. The whole story of the Army Service Corps in the Balkans offers a very striking example of its initiative, its resourcefulness and, it must be

INTRODUCTION

added, of the tact and good nature of all ranks in working with foreign allies and among strange nationalities.

Passing from Salonika eastward we reach our next sphere of operations in Egypt and Palestine. There the conditions were so unusual as to be of extraordinary interest, and it may fairly be conceded that the Royal Engineers, who carried the railway and the water-pipe line across the desert, displaying moreover almost Mosaic skill in the discovery of hidden water-supplies, were the heroes of the campaign. But man and beast cannot live by water alone, and the task of maintenance by food and forage taxed the utmost skill of the Army Service Corps. In the desert itself little use could be made of mechanical transport, and the Corps was compelled to fall back on camels. These were nothing new in British campaigns, 30,000 having been employed in the first Afghan War alone. But the losses in those operations were appalling, for not only were the beasts much neglected but the Indian camel simply could not or would not live in Afghanistan. In the desert campaign of 1884–5, again, camels were found wanting, but once more very greatly because they were improperly treated and because there were not nearly enough of them. Still Charles Napier, by incessant care and vigilance, had contrived to keep his camels in good order in Sind, and the Army Service Corps proved that it could do as well as Charles Napier. In all 72,000 camels—say a hundred and sixty miles of camels in single file, nose to croup—passed through the Camel Transport Corps, and the casualties among them only slightly exceeded 10,000 from all causes, which, in the case of so delicate an animal, is an astonishingly low figure. Further, in provision against the rough tracks of the Judæan hills, there were organised, as something of a novelty[1], two ass companies, each 2000 strong, in which the casualties during two whole years' work were

[1] Asses had been used before, notably in Abyssinia and China, but never on so large a scale.

INTRODUCTION

only two hundred and sixty-eight, a number which, as Colonel Beadon remarks, reflects great credit on those who had the care of them. But, as Wellington always insisted, drivers are a not less important matter than beasts, and the Army Service Corps had taken his teaching to heart.

Once clear of the desert, it was possible to employ wheeled transport in general and mechanical transport in particular; but the utmost powers of the Army Service Corps were strained to maintain the troops in the pursuit of the enemy after the capture of Gaza, at a distance from the railhead. They did it somehow, though hampered by heavy rain which reduced much of the country to a morass. There were pitiful cases of camels sunk girth-deep in mud and abandoned, and there was sad wastage of drivers. But by combining every possible means of transport the troops were fed; and the advance from Gaza–Bir Saba to Jaffa–Jerusalem was covered in one bound, which meant nothing less than that a single battle had done the work of two, to the great economy of human life in the victorious army.

After Armageddon mechanical transport came into its own with astonishing results. Three cavalry divisions were pushed forward to the chase, and these, in spite of the rapidity of their movements, the Army Service Corps contrived by great efforts to supply regularly. The foremost of them, the 5th Cavalry Division, with its armoured cars covered five hundred miles in forty days, and only halted fifteen miles north of Aleppo upon the conclusion of an armistice. But the strain upon the transport companies was terrific. They were at work day and night, and were so much thinned by exhaustion and sickness that some lorries were stopped from sheer want of men to drive them. Yet the survivors went on, and the lorries entered Aleppo on the same day as the troops. And it must be added that all the miscellaneous motor vehicles which spread wide towards the Hedjaz army on the east were driven by the Army Service Corps. Finally, to show how multifarious are the duties of the Corps, when Damascus was reached most difficult financial questions arose out of the confusion of the currency, which were satisfactorily met by the institution of a system of barter. It all sounds very simple, when done; but it must be remembered that these sudden and difficult problems must be solved and solved promptly by some one. They do not solve themselves.

Not the least interesting point in the campaign is to observe how, as the Army moved north, it kept opening up new maritime bases of supply on the coast, exactly as Wellington did, beginning at St Ander and ending at Bordeaux, on his march from Spain into France in 1813–14. For the rest, if we seek out the brains which thought out the means of overcoming all obstacles and the shoulders which were broad enough to bear the main burden of transport and supply, we find that they belonged to Colonel W. Elliott, who was always to be found at the post of greatest difficulty, whether it lay at the base or at the front. It is noteworthy too that, though out of nearly eleven hundred officers of the Army Service Corps in this sphere only sixty-eight were regular officers, yet all worked heartily together, whether they were of the New Armies or of the Territorials, Australians or New Zealanders, from the Indian Army or the Egyptian. And as the officers showed the way, so the men followed, to whatever race they might belong. So good and so sound had been the work of Redvers Buller.

Mesopotamia, which demanded at first one hundred men to guard the end of the pipe-line, and at the last 420,000 men, presents perhaps the most remarkable example of our methods of waging war. The campaign was supposed at first to be merely an Indian concern with which England had nothing to do. Actually in a confidential summary of the military situation in all parts of the world, which was submitted to the Cabinet

INTRODUCTION

in December 1914, the name Mesopotamia does not occur. How any sane man could conceive of it as a purely Indian concern is frankly unintelligible. White troops were engaged and could not be kept up to strength from India. These white troops required their own particular diet, parts of which—for instance, jam—could not be supplied from India. The campaign was a river campaign and the necessary river boats could not be supplied from India. Furthermore, it was contrary to reason and experience to entrust the conduct of military operations upon any great scale to the Indian Government. That Government had invariably made a mess of any important war; and Lord Kitchener at least should have known it. Perhaps he did know it, in which case his careful shrinking from anything to do with Mesopotamia is the more to be marvelled at.

There is no occasion to recapitulate the dismal story of the earlier operations nor the shortcomings of the unfortunate Indian Supply and Transport Service. Suffice it that in one of the most trying climates in the world the men were starved and their movements were crippled even to disaster from sheer neglect of the business of transport and supply. Never were fighting soldiers more infamously treated by their distant masters.

Upon a scene of utter chaos the Army Service Corps entered in September 1916 with instructions to reduce it to order within two months, when operations were to be renewed. Everything had to be started anew from the very beginning; and, to increase the difficulties, more troops were continually pouring in. The transport consisted of river barges, army transport carts, lorries, motor vans and camels; and had the supply officers not known the capabilities of each they could never have combated their difficulties with success. "Seldom," says Colonel Beadon, "have the advantages of the union of transport and supply been more clearly demonstrated"; and this is a point which cannot be too strongly emphasised.

INTRODUCTION

The gigantic task accomplished by the Army Service Corps in Mesopotamia must be read at length in Colonel Beadon's summary, which itself is none too long. Perhaps the most noteworthy detail in the whole of it is the performance of the mechanical transport when acting as combatant flying columns. "In a war of movement," as Colonel Beadon says, "the Corps came into its own as the dominant agent in the mobility of the Army. On the efficiency of its fast moving mechanical transport columns the operations depended. These columns in fact constituted a new auxiliary arm." They not only maintained the troops but carried them whither they were required for strategic and tactical purposes.

The politicians at home no sooner realised the power of this new arm than they set it to perform impossible tasks. But that is the way of them. They need much to convince them that soldiers do not live on air, and they have an idea that petrol comes down from heaven.

In East Africa the difficulties of supply and transport were perhaps greater than in any other sphere, the operations being carried on in, to all intent, a savage country. So-called roads were no more than tracks, turning to morass in the rainy season and to deep sand in the dry.

The Army Service Corps did not come upon the scene until January 1916, when it found much disorder among the transport and indeed no certain record of the transport that existed. However, General Smuts decided at all risks to advance at once, allowing no time for preparation; and his movements were rapid and successful. But the efforts of the transport to keep pace with him over such a country were terrifically costly. One movement of 28,000 men during three months cost the lives of exactly 28,000 oxen, chiefly owing to the plague of the tsetse fly. Sand-fly sickness equally assailed horses, mules and men. "The life of a mule or an ox was not usually more than six weeks." When after a

INTRODUCTION

time mechanical transport arrived, the white drivers fell down so fast from malaria that it was necessary to train natives of Africa and India, and to import Chinese as artificers. All of these of course required to be taught in their own language and to be fed with their own diet, which were neither of them easy tasks.

On the whole it should seem that the enemy chose the better part in relying mainly upon human carriers for transport. But he had first choice of these as he retired through the districts of the various tribes, and he would and did impress them by force without fear that any questions would be asked; whereas political objections were raised to the employment of carriers by the British. Latterly these political objections were to some extent waived, but it was then rather late in the day. The campaign was full of instruction, for hardly since Braddock's time had the British Army been called upon to contend with European commanders in a savage country. In the Cameroons, of course, the conditions were the same, but the Army Service Corps was not so deeply concerned in those operations.

Lastly, we come to the campaigns in North Russia, which were initiated in the casual fashion so dear to British politicians. The officers present of the Army Service Corps were consequently much overworked, and the more so because it was found necessary to feed 100,000 of the population. A certain number of ponies were bought locally, also wagons which in winter gave place to sleighs; and actually 1500 troops and 400 tons of supplies were sent on sleighs over a route of 300 miles. When the year 1919 came in, it was judged advisable to form a Reindeer Transport Corps of 2000 reindeer, 500 sleighs and 1000 Laplanders; and a complete battalion was thus moved over a distance of one hundred and thirteen miles in sixty-six and a half hours without a single casualty. Before the thaw came in the spring the Army Service Corps started a small factory for the construction of local carts, and thus was able to meet the change from winter to summer conditions. But even so it was necessary to improvise pack transport, with saddles put together as best they could be and with peasants for drivers. It was to make bricks without straw, but the bricks held together notwithstanding. Later, dogs imported from Canada were also used to draw sledges, but were not greatly favoured, for their carrying capacity was small, and, except in harness, they were dangerous to handle. Dogs, however, were no novelty as transport animals, having long since been used for military purposes in Canada. It was the reindeer that prolonged the list of transport animals employed by the British soldier. Horses, ponies, mules, asses, camels, dromedaries, oxen of every description from the South African to the yak, men—British sailors, British soldiers, Kaffirs, West Africans, East Africans, Chinese, Tartars—all of these had been used as transport animals; but the reindeer never until the twentieth century. So far as I know the llama alone remains to be employed in the service of the British Army.

Altogether the achievements of the Army Service Corps in the late war strike me, who have followed pretty minutely the many campaigns of the British Army, as nothing short of marvellous. The Army of course would have been absolutely powerless without it. In the first place it was the Corps's representatives at the War Office, one and all of high professional calibre, who by keen foresight had made everything ready for the Expeditionary Force and by remarkable moral courage prevented any trouble over the food supply at home upon the opening of hostilities. In the second we find the spirit of initiative, acceptance of responsibility and readiness of improvisation pervading the Corps in every sphere of operations. It mattered not whether the scene were the waterlogged plain of Flanders, or the mountains of Italy and Serbia, or the sands of Palestine, or the vast

INTRODUCTION

tropical jungle of East Africa, or the dreary banks of the Euphrates and Tigris, or the frost-bitten wastes of Archangel—whether on the equator or in the Arctic Circle—whether the thermometer stood at 120° Fahrenheit or at 50° below zero—whether there were roads or no roads—whether the approaches were safe or swept by shrapnel shell and machine-gun bullets—there was the Army Service Corps with but one thought governing brain, heart and limb—to keep the fighting men in good fettle for action or perish—as eight thousand did actually perish—in the attempt.

I have weighed my words carefully before I say that Redvers Buller, who made the Army Service Corps, wrought not less towards the winning of the late War than Herbert, Earl Kitchener himself.

In recognition of its good work the Corps was made the Royal Army Service Corps; and it might have been expected that the sphere of its usefulness would have been expanded, so that in future it should control railways and inland waterways on the side of transport, and include clothing, as well as food, fuel and forage in the domain of supply. Any such expectations were rudely disappointed. It is the misfortune of our Army that, as soon as it has been brought to high efficiency by a great war, it is instantly pulled to pieces by the nation. The English always assume that wars will cease because they find them inconvenient, forgetting that the excellent Society of Friends, founded in the seventeenth century, has failed altogether to check war, and that the Society for Universal Peace, which came into being after Waterloo, has not left behind so much as its name. However, on the advent of peace after a mortal struggle, the British Army is always pared down to a shadow, and there ensues a frantic struggle for survival among the units which

INTRODUCTION

compose it. In old days the infantry and cavalry had things all their own way, with remarkable results. Within two years after the close of Marlborough's wars the Board of Ordnance could produce neither guns nor gunners to quell the Scottish rebellion of 1715. Within a year of the end of the Peninsular War it could supply Wellington with gunners for no more than forty-two guns and with insufficient drivers even for these, for the campaign of Waterloo. Only one year before the Crimean War the Artillery were not in a position to put more than six batteries into the field. It was long before the Artillery and their later comrade, the Engineers, rose from their inferior stations. They were a peculiar people. Their officers did not purchase their commissions nor their steps; the men were not clothed by their Colonel; and both Corps were subject not to the Commander-in-Chief but to the Master-General of the Ordnance. In America, fifty years after the Royal Regiment of Artillery had been formed, grave doubts were raised whether one of the ablest officers in Europe might command a small mixed force of 3000 men, simply because he was an artilleryman. Long after that no artillery officer, much less an engineer, commanded even a small expedition in the field. In 1855 Artillery and Engineers were placed on the same level with the rest of the Army under the Commander-in-Chief, and in 1870 the abolition of purchase removed the last differences between them and the Cavalry and Infantry. Not until then did Artillery and Engineers come into their own. Lord Napier of Magdala, Sir Gerald Graham and Lord Kitchener broke the spell for the Engineers and Lord Roberts for the Artillery. But it had taken a century and a half to establish their position.

In the scramble for survival which follows upon every great war, seniority counts for very much. Occasionally extreme efficiency may supplant it. I doubt if the disbandments of infantry after Waterloo would have

INTRODUCTION

stopped at the 95th Regiment of the Line but for the fame which it had won in the Peninsula. But that regiment (now the Rifle Brigade) had been chosen by Wellington to lead the march of the British troops into Paris in 1815, and was moreover a peculiar corps, so that it was spared. On the same principle some consideration might have been shown to the Royal Army Service Corps in recognition of its extreme efficiency. But it had been in existence only thirty years and had not served the long apprenticeship of the Artillery and Engineers. Like them, its predecessors had belonged to a different department—the Treasury—before it was joined to the War Office in 1855, and, unlike them, it was neglected and mishandled for more than thirty years until it found a saviour in Sir Redvers Buller.

In the bitter struggle for existence, therefore, it fared ill. Had it possessed at the War Office such a champion as Sir Frederick Clayton, who saved it after the South African War, things might have gone differently; but apparently it did not. Possibly the officers selected by the Army Council to represent the Corps at headquarters were not those best fitted for that particular function, or did not realise what was expected of them. It may be deemed presumptuous for a civilian to express an opinion upon such matters, but it seems to me that the Army Service Corps, being youthful, has fallen into the error of following a fashion which in the rest of the Army is happily obsolete. I remember the time when in practically every regiment in the Army an officer who sought admission to the Staff College was viewed with some suspicion, occasionally almost amounting to contempt, by his fellows. This was in a way natural, for the Army during the greater part of its existence was only kept alive by regimental feeling. It was not, properly speaking, an Army at all, but only a collection of regiments. The Army Service Corps could not but inherit the craving for a powerful *esprit de corps* within

INTRODUCTION

itself; yet surely it made a grave error in excluding its graduates of the Staff College from posts within the three branches of the Directorate of Supplies and Transport at the War Office. Such exclusion must be construed either as an opinion that staff-training is no qualification for the higher duties of the Army Service Corps, which is not merely wrong but childish, or that the Corps does not send its best officers to the Staff College. Either construction is fatal to the reputation of the Corps in the Army. Furthermore the chief posts at the War Office are almost wholly filled by graduates from Camberley and Quetta, so that a graduate from the Army Service Corps would enter the charmed circle not as a stranger or an intruder but as an equal and a fellow, with infinite advantage not to the Corps alone but to the military service at large. Not all of Sir John Cowans's successors in the post of Quartermaster-General shared in his wise appreciation of the Army Service Corps. Sir Redvers Buller, when recreating the Corps in 1888, had written, "I want to officer my new organisation with men who will have the same prestige and position as officers of the combatant branches...they must have no disabilities and a full military career must be open to them." This ideal has never yet been fully realised, not, perhaps, wholly without blame to the Corps itself. In the Army at large, moreover, its combatant status is not recognised as it should be, though the nature of its responsibilities and the tale of over 8000 officers and men who lost their lives in the late war should be sufficient to justify it.

Next, in July 1919, it was decided that the special pay, which had attracted such excellent officers before the war, should be withdrawn from all except a small proportion who had been specially trained to mechanical transport. This was virtually a breach of faith, and was the more galling because the Royal Army Service Corps alone was subjected to this deprivation. So much damage

INTRODUCTION

was thereby done to the Corps that in 1925 the authorities agreed to restore two-thirds of the former allowance. But this is not the fashion in which a highly skilled body of men, of proved worth and of vital importance to the Army, should be treated.

Next came the cruellest blow of all. Prior to 1914 the Army Service Corps contained practically the whole of the mechanical transport of the Army. In the second year of the war new mechanical vehicles, represented first by the tanks, came into being, and what may be called fighting vehicles were added to transport vehicles. It was then decided that the fighting vehicles should be committed for storage, issue and repair to the Ordnance Department, and transport vehicles to the Army Service Corps; and this arrangement acted with perfect smoothness.

In October 1927 the Army Council ordained that the whole of the research, experiment and other functions formerly undertaken by the Army Service Corps in respect of mechanised vehicles should be transferred to the Ordnance Department; only the vehicles of the Army Service Corps itself being excepted. This decision spelled disaster to the Army Service Corps, for it ruined all its hopes of growth and expansion. The change involved a reduction of establishment; and, since the Ordnance Corps did not possess the men to perform the new duties which it had appropriated, it annexed a number of Army Service Corps officers who could perform them. It is difficult to understand what object to the Army and the nation was gained by this change. If centralisation of repair and provision of mechanised vehicles were desired, it was not achieved and could not be achieved, for this control was not and hardly could be taken from the Army Service Corps in respect of its own vehicles. Moreover, the Ordnance Department with artillery and fighting vehicles under its charge had already plenty to do; and to depress and discourage the Army Service Corps means fatal mischief to the Army.

INTRODUCTION

To a mere outsider it seems lamentable that a young ancillary service of proved importance and value to the Army should be thus harried and undermined for no public advantage and that it should be deprived of functions to which its organisation, and its organisation alone, had proved equal under the stress of war.

One result of all these alarms and incursions has been so far to unsettle the Army Service Corps that the old question of divorcing supply from transport has again been broached. Once for all such divorce must never be. No amount of specious argument can do away with the principle based on the solid experience of the past, that the people responsible for the load should be responsible for the wagon, and that those responsible for the wagon should be responsible for the load. The soundness of this principle was demonstrated again and again during the late war, and must not be abandoned. It is idle to argue that the sampling of meat and the repair of an internal combustion engine are incongruous functions. They are not more so than the demolition of a bridge and the opening of a water-supply by the Royal Engineer. In these days of demagogues it is very common to see old exploded fallacies brought forward as novelties and glorified under the name of progress. Such conduct is wicked and dangerous enough in political life. It should be eschewed as poison by soldiers.

But though the career of the Royal Army Service Corps since the war has been disappointing, it is to be hoped that this history may do something to enlighten the public as to its value and perhaps even to instil into military officers some conception of the indispensability of the Corps to the Army at large. Within the Army itself this seems to be imperfectly realised. In the official history of the Mesopotamian campaign, for instance, no distinction is drawn, in the matter of Supplies and Transport, between the work of the Army Service Corps, and that of the Indian Supply and Transport Corps.

INTRODUCTION

Consider what an opportunity the writer has missed! He had to describe the breakdown of the unfortunate Indian Supply and Transport Corps, a helpless, resourceless body of men, who failed dismally because they had always been despised and neglected, never trained to their business nor taught that their calling was one of the highest and most important. And it seems (apparently) never to have occurred to the author that if Sir Redvers Buller had not taken the old Commissariat and Transport Corps in hand and put new life and spirit into it, its failure would have been as conspicuous as that of the Indian Supply and Transport Corps.

I am familiar with Napoleon's impatient exclamations, "Don't talk to me about 'supplies'! Twenty thousand men can live in a desert." But it always seems to me (if a civilian may be pardoned for saying so) that British officers should study Napoleon's campaigns with the greatest caution and reserve. I am not so foolish as to decry the great captain, but for British officers he is a very dangerous model. He began his career as the General of a bankrupt State and a blackguard Government; and it was his duty to make war support war. He did so to the end, living on the enemy's country and extorting enormous sums from them. His principle was to squander men in order to save money, and no one knows how many men he marched to death and starved to death. He began heavy overdrafts on his conscript account, so to speak, in 1806; and recruits from all Europe could not keep his ranks full. Moreover, his exploits, though dazzling, were never final, and the discipline of his army, from the necessity of marauding in order to live, was always bad. He scared his enemies into submission for a very brief space, but they took up arms again at the first opportunity. His only decisive campaigns were those of 1812–14 and of 1815 when he was decisively beaten.

Now the English practice is precisely the opposite. We squander money to save men. In an European war

INTRODUCTION

we practically always start in a friendly country because otherwise we cannot start at all[1]; and to live by requisition in a friendly country is fatal because the population speedily becomes more dangerously hostile than in an unfriendly one. Hence we have made it a rule to pay our way; and in order at once to conciliate the inhabitants and to preserve discipline, our greatest generals have always devoted immense attention to the feeding of their men. They contrived to do so even with the imperfect instruments that lay to their hand. From their experience after many painful failures we at last evolved the Army Service Corps, a Corps exactly adapted to our needs, unlike any other such Corps in the world and—from 1914 to 1918—at least equal and most probably superior to any other.

It may be said that it took two hundred and fifty years to make that Corps, and no policy could be more suicidal than to allow it to decline. Mobility counts for more than ever it did in war and the Royal Army Service Corps stands for mobility. It must not be slighted nor jostled aside nor sacrificed to petty jealousies from within or greater jealousies from without. It must be treated, as Sir Redvers Buller insisted, as an integral part of the combatant Army, with a full military career as open to its members as to cavalry, infantry and artillery. It should have its equal chance of expansion and progress, so that its officers may delight in advancing its efficiency. Will any man be bold enough to deny that there were in 1914 as good brains, as accomplished minds, as clear heads and as resolute wills in the Army Service Corps as in any branch of the Army? It is imperative that the Corps should always possess such men, and many men of the same stamp. It has been my fate to make some study of the British Army's campaigns past and present, and I say emphatically that at present our Army without

[1] The campaigns of the Crimea and Gallipoli are the exceptions to this rule, and are sufficient to prove it, see p. xxxi.

INTRODUCTION

the best possible organisation for mobility and maintenance is naught. It is like a motor car without petrol—comely perhaps, well designed, well engined, but inert and lifeless. Such an organisation we possess in the Royal Army Service Corps. To preserve its name without maintaining its efficiency and prestige is to expect a motor car to run on water poured into the petrol tank from a petrol can. Encourage it, foster it, speed it, and it will render in future wars as in the past, devoted and transcendent service.

JOHN FORTESCUE

CHAPTER I

"AFTER SOUTH AFRICA"

As recognition of its work in South Africa, the Army Service Corps was honoured by the appointment of H.R.H. the Duke of Connaught as its Colonel, notification in the *London Gazette* being dated the 2nd of September, 1902. Early in that year Colonel F. T. Clayton, who, since his return from South Africa at the end of 1900, had held the command of the Army Service Corps at Aldershot, was sent to the War Office as Assistant Quartermaster-General for the Corps. For the transport and supply services the appointment was of importance in that it was the first occasion since the re-organisation by Sir Redvers Buller that the post was occupied by an officer belonging to the Permanent List of those services. The original holder in 1889 had been a Colonel Reeves, a former officer of the Commissariat and Transport Staff who had been transferred to the Supernumerary List of the Army Service Corps on its formation, and his work and enthusiasm for the new régime deserve to be remembered with gratitude. On the expiration of his term, however, it was considered desirable, in order to hold the balance between the officers of the Supernumerary and Permanent Lists—none of the latter being then sufficiently senior for the appointment—to bring in an officer from outside. Accordingly Colonel Burnett of the Royal Irish Rifles, who had been Assistant Adjutant-General in the Aldershot Command, took the position and was subsequently followed by Colonel Raper of the North Staffordshire Regiment and by Colonel Auld of the Northumberland Fusiliers, who was appointed during the South African War.

No better selection than that of Colonel Clayton could have been made to succeed the latter. The new Assistant Quartermaster-General was a man of strong, resolute character and he had unbounded faith in the future of the Army Service Corps. Joining the Commissariat and Transport Staff in 1883 as an attached officer from the Royal Warwickshire Regiment, Colonel Clayton saw active service a year later on the Bechuanaland Expedition under Sir Charles Warren when he organised the ox and mule transport for a column of some five thousand mounted troops. In 1889 he was transferred to the Permanent List of the Army Service Corps, and, after a spell as Deputy Assistant Adjutant-General in China in 1895, was sent on the Ashanti Expedition, when the transport consisted of some 20,000 carriers. A period as an instructor at the Army Service Corps Training Establishment at Aldershot and command of the Corps at that station intervened before the South African War, on his return from which Colonel Clayton resumed the Aldershot post until called to the War Office. In his nineteen years of experience of transport and supply he had thus seen active service on three occasions and had held the most important appointments which the Corps could offer. He lost no time in bringing to the notice of the War Office authorities the promises which had been made in 1889 as an inducement to regimental officers to transfer, which had not up to then been fulfilled. As a matter of fact they had been well-nigh forgotten.

The memorandum submitted to the Quartermaster-General, Sir Charles Mansfield-Clarke, in January 1903 was a landmark in the history of the Army Service Corps; for it was the first real attempt made to assert its status. And its reception was encouraging. Colonel Clayton began by recalling the position of officers on the re-organisation of 1888 and this may be briefly summarised. In place of the Commissariat and Transport Staff which was abolished, the Army Service Corps was established as a combatant branch. Regimental and Corps pay on similar lines to those of the Royal Engineers were issued in lieu of the previous high Departmental rates and allowances. And finally thirty appointments on the staff were reserved for Army Service Corps officers. Of the two classes embodied in the new Corps, namely the former officers of the Commissariat and Transport Staff and the combatant officers who elected to be transferred or subsequently joined, the first formed the Supernumerary List and the second the Permanent List. The Supernumerary officers had been well provided for in that they had been given substantive rank in the Army instead of their previous honorary rank, while their emoluments were adjusted on a higher scale than those of the combatant officers. At the time—1903—only nineteen of the former category remained, and since all these were due to disappear in the ordinary course of events by 1910 no review of their position appeared necessary. As regards the officers on the Permanent List proper the question was of quite another kind. On the re-organisation of the Commissariat and Transport Staff there were seventy-one officers attached from various regiments in the Army and among the seniors there were many captains of considerable length of service. These officers had been invited to join the Permanent List by the inducement of more rapid promotion than they could have hoped for within their own units and excellent prospects of employment on the staff. It was these advantages which they had to weigh against the loss of the high rates of pay and allowances which they had enjoyed when merely attached to the Commissariat and Transport Staff. About one-half of the number accepted the terms and transferred to the Army Service Corps.

The same prospects had been held out to induce officers to join since, but, as far as chances of staff employment were concerned, they had never been fully realised owing to the fact that the Supernumerary List officers had always to be included in selection for the appointments in question up to the introduction of what was known as the Army Corps system after the South African War, while by this system the number of appointments to be held by the Army Service Corps was much reduced. Thus the prospects which encouraged the original officers to transfer and subsequent officers to join were in process of diminishment and bore a very different complexion from those formerly held out. Colonel Clayton proposed to meet this grievance by the creation of certain high appointments, peculiar to the Army Service Corps, which would thus give the necessary goals at which officers could aim: and for these he suggested posts for two major-generals, one to be the Inspector-General of the Army Service Corps at the War Office under the Quartermaster-General and the other for the important post involved by the charge of the Reserve Supply Depot at Woolwich in which were stored the necessary reserves of supplies for the whole of the Field Army on mobilisation: and in addition one brigadier-general as Director of Supplies and Transport in the Aldershot Command where the Army Service Corps had a strength of some two thousand men and where their training establishment was situated. These appointments were not proposed as an immediate measure but were to be given in due course as officers of the Permanent List became senior enough to fill them. As the Army Service Corps had no provision at that time for any general officers, the suggestions were at least reasonable and were supported by the Quartermaster-General. Sir Charles Mansfield Clarke at the same time took the opportunity to point out in a memorandum to the Military Secretary the desirability of Army Service Corps

AFTER SOUTH AFRICA

officers competing for the Staff College so as to be available for staff employment as officers from any other arm of the service and he emphasised how the real interests of the Corps would be thereby strengthened, adding "for it will prevent the possibility of the accusation which has been made that officers not properly qualified were being employed on staff duties". Later events proved how prescient was this warning. But perhaps most satisfactory of all from the Army Service Corps point of view was the statement of the Quartermaster-General that the Corps had been the first successful body to grapple properly with the difficult duties of transport and supply and that it had recently come through a severe test in South Africa with satisfactory results. In backing the Quartermaster-General the Military Secretary, Sir Ian Hamilton, recommended to Lord Roberts, the Commander-in-Chief, that as regards staff appointments the officers of the Army Service Corps should be considered on exactly the same footing as those of the rest of the Army, and he also gave it as his opinion that the time had come when the claims of the Corps in this respect could no longer be resisted. It is of interest to note that Lord Roberts submitted the case for the opinion of the Permanent Under-Secretary of State, Sir Edward Ward, who had himself been one of the Supernumerary officers of the Army Service Corps and obtained from him the strongest recommendation that the proposals should be carried into effect. The matter then went forward for the sanction of the Treasury. Financially there was little increase to the public expenditure. Indeed the new appointments actually made some small saving on the effective votes, as one Assistant Quartermaster-General at the War Office and four colonels on the staff disappeared before they came into force. In June 1903 their Lordships of the Treasury notified their approval and in their reply inserted a hope that it might "soon be found practicable to give Army Service Corps officers a larger

AFTER SOUTH AFRICA

share in the higher commands which are filled from the Army as a whole ". It seems possible that this aspiration on the part of their Lordships was inspired by the knowledge that the training of the Army Service Corps officer was such as to inculcate habits of economy.

But any hopes built on this happy outcome were destined to be dispelled within a few months, for at the end of the year the "Esher" Committee was formed with the object of making recommendations for the reconstitution of the War Office. Their report furnished early in 1904 made proposals which were far-reaching in their effect upon the Army. The foundations of a General Staff were laid, and administrative work was decentralised and divorced from executive military functions. The recommendations made as regards the Department of the Quartermaster-General at the War Office were not without interest. Transport and Supply were to be placed under separate Directors in order to follow what was described as "the arrangement necessary in the field where there should be a Director of Transport and Remounts and a Director of Supplies". It was, too, considered that the Director-General of the Army Veterinary Services should be under the Director of Transport and Remounts at the War Office, and that the Quartermaster-General's branch should be relieved of all work in connection with barracks except the custody, equipment, appropriation and hire of buildings to supplement barracks. A Directorate of Movements and Quarterings, which would comprehend the latter duties, and also include a section dealing with the question of employment of railways in time of war, was proposed, while it was urged that the Army Ordnance Department, in so far as its responsibility for clothing, equipment and ordnance stores as distinct from arms, ammunition and vehicles was concerned, should be transferred to the sphere of the Quartermaster-General. From the purely Army Service Corps point of view the most ominous feature of the

AFTER SOUTH AFRICA

report was the doubt expressed as to the compatibility of its twin functions of transport and supply, and, while the necessity for an adequate number of officers trained in supply duties was recognised, it was doubted whether it was desirable that all officers employed in the management of transport should be so trained. In this last respect the report of the Committee was anything but convincing, but on the other hand the proposal to place supplies and clothing under one head, following the practice in Continental armies, had much to commend it, although it was never adopted. But certain other of the recommendations were put into practice with satisfactory results.

The combination of transport and remounts was, without the inclusion of the Veterinary Department, tried for a short time but did not last. When the Great War came the Army Service Corps duties were divided as follows: supplies and quarterings under one directorate and transport and movements under another. Remounts were a separate branch.

As a result of the recommendations, the three Army Service Corps appointments which had been sanctioned by the Treasury were negatived and, moreover, on the re-organisation of the staff, the thirty posts given by the Royal Warrant of December 1888 were lost. This decision, which placed the Corps in a far worse position as regards extra-regimental employment than had been anticipated, was felt to be a breach of faith and caused much discontent and disheartenment at the time. Yet looked at from the broadest point of view it was probably the best thing that could have happened; for the Army Service Corps was placed in precisely the same position as the rest of the Army as regards service on the staff and bidden to send its officers to the Staff College if they wanted such employment. It was true that at that time the Corps had no graduates of the Staff College, but there was every reason why they should have, both for the sake of the Corps and the Army. The ruling, therefore, furnished a direct stimulus to that end. Again it could not be expected that a privileged position in respect to staff appointments could, with changing circumstances, remain with any one branch of the service for all time. Such position was bound to be a cause of resentment to the rest of the Army, and as a matter of fact was already felt to be one. Colonel Clayton wisely recognised that there was no case to fight and devoted his energies to finding some means of compensation. To this end he obtained sanction for the creation of the appointments of Assistant Director and Deputy Assistant Director of Supplies and Transport at the Headquarters of Commands under the major-general or brigadier-general in charge of administration, which arrangement fitted in with the new system by which the training of the troops was separated from their administration. This measure gave the Army Service Corps control of its own affairs within Commands, at the same time giving some opening in extra regimental employment; but it did not give any Army Service Corps officer the prospect of rising higher than a colonel since the Assistant Directors of Supplies and Transport were of that rank. This last question was re-opened in 1904. In his memorandum Colonel Clayton traversed the whole ground since the formation of the Army Service Corps and drew special attention to the fact that since the general officers which had been sanctioned by the Treasury in the previous year had never been created, some other means should be found for putting the Corps on the same level as other branches of the service as regards higher appointments. For such means the moment was ripe. Reference has been made to the decentralisation of work within Commands and by this means the General Officer in Command was relieved of his administrative work in order to devote the larger part of his time to the supervision of training. The training of senior Army Service

Corps officers adapted them specially for the charge of the administrative functions and it was proposed that they should be eligible equally with officers of other arms, thus giving opportunities of promotion to general officer's rank.

Careful consideration was given to this proposal and the Army Council approved it, notifying the Selection Board that it should act on the principle of considering Army Service Corps officers when suitable for higher administrative appointments and for promotion to the rank of major-general. Most promptly and honourably was that policy carried out. Early in 1905 Colonel C. E. Heath was sent to Aldershot as Brigadier-General in charge of Administration, and on vacating this post he was promoted to the rank of Major-General and sent to the War Office in 1907 as Director of Transport and Remounts. He was not, however, the first major-general in the Army Service Corps, for Colonel H. N. Bunbury, the senior regimental officer on the Permanent List, received that rank in 1906 when he went to Ireland as Major-General in charge of Administration. Colonel Hadfield was likewise promoted in 1908 for a similar position in the South African Command. Thus within three years of the decision being given the Army Service Corps had three major-generals, while in 1909 Colonel Clayton himself attained that rank and was sent to South Africa to relieve General Hadfield in 1911.

These appointments did much to strengthen and enhance the position of the Army Service Corps, the more so in that they were, in the cases of the major-generals in charge of administration and in the head of the Remount Department, appointments which were open to the whole of the combatant portion of the Army and thus served to break down any sense of departmental isolation. In this respect they were far more effective than the original proposal to create appointments specifically for

AFTER SOUTH AFRICA

general officers of the Corps and it was due to Colonel Clayton's pertinacity and courage in asserting the interests of his branch, and above all his refusal to be disheartened when his original projects were vetoed after being approved, that matters turned out so happily.

During this period the Corps made considerable strides both as regards its organisation and training over anything that had hitherto been reached in the services of transport and supply. As a career it was able to offer very definite attractions once the question of promotion to and employment in the senior grades of commissioned rank had been resolved. The higher rates of pay, though seemingly insignificant enough to-day, were an inducement to many.* The provision of a horse at the public expense likewise made for popularity, while, to most, the greater measure of responsibility enjoyed by junior officers as compared with those in other branches, the Royal Engineers excepted, was a decided advantage; again with mechanical transport in its military genesis a proportion of aspirants for mechanical knowledge was always ready to come forward.

The result of these conditions was that the supply of candidates for commissions greatly exceeded the demand. The Corps at this period was drawing its officers in approximately equal numbers by direct entry either from Sandhurst or from the Militia and Special Reserve, with a few from the Universities, and by transfer from other branches of the Regular Army. The Sandhurst cadet or Militia or Special Reserve officer had to pass very high on the list to get a vacancy, while, as regards the transfers from regiments, a considerable proportion of candidates were eliminated before completing their year's probation. The standard of officer recruits was in

* In addition to the ordinary regimental rates as drawn by the cavalry and infantry corps pay was issued as follows: Second-lieut. 2s.; lieut 2s. 6d.; captain, 3s.; major, 4s.; lieut.-colonel, 6s. per day.

AFTER SOUTH AFRICA

fact one that would bear comparison with any other time and, although the training received by them was imperfect in some respects, it nevertheless embodied assets the importance of which can scarcely be over-stressed. And these lay firstly in the practice of sending out the second-lieutenants at the conclusion of their course at the training establishment to carry out on their own the entire duties of supply and transport for cavalry and infantry brigades both on divisional training and Army manœuvres, which duties in some way actually presented more difficulties than did the conditions of active service. In any case there was ample scope for initiative and foresight under circumstances in which the troops were continually on the move. Secondly, officers were taught organisation from the moment of joining, and in this respect may fairly claim to have possessed in the junior ranks a knowledge not exceeded elsewhere in the Army.

There was every reason why this should be so, for in the full tide of its fortunes the duties which fell to the lot of the Corps were more comprehensive than is usually remembered.

In addition to the twin services of transport and supply there were those of remounts, barracks and the provision of the greater proportion of Army clerks.

The remount service has a history worth recalling. In July 1891 two companies were added to the establishment of the Army Service Corps for the purpose of carrying out the executive duties at the two remount depots in England and Ireland which were situated at Woolwich and Dublin respectively. These units, each of which included an Army Service Corps quartermaster, were under the Inspector-General of Remounts at the War Office and took the place of the *personnel* previously found from the cavalry and Royal Artillery. They were first shown in the Army List for September 1891 as " A " and "B" Remount Companies,* and so remained until March 1904 when an increase was sanctioned and given effect to at the end of that year in the shape of "C" and "D" Remount Companies at Lusk and Dublin.

Seven years later the four units had their nomenclature changed to "AA", "BB", "CC" and "DD" Companies respectively. As has been noted, Major-General Heath of the Corps was Director of Remounts from 1907 until 1911 when he was succeeded by Major-General Birkbeck, a cavalry officer. The new director had not been long in the post before he recommended certain changes which had the effect of diminishing the monopoly held by the Corps as regards the executive duties of the companies, but his proposal was in every way reasonable, being simply that their *personnel* should not be drawn wholly from the Horse Transport Branch but also from the cavalry and artillery. The units were to remain part and parcel of the Corps and men from other arms were to be transferred. This proposal was adopted.

The work of the Remount Department was so successful during the Great War that it would have hardly seemed necessary to have disturbed the principles of its organisation apart from the inevitable reductions. But economy from 1919 onwards dominated everything else, and it was discovered that some trifling amount could be saved by substituting civilian *personnel* for soldiers, thus joining in the then fashionable pursuit of demilitarisation. Accordingly, this measure was partially carried out—partially only because it was necessary to hold some

---

* The establishment in detail consisted for each company of:
1 Company Serjeant-Major.
1 Company Quartermaster-Serjeant.
1 Farrier Quartermaster-Serjeant.
3 Serjeants.
3 Corporals.
3 Lance-Corporals.
4 Shoeing Smiths.
50 Privates.

personnel disposable for staffing the remount depots overseas, and the civilians were under no obligation to serve outside the United Kingdom. The risk of the latter going on strike was accepted, and Woolwich remained the only depot to be staffed by soldiers—some eighty being there employed. But even this arrangement was not destined to remain long in force, for ten months later Sir Noël Birch, an artillery officer, who had in the meantime succeeded General Birkbeck, advocated the suppression of all military *personnel* and, when this policy was agreed to by all other branches concerned, presented the Transport Directorate with the *fait accompli*. Thus, without opposition, a portion of the Corps was suppressed and a civil organisation put in its place. It was admittedly a difficult question to fight because the Corps did not then control the Remount Department. It merely provided the subordinate *personnel* to do the work for the Army in general. But the precedent was highly dangerous for the structure of the Corps and it might well have been questioned where the process of demilitarisation was going to stop. There were indeed almost as good or as bad reasons for the substitution of civilian bakers and butchers in the Supply Branch on the score of economy, or, carried to its logical conclusion, the suppression of the whole Corps, as the transport and supply services could assuredly have been carried out cheaper in peace time by contract.

It might be contended, with some superficial show of logic, that the claim of the Corps in the Remount Department was no very substantial or even desirable one, especially in view of the fact that the Corps was becoming increasingly mechanical and decreasingly concerned with horses. But such contention can stand no detailed examination. The title was perhaps the best of all titles, that of possession, while the claim to continue in possession may be based upon the fact that the duties had been successfully carried out. It may be asserted that the executive duties of the Remount Department more properly belong to the Army Service Corps than to any other branch of the service, since for good and sufficient reasons the Veterinary Branch is excluded. In the first place it is purely administrative and not one which should encumber the fighting arms. Secondly the mechanical trend was common to the cavalry and artillery, and it may well be that the Army Service Corps, in the nucleus pack transport organisation maintained against the requirements of "small wars", will remain the last to keep any establishment of animals in the Army.

The executive functions of the Barrack Department had been vested in the Corps since the abolition of "control" and involved the responsibility for the allotment and equipment of quarters for the troops—other than upkeep of buildings and fixtures therein, which latter pertained to the Royal Engineers. The duties were carried out partly by military *personnel* in the shape of barrack officers and partly by civilian *personnel* in the shape of barrack wardens and labourers whose scope included the charge of what were termed "expense stores" where the necessary furniture, utensils and bedding were kept for issue to units, and the coalyards from where the fuel was distributed. It cannot be said that this prosaic task gave the officers or military clerks concerned much, if any, training for war, but at all smaller stations the duties were combined with other work, either in the nature of transport or supply or possibly both. In this way, therefore, it made for economy, while it certainly made for a stringent administration, and afforded instruction to officers in the interior economy of military institutions, very necessary in view of the valuable nature of the articles affected. It was not uncommon to find a junior officer—a subaltern or captain—charged with direct responsibility for barrack stores worth several hundred thousand pounds or more. In this direction as in others

AFTER SOUTH AFRICA

no branch of the public service obtained responsible supervision at a cheaper rate than did the Army.

In February 1905 an innovation was made as regards the administration of barrack work at the Headquarters of Commands in the United Kingdom and this consisted of the appointment of a District Barrack Officer—a retired Army Service Corps officer—to supervise under the Assistant Quartermaster-General the duties throughout the Command. This system has stood the test of time and still obtains.

It may be frankly admitted that barrack duties have always been unpopular in the Army Service Corps, because they were considered to have little bearing on the duties of the Corps in the field and moreover involved much purely office work. This sentiment was healthy enough in itself, but may yet be deemed shortsighted. For had those same duties been removed from the sphere of the Corps, a reduction of establishment would have inevitably followed, with the result that a lesser number of regular officers and military clerks would have been available on mobilisation when barrack duties were turned over to those on the retired list. In addition, there were responsible posts to be filled at the War Office in the Directorate of Quarterings, for which some practical experience of detail was obviously the best of all qualifications and would therefore naturally fall to Army Service Corps officers. They did so fall—as regards the Director and the staff officers—during the Great War, following which other interests were considered and officers, however able, yet not possessing the same qualifications, were found employment in what was in fact almost a special department of the Corps.

Finally some allusion may be made to the clerks' section which became part of the Army Service Corps during the South African War, having formerly been a separate body of staff clerks. The decision to incorporate this on the general list of the Supply Branch was a wise one, and its efficiency steadily rose. The work of the military clerk is perhaps the least spectacular in the Army, but in the case of the Corps clerks it was of a special importance, for from among them were found almost the whole of the *personnel* necessary for Staff offices and they were therefore concerned, and very vitally concerned, with the preparation and distribution of orders to the troops. At Army, Army Corps, Divisional and Brigade Headquarters, or in other words in the higher fighting formations, as well as in the administrative offices, they were engaged upon duties which demanded a high standard of intelligence and loyalty and often no little initiative. Many general and staff officers bear witness to the debt they owe to the service of their clerks, many of whom possessed a knowledge of regulations, routine orders and procedure not surpassed elsewhere in the service, and a method and accuracy that was of high import under active service conditions when even a slight error of a figure or letter might have disastrous consequences.

The training of these men fell to the Army Service Corps, and seldom has training been better justified by its ultimate results. Lance-corporals and corporals were quite early in the Great War occupying positions far above their permanent rank and in most cases with credit. From one disability the clerks' section did suffer in 1914 —and that was common to the whole Army—it was too few in numbers.

In 1906 Mr Haldane came into power as Secretary of State for War and commenced the series of reforms so pregnant for the future of the British Army, and to which Lord Haig paid so generous a tribute at the close of the Great War. The crowning achievement was the organisation of the Territorial Force, and, from the point of view of all administrative services in the Auxiliary Forces, it meant a change from chaos to ordered progress. The principles of these reforms are of common knowledge

AFTER SOUTH AFRICA

and as commonly appreciated to-day, tried out as they have been in the furnace of war, but their bearing on the Army Service Corps may be reiterated. On the 1st of April, 1908, a transport and supply service came into existence as far as the divisional formations were concerned and the cadres of this were carefully nursed and trained by their regular comrades. Little difficulty was experienced in the recruitment and officering by zealous professional men, who sacrificed much of their leisure in undergoing courses of instruction at the training establishment at Aldershot and their Saturday afternoons in riding, driving and other Army Service Corps duties at the regular depots. An admirable spirit existed in spite of certain discouragement from outside the ranks of the Army, and the fundamental secret of this lay in the facts of their close touch with the regulars and that they were identified in peace with the higher formations they were to serve in war. To each divisional transport and supply column a regular adjutant and a proportion of regular non-commissioned officer instructors were appointed.

These conditions represented a marked advance on any which had previously obtained as regards administrative troops in the Auxiliary Forces. Prior to 1908 arrangements for transport and supply in the old Volunteers had been of the sketchiest. There had existed certain Army Service Corps companies but they had never been in any satisfactory state owing rather to lack of organisation than to any other cause. Individuals who were shown as belonging to those units were also borne on the rolls of the battalion which furnished them, or in other words the battalion spared those whom the Army Service Corps company gained—a system which hardly conduced to commanding officers supplying the most suitable men.

At one time there were thirty-four volunteer infantry brigades, some of which possessed "Supply Detachments" and some of which did not; while as concerned

AFTER SOUTH AFRICA

eighteen brigades of yeomanry, there was absolutely no provision in this respect whatever.

It could not be expected that order could be brought into this administrative chaos at once. The Army Service Corps of the Territorial Force took some time to find its feet—the regular adjutants, for example, were not appointed until 1911, but for the six years preceding the Great War, it made steady and ordered progress.

Between the war in South Africa and the Great War only one opportunity of active operations and that on a modest scale was afforded the Army Service Corps. This occurred in Somaliland in 1909, when the transport and supply services were for the first time in that country undertaken by the Corps. Upon previous expeditions, the preceding one being in 1904, these duties had been in the hands of the Indian Army, although a small proportion of Army Service Corps *personnel* had taken part.

The campaign, if such word can be justifiably applied, was of no importance in itself, but it did serve to give those who took part in it some experience of desert operations and of camel transport, an experience which was usefully digested, while the practice in organising maintenance services in a country without roads and railways was not without value.

Major G. E. Pigott was appointed Director of Supplies and Transport with Captain N. G. Anderson as his assistant, the command of the troops being vested in Colonel J. E. Gough, Inspector-General of the King's African Rifles, who had under his command four battalions of the King's African Rifles and the 113th Infantry of the Indian Army, in all some three thousand men. British Somaliland, about 58,000 square miles in extent, consists of a maritime strip of arid coast, backed by a range of mountains running parallel and often intersected by inland plains. To the south there is a raised plateau with subsidiary hills lining the water drainage.

The nature of the country varies between that of a sandy desert occasionally intersected with ravines and wildernesses of thorn and scrub. In some parts it is even comparatively fertile and the climate on the whole is not unhealthy, although very hot on the coast plain. The only articles of supply produced locally are ghee, meat, vegetables and grass, so the larger proportion of requirements of the troops had to be imported. The seaport of Berbera, with very indifferent landing facilities, was the base, and inland from there the route ran south to the foot of the Sheikh Mountains, which portion was practicable for wheeled transport. Traversing the pass the route continues to Burao, some forty miles south by east of Sheikh, and nearly ninety from Berbera. From Burao on to the Ain valley at Wadamago is a further eighty miles. The first duty of the supply authorities was to collect a reserve of supplies for the force to be employed and secondly to organise the necessary transport in accordance with the operations projected. At the beginning of January 1909, there were rations available for *personnel* amounting to seven hundred, and some two hundred and fifty camels, two hundred mules and two hundred and forty ponies for only some three and a half months, but by the middle of the month this had been increased to six months for all troops in the country, and in view of the forward movement which had been planned an important supply depot was opened at Burao, where a four months' reserve was accumulated. Most of the articles were, to save delay, obtained from India.

On the 22nd of January, 1909, the 1st and 6th Battalions of the King's African Rifles stationed at Burao left for the Ain Valley, which was at that time threatened with a raid on a large scale. They carried seven days' supplies with the necessary stores on a hundred and seventy-one camels, which took them through to Wadamago, where reserves were kept up by means of a system of convoys leaving Burao every third day carrying three days' supplies. Some difficulty was experienced in getting the number of transport animals required and the rates had to be raised accordingly. Armed natives were also employed as escorts at eight annas per day on the scale of one for every twenty-five animals. Meanwhile reinforcements in the shape of the 3rd and 4th Battalions of the King's African Rifles being due in February, purchases of camels were made up to the number of seven hundred and fifty, the majority coming from Berbera, Burao and Bulhar. The acquisition of these took some little time but when completed it enabled seven days' forage and rations and two days' water being carried in the field on Government transport. On the 14th of February the last units arrived in the country, proceeding a week later to Burao, after they had been fitted out with transport: the 4th Battalion remained at Burao while the 3rd went on to join the Ain column. Thus there were now some sixteen hundred men and thirteen hundred animals, including ponies, mules and camels, to be maintained some eighty miles from the advanced base at Burao, while at the latter, including detachments therefrom, were some seven hundred men and three hundred and sixty animals—numbers which do not sound very formidable from the supply point of view, but which, bearing in mind the improvised nature of the transport formations and the reliance which had to be placed on hiring, presented circumstances requiring care and foresight.

As far as the operations were concerned, little fighting beyond small affairs between native scouts and the dervishes took place, and for six months the troops were employed on reconnaissances and in moving to areas threatened with raids. In mid-April the Ain column moved from Wadamago to the district eastwards; its reserves of supplies were accordingly raised to thirty-six days; five months later the 4th Battalion of the King's African Rifles was sent up to Wadamago and, as a consequence of all the field troops now being in the forward area, a new advanced depot was arranged for at Eildab, twenty miles east of Wadamago. It was at that time the intention to carry out some far-reaching operations, and supply arrangements were made accordingly, but owing to the refusal of the powerful Dolbahanta tribe to carry out their share in the scheme the plans did not eventuate and at the end of October the forces were concentrated at Wadamago and preparations for the evacuation of the Ain Valley put in hand. On the 18th of November all supplies in the country were ordered to be reduced to two months' and all orders for the delivery of grain and African rations cancelled; in the following month the Ain column was back at Burao, the 127th Baluchis coming out in relief of the home-going units. Activities which had lasted almost exactly a year had never at any time promised much excitement. Nevertheless they gave the transport and supply some useful practical experience in a difficult country, although it may be considered a matter of regret that there was so restricted a *personnel* to profit by it. All the fatigues and discomforts incidental to such service were involved. There were no tents with the field force except four or five for the use of the hospital, and the allowance of baggage was limited to what could be carried on the march. The labour involved by the necessity of storing water was heavy and continuous and the troops were, except during the rains, on a short allowance of water, which was in itself of very unpalatable quality. Certain points of interest may usefully be noted. The Army Service Corps was responsible for ordnance services in addition to its own, a conductor and a staff serjeant of the Army Ordnance Corps only being provided to assist. An attempt was made to use mechanical transport in the shape of a tractor which, with its crew and some trucks, was sent out in June, but this experiment proved unsuccessful and they were ordered home in October. The chief interest lay in the organisation of camel transport for columns operating in country where water was scarce, and useful information was collated by Major Pigott on this subject. An average of 3330 camels per month were hired from January to November 1909, of which one hundred and sixty-four were lost, including nine killed in action. The Somali baggage camel, of which seven thousand were afterwards employed with the Egyptian Expeditionary Force during the Great War, is a small and wiry animal, capable of prolonged exertion on scanty food and water, and used to grazing rather than grain, and requires five hours' uninterrupted grazing per day. It can carry a load of four hundred pounds, and as it cost only sixty rupees to purchase the rates at which it was hired may be deemed high.* These rates were, however, regulated strictly in accordance with the supply and, bearing in mind that they included the services of a skilled driver who was required to proceed into areas where the danger element was not negligible, were not in fact excessive. At the same time familiarity with expeditions in Somaliland brought home to those who were concerned with the maintenance of the troops the relative expense involved; and not a little of the work was involved by efforts to keep within reasonable bounds the rapacity of the Indian contractors at Berbera.

The services of the Corps were recognised in Colonel Gough's despatch by the statement that the Director of Supplies and Transport had "an exceptionally difficult task" but that "his arrangements were excellent".

* In expeditions in Somaliland during 1902–4 camels could be purchased for from 35 to 40 rupees. The 1909 rates for hiring from Berbera to Burao ranged between 7 and 9 rupees per camel.

BIBLIOGRAPHY

1. "The Army Service Corps of the Territorial Force." By Colonel P. E. F. HOBBS, C.M.G. From the *Journal of the Royal United Service Institution*, June 1914.
2. Despatch dated 9. 2. 10, by Colonel J. E. GOUGH, V.C., Inspector-General, King's African Rifles.
3. "Somaliland Operations 1909." By Major G. E. PIGOTT, D.S.O., R.A.S.C. From the *Royal Army Service Corps Quarterly*, January 1911.
4. *Somaliland*. By ANGUS HAMILTON. Hutchinson and Co. 1911.

CHAPTER II

THE EARLY DEVELOPMENT OF THE MECHANICAL TRANSPORT

ROAD mechanical transport was first used in war as far back as 1870, when the German Army employed two traction engines between Metz and Pont à Mousson for the conveyance of stores and the evacuation of wounded.

In the British service, steam traction engines had been for many years employed by the Royal Engineers, and in 1885 the driving of such vehicles formed part of the course of instruction undergone by young officers at the School of Military Engineering at Chatham. On the outbreak of the South African War, Major Templer of the King's Royal Rifle Corps, who was attached to the Royal Engineers, took out a number of traction engines driven for the most part by civilians. A base workshop was established at Cape Town, and a considerable amount of transport work was effected, especially in the nature of moving heavy engineer stores in the large towns.

There were also in South Africa during the operations two detachments of electrical engineers raised by Major Crompton, a volunteer officer, these units being equipped with portable electric lighting and searchlight sets drawn by steam tractors. The first of the detachments was taken out by Captain F. L. Lloyd, R.E., who had previously been Chief Instructor at the School of Submarine Mining at Plymouth, and the second by Major Crompton himself. Both rendered excellent service and

DEVELOPMENT OF MECHANICAL TRANSPORT

on many occasions assisted the Royal Artillery to move their heavy guns.

During this period the whole question of the use of mechanical transport for military purposes was occupying the attention of the War Office, with the result that in 1900 a Committee was set up entitled "The Mechanical Transport Committee", Captain Lloyd being appointed secretary. The first chairman was the Financial Secretary of the War Office, but he was shortly succeeded by Lord Stanley, now Lord Derby. Colonel Crompton was appointed one of the original members and Lieut.-Colonel H. C. L. Holden, R.A., joined shortly after its formation. The Committee included a President and three members, the latter consisting of representatives of the Quartermaster-General's branch, and of the departments of the Director of Fortifications and Works and of Equipment and Ordnance Stores. Power was given to add to this number and in December 1900 four sub-committees were formed representing "Experimental and Motor", "Royal Artillery", "Royal Engineers" and "Army Service Corps". Colonel C. E. Heath and Lieut.-Colonel F. T. Clayton both served on the latter.

By 1902 the *personnel* of the main Mechanical Committee included Lord Stanley, Colonels Smith and Crompton, Lieut.-Colonel Elmslie, Captain Nugent, with Colonel Wace as an associate member.

Activities may be said to have begun with the issue of a memorandum from the Adjutant-General on the 29th of November, 1900, which was passed to the Committee as an instruction. This document, in its way historic, called for consideration of the reports on the steam transport in South Africa, the extent to which mechanical transport could usefully be applied to military purposes in countries with and without good roads, and the relative cost of such transport and of other means of transport now in use. The Committee were also asked to state their recommendations as to the engines and vehicles suitable for service in the Army and the provision and organisation of the *personnel* required in each case.

The principal feature of the early deliberations was the finding that mechanical transport came within the province of the Army Service Corps rather than within that of the Royal Engineers or any other branch, and consequently it was recommended that all mechanical transport and *personnel* should be taken over. The history of the Mechanical Transport Branch of the Corps may therefore be said to have started in 1902.

Two incidents about this time deserve mention. A demand having been received from South Africa for mobile searchlights, the matter was referred to the Committee who arranged for the construction by the Wolseley Company of six mobile searchlight plants consisting of the then standard Wolseley chassis, carrying a small independent internal combustion engine and dynamo. These were fitted on solid tyres and sent out to the army in the field. A few motor cars were also purchased for experimental work and handed over to the Army Service Corps at Aldershot, which looked after them and provided them with drivers, their employment being directed by the Committee.

In the late summer of 1901 trials of lorries for military purposes were organised on a somewhat extensive scale. It having been laid down that petrol ought not to be used for such vehicles, the lorries sent to be tested were mainly steam driven, the only internal combustion engine being entered by the Milnes-Daimler Company: this ran on paraffin after having been started by petrol. The two best performers were built by Thornycroft and Foden, and these were bought and sent out to South Africa for further trial.

During the following years the Committee continued to purchase and experiment with various types of motor

MECHANICAL TRANSPORT

cars, while attention was devoted to both lorries and tractors, using internal combustion engines with petroleum as motive power. The use of cars for staff purposes was specially encouraged and on the manœuvres of 1903 and 1904 both service cars and those belonging to private individuals were employed.

It was in 1902 that Captain M. J. Mayhew suggested the formation of Motor Volunteers and, contrary to the commonly held opinion that the War Office is impervious to new ideas, the proposal was welcomed. In giving their sympathy and assistance the Mechanical Transport Committee instructed Captain Lloyd to help Captain Mayhew, and during the Army manœuvres of 1903 the Volunteers were utilised with success and had the encouragement of being inspected by Lord Roberts at Marlborough.

In 1903 the branch known as the Inspectorate of Mechanical Transport came into being, Major W. E. Donohue being appointed Chief Inspector, with the object of securing the upkeep of the growing numbers of vehicles and to act as the executive of the Committee. From this period onwards the work of the latter and the inspectorate were so closely connected that development can most easily be followed by some examination of the activities and growth of Major Donohue's department.

In 1902 at the time when the Army Service Corps took over, there existed, under the general heading of "Inspectors", officers in various branches of the service where machinery was in use, such as the Royal Artillery, Royal Engineers and Army Ordnance Department. These officers devoted their whole time to technical engineering matters and were known in the Royal Engineers as "Inspectors of Royal Engineers Machinery" and in the Royal Artillery and Ordnance Department as "Inspectors of Ordnance Machinery". Their duties were primarily to act as technical advisers and generally included keeping in touch with commercial progress and considering its relation to military requirements; preparing specifications for new material and stores; supervising and safeguarding the interests of the service in connection with the construction and purchase of machinery; advice relating to the suitability, condition and upkeep of machinery and the preparation of estimates for maintenance charges.

In order to bring the Army Service Corps Mechanical Transport into line with the other technical branches, the new Inspectorate was established in conformity with the above lines, and its head served in the dual capacity of technical adviser to the Director of Transport at the War Office and of chief technical mechanical transport officer in the Army Service Corps. For the purpose of administration, the Assistant Director of Transport at Army Headquarters was a member of the Mechanical Transport Committee. Major Donohue had on his staff two assistant inspectors, the establishment being subsequently increased to seven, although no more than five were actually appointed prior to 1914.

The first mechanical transport unit to come into existence was No. 77 Company Army Service Corps, which under the command of Brevet-Major C. E. I. McNalty was formed at Chatham in 1903. A dozen traction engines were taken over from the Royal Engineers and also one Bush car. At the same time the traction engines on charge of the engineers at Malta and Gibraltar were also transferred, being treated as portions of No. 77 Company.

Later in the same year a start was made at Aldershot and the Curragh by detachments being sent from Chatham, but it was soon found that this system was cumbersome and uneconomical, and consequently the Aldershot detachment was shortly afterwards re-organised as No. 78 Company, while the Malta group was made independent of its original parent.

MECHANICAL TRANSPORT

In such manner were the foundations of an organisation laid which, a decade and a half later, was to muster some 150,000 officers and other ranks.

The year 1904 was one of continued progress. The Committee were engaged in pursuing their experiments with tractors, the guiding principle being the use of petroleum and internal combustion engines. As a result the Hornsby-Ackroyd internal combustion tractor was produced. Certain Foden and other steam lorries were purchased and also some further motor cars, mostly Wolseleys. In addition, various members of the Committee and the Secretary visited from time to time all localities in England and on the Continent where tractor or car trials were being held or where information was received that foreign Governments were manufacturing tractors. On the executive side a new company was formed from the nucleus which had been sent to the Curragh and the Inspection Branch was transferred from Chatham to Aldershot.

Until 1905 little or no system had obtained with regard to the testing and training of recruits. A man desirous of enlisting in the Mechanical Transport Section of the Army Service Corps presented himself at the Headquarters of No. 77 Company with such credentials as he was able to obtain, and if he was considered sufficiently skilled from a technical point of view he was accepted.

On the development of adequate premises and accommodation at Aldershot between 1905 and 1906, proper testing was carried out, and the training of recruits put on a correct footing. All recruits joined there and received their preliminary training in drill and musketry. A workshop, which was set up at this time, dealt with the periodical overhaul of vehicles owned by the War Department, and was also used for the purpose of testing recruits. The latter in fact in collaboration with the permanent staff provided the labour necessary to carry out the overhauls.

A small Stores Section was instituted, but this was mainly concerned with supplying workshop requirements, for the reason that very few repairs were carried out in the companies. New vehicle parts were ordered through this section, which was directly under the control of the inspector in charge of the shop. With the increase of vehicles, however, it became necessary to keep technical records, and with the purchase of different types it was also necessary to establish a drawing office with technical *personnel* for preparation of the drawings and specifications of the new vehicles.

In 1903 too the Hornsby-Ackroyd caterpillar was inspected and reported on by the Mechanical Transport Committee with the result that the Hornsby-Ackroyd tractor which had already been introduced to the service was converted to a caterpillar, and a vehicle on the same principle but of a lighter type constructed. This event, hardly noticed at the time, marked the beginning of a new epoch in military transport which was destined to have a profound effect on the science of war.

It had now become clear that mechanical transport in one shape or another was likely to increase rapidly, and in 1906 its development was so far anticipated, that at the end of that year a scheme was evolved whereby a certain proportion was included in the mobilisation establishments of the Field Army. In this scheme provision was made whereby supplies and ammunition for one cavalry division and six divisions could be staged by mechanical transport on the assumption that by such means twice the distance as could be covered by horse transport daily could be achieved. The assumption was a modest one but even as such it made a very definite advance on any previous arrangements for maintaining a fighting force in the field.

The immediate outcome of this policy was the necessity for trained *personnel* and vehicles. In the case of the former the first step was to give the necessary instruction

MECHANICAL TRANSPORT

to serving Army Service Corps officers. A syllabus was accordingly prepared, and in 1907 Captain T. M. Hutchinson, A.S.C., who had previously commanded the unit in Ireland, and the value of whose subsequent labours can hardly be over-stated, was appointed to conduct courses at the training establishment at Aldershot. These courses also formed part of the normal curriculum for all young Army Service Corps officers joining, and from among them those who showed special aptitude for the work were selected for a further advanced course of nine months' duration. At the end of this latter a proportion was again eliminated and the best were sent as apprentices for a period of from twelve to eighteen months to certain of the great engineering firms in the country in order to obtain a sufficient grounding in general shop practice.

In the case of vehicles, arrangements were made for augmenting these on mobilisation by "earmarking" a certain number in civilian employment, a small subsidy being paid to the owners. Meanwhile efforts were made to evolve a satisfactory form of internal combustion tractor, as it was realised that the steam vehicle had several inherent shortcomings which rendered it unsuitable for general use by the transport services. At that stage, however, these efforts were unsuccessful and for the time being they were abandoned.

In other directions progress went steadily forwards. The increase of the organisation demanded that the administrative and technical headquarters should be overhauled. Regimental and purely transport matters, as distinct from mechanical, were placed apart from the Inspection Branch: the commandant of the training establishment assumed much of the work which had hitherto been carried out by the War Office: the depot company at Aldershot took over the workshops, the Inspectorate Branch confining itself to all questions of inspection.

In 1906 Major Lloyd vacated his appointment as Secretary to the Mechanical Transport Committee and was succeeded by Captain R. K. Bagnall-Wild of the Royal Engineers.

The future of mechanical transport then being assured, it was of importance to observe developments in civil life, adapting and moulding them if possible to military requirements. This phase is a noteworthy one as the well-founded maxim of accepting the "transport of the country" could not be followed, inasmuch as mechanical transport was limited in commercial use both as regards vehicles and accepted design. Neither was it practicable to manufacture and maintain vehicles wholly for military service, although some consideration had been given to this aspect. At that period, therefore, the Army was unable to follow the usual method of accepting established practices and adapting them to its use. But it did keep abreast of commercial development and at times was even ahead of it. One factor which dictated caution was that which concerned petrol supply in event of war and, since this could not be guaranteed, it was essential to test out steam vehicles and the use of paraffin in internal combustion engines. Great efforts were, in fact, made to produce a paraffin carburettor, while some £5000 was spent by Colonel Crompton in an endeavour to produce to his designs a satisfactory "long range" medium size tractor for Army purposes. Attention was also devoted to the internal combustion Thornycroft tractor. During the opening decade of the twentieth century over £30,000 was spent by the Mechanical Transport Committee on experimental work—in those days a considerable sum, yet all too small when the expensive nature of the work is considered. Although the strides that were then being made in design and construction often made models for trial out of date almost before they were completed, the initiative and enterprise shown proved of great value, and there is little

MECHANICAL TRANSPORT

doubt that the close touch maintained by the Committee and the Inspection Branch with the outside motor world was mainly responsible for the success that attended the employment of mechanical transport in the early days of the Great War. Suitable vehicles, and oils and accessories had been carefully selected and arranged for against the future.

Parallel with the foregoing activities, dealing almost entirely with steam and paraffin vehicles of the traction engine type, a watch had been kept on the progress in civil transport of the internal combustion lorry using petroleum spirit. A few lorries were bought annually from 1904 onwards, while at the same time mechanical transport companies were established to form nuclei for the formations for the field.

One of the earliest trials of the application of mechanical transport on a large scale to war purposes took place in Essex on the 18th of December, 1908, when the General Officer Commanding Eastern Command—Lieut.-General Sir Arthur Paget—arranged with the London General Omnibus Company for ninety-four of their vehicles to assist in a concentration of troops at Shoeburyness. The test was effected under service conditions over heavy roads in bad weather and was pronounced a success. Mr Haldane, then Secretary of State for War, referred to this experience when speaking in the House of Commons in March 1909 on the Army Estimates, when he indicated the provision made for additional mechanical units and a corresponding reduction in the Horse Transport Branch of the Army Service Corps. He also announced the intention of the authorities to carry out a further trial for which arrangements were made by Mr du Cros, M.P., and the executive members of the Automobile Association. This experiment subsequently took the shape of a demonstration of the possibilities of transporting rapidly from London to Hastings a battalion of Guards complete with their field equipment.

The favourable result of these and other trials, together with the reports of officers detailed to follow mechanical transport in various manœuvres both in the British and in Continental armies, led to the conclusion that the steam vehicle could be abandoned, except in certain cases for which it was peculiarly fitted, and the internal combustion engine substituted for it and employed in general use. This decision was taken at the end of 1910. It had been largely influenced by a visit paid by Colonel G. R. C. Paul, the Assistant Director of Transport at the War Office, to the French manœuvres of that year. The French were then trying out schemes for extending the radius of action of an army by supplying it with food, ammunition and other necessities from railhead by means of internal combustion lorries.

On his return from France, Colonel Paul wrote a memorandum to the Quartermaster-General describing the British system, in which steam vehicles were mainly employed, as being "archaic and a relic of the stone age".* The result was that in 1911 steam engines were eliminated in so far as the field units went and the internal combustion lorry introduced in large numbers to the Army. Details of the new organisation in its application to the maintenance of the troops in war can more properly be given in the ensuing chapter.

Right up to the outbreak of war experimental work was carried on. In July 1914 a demonstration of gun-towing was for the first time carried out, being held in the Northern Command under Colonel Earl Fitzwilliam with 30 H.P. Sheffield Simplex cars and 15-pounder guns of the West Riding Royal Horse Artillery. The idea was to repulse an imaginary enemy landing at Great Grimsby eighty miles away, the advanced ammunition party having a journey of one hundred and eighteen miles to complete before they pick up their loads and rendezvous

* In 1910 the Second Division at Aldershot had been completely mobilised and an opportunity given for trying out the steam tractors.

MECHANICAL TRANSPORT

with the guns. The average pace-running time was twenty-one miles per hour, the whole journey occupying between five and six hours as compared to fourteen hours by rail or between four and five days using horse transport. The guns were manœuvred by the cars right into the battery positions off the road, and after a critical examination by Lieut.-General Sir Herbert Plumer and his staff, were pronounced to be none the worse for their rapid transit, either as regards their sights or other component parts, or the special couplings for the cars, which themselves only took two and a half minutes to fit or dismantle. Altogether it was clearly demonstrated to be a satisfactory arrangement under the conditions naturally imposed by the limitations of a standard touring car not designed for artillery work over bad roads or shell-torn country.

Slow internal combustion tractors of the caterpillar type came into use soon after the commencement of hostilities. It had been fully realised that specialised haulage was necessary for such vehicles as guns, ammunition wagons and other transport of a technical nature which might require to leave main roads and cross soft or uneven ground, and possess in addition a wide radius of action.

With the growth of number of units, the establishment of workshops was taken in hand. The first was set up in tents during the manœuvres of 1905, and in 1909 a Base Mechanical Transport Depot with a workshop attached was formed near Bisley. The type of shop and on which department should fall the responsibility for repairs subsequently became a matter of policy and the question of the amalgamation of the Army Service Corps and Army Ordnance Department was mooted and a Committee appointed to consider the matter, the Chief Inspector of Mechanical Transport being appointed a member. The recommendations of this Committee were to the effect that, as the Army Ordnance Department had workshops of considerable size in almost all Commands, that department should undertake the overhaul as opposed to running repairs of vehicles, but that the existing Army Service Corps shops at Aldershot, Chatham, Bulford and the Curragh should not be handed over but should be retained for the purpose of carrying out the running repairs.

In making these proposals the Committee were doubtless influenced by considerations of economy, but from every other point of view shops dealing purely with mechanical transport were desirable, especially because they needed to be staffed by officers who were trained engineers, specialised in mechanical transport practice. However, under the compromise reached, Army Service Corps workshops, even if limited in scope, were definitely confirmed as part and parcel of the organisation.

The type of workshops to be employed in the field was a question which was given attention and it may be recorded that the post-war equipment and *personnel* of the mobile workshops was much the same as that originally recommended and accepted. The equipment having been settled, it had to be decided how it was to be carried, and the mode of carrying the tools altered as the type of vehicle in use altered. At first steam traction engines were in vogue, followed later by steam lorries. Then came the light tractor and subsequently the petrol lorry. The type of workshop vehicles purchased in the early stages was naturally found to be unsuitable later when lorries came to be almost universally employed. It was decided, for instance, that each company should have a mobile workshop carried on a trailer hauled by a tractor. Subsequently this was found to be insufficiently "handy" and it would undoubtedly have been the wiser course to have discarded it then and there instead of retaining it and attempting to improve its inherent defects to keep in line with vehicle development. It was not, in fact, until the Expeditionary Force was overseas

MECHANICAL TRANSPORT

that new types were brought into use. The criticism is perhaps somewhat captious, because, with only limited funds available and the period being one of transition, caution was obviously dictated.

In 1911, after the internal combustion engine had been adopted, the war establishments necessary for the new field organisation were published. They involved the provision of some fourteen hundred lorries for the Expeditionary Force, of which about nine hundred were needed to supplement those already in the service. It was clearly desirable that these vehicles should be all of one make, or at least as few makes as possible, in order to reduce the stock of spares to be supplied and to be carried with units, and to facilitate repairs and interchangeability of parts in the field. By 1911 two schemes had fructified in order to arrive at some form of standardisation, the first being known as the "Provisional Subsidy Scheme", and the second as the "Main Subsidy Scheme".

In conjunction with the automobile manufacturers a specification for a lorry was evolved which introduced a considerable amount of standardisation as between various makes and which was suitable to Army requirements. At the same time it did not restrict the individuality of designers or render their products unsuitable for the civil market. The intention was that as the vehicles were produced, a certain number of them would be acquired by the Army for its current needs and the rest when required on mobilisation should be withdrawn from the civilian owners, who had been encouraged to purchase the type required by means of an annual subsidy being paid to them. As it was foreseen that it would require several years to produce this "subsidy" type in sufficient numbers, steps had to be taken to fill in the hiatus. This was achieved by the "Provisional Subsidy Scheme" which consisted of the compilation of a register of vehicles in the hands of civilian owners who were subsidised to deliver their vehicles to the War Department on mobilisation; and, to ensure that these should be fit for service if called for, an inspection system was inaugurated, whereby each vehicle was regularly examined every six months. Owners of suitable vehicles were called upon and asked to enter the scheme. Their drivers were also approached with a view to their joining the "Special Reserve" of the Army Service Corps which was then established, for it was clearly of little practical use to provide a reserve of vehicles unless the necessary *personnel* was available to drive and maintain them when called upon. As regards the officers, a certain number of qualified automobile engineers and others in close touch with the motor engineering world were prevailed upon to take commissions, while the men were enrolled from among qualified drivers, who had no obligations laid upon them beyond that of reporting for duty in the event of the outbreak of war. For this liability they were paid an annual bounty of £4 and in the majority of cases after mobilisation remained with the lorries they drove in peace time. They were known as the Category "C" reserve and when called to the colours were paid at the rate of six shillings a day—a scale which was eventually to be the cause of some complications.

For the handling of the Subsidy Schemes Captain H. N. Foster, A.S.C., was, in 1911, appointed as "Inspector of Subsidised Transport" with his Headquarters at the War Office. He was given a staff of six assistant inspectors, who were posted to various parts of the country to carry out the six-monthly inspections and to supply data to maintain the Headquarter Registers, and he was also charged under the Director of Transport with making arrangements for the receipt and despatch of the vehicles in the event of mobilisation.

During that period much work was thrown on the branch presided over by Major Donohue by reason of new types of vehicles being produced by makers to

MECHANICAL TRANSPORT

conform to the "subsidy" requirements. As a result of road running experience, a number of defects in components of the vehicles came to light, and these defects required to be traced to cause and overcome—very often a difficult matter, as the makers' policy was not to bear the burden of experimental costs by the introduction of new models. The increase in the number of Army Service Corps companies also threw an additional burden on the Stores Section and to meet this a small extra staff of civilian storekeepers was authorised, although the rates of pay were so meagre that few suitable men were attracted. For the rest, the clerical staff came from the Supply Branch of the Corps and were therefore, as far as mechanical transport was concerned, non-technical.

Yet when all is said, looking back at the ten years which preceded the Great War, it is remarkable how much prescience and foresight was shown. From the Mechanical Transport Committee downwards the pioneers of the enterprise threw themselves into the work with faith and with enthusiasm, and Transport Corps of the Army will be the first to admit the debt owed to those who were actually outside its household and who were destined in the years of war to render services still more distinguished.

The sands in the hour glass were running low when, in the summer of 1914, arrangements were put in hand for the mobilisation, transfer overseas and maintenance overseas of the mechanical transport allotted to the Expeditionary Force. The anticipation was even more fortunate than its sponsors could have dreamed when they put their hands to this task.

It had become apparent that the numbers of subsidised vehicles would be inadequate to meet requirements after mobilisation and that ways and means of replacement quite apart from enhanced establishments must be sought. Therefore impressed vehicles of other makes and types needed to be considered, particularly in relation to the provision of spare parts. Under the "Provisional Subsidy Scheme" and impressment on mobilisation, numerous makes of vehicles could be gathered in and an arrangement was made with the Chief Inspector of Subsidised Transport whereby the types impressed would be notified to the Inspection Branch Stores before the vehicles left the country for overseas in order to maintain the provision of spares, which would otherwise have been impossible. This information required analysis, so that forms, schedules and order sheets were prepared in readiness, but as matters turned out there was insufficient time and staff before mobilisation to complete the matter, although, subsequent to mobilisation, the leeway was soon overtaken.

As regards spare parts in general, a schedule had been compiled on an "order" basis. It was decided that for every ten vehicles of a type one set of "unit components" plus smaller detail parts should be provided. The scheme followed closely the practice of the London General Omnibus Company, and the underlying principle was to remove an engine, gear box or back axle and replace by another complete and in good order, the defective item being subsequently repaired. At that time the London General Omnibus Company was in the van of progress in these matters, and the method suited their conditions of working, as all their vehicles were alike, running on good London roads and returning to the same well-ordered garage every evening.

In effect what was known as the "Ten per cent. Schedule" meant that ten out of eleven vehicles were kept on the road, and it was the most practical scheme that could be adopted at the time.

The "lay out" of a Base Mechanical Transport Depot was a further matter that had been considered and the area required had been calculated as early as 1911, being modified as ideas on the subject changed.

MECHANICAL TRANSPORT

Such, avoiding technicalities, was the general outline of what was accomplished towards the creation of a mechanical transport service prior to 1914. In view of the progress made between 1914 and 1918 it might in these times seem even leisurely. But it is usually the first stage that is the most wearisome and exacting, and it is indeed rare that the pioneers themselves reap the results of their labours. To this last condition this case was a happy exception, for those who had toiled so patiently to construct the new organisation had the satisfaction of controlling and developing it as no unimportant contribution to victory. That progress was hastened and enhanced by experience in the field was a circumstance common to all arms and branches of the service. But it may be emphasised without fear of contradiction that the foundations had been well and truly laid and that no whit of the energies and efforts that had been devoted to their consummation had been unfruitful.

The system of higher control up to the outbreak of war may now be re-stated—for there will be occasion to record at a later stage the changes brought about by the vast expansion found necessary.

Mechanical transport was controlled by the War Office Mechanical Transport Committee through the Transport Branch of the Department of the Quartermaster-General, which dealt also with questions of animal transport. The actual executive work was carried out by the various Army Service Corps Mechanical Transport Companies in Commands under the instructions of the Assistant Directors of Supplies and Transport at the Headquarters of those Commands.

It was a modest enough conception for the direction of so great a matter. That it sufficed to launch the new organisation is now a fact of history.

For purposes of comparison it is useful to glance at what had been accomplished during the same period by certain foreign armies.

As early as 1897 the French War Minister formed a Mechanical Transport Committee composed of technical officers of all arms, and from 1900 to 1905 various types of vehicles were tried. During the manœuvres in 1906 in addition to motor cars requisitioned for the use of the staff, a number of lorries were employed in carrying water.

In 1907 the Automobile Club of France, at the request of the War Office, collected forty lorries with a carrying capacity of two tons each, and these vehicles were used to convey supplies for the 18th Army Corps, when from the supply centre at Bordeaux the lorries had to traverse from sixty to ninety miles daily to reach the regiments.

The test was satisfactory, but the conditions were not those that would exist in war, for the lorries were new and consequently not likely to need repairs, while the drivers were picked men and the roads in a perfect state, neither cut up nor blocked with vehicles.

The 7th Army Corps employed three Renard trains, these consisting of a vehicle called a locomotor on which was mounted a 75 H.P. internal combustion engine which transmitted power mechanically not only to the driving wheels of the locomotor but to one pair of wheels on each of the trucks behind it. These did all that was required of them.

Trials on an extensive scale took place in 1909, the largest class examined consisting of lorries with a useful load of from two to three tons and, shortly after, the military authorities called for tenders with a view to producing a vehicle equally suitable for peace or war.

The following year a credit of £40,000 was passed by the Budget Committee for the purpose of subsidising private firms and individuals to place their vehicles at the disposal of the military authorities in the event of mobilisation.

The French organisation, as will be shown in a later chapter, differed in certain respects from the British, but generally speaking the progress made up to 1914 was about equal for the two Armies when their proportionate size is taken into consideration.

The Germans, as might have been expected, dealt with the problem in their usual thorough manner but almost regardless of expense. Premiums were paid for the most satisfactory vehicles from a military point of view. In the 1907 manœuvres both lorries and tractors were used for supply purposes and the success of the motor bicycle led to the formation of a Motor Bicycle Corps.

At the Posen siege exercises also held in 1907 sixty mechanical transport vehicles were used to convey material from Berlin. The light column consisted of lorries carrying a useful load of $1\frac{1}{2}$ tons and a certain number of road trains: the heavy column consisted of traction engines each hauling two or three wagons, the useful load for each train being $13\frac{1}{2}$ tons: there was also a tractor hauling a mobile workshop.

These trials lasted seven weeks and were very severe, but as no adequate arrangements had been made for the supply of fuel and water *en route*, many delays were experienced. The light column was, on the whole, deemed to be best, although it is interesting to note that the English traction engines used gave excellent results.

On account of the importance of ascertaining the behaviour of mechanical transport under unfavourable winter conditions, a trial had been run during November and December 1907. The roads traversed were in many cases very bad and were sometimes covered with ice. No practical conclusion was, in this case, reached, as the experiment terminated abruptly at an early stage owing to the conditions due to the melting snow on the roads.

Like the British, the German authorities collaborated with their leading lorry manufacturers to modify their standard types so as to be suitable to military requirements. The steam lorry was not manufactured in Germany to any extent. A subsidy was also paid for a lien on private vehicles, but these were liable to be called out on manœuvres when their owners were paid a fuel allowance, and the military authorities were empowered to examine them whenever they chose to do so.

The Germans also made extensive use of motor cars, trying out an armoured type at an early stage.

In their conceptions of the use of mechanical transport for conveying infantry they were ahead of the British, as was discovered early in the war, when they constantly supported their cavalry divisions with infantry in lorries, but otherwise it cannot be claimed that they had progressed farther, especially in view of the more authoritative position held by their Ministry of War.

The Austro-Hungarian Army was in no way behind the German—in fact in certain respects it might be said to have been ahead of it. By 1911 an internal combustion engine lorry had been evolved capable of carrying a load from 2 to $2\frac{1}{2}$ tons at a rate of seven miles per hour. The fuel used was benzine which—an important factor—was produced in the country. There was also a heavier type of lorry tractor, driven by a benzine motor, which carried a load of 2 tons and in addition drew two or three wagons, which together brought up the carrying capacity to 8 or 9 tons: the daily march of this vehicle was about forty miles.

The Austrian Mechanical Transport was organised in columns each carrying one day's supplies for a division, but generally speaking mechanical transport was considered more suitable for work on the lines of communication and not employed in conjunction with horse-drawn transport. The importance of establishing fuel depots, stationary and mobile repair shops and of maintaining a reserve of vehicles ready to replace casualties was fully realised.

There was a Motor Volunteer Corps organised on similar lines to the British Army Motor Reserve.

The Italian War Ministry started experiments in 1898

but up to 1907 these proved inconclusive and a waiting attitude was adopted until November 1909 when a scheme for a competition was issued. This was limited to internal combustion engine lorries of one ton and two tons carrying capacity, burning benzine, alcohol or benzol and manufactured by Italian firms. Various detailed specifications were laid down and £140,000 was charged to the 1910–11 estimates for providing up to six hundred vehicles. Largely as a result of this judicious expenditure, the Italian Army was equipped at the outbreak of war with a Fiat vehicle which rendered excellent service. Indeed their mechanical transport service was in some respects the most efficient part of their Army.

As in England and Austria, a Motor Volunteer Corps was organised, while for the purpose of manœuvres lorries were hired from civil sources.

BIBLIOGRAPHY

Notes on the Early History of Mechanical Transport to 1906. By Colonel F. L. LINDSAY LLOYD, C.M.G., C.B.E.

Mechanical Transport in the Army prior to 1914. A Note by Colonel H. N. FOSTER, C.M.G., C.B.E.

The History and Development of Mechanical Transport, R.A.S.C. Prepared from various sources by the Directorate of Supplies and Transport, War Office.

"Mechanical Transport for Military Purposes." By Captain H. R. HAYTER, A.S.C. From *The Journal of the Royal United Service Institution*, June 1910.

CHAPTER III

THE EVE OF THE GREAT WAR

For any understanding of the work of the Army Service Corps, and still more so of the success which attended its efforts in the course of the world-wide campaigns which were undertaken by the British Army from 1914 onwards, it is necessary that the main principles of its organisation should be described. It was almost exactly three years before war broke out that the organisation was re-modelled and re-cast to meet the new conditions which the general use of mechanical transport had imposed. The measures then adopted proved fully equal to modern requirements and indeed may be claimed to have anticipated them. In respect to its maintenance services, no army in Europe was better equipped.

Before directing attention to the advantages of the new system it will be well for purposes of comparison to summarise the main features of those systems which had, up to then, obtained. Road transport consisting wholly of draught or pack animals was, if the first line or regimental transport is excluded,* organised normally in three echelons for the purpose of conveying ammunition, food supplies and stores. The first echelon moved in close proximity to the fighting units for which it carried the baggage and one or sometimes even two days'

---

* This transport in the hands of units was such as was at all times required by them during fighting or normal movement and consisted of ammunition mules, water carts and a Maltese cart for medical stores, together with limbered wagons for tools, etc., and travelling kitchens.

supply of food and oats, and joined those units at the end of the march or at any rate every night. It was refilled from the echelon immediately in rear and during an advance was not expected to go back for that purpose, while, since much of its work had to be effected off the roads, it was organised for such movement. The primary duty of the second echelon was to replace the expenditure of the first, while the third or subsequent echelons were in the nature of a mobile reserve. There were, then, four to five days' supplies of foodstuffs and such quantities of ammunition as might be required for heavy fighting, mobile on wheels, thus endowing the Army with power to manœuvre with some freedom.

This system had been in vogue for many years in more or less the same form but had never received a real practical test in European war or even on manœuvres on a large scale. In 1870-1 the German armies were supposed to have mobilised complete with their transport but owing to the railways being fully occupied in moving fighting troops and their impedimenta into the areas of concentration the transport had not assumed the shape intended when the initial advance took place. Consequently recourse was necessarily had to whatever transport existed locally and vehicles of all descriptions were hurriedly pressed into the service by the field units, and the system conceived was never employed in its entirety by the armies at large.

The British system was tested up to a certain point during the South African War of 1899-1902 but it was only on the Natal side that the organisation was really given full play and there the small army was so close to the railway line that the test was of limited practical value. The Army manœuvres of 1910 however revealed, as manœuvres have a happy knack of doing, certain weaknesses in the maintenance system which appeared to render it unsuitable to the exacting demands of modern war. For it showed clearly that it would be impossible to supply the troops with fresh foodstuffs, in the form of meat and bread, owing to the time taken by their transfer from the rearmost echelon to the front, which, occupying from three to four days, rendered these commodities often unfit for consumption before they reached their destination. The organisation had been originally based on the issue of preserved supplies, and had been designed at a time when railways were scarce and their capabilities as lines of supply little understood; and before road mechanical transport existed.

It could not be calculated that for a European War the Army could subsist on preserved rations, and, as local supplies would obviously be inadequate for any large force over any long period, the transport formations would need to be organised for maintenance wholly from the rear.

Given good roads, such as might be expected in most European countries, one echelon only of comparatively fast moving mechanical transport, used as a prolongation of the railway system, could be expected to keep the first echelon of horsed supply wagons filled daily with fresh provisions at a distance of some forty miles from railhead, thus making a "turn-round" of eighty miles which could be taken as the normal maximum. Such method would enable one echelon of transport to be dispensed with and ensure a daily supply. But it provided the solutions to problems far more complex. Even when working at its maximum theoretical efficiency the disadvantages of the old system were manifest. In practice it was highly improbable whether that efficiency could generally be obtained. In the first place such an enormous mass of horses and vehicles as would be required for the large armies that might be expected to operate in modern European war would be difficult to mobilise in the concentration areas and when mobilised would be still more difficult to manœuvre. Again the armies themselves would almost certainly be formed up and move in considerable depth. There might well be some three divisions or some sixty thousand men and eighteen thousand animals on one road which would involve a distance of some forty-five miles from front to rear. Under such circumstances, in a country where food supplies were scarce and where the railway lines had been destroyed, the problem of supply would be wellnigh insoluble. At best any advance would be slow while the difficulties of a strategic retirement or change of base would involve insuperable difficulties. The many disadvantages of horse transport in itself are obvious. The horses and the large amount of *personnel* required per ton of useful load consume a relatively large percentage of the total load carried while the columns are long and vulnerable. In short the situation created by the provision of an ample scale of transport in order to render the Army in the field mobile had become such that it was almost certain to have the contrary effect to that intended. Great unwieldly bodies of animal transport in rear of the Army would fatally restrict the freedom of manœuvre of the latter, even if they were able to ensure that it did not starve or want for ammunition. The system, which many were accustomed to regard as something sacrosanct and eternal, was therefore drastically remodelled.

The transformation of the transport and supply services with which the British Expeditionary Force ultimately took the field was gradual, being spread over the years 1904 to 1912. In the former year the General Staff at the request of Colonel Clayton interested itself in a number of transport and supply problems which had been set by the Chief of the General Staff of the Fourth German Army Corps as a winter exercise for the training of officers.* Colonel Clayton followed this up in the ensuing year with an enquiry in regard to supply reserves in case of war. A Committee set up for the purpose

* *Supply Service in the Field from the point of view of the Staff in Higher Commands*, by General Von François.

addressed itself to the Admiralty to ascertain what shipping arrangements would be made in the event of mobilisation, and this naturally raised the whole question of policy as to what preparations should be made. It took some four months for an understanding between the two departments to be reached, but when a settlement had been arrived at the maintenance services of the Expeditionary Force began to take shape. The General Staff proceeded to draft the volume of Field Service Regulations dealing with organisation and administration, the supply and contracts directorates prosecuted enquiries as to sources from which foodstuffs could be obtained, while the transport directorate drew up the scales of baggage and equipment to be carried by transport in the field.

Among the various recommendations made, certain may be noted. Tender forms, fully made out for the articles of supply urgently required at the beginning of a campaign, were to be kept ready for immediate issue. Sufficient experienced Army Service Corps officers or duly qualified civilian inspectors were detailed in peace time for carrying out inspections of supplies during manufacture by the contractor, at the Supply Reserve Depot and at the ports of embarkation. Enquiries were to be addressed to the Canadian Government to ascertain the quantity of hay, grain and other commodities immediately available from time to time for shipment to Europe in the event of war.

When the first draft of the new volume of Field Service Regulations dealing with organisation and administration became available, it was at once apparent that, in spite of the great advance achieved in the matter of co-ordinating the various services of maintenance of an army in the field, the services themselves were inadequate to meet requirements. The Chief of the General Staff therefore decided to hold a War Office Test Staff Tour at which all the services for an Expeditionary

THE EVE OF THE GREAT WAR

Force landing at two base ports—Portsmouth and Dover were selected—were to carry out their functions, and for this purpose situations were provided which were in fact very similar to those which the British Expeditionary Force had eventually to meet in August 1914 including even a hasty retreat. Colonel Clayton was appointed as Quartermaster-General of the imaginary force while Generals Henry Wilson and C. E. Heath were on the Directing Staff. A number of Army Service Corps officers participated, including Colonels T. D. Foster, P. E. F. Hobbs, A. Long, Majors E. Carter and P. O. Hazelton, and Captains H. R. Hayter, W. K. Tarver, and H. F. P. Percival, in addition to representatives of the army medical and ordnance services and other administrative corps.

The results of the tour proved that much remained to be done before the transport and supply services could be regarded as perfect, and it was decided that Colonel G. R. C. Paul, who had just gone to the War Office as Assistant Director of Transport, should undertake an intensive study of the methods in force in Continental armies with a view to introducing a more modern system.

The enquiries on these lines were hardly completed when the General Staff put forward proposals for the re-organisation of the transport and supply establishments for war in such a way as to produce a material reduction of the expenditure thereon. The object of these suggestions was to make further funds available for the fighting arms, and among the outstanding features were the disbandment of twenty-four regular horse transport companies and their replacement by "special reserve" companies, and the reduction of the colour service of the horse transport *personnel* from two years to one. Past history was to be repeated in that the commissariat and transport cadres were to be eliminated as much as possible from the permanent peace establishments.

General Sir Douglas Haig as Director of Staff Duties was the sponsor of the new scheme, which Generals Clayton and Paul naturally felt it their duty to oppose, and in this opposition they were supported by the Quartermaster-General Sir Herbert Miles. The matter was referred to the Army Council and as the latter could not agree it was referred to a Committee.

Meanwhile General Paul realising certain weak points in his proposals, which then held the field, determined to recast his ideas and it was on this basis that agreement was finally reached. The General Staff expressed itself as willing to consider any further scheme which might be put to them. General Paul then submitted in December 1910 a memorandum the importance of which merits a full measure of quotation.

There can be no doubt but that our existing Supply system is obsolete.

It appears to have been originally based on the issue of preserved supplies and to have been conceived when War Establishments were intended to embody operations in all parts of the world and at the time of its inauguration Mechanical Transport was a negligible quantity and the capacity of railways as lines of supply little understood.

This system which provides for the transfer of food supplies and oats from the Advanced Supply Depot to the Mechanical Transport Section of the Park, thence to the Horse section of the Park, to the Supply and Transport Columns, to the Second Line Transport and finally to the man and horse cannot possibly be suitable for operations in Western Europe for which contingency War Establishments now alone provide.

In such a theatre of war modern ideas demand a more or less continuous provision of fresh meat and fresh bread.

The re-organization called for in the Supply system to meet present requirements demands a corresponding re-organization of the Transport system in the consideration of which full advantage should be taken of the great progress made in Mechanical Transport and of the many railway systems which exist in Western Europe.

The use of fast Mechanical Transport immediately behind the present Second Line Transport will enable fresh supplies to be conveyed rapidly from distant parts in rear, and its employment will to a very great extent relieve the present congested state of the roads immediately behind the fighting troops which is a source of much danger. To further ensure this end all driving and slaughtering of cattle has been removed from the vicinity of the troops, but it is important that units should themselves still be prepared for emergencies to kill and dress sheep or cattle.

The proposals are as follows:

(1) All fighting units to carry a reserve ration (iron ration) on the man or horse in addition to the present emergency food.
(2) Regimental Transport to consist of the First Line Transport plus water tank carts and travelling kitchens.
(3) All other Regimental Transport to be grouped by Divisions and to form units of the Army Service Corps. These A.S.C. units to be capable of division for Brigades, etc., each battalion's or other unit's baggage and equipment being as a rule carried on the same vehicles. The Supply wagons will as now carry one complete day's supplies and forage plus an extra grocery ration. Meat (fresh, refrigerated or frozen) will be carried in specially constructed meat wagons (horsed).
(4) The Supply wagons of the above A.S.C. units to be replenished daily from the railway by Mechanical Transport convoys of fast motor lorries. The carrying capacity of motor lorries for the Cavalry and Army Troops to be 30 cwt. and for all other formations 3 tons.
(5) The motor lorries and light tractors required to complete the numbers necessary for mobilization to be obtained by means of a Subsidy Scheme.
(6) Special motor lorries or horse-drawn vehicles to be built for the conveyance of fresh meat which will be carried in quarters suspended from the roof of the vehicle.
(7) The driving and slaughtering of cattle and sheep to be removed from the vicinity of the troops.
(8) Field Bakeries and Field Butcheries to be established on the railway line and capable of turning out daily 22,500 rations of fresh bread or fresh meat.
(9) All other supplies to be sent by rail from the Main Supply Depot to the Regulating station, whence they will be forwarded daily to the Railway Refilling point, to which point the fresh bread and meat will also be sent.

(10) Separate Supply Columns and Parks to be provided for the Cavalry Division and for Army Troops.

(11) Exploiting Detachments have been added to the Train of Brigades and other formations. These consist of one officer, and six to eight other ranks mounted on bicycles whose duty it will be to proceed whenever practicable with the Advanced Guard and obtain such Supplies as hay, fuel, wood, and fresh vegetables. They are also available for general requisitioning duties.

(12) Six reserve convoys (horsed) capable of carrying two days preserved rations for the whole force to move in rear of the fighting troops at least thirty miles behind and in such a position as not to interfere with the free passage of the Mechanical Transport. These reserve convoys are considered necessary in the event of Railway or Mechanical Transport not being available from unforeseen causes such as abnormal weather, heavy floods and snow. This horse transport will also furnish immediate replacement of any heavy casualties at the front when time does not admit of replacement from the Transport Depots.

(13) The whole of the Divisional Ammunition Column to be converted into Mechanical Transport Ammunition Parks.

(14) The system of demanding supplies will be as follows: General Head Quarters will telegraph to the Representative of the Inspector General of Communications at the Regulating Station every afternoon stating the time and place that the supplies for each Division or other formation should arrive at certain rendezvous points on the following day. The Inspector General of Communications will use any Railway Refilling points which may seem best to him, but the distance to the rendezvous should not exceed forty miles. On the arrival of the motor lorries at the various rendezvous they will be met by Staff Officers from General Head Quarters, who will direct them to the refilling points for the various Divisions, etc. These refilling points should not be more than seven miles further on. After refilling the horsed supply wagons at the refilling points, the Mechanical Transport will return to the next day's Railway Refilling point.

The advantages claimed for the re-organization of the Supply and Transport Services in the field are as follows:

(a) Increased mobility of the Expeditionary Force generally.

(b) Clearance of roads in rear of the fighting troops.
(c) Regimental Transport officers, Brigade Transport officers and Divisional Baggage masters are no longer required from the establishment of fighting units.
(d) Substitution of fast moving motor lorries carrying one day's supplies only for the present slow and cumbersome Transport and Supply Parks.
(e) Abolition of the present Transport and Supply columns (horsed) carrying one day's supplies.
(f) Present Second Line Transport controlled by specially trained Transport officers of the Army Service Corps (the drivers are already provided by that Corps).
(g) Proper organization for exploiting local resources.
(h) Delays in refilling obviated.
(i) Reduction of A.S.C. *personnel* required on mobilization.
(j) Reduction of horses required for Transport in the field.
(k) Provision of good and regular facilities for evacuating sick and wounded.
(l) Driving and slaughtering of cattle removed from the vicinity of the troops.

The moment for such re-modelling was particularly apt. Past experience had shown conclusively that, to provide transport on the scale required for war, recourse must be had to that type generally in use by the civil community in peace. In this respect in relation to the projected reforms Great Britain was in a happy position for here more than in any other country in Europe had mechanical transport driven by the internal combustion engine been adopted for commercial employment. There was no question but that lorries would be available on mobilisation and could be obtained with ease and it remained only to standardise such portion as would be required by the Army; for it could not be expected that those in ordinary use would altogether meet military requirements, although they could as a temporary expedient be made to serve. The subsidy scheme was therefore introduced, by which means the nine hundred vehicles needed to complete the Expeditionary Force of one cavalry and six infantry divisions conformed

THE EVE OF THE GREAT WAR

to certain specifications and were kept in running order.

As has been shown, mechanical transport in so far as the Army Service Corps was concerned started in 1902 but was given five years to develop and did not appear in war establishments until 1907-8. In these establishments mechanical transport had been introduced by making two sections of the Transport and Supply Park (third line transport), originally consisting of eighty horsed general service wagons, into mechanical transport sections consisting of heavy traction engines, seven to each section.

In War Establishments the words "Expeditionary Force" were for the first time printed on the cover and gave the first definite idea as to the use of the force, viz. in a civilised country with a temperate climate.

The new organisation thus left untouched First Line or regimental transport, and the Second Line transport or "Divisional Train", to give the new nomenclature, and the Divisional Ammunition Column, since both forms were liable to work off the roads for which no mechanical vehicle was then adapted or even in sight. The whole of the echelons in rear were swept away and replaced by two mechanical transport companies for each division, the one to carry supplies and stores to the divisional train and the other to carry ammunition to the divisional ammunition column. In connection with this last formation a certain anomaly was maintained in that it remained an artillery and not an Army Service Corps unit. The reasons for this were that it enabled the ammunition supply direct to the troops who required it to be immediately in the hands of the greatest users, that is the artillery themselves, while, moreover, the unit provided a useful reserve of *personnel* and horses in close proximity to the batteries.

There was a certain hesitation, perhaps very natural at that time before mechanical transport had fully proved

THE EVE OF THE GREAT WAR

itself, to trust unreservedly to it being able at all times to fulfil the functions designated for it. And it was therefore held to be desirable as a margin of safety to have mobile a two days' reserve of preserved food and of grain carried in horsed transport. Since mobile warfare was envisaged the principle was sound, even had no doubts existed as to the working of the mechanical transport. The supply system was based on the desideratum of providing fresh meat and bread daily, while the individual soldier carried only one reserve ration on his person. If for any reason this ration was required to be used, there was no immediate means of replacing it, unless it could be obtained from some movable magazine. There was, however, a far more important use to which the bulk of these preserved rations might be put, for the time of their consumption would probably be either after a general engagement, when a forward movement in pursuit would be better carried out if extra preserved rations were available for issue to men or horses, or when it was necessary to make a sudden movement to a flank involving a change of the line of communication.

The static conditions which obtained for the longer part of the time in the main theatre of the Great War naturally modified the whole *raison d'être* of the reserve parks.

The more evident advantages of the re-organisation which has been described in detail above may be re-emphasised as "the speeding up" of the whole movement of the Army in the field owing to greater certainty and rapidity of supply: the clearance of roads in rear of the fighting troops; and a large reduction of the number of Army Service Corps *personnel* and horses required on mobilisation. And these were in themselves substantial enough. The first two are of special import because they mark a considered and determined effort to attain real mobility and freedom of manœuvre, which since Napoleonic days, when armies lived to a great extent on the country, had been conspicuous by its absence. That the British Army should give a lead in this matter was only to be expected since more than any other in Europe it needed to seek the highest degree of mobility in order to counterbalance its numerical inferiority. It is significant that the initial steps were taken in the direction of the transport and supply services.

Once the new system had been determined upon, the necessary steps were taken to form the cadres of mechanical transport units required on mobilisation by the Expeditionary Force. These consisted of eight supply columns of which one was for the cavalry division and one for Army troops and eight ammunition parks to correspond; three depot companies, one for the home base, one for the base overseas and one for any advanced base overseas. Much consideration had been given previously as to whether steam or internal combustion engine vehicles would be adopted, and in the earlier stages the former were contemplated. But the rapid strides made by the petrol-driven forms of transport decided the matter in favour of the latter before the new organisation was finally adopted. The carrying capacity of lorries allotted to the cavalry and Army troops was 30 cwt. and for all other formations 3 tons.

The practical working of the system introduced may most clearly be shown in diagrammatic form which explains itself. The plan on page 81 shows the method in so far as supplies were concerned. For ammunition the principles were similar except that as already noted the Divisional Ammunition Column, which dealt with ammunition for the division as the divisional train did for supplies, was an artillery unit.

The general result of these dispositions was to relieve the Divisional General of a responsibility and anxiety which under the previous system could not fail to affect the arrangements for the movements of his command.

THE EVE OF THE GREAT WAR

On the other hand the functions of the lines of communication were modified by reason of the fact that communications were no longer lines terminating at a well-defined point or points on a railway system, but were extended on a more elastic basis to road points varying day by day and known as "rendezvous" between which and "railhead" the mechanical transport formed the link. Consequently on the staff of the lines of communication devolved measures of protection of a more extended character than was formerly the case.

To a limited extent the new system was tried out during the manœuvres of 1912, when, from a purely regimental point of view, the Army Service Corps gained valuable experience, but for the first time in the history of the Army the scheme arranged for the Army exercise of 1913 rendered possible a complete test of the transport and supply system. The scheme for the manœuvres was an eminently practical one, designed to afford a trial of the working of General Headquarters at war establishments: an approach march of one cavalry division and two armies, each of two divisions, marching on one road with the supply of the above force—the supply services being confined to the same roads as those on which the troops marched. The various movements comprised an advanced guard action, deployment of one force for an attack on an entrenched position, the organisation of the subsequent pursuit and the breaking off of that pursuit followed by a sudden change of direction. To these main movements the services of maintenance had to conform as an integral part of the forces engaged which numbered some forty-two thousand men and fourteen thousand animals. For all practical purposes these services of maintenance resolved themselves into matters of supplies and transport. Questions of ammunition were not involved and the procedure as regards medical services was necessarily improvised. Nevertheless valuable lessons were gained, especially as regards co-operation between the staffs of the various formations and the executive officers of the divisional trains, and in the practice of moving large masses of transport in congested areas, while the fact that there were two divisions marching on one road furnished material for instruction relating to the selection of the "rendezvous" and "refilling" points. It was well that this was so for it was at the same time the first and last opportunity that the Regular Army was to get of familiarising itself with the re-organisation before the Great War. As a result of the experiences obtained an important modification was made. The horsed cavalry divisional train was abolished and the small organisation known as Headquarters Cavalry Divisional Army Service Corps consisting only of four officers and twenty-two other ranks substituted. Thus between the first line transport of units and the mechanical transport of the supply column the horsed echelon of second line transport disappeared. This link was made good in so far as supplies were concerned by two mechanical transport companies being allotted to the supply column instead of one as previously. The radius of action of supplies from railhead was thus greatly enhanced. The baggage portion of the divisional train was included in the first line transport of units. Each mechanical transport company delivered to the troops direct in turn, working from railhead. The cavalry division might normally be expected to be situated in advance—perhaps even some distance—of the remainder of the force, though it might well have to use the same railhead. Therefore its supply column would have a much farther distance to go each day from the ordinary divisional supply column, and it was quite conceivable that with only one mechanical unit the cavalry might be without food for a day. Again delay might occur before the supply column could discharge its supplies and return to railhead owing to difficulty of locating the units of the cavalry division. These contingencies were exposed during the Army exercises of 1913 and in consequence the necessary change was embodied in the War Establishments published at the beginning of 1914. Army corps and General Headquarters troops which in the war establishments of 1914 were of comparatively modest dimensions were provided for by mechanical transport units in the shape of corps troops and General Headquarters troops supply columns. No horsed echelon was interposed, as it was assumed that these troops would normally be near railhead, while if attached to divisions they could be maintained through an increase of the divisional transport formations.

Such then were the reforms which were introduced in the Army Service Corps principal field formations prior to the Great War. They had only been completed and tested just in time; but they brought the maintenance organisation for the field Army abreast of all modern conditions. They were, moreover, susceptible of adaptation to all sorts and conditions of warfare as was subsequently proved in practice.

After General Paul and his associates had laid down the framework of the maintenance arrangements for the Expeditionary Force, the various administrative branches of the Army occupied themselves with the details of the scheme. In connection with those appertaining to supply the chief credit belongs to Colonel S. S. Long, whose services during the War as Director of Transport and Supplies there will be occasion to recall in a later chapter. In his task he was ably assisted by Major W. K. Tarver and Captain W. H. P. Law.

Colonel Long took charge of the Supply Reserve Depot at Woolwich in July, 1909, having previously been Commandant of the Army Service Corps Training Establishment at Aldershot.

Under the old arrangements in force, before the reorganisation of the transport and supply services was taken in hand, a bakery company, field butchery and five depot units of supply were to be mobilised for every division which took the field, whilst supply for thirty days' requirements of the Expeditionary Force in preserved meat, biscuits, medical comforts, compressed forage and hay was held at the Supply Reserve Depot. It had been arranged that as soon as mobilisation was ordered the Supply Reserve Depot would at once despatch priority telegrams to contractors and others to submit tenders for further requirements, while as regards meat it was proposed that live cattle should be purchased and shipped to the Continent, and the whole scheme presupposed that, in the event of war, conditions in England would be more or less normal.

So far as calling up the Territorial Army and the formation of any additional bodies of troops was concerned, it was taken for granted that they would be fed and maintained under the same arrangements as existed during peace time, namely, by means of contractors for the supply of the necessary bread and meat, their grocery rations being obtained through the contractors for their regimental institutes.

Based on these premises the supply instructions covering the mobilisation of the Expeditionary Force only consisted of some dozen typewritten foolscap pages.

Some few months after taking up his duties at the Supply Reserve Depot Colonel Long, after a study of the position, considered that the arrangements in force were inadequate. He therefore made certain suggestions which might hasten the flow of supplies generally. He then addressed himself to the question of bread and meat. In a memorandum to the War Office, he pointed out that although at the outbreak of the War it might be possible to obtain sufficient live cattle for the maintenance of an army in the field, the supply would quickly give out, the price of meat become enormous, and that the system was neither feasible nor practicable, although it obtained in all other countries.

THE EVE OF THE GREAT WAR

He proposed that instead, at the base or bases selected abroad, should be held a frozen meat ship which would act as the Base Meat Depot and from which all the requirements of the fighting troops could be met, the daily requirements being despatched per rail and road to the fighting troops in front.

These suggestions met with some opposition in the War Office, it being held that the meat would not keep beyond a day or two if taken from cold storage; while the Finance Branch based their objections on the cost which would be incurred owing to the heavy demurrage.

The first of these objections was disproved by a simple test made on manœuvres, while the second only needed a small calculation to show its inaccuracy. The demurrage on a ship was only £100 to £150 a day and even were she kept three months, this would only add $\frac{1}{4}d$. per pound to the price of the meat; whereas such meat if supplied to the troops by means of live cattle would cost the country three or four times the price of frozen.

After lengthy arguments, therefore, the system was adopted and the War Office became direct purchasers; the contractor was eliminated and the meat supply satisfactorily ensured.

The bread question was then taken in hand. It was proposed that the bakery companies should be located at the base or bases or at convenient spots on the lines of communication: the bread as baked and cooled was then to be packed in what were known in the trade as "offal sacks", cheap, loosely woven, jute sacks, which were used in the butchering trade for packing offals in for despatch to factories which deal with such commodities, the sacks being only used once and purchasable at that time on the market at 4s. per dozen. Experiments showed that each of these offal sacks would hold fifty $2\frac{1}{2}$ lb. loaves, equal to a hundred men's rations, ten sacks being required for the bread supply of a battalion, and therefore easily and expeditiously handled.

THE EVE OF THE GREAT WAR

Here again objections were raised on the ground that this system would be costly and wasteful. As in the case of the meat therefore an experiment was tried on manœuvres, the bread being sent from Aldershot direct, in lieu of a bakery unit being sent to the manœuvre area. The trial proved that this method was more economical and efficient and it was accordingly adopted, a reserve of sacks being sanctioned for the Supply Reserve Depot to meet initial requirements.

By 1912 the scheme for the transport and supply services of the Expeditionary Force was well advanced. One of the English ports was specially earmarked as a Home Base Supply Port from which all the supplies required for the Army should be despatched; this port was to be kept entirely independent of those used for the despatch of troops and other war requirements. After some discussion, Newhaven was earmarked for the above purpose. It was then suggested that the requirements of the Expeditionary Force should be met by direct War Office contract, and that arrangements should be worked out for everything to be bought direct from manufacturers or on the open market, all agents, middlemen and contractors overseas being eliminated.

At the same time careful instructions were drawn up in connection with supplies for the Expeditionary Force, from the Director of Supplies of that Force down to the officer in charge of any depot, and even to orders and instructions to a ganger in charge of a gang of labourers.

These were all carefully filed in portfolios so that they could be issued at once to everyone affected.

At this time Colonel Long had interviews with all the railway officials concerned, and arranged with them as to what goods yards would be used in London, the quantities of rolling stock which would be necessary to meet requirements and other details.

It will thus be seen that by the end of 1912, so far as the Expeditionary Force was concerned, the supply arrangements were well forward and that it was possible for the necessary preliminary supplies to be on rail and pouring down towards Newhaven ready for shipment overseas even before the troops themselves were ready to take the field.

On the 1st of January, 1913, on the retirement of Brig.-General Bourcicault, Brig.-General Long took up the duties of Director of Supplies at the War Office, and shortly afterwards assumed also the duties of Director of Quarterings.

The new supply scheme for the Expeditionary Force being then practically completed, he turned his attention to the question of supply requirements for home defence should a national emergency arise.

As already pointed out, in working out the requirements for the Expeditionary Force, the Supply Directorate had the whole-hearted support and assistance of General Wilson, the Director of Operations, whose branch had however nothing to do with home defence, the responsibility therefor resting with the Director of Military Training.

As to what was likely to happen in the event of a general mobilisation as far as foodstuffs were concerned, the details of the scheme had not been completed. Generally every Command was expected to enter into the necessary local contracts for the supply of bread and meat, while regimental arrangements were to be made by units for the necessary groceries. It had been pointed out that while under the existing system in peace time the food requirements for every regimental depot or small detachment throughout the country were met by means of local contracts, in an immense number of instances the contractors were either butchers or bakers in a comparatively small way of business, and were in a position to carry out quite easily such small contracts for the supply of anything from fifty to a hundred men; but that on mobilisation quite a different state of affairs was

THE EVE OF THE GREAT WAR

bound to occur. Depots would probably expand with great rapidity from a comparatively small number to many hundreds, so that there was a great danger that the contractor would not be able to meet requirements which, after all, had never been contemplated. Also very possibly owing to rising prices he would default in his contract. Then again, as all contracts to be made were local ones, there would be an immense number of contractors all in competition with each other, and with Commands equally in competition. The great food magazines, such as those of frozen and refrigerated meat, and flour, were not spread evenly throughout the country, but located in certain large centres, so that the country would find that not only were General Officers in Command in competition with each other in making contracts for the supply to the troops under their command, but there would be at the same time a further competition of naval purchasers, and last, but most important of all, the great central purchasing by the War Office for the Expeditionary Force. This would undoubtedly react upon the general markets, and prices would be bound to soar in all directions, owing to contractors and speculators buying largely to sell again on a rising market, whilst importers and those holding stocks would still further complicate and embarrass the situation by holding on to their stocks when it was obvious that by so doing their profits were bound to be enormously increased.

A scheme was therefore worked out under which it was proposed that the instant that mobilisation was ordered all peace contracts in existence should cease and that the War Office should become entirely responsible for the feeding of both the Expeditionary Force and all troops in the United Kingdom. It was decided that, in addition to the great base depots which had already been designed at London, Bristol and Liverpool, an additional number of depots should be earmarked throughout the country—Glasgow, Leeds, Northampton, Reading and

Dublin. These five great depots were to be carefully surveyed during peace time, their exact position and size noted, and an agreement made with the railways as to what additional railway sidings should be laid if the necessity arose; the amount of the local cold storage or other buildings which would be required was to be noted, so that they could be either requisitioned or hired immediately the necessity arose. The plan was that the instant mobilisation was ordered the officers in command of the necessary staff required for these depots, who would be previously earmarked, would come to the War Office, receive their boxes of documents and instructions which had previously been drawn up and then proceed direct to their depot and put the scheme in force. In the meantime, the Contract Branch at the War Office, being in possession of all the details of the requirements of each depot, would make the necessary direct purchases and arrangements for immediate despatch to all depots.

It was anticipated that before the depot was in possession of its requirements and had got into smooth running order, a week would elapse. General Long's proposal was that during this interregnum between the time mobilisation was ordered and the depot was in a position to feed the whole of the troops based upon it, every officer commanding a unit should be authorised to make the best regimental arrangements he could for the local rationing of officers and men and animals, charging in his pay lists 1s. 9d. for every man and 2s. per diem for every horse. He pointed out that by means of his scheme it was possible to move at a moment's notice troops in any direction desired, or to concentrate them in large bodies at any particular point without trouble or confusion, as under the plan rations would be always available, the essence of the scheme being that each depot was always to hold a reserve of rations sufficient for the supply of a definite number of troops for one month.

Owing to the shortage of Army Service Corps officers, a number of those retired were earmarked to take charge of the various depots, and directly after the despatch of the general instructions, these officers were summoned to a conference at the War Office in order that General Long might personally explain to them all exactly what their duties would be. It is interesting to note that these officers assembled at the War Office only about one week before the 4th of August, 1914. With the declaration of war, all this work came to fruition. The Expeditionary Force left England absolutely to programme; the first soldier to land in France was an Army Service Corps officer, Captain C. E. Terry, in command of the supply detachment for the first overseas base, and the ships bearing supplies were being unloaded actually before the arrival of troops. Similarly the great main supply depots at home came into being, and within a few days again the mobilised territorials and reservists were being fed and maintained without confusion or loss.

During the first few days of that momentous period the transport and supply directorate, like the Prussian War Minister von Roon in 1870, had little to do but to watch and see its schemes come into operation, working smoothly as they did with practically no material alterations or amendments from the start to the finish of the Great War.

In the year 1913 some experiments were made on Salisbury Plain as to the food values of certain commodities. Somewhat similar experiments had a short time previously been carried out in the United States. A Committee then assembled at the War Office, consisting of medical authorities, the Director of Supplies, a representative of the Adjutant-General's Department and a finance representative, for the purpose of ascertaining what would be the best balanced ration for troops on active service, and also for an emergency ration. As regards the latter, it was agreed that the then approved emergency ration consisting of some 12 oz. of chocolate was not satisfactory, and instead, it was approved that for an emergency ration every soldier should carry a small 1 lb. tin of preserved meat, 1 lb. of small biscuits tied up in a little bag, and a packet containing a grocery ration of sugar, salt and tea. The approved active service ration for a soldier during the South African War and subsequently, had been 1¼ lb. of bread or 1 lb. of biscuits, ¾ lb. of preserved meat or 1 lb. of fresh meat, 3 oz. of sugar, 4 oz. of jam, ⅙ oz. of pepper, with 2 oz. dried vegetables or fresh vegetables in lieu when available.

There had always been complaints that, although this ration seems a good one, it was insufficient. The real cause probably was not that it was insufficient, but that it lacked fats. The Committee assembled at the War Office, and, with the evidence of the experiments which had been carried out before them, came to the conclusion and recommended that the ration should remain as it was, but that to it should be added 3 oz. of cheese and 4 oz. of bacon, thus providing the required fats. This was the ration which was approved for issue when the War broke out, and which, as a matter of fact *was* issued, although later on, owing to its excellence and its being almost invariably forthcoming, the Authorities were able to cut it down slightly, particularly for those troops not strenuously employed.

It will now be apposite to give some account of the Supply Reserve Depot at Woolwich. This organisation, which at all times, in view of the widely disseminated situation of the British Army, was an important one, was destined to play a basic part in relation to supplies for the great armies which took the field between 1914 and 1918, and therefore demands that some account of its origin and history be inserted.

The genesis of the depot went back as far as 1878 when the need for a reserve of foodstuffs both for the *personnel* and animals of the Army was felt. Previous shipments of supplies from home for military forces overseas had been made by the Admiralty and the Ordnance Department—shipments of flour, salt beef, salt pork, peas, chocolate, sugar, beer, rum, hay and corn having been made by the former, and lamp oils, cotton wicks and coals by the latter. It is not without interest to record the destinations of these articles marked for "Army Service" in the year 1835. Gambia, Sierra Leone, Gold Coast, Bahamas, Bermuda, China, Cape of Good Hope, Gibraltar, Honduras, Hudson Bay, Ionian Isles, Jamaica, Malta, Mauritius, New Zealand, Newfoundland, New South Wales, Nova Scotia, St Helena, Van Diemen's Land, South Australia, Western Australia, Windward and Leeward Islands and Colonies, which would seem to indicate that the British Army was far more scattered over the face of the globe than it is to-day. Some tragedies are envisaged by a perusal of old records. In January 1836, the ship *Elphinstone* sailed for Van Diemen's Land with 2000 gallons of rum to replace a similar quantity lost on the *George the Third*: while the record of a shipment of salt pork to Antigua in November 1836 is completed with the note: "This vessel was totally wrecked near Weymouth on November 28th 1838". The first bulk shipment made to the Crimea was by the transport *Hope* which sailed from Deptford in March 1854 with a cargo of biscuit, barley, rice, salt meat, sugar, tea, cocoa, coffee, milk, rum, potatoes and chocolate. This ship was followed a week later by the *Alcides* which set out for the seat of war with the curious freight of some 60,000 gallons of porter and 2700 of ale.

A system of sending out provisions from a fixed military centre at home being recognised by 1878, small quantities of a few of the commodities required on mobilisation were that year placed in reserve in Woolwich Dockyard under the control of the senior commissariat officer of the Woolwich garrison. The department

THE EVE OF THE GREAT WAR

thus formed was named "The Commissariat Reserve Stores" and Lieutenant and Commissary J. Steele with a small staff was placed in direct charge. The utility of this organisation was quickly proved in the Egyptian campaigns of 1880 and 1882 and it was accordingly decided to enlarge it. By 1888 it had come to be considered of such importance that an officer of the Commissariat and Transport Staff, Commissary-General Robinson, graded as a Deputy Adjutant-General, was appointed to its control. At that period the depot was established as the supply centre for any expeditionary forces overseas and garrisons abroad generally, and its reserves were regularly turned over by issues to the troops at home. The general idea was to maintain stocks of those articles not immediately available from trade sources on emergency by reason of their not being common in civil use or because they were required in a special form of packing by the Army.

In 1899, when Colonel W. Dunne was in charge, it was decided to despatch to South Africa a reserve of three months' supplies for the force sent out, and the figures give some idea of the needs of the comparatively small army provided for at the opening stages of the campaign. There were included 4000 tons each of preserved meat, biscuit and flour, 1000 tons of jam, 750 tons of sugar, 400 tons of compressed vegetables, 110 tons of salt, 80 tons of coffee and 40 tons of tea, with 35,000 tons each of oats and hay, which seemed formidable enough figures at that time but which were destined to shrink into insignificance as compared with those of fifteen years later. The receipt, issue and despatch of the bulk of these was made through the Supply Reserve Depot, where a large proportion of the supplies received from contractors were repacked. During the period of the South African War the output averaged some 350 tons a day.

In 1903 the appointment of the officer in charge was made, that of Assistant Director of Supplies, Colonel

A. W. Collard being the first to hold it. He was succeeded by Colonel S. H. Winter in 1906 and three years later, as already shown, Colonel S. S. Long filled the post. Under the direction of these officers, and especially of the last, the depot reached a high stage of scientific organisation. With the establishment of the Expeditionary Force under the Haldane reforms it was required to make provision for a total of 160,000 men and 50,000 animals for a period of thirty days and as matters eventuated there seldom had been a wiser measure of foresight in the annals of British military administration.

The obvious difficulties were to combine the maintenance of these reserves with the necessary economy. In peace time the soldier's daily ration at home stations consisted simply of 1 lb. of bread and $\frac{3}{4}$ lb. of meat, while the officers received no rations at all. On mobilisation both were wholly fed by the Army Service Corps. On the other hand, in normal peace times, groceries were issued to troops abroad: these, however, were in such small quantities that they did not provide sufficient turnover for large reserves. The situation was met by a reserve of cases, sacks and other forms of packing being kept ready for filling at short notice. These articles were all marked with a green shamrock, which was then the identity mark of the Supply Reserve Depot. Preserved meat, which by reason of expense and also because it was not desirable to issue it too frequently to the troops in peace time, was "turned over" under what was known as the Admiralty system. Under this arrangement a three years' contract was placed for three equal annual bulk deliveries. The first of these deliveries was held in the depot for one year and then withdrawn by the contractors and replaced with newly canned meat; the annual withdrawal and replacement was repeated twice, the third delivery being held for reserve and issue in the ordinary way. Hay, by reason of its bulk and the consequent expense of moving it, gave rise to another difficulty. This was met by compressing. Of interest in the turnover of hay were issues made to H.M.S. *Ascension* as the Isle of Ascension was shown on the Navy List, these being required for the cattle held for milk and slaughter.

Reserves of all supplies held were augmented in 1905 and again in 1911, when the former figures were almost doubled. Yet even then the latter did not fully meet the requirements of the Expeditionary Force because of the impracticability of turnover, and detailed arrangements were therefore made for the balance by emergency contracts through brokers and by direct purchase on the market.

In 1912 with its rising importance the administrative control of the depot was transferred to the supply directorate at the War Office and it was at this time that the attention of Colonel Long was drawn to the suitability of the site of the Deptford foreign cattle market for use in event of war when Woolwich Dockyard was likely to prove inadequate. With its river frontage of over 1000 feet, its 32 acres of covered storage and its proximity to the principal victualling depot of the Royal Navy at the Victoria Dock, it was an ideal situation and arrangements were accordingly made to explore all its possibilities and definitely earmark it for use in war, especially as the Deptford cattle trade was in a state of dissolution and the market was only being used as a storehouse by the City of London. This historic spot, where Peter the Great had once worked, was actually taken over seven weeks after the outbreak of war but was not purchased by the War Office until after the close of hostilities.

On mobilisation in 1914 the staff of the depot at Woolwich Dockyard consisted of three officers of the Army Service Corps and thirty-five civilian subordinates, with casual labour which averaged some eighty men a day.

The eve of the Great War is an apt occasion to recall in brief the existence of the Army Service Corps of the

THE EVE OF THE GREAT WAR

Dominions, which, modelled on that of the Imperial service, were to play a proportionately equal part in France, the Dardanelles, Egypt and East Africa. If distinctive mention is not made of these when the operations come to be described later it is because their activities were so intimately fused with those of the parent body that to all intents and purposes they were one and indivisible. There is one exception to this condition, and this lies in the campaign which was conducted in German South-West Africa in 1915, which, except for the presence of some artillery and armoured cars, was conducted entirely by the Union of South Africa under the leadership of General Botha. Some short account of these successful operations will be given at a later stage.

The Army Service Corps of the Dominion of Canada had been formed as a result of experiences in the South African War. Colonel Lyons Biggar was the officer who was directly responsible for its birth by organising in 1900 companies at Kingston, Toronto, Guelph, Ottawa, Hamilton, Montreal, Sherbrooke, Quebec, St John (New Brunswick), Winnipeg and Kentville (Nova Scotia). These units formed portion of the Canadian Militia, for which they carried out the transport and supply services during the period of twelve days' annual training.

The Army Service Corps of the Permanent Forces was not authorised until 1903 and the following year the first detachment was formed by Captain Dodge at Kingston. It was a modest beginning, for only one officer and fourteen other ranks were included but when shortly afterwards Halifax was taken over by the Dominion authorities this number was doubled. By 1906 the strength had increased to fifty, which made provision for three officers including a major, and shortly afterwards a fixed establishment was laid down which included thirteen officers with a Lieut.-Colonel as the senior one and one hundred and fifty-one other ranks. The Corps was scattered in small detachments all over the Canadian Dominion where troops of the Permanent Forces were stationed and, in so far as its numbers allowed, it carried out precisely the same duties as appertained to the Army Service Corps of the British service, including the responsibility for training the second line units of its own branch. From this small nucleus developed the numerous and powerful body, which so efficiently carried out the maintenance services of the Canadian Expeditionary Force in the field in France and, as in the case of similar Corps in the sister Dominions, the fact that its methods were based on those of the Imperial Army made for smooth and harmonious working.

The Australian Army Service Corps was on somewhat more ambitious lines and had a history somewhat older than the Canadian. Prior to Federation the defence forces were raised and maintained by each State separately, and to Victoria belongs the distinction of having formed the first transport and supply unit. In 1887 a company known as the Ordnance, Commissariat and Transport Corps came into being, its name being changed into Commissariat and Transport Corps two years later when the ordnance duties were removed. In 1892 the nomenclature Army Service Corps was adopted. New South Wales followed close behind, its first company being raised by Captain D. Miller in 1891: a second was added in 1896, and a third in 1899. All passed under federal control in 1901, and as a result of re-organisation of the Commonwealth Forces, according to a scheme prepared by General Hutton following the war in South Africa, by which six brigades of light horse, three brigades of infantry and certain garrison troops were to provide for the defence of the Dominion, a permanent Army Service Corps came into being. This was designed to provide a permanent cadre for the supply columns which were organised for each of the higher formations, and consisted of eleven officers, the senior being a major, four warrant officers, and two hundred and twenty-one other ranks, which were distributed in varying strength among the supply columns. A notable feature of this was the fact that unlike the Canadian Permanent Army Service Corps, the Army Service Corps consisted of field rather than garrison troops. The Assistant Quartermaster-General at Headquarters of the Defence Ministry controlled the Army Service Corps, while in each district the Deputy Assistant Quartermaster-General was responsible for them. The supply columns were distributed by States thus: New South Wales, five; Victoria, four; South Australia, one; Queensland, two; Western Australia, one; Tasmania, one. Sixteen days in camp each year formed the annual training. With the Easter camps and a certain number of night drills on the same principle as that of the Territorial Force, a certain standard of efficiency had been attained in 1907. Some modifications subsequently took place in the higher formations subsequent to that date, which increased the number of supply columns, and for purposes of comparison it may be stated that the Light Horse Brigade, being the equivalent of the British Mounted Brigade, an organisation existing at that time, had almost precisely similar provision made for its transport and supply services. The Infantry Brigade being the highest formation of that arm was equal to what British Army phraseology terms a brigade group—that is the brigade of infantry had its proportion of divisional troops. For this reason the supply column was somewhat larger than the Army Service Corps company for an infantry brigade on the home establishment. The duties were of course identical.

When the new system at home was adopted in 1912 the Australian authorities lost no time in recasting their own. Since no mechanical transport existed it was impossible to model on British lines, but at the same time it was possible to adopt the principles. The first line

THE EVE OF THE GREAT WAR

transport of units was therefore fully completed. The old supply columns were re-formed as "trains" carrying one day's supplies, and supply columns, whose purpose was to run between railhead and refilling point and replenish the trains daily. Owing, however, to the distances from railhead at which operations took place, and the fact that they were necessarily animal-drawn units, the latter carried three days' supplies. Reserve parks were provided for British lines.

The Army Service Corps of the Dominion of New Zealand was only in its embryo stage in 1914 and nothing beyond projects for its formation and the enlistment of the necessary *personnel* existed. The outbreak of war and the departure of New Zealand expeditionary troops necessitated some rapid improvisation, which, carried out according to the organisation of the Imperial service, ultimately reached a high degree of efficiency.

In South Africa very similar conditions obtained. The Defence Act of 1912 had only commenced to operate and only two of the brigade trains which had been therein provided for had received any training. The remainder were in process of formation. There was a small nucleus of trained transport and supply *personnel*, including some few who had been obtained from the Imperial service, which was employed on duties in connection with the permanent and police force training camps. Remounts were combined with transport.

During the course of the Great War, the South African Army Service Corps was in some respects more highly tried than that of the sister Dominions in that they played a rôle more independent of their British comrades.

The eve of the Great War found the Army Service Corps, like the remainder of the Army, scattered throughout the world in every British garrison, with the exception of India. At that time it numbered five hundred regular officers and six thousand other ranks, having doubled its size since the beginning of the South African War.* It had certainly more than doubled its efficiency, and not only in the sense of scientific organisation, for the *personnel* throughout was vastly better trained in the course of the period 1902–14, perhaps one of the most fruitful in British military history. The Corps Training Establishment at Aldershot was firmly consolidated and the education given to young officers and recruits in the depots was thorough and practical. The work of the instructional staff at Aldershot reached a high standard—among its activities being the conduct of an excellent professional magazine, unhappily allowed to die in 1928; and that staff deserves to be had in remembrance not only by those who benefited by its labours, but by the whole Corps for whom so much was done to prepare for the task ahead. In this last connection also the name of Captain H. F. P. Percival should be specially recalled as perhaps the most highly educated professional soldier then serving in the Corps. As adjutant for some years of the important station at Woolwich, he was directly concerned with the initial training of the young officers: in the Transport Directorate at the War Office he bore a large share in the re-organisation of the field system; and subsequently as an instructor at the Staff College he expounded that system to the Army.

* The distribution of companies was as under:

	Home	Abroad
HORSE TRANSPORT		
Depot companies	3	—
Higher establishments	33	—
Station companies	2	—
Mediterranean companies	—	3
South African Companies	—	2
MECHANICAL TRANSPORT		
Depot	1	—
Service companies	20	—
SUPPLY		
Depot	1	—
Service companies	4	—
REMOUNT COMPANIES	4	—

Among the more senior whose names there will not be the occasion to recall later must again be mentioned pre-eminently that of Brig.-General G. R. C. Paul, who as Assistant Director of Transport was principally responsible for the reforms of 1912, but who did not survive to see the results of his labours. To him both the Army Service Corps and the Army are deeply indebted. Although stricken with a painful and incurable disease, he toiled indefatigably until the end, thinking only to serve his country and seeking no other reward but that of duty well done.

Incompetent and indifferent officers there were—and what human organisation has ever lacked them?—but they were few in number, which fact was confirmed by subsequent experiences in war—that great exposer of fraud. At this epoch, too, the Corps was beginning to produce its quota of graduates of the Staff College, although it had not perhaps reached the stage of assessing those so qualified at their proper value.

There had emerged, also, a body of warrant and non-commissioned officers accustomed to a large measure of individual responsibility and imbued with a strong *esprit de corps*. Although somewhat handicapped in the Horse Transport Branch by the short term of colour service—two years as compared to ten on the reserve—the rank and file were well trained in their duties, possessing a marked solidarity which was to show itself to advantage in the field. No better proof of this happy state of affairs exists than in the smoothness with which the cadres were expanded on mobilisation and the units multiplied during the period following it. The little leaven that existed in the nucleus of regulars succeeded in leavening the whole.

To some extent training suffered by the necessary dispersion of the Corps. Abroad, comparatively small detachments served in Sierra Leone, Bermuda, Jamaica, Mauritius, Singapore, north and south China and Cyprus, while Gibraltar, Malta, Egypt and South Africa were the larger foreign stations. But at home between one-quarter and one-third of the Corps was permanently at Aldershot, while Woolwich, Bulford, Portsmouth, Devonport, Colchester, the Curragh and Cork contained the bulk of the remainder. At all these places there was continuous contact with comparatively large bodies of troops, while the frequency of Army manœuvres on a considerable scale furnished possibly a more adequate preparation for the administrative than even for the fighting troops. If then those scattered in out-stations and districts both at home and abroad suffered from being unduly tied to their offices and in being concerned with peace-time routine, with all the fatal habits that such routine, especially on the administrative side, is apt to engender, the Corps as a whole had advanced far beyond the old departmental conception of transport and supply. It was definitely a military body and developing on the lines marked out for it by its creator. The accuracy with which accounts were kept had ceased to be considered the only hall-mark of efficiency. The maintenance of the Army on mobile operations was the aim and end to which attention was directed, and the doctrine with which the *personnel* throughout was inculcated. Nor is it open to reasonable doubt that this outlook and the standard consequently attained were the direct outcome of the superior status that had been given in 1889, which removed the services of transport and supply from the position of a kind of appendage to the body military and scarcely belonging to the household of the Army. The fruits of this policy were not indeed limited to the Regular Forces, for as has already been shown—though it will bear re-emphasis—the Haldane reforms brought the second line troops to a stage never previously attained, and, as far as their Army Service Corps was concerned, made them well versed in carrying out their duties for the divisions of which they were an integral part.

THE EVE OF THE GREAT WAR

It is, then, no mere hyperbole to claim that the outbreak of the War found the Corps equipped, both as regards *personnel* and material, in no manner behind any other branch of the Army which it was called upon to serve, and did indeed serve with devotion and perseverance, on the battlegrounds of the world.

TRANSPORT SYSTEM FOR SUPPLIES

		Rations Men	Animals
	Troops. On man: 1 reserve ration and 1 emergency ration	1	
	On horse: current day's oat ration.		1
Maximum about 15 miles	*Regimental transport: 1st line.* The current day's ration.	1	
	Divisional train. Supply section and 1 extra grocery ration	1	1
Refilling point	For divisional train		
	In front of lines of communication	3 (1 emergency)	2
Maximum 40 miles	*Divisional supply column mechanical transport* (returning to railhead same day)	1	1
Rendezvous*	Reserve park, horse transport (marching parallel if possible to mechanical transport)	2	2
Railhead	Divisional supply columns refill	1	1
Regulating station	Rail		
Advanced base	Advanced or main supply depot	Variable	
Oversea base	Reserve supply depot	Variable	

* The rendezvous was the point at which the divisional supply column was met by a representative of the division concerned and taken by the shortest route to the refilling point where the next transfer of loads took place, namely from the lorries to the divisional train.

BIBLIOGRAPHY

1. *The New Transport System. Its Principles and their Application.* By Lieut.-Col. E. E. CARTER, C.M.G., M.V.O., *p.s.c.* A lecture delivered at the R.U.S.I., March 6th, 1912.
2. "Notes on Recent Developments in Road Transport." By Colonel G. R. C. PAUL, C.M.G., A.D.C. From *The Army Review*, July 1911.
3. "The Services of Maintenance in the Field—Some Object Lessons from the Army Exercise 1913." By Colonel E. E. CARTER, C.M.G., M.V.O., *p.s.c.* From *The Army Review*, April 1914.
4. *The Canadian and Australian Army Service Corps.* Various articles from the *R.A.S.C. Quarterly*, 1905, 1906, 1907, and *The Commonwealth Military Journal*, October 1913, and material furnished by Dominion authorities and Lieut.-Col. N. C. HAMILTON, D.S.O., O.B.E., R.A.S.C.
5. "The Supply Reserve Depot. Its history and functions." By S. S. M. A. W. FLOOD, R.A.S.C. From *The R.A.S.C. Quarterly*, April 1926.

CHAPTER IV

THE BRITISH EXPEDITIONARY FORCE

EMERSON once wrote that the most remarkable thing about the city of London was its size. In a sense a similar remark may be applied to the operations of transport and supply with the British Expeditionary Force in France and Flanders. For except during the opening and concluding phases of the long-drawn-out struggle there was no movement demanding any special subtleties in the feeding of the troops or in conveying the wherewithal required by them to live and fight. It is for this reason, therefore, that the activities of the Army Service Corps call in their narration for a treatment differing from that adopted in other fields where static conditions did not prevail or only prevailed spasmodically. In the latter the maintenance services were for the most part so continually and closely identified with tactical or strategical situations that the story of their accomplishments emerges naturally in the story of the movements of the troops engaged; while even work at bases and on lines of communication differed not only in degree but to some extent also in nature from that in the main theatre of war.

In France the bases were large modern towns with ports equipped to a greater or lesser degree with facilities for dealing with stores and supplies in bulk and although a scientific organisation was demanded to ensure the necessary output, there were not the primitive difficulties that had to be overcome in Gallipoli, Mesopotamia or in East Africa, or even in the Balkans. Again, the lines of communication were short. While requiring an intensive exploitation, they were yet provided with efficient railway systems and an excellent network of durable roads. Obstacles to the passage of transport in the sense of impassability of routes existed only in the forward areas which had been devastated by fighting, and there again the distances were short. A further favourable circumstance was the proximity to sources of supply in the United Kingdom and the fact that the passage to and fro was not threatened in any serious manner by enemy submarines. Consequently there was at no time the anxiety as to ways and means as existed elsewhere. And finally it may be observed that the Army took the field equipped with a scale of transport applicable to mobile warfare, which scale was generally maintained with the growth in its numbers. Modifications and economies were made from time to time, when it became clear that the stabilised conditions were likely to persist, but it was never contemplated to effect such reductions as might compromise any great forward movement. Establishments thus remained on a generous scale, so much so that surprise and even criticism was evinced at times in foreign quarters that so extensive a *personnel* could be spared in the non-fighting branches.

Yet giving due weight to all these considerations, it still remains that the task achieved was a formidable one and that the manner of its achievement was in every way creditable to the organisation responsible for it. That the troops were better "found" than ever previously in history had an important share in maintaining the spirit of the citizen armies of the British Empire in the terrible ordeals through which they passed.

The Army Service Corps had evolved a system which so fully proved itself that in most essential respects it was unchanged from start to finish—in a campaign where other arms and branches had, almost without exception, to recast or modify their ideas or their organisation, or where new arms needed to be created. That aspect alone was noteworthy, especially in view of post-war events when this prescience seemed to be forgotten. But the work of those who were responsible for the Corps' preparation for war involved more than the element of immutability of method, for that method itself was designed to be worked by those who could have had but scanty training or experience of military affairs. And therein lay its supreme virtue. Such simplicity spelt easy and rapid expansion—the fundamental justification for the permanent upkeep of any military body.

The transport and supply services could not and did not expect to command the best of the splendid material which offered itself for the New Armies—at any rate not the best in the physical sense. It would have been even improper had they so expected. But they did incorporate a devoted and competent body of officers and men, which quickly assimilated their duties and generally carried them out in an adequate manner, often during the later stages of the war under the handicap of years which, prior to 1914, would have been held too great for active service. The leaven of regular officers was from 1915 onwards increasingly minute, the greater proportion being employed in ranks either one or two above their permanent ones. From these were found practically the whole of the *personnel* for the transport and supply directorates and they were therefore the architects of the great machine which was evolved for the provisioning of some two million four hundred thousand men and four hundred thousand animals—the size attained by the Army in France by November 1918. The bulk of the executive work was done by those who had prior to 1914 no experience of military affairs. That such condition was common to the whole Army detracts no whit from what was accomplished by the

Army Service Corps. And it was accomplished in the main by the co-operative effort of many rather than by the outstanding services of the few. Nevertheless individual capacity is bound to emerge in the undertaking of any organisation, however decentralised, and events brought forward officers competent to build up a vast administrative machine. Brig.-General C. W. King who went out as the Original Director of Supplies was at an early stage replaced by Major-General Clayton on his return from South Africa in September 1914. There was then an idea of creating a combined Directorate-General of Supplies and Transport at General Headquarters, but this was dropped when General Clayton was appointed to the responsible office of Inspector-General of Communications with headquarters at Abbeville in January 1915. This post which carried with it the rank of Lieut.-General was the highest ever attained by an officer of the Army Service Corps, and was held by General Clayton with distinction for two years. Brig.-General E. Carter succeeded General Clayton as Director of Supplies and remained in that capacity until the end of the war. On the transport side the original Director was Brig.-General F. C. Gilpin, but he returned to England in November 1914, when his place was taken by Brig.-General W. G. B. Boyce, a strong and able organiser, who possessed that merit somewhat rare in the British Army of knowing when to dismiss subordinates who, however agreeable in other respects, did not satisfy him professionally. Like the Director of Supplies he remained at the helm for the rest of the war.

Under the aegis of these men grew up a vast organisation, which by November 1918 employed a *personnel* of some 150,000 officers and men. In order to be able to appreciate the magnitude of this task, before proceeding with the narration of any activities of special interest or importance, the work of each branch may be summarised.

THE BRITISH EXPEDITIONARY FORCE

The duty of the directorate of supplies was complicated by the fact that provision was required to be made for the numerous varieties of foodstuffs on account of the presence of many different races in the British armies. The care needed in the issuing and accounting for supplies will be gathered from the fact that the scales of rations included quantities varying between one hundredth part of an ounce to one and a half pounds.

Table showing development of Supply Depots

		Highest daily feeding strength	Highest monthly issues Petrol (gall.)	Fuel (tons)
Boulogne	1914	65,919		
	1915	311,242		
	1916	381,620		
	1917	692,423		
	1918	670,266		
Le Havre	1914	214,565	338,091	
	1915	383,689	517,208	
	1916	416,958	909,188	
	1917	138,107	250,466	
	1918	233,005	225,610	
Rouen	1914	16,918	222,011	
	1915	213,098	397,738	8,472
	1916	1,056,151	2,956,442	18,423
	1917	1,234,612	2,833,060	20,453
	1918	1,294,936	4,673,024	14,186
Marseilles	1914	27,477		
	1915	52,200		
	1916	34,150		
	1917	51,800		
	1918	58,400		
Dieppe	1916	7,572		
	1917	11,327		60
	1918	24,295		60
Calais	1915	188,000	282,503	422
	1916	361,000	2,081,650	1,337
	1917	606,700	3,636,961	1,931
	1918	665,110	7,918,384	369
St Valery	1917	11,617		
	1918	13,933		
Cherbourg	1917	6,047		
	1918	13,745		

Starting with Base Supply Depots at Boulogne, Le Havre and Rouen and at St Nazaire and Nantes during the few weeks when the former were evacuated, the development of the situation brought into being other Base Supply Depots at Marseilles, Dieppe, Calais, St Valery-sur-Somme and Cherbourg. In these, bakeries, cold storage installations, forage depots, sheep and goat farms, petrol depots and mineral water factories all grew from small beginnings into huge proportions, as may be inferred from the table on p. 87. Originally an Advanced Supply Depot had been arranged for at Amiens but railway conditions and the rapid advance of the enemy in the early stages prevented it from working. Consequently a fortnight after the occupation of Amiens the supplies had to be evacuated to Le Mans, one hundred miles southwest of Paris, which for some weeks fed the whole of the Expeditionary Force. Afterwards Advanced Supply Depots were opened at Orleans for the Indian troops on their arrival in the autumn of 1914, at Abbeville and Abancourt and at Outreau. The record output was reached at Abancourt on the 16th of February, 1917, when supplies were loaded representing 1,236,114 rations.

The chain of supply depots from the bases to the front was completed by Field Supply Depots in Army areas; the general functions of these was to hold certain reserves of rations for men and animals to make up any deficiencies that might be found at railheads, and likewise to take in any surpluses that might be found at the latter. Normally each of the five British armies was allotted two of these depots, but as many as thirty were opened when occasion demanded. The most important of these installations were at Wardrecques, Bethune, Doullens and Barlin.

Bakeries were established at all the Base Supply Depots except St Valery and Cherbourg and also at Etaples. Originally these units were equipped with the familiar "Aldershot" ovens but early in 1915, in view of the increasing requirements, these gave way to the "Perkins" ovens. In the process of evolution these were in turn superseded by a larger type and "Hunt's" ovens were gradually put in all the great bakeries.* Efforts were continually made to economise man power by the introduction of machinery for the various processes of mixing, dividing, scaling and moulding, while women from Queen Mary's Army Auxiliary Corps were also employed with most satisfactory results.

The demand for petrol for aircraft and mechanical transport grew to dimensions which had up to then never been contemplated. As is shown by the figures the largest depots were established at Calais and Rouen. Attached to these were refilling and repairing plants as well as can-making and case-making factories. Aerial ropeways kept the depots in constant touch with the refilling plants and, by the saving of transport thus effected, paid for the cost of their erection in less than two months.

As regards fuel, in the early days of the campaign the coal requirements were met from England supplemented by local purchases in France. In the summer of 1915, however, the French Government was compelled to prohibit local purchases of coal owing to the necessities of the French munition works. Rolling stock had then become so short on the railways that it was impracticable to send it up from the bases, so the expedient was arrived at by which the British authorities drew their requirements from the Bruay mines, while an equivalent quan-

* The following figures show the growth of demands in the larger bakeries in lb. per month (highest issues)

	Boulogne	Le Havre	Rouen	Dieppe	Calais
1914	1,598,944	1,969,325	2,406,113	—	—
1915	7,950,682	10,147,460	5,145,736	—	3,868,898
1916	10,694,650	12,113,513	8,484,687	9,300,000	8,051,760
1917	17,346,498	11,109,519	7,096,564	15,000,000	11,882,866
1918	21,658,847	9,263,930	9,073,375	12,357,150	13,146,984

The highest combined output on any one day was 1,735,418 lb.

tity was replaced by sea at St Malo, Brest and Cherbourg. During the course of the war 1,330,000 tons were thus drawn from French mines and replaced, while in addition some 858,000 tons were imported to the Base Supply Depots from England for the use of the British armies.

In so rich an agricultural country as France it was found possible to make extensive local purchases of various commodities. Hospitals obtained large quantities of fish, eggs, milk and fresh butter, while forage was also bought on a large scale, a total of some one hundred and sixty-two million francs thus being disbursed.

An important branch of the Directorate of Supplies was the Investigation Department, which exercised an economic control over supplies, keeping, by means of certain forms and returns, a complete check from the bases to the front. The importance of this will be realised by the fact that some £80,000,000 worth of supplies were accounted for yearly. The officers of this department were actuaries, accountants or business men of experience who paid regular visits to the various supply depots on the lines of communication and in the armies in an advisory capacity. Nor in the efforts made for economy was salvage overlooked. Skins, tin and solder from old petrol cans, flour sweepings, waste oil and bottles, to cite some few articles, were all turned to account. Labour-saving devices were developed when practicable, instances being that of the sack-filling machines and old lorries converted into coal elevators.

On the transport side the scope was no less comprehensive. Starting with 950 lorries and 250 motor cars with the original Expeditionary Force, the directorate dealt at the time of the Armistice with no less than 33,500 lorries, 1400 tractors and 13,800 motor cars, in addition to many thousands of motor bicycles. By the system obtaining in 1914 all heavy repairs to mechanical vehicles were executed in the workshops of the Army Ordnance Department at the bases, light running repairs only being effected in the mobile workshops of the Army Service Corps. As early as October, however, it became clear that these arrangements were inadequate as the already burdened Ordnance Department could not cope with the work; and accordingly the whole of the heavy repairs were taken over by the Army Service Corps, to whom indeed they properly belonged. Thus operation was directly identified with maintenance, and the results were in the highest degree satisfactory. Four heavy repair shops were ultimately established in all, these being located at Paris, Le Havre, with two at Rouen. Lorries were dealt with at Paris and Rouen, motor cars and ambulances at Le Havre and motor cycles and cycles in a separate organisation at Rouen. In addition a Retrieving section was formed to produce from damaged stock or by manufacture items of which the Base Mechanical Transport Depots were short owing to the non-delivery of stores demanded from England.

A Base Mechanical Transport Depot had been provided for in the war establishments of the Expeditionary Force and on a small scale its capabilities had been tested in Army manœuvres. In the field the *Personnel* or Reinforcements Branch increased rapidly from a few score "details" to a floating population of between 1000 and 1500 men and an organisation which could train, equip and despatch to the front over 2000 men per month. In the spring of 1915 a second Base Mechanical Transport Depot was found necessary and was eventually established at Calais. These two establishments supplied the necessary spare parts for a large number of makes and types of vehicles.

Between the outbreak of war and June 1915 the Advanced Mechanical Transport Depot made several moves, but the most important was from Rouen to Abbeville, where it remained until April 1918 when, owing to the intensive air raids on that place interrupting the work, it was located at Calais. The duties of this unit were to receive and deal with all demands for spare parts, tyres and accessories for all mechanically propelled vehicles with the armies at the front and also for such workshop tools, equipment, and material as were not furnished by the Army Ordnance Department, demands being received through Army Service Corps mechanical transport units who were responsible for the maintenance of all mechanical transport vehicles. During the first few months of the War the general condition of the mechanical vehicles naturally suffered owing to the mobile nature of the operations, and early in 1915 a systematic technical inspection was introduced and maintained throughout. The procedure proved necessary to keep vehicles up to an efficient standard and opportunity was taken by the technical inspecting officers to instruct officers and men of the various units in the special points requiring attention in the upkeep of each vehicle, new formations being visited as soon as possible after their arrival in the theatre. A Census Branch was also organised at the Headquarters of the Transport Directorate to afford an efficient check on the registration and number of every War Department vehicle, excluding motor cycles. When this census was first struck in July 1915 the total number of vehicles with the Army in France was 9845. By March 1919 the figure stood at 59,840. The practical use of this census was two-fold; on one hand a complete history was kept of the whereabouts of a vehicle from the time it entered the country up to the time of its official disposal; and on the other hand any vehicle could be traced by referring its War Department number to the census, while in the case of accident reference established the name of the unit in whose charge the vehicle was borne.

While in the early stages the demand for skilled drivers was easily met, it soon became necessary to train *personnel* for this purpose, as owing to the strain put on the resources in the United Kingdom by demands from new theatres of war it was not always possible to despatch adequately trained reinforcements. Small schools were therefore set up at Rouen and Calais, but in 1916 these were merged in a Central School of Instruction designed to deal with fifty officers and two hundred and six drivers at a time. The total number trained in France amounted to nearly 10,000.

The horse transport was based on two main depots. The Base Depot was located at Le Havre and here all supply and horse transport reinforcements of *personnel* were located and the training of young soldiers was continued. The Advanced Horse Transport Depot was at Abbeville, its main duties being to provide complete "turn outs", that is, man, vehicle and animals to units and teams of animals with harness, trained for special purposes.

Record should not be omitted of the organisation of labour. This was at one time a purely Army Service Corps responsibility, when in the early stages Army Service Corps Labour Companies were formed for work on the lines of communication, where they were employed partly by the Director of Supplies and partly by the Directorates of Works, Railways and Ordnance. In 1915, however, demands for labour became so great that Royal Engineer and Infantry Labour Units appeared on the scene to be followed a year later by miscellaneous additions in the shape of South African natives, Cape Boys and British West India Regiment and Bermuda Garrison Artillery. Subsequently contingents of Egyptian, Chinese, Indian and Fijian labour arrived and it was decided to form a Labour Corps proper, to which the Army Service Corps Companies were transferred. The huge organisation thus formed, amounting in 1918 to a quarter of a million men, was for some time ably controlled by an Army Service Corps officer in Brig.-General E. Gibb, who in 1929 became Director of Supplies and Transport at the War Office, where prior to the War he had done admirable work in the Transport Directorate.

Such in short was the field covered by the Army Service Corps; and the figures that have been given allow some appreciation of its magnitude. Yet figures standing by themselves or with a minimum of explanation are necessarily dry and uninspiring. It is therefore proposed to elaborate them by directing attention to executive features of general interest. We may revert in the first instance to the Directorate of Supplies, whose problem differed from the organisation of the same nomenclature at the War Office in that it was essentially one of distribution as against the more complex task of provision and distribution carried out from London.

For the purposes of supply, northern France was divided into two districts, northern and southern. The northern lines of communication included the major ports of entry of Calais and Boulogne and were responsible for the feeding of three of the five British armies in the field; on the southern line were the three major ports of Rouen, Le Havre and Dieppe, which had a similar responsibility for the remaining two. By reason of the proximity of the northern bases to the front there was, until an advanced depot was opened at Outreau, some slight difference between the organisation of the northern and southern lines; and this lay in the fact that, on the first, supplies went practically straight from the Base Depot to the railhead,* while, on the second, it went in bulk to the Advanced Supply Depot at Abancourt, from whence it was re-consigned in "pack trains" or in other words railway trains, capable of meeting the needs of two divisions daily. These trains then proceeded to railhead and from thence onwards the distribution on both lines was identical, the divisional supply column working from railhead to refilling point where the horsed wagons of the

* Actually the route was to a "regulating station", where the loads were re-packed on "divisional pack trains".

divisional train were replenished. A further distinction between the northern and southern lines was involved by the former receiving all kinds of foodstuffs and commodities at the same ports, while the latter specialised, in that each port dealt exclusively with one article such as petrol or forage or preserved supplies.

The maxim of von Moltke that "no army food is too expensive" was faithfully observed throughout by the War Office, but early in 1917, when the necessity for economy was becoming more and more accentuated, a radical amendment was made as regards the ration scale in France. Two rations were established: one for the troops on the fighting front and another and slightly lower for those on the lines of communication. The comparative cost of these was about one shilling and tenpence as against one shilling and sevenpence per man per day.* Issues, however, were elastic, adapting themselves to season and locality, and there was also a system of substitution to add variety to the food. Sardines, tinned herrings or veal were among other things which took the place at times of preserved meat, as did sausage in lieu of bacon on occasions. But, as already noted, the real complications for the supply authorities lay in the presence of the cosmopolitan host that went to compose the forces of the British Empire, and here conflicts of

* The normal daily higher scale ration was as under:

Meat, fresh or frozen	1 lb.
Bacon	4 oz.
Bread	1 lb. or 10 oz. biscuit.
Butter	2 oz. (3 times a week).
Jam	3 oz.
Tea	⅝ oz.
Sugar	3 oz.
Condensed milk	1 oz.
Cheese	2 oz.
Oatmeal	2 oz. (3 times a week).
Potatoes	2 oz.
Fresh vegetables	8 oz. (or 2 oz. dried vegetables)
Tobacco or cigarettes	2 oz. (once a week).
Matches	1 box (3 times a fortnight).

With salt, pepper and mustard: also rum at the discretion of the G.O.C.

religion, taste and custom had to be met and appeased. The Indian *personnel* for example demanded a ration which included *atta* or native meal, *ghee* or the native substitute for butter, *dhal* or split peas, besides certain spices and condiments. The Fijians employed in the Labour Corps had their own special requirements, as had also the Chinese, among them being nut oil. Lentils and cheese were components of the Egyptian scale. There was also a separate diet for the enemy prisoners, which consisted of the not ungenerous scale of 9 oz. of bread, 6 oz. of fresh or frozen meat five days a week and 10 oz. of salt herrings or sprats on the other two days. Coffee, tea, sugar, potatoes and other vegetables, rice, oatmeal, jam and cheese were also issued in proportions naturally somewhat lower than those for British troops but at the same time amply sufficient for a healthy existence; the German black bread was after a time made and substituted for the standard kind, which resulted in a considerable economy.

As foodstuffs were provided from time to time to meet the needs of French, Belgian, Portuguese and American troops, the work of distribution and accounting was immensely complicated; one Base Supply Depot alone supplied seventeen different diets, while the hospitals required special and varied articles at all times. In comparison to the needs of man, the animals were a facile proposition—here it was more a question of bulk, and a simple calculation for 400,000 animals at an average of some twenty-five pounds weight of food per day will show the quantities to be handled.*

Up to 1916 the whole work of transport from the time a supply ship reached port was carried out by the Army

---

* The daily ration for horses and mules was as under:

	Oats	Hay
Heavy draught horses	17 lb.	15 lb.
Officers' mounts and other horses and mules of 15 hands and upwards	12 lb.	12 lb.

Service Corps, but in the autumn of that year a change was inaugurated by which the unloading was placed under the newly created Directorate of Transportation and the handling by the Directorate of Labour. The reasons which led to the formation of the latter have already been touched upon, but the former important innovation, so closely bound up with the work of supply, demands some words of introduction. The original arrangement by which the French authorities assumed the responsibility for British rail transport required revision, as the rolling stock and permanent ways had fallen into very bad condition, while the French *personnel* was steadily reduced by calls made upon it for combatant service in the armies. Replacements of every kind were needed, while both men and material were lacking, and the French were therefore forced to call upon the British to take a share in railway transport work. In November 1916 therefore, the appointment of Director-General of Transportation was created and the functions of this official were to control railway transport from the ports to the troops, to provide rolling stock and material of all kinds and to be responsible for railway and road construction. Under him a Directorate of Docks was set up, as a change in the method of working at the ports was imperative in order that a more rapid discharge of vessels might be effected. Until they passed into the hangars of the Base Supply Depot supplies did not, under the new system, come into the hands of the Army Service Corps, but when they did so pass they remained in its charge until they were handed over to representatives of the actual units destined to consume them. As soon as a supply ship touched a base port it was caught up in the toils of a very complete system. The duplicate invoices of the cargo were checked and returned as receipts to the port of departure, while the originals of the invoices became the first link in the chain of accounting that lasted until the supplies were consumed or destroyed. Every commodity was stacked so that it could be counted swiftly and easily and to this end every stack had hanging to it a tally board, containing the letter of the shed or hangar and the number of the block in which it was situated. Additions to or withdrawals from any stack or block were recorded on the tally board so that a complete inventory could be effected in the shortest time. The check on the stacks themselves apart from the tally boards was facilitated by the manner in which they were built up, and in harmony with the perfection of detail which marked the whole system a special manual entitled *The Stacking and Storing of Supplies* was drawn up. This manual indicated by means of section illustrations the manner in which cases, sacks and bales could be piled up so as to expedite accounting and unpacking, one chapter showing the spaces required for storing and stacking rations for a given number of men and horses, so that it could be seen at a glance how many troops could be fed. The convenience of this method and order will be realised by the statement that in one single hangar at Le Havre no less than 80,000 tons of various articles of supply were stored at one time. The building in question was more than half a mile in length and over six hundred feet wide.

For the purpose of illustrating procedure forwards some further detail may be given. So complete a check was kept on every pound incoming and outgoing that a Base Supply Depot was able to forward to the Advanced Supply Depot a "daily stock" telegram, which notified the precise amount of supplies on hand and what was due to arrive the following day. This was achieved by the section officers in charge of each group of commodities balancing his receipts and issues daily and rendering to the Base Depot Headquarters every evening the amount he had on hand the preceding night, the day's receipts and issues, the transfers or issues for local troops and the "remains" at the time of making the report. The sum

THE BRITISH EXPEDITIONARY FORCE

of these daily "states" furnished the information for the "daily stock" telegram.

By means of this information the Deputy Director of Supplies, who was located at the important distribution centre that lay in the Advanced Base, was cognizant at all times of what he could draw upon in the event of a sudden increase of ration strength at the front. From the Base Supply Depot the supplies were forwarded in bulk in complete trains of bread, meat, flour, petrol or groceries, and these trains with the exception of those carrying groceries went direct to the railway regulating station, where their freight was re-packed on to the divisional pack trains. The grocery trains with their numerous comparatively small items were unloaded at the advanced depot and their contents sorted out according to divisional needs. One reason why there was such a constant procession of "bulk" trains out of the Base Supply Depots was the necessity for a quick turnover at the ports because vessels were entering every day and a congestion of shipping would be fatal. The average number of trains loaded daily at the Abancourt depot, when it was working to its normal capacity, was twenty-one, which meant that rations for 840,000 men alone were forwarded every twenty-four hours. Over one period of two months the number reached 1,300,000. The system of handling and despatch from the advanced depots was a model of time and labour saving. All supplies were loaded and unloaded in a shed flanked by railway sidings, the groceries being loaded on to the platform, where each separate commodity had a numbered section, each section holding thirty days' requirements for one division. On the opposite side of the shed were marshalled the empty grocery trucks destined for the divisional pack train, each truck being drawn up alongside the section from which it was to be filled. In charge of the operation for each train was a "Loading Officer", who was furnished every morning with a form containing a list of the articles and quantities to be packed, and these were in turn checked by a "Checking Officer" after having been loaded. On every truck was placed a number indicating the division for which the contents were destined and this enabled the "make up" of the divisional pack trains to be effected smoothly at the regulating station, as a corresponding group of trucks bearing the same number, and conveying the foodstuffs other than groceries, was attached behind. The train thus completed proceeded to railhead with a series of waybills, one being signed by the "Railhead Supply Officer" who sent it back to the Advanced Supply Depot as a receipt for the goods. A five days' reserve of supplies turned over monthly was kept at railheads as a precaution against any breakdown in transport.

At the regulating station a complete set of "divisional pack trains" was required to be handled every twenty-four hours and normally left for the front in the evening so as to arrive at railhead on the following morning; no train returned empty, as it was used to convey stores to be salvaged or renewed. From railhead onwards supplies passed through the hands of the field transport proper, being taken over in the first instance by the lorries of the divisional supply column, and dealt with after the manner detailed in the chapter dealing with the organisation of the road transport as drawn up prior to the war. At times, from the fact of railhead being in close proximity to certain of the divisions served, either for the reasons that they were in rest or otherwise, it was found possible to dispense with the mechanical transport and draw direct with the divisional train.

The duties of the Railhead Supply Officer bore an importance higher than that usually assigned to a subaltern, in that he was the final distributing authority to the divisions, sometimes as many as ten or twelve being served by one railhead. Demands on him were made by the Senior Supply Officer of each division, and he was also responsible for notifying the Headquarters of the Army concerned of the daily feeding strength for which indents were made as well as the situation of his reserve of supplies. Based on this information Army Headquarters submitted their requirements to the Advanced Supply Depot, and naturally casualties made their requirements vary at times from day to day.

Mention has already been made of an Investigation Department. Started in 1914 its activities were originally confined to the Base and Advanced Supply Depots, where its representatives acted as auditing officers and in tracing loads of supplies which were lost on rail in transit. In the pre-War regulations it was laid down that there should be no accounting for supplies subsequent to their leaving the Advanced Supply Depot as it was considered that the Army Service Corps would be unduly hampered in its task of feeding the troops. As far as mobile warfare is concerned the wisdom of such provision was incontestable, for every supply officer knows how his difficulties are augmented on peace manœuvres by the necessity of detailed accounting when the troops are on the move and frequently scattered in small detachments, under which circumstances his constant supervision is impossible. Sacks for example were a "bugbear" on such occasions to the Army Service Corps subaltern, and few have escaped having to pay for deficits caused through no faults of their own and indeed very often caused by their determination to feed the units at any cost. The injustice of this went far to confirm the saying that prior to 1914 the British officer "paid for the honour of serving". In this connection the counsel of the old Supply Officer learned in the ways of the Financial Department was singularly apt: "If you must lose something lose more than you can pay for. If you lose about £20,000 worth they will have to write it off. Governmental financial authorities are always penny wise and pound foolish".

In France, where static warfare prevailed, there was obviously no reason why accounting in proper form should not be carried out and in the summer of 1915 the Investigation Department accordingly extended its ramifications into the Army areas with the result that marked economies were effected. Some idea of the scope of the work may be gathered from the fact that the department received a copy of the daily indent for rations made out by each unit of the Expeditionary Force—a number which attained nearly 60,000, a copy of every receipt for supplies delivered and of each waybill used throughout the traffic system. By these means it was possible to reconcile issue with receipt and as a consequence there was rarely more variation than one per cent. in surplus or shortage in any commodity, and in most instances far less.

In few directions are the lessons to be drawn from the War of more import than as concerns the administration, maintenance and operation of mechanical transport. It was for all practical purposes the first occasion on which it had been employed on active service and its development was accordingly rapid, eventually attaining a high degree of scientific organisation, the main outlines of which have already been recorded.

Some elaboration of this is now required.

With the original Expeditionary Force in August 1914 the Director of Transport had under him a Deputy Director for the Lines of Communication (the latter having his representatives at the bases) and also an Assistant and Deputy Assistant Director with him at General Headquarters. This modest staff was steadily augmented until it finally attained considerable proportions. The Director had then directly under him at General Headquarters a Deputy, four Assistant and four Deputy Assistant Directors and a Chief Inspector of Mechanical Transport, while representing him on the lines of communication were two further Deputies, one for the northern and one for the southern line, the first having five Deputy Assistant and the latter four Assistant and two Deputy Assistant Directors. Thus the headquarter organisation included no less than twenty-four administrative staff officers. With each of the five armies was a Deputy Director who was charged with the duties of both supplies and transport and who had with him a Deputy Assistant Director of Transport. The Cavalry Corps and General Headquarters troops each possessed an Assistant Director of Supplies and Transport and a Deputy Assistant Director of Transport, while the Tank Corps possessed an Assistant and Deputy Assistant Director. Finally the Forestry Corps had a Deputy Assistant Director, making seventeen additional officers charged with transport duties, of which nine were also concerned with supply.* In round numbers it may be noted that some seventy Army Service Corps officers were thus employed on the administrative staff of their own directorates in France alone—a point that should not be overlooked. For since the majority were regulars they formed a not inconsiderable proportion of the total of five hundred who were serving at the outbreak of war, and who were necessarily scattered throughout the different theatres and in the United Kingdom, and a high proportion of those available in the British Expeditionary Force, a further number of the most efficient being required for the Staff of the Army. While the experience thus gained was invaluable, justice demands that it should be emphasised that nearly all the executive duties with units were carried out by Territorial and New Army *personnel*, services to which their professional comrades will not fail to pay tribute.

Reverting to the great establishments upon whose industry and efficient administration the mobility of the Army so largely depended, some account of the activities

* The organisation of the supply directorate has not been given as it followed very similar lines to that of the transport.

and of the system prevailing in a Base and Advanced Mechanical Transport Depot and a Heavy Repair Shop and the Advanced Horse Transport Depot, may now be given. For the first of these the work of the organisation at Rouen may be taken as an illustration. No. 1 Base Mechanical Transport Depot had, as has been noted, been provided for in the original establishments of the Expeditionary Force and it came into being on the 5th of August, 1914, when it consisted of a permanent staff of seven officers and ninety-one other ranks. By 1916 this had increased to twenty-five officers and some five hundred other ranks, while during this expansion the store accommodation grew from one shed, approximately sixty feet by thirty, to a covered area comprising over 20,000 square yards. The branch dealing with vehicles which began with five lorries and two cars developed into a reserve vehicle park with a reserve of over a thousand vehicles ready for instant despatch to the front.

In the early days spare parts for the vehicles in France were supplied automatically to the base depot on a scale known as the "ten per cent. schedule", which had been drawn up on expert commercial advice and accepted by the Mechanical Transport Committee. In practice, however, this scale was unnecessarily large, and the principle of automatic supply presented considerable difficulties. Masses of stores were sent over in unequal proportions, resulting in large surpluses of articles for which there was little or no demand, and as no advice was given of these automatic consignments it was often impossible to distinguish between items definitely ordered and those supplied automatically. As a consequence within a few months a reduced scale, based on the three most important units of supply for any number of vehicles above one hundred, was introduced in lieu of the former plan, by which ten of the most important units of supply for every hundred vehicles in the field were maintained. At the same time the use of detailed advices with each consignment was introduced. These measures did much to remedy the confusion that had arisen.

Another difficulty was that of nomenclature. Different makers used different names for the same article and some even changed the names of their manufactures from time to time. As it was obviously impossible to induce makers to standardise the names of parts this had to be done in the Base Mechanical Transport Depot, and work on this commenced in 1915. It took two years to compile vocabularies for every type of vehicle in use in the Army and the magnitude of the task may be gauged from the fact that it had been estimated by experts that it would take five.

The minimum stock of stores held in France to maintain vehicles in running order was calculated at two months' requirements, based on actual demands received from field units during the previous two months—stock including, besides that held, what had been ordered but not delivered. In the "Provision and Demand" office, records of all demands and orders were kept on order cards showing those totalled up to date, receipts and either stock in hand or outstanding. These order cards were distinct from the ledger cards kept in each store group which recorded receipts and issues only. Every demand received was scrutinised for errors and entered on its order card and if the state of the stock necessitated it an order was placed on England. The demand itself was passed to the store group concerned, of which the officer in charge notified the "Provision and Demand" office whether it could be met in full or in part. The latter passed the information to the unit concerned and gave the probable date of the completion of the consignment. In the store group the stores on demand and available were counted out by the storeman, who at the same time checked the balance of the particular stock, and then sent the issues with their vouchers to the depot central packing shed. There the articles were again counted, packed in strong cases and sent by road or rail to the consignee.

This system provided for a cross check on practically every figure where there was a possibility of error and also for a continual stocktaking.

The *Personnel* Branch began to operate on the 13th of August, 1914, when the first reinforcements were left at the base by divisional supply columns, and it was responsible for the whole of the reinforcing of mechanical transport until April 1917 when No. 2 Base Depot at Calais took a share in the task. Over 200,000 arrivals and departures were recorded in the *personnel* office, and the card index which was kept contained complete records, personal, medical and technical, of over 100,000 men. This work was complicated by the fact that about thirty trades were represented and the men had to be registered in different categories of which lorry drivers, car drivers, steam engine drivers, fitters, blacksmiths, wheelers, electricians, boiler-makers and motor cyclists formed the largest. In addition to the Imperial troops there were Canadian, Australian, New Zealand and South African *personnel*, involving the necessary subdivisions in each trade category and thereby involving much additional clerical work.

Reinforcements arrived either in the shape of drafts from England or as casuals from a hospital or unit, all drivers being tested and if necessary being put through a course of training at the School of Instruction, which originated at the depot, but was in 1916 formed as a separate organisation at St Omer.

The reserve vehicle park was originally embodied in the Rouen depot by the inclusion of a small detachment as a nucleus, in 1914, for as soon as mechanical transport units began to disembark casualties occurred among their vehicles, often in the process of disembarkation. Any vehicle too much damaged to proceed with its unit was then taken over by the vehicle park and there put in order at an improvised workshop, which was in fact the forerunner of the heavy repair shops. By the end of 1918 the reserve vehicle park comprised four separate divisions—two for new and repaired vehicles, one for German vehicles and one for those awaiting despatch to England, the majority of the latter having to be overhauled before being consigned.

Finally some figures of tonnage and items will best assess the scope of the Base Mechanical Transport Depot. The maximum monthly average of items demanded by units on any one year was 20,500 in 1918, during which period the tonnage received averaged 2515 per month and that despatched 1900. The gross number of items demanded by units from the beginning of 1915 until December 1918 reached the figure of 844,800, those for tonnage received and despatched being 96,240 and 66,440 respectively.*

The establishment for the northern line located at Calais was organised on a similar basis but dealt with all American makes of vehicles, of which sixteen types were in use, while in 1916 a Portuguese section was added. On the 11th of August, 1918, during an intensive air raid some sixty bombs of various descriptions were dropped on the town and a conflagration was started in the depot which could not be arrested until a large portion had been destroyed. The spare parts of approximately 19,000 cars and lorries were lost in this fire, together with the whole of the ledger cards and records of fourteen makes of vehicles. The difficulty of obtaining assistance during this fire was accentuated by the fact that the depot camp was also hit by three bombs, eight men being killed and twenty-seven wounded.

* A comparison of the gross figures for No. 2 Base Mechanical Transport Depot at Calais is of interest. The depot was opened in August 1915 and up to the end of 1918 had dealt with the following:
Items demanded by units: 509,521.
Tonnage figures only exist for 1917 and 1918 and amount for those two years to 8946.

Fortunately three large store hangars and the central stores offices were saved and the provision cards were therefore able to be utilised to ascertain the approximate stock on hand at the time of the fire. By the 14th of August a complete replacement order for the whole of the stock lost, an order comprising nearly a thousand sheets of typewritten foolscap, was furnished and despatched by special messenger, while all units in the field were ordered to return to the Depot every spare part they might have in their possession belonging to the makes lost. As a consequence of these measures by the 20th of August some 1600 cases had been received from England and 3000 from field units, while by the end of September 13,000 cases and packages had arrived from the Home Mechanical Transport Depot and the situation was again normal. The estimated value of the material destroyed was between one and one and a half million pounds.

Calais was subject periodically from 1916 onwards to severe hostile air action and in this connection the depot fire brigade, composed largely of experienced firemen, was kept fully employed, turning out for no less than ninety fires in the area, forty of which occurred on premises occupied by the French and Belgian Governments or private individuals. One member of the brigade received the Meritorious Service Medal and three others the Croix de Guerre for their gallantry in fighting fires, and the official thanks of the French authorities for the valuable services rendered were conveyed to General Headquarters.

In August 1914 the establishment of an Advanced Mechanical Transport Depot was five officers and one hundred and three other ranks: a year later this had risen to nine officers and two hundred and fifty-four other ranks, while the fact that the 1st and 2nd Advanced Mechanical Transport Depots had been merged into one, so organised that they could operate separately if desired, gave the organisation a strength of eighteen officers and five hundred and eight other ranks. In April 1917 two hundred members of Queen Mary's Army Auxiliary Corps replaced a hundred and fifty men. The depot commenced to function at Amiens, but consequent on the changes in the military situation moved to Rouen on the 27th of August, 1914, and three days later to Le Mans. Thence it returned to Rouen in the ensuing October, going to Abbeville in June of the following year, where it remained until the 1st of April, 1918, then repairing to Calais and finally being again located at Abbeville. These vicissitudes were anything but helpful towards the complex duties of the unit, but the fact that in the move from Abbeville to Calais, over a thousand tons of material were moved in eighty-seven hours with a loss of only some £57 worth, and operations started at the destination within forty-eight hours of the departure, speaks for itself. A stock of spare parts, tyres and accessories was maintained on a basis of ten days' requirements as a minimum, and thirty days' as a maximum, calculated on the demands received from units on the previous thirty days, items only being kept in stock for which more than three indents were sent in per month. That spare parts for 43,761 vehicles of three hundred and seventy-seven different types were provided from this depot gives some measure of the complexity of the task of detailed issue.

The system of the repair of mechanical transport obtaining between the Army Service Corps and the Army Ordnance Department when the British Expeditionary Force took the field has been noted above in addition to the fact that the conditions of active service quickly showed the system to be impracticable. In view of post-war reactionary measures in this important department the subject may be somewhat further expounded.

As soon as operations began and vehicles became casualties, requiring considerable repair, they were handed over to the Army Ordnance Department at Rouen and Amiens. But even within a few days the accumulation awaiting attention became serious, especially owing to the fact that many of the lorries which had been impressed had started off in a none too satisfactory condition. It became essential, if the transport was to be maintained, for the Base and Advanced Mechanical Transport Depots to harness themselves to the work of repair in addition to their legitimate duties and for certain French civilian shops to be called into play to assist, these latter being taken over by the Transport Directorate. In spite of these measures the number of vehicles requiring treatment continued to increase rapidly and a further number of French shops in Paris were taken over for medium repairs which should have properly fallen to the Army Ordnance Department.

Early in October 1914, it became clear that these makeshift arrangements were inadequate and were likely to become still more so. Accordingly it was ruled by the Quartermaster-General that, in addition to doing the light running repairs, the Army Service Corps should take over the whole of the heavy repairs, and with the matter thus regularised the maintenance of the mechanical transport went from strength to strength. It was only to be expected that it should have done so, for in that Corps was embodied all the best mechanical transport experience that the Army possessed, while that experience was continually being reinforced by some of the ablest brains in the motor world who naturally offered themselves in the branch in which their services could be most fully utilised. In the hands of the Corps, too, were all the base mechanical transport establishments and the training of the mechanical transport *personnel*. To have kept repair separate would inevitably have led to overlapping and waste of man power and energy, even if it had led to no worse consequences. Finally there was the stimulus given by identity of the body charged with repairs with that of the body in whose hands the vast bulk of the operation lay, the value of which needs no emphasis.

The First Heavy Repair Shop, Army Service Corps, developed from that which had originally started in Paris and this gradually extended so as to be capable of dealing with three hundred vehicles at a time. The second unit of this nature was opened at Rouen in February 1915 and the third at St Omer in May of the same year, all three having the same establishment. No. 4 Heavy Repair Shop formed at the end of 1915 at Rouen was the Retrieving Section, the work of which was carried out by German prisoners of war under British supervision. By March 1919 stores to the value of over £800,000 had been turned out by this unit. In November 1917 yet another shop was found necessary and accordingly No. 5 was organised, although it did not actually carry out its functions until August 1918 as its original situation at Dunkerque became untenable owing to enemy action. It was then re-established at Rouen.

In the early stages of these establishments the main essential was to put vehicles in running order as quickly as possible. In most instances the body was not removed from the chassis and any item requiring overhaul, such as an engine or back axle, was completely removed and replaced by another drawn from store. This enabled a large output to be obtained with a limited number of artificers. As the shops increased in number, and greater facilities were given them, it was usual to strip vehicles entirely except in the case of a comparatively small proportion, which could be dealt with by repairing one or more parts only without touching the rest of the chassis.

As regards general procedure a vehicle on arriving was delivered over to the car or lorry park where it was thoroughly inspected, a report of the repairs necessary being sent to the Commanding Officer and filed pending a vacancy in the shop. In the meantime all movable equipment was taken out and the magneto sent to the special magneto department for examination, testing and safe custody. If the drivers of vehicles undergoing repair were found to be inefficient they were despatched for further training to the Central School of Instruction.

Immediately a vacancy arose in the repair shop the selected vehicle was towed there from the casualty park. Its body was removed and the chassis cleaned and washed: the engine with fly wheel and clutch was then taken out as a complete unit, fixed to an adjustable wheeled frame and taken to the engine unit section. A similar course was followed with the gear box, back axle, radiator and the other minor details, each being sent to its particular section of the shop. After the engine had been repaired and re-assembled its moving parts were "run in" by power taken from the shafting. It was then sent to the "Test Branch Department", which had accommodation for six engines, and with its own magneto refixed was tested for brake horse power exactly as when first built. If it failed to indicate its full power it was returned to the repair shop and was not allowed to pass out until it had attained its original efficiency.

After passing inspection the various components of an engine and transmission were sent to the stores from which they were issued to be re-erected in their chassis, which had meanwhile been overhauled and repaired. A test body loaded to the full carrying weight of the complete vehicle was then put on and a searching road test given. If this was passed satisfactorily the proper body was fitted, final adjustments made and the vehicle inspected by the "Inspections Branch Mechanical Transport"—an organisation entirely distinct from the repair shop. If satisfactory the vehicle was classed according to its condition and passed on to the reserve vehicle park to be re-issued in replacement of another casualty.

THE BRITISH EXPEDITIONARY FORCE

From 1914 to the end of 1918, 6691 lorries and tractors, 7074 motor cars and ambulances and 12,734 motor cycles and sidecars were dealt with in Nos. 1, 2, 3 and 5 Heavy Repair Shops.

In conclusion, something may be recorded as regards the principal installation devoted to animal transport. This existed in the Advanced Horse Transport Depot which, in the shape of No. 14 Company Army Service Corps, disembarked at Rouen on the 11th of August, 1914. At that time its strength was but five officers and fifty-nine other ranks, Royal Artillery and Royal Engineer sections being added a month later when the total establishment then reached sixteen officers and three hundred and thirty-five other ranks. For a short time this unit carried out its duties at Le Mans but was then moved to Abbeville, where it remained for the rest of the campaign. By the time of the armistice the strength of the depot was 2462 all ranks, with some 2000 animals and 1600 vehicles. The duties carried out were of a varied character but the most important lay in those concerned with providing units with complete "turn outs", that is, driver, animals, vehicles and harness complete. This was necessary in the case of units requiring replacements and also to meet special demands, such as for newly formed units or for divisions arriving in France without transport or with incomplete transport.

Among other functions was the reception of "turn outs" evacuated for any reasons from the front, the animals being if necessary re-conditioned and any light repairs being done to vehicles or harness. Local transport duties were also undertaken, over five hundred vehicles being employed daily. This enabled animals to be worked into good condition before despatch to field units. A further important duty was the training of infantry transport drivers, many of whom possessed but little previous experience with horses, while from May 1916 onwards large numbers of transport drivers of the newly formed Machine Gun Corps were likewise put through courses of instruction. Transport courses were held every month, attended by five officers and twenty other ranks from each of the armies.

The scope of the work of the depot may be gauged from the fact that during the course of its existence nearly 90,000 animals, 25,000 vehicles, with a *personnel* in charge of the latter amounting to some 45,000, were issued. In addition 20,000 complete "turn outs" were supplied.

BIBLIOGRAPHY

The Business of War. By ISAAC F. MARCOSSON.

Report of the Directorate of Transport British Armies in France and Flanders.

CHAPTER V

THE BRITISH EXPEDITIONARY FORCE (*continued*)

In the preceding chapter, necessarily somewhat statistical, it has been the aim to present the sum of the task accomplished and at the same time to elaborate it by directing attention to certain important parts of the machine which generated the power by which the Army existed and made war. The activities, which constantly and more directly touched the action of the fighting troops, may now be indicated: and towards this purpose no complete or continuous record of the tactical or strategical operations is demanded, for any attempt to describe step by step the part borne by the Army Service Corps in these operations would inevitably lead to an undue degree of repetition. During the greater part of the four years and three months' campaigning, matters were, to use a colloquial term, "much of a muchness". While stabilised warfare lasted, the work of the Corps in the forward zones was incessant and hazardous to an extent greater than is usually supposed. It was, too, maintained at a high standard of efficiency. But it was of a nature that in all essential respects showed little change and therefore does not lend itself to any continuous narrative of sustained general interest.

In the official volumes, owing to lack of interest displayed by the average reader towards them, little room can be found for the work of the maintenance services. The matter is therefore almost wholly confined to the doings of the fighting troops, the priority of whom is evident. Nevertheless, it may be questioned whether a method which gives a reasonable proportion of attention to the administrative side would not have greater value for the future. Now that war has become so much a matter of organisation, superiority in this direction is, given equal courage on the part of the contestants, the most potent factor in deciding the day. Again, in the realm of tactics, changes and modifications occur with kaleidoscopic rapidity as new weapons or their antidotes are evolved, and interesting as it may be to study the manner in which previous generations fought or in which previous commanders ordered their battles, quite apart from the epic of heroism embodied therein, the process leaves much to be desired as concerns measures required for the present or possible in the future. The supreme value of history lies in what it can teach for guidance in the years to come. In this respect full value is obtainable from strategical lessons of the past, since they are subject in only a minor degree to such evolutions as those of tactics. But strategy on the Western Front during the years 1915, 1916 and 1917 can hardly be said to have existed: even the grand tactics of trench warfare were crude; and this being so, the case for finding room in the official records for some fuller account of the machinery of the vast organisation which supported the armies in the field is emphasised. The principles of administration in the field are constant, involving as they do the provision and distribution at the right time and in the right place of everything needed by the army to live, move and fight; but these principles, like those of strategy, vary in their application. In the last and greatest of wars, the bulk of material, stores, supplies and munitions was unprecedented, but it was the advent of the internal combustion engine which revolutionised ways and means and opened avenues which are as yet in their early stages of exploration. In this respect experiences from 1914 to 1918

THE BRITISH EXPEDITIONARY FORCE

are basic and merit all the study that can be devoted to them.

Within defined limits of space one of two courses may be adopted in recording the achievements of the Army Service Corps. The first lies in setting out in chronological sequence the doings of its various branches and special units of those branches during the campaign; and the second, of throwing into relief what appear the more noteworthy or instructive episodes or activities during the important phases, and allowing the rest to be taken for granted. The advantage of the former method would be that a representative body would be brought "into the picture", but on the other hand the canvas would be unduly crowded, so that, whatever use it might have for purposes of reference, the features of most consequence might be obscured. For this reason the second method has been chosen.

The War in France and Flanders falls naturally into three main periods. There was the initial epoch of mobile operations, which, as far as the British Expeditionary Force was concerned, lasted from the 12th of August, 1914, when the troops began to arrive in France, and the 16th of September, 1914, when the line on the Aisne was ordered to be strongly entrenched.* The dreary years of stabilisation followed until the summer of 1918 and the precise date when this state of affairs may be said to have terminated is difficult and perhaps a little invidious to fix. From August 1918 onwards, however, operations were developing into a general pursuit on a gigantic scale following a break through.

The most lively interest is inevitably attached to the first and last periods.

With the original Expeditionary Force of six divisions

* The following is the extract from the *Official History* on this subject (vol. 1, p. 374): "Sir John French's operation orders for the 16th of September ordered the line held by the army to be strongly entrenched. ...His orders proved to be the official notification of the commencement of trench warfare".

and a cavalry division, army and lines of communication troops,* were mobilised thirty-four horse and nineteen mechanical transport companies; three remount depots and sixty supply units of various sizes, figures, amounting to some 15,000 all ranks, which give some measure of the participation of the Army Service Corps in the regular field army.† The initial movements, which effected a concentration of four divisions and the cavalry division in the neighbourhood of Le Cateau on the left flank of the Fifth French Army was completed by the 20th of August, when an advance northwards was carried out to

* The 6th Division did not embark for France until the 8/9th of September.
† These units were
HORSE TRANSPORT:
    Headquarters Cavalry Divisional A.S.C.;
    1st–6th Division Trains;
    Army Troops Train;
    1st–6th Reserve Parks;
    Advanced Horse Transport Depot;
    Base Horse Transport Depot.
MECHANICAL TRANSPORT:
    1st–6th Divisional Supply Columns;
    1st–6th Divisional Ammunition Parks;
    Cavalry Supply Column;
    Cavalry Ammunition Park;
    5th Cavalry Brigade Supply Column;
    5th Cavalry Brigade Ammunition Park;
    Army Troops Supply Column;
    Advanced Mechanical Transport Depot;
    Base Mechanical Transport Depot.
SUPPLY:
    1st–6th Field Bakeries;
    1st–6th Field Butcheries;
    1st–8th Railway Supply Detachments;
    1st–8th Bakery Sections;
    1st–30th Depot units of Supply;
    Central Requisition Office;
    Branch Requisition Office.
REMOUNTS:
    Nos. 1 and 2 Advanced Remount Depots;
    Base Remount Depot.

The Army Service Corps had too to provide in addition the whole of the transport *personnel* for the Field Ambulances, as well as that for headquarter formations such as divisions, brigades, etc.

THE BRITISH EXPEDITIONARY FORCE

Mons, where the first action was delivered three days later. Sir John French's operation order instructing this move, fixed rendezvous for the supply columns on the 21st of August at Douzies for the cavalry, Boue for the First Army Corps, and Landrecies for the Second Army Corps and army troops. The progress of the supply arrangements may conveniently be followed from the operation orders issued by General Headquarters and the Army Corps. By the 28th of August the supply railheads were back at Lamotte Breuil (cavalry), Attichy (First Corps) and Compiègne (the remainder), the latter place being over one hundred miles from Mons. It was with great difficulty that the troops were fed during the retreat, as they were almost continuously fighting and marching and could not in many instances be found by the transport columns; in addition, difficulties were accentuated by the congestion on the road caused by refugees. But one fact became abundantly clear, and that was that, had the old transport and supply system in vogue before 1912 attempted to have dealt with the situation, the confusion inherent in a retreat under heavy pressure would have been many times increased, and the troops probably not fed in any manner at all. As it was, with the limited number of roads at the disposal of the army, the staff had anxious moments in clearing them of transport to allow of the passage of troops.

The military situation had then become such that the bases which had been organised at Boulogne and Le Havre were no longer safe—indeed the advance of the enemy had already dispossessed the British of the Advanced Base at Amiens. The contingency had been foreseen by the Quartermaster-General's Department on the 24th of August, the day after the fighting at Mons, and from that date all further movement of men and stores to the two former ports had been stopped, and the difficult undertaking of a change of base when the army was heavily involved had to be carried out with the minimum of warning. By the 27th of August, Boulogne had been cleared of stores and closed as a point of disembarkation: on the 29th St Nazaire on the River Loire was selected in lieu. At that time there were 60,000 tons of stores in Le Havre, also 15,000 men and 1500 horses all awaiting transfer to St Nazaire. By the 5th of September, every pound of stores and supplies had been removed from Le Havre, the whole of the *personnel* having been evacuated two days previously. Despite this effort, in itself no mean feat of organisation, some days were bound to elapse before the huge accumulation could be landed, and the new base put in working order for the despatch of what was needed at the front by a longer line of communication which then ran by two railway routes—one via Saumur and the other by Le Mans—to Villeneuve St Georges, just southeast of Paris, where there was one route to a varying railhead.

The retreat of the British Army continued until the 5th of September, having lasted thirteen days, during which time the troops marched some two hundred miles and then found themselves south-east of Paris. On the following day Sir John French passed to the offensive, crossing the Marne on the 9th of September and the Aisne on the 12th in pursuit of the enemy. North of the Aisne River the line was stabilised, and the British troops remained in this position until the 8th of October, when, with the exception of the cavalry who marched, they commenced entrainment for the north to take their place on the left of the French line.

It was just after this that Major-General Clayton relieved Brig.-General King as Director of Supplies, the latter being invalided to the United Kingdom. The most energetic action was taken to put matters on a proper footing and to provide for the steadily increasing strength of the army, which by the middle of September had attained figures of 240,000 British, 25,000 Indians, and

100,000 animals. The heavy fighting around Ypres and the uncertainty as to how that fateful struggle would end made the period one of the most critical of the whole war. Emergencies were provided for by having *en cas mobile* trains loaded with supplies standing by ready to move at short notice. The maintenance of the Indian troops was a source of embarrassment as it was desirable to meet their tastes as far as possible and to supply them with the special foodstuffs demanded by caste prejudices, especially in view of the unusual conditions with which they had to cope, and did cope so gallantly at a time of crisis. But unfortunately the Indian contingent was sent scantily provided for as regards supply *personnel* and this fact gravely handicapped the efforts to meet their needs. Further complications ensued through the inferior quality of supplies which accompanied them and the lack of system by which they were packed. The tea and hay, among other articles, were quite unfit for issue, while packages alleged to contain salt were strongly adulterated with sodium sulphate. Various commodities and even consignments of the same commodity were put up in different ways, thus rendering stocktaking almost impossible or at best a lengthy process. Again the barley, which was the accustomed ration for the animals and which had accompanied them, became violently unpopular once oats became available, and the latter were consequently demanded by the Indian cavalry. These and many other details unduly perplexed the supply directorate which was then inadequately staffed. In addition, there were delicate questions to be solved in relation to the French. At one time it was feared that all imported supplies were to be deemed as liable for customs duty while the "octroi" payable on local produce brought into towns was actually insisted upon. Nevertheless the co-operation of the French authorities on the whole left little to be desired, provided they were treated with tact and discretion.

When the battle of Ypres had died down and the necessary reliefs of the exhausted troops had been carried out, the army lay on a compact front from the La Bassée Canal at Givenchy to opposite Wytschaete, a distance of twenty-one miles. General Headquarters was located at St Omer and Advanced General Headquarters at Bailleul. Both sides required time to draw breath and reorganise after their heavy losses—those of the British amounting to over 54,000 killed, wounded and missing. What these casualties spelt to the field ambulances is at times apt to be overlooked in the more dramatic events elsewhere. Although these units pertain to the Royal Army Medical Corps, their transport, both horse and mechanical, which forms in fact about one-sixth of their *personnel*, is wholly found from the Army Service Corps, and may equally be recognised with the medical officers and orderlies for its devoted work. The main centre of medical activity was at Ypres, various advanced dressing stations being located on the Menin road and at St Julien and Wiette, and the wounded were brought back from the regimental aid posts in horse and motor vehicles whence they were evacuated as soon as possible by motor ambulances to the ambulance or ordinary trains. By mid-November five motor ambulance convoys of thirty to forty vehicles each were in France.*

If no very complex one, in spite of certain difficulties experienced in the movement of supply and ammunition columns to refilling points owing to lack of co-ordination between the Allies,† the task of the normal transport

* No. 2 Motor Ambulance Convoy did not arrive in France until the 14th of October. It was quickly followed by No. 3, on the 15th, No. 4, on the 28th, and No. 5, on the 11th of November.

† The French used a system of circular routes for the supply of their troops without regard to the British in the vicinity, and frequently changed the routes without notification. Thus it sometimes happened that motor transport met "head on" on the Belgian roads paved only for the width of one vehicle, with deep mud on either side, and great delays ensued.

units was one of unremitting labour. Though well served by railheads, there was an increasing volume of material in the shape of engineer, ordnance, and other stores to be carried into the forward areas for the purpose of ameliorating the situation of the troops.* Even at that static epoch the necessity for ample transport establishments was apparent and, whatever was not provided by pre-War foresight, transport certainly was, and moreover in scientifically organised formations. But when in the history of war has a commander ever been known to aver that he had too much transport? Any instance is far to seek, since it is the equivalent of saying that he had too much mobility, and it is of interest to note that in the *Official History of the War* it is stated that as far as trench stores, such as timber and sandbags went, there was insufficient transport to deal with the quantities reaching railheads.† Had Army Service Corps establishments been of a less liberal nature the work of consolidation would have been grievously handicapped.

There is no call to linger over the events of the year 1915. From the point of view of operations the period was marked by the offensive enterprises of Neuve Chapelle and Loos in March and September respectively, and the

* Railway lines radiated conveniently from St Omer and Hazebrouck. During the critical period of the battle of Ypres, supply railheads were as follows:

On the Hazebrouck-Lillers-Bethune line—
  Steenbecque for the Cavalry Corps.
  Choques (west of Bethune) for the Indian Corps.
On the Berguette-Armentières line—
  St Venant for (III) Army Corps—19th Infantry Brigade.
  Basse, Boulogne (near Merville) for (IV) Corps.
On the St Omer-Hazebrouck-Armentières line—
  St Omer for General Headquarters and Royal Flying Corps.
  Hazebrouck for (I) Corps.
  Strazeele for (II) Corps.

The ammunition railheads were at Aire and Arques, both on the St Omer–Berguette line.

† Vol. III, p. 6. *Official History of the War*—Military operations in France and Belgium, by Brigadier-General J. E. Edmonds, C.B., C.M.G., p.s.c.

defensive battle known as the Second Battle of Ypres in April.* Disappointing as these were in material results, they served the purpose of giving the rapidly increasing army experience which could not be obtained except at the price of errors and sacrifice.

While this condition naturally applied more to the fighting than to the administrative troops, the lessons gained had their value in enabling the latter to improve ways and means and to adjust their methods to meet the needs of the troops in the new style of warfare. At the same time the maintenance services were expanding and developing their machinery to meet the growth of the army and laying securely the foundations of a system which even the subsequent transfer of their most skilled *personnel* could not throw out of gear. At the end of December 1914, the British Forces comprised eleven divisions and five cavalry divisions: a year later the numbers stood at thirty divisions and five cavalry divisions. They had at one time been even higher but the Indian Corps and four British divisions had been despatched to Mesopotamia and Salonica respectively during the last quarter of the year.

Proportionate with the increase in the higher fighting

---

* The following extract from the *Official History*, vol. III, p. 266, suffices to describe the work carried out by the Corps in the Ypres Salient at that time: "The dangers and hazards of getting ammunition and supplies into, and the wounded out of the Salient each night were immense. The columns were brought to a certain rendezvous and then taken over by guides who knew how to avoid the areas most favoured by the German artillery. By careful observation of the areas and routes that the Germans shelled—of course on a methodical programme—it was possible after a little time for the R.A., R.A.S.C., and R.A.M.C., and the regimental transport which had to go back across the canal, to the refilling points, to bring their columns through without heavy casualties; but shelled the enemy never so furiously, the transport moved slowly and deliberately, without lights, never pausing on its way except to avoid a shell hole or clear a lorry that had been hit. So ammunition and supplies were brought up and wounded got away. It was a marvellous display of cold-blooded courage and discipline which greatly impressed those who heard although they could seldom see the long procession of vehicles that went up night after night".

formations in the shape of divisions was the growth in Army Corps, army and lines of communication troops, and for the Army Service Corps these accretions involved more than additional mouths to be fed and a greater bulk of stores and supplies to be transported. For among the most prominent of the measures taken to strengthen the army was the creation of a numerous and powerful heavy artillery for which the Mechanical Transport Branch was called upon to provide its means of mobility. In this direction responsibilities continued to grow until the end of the campaign.

Two major operations stood out in 1916—that conducted in defence of Verdun from February onwards by the French, and the battle of the Somme which was initiated by Sir Douglas Haig on the 1st of July. Conceived on a more extensive scale than anything up to then undertaken by the British Army, the preparations carried on for months previous were enormous and entailed continuous and heavy work for both horse and mechanical transport. Great dumps of supplies, ammunition, engineer and other stores of every description were built up in the forward areas, while material for road construction involved shifting thousands of tons. In this prosaic but essential work the non-divisional horse transport units such as the reserve parks were kept fully employed, with such others as could be spared from their normal duties of maintenance.

By the middle of the year the man-power situation was causing anxiety at the War Office. The results of the recently introduced Conscription Bill were yet to make themselves felt, while heavy casualties were anticipated in the operations that were being undertaken on the Somme. It was obvious that some re-distribution of the *personnel* serving in the army would be necessary, though it was not fully grasped at that time how drastic a form this would eventually take.

The Directorate of Supplies and Transport at the War

Office had, for some time past, been seriously considering its commitments, for it realised that the time was coming when it would no longer be able to count on being treated generously in respect to man power. The question was first approached from the point of reductions in the scale of transport. In the United Kingdom—the great base upon which all the Expeditionary Forces depended—matters were already cut very fine: all transport was fully and continuously employed. In other theatres local resources were already being exploited to supplement British *personnel*, and moreover, with the exception of the Balkans, the operations were of a mobile or semi-mobile nature, thus vetoing any overhaul with a view to reduction of establishments which had been carefully worked out.

The army in France and Flanders was in a very different situation. A stalemate existed, and although it was both desired and hoped to break up the war of position, extensive movement was unlikely for some time. Moreover it was in France that the Army Service Corps attained formidable numbers that might make some process of re-organisation worth while.

The strength of the Corps under Sir Douglas Haig on the 31st of July, 1916, was 3396 officers and 119,493 other ranks out of an army of 1,565,800 or 8 per cent. of the whole,* and of these over 20,000, chiefly of the Mechanical Transport Branch, were serving with fighting arms.

It will be remembered that the original establishments of the Expeditionary Force had furnished a horsed reserve park for each division to carry two days' supplies as a measure of security in case the normal flow was for any reason interrupted, and to give the army more free-

---

* The detail which included the Dominion Army Service Corps was as follows:
Supply 32,699.
Horse Transport 32,511 (of which 3075 were artificers).
Mechanical Transport 54,283 (of which 9515 were artificers).

THE BRITISH EXPEDITIONARY FORCE

dom of manœuvre. As early as 1915 the War Office called for reductions in this direction and, as a result, the scale was reduced to two reserve parks for each Army Corps of three divisions. As it was not at that stage realised that static warfare had set in as a semi-permanent condition, General Headquarters was naturally unwilling to go further. A year later, however, the reserve parks were down to a scale of one per two divisions, thus effecting a saving of 271 officers and men, and 358 horses for every division in the field.

In 1915 also an effort was made to reduce the *personnel* of divisional supply columns and ammunition parks which was based on the scale of three and a half men per lorry in the case of the former, and three and a quarter men per lorry in the case of the latter. These figures were lowered to two and a quarter in each case—a material economy, as there were at that time over 40 divisions in France.

It was not until July 1916 that the question was put to the Expeditionary Force as to whether some decrease could not be made in the divisional trains, the constitution of which formations had, naturally, been based on mobile warfare. There were, for instance, included the officers necessary for requisitioning on an extensive scale—obviously no very complicated matter with the army unable to advance, while the scale on which requisitioning could be carried out in the occupied areas was strictly limited. The outcome of the proposals effected a reduction of 200 transport officers.

Meanwhile similar steps were in train as concerned the supply *personnel*. In May 1916 the matter was opened up by a communication from the Director of Supplies at the War Office to the Inspector-General of Communications in France offering to replace 5500 category "A" men employed under the direction of the latter by those of lower category from the United Kingdom. It was, too, represented that a clean sweep in this respect was desirable as soon as substitutes could be found.

This proposal initiated the system under which wholesale transfers were subsequently effected.*

At the same time consideration was given to economy from reductions in the establishments of existing formations. Supply units on the lines of communication had originally been provided for on the basis of five depot units of supply—each consisting of one officer and thirteen other ranks—for each division. These small units were very handy and in certain theatres were almost indispensable in that shape, but they had been contemplated for a force of six divisions and it was obvious that for between forty and fifty divisions the same proportion was not required. It was therefore decided to re-organise on an Army Corps basis, and accordingly a new unit entitled a Lines of Communication Supply Company was formed for every Army Corps of three divisions; and by this means some two hundred officers and eleven hundred other ranks were dispensed with or made available for other purposes, for it was at the same time found possible to make adjustments of a similar nature with regard to the field butcheries and bakeries.

While the sum of these preliminary measures was substantial, it is not only for that reason that attention has

* During 1917 many thousands of horse transport drivers were so transferred, large numbers coming from the Divisional Trains. These were assembled in the Army Service Corps Base Depot at Havre and were drafted to battalions after very brief training at Infantry Base Depots. The spirit of these men returning "up the line" in their new rôle was wholly admirable and in this connection one small incident is worth relating.

In the autumn of 1917 some battalions of the 60th Rifles had after a gallant resistance been overwhelmed by a crack German Marine Corps near Nieuport. These units had recently received large drafts of ex-Army Service Corps drivers, and the adjutant of one battalion who survived the fight wrote to the Officer Commanding the Army Service Corps Depot at Havre, asking whether it could be arranged that further men from the same source could be provided for the re-constitution of the unit, as those which had previously been incorporated had conducted themselves so splendidly in face of the enemy.

been directed to them. For they serve to demonstrate also that the Army Service Corps had no intention or desire to assure its own position at the expense of wider needs, but that it was at a comparatively early stage alive to new circumstances, and in some cases may even be said to have anticipated them. Yet in contradiction to the ideas held in certain quarters as to the physical demands made by the work of the Corps in the field, a great deal of that work could only fairly and effectively be performed by those of a high standard of bodily fitness. The duties of the Divisional Army Service Corps, which in the form of the horsed train consisting of some thirty officers and over seven hundred other ranks, was of a specially strenuous nature. Moving as it did, mostly by night, into the forward areas, over roads or tracks difficult enough in themselves but also constantly searched by enemy shell fire or aerial bombing, its task had, whatever were the conditions, to be performed regularly every twenty-four hours. The fact that there could be no respite made that task a heavy mental and bodily strain—mental, because whatever punishment it received from the enemy it had no opportunity to retaliate, but had to deliver its loads to the troops—physical, because of the long hours over difficult ground added to what every mounted man knows, that, with animals to be cared for, the work is but half done when he re-enters his billet or bivouac.

The service was indeed one demanding no mean standard of discipline—the horsemastership was in fact not excelled in any other branch of the army, and the greater part of the casualties in the ranks of the Corps was sustained in the divisional trains and field ambulances. Yet its duties involved more hard toil than glory. In their stubborn monotony they do not lend themselves to any picturesque or romantic story such as attracts public attention or public fancy. The work was, as all sound work should be, its own reward.

There are none, however, who participated in those activities but would desire to pay tribute to the thousands of noble animals who played a humble and yet an important part in the maintenance of the armies and the saving of the wounded. The transport service knows them no longer, and for them it is well. But the passing of the horse has removed a certain humanising influence of which nothing can take the place.

With historical records available of hundreds of Army Service Corps units which served in France,* the natural course would be to take refuge in generalisations. For to cover the doings of even a fraction would far exceed the limits of space, even if such narration had any real utility; while on the other hand it would seem invidious to select any one or two for special mention, when all were doing similar work in a very similar manner.

But this last risk must be accepted, if only to indicate to those who may belong to a post-War generation the place which the horsed divisional train had in the scheme of things. The 9th Divisional Train is taken, not because it was necessarily more efficient than any other (although it was a very efficient unit), or because its career was more adventurous, but simply because it was the first New Army train to take the field and may therefore be considered as the prototype of those formations.

Consisting of Nos. 104, 105, 106 and 107 Companies Army Service Corps it came into being in August 1914 and commenced the work of feeding its division at Bordon in January 1915. Under the command of Lieut.-Colonel R. P. Crawley, the train accompanied its division to France in May 1915, and from thence onwards no single instance occurred of the troops failing to receive their supplies regularly owing to any breakdown of its Army Service Corps.

* The majority of the records were compiled by 2nd Lieutenant R. Victor Beveridge and Lieutenant R. G. Jolley, A.S.C., to whose work the author is much indebted.

Up to January 1916 the normal supply system was in vogue, the divisional supply column drawing in bulk from railhead and dumping on the following morning at refilling points, where the supplies were loaded in detail on to the train wagons and thence delivered to the troops. From February onwards the mechanical transport echelon was as a rule dispensed with, and the system of the train wagons drawing in bulk from railhead, dumping at refilling point and then refilling in detail, was adopted. This course was only made practicable by the proximity or comparative proximity of railhead to the troops.

In September 1915 when preparations were being made for the Loos offensive, it became necessary to devise some scheme for keeping transport as much as possible off the roads, and accordingly the tailboard system of loading into wagons was utilised. This consisted of drawing up both lorries and horse-drawn wagons tailboard to tailboard in a suitable field and transferring the loads without dumping the supplies on the ground.

The first forward dump was put up near the Fosse, in Annequin, a few nights before the offensive commenced, and consisted of 10,000 iron rations in boxes. These were taken forward during three successive nights and placed in carefully camouflaged stacks near the Fosse. On the fourth night they were removed to Cambrin, where they were handed over to the custody of the battalions.

This particular consignment happened to come in very appropriately, though not for the 9th Division, by whom they were handed over to another division which, owing to leaving their cookers behind by an error of judgment, arrived to support the attack without rations.

In July 1916 when at Sailly Laurette the supplies came direct to refilling points on barges, being off loaded to a covered shed on the bank of the canal, and under these circumstances the whole proceedings were slow.

On the eve of the first Somme offensive in 1916 the train was quartered at Grove Town, near Bray, where it refilled direct from railhead, the railway siding running along the road upon which the wagons were drawn up. Two reserve dumps of iron rations which had been taken over from the 30th Division at Maricourt were advanced later to Nord Allée in Montauban, to Carnoy Valley and subsequently to a point just south-west of Longueval, these moves involving casualties to three officers, five other ranks and a number of horses.

In September 1916 four forward dumps of iron rations were put up on the Vimy Ridge, the two in the right divisional sector being conveyed by light railway from St Eloi through the Zouave valley by night, and those in the left divisional sector being also taken by night by horse transport to Souchez to positions swept by machine-gun fire and within four hundred yards of the enemy lines.

Towards the end of March 1917 three reserve dumps were placed in position for the Arras offensive, the most forward of which, to serve the troops engaged, being located near the candle factory at St Nicholas, where it was much damaged by shell fire before the operations started.

For the attack from the Frezenberg Ridge in September of the same year, four forward dumps of iron rations and water were established at Kit and Cat, Bavaria House, Grey Ruin, and at Railway Copse in Cambridge Road, the supplies being conveyed as far as wheels could go and thence taken on by infantry carrying parties. They suffered much from enemy action.

On the morning of the 21st of March, 1918, the intense enemy bombardment swept practically every road with 5·9 inch shell and shrapnel and gas masks had to be worn while delivering supplies. The retreat began at

2 p.m. but forty drivers of the train were, under the command of Captain Hilton Simpson, left behind at Nurlu for the defence of the Nurlu–Fins road until the following day. For the next ten days the transport companies covered an average of twenty-five miles every twenty-four hours, certain of the movements being carried out by night, and they were usually under orders to move at fifteen minutes' notice. Consequently the horses were compelled to remain in harness for practically the whole of this period, grooming being done while awaiting orders for delivery of supplies, and pieces of harness being removed for this purpose. In spite of these conditions there was no single case of gall or rub in the whole train, although there were a number of casualties among the animals from enemy artillery and aerial bombs. Four baggage wagons were destroyed by shells, but otherwise there were no losses among the vehicles. Although there were no traffic controls, march discipline was splendidly maintained throughout and there was no serious case of congestion or blockage.

But the most satisfactory feature of those troublous times was the close touch maintained with the fighting troops of the division under the circumstances of difficulty due to a retreat under pressure of the enemy. Intercommunication between train companies and the first line transport of their brigades was maintained by means of orderlies, and communication was at all times kept up between Divisional Headquarters and the headquarters of the train. By these means the delivery of rations was much facilitated.

After one day's rest at Talmas, the 9th Divisional Train had a four days' march by road to the Ypres sector, arriving there four days before the German offensive on the line of the River Lys, and thus found itself once more in the centre of events.

Such, for there is no necessity to follow its fortunes any further, was the typical rôle played by the Army

Service Corps of the division. In this particular instance the casualties in *personnel* were not heavy,* but casualties are not always the surest gauge of the physical demands made upon the *personnel* or the quality of their work. That quality may best be appreciated by contrasting the order, discipline and regularity of the maintenance arrangements which normally prevailed during the course of the Great War with the confusion and chaos so common in past campaigns, when the transport and supply services had been neglected in times of peace.

Paradoxically enough the conditions of position warfare in France in no way diminished the part taken by transport in general.† In some respects it actually enhanced it, and the reasons for this are worth some brief emphasis. In the early stages following stabilisation the most optimistic views prevailed regarding possibilities of a "break through". Nor were these views confined to any one army. Masses of cavalry were retained in hand to exploit success that never came to the extent that could be exploited by cavalry. Even the comparatively limited objectives, which were set as the task of the infantry in the plan of battle, were rarely obtained until the conditions of the modern battlefield were sufficiently comprehended. And such comprehension was slow in coming. The methods by which the Germans owed their initial successes in the spring of 1918 are well known. Yet even those successes, and they were probably up to that time the greatest in the tactical sense which had been obtained on the Western Front, were very limited.

What was the primary reason for their limitation?

It may be supposed that after the defeat of the Fifth

* Up to and including the Lys battle there were one officer killed and six wounded, four other ranks killed and twenty-six wounded.

† The following extract from the *Official History*, vol. III, p. 355, is apposite in this connection: "The control by the higher commanders of the actual fighting when once it had begun remained almost negligible; and their efforts were then best directed to ensuring the provision of ammunition, rations, water and the special stores and material required so that their men might fight to best advantage".

Army at the battle of St Quentin or of the French a little later on the Aisne, the enemy had an unparalleled opportunity for effecting something decisive. Tactically the German troops were superior to their enemies on both those occasions, and it was eminently desirable from the point of view of their High Command to press to the utmost the advantage they had obtained. That they were unable to do this was not so much due to the positive resistance which they encountered, but because they could not continue to push forward sufficient means of overcoming such resistance as existed. It was obviously useless pushing forward infantry and machine gunners if the necessary means to support them in the shape of ammunition, supplies and artillery could not be brought forward simultaneously. But in fact even the infantry could not be pushed forward rapidly unless roads existed over which they could be transported by motor lorries. In the case therefore where the *morale* of the defenders still held there was exemplified in every great battle in the west that, whatever the initial success on the part of the aggressor, the impetus died away as soon as the attacking troops outran their means of support. And the conditions of the modern battlefield, with great areas over which the advance is to be made devastated by the powerful explosives hurled by both sides, made such means of support a complicated and difficult problem. In fact the mobility which was the key to the situation was most difficult of attainment.

The problem of continuing, and extending, an initial success into a victorious general action lay fundamentally in transport, and transport in the sense of capacity to move large bodies of men rapidly from one part of the line to another, and to develop forward communications with the advance of the troops so that they should be able, even after a considerable advance, to give battle to the enemy under the same or approximately the same conditions as they did at the beginning of their forward movements; that they should be supported by the same amount and weight of artillery, by the same number of tanks; that they should be as easily and as quickly fed, and finally that they should equally receive all machine guns, trench mortars, ammunition, and other assistance as was available for them at the outset. There was, in addition, the further consideration which lay in sufficiency of men to prosecute an initial success. There again the question of movement was involved. But, since the losses at the beginning of an advance were comparatively small in proportion to those suffered at the later stages when the enemy had retreated on to his material and the attacker had outrun his, this aspect was by no means the dominating one. The trouble was that the fresh troops which took the place of those who made the initial thrust were not supported and could not be supplied in an equal measure. To support them in an equal measure was the problem to be overcome, and that in its essence was a question of transport.

The Allied offensives during the last three months of the struggle demonstrate the improved methods by which the difficulties were overcome. But it would be unwise to draw any full conclusions, since the operations in question were facilitated by the falling *morale* of the enemy and the untrustworthy condition of certain of his divisions.

Now the considerations which have been touched upon above open up the wide field of what may be termed the tactics of transport, in that its manipulation in the battle and not the rearward zone is concerned. It is an aspect to which but little attention had been given, because the circumstances as obtained in France between 1915 and 1918 had not been previously contemplated. Second line transport had been conceived as something that carried out its functions comfortably removed from the rougher activities—indeed mobile warfare demanded that it should be kept well clear of the fighting troops in order to avoid hampering their power of manœuvre when they were dependent on a limited number of roads as would normally be the case in a civilised country.

On the other hand, the more methodical and leisurely processes of position warfare required closer association and touch between the actual combatants and the machinery which purveyed the wherewithal to fight and to continue fighting. In this respect the task of the transport was enhanced in much the same way as that of the Royal Engineers. Both were important auxiliaries on the spot.

There is no place to pursue this argument here, but it may be well to recall the fact, somewhat obscured as a rule, that the Army Service Corps was during the Great War, as it still is theoretically, the Transport Corps of the Army, and not an organisation concerned wholly or even primarily with the carriage of loads emanating from its own Supply Branch. As will be shown later, in the Mesopotamian plains, where movement was not restricted by roads, there was a very proper appreciation of the tactical use of transport.

What is alternatively known as the battle of Passchendaele or the third battle of Ypres, in the autumn of 1917, put the mechanical transport to the severest test it had up to that time experienced—in that it was during the course of these operations that the heaviest concentration of artillery fire was experienced.* In the later

* As instancing the nature of the work the following notification awarding the Distinguished Conduct Medal to Corporal A. R. Wadsworth of the 15th Ammunition Sub-Park is given, as typical of many similar instances: "On the night of July 14th, 1918, a number of ammunition lorries were held up outside Ypres owing to heavy shell fire. One of the Company's lorries was hit by an incendiary shell and set on fire. The ammunition began to explode and eventually three of the Company lorries were completely destroyed together with twelve Siege Park lorries in front. This N.C.O. saved the other four by reversing them out of danger. When rescuing the fourth vehicle he had to remain for two and a half hours in a ditch owing to the explosions taking place in the Siege Park vehicles".

phases, the roads upon which many of the more important formations had to depend for their maintenance were without foundations, being a mere crust laid upon a soft clay subsoil and designed only for farm traffic. Owing to continuous rain these quickly became veritable sloughs, especially the Hell Fire Corner–Westhoek–Zonnebeke and Ypres–Wieltje roads—more than 100,000 troops being dependent on the former.

The successful work of the mechanical transport under such conditions proved that upon this service could be placed a reliance previously unimagined, for, provided stone and timber were available, even the most elementary track could be made temporarily fit and maintained so in spite of the most intelligent direction of enemy artillery fire against nodal points. The elasticity of road transport and its susceptibility to control enabled it to take full advantage of the lulls in hostile fire, while shell holes were quickly filled in with rubble dumped from lorries. It was thus found that mechanical transport could operate effectively, while light railways were almost completely immobilised.

During the winter of 1917–18 an important re-organisation of the mechanical transport took place as a measure of precaution against possible railway breakdowns. The policy adopted involved the principle that the vehicles were to be "pooled" for common use and, save in a few isolated instances, were not to be specialised for any particular service. In place of ammunition sub-parks, army divisional and corps troops supply columns, auxiliary patrol companies and similar units, mechanical transport companies were organised on a universal establishment of a headquarters and number of sections of sixteen lorries each. Divisional mechanical transport companies consisted of five sections and those of corps troops of two sections each, and these units were allotted in the proportion of one to each division and one to each corps troops. One company was allotted to each Army Headquarters for army troops and one to General Headquarters for G.H.Q. troops. These measures secured a large economy in vehicles as well as in *personnel*, and were based on the practice in the French Army by which "pooled" vehicles, if scientifically used, produced a greater output of work per vehicle than in the case of those affiliated exclusively to units. The balance thus obtained was put into a general reserve, a portion of which was placed on one side to provide replacements, the number retained for this purpose being calculated upon the requirements of 1917. The General Reserve was formed into General Headquarters reserve companies and in the first place eight and subsequently twelve of these came into being, each comprising a Headquarters and six sections.

This new grouping fully justified itself during the retreat and subsequent advance of 1918 when mechanical transport filled the breach made by the breakdown of the railways, and it may even be considered surprising that some such organisation had not been evolved at an earlier date. The original allotment had been admirably suited to a small force, but with the growth of the army it became extravagant, especially as the conditions of affairs were static and a considerable proportion of divisions was out of the line and at rest. Even allowing for contingencies of movement, and it was indisputably wise to so allow, it would have made for greater economy and no less efficiency to have carried out a certain re-grouping with a view to a high degree of centralisation of transport resources. In this connection the system which obtained in the French Army at the outbreak of war may be noticed. By the organisation of their mechanical transport, published in 1913, the basic unit was a self-contained section of twenty vehicles, sections being devoted to various services in three main divisions—those in use by armies, General Headquarters and what was known as the "Parc de Réserve" of each army, which dealt with such needs as those of heavy artillery and aviation. A large General Headquarters pool was formed as early as 1915, and in August 1918 consisted of 11,000 vehicles capable of transporting 200,000 men. Four sections constituted a group, and five to six groups a *groupement*.

In respect to the manner in which it was maintained and in its capacity to meet every call made upon it, the Army Service Corps mechanical transport was not excelled elsewhere, but its "mass" movement was not, until the re-organisation took place, as scientifically operated as that of the French, who from the time of the battle of Verdun in February 1916 introduced a definite system of control which produced most effective results. That the French Army should have been somewhat ahead of the British in its conception of the uses of mechanical transport in bulk was only to be expected, since greater opportunities had been vouchsafed it prior to the War of considering the problems likely to arise. A subsidy scheme had been introduced as early as 1908 and in the course of the ensuing four years 6000 vehicles were put into use. The movement of *personnel* had been the object of study far beyond what had been contemplated in the British service, which in fact up to the latter part of 1916 possessed no mechanical transport formations solely available to move even a brigade from one army area to another under the direction of General Headquarters. Strategic moves were normally carried out by rail or march route. Provision, it is true, had been made for an auxiliary omnibus company, of about fifty vehicles, to be stationed in each army area for the conveyance of troops within that area under direction of the Army concerned, but this arrangement far from responded to more than comparatively local requirements. The need for a more far-reaching system soon made itself apparent.

It was, therefore, decided to place all the omnibus

companies in France under one command to be operated by General Headquarters—the unit to be known as the Auxiliary Omnibus Park (Mechanical Transport). This re-organisation began during the winter of 1916 and the formation was finally established by the spring of the following year, being commanded in the first instance by Lieut.-Colonel G. L. H. Howell, A.S.C., who was transferred from the 13th Corps Ammunition Park for that purpose.

The five existing omnibus companies were concentrated at St Valery-sur-Somme during October and November 1916 and two companies were then added to them, one of these latter consisting of charsabancs and the other of troop-carrying lorries. The strength of the whole then amounted to some six hundred and fifty vehicles manned by some eighteen hundred of all ranks, and its capacity was that of the dismounted troops of a division, the headquarters company conveying the divisional troops and each of the remaining companies half an infantry brigade. The work of preparation was severe, as it entailed the conversion of lorries to troop-carrying vehicles, while a high proportion of the buses were in so bad a state as to be practically immobile. It was only by dint of very hard work that everything was ready in time for the concentration at Amiens in March 1917. The seven companies of the park were then located at intervals on the main trunk road through Amiens–Doullens–St Pol to the Ypres sector and all orders for its operations were transmitted from the General Staff at General Headquarters direct to the Park Headquarters, being normally sent by telephone and confirmed by despatch rider. A combined traffic embussing and debussing map was drawn up for the whole front, showing army areas, direction of traffic on all roads and all embussing and debussing points, which were numbered and also marked on the ground. There were a large number of these points, every army area being allotted a sufficient number

THE BRITISH EXPEDITIONARY FORCE

to ensure movement of troops wherever they might happen to be located.

When the system had become properly established, moves of divisions were effected smoothly and rapidly—the bus columns being available to move within one hour of the receipt of their orders, while the actual process of embussing and debussing a division seldom took more than half an hour. The record for a brigade was four and a half minutes. During the enemy offensive of 1918 many of the moves were of a vital nature, and had an influential bearing on the operations. Among such as are worthy of record may be mentioned the move of the 12th Division from the First Army into the gap at Albert in March 1918, the move of a Guards Brigade into the breach near Strazelle during the same critical period, and the move of a large portion of the Canadian and the Australian Army Corps from the Arras sector to Amiens for the offensive in 1918, this last being carried out largely by night. In the course of these undertakings the bus drivers were often at the wheel for periods up to sixty hours at a stretch.

For its services during the 1918 offensive the Auxiliary Omnibus Park was mentioned by name in the despatches of the Commander-in-Chief, being the only Army Service Corps unit in the British Expeditionary Force to receive that distinction during the course of the War.

As illustrating what could be accomplished in the way of troop movement by a highly organised road transport service, the instance of the French effort following the retreat of the Fifth British Army at the battle of St Quentin may be quoted. In a period of over twenty-four hours between the 22nd of March and the 2nd of April the French actually had on motor lorries 100,000 men completely equipped and three divisional artilleries including their horses. The movement in question necessitated 18,000 trips of 300 kilometres each and a total of 11,200 lorries were used. During the same period eight complete divisions were moved by rail and the equipage of fourteen. Following this operation the proposal was put forward by French General Headquarters that a reserve of 24,000 lorries should be formed from the various Allied Armies and placed under the command of Marshal Foch. It was not intended that the vehicles should remain inactive: they were merely to be earmarked and remain performing their ordinary duties until called up.

There were grave practical objections against this scheme, but it was nevertheless attractive, since its immediate objects were to ensure transport at any given moment of ten divisions complete with all their artillery, and to provide for the supply of forty divisions operating more than fifty kilometres from railhead. The first of these aims would have involved 11,200 vehicles and the second 12,800.

While in 1917 the British effort in Flanders dominated all else, the advance to the Hindenberg line in the early spring, after the voluntary withdrawal of the enemy, had kept the transport and supply services more than normally active in so far as the Third and Fifth Armies were concerned, and this unexpected forward movement once more emphasised the wisdom of maintaining intact ways and means of mobility through a long period of stagnation.

The history of the last year of the war is a tale familiar even to cursory students of military history. The long swaying struggle, which began on the 21st of March and ended on the 11th of November, may be divided into two periods, the first of which may be said to have ended on the 18th of July when the Allied counter-offensive, which marked the break-up of position warfare, was launched under Marshal Foch.

The German offensive of 1918, which closely followed the re-organisation of the mechanical transport, showed clearly the advantages of the new system. The enemy thrust was directed against certain vital railway centres behind the Allied front and the over-running of such important lateral lines as Amiens–Achiet–Arras and the interruption by shell fire of the line Hazebrouck–St Pol–Amiens–St Just interfered seriously with efficient rail working. Owing to the difficulty in finding return circuits for empty rolling stock, congestion and delays occurred in the main forward lines, and it became necessary to select railheads far back. At the same time heavy additional demands were made on the railways for stores for the construction of rear lines of defence, the evacuation of casualties and material of all kinds from areas threatened by the enemy.

Demands were also preferred on the British for maintenance of French, American and Portuguese troops, and for feeding civilians. Under these circumstances the railways became hopelessly overweighted and the situation had to be met by Mechanical Transport.

It was during the fighting in the spring of 1918 that Private R. G. Masters of the Army Service Corps, a driver attached to the 141st Field Ambulance, won the Victoria Cross on the 9th of April near Bethune, the award being announced in the *London Gazette* of the 8th of May, 1918, as follows:

For most conspicuous bravery and devotion to duty. Owing to an enemy attack, communications were cut off and wounded could not be evacuated. The road was reported impassable, but Private Masters volunteered to try to get through, and after the greatest difficulty succeeded, although he had to clear the road of all sorts of debris.

He made journey after journey throughout the afternoon, over a road consistently shelled and swept by machine-gun fire, and was on one occasion bombed by an aeroplane.

The greater part of the wounded cleared from this area were evacuated by Private Masters, as his was the only car that got through during this particular time.

On the eve of the offensive, which, so far as the British armies were concerned, started on the 8th of

August, Field-Marshal Sir Douglas Haig disposed of fifty-six divisions and three cavalry divisions. Although a strength of sixty divisions was subsequently attained, the zenith had been passed, for, in the previous year, there had been sixty-two divisions and five cavalry divisions. At the date of the Armistice the ration strength may be recalled as 2,360,400 men, of which 1,157,080, or approximately half, were combatants, figures which not only indicate the size of the administrative machinery necessary to support the fighting arms, but which also emphasise the immensity of the task of supply.

From the late summer onwards there was an unbroken record of victory, and events moved with almost incredible rapidity. The Hindenberg line was smashed at the end of September and early in the following month the German right wing in Flanders was driven in, and the coast cleared. On the 17th of October the 59th Division entered Lille and the general alignment of the British armies ran from along the Scheldt north of Valenciennes to the south of the latter town. The onward sweep of hundreds of thousands of men and thousands of guns in face of a German resistance, still obstinate, and over a devastated country, was indisputably the greatest military operation of all time, and it may be therefore somewhat in the nature of bathos to interject details of the material support which made that advance continually possible, even if such details could be given with reasonable brevity. Sufficient has, perhaps, been said as regards the constitution of the Army Service Corps in France, of its practical work and of the modifications introduced in its organisation to meet new or anticipated needs, for those details to be visualised. The results speak for themselves.

The elasticity of the system and the foresight which had always characterised its practical working enabled the strain to be taken with effort certainly, but yet without disorder. And it is just because of this last circumstance that recognition of what was then accomplished is not always forthcoming.

To appreciate the task is fundamentally a matter of time and space as most military problems are, but time and space involved with such weight of material to be pushed forward and distributed as had never up to then been contemplated.

On the last day of actual hostilities, the Allies had reached the Meuse with their centre from Charleville to Rocroi, the British Second Army being south of Ghent with the Fifth and a portion of the First in Artois, the remainder of the latter was in Picardy. The Fourth Army entered Mons on the 10th of November, and the Third Army was east of the Valenciennes–Hirson railway. The whole mass had been thrown forward between fifty and sixty miles, as the crow flies, from the Hindenberg line.

The question as to what extent Marshal Foch could have continued the pressure had the enemy succeeded in disengaging himself with a view to standing on the Rhine, is one the solution of which depended on the degree of resistance which he could there have offered, and, as far as the northern portion of the front was concerned, the extent to which the railways in Northern France and Belgium could have been put in working order in a short space of time. The Allies could not indefinitely operate at a distance from their railheads, and the events of the three months preceding the 11th of November had put a strain on the Army Service Corps mechanical transport formations, both as regards men and material, that could not be maintained at the same tension for a much longer period. The *personnel* were exhausted and the vehicles knocked about. The first fortnight of November marked the highest point of service and effort. The speed with which the enemy was driven back left the railways behind, and both supplies and ammunition had to be carried over execrable roads in bad weather. Bridges had everywhere been destroyed; the routes were strewn with bodies of the enemy dead and the wreckage of war. At times, owing to delay action mines and other causes, the supply trains could not reach their railheads, while supplies had constantly to be drawn by night. Had the further problem been merely one of feeding the troops, it could most certainly have been solved, but to have brought forward the vast quantities of ammunition and battle stores required for mounting offensives in face of serious resistance, would have demanded more than could have been achieved in view of the destruction done to the roads and railways by the retreating Germans. It was, in fact, recognised early in October by the Allied High Command that a prolonged winter campaign would have been impracticable, and the necessary measures were under review for a methodical advance in the following spring, when the forward lines of communication had been put in order.

For the advance to the Rhine following the Armistice the British Second Army was selected, and it is of interest to glance at the journeyings of a divisional mechanical transport company serving a division of the Army of Occupation, as by so doing the feeding of the troops in the march forward will be made clear. No. 496 Company Army Service Corps allocated to the 29th Division moved on the 12th of November to St Genois, the railhead being at Sweveghem, east of Courtrai. The division then lay in the Renaix area at a considerable distance by road from railhead, owing to the detours necessary to conform to traffic circuits, and to meet the situation a reinforcement of sixty lorries was added to the existing strength of the mechanical transport company, which was required to find as many as forty-two vehicles for the conveyance of baggage alone.

Railhead was next located at Vichte and then on the 22nd of November at Oudenarde—an advance of twelve miles—while divisional dumps of supplies were being pushed forward so rapidly that by the 28th the gap to be bridged by the lorries had widened to close on a hundred miles. The roads were in the last state of disrepair, and conditions in other respects adverse, owing to the short period of daylight and dense fogs, which made it difficult to trace direction in a strange country.

The continuity of supply was, nevertheless, satisfactorily maintained, the available lorries being divided into three groups of thirty-five vehicles each, and three days being allowed for every convoy between drawing at railhead and dumping. In this manner deliveries were invariably effected without any serious irregularity.

After the 29th of November the situation was relieved by the transfer of divisional railhead from Oudenarde to Namur, although even then the distance from the troops approached twenty-five miles as their advance towards Cologne moved via Spa–Malmedy–Montjoie–Zulpich while railhead went on the line Amay–Pepinster–Rotgen and Duren, but no abnormal difficulties were encountered as the roads were good and weather conditions had improved.

After leaving Renaix on the 29th of November the divisional mechanical transport company was located successively at Namur, Huy and Pepinster: the German frontier was passed on the 4th of December, on which date Company Headquarters was established at Rotgen, and after halts of a few days at Duren and Horrem, the Rhine was crossed on the 14th of December and the journey brought to an end at Dellbruck in the Cologne bridgehead.

Relative to the last year of the war one aspect of the higher administration cannot be passed over in silence, the more so as very little is generally known concerning it. While not solely an Army Service Corps matter, it was chiefly such, and its repercussions on transport and supply threatened at one time to be serious.

Shortly after the appointment of General Foch to the command of the allied armies the question arose as to

THE BRITISH EXPEDITIONARY FORCE

the expediency of the appointment of a similar authority for the co-ordination of the rearward services. It was pointed out that a Commander-in-Chief was unduly handicapped if he had not complete control of those services; and that moreover the step involved no loss to national "amour-propre" in that nations which had entrusted the lives of their soldiers to a foreign general should not object to entrusting less, providing greater combined efficiency could be thereby obtained. In its logic the contention was characteristic of the Gallic mind, but it lost sight of the fact that Britons are among the last to be governed by logic, while it is an undoubted fact that human kind are so constituted that they are often prepared to give their lives when they are not prepared to give their property. In any case the proposal was not one which could commend itself to the British Army, better "found" as it was in most material respects than its French ally, and the case was not therefore pressed on the original line of argument.

In May 1918, however, the matter was again raised from a somewhat different angle and through a different agency. It took the shape of a letter from General Pershing—the American Commander-in-Chief to Lord Milner, Secretary of State for War, in which was enclosed an agreement which had been arrived at between the French and American Governments. This document, to which the British Government were invited to adhere, laid down as follows: Firstly that the principle of unification of "military supplies and utilities for the use of the Allied Armies" be adopted; and secondly that in order to apply this principle a Board, consisting of representatives of each of the armies whose unanimous decisions should have the force of orders, be constituted. Theoretically, of course, there was much to be said for this proposal, and its sponsors did not hesitate to say it. It was urged that a great economy in administrative *personnel* would be effected. Both British and French had passed their maximum fighting strength, and a point would eventually be reached when their rearward services would be out of all proportion to the combatants which those services would be required to maintain. The deficit in fighting men could only be made good from America, who would all the time be engaged in bringing "non-fighting" troops across the Atlantic for the purpose of building up a complete and separate rearward organisation of her own. It was difficult to have imagined anything more wasteful, and therefore in so far as man power was concerned there was a strong case for some measure of co-ordination of resources.

But the economies and advantages accruing need not be laboured. What the American proposal advocated towards them, in so far as Army Service Corps interests and responsibilities were concerned, was the "pooling" between the Allies, including the Belgians and such Italian troops as were serving in France, of mechanical transport vehicles, of depot accommodation and of all articles of supply common to the different armies.*

It would have been very easy for this suggestion to have been negatived on the grounds of its obvious practical difficulties, quite apart from the fact that the British Army was satisfied with its own *status quo* in the directions named. The problem, however, was not so simple as it might have appeared, for it was out of the question to flout abruptly the opinion of two great allies at the very crisis of a life and death struggle. With a fine loyalty to the common cause America had made a sacrifice of national pride in permitting a measure of incorporation of certain of her divisions in the British and French armies, while she had met in the most wholehearted spirit the demands that infantry and machine gunners should take precedence in her transportation

* Among other counts suggested for co-ordination were: Construction and allotment of dock accommodation, Distribution of labour and of railway engines and rolling stock by "pooling".

programme, thus postponing the time when she could build up her own higher formations complete. To have responded to such an attitude with an abrupt *non possumus*, concerning measures of which the principles were indisputably sound, would not only have been churlish but even impolitic.

To British General Headquarters in France the American scheme was anathema, and such opposition was natural enough, for it appeared to threaten to deprive the British Army of something which it already possessed and to offer doubtful advantages in lieu, for in "pooling" material resources the richest of the partners stood to lose. But Lord Milner was obliged to take a longer view and in that view he was supported by the Quartermaster-General Sir John Cowans. In reply to General Pershing, therefore, he expressed his hearty accord with the aims set forth, at the same time indicating certain doubts as to what extent co-ordination would be practicable. In reiterating the scope and powers of the proposed Board as understood and accepted by the British Government, the Secretary of State agreed to nominate a representative.

The Board was established early in June, an Army Service Corps officer being appointed as British member* with a small staff. Special quarters were provided at Coubert, some twenty miles south-east of Paris. Colonel Payot, as President, was a man of great ability and force of character, both of which qualities he used to

---

* The members of the Board were:
AMERICA: Colonel (afterwards Brig.-General) Charles G. Dawes.
FRANCE: Colonel (afterwards General of Brigade) Charles Payot. Director of Rearward Services to the French Army (a post somewhat corresponding to that of the British Quartermaster-General in the Field).
GREAT BRITAIN: Lieut.-Colonel R. H. Beadon, A.S.C. (from Staff of Supreme War Council, Versailles), June to September 1918; Major-General R. Ford, late A.S.C., D.Q.M.G., G.H.Q., France, October–November 1918.
ITALY: General Merrone.
BELGIUM: Lieut.-Colonel Cumont.

the full in the attempt to subordinate the Board to the Generalissimo, and thus succeed where earlier and more direct efforts had failed. Backed by a profound knowledge of all details of administration, a logical and lucid power of expression and by American sympathy for the principles of co-ordination, the French representative strove to make the Board an agency for placing material resources at the disposal of Marshal Foch.

The situation became one of extraordinary delicacy. On the British side there was, indeed, no lack of will to support the Supreme Command at the crisis of the war, but the British conception of how such material support might most conveniently be given was that each ally should freely assist the others by utilising the resources which could be spared after its own particular needs were satisfied. Between this and the French contention, that all resources should be thrown into a common pool, compromise was difficult. Moreover, the British Government had only participated in the Military Board of Allied Supply on the distinct understanding that its resolutions were the united decisions of the Governments concerned and not of the Generalissimo, while there existed the safeguard that no resolution taken had the force of an order unless it had been agreed to unanimously by every member of the Board.

A crisis, which might well have involved serious consequences, was averted by the loyal action of the American representative. Colonel Dawes, who was destined in after years to become Vice-President of the United States and its ambassador in London, and to whose ardent faith in closer union of the Allies the inauguration of the Board was largely due, was a man of quite exceptional breadth of mind. Although personally in accord with his own Commander-in-Chief—General Pershing —that Marshal Foch should control the Board, he was not prepared to go beyond the terms under which the British had agreed to participate, and his attitude saved the situation. Among his many qualifications Colonel Dawes possessed three of special virtue at that epoch. He was tenacious without being obstinate, patient without being procrastinating, and while thoroughly American he had an understanding of the British mentality. In this last respect Colonel Payot was conspicuously lacking: he had, moreover, an intellectual contempt for minds less quick and comprehensive than his own, and did not trouble to hide it.

Fortunately for Allied relations, however, the Board continued in being and was even able to accomplish useful work. After an attempt to interfere with the British forage ration had been defeated, the American scale was lowered to correspond to the former, whereby shipping was economised. An inter-Allied reserve of lorries was formed, available for troop movement, and regulations on the handling and circulation of mechanical transport on a large scale agreed upon between the armies, after a school had been set up for teaching a uniform system. Ammunition between French and Americans was "pooled" along the front.

These and other measures towards a more efficient use of combined resources without interfering with the internal administration of any one of the armies were either adopted or put in hand, and concerning them there is no call to dilate. The Board was, however, only in the early stages of its purpose when the war ended, and had the campaign continued into the following year it would have been able to have rendered valuable services, especially when it is borne in mind that more and more would dependence have to be placed on American resources.

That any proposal tending to "pool" transport and supplies should have been looked at askance by the directorate at the War Office and by its representatives at General Headquarters in France was natural. But it was fortunate that in Lord Milner there was as Secretary of State a sagacious and far-seeing administrator, who saw the issues and their possible consequences, and was able also to impress them on Sir John Cowans and General Crofton Atkins, and secure from them such co-operation that the matter was handled in a manner which protected British interests and at the same time met reasonable demands from allies in a reasonable spirit. In this sense the lessons to be learnt from the history of the Military Board of Allied Supply should not be overlooked, for it is certain that in any similar circumstances in the future similar questions would again arise.

The solution adopted in 1918 was a compromise such as was the Supreme War Council at Versailles before unity of command was achieved, and it may be supposed that, had 1919 still found the Allies fighting, that compromise would likewise have eventually reached its logical conclusion.*

The wrangles of Boards and Committees are dull and uninspiring as compared with the actions of men in the fields of practical endeavour, and in concluding this survey of events in France it is fitting to return to mention of the troops themselves.

No special distinctions have been, or indeed can properly be, drawn between the activities of the Army Service Corps of the Imperial Army or that of the Dominions, which latter bore no small share in the common task.

On the lines of communication were four Canadian, five Australian, and one New Zealand field bakeries; three Canadian, five Australian, and one New Zealand

---

* The views of General Dawes in this connection were expressed in a story related by him as coming from Mr Dwight Morrow: "A father was telling his little boy a story. He said, 'The alligator had his mouth open and was about to close it on the turtle when the turtle suddenly climbed a tree and hid himself in the foliage'. 'But, papa', said the little boy, 'a turtle can't climb a tree.' To which papa replied, 'But *this* turtle *had* to'."

GENERAL SCHEME OF SUPPLY
from the Base to the Trenches
BRITISH EXPEDITIONARY FORCES

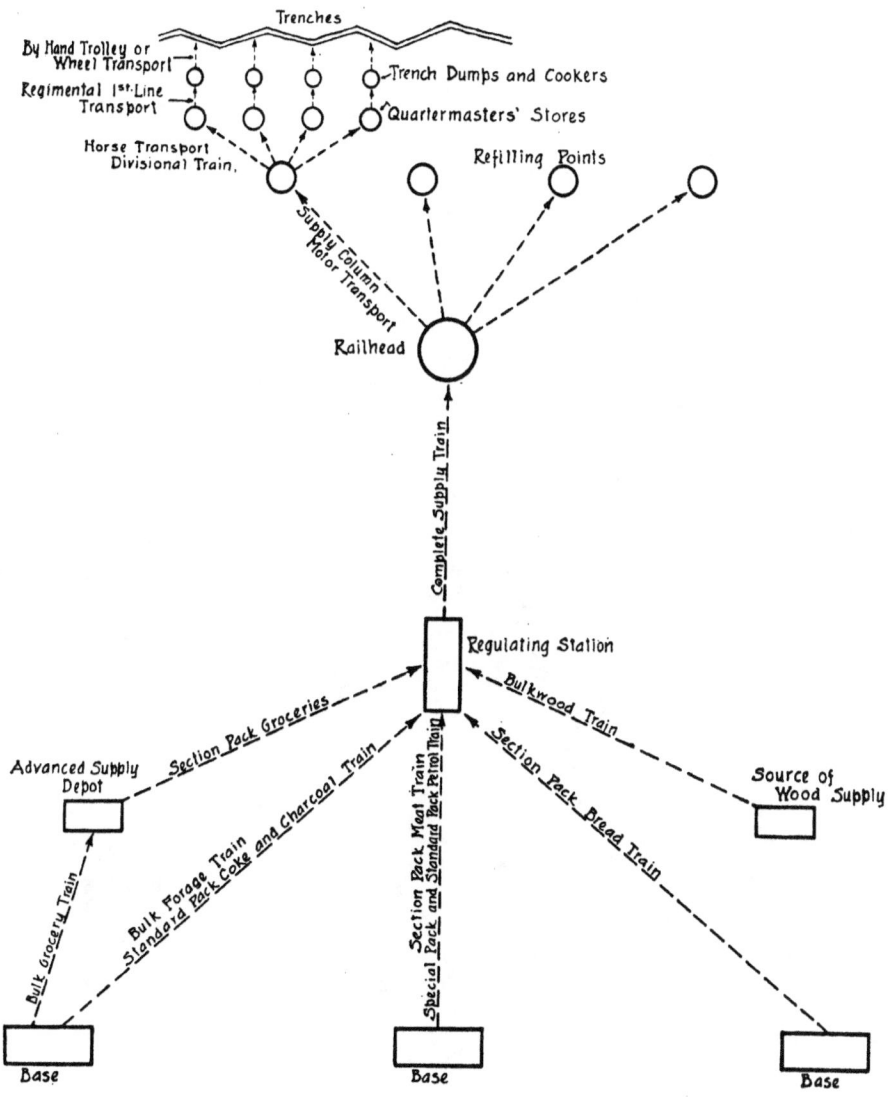

THE BRITISH EXPEDITIONARY FORCE

field butcheries; fifteen Canadian, twenty-five Australian, and five New Zealand depot units of supply. In addition to the Dominion horsed divisional trains, mechanical transport was provided in the shape of divisional and corps companies, and there were also some few auxiliary horse transport companies. South Africa had no distinct units of her own, but she sent some 2000 Cape Boys for work in horse transport units, in which they proved as satisfactory as did the infantry battalion of the same material which served in Palestine.

The organisation throughout was the same as that obtaining in the British service, which made corresponding units interchangeable, and thus facilitated administration.

In round figures the casualties of the Army Service Corps in France amounted to nearly 10,000, including some 3700 dead.

BIBLIOGRAPHY

Official History of the War. Vols. I–IV. "Military Operations in France and Belgium." By Brigadier-General J. E. Edmonds, C.B., C.M.G., p.s.c.

The Auxiliary Omnibus Park. By Captain C. B. Cockburn, O.B.E., Royal Army Service Corps.

"The Campaign of 1918 in France." By Major T. E. Compton. From the *Journal of the Royal United Service Institution*, February 1920.

CHAPTER VI

THE OPERATIONS ON THE GALLIPOLI PENINSULA

THERE are few if any campaigns waged by the British Army which have lent themselves less to the operations of transport than the expedition to the Dardanelles. That expedition indeed would seem to furnish a classic exception to the familiar aphorism that "war is movement." Neither does the definition of the task as the siege of the great fortress that was the Gallipoli Peninsula suffice to represent the case, for two conditions normally obtaining in siege warfare were absent. Firstly the besieged were not completely cut off, and at all times had both land and sea communications with their bases of supply; and secondly the besiegers themselves lacked freedom of manœuvre and were in fact clinging precariously to the outer defences which they had seized at great cost, and from which it was at the same time impossible to advance and difficult to retreat. The situation was without parallel in the history of modern war and possibly of any war.

Whilst it is always easy to be wise after the event, there is no doubt but that the operations were initiated under certain misconceptions which should have been avoided if those concerned had known their business. Into the controversies which have been aroused over the matter there is no place to enter here, but one minor aspect may be recorded as illustrating the curious ideas which prevailed when the expedition had been decided upon early in 1915.

OPERATIONS ON THE GALLIPOLI PENINSULA

The Director of Transport at the War Office received a telegram from a general officer, whose division had been put under orders for the East, asking if he was aware that instructions had been issued for the troops to proceed without transport, which including the first line or regimental was all to be left behind. Very naturally General Long was surprised and perturbed by this information, of which he had previously no inkling, for while he was unaware of the details of any tactical or strategical projects, he was at the same time, as Director of Supplies, responsible for feeding the army to be landed on the peninsula and had made arrangements accordingly. On enquiry it was ascertained that orders to the effect indicated had actually been issued by Lord Kitchener, the Secretary of State for War, who had laid down that as the troops were to be landed on the beach, and would only have to walk across the peninsula, no transport was needed.

Now among Lord Kitchener's qualities, and they were both numerous and eminent, knowledge of transport matters was not included. As regards this deficiency the Army Service Corps had considerable experience in South Africa, and mindful of this General Long proceeded to interview the Secretary of State. By the simple analogy of the impracticability of a battalion of Guards encamped in St James Park drawing their water from the lake, if it was drinkable, by means of their mess tins, reinforced by the reminder that on active service a properly organised supply of ammunition was essential, Lord Kitchener was persuaded to agree to a quota of transport accompanying the troops.

On the 10th of March, 1915, it was decided to send the last regular division—the 29th—to the Mediterranean, and instructions were accordingly issued to prepare it for service in that theatre. As a further illustration of the vagueness and confusion which existed as to the nature of the terrain in the intended theatre, the following incident may be cited. The 29th Divisional Supply Column was equipped with 3-ton lorries, the standard vehicle in such unit for service on the Western Front, and the uselessness of sending these vehicles was realised. But the Intelligence Branch of the Staff not having been informed that military operations on the Gallipoli Peninsula were contemplated could not say whether the roads were at that season fit for any form of mechanical transport, or indeed whether there were any roads at all. In the absence of definite information, it was decided, as a compromise, to provide 30-cwt. lorries, and new war establishments were hurriedly drawn upon that basis. Not until many months afterwards was it known that General Maxwell, who was commanding in Egypt, had informed Lord Kitchener on the 7th of March that "all our information indicates that there are no roads...it therefore seems that pack transport is necessary".

In addition to the 29th Division from England the forces for the original landing comprised the Royal Naval Division and the Australian and New Zealand Army Corps, amounting to some 60,000 men and 13,000 animals, exclusive of the French contingent numbering 17,000 men and 3500 animals. Leaving Mudros on the night of the 24th of April these troops at the price of terrible losses succeeded in getting a foothold on shore— the 29th Division at Helles and Sedd el Bahr and the Australians and New Zealanders at Ari Burnu north of Gaba Tepe. By the 1st of May the French were landed on the right of the 29th Division, and the Royal Naval Division and an Indian Brigade, which had been sent from Egypt, had also commenced their disembarkation at the toe of the peninsula. On this date the allied line had progressed under two miles from Helles, while at Anzac, the foremost troops were hardly established more than 1500 yards from the shore, the country being exceedingly rugged and broken.

In such a situation transport and supply arrangements could not follow any recognised system. Although it had been hoped that the first day's fighting would lead to a considerable advance, the decision as to the number of animals and vehicles to be landed depended largely on the questions of water supply and roads, while to land any number of horses and mules in view of the reported shortage of water might well serve no useful purpose. Again, it was impossible to land animals in the first instance without a serious reduction in the rate of landing fighting troops. These difficulties were met by a temporary re-organisation of the system of food and ammunition supply; animals were cut down to a minimum; officers' kits and men's blankets were left behind; and, in the case of an advance, supply and ammunition vehicles were to be refilled from specially loaded storeships which would land their cargoes at convenient points on the coast.

In accordance with these arrangements the units were allotted to transports, all surplus animals and vehicles being left in Egypt. Troops were provided with two hundred rounds of ammunition and three days' food with which to land, and in addition each transport was instructed to put ashore a reserve of three hundred rounds of ammunition and seven days' food for every man disembarked. The covering force was designed to land without horses or vehicles of any kind, man-handling its machine guns and such stores as were absolutely essential. Regarding the water supply nothing was left to chance. A condensing steamer had been chartered by the War Office, a large tank steamer had been hired at Port Said and skins, tanks, oil tins, and other receptacles were collected in large numbers for the purpose of storing water on the beaches or sending it forwards. As matters turned out, except at Anzac, fears of an insufficient natural supply of water proved groundless, although difficulties were experienced in the early stages until those supplies were found. On the 26th of April some good wells were discovered in the low ground north of Morto Bay, but the rationing and ammunition supply was for the first three days an anxious problem, as very few transport animals had been landed. The work of transferring stores, supplies and ammunition to the beaches, both at Helles and Anzac, had proceeded well in spite of incessant hostile fire on the anchorages, and as early as the evening of the 26th certain localities were beginning to assume the appearance of large supply depots.

While the Australians and New Zealanders were maintaining themselves with great bravery in the positions so hardly won and were even fighting for more elbow room, an attempt was made to get forward on the Helles front. This led to what is known as the First Battle of Krithia, which took place on the 28th of April. The troops had been warned that their emergency rations, which had been taken ashore in their packs, might have to last for two days instead of one owing to the impossibility of getting supplies forward until the evening of the 28th, but as many of the men had thrown these rations away in the course of their strenuous efforts on landing, the effect of this warning was merely disheartening. The disembarkation of the administrative troops of the 29th Division was not completed until the 5th of May, and until this was achieved it was impracticable to count on a regular and even flow of all that was required at the front.

In an operation of such a nature conditions could scarcely have been otherwise, for in contradistinction to the more orthodox forms of campaign, where administrative corps prepare in advance the bases and to some extent the lines of communication for the maintenance of the fighting troops, the latter were compelled to extend themselves to the uttermost before anything could be done to assist them from the rear. The tests to which they were put were doubly exacting in that not only had

GALLIPOLI PENINSULA

the resistance of the enemy to be overcome, but the normal help from administrative sources in overcoming that resistance could not be given.

From the 28th onwards matters began to mend in so far as transport was concerned, for an organisation known as the Zion Mule Corps (containing seven hundred and fifty pack mules), which had been formed in Egypt of Russian Jews who had fled from Palestine, began to disembark, and during the First Battle of Krithia some of its animals were engaged in taking ammunition forward. This unit, the first to be so employed on the Peninsula, for the most part served with credit during its eight months' sojourn there. Commanded by Lieut.-Colonel J. H. Patterson, a reserve officer who had under him five British temporary officers who had thrown up their employment in Egypt to join, and eight Jewish officers selected from among the refugees, the Corps numbered some five hundred all ranks divided into four troops. Unfortunately after leaving Lemnos two of the latter were detailed for Anzac and thus passed outside the control of their own headquarters, and therefore from the support and direction to be derived from such association. As a consequence they failed to come up to expectations under conditions extremely trying to even the best disciplined troops, and after a fortnight were returned to Alexandria for disbandment. The headquarters and two troops which went to Helles fared very differently and were destined to see the matter through to the end.* Arriving as a battle was raging, they were called upon at once to take up ammunition and supplies to troops engaged, being piloted in the first instance by Major E. R. O'Hara, A.S.C., the Deputy Assistant Quartermaster-General to the 29th Division, who at all times distinguished himself by his presence where most

* The strength of the Corps in December 1915 was five British Officers, two Jewish Officers and one hundred and twenty-six rank and file.

needed, by his habit of personally supervising the execution of his instructions and even of participating in the actual manual labour of the convoys in delivering to the troops. The example thus given by one of the divisional staff officers did much to stimulate and encourage the young and inexperienced unit in its early trials, inherent in the conditions of working by night in an unknown country, constantly subjected to heavy shell fire, with a great battle proceeding in the vicinity.

During the fighting on the 1st of May, one of the men, Private Groushkonsky, distinguished himself greatly, for when a hail of shrapnel descended on the convoy and stampeded many of the mules this plucky youth, though shot through both arms, held on to his plunging animals and succeeded in delivering his loads of ammunition to the troops engaged. He was awarded the Distinguished Conduct Medal.

That the Commander-in-Chief recognised the services of the Zionists was shown by a letter written by him in reply to a query from an American Jewish paper as to whether such a unit as the Zion Mule Corps actually existed. Sir Ian Hamilton wrote that "the officers and rank and file have shown great courage in taking water, supplies and ammunition up to the fighting line under heavy fire".

British reinforcements in the shape of the 42nd East Lancashire Division made their appearance early in May, commencing their landing on the 6th instant, while four days afterwards the 52nd Lowland Division was notified as having been put under orders, and it eventually came out in June. With a second French division which arrived during May there was therefore in prospect a large army on the peninsula and certainly numbers much greater than had originally been contemplated. Before, however, proceeding with the narrative of events following these accretions of strength, it will be well to summarise the transport and supply situation as it stood at the end of April, when the first and most delicate situation had been met.

In the great port of Alexandria the Mediterranean Expeditionary Force had a first-class base whose sole disadvantage lay in its distance from the theatre of operations. To the advanced bases at Imbros and Mudros on the island of Lemnos the distances were six hundred and eighty and six hundred and fifty miles respectively. From Imbros to Helles was fifteen miles and from Mudros to Helles sixty miles, figures which were, over a sea route, bound to be a cause for anxiety when the difficulties of building up reserves on the peninsula are considered, quite apart from possibilities of enemy action against the communications. Although Port Mudros provided a fine natural anchorage, it lacked certain qualifications indispensable for a military base. There were no jetties and none of the appliances usually found at a shipping resort existed, while, on shore, water presented a difficulty. But in spite of these drawbacks it was developed as the headquarters of the line of communication in a manner which reflected the industry and energy of those concerned. Piers were constructed; the water supply was put in order; roads were made; stretches of light railway were introduced and stores and camps set up. A large Supply Depot and a Horse Transport Depot were established.

At Imbros there were Advanced Supply and Horse Transport Depots and a frozen meat ship which was used as a store.

In a sense Mudros was comparable to a regulating station as known on the Western Front, while at the far end the Army Corps dumps of supplies on the beaches could be likened to railheads except that they were continually under hostile shell fire. In the forward zones there were Army Corps Supply Depots at Helles, Anzac, and ultimately at Suvla and also a field bakery at the former place, where the *personnel* had the unusual experience of carrying out their duties under fire.

From Mudros Brig.-General Koe, the Director of Supplies and Transport, personally dealt with Helles, but his control over affairs at Anzac, and subsequently at Suvla, was effected through his representatives at Imbros.

At the end of April the total strength of the Mediterranean Expeditionary Force was 86,000 men and 31,000 animals, 25,000 of the former and 14,000 of the latter being in Egypt. For these, rations were in hand for twelve days plus a six weeks' reserve, while outstanding demands which were due to arrive by the 7th of May amounted to an additional thirty days. The supply authorities were therefore leaving nothing to chance, and it is sad to recall that their precautions were enhanced by the unexpected severity of the casualty lists. The question of hay, which it was impracticable to resolve by shipments from the United Kingdom, was met by obtaining 10,000 tons from India supplemented by quantities of tibbin from Egypt. Crushed maize and barley were provided in lieu of oats.

On the transport side mechanical units which had been sent out from England were employed in Alexandria. An Indian mule cart train, which had arrived from France, and which consisted of some seven hundred carts and fifteen hundred animals, was in course of being distributed amongst the 29th Division, Anzac Corps and the Indian Infantry Brigade, where it was available to work forward from the beaches either by wheel or pack. For the rest the Zion Mule Corps, as already shown, had commenced its functions, but it had not been found possible to get the sections of the divisional trains which dealt with carriage of supplies landed on the peninsula. In view of the cramped position of the troops and their proximity to the beaches, the presence of such transport formations was indeed hardly called for at that time.

At the risk of labouring events of the preparatory stage it will be instructive to recall the anticipations of their task conceived by the Army Service Corps prior to the disembarkation of the troops. Optimistic as these seem in the light of subsequent disappointments, they yet merit study as indicating the nature of the measures required on the part of transport and supply in such operations as were then projected. That matters did not go according to plan actually lightened the work of maintenance in that the distances over which supplies, stores and ammunition had to be conveyed to the troops were negligible.

For the 29th Division the position envisaged on the evening of the second day following disembarkation was that there should be seven days' supplies on beaches—the supply portion of the divisional train there refilling and proceeding daily to its troops up to about one mile beyond Krithia. Following this it was intended that a second echelon of transport in the shape of the baggage section of the train should be interposed to act as a supply column. The reserve of supplies on the beaches was, as a precaution against the weather interfering with landing operations, maintained continually at seven days. As a supplementary transport measure one hundred and fifty Indian army transport carts were allotted, but these, as events turned out, did not arrive on shore until nearly a week after the original landing on the 25th of April.

For the Royal Naval Division designed for a demonstration off Bulair no auxiliary transport was required, but one battalion which it was intended to throw ashore to give colour to the feint was provided with fifty pack mules in addition to its first line transport.

In the case of the Australian and New Zealand Army Corps, the supply preparations were regulated on a similar basis to those of the 29th Division, but having in view the difficult nature of the terrain over which operations were contemplated, two hundred and fifty pack mules from the Zion Mule Corps were allotted and two hundred Indian army transport carts, whose mules could be made available for pack if required, were earmarked; some pack donkeys purchased in Egypt were also provided. In all cases seven days' forage was to accompany every animal landed.

During the early part of May there was heavy fighting on both the Anzac and Helles fronts, more especially on the latter, where the action known as the Second Battle of Krithia took place on the 6th–8th of May. It was hoped that this offensive delivered with all the strength then at the disposal of the Allies would have enabled the commanding position of Achi Baba to have been reached, but as a result of three days' fighting which cost some 6500 casualties, the line had nowhere advanced more than six hundred yards when it was then only about two and a half miles from "V" beach opposite Sedd el Bahr at the toe of the peninsula. Achi Baba, which had been the objective on the day of the original landing, was still a further two and a half miles distant. As the total front from sea to sea was but three miles, it will be realised how cramped was the position of the troops.

In the Anzac area, however, the situation was even worse, for the line at its farthest point from the coast was but fifteen hundred yards and the nature of the ground was still more inimical to progress.

Under these circumstances "supply" presented few complications on the spot and "transport" none. There was only the question of moving an insignificant distance forwards what had been landed on the beaches. This involved hard and unpleasant work but it did not call for any particular subtleties to perform it.

From the point of view of higher administration the supply directorate was not without its anxieties. For while Alexandria served as the main base, the communications of the force were not confined to those stretches of sea between Egypt and the peninsula. They extended back to the English ports and a voyage from Southampton or Avonmouth to the Aegean might be reckoned, as a rule, to take more than a fortnight, while one from Marseilles would take fully a week. Nor was the number of days required for the passage from Great Britain to the zone of active operations dependent solely upon the period occupied by the sea voyage. Transhipment was almost always necessary before reaching the final destination and in some cases there was a double transhipment, once in Egypt and a second time in Mudros harbour or at Imbros. Rarely did a consignment of supplies take less than three weeks to find its way from Great Britain to the shores of the peninsula on to which it had to be unloaded by night. Careful provision for the various commodities required was therefore at all times necessary.

The events in the Helles area during July call for little comment. A forward movement essayed in the middle of that month met with no success and it was evident that the enemy had considerably strengthened his defensive system. At Anzac, where reinforcements in the shape of certain mounted units without their horses had arrived during June, stalemate also existed, and, although better protected by deep gullies, the discomfort of the troops was even greater than that of their comrades to the south, for the provision of adequate quantities of water occasioned great difficulties. Supplies had to be brought from Egypt and Malta, the demands on the latter place being so heavy that a serious shortage occurred. Water which had come out as ship's ballast from England was in some instances consumed by the troops, and, during the concluding stages of the campaign, the army depended largely on a slow-steaming tank ship which brought Nile water to the peninsula at the risk of being torpedoed.

Much strenuous work was put in to improve the communications in this zone, a network of tracks being spread throughout the position and sheltered magazines for ammunition and supplies created. Fortunately the weather during this period was fine and favoured the landing of stores.

Meanwhile the British Government was in course of making up its mind as to whether Sir Ian Hamilton's request for reinforcements could be met. It was finally decided that the army would be augmented by three complete divisions and the infantry of two Territorial Divisions, all to come from the United Kingdom between the 10th of July and the 10th of August. At the end of July the 13th Division began to make its appearance at Helles, where it relieved the 29th Division in the line in the first instance and was subsequently sent north to Anzac to take part in the offensive on the 6th of August. The 10th Division less one brigade and the 11th Division were on the evening of that day landed in and south of Suvla Bay, so that, with an offensive from Helles timed simultaneously, three different onslaughts were made on the Turkish positions. The Suvla operations were among the most disappointing of the enterprises undertaken during the course of the War in that they represented the greatest lost opportunity. Although the surprise of the Turks in this area was carried out as contemplated and the infantry of the 53rd and 54th Divisions were rapidly put ashore in support of the original troops, various causes, the questions of water and ammunition supply being among them, conspired to make the whole undertaking hang fire. Nor can the failure be imputed to any lack of preparation. As far as was humanly possible every measure to ensure success had been taken. But from conception to execution is a long step and in this case there was a faltering in making it. At two of the beaches, owing to the landing craft going aground some distance from the shore, there were great delay and inconveniences, and the precious time lost was never regained. The whole programme for the disembarkation of transport animals got seriously in arrears—by 2.45 p.m. on the 8th of August there were only one hundred and sixty transport mules ashore,* and this shortcoming reflected gravely on the general situation. Food supplies and ammunition as well as water had to be carried from the beaches to the front line by hand, a state of affairs which greatly depleted the fighting ranks, while some units which had taken part in the advance on the afternoon of the 7th returned to the beaches for water.

A distinguished critic has written that "something undoubtedly went wrong after the disembarkation had been most successfully effected". Yet this partial truth really obscures one of the principal causes of failure. Truly enough the disembarkation of the fighting troops had been successfully accomplished, but the ways and means to support them and to enable them to advance were conspicuously absent. On August 7th the enemy resistance was such as could have been easily overcome had the assailants been able to get forward. That they did not do so must be imputed, not to the lack of any will to do so, though the troops were in fact somewhat weary after their night landing, but to the fact that except for the legs of the infantry they had no means of mobility. The individual soldier is more than sufficiently loaded with his rifle and pack for an attack on the enemy, without being required in addition to fetch and carry supplies, water and ammunition from the rear, quite apart from the dispersion involved by such a situation.

Had it been possible to have assisted the Ninth Army Corps in the early stages following its landing with

* As indicating the progress made in this respect, the following figures are significant:
By August 16th, 1950 mules and 177 carts were landed
 „   17th, 2056 „   „ 202 „   „   „
 „   21st, 2324 „   „ 202 „   „   „
Up to the last date sixty mules were killed and one hundred and thirty-three wounded.

adequate rearward services to send forward all its needs promptly, it may be believed that history would have been written very differently. It was over two thousand miles from England to Suvla and two or three miles from Suvla to the tactical objectives whose possession might well have decided the campaign; but it was those two or three that made the difference.

With a curious but yet common neglect, this aspect of the affair is one which is usually overlooked. Lack of energy on the part of the Corps Commander, failure of subordinate commanders to appreciate the vital need of getting forward, the rawness of the troops and their inability to find water on the spot, have all been reasons offered to explain the fatal delays occasioned on the 7th and 8th of August, 1915. But the fundamental reason was that a part of the army machine was lacking and in that part lay the means of mobility. With its ultimate provision the tactical opportunity was gone, and the further attempt to seize it in the battle of the 21st of August was in vain.

Under these circumstances it is pardonable to recall Lord Kitchener's original conception of the operations as noted at the beginning of this chapter.

The details of the work in the Suvla area call for no special comment beyond the fact that it was there alone on the peninsula, except for a few four-wheel-drive lorries for the artillery at Helles, that mechanical transport was employed—a detachment of twenty 30-cwt. lorries, Ford cars and motor ambulances proving useful on the comparatively flat ground.

As a result of events in August Sir Ian Hamilton asked for further reinforcements. His request was met to the extent of a second Australian division which proceeded to Anzac and a dismounted division of yeomanry which went to Suvla, but drafts amounting to some 45,000 men to make good the wastage in the depleted battalions could not be spared. Possibilities of any further great efforts were therefore ruled out and the autumn was from the operational point of view uneventful. A disquieting feature was that the health of the troops was unsatisfactory. Disease had been playing havoc in the ranks ever since the warm weather had come in May and even when men had not actually to be invalided their fighting potentialities were appreciably diminished. The discomforts arising from insufficient water, especially at Anzac, the nerve-shattering effects of a persistent and harassing shell fire, and the debility resulting from the lighter forms of sickness, by which practically the whole force was affected, made it necessary for whole brigades and even divisions to be relieved and sent to Lemnos or Imbros to recuperate, which greatly reduced the ration strength of the peninsula.

On the administrative side, however, quite apart from the work involved by these comings and goings, the period was an active one. Suvla Bay was transformed into a fairly satisfactory base, two landing places having been constructed near Gazi Baba and another one between "D" beach and Nibrunesi Point. Light jetties were also erected north of Ari Burnu. Roads were laid out at all points within the lines, water arrangements were developed as far as circumstances would permit and dumps of supplies accumulated in the vicinity of all landing places. These measures undertaken for the security and comfort of the army were not without their influence on the enemy, for the display of so much energy went far to convince him that the Allies intended to see the matter through to the end. But other and probably wiser counsels were to prevail.

Before dealing with the final stages, one incident affecting the Army Service Corps should not be left unrecorded. On the 13th of August H.M. Transport *Royal Edward* carrying drafts from Egypt was torpedoed by a German submarine as she was approaching Kandeliusa Island off the Gulf of Kos. Among the fourteen hundred troops on board were some three hundred men of the Corps, the majority of whom were elderly and physically unfit for service in the infantry. Most of these perished, but the testimony of survivors to the magnificent discipline of the troops in that unhappy vessel and the calmness and order with which they met death deserves to be placed on a level with the heroic story of the wreck of the *Birkenhead*.

The last and by no means the least of the trials to which Sir Ian Hamilton's army was subjected was the storm of the 27th of November, when a hard frost and a blizzard followed twenty-four hours' torrential rain. The troops at Suvla especially suffered, in consequence of the lack of protection in that area, and all means of communication were for the time being interrupted, several soldiers being drowned in the rush of waters. Drenched as they were by the deluge and floods the troops afterwards suffered terribly from the cold, and the casualty list included nearly 50 per cent. of the sorely tried 29th Division, over two hundred men succumbing, while 10,000 sick in all had to be evacuated from the peninsula.

Much damage was done to the piers and unsubstantial breakwaters on which supplies so much depended, and for some time facilities for landing and embarkation at Helles were greatly reduced. Numbers of barges and other kindred craft foundered or were seriously injured.

For the supply directorate the period was a most anxious one. Reserves on shore dropped fast,* and it

---

* In the first week of November there were in the various areas rations and forage as under:

   Helles 35 days' rations for 35,000 men
      13 days' forage for 6,500 animals
   Anzac 32 days' rations for 45,000 men
      10 days' forage for 2,500 animals
   Suvla 35 days' rations for 60,000 men
      10 days' forage for 4,000 animals

was only by the display of the utmost energy that many special commodities, required by the troops owing to the conditions, were provided. Yet with all the precariousness of the position and the lengthy and complicated lines of communication, there was never any question of a breakdown of supply. The temptation to compare the situation of the army in this respect to that obtaining in the winter of 1854-5 in the Crimea, to which attention has been directed in the preceding volume, is irresistible. For in certain respects the conditions in the Crimean Peninsula were similar to those in Gallipoli. Both expeditions were besieging a great fortress in eastern Europe, the objective in each case being on the outer fringe of the enemy's coast, and consequently in both cases the communications were at the mercy of the elements. Administrative problems were then alike in their nature. It is a matter for thankfulness that, with all their trials, Sir Ian Hamilton's troops were at least spared what their predecessors were called upon to endure through the neglect and ignorance of the authorities in England and their failure to provide adequate military administrative services.

On the 16th of October General Sir Charles Monro had succeeded to the command of the Mediterranean Expeditionary Force and on the 3rd of November he gave his opinion to the Government that evacuation should be carried out. At that time, this judgment was considered in many quarters to be a counsel of despair. It was pointed out that it was due not only to the greatness of the prize to be won but also to the valour and tenacity of the troops that the enterprise should be pursued to the end, and that moreover the moral results of its abandonment would be more harmful to the allied cause than the material effects of its continuance. And certainly in nine cases out of ten it is truer wisdom that a bad plan should be carried through rather than changed once the realm of execution is entered. Yet how simple would be the direction and control of human affairs if inviolable rules could be formulated for their conduct. It is just because all rules are fertile in exceptions that life is such a complicated affair. General Monro's recommendation demanded a high moral courage, and although the British Government hesitated to confirm it and invoked the opinion of Lord Kitchener, who was sent out for the purpose, it was finally upheld.*

The evacuation was envisaged in three stages. In the first all troops, animals and supplies not required for a long campaign were to be withdrawn. In the second, all men, guns, animals, supplies and stores not required for defence during a period when the conditions of weather might retard the operation or interfere with the programme contemplated were to be evacuated. In the final stage when the troops on shore were to be embarked with all possible speed, such guns, animals and stores as were needed up to the last were to be abandoned.

The Suvla and Anzac areas were first taken in hand—indeed it was not until after their successful evacuation that the retirement from Helles was sanctioned, and every practicable step was taken to deceive the enemy even to the extent of landing a number of transport animals and pushing supplies to the front by day. Withdrawals were naturally effected by night.

The final act carried out on the night of the 19th–20th of December was wholly successful and, taking into consideration essential precautions, surprisingly little

* In his despatch on the subject dated the 6th of March, 1916, General Monro summarised the situation as follows: "The position occupied by our troops presented a military situation unique in history. The mere fringe of the coast line had been secured. The beaches and piers upon which they were dependent for all requirements in *personnel* and material were exposed to registered and observed artillery fire.... The position was without depth, the communications were insecure and dependent on the weather....At Suvla and Anzac disembarkation could only be effected by lighters and tugs....Yet notwithstanding the difficulties the Army was well maintained in equipment and ammunition. It was well fed; it received its full supply of winter clothing at the beginning of December".

was left to the Turks as booty. Fifty-six sorry transport mules were left at Anzac and such dumps of supplies as had to be maintained at both Suvla and Anzac until the last moment were destroyed by puncturing the tins, soaking contents in paraffin and fixing automatic arrangements for firing.

The operation at Helles, which was completed on the night of the 8th–9th of January, 1916, was equally prosperous, being, like the other two enterprises, favoured by calm weather. But in this case a considerable amount of supplies, material and animals had to be left behind, the latter being destroyed before the troops embarked.

To have made away with the whole of the accumulation of supplies before the evacuation of *personnel* was complete was naturally impossible, for it would have involved the risk of betraying the movement to the enemy. As it was a large proportion of the most valuable commodities were saved. For the rest the quantities destroyed on shore were considerable. At Suvla they included nearly a million and a half rations of preserved meat, over a million rations of biscuit and 100 tons of bacon, besides large amounts of forage, and other commodities. In Anzac the loss was not quite so great but it nevertheless included some sixty items, the largest of which ran to over 350 tons. Yet when it is remembered that the daily average of consumable supplies which were required to be landed on the peninsula by the Army Service Corps was 763 tons, it may well be believed that matters in this respect were cut as fine at the end as reasonable precautions would allow. The mechanical transport and practically all the vehicles were saved.

To have incurred far greater material losses would have been well justified in the achievement of what was at the time described by a German writer as "a hitherto quite unattained masterpiece".

Numerically the Army Service Corps was not strong

on the peninsula; the bulk of its work lay on the lines of communications, especially at Mudros and Imbros.

Four muled divisional trains—those of the Royal Naval Division, partly composed of marines, the 29th, 42nd and 52nd—were at Helles and also an Advanced Transport Depot, but at Suvla the Indian mule cart train with over 2500 animals carried out the bulk of the work. In addition to the field bakery at Helles, there were a number of depot units of supply in all three areas. There was also a motor boat company of thirty-five vessels, to which further reference will be made in dealing with the Egyptian Expeditionary Force.

But if the Corps bore little share in the glory and sacrifice of the fighting troops, it nevertheless did all that was required of it in their service.

Before ending the account of the Dardanelles Campaign it will be convenient to record the formation of what was known as the Levant Base in the summer of 1915, if only to link up with the chapter dealing with the fortunes of the forces in Egypt and Palestine where, in so far as the Army Service Corps was concerned, a large proportion of the *personnel* from Gallipoli was destined to betake itself.

Following the launching of the Mediterranean Expeditionary Force, and with the possibility of adventures in the Balkans in addition to pre-occupations in Egypt itself and further east, it was decided to form a Central Base on which the British Forces in the Eastern Mediterranean could depend. As Director of Supplies and Transport for this organisation, Brig.-General R. Ford was sent from France, and he had a useful share in much of the "spade work" which was to bear such fruits in the campaigns of General Murray's and General Allenby's armies. Being commander of the British troops in Egypt and therefore responsible for the internal security and external defence of that country, General Sir John Maxwell had a full task, and it would have been obviously impracticable to have laid upon him any responsibility for great Expeditionary Forces operating at a distance. The Levant Base therefore continued in being for six months, when on the return of the Gallipoli army and with the higher degree of independence assumed by the Salonika Expedition, it was no longer required as a distinct organisation.

But its existence had been thoroughly justified for much was accomplished in the way of putting Egypt on a proper footing as a Base supported not only on the products of that country itself but also on those of India, Ceylon and even farther East. A measure of assistance was also given to Mesopotamia.

In Egypt the whole system of purchasing supplies was put on an economical basis and a Local Resources Board formed, which not only met the demands of all departments both civil and military, but also had the last word as to the making of contracts.

The whole of the waterways, with the exception of the Suez Canal, were taken over by the Inland Water Transport Committee, of which certain members of the Egyptian Government service, representing Canals and Irrigation, were members, and it is interesting to note that this form of transportation, in contradistinction to the system prevailing in France where it was under the Directorate of Railways, was in the hands of the Directorate of Supplies and Transport.

An innovation was started at Port Said, where the cold storage plant belonging to a civilian firm was requisitioned and, with the assistance of experts sent from England as officers and in subordinate capacities, the whole supply for Egypt, Gallipoli and Salonika was handled. By this means a sum estimated to be in the neighbourhood of £750,000 per year over the previous contract was saved to the public.

Finally preliminary steps were taken to put in hand the formation of the Camel Transport Corps, concerning whose work there will be occasion to dwell in dealing later with the campaigns in the Western and Sinai Deserts and in Palestine.

BIBLIOGRAPHY

1. *Official History of the War.* Military Operations—Gallipoli. Vol. I. By Brig.-General C. F. Aspinall-Oglander, C.B., C.M.G., D.S.O., p.s.c.
2. *The Dardanelles.* By Major-General Sir C. E. Callwell, K.C.B.
3. *With the Zionists in Gallipoli.* By Lieut.-Colonel J. H. Patterson, D.S.O.

CHAPTER VII

THE BALKANS AND THE BLACK SEA

THE first proposal for engaging in military operations in the Balkans originated from political sources as early as January 1915, from which date, as Sir William Robertson has written, "it periodically competed against and eventually supplanted the expedition to the Dardanelles". During the year events moved steadily in the direction of intervention owing to the ill-success of the measures which were being taken to secure the adhesion of Greece and Bulgaria. The former remained a doubtful neutral, while the latter inclined more and more in the direction of the Enemy Powers, and by the end of September her intentions had become clear. The Allies still cherished the hope that Greece, according to her treaty obligations, would place herself at the side of Serbia, and to enable her to do this Great Britain and France promised a contingent of 150,000 troops, the advanced guard of which force consisting of one British and one French division were put under orders to proceed from Gallipoli to Salonika at the end of September. But anticipations as regards action by the Greek Government, despite the efforts of M. Venizelos, proved illusory, as the King negatived the decision of his Parliament and declared for neutrality. Since the Serbs could not be left to perish, although, as it subsequently turned out, it was too late to save more than a portion of their army and any of their country, the Allies decided to proceed on their own account. It was under these somewhat unfortunate auspices that what has been commonly but inaccurately described as the Salonika Force was launched.

On the 30th of September, 1915, the British advanced party, conveyed by H.M.S. *Scourge*, entered Salonika harbour. It consisted of Brig.-General Hamilton and six other officers from General Headquarters Mediterranean Expeditionary Force including Lieut.-Colonel O. Striedinger, A.S.C., Assistant Director of Supplies and Transport, and its instructions were to prepare for the eventual arrival of five British divisions. Since Greece was a neutral, the party was liable to arrest and internment, but this fact did not deter it from inspecting the facilities of the port, choosing sites for camps and headquarters and office accommodation and making enquiries as regards the purchase of supplies. It was an unconventional beginning to a great military expedition, although the position of the officers received some regularisation two days later when their credentials reached the British Consul. In the meantime excellent preliminary work was done, Colonel Striedinger, in the absence of any accredited representative of the "Q" staff, undertaking the renting of hotels and houses and choosing the location of a Base Supply Depot at Dudular about three miles outside the town, where the Uskub and Dedeadatch railway lines unite before separating again for their destinations. With the assistance of the Consul local merchants were notified of supplies required, and on the 3rd of October the first offer of 2000 tons of hay and 600 tons of barley was accepted. A telegram was despatched to Egypt asking, somewhat optimistically, for a hundred and twenty lorries, two field bakeries, and butcheries and ten depot units of supply as a preliminary instalment of Army Service Corps *personnel*.

On the 5th of October H.M.S. *Albion* arrived with the first of the troops, two battalions, and these were followed rapidly by other units of the 10th Division. The disorder in which troops of all arms streamed into Salonika accentuated the lack of transport: first came the infantry with no transport at all: then came huts, ordnance stores and baggage of regiments which were not due to arrive until some days after: then a supply ship followed with seven motor lorries and two drivers. On the 10th of October however the first line transport of units with a number of extra horses arrived and this enabled some measure of order to be attained. The first battery made its appearance a day later. It was not however until the 28th of October that the disembarkation of the division was complete with the exception of the ammunition column which was sunk by a submarine off Volo. A few Army Service Corps units had also reached Salonika, but both transport and supply *personnel* were woefully inadequate in numbers.

The situation as regards supplies at this time may also be noted as demonstrating the energetic action which had been taken by the authorities both in Egypt and on the spot. By the end of October three ships containing respectively 800,000 rations, a quantity of forage and 900 tons of frozen meat, with 400,000 rations were safely in port, in addition to the quantities which were included on troop transports. Local resources had also been exploited. During the first fortnight of the month Colonel Striedinger had bought no less than 16,000 tons of hay, 21,000 tons of fuel wood, 200 tons of oats and 14 tons of potatoes, besides making provision for the issue of fresh meat up to the 6th of November, and this in spite of every obstruction from the Greek Government, which, by the 14th of October, had put a ban on further purchases. The French army then demanded frozen meat, and, since the British commissariat was invariably better placed in that respect than that of their Allies, the demands were met. The co-operation of the Allies with regard to supply services was most cordial throughout. The British were in a position to provide the bulk of the frozen meat required by all nationalities, while the

French, on the other hand, came to the rescue on at least one occasion by a loan of petrol when many of the British lorries were actually at a standstill. In the early stages medical comforts were the most noteworthy scarcity.

Meanwhile the organisation of the Base Supply Depot was being pushed forward. Railway sidings were run out of the depot and hutments constructed, but it was not until the 28th of October that supplies could be despatched from the port to the depot by road as a stream crossing the route was not safely bridged until that date. The baking of bread presented some difficulty, as the "Aldershot" pattern oven proved unsuitable. The wet and stormy weather that was experienced for practically the whole of the month washed away the sods covering the ovens, so, pending the arrival of "Perkins" ovens, arrangements had to be made for the baking to be done locally. The shortage of tarpaulins for covering supplies added to the embarrassment, and the sum of all these conditions was sufficient to make the task of the supply and transport directorate thoroughly unenviable and in some respects similar to that which, as shown later, prevailed at Basra in 1916.

In the port itself the quays were so congested with transports that it was impossible for some weeks to bring supply ships alongside. They had to be discharged into lighters, transferred from the latter to trucks on a small railway jetty and then pushed by hand two hundred and fifty yards to the railway siding where they were taken over by hired carts or lorries. As this laborious process had frequently to be undertaken by night and day the supply *personnel* was gravely overworked, and finally the jetty itself subsided under the weight of the supplies handled.

On the transport side the troubles were, for some time, even greater. For reasons best known to themselves the Greeks were mobilising and therefore requisitioned most of the available horses and vehicles. Some small dock vans, drawn by half-starved ponies, and only capable of a load of 8 cwt., were obtained at exorbitant prices, and even then it was necessary to place guards over them to prevent them from being seized together with their loads *en route*.

It had originally been intended to push a brigade group of some 5000 men and 1400 animals up to Doiran by rail on the 20th of October, but the Greek authorities refused permission for the move until the 29th, when two battalions took over the front which was then being held by the French between Kosturino and Lake Doiran. The remainder of the division was sent up to Serbia on the 12th of November and the following days and took over the French line eastwards from Kosturino. Up to then the sequence of events had been as follows. The arrival of the British 10th Division was simultaneous with that of two French divisions under General Sarrail, whose force was subsequently augmented by another division. These three divisions were then moved into Serbia under the arrangements made between the Allied and Serbian Governments, which was to the effect that the French forces were to protect the railway between Krivolak and Veles and to ensure communication with the Serbian army, whilst the British were to maintain the position from Salonika to Krivolak and to support the French right. If communication with the Serbian army could not be opened, the Allied Forces were to be withdrawn.

The task of moving troops into Serbia and maintaining them there presented many difficulties, but before attempting to show how these were overcome it will be convenient to summarise the Army Service Corps units which were available at the end of October. In addition to the Supply and Transport Directorate presided over by Colonel Striedinger, these consisted of the *personnel* of the Base Horse Transport Depot, the

29th Reserve Park, the 29th Divisional Supply Column (No. 244 Company), a field bakery and seven depot units of supply. The reserve park was a strong unit of over five hundred all ranks with six hundred and seventy mules and a hundred and fifty-two wagons, while the mechanical transport company had a hundred and twenty-five lorries. There was also the 10th Divisional Train which had previously been the 52nd Divisional Train, and which, since the 10th Division had left its train transport in England when proceeding to the Dardanelles, was sent from Egypt to make good the deficiency.

The sphere of action of the British force was roughly within the area Guevegli–Doiran–Tatarli–Robrovo—the railway serving this running from Salonika to Guevegli or Doiran itself. This line, with the exception of a small portion in Serbia, was in Greek hands, and the consequent slackness and delays in its direction gave cause for anxiety during the first fortnight, after which the British and French authorities took over a measure of control: no road existed between Salonika and Doiran. For road transport the main artery of communications was the route from Doiran to the town of Strumitza, which for the first six miles of its length ran alongside the lake and was flat and well surfaced: thence it proceeded to Hasanli where the Advanced Supply Depot was subsequently formed: five miles farther brought it to the top of the Dedeli Pass, a winding gorge with numerous stone bridges crossing the stream. From the bottom of the pass—sixteen miles from Doiran—the route wound up the mountain side via Robrovo to Strumitza, which was practically the farthest point reached by wheeled transport. The first detachment of British troops detrained at Guevegli, which was then one of the French railheads, and marched over the heavy road to Hasanli where the main route was joined. Subsequently the remainder of the division detrained at Doiran, which became the British railhead. The maintenance was effected by using the 29th Reserve Park with its mules in the rôle of a divisional supply column from this railhead to Hasanli and thence onwards to the Dedeli Pass where a refilling point was located: the train wagons then worked forward in the normal manner to the Robrovo Valley, whence supplies were carried to the troops in the hills by pack animals moving during the night only. Later the motor lorries of No. 244 Company Army Service Corps were brought up to operate the stage between Doiran and Hasanli as the "turn round" journey from the former place to Dedeli involved a daily trip of twenty-four miles and for the mules this could not be kept up indefinitely. This system worked without a hitch, but the weather conditions and the disintegrating roads made the constant movement of the convoys exceedingly trying. Towards the end of November a blizzard was encountered with several inches of snow, followed by severe frost and a strong north wind which lasted about a week, and consequently there was a great deal of sickness among the drivers and animals.

It was now evident that the power of resistance of the Serbian armies was broken and that the Allied troops could afford them no material help—in fact their own position was becoming precarious owing to a large German-Bulgarian concentration in the Strumitza Valley. It was, therefore, decided early in December that a withdrawal was advisable, and the 10th Division, as the pivot upon which the movement was effected, was compelled to hold its ground until the French left was brought back. On the 6th, 7th and 8th of December the British were heavily attacked by superior enemy forces, but were able to extricate themselves and withdraw to Greek territory without great losses and without continuous pressure from the Bulgarians. Meanwhile the disembarkation of further troops at Salonika was being carried out, and the Greek authorities through their representative from Athens were informed of the intention to construct a defensive line within their boundaries, which intimation they received in good part, even commencing to withdraw their own detachments farther to the east where they would not hamper the plans of the Allies.

During these events the Army Service Corps were labouring with the arrangements for the backward movement. The probability of retirement had been envisaged by the 1st of December and the prior consideration was to ensure that the limited communications would be clear for the passage of troops in the event of retreat under pressure. In order therefore to avoid congestion from supply wagons moving on the single main road to Doiran, reserve dumps of supplies were located at different points between Hasanli and Tartali, which step also had the further advantage of allowing all surplus wagons and Army Service Corps equipment to be sent south by rail. To enable this to be done the baggage wagons were withdrawn from the units to which they were attached and for four days a double quantity of rations was sent forward; at that time the animals of the divisional train were working as much as eighteen hours a day and travelling on an average twenty miles heavy going, for the roads had by then become almost lakes of mud. Six mules were required normally for each general service wagon and at certain spots ten or even twelve were necessary. Specially serious work was involved by the need of evacuating sick and wounded, and the fact that much of the movement had to be done at night made it the most strenuous of the whole of the first period. However, the objects were achieved and all general service wagons and surplus harness got clear, only limbered wagons and Maltese carts being retained. The transport and supply arrangements in advance of the base, other than those under divisional control, were carried out under great difficulties by Major Beuttler.

But these tasks were only a prelude to the delicate operation of converting the divisional train and reserve park into pack transport, for it was only by this means that the troops could be provided for in the mountains in the event of their having to be extricated in face of enemy action. An ample supply of pack saddles, provided from local sources, had been sent up from the base, and six small pack units were formed from the divisional train complete with officers, n.c.o.'s and artificers to accompany the field artillery brigades and the field ambulance. In a similar manner the reserve park found pack transport to work with the divisional ammunition column. These measures played an effective part in the disengagement of the division which was concentrated near Doiran station on the 11th of December. The retreat proper began the following day and as the railway was fully occupied in getting away guns and vehicles, and was in any case unequal to moving the whole force at once, the troops had, in the absence of roads, to make their way back to Salonika by such mountain tracks as were available. All the transport had to pass through two difficult gorges with awkward fords, and it was only by the greatest efforts that the passages were accomplished. The rearguards especially suffered from these conditions as heavy rain began to fall, but the fourth day saw the bulk of the force back at Salonika. One of the most embarrassing situations in which troops can find themselves had been successfully surmounted. For the transport, however, there was no interval of rest, in that the change from pack to draught had to be carried out in a few hours, and mules which had arrived in camp in the morning wearing their pack saddles were hauling supplies in wagons during the afternoon while orders were immediately issued for the division to take up a new position.

Meanwhile activities at the base had been incessant. Gangs of Greek labourers were employed in off-loading the ships and in the supply depot, and preparations were made for the arrival of further divisions notified as *en route*. Local pack saddles, which proved so efficient up the line, were purchased and establishments were drawn up for placing the force on a pack transport basis which involved despatching detailed demands to the War Office for the additional *personnel*, animals and equipment needed.* A motor ambulance convoy of fifty vehicles had arrived on the 6th of November, a somewhat premature appearance in view of the shortage of other forms of transport and it had evidently been sent in ignorance of the conditions. The provision of hay and fuel wood presented difficulties, as the Greeks continued to obstruct, and it was necessary for General Sir Bryan Mahon, who was in command, to make representations on the subject to the British Minister at Athens.

As an example of the obstacles encountered, the episode of the Nehamas barn may be mentioned. Several hundred tons of hay had been bought and paid for locally and were stored in this barn under a British guard. The Greeks forbade its removal and added a sentry of their own to enforce the prohibition. The wily vendor of the commodity then offered it to the French who bought it in good faith and sent another guard to see that it was not removed by anyone else. The outcome of the incident is lost in oblivion, but the three sentries watched one another for several days without giving rise to an international incident.

* What this involved may be gathered from the following numbers of vehicles and mules required for each division (exclusive of any Army Corps, Army or lines of communication transport).

Maltese carts	183
Water carts	48
Limbered G.S. wagons	274
Army transport carts	526
Mules	3897

(including 2773 mules for pack, and these figures only allowed for a compromise between pack and draught transport. The off-lead mules in all teams carried pack saddles which were found invaluable when wheeled transport could proceed no farther).

With regard to fuel wood some enterprising individual in England cabled that it might be advisable to utilise olive trees for the purpose, ignorant perhaps of the fact that the value of the mature olive tree amounted to some £80.

The Greeks prohibited the sale of petrol in the early days and placed the inevitable guard over the entrance to the premises of the Standard Oil Company, which held the only considerable stocks. This establishment happened to be next door to one of the smaller British depots and all the immediate requirements were therefore pushed over the wall, thus eluding the vigilance of the sentries.

Apart from hay and wood, however, the main articles of supply were steadily pouring in, despite the shortage of shipping. Praiseworthy as these efforts were, and their detail should be known to be adequately appreciated, reinforcements began to arrive into Salonika so fast that the supply *personnel* found it almost impossible to keep pace with the work, especially as many of the transports arrived without any reserves of rations on board. This was remedied later by the troops leaving France carrying with them twenty days' landing rations and fifteen days' forage, but for the first three months it was never found possible to build up any reserve and the army was compelled to live from "hand to mouth". When the five divisions were landed by the 15th of December the supply depots only held reserves up to the 17th of December.

A further difficulty was the congestion of stores at the docks. Only those urgently required for consumption could be dealt with, and the quays were packed to the eaves of the customs houses with commodities which would not be needed for weeks.

Yet taking into consideration lack of preparation and hasty organisation of the expedition the success achieved was creditable and may be imputed to the skilled direction which the Supply and Transport Directorate enjoyed, together with the unflagging efforts of all ranks. On the 5th of November the head of the 22nd Division disembarked, while two days later the belated 29th Divisional Ammunition Park which had been allotted to serve the 10th Division began to come in from Mudros, which gave a welcome accretion of some seventy lorries: the same day also saw an additional depot unit of supply. On the 9th of November the Army Service Corps received even more substantial reinforcements in the shape of the 22nd Field Bakery, 54th Field Butchery, a railway supply detachment and five further depot units of supply. By the middle of November the 22nd Division had landed and this was shortly followed by the 26th together with the necessary corps *personnel* to admit of the staffing of the base and lines of communication for the large army in process of assembly. These last consisted of three field butcheries, two railway and two railhead supply detachments and twenty depot units of supply, but transport still remained short. The 27th and 28th Divisions were disembarked and concentrated outside Salonika by mid-December, and there the first phase of the campaign may be said to have ended.

No justification is needed for having occupied a considerable proportion of the space available for this chapter with the events of the opening ten weeks, since they were from the administrative standpoint by far the most trying of the three years spent in this theatre of the War. Certainly they demonstrated the power and the will of the Army Service Corps to improvise and to adapt themselves to new and unforeseen conditions. Under the circumstances there was little confusion—at any rate little confusion which affected the fighting troops, who were fed with punctuality and regularity. The measure of the success attained may perhaps best be realised from a perusal of the despatch of Sir C. Monro who was at that time in command in the Eastern Mediterranean.* Satisfactorily as this reads, it cannot be contended that as an operation of war the inception of the Salonika adventure was one upon which the Allies could congratulate themselves. Like most expeditions undertaken for political rather than military reasons it was undertaken too late, and once launched, involved increasingly serious commitments which were a drain on the shipping and other resources of Great Britain.

Yet, when all is said, those who served on that front bore their full share in the War, in that their presence enabled the remnants of the Serbian Army to be brought once more into the field, secured the adhesion of a large part of the Greek nation and eventually won a great victory. But had none of these things been, the expedition would yet have been redeemed in the eyes of posterity by the patience and steadfastness of the troops and the British capacity for improvisation and adaptation. In this last sense the episode may be deemed to have provided almost unique experience for the administrative services called for the first time to officiate in the Balkans.

Two incidents in which the mechanical transport were concerned during the period dealt with above may be recorded as exemplifying the varied and arduous duties

* The paragraph covering the work of the Corps read as follows: "From the date on which the 10th Division first proceeded into Serbia until the date of its withdrawal across the Greek frontier personnel, guns, supplies and material of all kinds had to be sent up by rail to Doiran and onwards by march, motor lorries, limbered wagons and pack animals. ...The evacuation of the wounded and sick had to be arranged on similar lines, yet the requirements of the troops were fully satisfied. The majority of the Divisions were sent without Trains to Salonika, most units without first line transport; in spite of this, part of the force was converted into a mobile condition with very little delay. The complications presented by the distribution and checking of animals, stores, supplies and ammunition discharged from ships on to the quays with insufficient accommodation or store houses and with crude means of ingress or egress therefrom and served by a single road which was divided between the French and ourselves constituted a problem which could only be solved by officers of high administrative ability".

which the Corps was called upon to perform. Late in October two lorries and a Studebaker car left Salonika by train with Lady Paget* with orders to travel to Uskub one hundred and fifty miles north-west and rescue Lady Paget's hospital unit, which was in danger of being captured by the advancing Bulgarians. With the exception of the car which pushed through to its destination, these vehicles were unable to get beyond Gradsko, as the enemy blew up the line, and they accordingly made for Monastir, where they reported to the British Vice-Consul, who employed them northwards towards Babouna and Prilep conveying *personnel* to the hospital at the latter place. Early in November they left Monastir for Debra some ninety miles north-west on the Albanian frontier to meet the Naval Mission under Admiral Troubridge and the Scottish Women's Hospital and other medical units with the Serbian army, where their presence was of great service. Three weeks later when the blizzard was at its worst one lorry became "bogged" between Struga and Monastir and was captured by the Bulgarians and used by them until retaken by the Serbians a year later, and brought into use with its original company once more.

Lieut. Hastings Thomas, A.S.C., had likewise an adventurous time with a convoy of twenty vehicles which with forty from No. 245 Company Army Service Corps, which began to arrive on the 14th of November, were lent to the Serbian Government on the 20th of November and proceeded to Monastir. This party enjoyed the experience, rare for British soldiers during the War, of being fed by their Allies free of charge—indeed the Serbians were also desirous of paying them, but this last offer was declined. The lorries were employed in taking supplies and on one occasion some £2000 in coin

* In addition to Lady Paget the party consisted of Corporal Bakers in charge and Privates Smith, Turner and Phillips of No. 245 Company Army Service Corps.

from Monastir to Struga and Ochrida and in evacuating refugees from the latter place over villainous roads—the journeys being made more difficult from the fact that many of the drivers were comparatively inexperienced, while the weather conditions were indescribable. Nevertheless valuable work, including the conveyance of the British Naval Mission from Struga to Monastir by night in a blinding snowstorm, was accomplished. Three lorries were lost on the road and their drivers narrowly escaped capture, only turning up at Florina about ten days later, after having been cut off by the Bulgarians and experiencing great hardships. At the end of November the Serbians were compelled to leave Monastir, and Lieutenant Thomas exerted himself to save some of their transport, the difficulties of which will be realised inasmuch as for one stage of the route, before entering Florina, it took six days to cover eight miles and this was only effected by the assistance of oxen to drag the vehicles over the softer portions of the road. All the British and seven Serbian lorries were, however, successfully brought over the Greek frontier.

On the 23rd of November the Supply and Transport Directorate, which had been carrying out its functions as a skeleton organisation from the start, received a much needed reinforcement in the person of Colonel P. C. J. Scott, who took over two Deputy Assistant Directors and a complete staff of clerks, and on the 14th of December Major-General Koe came from Gallipoli to investigate the transport requirements of the force: in August 1916 he was appointed Inspector-General of Communications, the second Army Service Corps officer to hold such post.* By the 20th of December the ration strength of the army had reached 90,000 men and 25,000 animals. In spite of the fact that mechanical transport was still short, the chief anxiety at this time was petrol, and

* Lieut.-Gen. Sir F. T. Clayton was I.G.C., B.E.F., France, from January 1915 to December 1916. *Vide* Chapter IV, p. 86.

although every effort was made to expedite a supply, stocks were completely exhausted by the 26th of December and the situation was only saved by borrowing one day's needs from the French. Fortunately this was able to be returned the following day out of a shipload of 50,000 gallons which reached harbour safely.

From the beginning of January 1916 until the middle of April the Allied troops were holding their shortest line of defence, which, owing to the amount of barbed wire that extended from the River Vardar on the west through the valleys of Langaza and Bezik as far as Stavros on the east, was known as the "Birdcage". Of this front the British army held some twenty-four miles along Lakes Langaza and Beshik.

Salonika had now assumed the position of an entrenched camp—a very different rôle from what those responsible for the adventure had intended. Yet it was destined at the last to play the part of a Torres Vedras.

On the 30th of January, 1916, Brig.-General A. Long arrived to take up the appointment of Director of Supplies and Transport. The formations needed to complete the transport establishments were then coming to hand, and the position slowly easing. The ship, *Norseman*, conveying the train for the 26th Division had, however, the misfortune to be torpedoed by a submarine outside Salonika harbour in the early morning of the 21st of January. The excellent discipline of all ranks under the command of Captain G. O. Mitchell, A.S.C., enabled six hundred of the eleven hundred mules on board to be saved with the assistance of the Navy, and there were no casualties among the *personnel*. The Base Mechanical Transport Depot (598 Company A.S.C.) disembarked safely five days later and the advent of this important unit did much to relieve anxiety, despite the shortage of stores and spare parts. In February the 34th Reserve Park, the first Army Service Corps unit to be equipped completely with limbered general service wagons, followed. A further accretion, which was of great value in the particular terrain in which the troops were operating, was a quantity of Indian army transport carts in the shape of the 3rd and 31st Indian Mule Cart Corps.

On the supply side matters were likewise improving, though difficulties were still experienced with regard to certain commodities. In mid-January there were no oats in the country and by the end of the month petrol was again out, the position being saved in this case by drawing on certain Serbian stocks which had been stored in bond at Salonika. The most pressing need at this time was to form some kind of reserve of supplies with the divisions in the line as an ordinary precaution, but this was never achieved during the early part of 1916, as the transport could not suffice to do more than maintain them from day to day, while, owing to the lack of normal harbour facilities, it was only by the supply depot working continuously day and night, unloading ships as they came into port, that even that flow, amounting to 1000 tons a day, could be assured. Every sort of obstruction and a wholesale pilfering of supplies by the natives complicated matters. Army foodstuffs were openly sold in shops in Salonika, and the delicate relations with the Greeks made it difficult to take proper measures for some time.

By the end of February the ration strength of the British army was 120,000 men and 50,000 animals and as it was steadily rising, while material reinforcements in horse transport *personnel* could not be looked for from home, it became evident that steps were required to provide them from other sources. It must be remembered that the pack form of transport required in the mountains swallowed up such enormous numbers of men that the War Office could not provide them except at the expense of more urgent demands elsewhere. The voluntary system of recruitment at home had early in 1916 almost spent itself: the fighting troops everywhere were short, for which reason the administrative services were already being "combed". In Egypt a great campaign was just about to be initiated. In Mesopotamia Sir Percy Lake was fighting desperately to save Kut-el-Amara. In East Africa General Smuts was opening his offensive. With all these pre-occupations it was not surprising that the Salonika army was bidden to help itself as best it could and very rightly a proportion of that task fell on the broad shoulders of the Army Service Corps.

In view of events up to that time it seemed a hazardous step to enlist the help of the Greeks, who had shown themselves anything but complaisant to the Allied occupation, which was, in fact, an infringement of their neutrality. Yet, as is the case nine times out of ten, the bold course was justified and early in March 1916, in spite of the interdiction of the Greek Government, a start was made by the recruitment of a hundred muleteers at the pay of three drachmae a day. This number was increased shortly afterwards to two hundred and fifty, and detachments were sent to the field ambulances where they proved very satisfactory and consequently encouraged a continuation of the experiment, especially as with the advent of the warm weather malaria and dysentery began to ravage the *personnel* of the Army Service Corps, above all in the Struma area. By August there were twelve hundred and fifty muleteers serving in field units and a further eight hundred and fifty being trained in the Base Horse Transport Depot.

On the 9th of May General Mahon, who, as a Divisional Commander, had been in command of the British forces, left for Egypt and General Milne with the staff of the Twelfth Army Corps succeeded him. In the following month, a bombing raid gave General Sarrail, the Allied Commander-in-Chief, the excuse to declare a state of siege. This involved the taking over of all public departments from the Greeks, and the departure of

Colonel Massalas and other senior Greek royalist officers, who had long been thorns in the side of the Allied administrative services. These steps immediately improved the supply situation as far as local resources were concerned, but as a set-off against this a fire at the Main Supply Depot, which proved to be the work of incendiaries, destroyed some 5000 tons of hay and grain stuffs, with the consequence that for some period after, only half rations of hay could be issued. The cost of this incident amounted to nearly £40,000.

The Allied troops had remained in the "Birdcage" line until the end of April, during which time the natural fortifications of the position had been greatly strengthened. The German-Bulgarian army had taken possession of the mountains about Doiran and north of the Struma Valley but their main body had not crossed the Greek frontier, although the Greek garrison at Fort Rupel, an important point commanding the only passage through the Belashitza Mountains, had voluntarily surrendered the post to enemy troops. When it became clear that the enemy had no intention of attacking Salonika, the Allies began preparations for an advance towards the Struma early in May, moving over the mountains to the north of Lakes Beshik and Langaza and also up the main Seres road. The latter, which was the only real road running north from Salonika, was the route of the 10th and 28th Divisions which took up positions on the southern bank of the Struma River. The 22nd and 26th Divisions marched by the Narish–Kukus–Janes road and were aligned from the south of Lake Doiran to the Vardar River. These changes greatly influenced the transport and supply problem, for instead of the eight or ten miles to the original front it then became a question of some fifty miles with indifferent communications. This necessitated bringing the divisional trains up to the establishment sanctioned for mountain warfare, involving eight companies in each train, four being wheeled with limbered wagons or army transport carts and four consisting of pack mules—one company of each nature working in echelon for each brigade. While the authorities at the War Office exerted themselves to find such reinforcements as could be got together, an effort had to be made to exploit sources beyond those of Macedonia, and accordingly Cyprus was, through the agency of Major Sisman, A.S.C., asked to provide 3000 muleteers. By the 22nd of July over 1100 had been enlisted and the first detachment left at once with four hundred mules. A month later, of some 6700 drivers required to complete the special Salonika establishments, there were slightly over that number in sight including 2000 British promised from Egypt and the United Kingdom, and 2000 Cypriots to complete the demand from Cyprus. Arrivals of mechanical transport kept pace with these augmentations of strength. At the end of July, and none too soon, four companies arrived, for with the advent of the Serbian army at the same time on the Ostrovo–Dragamanci front, mechanical transport had to be provided for it.* Among these was No. 706 Company under Captain J. E. Davies, the majority of the *personnel*, including the commanding officer, having just come from the Cameroons, and they were at once plunged into a rush of work in a very different terrain, carrying supplies and ammunition for the Timsk Division during the advance to Ostrovo.

These new responsibilities, however, were by no means all, for during September the French found themselves in difficulties over the feeding of their troops in the Struma Valley and requested British assistance, which was accorded, and the provisioning of this sector undertaken until British troops took it over shortly afterwards. Meanwhile, however, a considerable proportion of trans-

* The Serbian Army 130,000 strong brought from Corfu had been concentrated at Mikra Bay near Salonika during July—a potent example of sea power.

port was loaned to the French, including two reserve parks and a mechanical transport detachment, and it was some months before this could be recovered from its borrowers. The situation as regards mechanical transport *personnel* was by the early autumn causing anxiety, since a deficiency of eight hundred drivers and over one hundred artificers involved a number of vehicles being out of action. Consequently for some weeks it was again only just possible to keep pace with the ordinary maintenance services. The artillery were then demanding that the shortage of drivers for their heavy batteries should be made good, in addition to the transport required for building up reserves of ammunition, in view of impending activities. There was a large accumulation of mails from the United Kingdom to be cleared. The Serbians were asking for assistance over and above what had been allotted to them. Meanwhile, owing largely to the strenuous conditions, sickness was rife amongst the mechanical transport *personnel*. One company, No. 338, which had landed on the 30th of June had two hundred and twenty of its *personnel* and all its officers in hospital with sandfly fever by the 6th of July. As on several other occasions, matters were getting down to bedrock for the Directorate of Supplies and Transport, when the divisional ammunition parks made their appearance early in October—an appearance doubly welcome from the fact that heavy fighting had started just before and continued throughout the ensuing two months.

Up to that time the fortunes of the army had been comparatively uneventful since the events of the preceding autumn. It has been seen how, after leaving the "Birdcage", the Allies had moved north and before their line had stabilised there had been a certain amount of marching and counter-marching during which the French and British troops were to some extent mixed up. An Allied offensive along the Vardar was then in contemplation, but it had to be abandoned because the Bulgarians anticipated it by attacking the Serbs on the left of the line during August. Preliminary operations in the Doiran region had, prior to that, led to the captures of positions known as Tortue Hill and Horseshoe Hill by the French and British respectively and following these an Italian division occupied a sector of twenty-five miles between Lake Doiran and the Struma Valley, thus breaking the continuity of the British front. It was not until November 1916 that the latter finally settled down on the line running from the Vardar to Doiran round the elbow made by the Krusha Balkan Range and down the long Struma Valley to the sea, a distance of about ninety miles, and this was held for a period of two and a half years. There were normally only four British divisions available for the line. The maximum number in the theatre was six, and that only for a short time, for the 10th Division left for Palestine in September 1917, while the 60th, which arrived at Salonika in December 1916, departed six months later.

The outstanding event of 1916 was the counter-offensive undertaken by Franco-Serbian forces during the autumn which carried the Serbian army into Monastir. In the course of this undertaking the Serbs, fighting in high tumbled mountainous country, accomplished one of the finest deeds of the war by the capture of Kaimakchalan, a crest of over 8000 feet—an accomplishment that may be recalled from the work of the attached Army Service Corps Ford units, which kept up their supplies and ammunition over precipitous mountain tracks. The only contact maintained between British and Serbian troops was in fact through the medium of the Army Service Corps mechanical transport, for the two armies never actually fought side by side—that is, their respective fronts never touched, the French always being in between.

During the long period of trench warfare which lasted

until the final victory in September 1918, and which was only broken by an abortive and costly offensive in April and May 1917, the supply problem was to all appearances straightforward enough, involving as it did deliveries and distributions more or less regular and constant. But there were circumstances making for difficulties which are not always obvious. The working margin was at all times close enough to cause anxiety, for, since the army was dependent to the far greater extent on imports, the enemy made very special efforts against the Allied shipping with his submarines; few zones were as dangerous as the waters round and about Salonika, and the losses were very heavy. On many occasions disaster was only averted by the timely arrival of a cargo to replace another or even two or three others which had been sunk. Again, the communications between the base and the front were unsatisfactory. The left sector held by the British, maintained as it was by the railway leading eventually to Doiran, was comparatively well off, but the Struma front usually held by three divisions was dependent on the single artery of the Seres road, and to maintain between 40,000 and 50,000 men with thousands of animals fifty miles from railhead over a single and very indifferent route, was not a task which could be contemplated with equanimity, especially as the state of stocks prevented any material reserves being built up in the vicinity of the troops, even if the tactical situation had made it safe to have done so. The story of the re-making of the Seres road to bear the immense volume of traffic which flowed along it for thirty months is a fine tribute to British thoroughness. Dozens of steam rollers were brought from England: the adjacent country was prospected for hard stone and quarrying started: a quantity of ox and buffalo transport and local labour was organised under Royal Engineer supervision, and hundreds of thousands of tons of "metal" were poured into the road. For months the work went on day and night, acetylene flares being lighted when darkness intervened. And when the work was finally finished and perfected by the middle of 1917 the road still swallowed up an immense amount of labour and material to keep it in repair. Over 2000 lorries, and hundreds of motor ambulances, motor vans, motor cycles and mule-drawn limbered wagons worked incessantly along the route, the memory of which is long likely to remain with thousands of those who belonged to the Army Service Corps and spent no small fraction of their lives moving up and down upon it. Before the road was taken in hand the mechanical transport vehicles were only able with great difficulty to get as far as Lahana—thirty-five miles from Salonika—where muled limbers took on and struggled forward, often with mud up to the axles of their wagons or to the bellies of their mules. There never was and never could be any real rest for the transport. Convoys were out at three in the morning and late at night under awful conditions of wet and cold in the winter and heat and dust in the summer. There was necessarily much sickness but as elsewhere the behaviour of all ranks was admirable.

Saturday, the 18th of August, 1917, was a day which will be long remembered by the Salonika army, for it was on that date that a fire broke out which destroyed a large portion of the town—actually about a square mile in a few hours. While only bearing indirectly on the life and welfare of the army it should not be passed over in silence because of the part played by the Army Service Corps in an event which will never be forgotten in the history of the ancient city. Curiously enough, two new fire engines had arrived a few days before and were in charge of the Corps—one being at the Base Mechanical Transport Depot at Kalamaria and the other at the docks. Both were on the spot almost at once with scratch crews, although neither was completely ready for service; they did splendid work, the driver of one remaining at his post without sleep from eight o'clock on Saturday night until six o'clock the following Tuesday morning, while one engine was in action for seventeen days and the other for ten, as once the first rush of the conflagration was over there were many sporadic outbreaks that needed attention. There were 80,000 homeless people with which to deal and although all the Allies took part in their evacuation along the Monastir road, it was the British mechanical transport companies which bore the largest share.*

As in every other field the Army Service Corps soon found itself involved in duties which though outside its normal rôle had not been allotted to any other branch of the Army. In December 1916 No. 33 Army Service Corps Motor Boat Section was authorised by the War Office. It was early in 1916, while the "Birdcage" line was in occupation, that it was decided to place a motor boat on Lake Langaza and another on Lake Beshik with the object of patrolling the lakes. These boats, armed with machine guns, were about thirty feet long and weighed four tons. To convey them to their destinations a useful vehicle to take the hull was improvised in the Base Horse Transport Depot out of a general service wagon, the standards and bolsters being strengthened and a twenty-five foot perch fixed, the engine being carried separately. On arrival at Lake Langaza the engine was dropped into its place, and by means of rollers and ramps the boat was lowered from its carriage into the water, this work being completed in about an hour.

The duties of these patrol boats consisted of keeping

* A correspondent writing at the time described this scene as follows: "An order was given over the telephone and forthwith from all directions our unrivalled transport service poured its innumerable lorries and motor vans into the town. Their order was simply to take up the refugees and hurry them out of danger. Up to that moment a rich merchant could not have hired a lorry for the evening for £1000. After it the tatterdemalions of Salonika were given all the care of a fine lady being handed into her carriage by her footman".

all native boats off the lake at night, no fishing being allowed between sunset and sunrise, and in preventing any fishermen from landing on the northern shores of the lakes. In March 1916 the Navy took over the work on Lake Beshik but were assisted by A.S.C. drivers and engineers; the A.S.C. boat thus relieved joined the other on Lake Langaza where both continued until the middle of June 1916, when they were transferred by wagon to Lake Tahinos. Moving by Stavros on the Gulf of Orfano, the convoy experienced something of an adventurous journey. Owing to an accident to one of the vehicles the journey of thirty miles occupied five days and it was necessary to caulk and repair the boats before launching them. The Navy then towed them across the gulf to the mouth of the River Struma, up which they proceeded under their own power for a distance of eight miles when it was impossible to proceed farther owing to the strength of the current. It was then determined to try and negotiate the river by means of the combined efforts of a part of the Surrey Yeomanry towing from the bank and Greek soldiers pushing in the water, and in this manner a further five hundred yards were made good in the course of three days. The attempt was then given up, but not before one boat was washed away downstream for some distance and holed in two places. When repairs had been effected the boats again resorted to land transport, and proceeded to a point on the southern shore of Lake Tahinos, opposite the village of Nehori. On the lake they did very useful work, the character of which may be illustrated by a few instances.

On the 25th of August, 1916, information was received that enemy parties were on the northern edge of the lake and as darkness set in the Army Service Corps patrol boat moved in towards the village where they had been located, and collected all the native craft. Outside the village of Patolinos the Bulgarians opened fire and one of the Greek boats in tow was shot adrift. It was promptly riddled with bullets to prevent it from falling into enemy hands. At Doksambo fifty native boats were got away when the Bulgarians arrived; at Ahinro one hundred were stacked and fired. Two days later orders were issued for the boom situated east and west of Doksambo to be destroyed and under cover of shell fire by night the patrol moved past the village and effectively carried out this task. On the following morning the Bulgarians located the boats and shelled them for two hours but without doing more damage than destroying the petrol tanks of one vessel. Later on, owing to enemy gun fire during the day from the mountains south-east of Seres, the patrols were carried out by night only. On Lakes Langaza and Beshik the boats were under the command of Lieutenant Swann, A.S.C., and were withdrawn in June 1918 and taken by road to Stavros, one being handed over to the officer in charge of fisheries at that place and the other returned to Section Headquarters at Salonika.

By the summer of 1918 the army was much depleted by sickness from its long sojourn in that unhealthy clime. The admissions to hospital from malaria over the three years 1916, 1917 and 1918 reached a figure of 160,000, and in August of the latter year influenza and pneumonia seriously ravaged the weary troops. The British strength at that time totalled 175,000, of which the effective numbers of fighting troops numbered some 60,000, of these only about half being infantry.

The health of the Army necessitated provision being made for periodical leave, a matter of great difficulty owing to the distance from the United Kingdom and hostile submarine activity in the Mediterranean. Eventually it was decided to send leave parties of 2000 men per week by train to Bralo in Greece, thence by the port of Itea—fifty miles by lorry, thence by steamer to Taranto and to England via Italy and France. This course necessitated the construction of a road from Bralo to Itea over the mountains and the constant employment of two complete mechanical transport companies thereon. Even then numbers of men never got leave at all after two or more years in Macedonia. Many of those still at duty were in a low state of health, which fact enhances the merit of the success that was now within their grasp. For the weariness of waiting and enduring was not destined to be suffered in vain. As in Palestine and Mesopotamia, victory, final and overwhelming, was the prize of one further effort.

Previous to this, the advent of the Greek National Army organised by M. Venizelos had produced a change in the British line. During the summer of 1918 the Larissa, Seres and Cretan Divisions took over the Struma Valley from the Seres road eastwards to the sea, and the 27th Division, which had previously held this line, was moved over to a section running westwards from the Vardar. The 28th Division moved a little to the west along the Krusha Balkan Range and took up a shorter line near Lake Doiran. Thus four British divisions were concentrated, if such a term can be applied to such a force with its units very attenuated, on a thirty-five mile front.

The story of the subsequent fighting in September is a familiar one. The rôle of the Anglo-Greek army was to await the result of the Franco-Serbian attack from the west and then attack the formidable positions east and west of Doiran, with a view to pinning the enemy to his ground and preventing him from sending reinforcements elsewhere. It was an exacting part and though successful could scarcely hope for the spectacular success of the principal movement elsewhere, but the conspicuous gallantry and self-sacrifice of the troops, both British and Greek, made it a vital contribution to victory. The British casualties amounted to nearly 4000 in the course of two days' fighting by three divisions so depleted by sickness that battalions only averaged some 400 rifles apiece. By the 21st of September, three days after the start of the battle, the Serbians had forged so far ahead that the Bulgarian communications were hopelessly compromised and their whole army in a retreat which only ended in its final surrender.

With its Allies the British army shared in the pursuit, and was in fact the first to enter Bulgaria. The 26th and 27th Divisions with the 14th Greek Division advanced along the Strumitza Valley, while the 22nd and 28th Divisions with the Cretan Division cleared the Belashitza Range from west to east. By the 29th of September the advanced troops were within fifteen miles of the Kresna defile north of the Rupel Pass, having marched some thirty miles, fighting most of the way. The possession of this important locality would have involved the surrender of thousands of the enemy but he anticipated this disaster by an armistice which came into force at 10 p.m. on that evening.

One of those accidents, the effect of which is incalculable in military operations, might well have proved the temporary salvation of portion of the Bulgarian army had it been known. The road from Doiran to Strumitza led over the Popchevo Pass, at the top of which was a narrow defile. Deviation on either side was impossible, and after some thirty lorries had passed the defile the road surface broke through, revealing deep sand beneath, quite impassable for mechanical vehicles and irreparable in less than two or three days. The lorries ahead could not get back, while those behind could not go forward.

In this emergency two reserve parks, which had been ordered to follow the pursuit, were hurriedly pushed forward, followed by a divisional ammunition column, which had been accidentally discovered exercising its mules at a roadside camp. Loads were transferred from lorries arriving at Popchevo, carried across the sand in mule-drawn vehicles and delivered to the few lorries on the other side. When the armistice came the limit of the radius of action of the transport echelons east of Popchevo had been reached, and had the troops attained their objective of the Kresna defile it was doubtful whether they could have been maintained for the following days in that position.

That the army could be thus thrown forward in pursuit emphasised once more the wisdom of retaining, even through a long and apparently hopeless period of stagnation, sufficient transport establishments to deal with mobile warfare and thus enable victory to be clinched. Nor should it be supposed that in default of the enemy capitulation at a comparatively early stage, the strategical pursuit would have necessarily been broken off through inability to push up supplies and ammunition. For the original instructions after that capitulation were for an advance to Widin on the Danube in order to undertake the invasion of Austria. The faces of the troops were already set northwards when orders were issued that the advance was changed towards the east to attack Turkey, and this movement began on the 10th of October. It was an operation that could only have been carried out by an army thoroughly well organised. The roads in Macedonia leading to the Turkish frontier were practically non-existent; at the best they were merely mud tracks. The railway between Doiran and Seres had been largely destroyed and could not be used. Had it not been for the presence of a large force of mechanical transport, and it may be added no little experience in the construction of Balkan roads, it would have been impossible to have concentrated on the Turkish frontier under six or seven weeks. As it was, in less than twenty days two British and one French division were assembled along the River Maritza ready to march on Adrianople. The troops had been moved two hundred and fifty miles. It is true that in this activity the Royal Navy played a worthy part. The bulk of the 22nd Division, which had marched down the Seres road to Stavros, was trans-

THE BALKANS AND THE BLACK SEA

ported by destroyers to Dedeagatch as well as large quantities of stores. The port of Kavalla was also utilised. But the fact remains that strategical considerations did not have to wait on the supply problem, as the history of war has so often demonstrated to be necessary before the maintenance services had been organised and trained to bring them into line with the troops they were required to serve. That the Commander-in-Chief of the British army in Macedonia recognised his debt in this respect may be gathered from an extract of his despatch dated the 1st of December, 1918—the tenor of which exceeded the usual somewhat formal wording employed in such communications.

"The work of all branches of the Royal Army Service Corps ",* wrote Sir George Milne, "deserves special praise. Their responsibilities include not only supplying the British Army requirements but also those of the whole Greek Army and a very large proportion of the Supplies for the other Armies in Macedonia. That in spite of difficulties by sea and by land the Supply and Transport Services of forces extending from the Black Sea to the Adriatic never failed for one day is a great tribute to the work of all ranks serving both with the British and with the Serbian Army and reflects great credit on the organising ability of Brigadier-General A. Long, C.B., C.M.G., D.S.O., Director of Supplies and Transport, and his staff. Large areas of country have also been brought under cultivation in order to supply the troops from local resources under the management of the Royal Army Service Corps."

Considerations of space have prevented more than an account of the early difficulties, of the later organisation evolved to meet the peculiar needs of the Balkan theatre and some few incidents to illustrate how arduous and comprehensive was the task. Yet there remains one further aspect for elaboration, if only for the reason that it had no real counterpart elsewhere.

* The prefix "Royal" had been conferred by Royal Warrant on the 27th of November, four days prior to the despatch.

The Army Service Corps mechanical transport units with the Royal Serbian Army came into being as a result of the Conference of Paris early in 1916. At this Conference it was estimated that the daily transport requirements of the re-organised Serbian army would be 1200 tons and an agreement was reached whereby the British and French should each provide half this amount, the Serbian administration from the point of view of material being carried out by the French.

The original British units, consisting of headquarters and six companies, were mobilised at Bulford between June and September 1916, the last of them disembarking in Salonika early in October.* Here they were joined by No. 605 Company which had previously been with the British Adriatic Mission and British Liaison Mission with the Serbians at Corfu. Lieut.-Colonel L. C. Bearne was placed in command.

Owing to the situation not having been clearly defined, the initial difficulty was the question of administrative control. It was first assumed by British General Headquarters in the Balkans that the units would be under Serbian authorities. The French, however, laid claim to the direction of transport and movements and when they undertook to provide all consumable supplies the position was finally adjusted on those lines, the companies in all other matters being under the Director of Supplies and Transport of the British Salonika army. The solution worked well in practice, for Captain Delest, the French officer responsible for the mechanical transport of the Serbs, was, like his successor Captain Cœurdercy, a man of courtesy and tact, and by his consideration at all times helped to overcome many difficulties and to create an organisation which ran very smoothly.

Lieut.-Colonel Bearne's command was concentrated at Mikra Bay, and the first company to take the field was

* These companies were as follows: Nos. 706, 707, 708, 709 (Fords); Nos. 688, 689 (Albions).

No. 605, which proceeded to Vertekop on the 17th of July where it carried out various duties for the Second Serbian Army. It was quickly followed by No. 706 Company and on the 23rd of August No. 688 Company went to Gorkop on the Vardar River where it was employed in feeding the Serbian Cavalry Brigade and certain attached French troops. Like No. 605 Company, No. 688 experienced great difficulty in the matter of sickness, for malaria and dysentery were prevalent, partly owing to the lack of mosquito nets and partly owing to the natural unhealthiness of the localities in which the units were operating. In September, No. 707 Company left for Verria, where it fed the Russian Brigade and from thence proceeded to the Third Serbian Army to take part with No. 706 Company in the operations at Gornichevo and in the neighbourhood of Lake Ostrovo, where they played a prominent part, earning a mention in a Special Order issued by the General Officer Commanding. With the difficulties arising from sickness and certain technical troubles, such as the unsuitability of the existing bodies of the Ford vans and the effect of the boulder-strewn tracks on the tyres, all these companies were, quite apart from the strenuous nature of their duties, put to an almost intolerable strain until the French completed a Decauville railway which enabled supplies to be transported to near Dragomanci for the troops operating in that area. Shortly afterwards Nos. 689, 708 and 709 Companies made their appearance. In the autumn offensive which culminated in the capture of Monastir on the 19th of November Nos. 706, 707 and 708 Companies were conspicuous for their services and it is no exaggeration to state that had no mechanical transport been available the results achieved would have been impossible, while the moral value at that time of the somewhat unexpected success was out of all proportion to the military gains, material as these latter were.

The conditions, and especially the road conditions, which prevailed during this winter campaign were excelled by few encountered by the mechanical transport anywhere during the course of the War. The vicinity of Ostrovo was composed of a deep mica-impregnated sand which was impassable in the wet weather while in dry weather it played havoc with the vehicles, not only by causing excessive low gear work but by getting into the working parts, and in addition it caused much discomfort to the *personnel*. Many of the tracks over which the vehicles had to pass were strewn with rocks and were roads only in name.

As the railway from Salonika was only negotiable as far as Exissou—the Bulgarians having blown up the viaduct at that place—the duties forward fell on the mechanical transport with what assistance could be obtained from a Decauville railway which ran from Exissou to Sakulevo.

At the end of November the command of the companies was taken over from Lieut.-Colonel Bearne by Lieut.-Colonel W. L. Sorel, and just after, a number of a hundred and forty Serbian drivers, who had been loaned during the previous September to make good British casualties, was withdrawn to a Serbian Mechanical Transport Depot which had been established at Salonika; their loss, in the depleted state of the units, was severely felt. Nor did the winter and early spring bring any relief to the tired *personnel*. The climatic conditions were unusually severe—a snowstorm occurring at the end of February 1917 which blocked all road traffic on the Monastir plain and for forty-eight hours suspended all the maintenance services. It was only by superhuman efforts that vehicles were eventually got through.

One factor, however, did make for assistance, and that was the amount of work put in by the Serbian troops and by local labour on the routes, an excellent mountain road being constructed up the mountain to Petalino to where supplies had to be delivered up to the advanced battalions.

During this period the Army Service Corps did not escape its share of hostile action by shell fire and by aircraft, involving material casualties to men and vehicles, and in this connection No. 688 Company, which was forced to carry out its daily transport duties over a road almost constantly exposed to enemy gun fire, had the honour of receiving as a unit the French Croix de Guerre. This instance is interesting for it was the first occasion during the War that a British unit was so decorated and the distinction remained to the end very rare.

It was in July 1917 that mechanical transport reinforcements arrived in the shape of four Ford units.* They were badly needed, for the existing companies were unable to cope with the "lift" of 600 tons per day, and were in dire need of rest and refitment. The original units were rested two at a time for a month.

At the end of 1917 Lieut.-Colonel C. L. St L. Tudor was appointed in place of Lieut.-Colonel Sorel who went to Salonika as Assistant Director of Transport. Opportunity was taken about this time to provide adequate musketry instruction for all ranks with results that were highly satisfactory.

To make good deficiencies, some Maltese, about a hundred and forty, were attached in 1918, but with few exceptions they proved to be quite useless as drivers, and were normally employed on fatigues or in some such trade as that of tailor, shoemaker or barber.

In May 1918 Nos. 880 and 881 Companies, which had been the last two to arrive, moved up from the Monastir plain to Petalino, 4000 feet above sea-level, which involved some of the hardest work up to then encountered as the grades were very steep and there were no level stretches whatever. There the daily run consisted of trips between two and five miles in length,

* These were: Nos. 819, 820, 880 and 881 Companies.

three to five times a day and at a height which varied from 3500 to 5000 feet above sea-level. On the 13th of September No. 880 Company carried 141 tons of supplies and ammunition to various places, which was a record for any Ford company and involved a mileage of 4500 being run by all the vehicles in the unit, there being rather under sixty available for duty.

The culmination of all efforts came during the final offensive in September, and while it is impracticable here to follow the movements of individual Army Service Corps units during the advance, which was for its size one of the most rapid in all the history of war, some figures of the distances involved may profitably be given.

Very shortly before the advance began the railway was opened to Monastir, but supplies had to be carried from there to Veles by heavy lorries, while the Fords worked the seventeen miles between Veles and Gradsko and the sixty miles between Veles and Kumanovo until the railway from Salonika to Veles was repaired. The repairs to the line north of the latter place took a long time, as the larger bridges over the Vardar and Morava Rivers had been blown up, entailing temporary wooden structures. The lines of communication therefore kept lengthening, and for some time the Albion lorries worked from Veles to Nish, a hundred and seventy miles, while the Fords worked from Nish to Cuprija, sixty miles, and all these distances were covered day in and day out over roads which were always indifferent and at places unfit for mechanical transport. This performance, inspired by the purpose of allowing the Serbian army to go forwards continually, speaks for itself. The Ford vans with their light tare weight, their high clearance and their powerful engines, although eventually shaking themselves to pieces, proved invaluable in operating over rough country with which no other form of mechanical transport could deal.

Largely by the efforts made by the transport the Serbian

THE BALKANS AND THE BLACK SEA

army was able, so to speak, to retake its country in its stride. From the time of the original break through at Sokol in September it took but forty-five days for the Serbian army to reach Belgrade, three hundred miles away, during which advance it had to fight continually, for after the Bulgarians had surrendered there were Germans and Austrians to be encountered. In their rapid advance the Serbians did not always wait for their transport, feeding as they could at times on the country and replacing their ammunition from captured arsenals. In the game effort to keep pace with the troops they were serving, many Army Service Corps drivers went on individually as far as their vehicles could carry them, to find themselves stranded in some desolate mountain track or wild unknown country. Weeks elapsed before some of these could be recovered from the remote villages in which they had been living on what was willingly spared to them by an almost starving population.

In all, the Army Service Corps contingent with the Serbians comprised 2400 all ranks, and they showed at all times a magnificent spirit in meeting difficulties and in their capacity for hard work and endurance. Relations with both Serbians and French were very cordial throughout, as is borne out by the warmth of recognition given in many Army Orders by the headquarters of the Serbian army.

The strength of the British army in the Balkans at the opening of the final offensive in September 1918 was 177,865,* of which, including the contingent with the Serbians, the Army Service Corps numbered 19,959.† The Corps left in Macedonia just under 700 dead.

The operations of the Royal Army Service Corps with the Salonika Force and the Army of the Black Sea from

---

* The ration strength for which the British army was responsible was 385,000 men and 120,000 animals, so the task of the Supply and Transport Directorate went considerably beyond purely British needs.

† These figures do not include Macedonians, Cypriots and Maltese who were employed with the Corps.

the date of the armistice with Bulgaria on the 29th of September, 1918, until the final evacuation of Constantinople on the 2nd of October, 1923, were so varied and far flung as to deserve being dealt with under a special heading. Partly owing to considerations of space, however, and partly owing to the lack of definite data due to the widely scattered and isolated operations of the force, it has been found impracticable to treat them in historical detail and a short outline of the general situation during those years is all that can be included.

Hostilities between Austria-Hungary and the Allies closed on the 4th of November, 1918, and by the 10th the British troops had joined hands at Rustchuk with the Roumanians on the left bank of the Danube. Sofia had been occupied, the landings at Dedeagatch and Kavalla had been completed and the advance towards Adrianople was in full swing. Operations were then being conducted along two lines of communications, respectively three hundred and two hundred miles long, through country which had been depleted of supplies through years of enemy occupation and the roads and railways of which were entirely disorganised.

Although there was no actual fighting, the administrative arrangements gave considerable cause for anxiety. Full advantage was taken of such supplies as the country and enemy magazines afforded, and yet another form of transport in the shape of bullock wagons, obtained from the Bulgarian Government, had to be employed, only shortly afterwards to be rendered useless by the almost entire absence of hay in the conquered territories.

Following the armistice on the Western Front the Allied fleet passed through the Dardanelles on the 12th of November. From that date the probability of a base at Constantinople became clear and as a consequence the importance of Salonika began to diminish, although for a year or more the large stocks accumulated there continued to be drawn upon and double handling at

Constantinople was avoided as far as possible. The supply problem ceased to be that of serving an army in movement.

But the army of occupation commenced to spread its tentacles rapidly over an area possibly greater than that ever previously covered by any army in history, and although sea communications greatly facilitated matters, fresh difficulties and complications constantly presented themselves. The evacuation of Macedonia, moreover, with its widespread detachments, usurped a large proportion of the *personnel* available, and constant demands for demobilisation during 1919 proved a disorganising factor. The continually increasing requirements of the civil population for additional quay space and storehouses, which had to be met, greatly embarrassed the supply service.

During the winter of 1918-19 the British troops were widely disseminated.

One division lay about Varna on the western shores of the Black Sea: another was based on Batum on the eastern side (seven hundred miles by sea from Constantinople) and carried out the occupation of the railway through Tiflis to Baku on the west coast of the Caspian (five hundred miles by rail from Batum). A supply depot at Enzeli in Persia on the south shore of the Caspian supplied this force.

General Denikin's White Russian Army, for the maintenance of which the British were largely responsible, was operating from Novorossisk on the north side of the Black Sea.

Army Headquarters and one division were at Constantinople itself and on the European side of the straits as far as Gallipoli. A further division was scattered on the Asiatic side from Ismid to Chanak with a brigade group along the Baghdad railway as far as Eski-Shehr (a hundred and fifty miles by rail from Constantinople) and Konia (four hundred and fifty miles by rail).

In Macedonia large detachments of troops were involved, operating base establishments of all kinds and providing guards for stores. Other detachments were in Crete, at Bralo and Itea in Greece and at Sofia in Bulgaria and elsewhere.

The total area thus covered by the army of occupation was some 300,000 square miles. Supply depots were established at Constantinople, Haidar Pasha (which was taken over as a going concern from the Germans on the Asiatic side of the Bosphorus), Chanak, Varna, Novorossisk, Batum and Ismid. These were filled up as most convenient either direct from England or from Egypt.

The troops in the straits were supplied by small craft from Chanak or Constantinople. A frozen meat store in the latter place was taken over and used for feeding all troops on the Bosphorus and Black Sea: this was kept filled up from the main store at Port Said which also continued to supply French and Hellenic troops at Odessa.

At that time over the whole area the British supply commitments were approximately as under. For the British troops 90,000 men's and 40,000 animals' rations daily, besides a varying number for local labourers, muleteers and similar auxiliaries. For the French and Serbs 15,000 tons of grain per month and complete rations for 70,000 Serbs per day. For the Italians 900 tons of flour and 30 tons of sugar monthly. For the Hellenic army almost all commodities for 200,000 men and 50,000 animals.

All these things considered it may be excusable to recall past campaigns, when such British commissariat as existed under civilian or semi-civilian control failed in the provisioning of even modest British armies, quite apart from hungry Allies.

During the years which followed 1918 innumerable issues of supplies were made to various famine-stricken areas, including the starving people of the Caucasus and the interior of Asia Minor, through various relief committees, to Red Cross Missions, to Allied Commissions, to British refugees from Odessa and elsewhere, to refugees' camps on Prinkipo Island, to Armenians, to Russian civil police and railway employees.

The demands for live sheep for Indian troops, of which six battalions were maintained from Batum, proved as usual to be a matter of considerable difficulty. No sheep or goats were available in the Caucasus area and they had to be shipped from Salonika to Batum where they arrived in miserable condition, sometimes as many as 50 per cent. of their number being lost from sickness during the voyage.

With the troops settled more or less into "occupation" quarters large quantities of transport vehicles became available for disposal. In addition to a consignment of lorries, cars, caterpillar tractors and a workshop which was sent to Denikin's force, numbers of vehicles were disposed of to the Roumanian Government, and, in order to spare as many mechanical transport drivers for demobilisation as possible, Turkish drivers who had been trained by the Germans were employed in Constantinople, while men of all nationalities were taken on as batmen, muleteers and in other occupations.

Meanwhile the Sultan had abdicated and there was no responsible Government representing the national will of the Turkish people, although Mustafa Kemal Pasha was gradually acquiring supreme power and collecting armed forces in Asia Minor.

From 1919 to 1923 the history of the Black Sea Army is one of gradual withdrawal, first, under a Turkish threat of renewed hostilities, from the Baghdad railway line, then from the Caucasus and finally from the whole area. A few anxious weeks were experienced before the Government decided to withdraw the troops from the Chanak defences, and renewed hostilities were only avoided by the exercise of great restraint by the British troops under considerable provocation, but no encounter took place. Stores and animals were disposed of or shipped elsewhere and *personnel* demobilised.

Thus the remnants of the old Salonika army trickled back to England, after a chequered existence as a separate force of some eight years, having earned the respect and goodwill of countless nationalities amongst which it had lived so long. Greeks, Georgians, Turks, Armenians, Russians, Roumanians, Serbs and Macedonians had all learned to trust and admire the friendliness, discipline, good nature and fair dealing characteristic of the British soldier in foreign parts.

From the point of view of the Royal Army Service Corps the experience was unique, the opportunities for improvisation and the necessity for re-organisation almost unending. But the willing work and loyal co-operation of all ranks and of the many varied nationalities employed during the eight years of operations contributed in no small measure to the success which attended the efforts of the British troops and the good name which the British Army left behind it in the Near East.

BIBLIOGRAPHY

The Army Service Corps in the Balkans. Compiled by Lieut. F. J. Kelly, A.S.C.
Salonika and After. By H. Collinson Owen.
History of the Mechanical Transport Units with the Royal Serbian Army. Prepared in the Supply and Transport Directorate, Salonika Force.

CHAPTER VIII

THE CAMPAIGNS IN EGYPT AND PALESTINE

THE campaigns undertaken by what was successively known as the Army in Egypt, the Mediterranean Expeditionary Force and the Egyptian Expeditionary Force may be divided into two distinct groups. There was the major series which was conducted east of the Suez Canal in the Sinai Peninsula, in Palestine and in Syria, and which culminated in the complete overthrow of the Turkish arms. The minor series consisted of the operations for the defence of the Suez Canal and the expedition against the Senoussi fought in the Western Desert which separates Egypt proper from the Italian colony of Tripoli. These last formed the prelude to the invasion of the Turkish Empire.

From the point of view of the transport and supply services both series are of high interest, for they demonstrate the wide range of duties that fell to the Army Service Corps and the adaptability of the Corps to meet such duties. If more formidable difficulties had to be met in East Africa and in Mesopotamia, in neither of these latter theatres were more diverse forms of transport called into use.

Administratively the defence of the Suez Canal presented little difficulty. The British forces were engaged in a passive rôle which lasted from November 1914 until early in 1916. The enemy offensive conducted in February 1915 had been inspired more from considerations of policy than with any real hope of success. It was easily repulsed and the main body of the Turkish army retired to El Arish, from which place it continued, for a period of some eighteen months, to hold out the threat of a renewed attack, and rumours of such renewal were in constant circulation. During this period defensive measures were extended and developed and the British forces were spread in a general north and south line parallel to the canal extending from Qantara in the north to Ain Musa in the south—a distance of approximately seventy miles. The defences consisted of a continuous series of fortified redoubts sited some ten miles east of the canal, to serve which roads suitable for 3-ton lorries were gradually constructed, as was also a series of light railways. Previous to the provision of these facilities, animal transport had been necessary on the eastern side of the canal. The canal itself formed, with the railway which ran parallel to it on the Egyptian side, the main arteries within the area, and when these were supplemented by a road which was built from Ismailia to Qantara and subsequently extended to Port Said, they fulfilled every requirement of lateral communications. In relation to these communications, one activity of the Army Service Corps is worth record and this consisted of the motor boat company which had been transferred from Lemnos to Ismailia on the evacuation of the Gallipoli Peninsula. This unit, which comprised some one hundred and forty all ranks, operated thirty-six boats of various descriptions and was used for the Embarkation Staff and other port officers on the canal and for the carriage of supplies and for patrol work, until later it was sent to Palestine where it provided detachments on the Dead Sea, the Sea of Galilee and at Haifa and at Tripoli in Syria.

In respect of numbers the Western Desert operations were unimportant, for at no time were more than 7000 men employed in active warfare. Nevertheless they may be noticed in that they furnished a typical example of the "small war" on which the British Army has so often found itself engaged and which involves not so much a struggle against the enemy as against the forces of nature. In this instance the use of light motor transport was an innovation as applied to a "small war", and the employment of camel transport on a considerable scale went beyond the normal Army Service Corps formations, which were otherwise adequate.

Geographically the operations ranged over a wide area, but these distances shrunk in proportion to the existence or non-existence of a water supply. Although the ground covered extended on the north from the outskirts of the Egyptian Delta to beyond Sollum on the borders of Tripoli, a distance of some three hundred and fifty miles, and British outposts faced a front which ended some eight hundred miles to the south, the actual points of contact were few and far between. The campaign proper therefore resolved itself into the securing of the port of Matruh, the re-establishment of the garrison at Sollum and the clearance of the Siwa oasis two hundred miles south-west of Matruh. The striking force allocated to these objectives was based for supplies on the great depot that had been established at Alexandria, where a special department was created to deal with it. Both rail and sea communications were used, the former proceeding from Alexandria as far as Dabaa and thence to Matruh eighty-five miles farther on by road; but owing to scarcity of water this route was hardly practicable except to mechanical and camel transport. Ten small steamers were employed upon the sea route to Matruh, which port possessed a serviceable natural harbour, landlocked and with sufficient depth of water. In order to escape the attentions of submarines the vessels left Alexandria at sunset, arriving early the following morning. Supplies were put ashore from ships to pier, the Egyptian Labour Corps undertaking the off loading. The transport of troops and animals was attended by unusual risks as the steamers were crowded, and large consignments of petrol were carried. At Matruh the water supply was scanty and unfit for drinking purposes. Requirements were, therefore, met from tanks brought by sea until a condensing plant was installed later. Except in this respect supplies presented little difficulty. Fresh meat in the shape of sheep was obtained locally, but prices rose so quickly that this commodity had eventually, like others, to be obtained on demand from the base.

The initial movements of the troops exposed the inadequacy of the existing transport, for which the waterless tracts of the desert proved unsuitable. If any horse-drawn transport could have wholly sufficed, that of the First Australian Divisional Train would have done so, for men and horses were used to similar conditions in their own country. During their time in this theatre this well-trained and hardy body did exceptionally fine work and on one occasion fought an action as a mounted infantry squadron. At the same time since the radius of action of the force was limited by the amount of supplies that could accompany it, lack of transport spelt immobility, and consequently after a successful action no question of a pursuit could be entertained as a return to the base was necessary. Accordingly the First Australian Divisional Train was withdrawn on the despatch of their division to France, and replaced by camel transport with the aid of which the hundred and fifty miles to Sollum were traversed. This was the first occasion in the Great War in which organised camel units were utilised on any scale and, as might have been expected, for any means out of the ordinary, a certain scepticism was manifested as to their value. But the advice of those who had had experience in Egypt and the Sudan prevailed and one thousand animals arrived at Matruh from Alexandria during the first week in February 1916, being followed later by a further similar number. In the course of the advance to Sollum supply depots were formed at Unjeila, one stage west of Matruh and, after the defeat of the enemy, also at Barrani—a point still farther west—where a ship was off loaded with some difficulty. Finally a depot, including a bakery section, was established at Sollum itself, where a pier was built by means of which stores could be put ashore without incurring the loss inseparable from the use of surf boats. The work of the camel convoys on these communications fully justified the faith of those who had been responsible for their introduction. On the 10th of February a convoy of eight hundred carrying some 22,000 men's rations and 7000 animal rations marched from Matruh to Unjeila, and similar convoys were despatched at intervals up to the 5th of March. After the occupation of Unjeila, camel transport continued to ply between that place and Matruh, and, as an example of stamina, a convoy arriving at the latter destination one morning left on the following one with a fresh load for the return journey—a distance of forty miles. For the next stage, that between Unjeila and Sidi Barrani, arrangements worked closely in accordance with the programme. On the 7th of March the British forces began to concentrate at Sidi Barrani and in spite of violent dust and wind over 2000 camels carrying five days' rations accompanied the column which marched out on the 9th. Two days later these supplies were replenished at Bag-Bag by the use of all the wheeled transport, withdrawn from units, which was able to negotiate that portion of the route, and this measure enabled one day's supply for the cavalry and three days' supply for the infantry to be pushed forward. In the course of these operations the camels were not watered until the 14th of March at Alim Tejid, the same day as Sollum was occupied, and they appeared little the worse for their enforced drought.

From Sollum took place the famous raid of an armoured motor car battery into the unknown country one hundred and twenty miles to the west with the object of rescuing the survivors of the steamships *Tara* and *Moorina* who were held there as prisoners. The incident was of interest from the supply point of view in that, without the availability of some two thousand gallons of petrol with the flying column, it could not have been successful.

The last operation of importance was the capture of the Siwa oasis two hundred miles south-west of Matruh. This was made possible by the use of light mechanical transport, which after a journey of two days deposited supplies at the point of concentration fifteen miles from Siwa. The expedition was thus enabled to refill, fight its battle and return to the base at Matruh within nine days of setting out from that place. In the remaining oases of the Western Desert the movements call for no comment. The fighting troops had little to do but show themselves, and the work of supply was effectively carried out from the Cairo depot and sub-depots established where needed. Camel transport was successfully used over this area.

Some space has been devoted to these minor operations since they were on a small scale a "dress rehearsal" for the transport and supply services in view of the performances to follow. As such they were invaluable.

Let us turn now to the counter-offensive which, under the command of General Sir Archibald Murray, was launched by the British army in Egypt and which was eventually destined to reach Aleppo in rather more than two years of strenuous campaigning. At the time this offensive started the main body of the enemy lay at El Arish, about one hundred miles east of Qantara, which latter place was the point of departure chosen for the advance. At that time it was only intended to go as far as Qatiya and possibly El Arish after the former place had been occupied, but as on other occasions it was found expedient to exploit success beyond original anticipations. Essential to movement across the Sinai Desert was the construction of a railway to accompany the army and of a pipe line communicating with the Sweet Water Canal. The railway put down was of the standard gauge and was begun in February 1916. It took two and a half months to reach Romani twenty-five miles distant, whence a branch was made to Mahemidiya. When work was resumed after the battle of Romani progress was made at the rate of fifteen miles a month. The total length from Qantara to Wadi Ghazze opposite Gaza was one hundred and forty miles and the capacity of the line was thirteen trains daily in a forward direction, of which six were "obligatory" in the sense that they were required for railway construction and maintenance, leaving only seven per day for supplies, stores and the movement of troops. For the water supply, until wells were located at various spots, the troops were dependent on the pipe line. At Qantara a plant capable of filtering 600,000 gallons a day was installed and the water was pumped through siphons under the Suez Canal into reservoirs on the east bank. Thence it was conveyed by steel pipes divided into four sections laid in the sand as far as El Arish, whence it was later extended to Rafah, from which point smaller lines radiated out to the front on which the army lay south of the Beersheba–Gaza line. The task involved by this construction was admirably carried out by the Royal Engineers. During the progress of the pipe line when water could not be pumped to railhead, it was carried from the last pumping station by water trains and from these trains distributed to the troops by camel convoys in small tanks known as "fanatis" of which each camel carried two, each holding twelve and a half gallons.

Meanwhile Qantara itself was developed towards the important rôle that it was destined to fill as a Base Supply Depot for an army which ultimately attained a strength of nearly 500,000 men and 160,000 animals. Wharves, at which ocean-going steamers could berth and unload with the necessary accessories in the shape of cranes and storage accommodation, were constructed, and the depot was thus enabled to have the supreme advantage of direct communication with the sea. As an indication of the size that this depot attained it may be recorded that at one time it contained some 120,000 tons of hay stuffs and 100,000 tons of grain stuffs, quite apart from food stocks for men. In Egypt there was held a minimum of sixty days' supplies for the whole of the Expeditionary Force. Concurrent with this preparation an organisation came into being which was to play no mean part in the success of the campaign. This consisted of the Camel Transport Corps whose initial operations in the Western Desert have already been noted; its formation was begun in December 1915 at a base near Cairo, and subsequently developed to the number of some 35,000 animals.

In past campaigns the camel had not always proved satisfactory. In Afghanistan in 1879–80 among the 70,000 transport animals lost a high proportion was camels. In the Egyptian desert in 1884–5, of 7000 purchased, over 4000 became casualties, while, of the remaining 3000, only some 1300 were effective after three months' work. In those days no transport service existed that was adequate for the task of organisation and supervision. A different state of affairs obtained in the campaign of the Egyptian Expeditionary Force. From December 1915 until December 1918 some 72,000 baggage camels passed through the Camel Transport Corps, of which 34,000 came from various Egyptian provinces and the bulk of the remainder from the Sudan and Somaliland, Algeria and India. Some few further statistics may be permitted. Just over 10,000 were killed or died and there were some 24,000 admissions to hospital, the greatest number of such at any one time being 3000. The highest percentage of the total strength unavailable during major operations was twenty-four. The fact that the camel is at all times a difficult and delicate animal to work, and that in this instance it was called upon to negotiate ground impassable to most other forms of transport and to face the risks and hardships of active service, enables the figures given to bear testimony to the efficiency of the *personnel* in control of the organisation. As regards the latter, some four hundred officers and five hundred non-commissioned officers, of which respectively one hundred and eleven and two hundred and eight belonged to the Army Service Corps, were posted, while from first to last some 170,000 Egyptian drivers saw service in the Corps, where the endurance of the fellahin was displayed at its best.

The Camel Transport Corps was organised in companies of 2000 animals each and these units were employed either as first line transport to divisions or in special columns. A very important share in the success of this new service was due to Colonel C. W. Whittingham, a reserve officer who left his post as Inspector-General of the Prison Departments in Egypt to raise, train and administer it.

The occupation of Sinai began in early April 1916. The northern portion of the peninsula consisted of a narrow coastal plain bordered with belts of sand dunes varying in breadth from five to fifteen miles. This zone was for the most part impassable for wheeled transport and was indeed heavy going for men. The central zone was a barren stony plateau, rising to a height of 3000 feet, and there the going was comparatively firm. In the south was a mass of rocky and precipitous mountains. The main advance in the north was extended by bounds followed by steady consolidation and preparation for the next move, except for one check administered by the enemy at Qatiya on the 23rd of April, when three and a half squadrons of yeomanry were surprised and destroyed. In this action Captain C. A. Bruce of the Army Service Corps, who was supply officer to the 5th Mounted Brigade, was killed. The battle fought at Romani in August opened the way to El Arish, and Rafah on the Palestine frontier was occupied in January. It had thus taken almost a year to cover the one hundred miles from Qantara, but the enterprise, while dissipating any idea of a further Turkish offensive against Egypt, had also brought the enemy within striking distance once more. The problem of supply during this period was, as has been shown, mainly one of railway communication augmented by camel transport, for wheeled traffic could not cope with the heavy sand and the few caterpillar tractors available were engaged on Royal Engineer services. The two cavalry and three infantry divisions which, with various auxiliaries, formed the British striking force were therefore grouped around the progressive railheads, while along the railway line were formed supply depots which were constantly pushed eastwards. With the occupation of El Arish another channel of communications was opened, for stores were forwarded by sea from Port Said and landed from surf boats. By the 31st of March, 1917, the railway had reached Rafah and the pipe line, in spite of the local water supply having greatly improved, had followed closely. But the construction of the railway had not entirely obviated the necessity of a road, and a sufficiently satisfactory method for the construction of such was discovered in the employment of wire netting laid on the sand and pegged down. Mounted troops were forbidden to use this track, as the hooves of the horses cut the wire, but it was of great value to infantry, while cars and ambulances could also be driven along it.

With the establishment of the Army on the southern borders of Palestine some re-organisation of the transport services became desirable. Accordingly the trains of the 52nd, 53rd and 54th Divisions and the Anzac Mounted Division, which had rejoined their divisions equipped with limbered wagons, were re-equipped with wagons, each having a team of four mules driven by long reins. As the operations proceeded and divisions were withdrawn for service in other theatres and fresh divisions arrived, trains were broken up and re-organised to meet the peculiar needs or establishments of the new formations, until there were ultimately fourteen formation trains operating, and also four auxiliary mule transport companies on the lines of communication. For all these units a base depot was established at Qantara and subsequently after the capture of Jerusalem at Ludd. Constant changes and shiftings, which were embarrassing in that they prevented any close identification with a particular division, were not, however, the sole disadvantage to which these trains were subjected. For at the time they were re-equipped on a wheeled basis it was decided that owing to the man-power situation they should only contain 50 per cent. of British Army Service Corps *personnel*, the balance being found from the Egyptian army. Of the 8000 men from that source who by the end of the campaign were employed in Army Service Corps units, including those of the Australians and New Zealanders, a large proportion were in the divisional trains, in which it should be recorded that they conducted themselves with every credit.

At about the same time as these measures were undertaken, two donkey transport companies were organised, for it was wisely anticipated that other forms of transport might find themselves restricted in their movements when once the army reached the Judean hills. Like the camel companies, each unit had an establishment of 2000 animals and one driver was allotted to every three: they accomplished some varied work, being employed at different times in carrying ammunition, ration water, entrenching tools, and stones for road making. The fact that the total number lost during 1917 and 1918 was only two hundred and sixty-eight speaks well for the manner in which they were cared for.

By a re-organisation of the army which took place at Rafah a fourth infantry division was formed from three yeomanry brigades which were not remounted on their return from Gallipoli; the force for the further advance, which was then decided upon, consisted of two mounted and four infantry divisions. On the 26th of March the First Battle of Gaza was launched, railhead then being at Rafah, eighteen miles from the scene of action. The troops gained their objectives but were unable to maintain themselves and consequently withdrew on the night of the 27th–28th of March. The severity of the hostile artillery fire made the approach of camel convoys with water supplies and ammunition a matter of difficulty, but the immediate maintenance of so large a force from so distant a railhead was stated by the Commander-in-Chief in his despatches on the battle to have been out of the question. In this last respect Sir Archibald Murray seems to have been under some misapprehension, for the supply work was normal and adequate and there is every reason to believe could have been maintained as such. Tactical and not administrative reasons decided the day at Gaza. The action was, in fact, an abortive one. The experience purchased was not, however, thrown away, and, accordingly, before a second attempt on Gaza was made, the railhead was extended to Deir El Belah, some twelve miles farther forward, from whence a light railway was taken to the coast. Reservoirs were also constructed on the Wadi Ghazze to hold 67,000 gallons of water; and on the 17th of April the attack took place. But the enemy had profited by the three weeks' interval to bring up reinforcements and strengthen his defences, and the result was a somewhat costly failure for British arms. It became clear that reinforcements, especially in artillery and infantry, were necessary before progress could be made and in reply to the representations of Sir Archibald Murray both were forthcoming; although the infantry which consisted of the 60th Division from Salonika did not arrive until June. In addition, from the same source, came two yeomanry brigades, which enabled a third mounted division to be constituted, while small French and Italian contingents also appeared on the scene. In prospect, too, by the early autumn was yet another infantry division composed of units to come from East Africa, Aden and India. These dispositions meant that the maintenance of three mounted divisions and six infantry divisions would need to be provided for in front of railhead—a task which would have strained the single line of railway to its uttermost. As an alternative to doubling it, therefore, stations were enlarged, additional crossing places made and extra engines and rolling stock taken into use. The Inland Water Transport Service was at the same time expanded and small craft under this organisation were employed to a great extent along the coast. The water supply, too, needed attention, for the curious situation had arisen in which out of 600,000 gallons pumped daily from Qantara only 36,500 gallons reached pipehead at Abu Bakra on the Wadi Ghazze, the remainder being required for the needs of the railway and the troops and labourers between the two points. Though considerable supplies of water had been found locally it was certain that these would diminish in the hot weather, and it was realised that the success of any offensive movement depended on the capture of Gaza or Beersheba with the wells intact. These engineering activities did not pertain directly to the Army Service Corps, but since they were basic to the functions of the transport and supply services, which were moreover responsible for distribution from railhead, it is necessary to set them out. From the supply point of view the strain placed upon a single thread of railway was a constant anxiety, especially since there was a total absence of local resources: and it may be recalled that along that single line was maintained an army as large as the British Expeditionary Force in France during the opening phase of the War.

In June 1917 General Sir Edmund Allenby succeeded Sir Archibald Murray as Commander-in-Chief and at once proceeded to move General Headquarters from Cairo to the desert front, from whence he energetically continued the preparations for the next offensive which had been initiated by his predecessor. Portions of the railway line from Qantara were doubled; from Rafah a branch line was built to Shellal, with an extension terminating at El Gamli, and a second extension to Karm in the direction of Beersheba—thus threatening the enemy left flank. Light railways were built to prolong the railhead at Deir el Belah to the positions in the Wadi Ghazze. By these measures it became possible to provide and accumulate everything required for an advance in strength. Reserve and advanced depots fed from the great base at Qantara were established throughout the wide area occupied by the British troops, notably at El Arish, Rafah, Khan Yunis, Deir El Belah, Shellal, El Gamli and finally at Karm, the last-named having to be formed in direct view of the Turkish positions and subject to attack by shell fire. This depot placed far forward proved of great value during the subsequent operations when, after the fall of Beersheba, it successfully met the needs of six divisions, the Imperial Camel Corps Brigade and a host of camel transport.

General Allenby, who had received reinforcements of the 10th Infantry Division and a further mounted division which enabled him to group his forces into two Army Corps, 20th and 21st, and the Desert Mounted Corps of three divisions, moved in October. Beersheba was surprised and captured on the last day of that month. Its fall was the prelude to operations which, driving in the enemy left flank, forced him to retire from Gaza and then gave him no rest until he had put some fifty miles between his former positions and the precarious line between Jerusalem and Jaffa.

The supply difficulties of the pursuit were augmented by the nature of the terrain, the communications and the weather conditions, but one feature was favourable, and that lay in the fact that the desert and the sand had been left at last and wheeled and especially mechanical transport could now be called upon. Up to that date there had been but little use for the latter. In Egypt and in the canal zone useful work had been done at the bases where metalled roads existed and a base depot for mechanical transport and stores had been opened at Alexandria. Later advanced depots were opened at Cairo, Ismailia, Qantara and eventually at Ludd. In 1916 a tractor company had been engaged in laying the pipe line, and, prior to the First Battle of Gaza, tractors had assisted in building up the supply dumps at Deir El Belah and Khan Yunis. These vehicles had also brought heavy guns into line on the Wadi Ghazze, but the first occasion on which mechanical transport was used to any material extent was on the Beersheba operations, when three companies were detrained at Karm and having successfully negotiated the unmetalled track towards Beersheba they rendered valuable aid on the Beersheba–Gaza and Beersheba–Hebron roads, and also in ammunition services in the course of which it was often possible to go across country as far as the gun positions. Just before General Allenby's first offensive there were with his army exclusive of his lines of communication up to and including Rafah, thirteen mechanical transport units, of which twelve were tractor companies (eleven of these being attached to the Army Corps heavy artillery) and also one Ford van company. On the eve of the action, however, three lorry companies were brought up from Qantara.

The country over which the next phase of the operations was conducted consisted of a wide coastal plain which to the east changed abruptly into a broken and mountainous region traversed by the Beersheba–Jerusalem road. The plain provided a sufficiently good surface for all kinds of transport in dry weather, but during the rains the surface broke up and the low-lying parts became an impassable swamp. In neither region was there normally a plentiful supply of water. The communications were confined to the metalled road running from Beersheba through Hebron to Jerusalem and an unfinished road connecting Gaza with Junction Station and Latrun, where it met the metalled highway which connected Jaffa and Jerusalem. In addition there were two narrow-gauge railways, one starting from Jerusalem and connecting Junction Station with Beersheba and the other going north from Gaza until it linked up with the first: both were considerably damaged by the enemy during his retreat.

Refusing the barren hills with their single indifferent road, the British army, abandoning its railheads, set out in pursuit. In order to facilitate supply two infantry divisions were recalled and a third handed its transport over to the pursuing force. By the 12th of November—Gaza had fallen on the 10th—the remainder of the army had advanced thirty-five miles beyond railhead and had secured the mouth of the Sukerieh, thereby obtaining a useful landing place for supplies sent round by sea. By the 14th it was sixty miles from railhead on its right and forty on its left and was in possession of Junction Station, Jaffa, Ludd, Ramleh and Latrun. These movements, carried out as they were while the weather was still extremely hot, and in face of a determined resistance by the Turks, constituted a brilliant feat of arms which brought the army to within five miles of Jerusalem by the 21st of November. It detracts nothing however from the heroic efforts of the fighting troops to record that they were only made possible by the efficiency and adaptability of the transport services. Immediately the Judean hills were entered pack transport was improvised so that the advance lost none of its impetus, and the brief pause before Jerusalem was entered on the 9th of December was devoted to measures which enabled the whole army to be concentrated and maintained on the front.

The work of supply over this period was the most

difficult of the campaign. It was successfully met by any and every means that could further a single purpose. While the weather had permitted, mechanical transport replaced the railway line; a succession of rainy days however reduced the country to a morass, and for a time all wheeled traffic except that on the Beersheba–Hebron–Jerusalem road came to a standstill. Camels working in three echelons along the sand dunes which fringed the coast saved the situation and the pursuit was able to continue. In places the camels sank up to their girths in mud and had to be abandoned. The wastage in drivers was high: but all the time the troops were able to go forward.

Meanwhile every opportunity had been seized upon to land stores on the coast. A depot was formed at Sukerieh, while the capture of Jaffa and its subsequent clearance to the north opened up another landing place. Thus by combining every possible means of transport the British troops were enabled to march and fight almost continuously. Every requirement for so doing had to be sent from behind, for the country itself was bare and the enemy had destroyed what supplies he could not remove. Had the army not been served by so comprehensive a system it would have been impossible to have gathered the fruits of the victory on the Beersheba–Gaza front. The enemy would have been given time to re-organise and the capture of Jerusalem in all probability only achieved at the price of costly and long-drawn-out fighting. As it was the Jerusalem–Jaffa line was, so to speak, taken by the British army " in its stride ". Seldom do the annals of war show a clearer example of the power with which a large army is endowed by having at its disposal highly organised and trained transport and supply services.

By the end of December 1917 fresh supply depots had been formed along the entire front from Jerusalem to Jaffa, while the capture of Jericho in February prolonged the line and enabled an advanced supply depot to be set up at that place capable of meeting the demands of any force sent beyond the Jordan. This last measure was of special value from the 21st of March to the 4th of May, when troops were sent east of the river to raid the enemy rail communications with the Hedjaz. From the Jericho depot the supply was effected by a combination of camels and motor lorries, the latter using the metalled road, constructed by the Turks, running from Ghoraniyeh Bridge to Es-Salt and Amman in Trans-Jordania.

Before fresh operations on a large scale could be resumed it was necessary to establish a more solid line of communications with Egypt than that which had been improvised to carry the army on to its existing front. Accordingly the desert railway from Qantara was double-tracked as far as Rafah and the single track carried forward to Rantie, passing through Ludd and Jaffa. The Ludd–Jerusalem branch was converted to a standard gauge line to increase its carrying capacity and when an iron bridge was subsequently built over the Suez Canal above Qantara, Jerusalem was directly connected with the Egyptian railway system; and produce could thus be run straight through from the Nile valley into Palestine. At the same time a series of light railways directed to the front was pushed forward from the main system in a similar manner to those which had been constructed previously to prolong the railhead at Deir El Belah. As road making and repairing kept pace with this railway activity, it became possible to form depots distributed over a wide area and capable of sustaining the needs of the whole army on the spot.*

General Allenby's original intention had been to continue his offensive in the spring of 1918, and had not

* The average daily tonnage of *supplies* despatched by rail from Qantara to Palestine was:

1918	Tons
June	1615
July	2026
August	2317
September	1732

events in France interfered he would have been able to have done so. But following the defeat of the Fifth Army under General Gough, the Egyptian Expeditionary Force was called upon to send two of its five British infantry divisions to the main theatre, while the others were depleted by the withdrawal of twenty-four battalions for the same purpose. In exchange he received the 3rd and 7th Indian Divisions and a number of comparatively raw Indian replacements, which necessitated some months being spent in training before extensive operations could be undertaken. From the Desert Mounted Corps nine yeomanry regiments were withdrawn and replaced by Indian cavalry units from France. Consequently the next forward movement was not made until the 19th of September.* The events which ensued, if an epic in the history of cavalry, were none the less so from the point of view of the Army Service Corps, and completed and crowned the three years' solid work which had been accomplished in the Egyptian and Palestinian theatres of war. Transport and supply preparations had been very thorough. As usual depots were established to the extreme forward limit, and ships were ready loaded at Port Said in order to be able to off load on the coast where necessary. It was known that little dependence could be placed on the railways to the north owing to damage by the enemy and that mechanical transport would have to work for the most part over unmetalled roads; it was on this basis that the maintenance scheme was prepared and mechanical transport carefully allotted to the various Army Corps, the vehicles being thoroughly overhauled. Considerable reinforce-

* The ration strength of the Egyptian Expeditionary Force at this date was:

British	226,000	Horses	74,800
Indian	111,800	Mules	39,100
Egyptians	128,950	Camels	35,000
		Donkeys	11,000
	466,750		159,900

ments had accrued in this direction since the Beersheba–Gaza battle and there were now available in the forward area no less than forty companies, of which nineteen were engaged in drawing the heavy artillery. It was well that this was so, for mechanical transport, hitherto in the background, was destined to come into its own.*

To recount the whole course of the happenings which followed the attack on the 19th of September would require a volume to deal with the administrative side alone. Within thirty-six hours of the start of the offensive the Turkish Seventh and Eighth Armies were broken and in full retreat, to which movement the Fourth Army east of the Jordan was forced to conform. The fighting resolved itself into a general pursuit and harassment of the flying enemy, amid which welter of events it will serve the purpose to indicate the more noteworthy incidents in the maintenance service. Two infantry divisions were affected—the 10th and the 7th—which went forward after the break through. The former, which had marched and fought its way for twenty-four miles and had reached a point north of Nablus by the evening of the 21st of September, was continuously supplied by mechanical transport moving up the Jerusalem–Nablus road. The 7th Division after fighting and marching for three days on the left of the line moved via Zimmarin on Haifa, where it arrived on the 29th, proceeding thence to Beirut ninety-six miles north and subsequently on to Tripoli in Syria— a further fifty-four miles—the total being accomplished in nineteen days. This formation was maintained by coastal landings made at Tyre, Sidon, Haifa, Beirut and Tripoli, the Camel Transport Corps co-operating until

* The total number of mechanical vehicles used by the Egyptian Expeditionary Force was as under:

Lorries	1601, of which 1450 were 3-ton
Cars and vans	1467
Ambulances	530
Motor cycles	1487
Tractors	288

mechanical vehicles could take up the work on the repaired coastal road which went north from Beirut and on the Haifa–Nazareth–Galilee road to Damascus.

East of the Jordan the cavalry division in pursuit of the Fourth Turkish Army was maintained by mechanical transport from the depot at Jericho and by its muled transport.

Finally the three cavalry divisions of the Desert Mounted Corps, which had poured through the gap made by the artillery and infantry, headed off the retreat of the enemy at El Fule and pursued the disorganised remnants to beyond Damascus where the Australian Mounted Division was left to secure the town after which it proceeded to Homs. One division, the 4th Cavalry, halted at Rayak on the 13th of October. The 5th Cavalry Division with its armoured cars only stopped on the 31st of October at the conclusion of the armistice, by which date it had reached a point fifteen miles north of Aleppo, having covered five hundred miles in forty days. The maintenance of these divisions, operating so far in advance of railhead, was only made possible by the absence of rain and the feasibility of employing mechanical transport, though often with great difficulty; also from the fact that supply depots could be opened up along the coast, in relation to which the most careful detailed arrangements had to be made daily as convoys were switched from day to day on to new bases. In addition, the Turkish light railway was made use of at Haifa and two small but valuable depots were established at El Fule and Samakh at the southern end of the Sea of Galilee. The latter depot was of great use to the cavalry around Damascus. Movement was, too, greatly assisted by enemy forage, captured during the advance which took place through regions where certain quantities were also obtainable locally.

But even with these facilities the supply of the cavalry divisions was a great and memorable achievement, in which the brunt was almost entirely borne by the mechanical transport. During much of this period the companies were working almost continuously day and night and there was consequently much sickness and exhaustion among the *personnel*. As the advance continued their numbers became so rapidly depleted that it became a matter of difficulty to provide one man per lorry. Indeed, when the lorries of the Fifth Cavalry Division arrived at Beirut, some became immobile from want of drivers, but the spirit of the men was magnificent and many of the sick remained at duty. Yet from one company alone one hundred and twenty-eight men were admitted to hospital during the early days of October and another company had one hundred and six sick out of a total strength of one hundred and sixty-one. During ten weeks from the 19th of September 57 per cent. of the *personnel* engaged with the three divisions of the Desert Mounted Corps were admitted to hospital. Yet all the time that the cavalry continued the pursuit the mechanical transport followed at their heels. Aleppo was captured on the 26th of October and, as was the case at Haifa and Homs, the lorries entered the same day as the troops; while from Aleppo a convoy was despatched to Alexandretta where in its turn a supply depot was formed. During this arduous work, in many places over ground which would ordinarily have been deemed impassable, an average of 81 per cent. of the vehicles was maintained on the road among the six lorry companies which participated in these operations. Even so, without the dry weather that obtained and the existence of certain main arteries in the shape of metalled roads, it was more than probable that the pursuing troops could not have been maintained and therefore that the victory would have been much less sweeping than it was.

In briefly surveying the administrative problems of the campaign with which the Quartermaster-General of the Expeditionary Force—Sir Walter Campbell—and his supply and transport directorate had to contend, some indication of the sources from which provision was made are necessary. So long as Great Britain retained unhampered command of the sea the question of supply presented no harassing question of difficulty as regards Egypt which was in fact a base for all Mediterranean operations; and the Egyptian railway system lent itself to a facile distribution. Suez was adapted as the entrepôt for supplies arriving from the east while Port Said was utilised for the Salonika army and as the Palestine Coastal Base. Rail and water communications ran from the Suez Canal near Ismailia to Cairo, where purchases from Upper Egypt and the Sudan were most readily assembled. Near Cairo similar communications existed with Alexandria, the main depot for arrivals from the west and Lower Egypt. In 1915 an Advanced Supply Depot was established at Zagazig; later to be replaced by Qantara. As the German submarine warfare developed in intensity the necessity of conserving shipping became a question of importance and consequently the army was forced to exploit local resources to their uttermost. Up to the spring of 1917 purchase in Egypt had been carried out mainly by a Military Local Resources Board which had a Government member. Subsequently the Egyptian Government took a fuller share in that a Supplies Control Board consisting of both civil government and military members was set up, its duties being to ascertain the crops of the country, to control civil consumption, to watch exports and to hand over any surplus in the country to the army at an agreed price. The Supplies Control Board, of which Colonel W. Elliott, A.S.C., Deputy Director of Supplies and Transport was a member, very wisely requested the Ministry of the Interior to undertake collection, since that department alone had direct authority over the provincial administration, and the work was most successfully accomplished, the inland water transport and the Egyptian

State railways assisting in the actual collection. It is pleasant to be able to record the exceptional zeal with which the local mudirs and their subordinates devoted themselves to this task, in which they were ably seconded by the goodwill of the fellahin. But the production and collection of these great quantities of forage and foodstuffs was a serious drain on the resources of Egypt. The Delta light railways and water craft were taxed to their fullest capacity in supplementing the Egyptian State system for the prodigious amounts required to be handled.*

Concurrently with these transactions, fuel wood at the rate of five thousand tons per month was obtained from the Government forests at Cyprus as was also timber required by the Royal Engineers; and from Cyprus also in the shape of foodstuffs were brought goats, grain, carob beans, dried fruit and potatoes. The Sudan Government helped by forwarding sheep, grain and cattle via Wadi Halfa and Port Sudan. Here the co-operation of Colonel Sir Edgar Bernard, Financial Adviser to the Sudan Government who had himself been an Army Service Corps officer, proved of much assistance.

Large industries were started and operated under the supply service, such as the pressing of tibben or the stalk of wheat into portable bales for pack transport, the milling of wheat, the manufacture of jam, biscuits and margarine. A large fishing fleet was brought into being at Lake Manzala; and fish curing establishments were set up at Port Said and Qantara where fish surplus to the needs of the hospitals was dried and smoked.

* In 1918 the Ministry of the Interior collected and handed over to the military authorities at the waterside or railway stations the following quantities:

	Tons		Tons
Wheat	30,000	Beans	12,000
Barley	30,000	Tibben	275,000
Lentils	6,000	Millet	25,000

Egypt also proved itself a fruitful source of supply for sugar, potatoes and fresh vegetables.

By these means it became possible to free the United Kingdom from being the main source of supply.

Upon the occupation of Damascus in October 1918 an interesting situation arose in connection with local purchase. The prices of certain commodities required being abnormally high, a system of barter was instituted by which supplies in possession of the army, such as petrol, tea and sugar which were almost impossible for the civil population to obtain, were exchanged for those commodities, chiefly medical supplies, which were needed by the army. Had these latter been purchased direct serious questions would have been raised by the financial authorities, who had fixed the maximum prices to be paid.

In the field of transport, activities were many which did not pertain specifically to the service of supply but which were carried out by the Army Service Corps. Mention has already been made of the motor boat company and of the tractor companies with the heavy artillery, while, as normally, all transport in the shape of field ambulances, ambulance convoys and station transport working with the medical service was found by the Corps. In addition to these were other forms outside the usual scope. The Rolls-Royce armoured cars which co-operated successfully with the Hedjaz Army through Akaba up to Maan and thence on to Damascus were driven and maintained by Army Service Corps *personnel*. Similar duties were carried out with the Ford car patrols used for reconnaissance work and to provide armed escorts for any special purpose.

The number borne on the strength of the Army Service Corps with the Egyptian Expeditionary Force shows how important a rôle the Corps played during the campaign. That number at its maximum, including Indians and Egyptians attached, amounted to 1094 officers and 53,286 other ranks, or over 11 per cent. of the whole Army. These figures include not only those employed with the striking force but also those on the lines of communications and in Egypt, on which country the Salonika force was also based, while among the officers there were over one hundred employed on non-Army Service Corps work on the staff of General Headquarters Army Corps and Divisions and attached to the infantry or Royal Flying Corps. There were in all only sixty-eight British Regular Army Service Corps officers, but no petty or invidious distinctions existed between these and their comrades of the New Armies, Territorials, Australians or New Zealanders, Indian transport and supply. All worked in harmony as one great and cohesive organisation.*

Nor were the other ranks one whit behind in this respect, though they contained less than 18,000 British *personnel*, of which 90 per cent. belonged to the New Armies or Territorial Force, the remainder being Indians and Egyptians.†

*Composition of Army Service Corps officers serving with Egyptian Expeditionary Force

Regulars	68
New Army	783
Territorials	110
Indian S.T. Corps	33
Anglo-Egyptians	51
Australian and New Zealand	49
	1094

Employment of Army Service Corps officers serving with Egyptian Expeditionary Force

Staff of G.H.Q. Corps Divisions	19
Supply and Transport Directorate	23
Attached to infantry	76
Attached to R.F.C.	12
Mechanical transport	273
Horse and mule transport	174
Camel	234
Supply	256
Miscellaneous	27
	1094

† Strength and distribution of other ranks of Army Service Corps in the Egyptian Expeditionary Force.

	British	Indians	Egyptians	Total
1. Horse transport	5390	2725	8,476	16,591
2. Mechanical transport	7856	—	977	8,833
3. Camel transport	238	—	19,423	19,661
4. Donkey transport	60	—	3,868	3,928
5. Supply	4273	—	—	4,273
Totals:	17,817	2725	32,744	53,286

Exclusive of Australian and New Zealand Army Service Corps.

This spirit and the results obtained were largely due to two facts. Firstly, that all had a common interest in upholding the traditions of a service which was not an ephemeral makeshift but was a recognised and integral part of the Army: secondly, that both transport and supplies were vested and united in that service. Nor will special mention of the Australian and New Zealand Army Service Corps be begrudged by their comrades in the Imperial Army. The necessary organisation was provided for the Australian and Anzac mounted divisions and also two small lines of communication supply units —depot units of supply. These latter were invariably to be found where supply activities were greatest in the forward areas.

Where so much able and, at times, even brilliant work was accomplished, it is a matter for delicate discretion to single out that of any individual. And generally administrative success depends more on the co-operation of many than on the insight or effort of any one man. Nevertheless it is incumbent on the historian to record individual services, especially when those services were signal and were moreover distinguished not by their ostentation but rather by their lack of it; for in these latter days honours fall most thickly on those who most diligently pursue them. Brig.-General G. F. Davies, the Director of Supplies and Transport, was fortunate in having as his Deputy Director one of the most capable and most enterprising officers of the Army Service Corps; and every credit is due to him in that he utilised the services of his subordinate to the full. Colonel W. Elliott who had previously served in the Dardanelles possessed a long pre-war experience of Egypt and the Middle East. But he was possessed also of foresight, a broad mind, and that love of responsibility which is one of the distinguishing marks of the able soldier. He had too studied his profession in no narrow departmental sense. Consequently on being called to high responsibility he was equal to every call made upon him, and they were many. For on almost every occasion when a specially difficult task had to be undertaken, that task was allotted to him. He directed the transport and supply services in the Western Desert in 1916 and also in the Eastern Desert when the main army advanced in September of that year, for it was not until August 1917 that the General Headquarters Staff moved up from Cairo after General Allenby had taken command. The problem of the exploitation of the local resources of Egypt, Sudan and Cyprus having then become of vital urgency, Colonel Elliott was sent back to Cairo to organise the military side of this important work: but immediately operations were about to be resumed by the initiation of the Third Battle of Gaza in October 1917, his services were again requisitioned for the advanced work at the Karm railhead—the pivotal point for the Beersheba turning operations. Again in the final advance it was on him that fell the brunt of the direction for the forward services, by the opening up as bases of the ports of Haifa, Beirut and Tripoli for the troops operating north to Damascus and on the Homs–Aleppo line. Thus this officer was invariably employed in the key position.

It is no detraction of the task achieved and of the obstacles overcome in Egypt and Palestine to state that the campaign was generously supported from home. Amid its many preoccupations elsewhere the War Office yet succeeded in meeting all the principal demands made upon it. Even so there were wide margins that could not thus be met and the manner in which local resources in both man power and material were adapted and applied towards the deficiencies was not the least creditable aspect of Army Service Corps administration.

While lacking the fierce intensity of the war in France or the strain and horrors of that in Mesopotamia, the campaign was nevertheless an arduous one in the physical sense for the transport and supply *personnel* with the

THE CAMPAIGNS IN EGYPT AND PALESTINE

army in the field. While battle casualties were comparatively light—the Camel Transport Corps, with two hundred and twenty-two killed or died of wounds and fourteen hundred and fifty-eight wounded, being the heaviest sufferer—sickness and disease took toll throughout, and especially in the last phase during the general pursuit. But throughout, the Army Service Corps did all that was asked of it and at times even more than was expected of it towards the decisive victory which was finally won, justifying the generous words which were applied by the Commander-in-Chief to their share in that victory "A triumph of organisation and perseverance".*

BIBLIOGRAPHY

1. *Official History of the War*. Military Operations in Egypt and Palestine.
2. *A History of the Transport Services of the E.E.F.* By Lieut.-Colonel G. E. Badcock, C.B.E., D.S.O.
3. "History of the Mechanical Transport of Desert Mounted Corps." By Major E. S. Baring-Gould, R.A.S.C. From *R.A.S.C. Quarterly*, April 1920.
4. "Supplies and Transport Egyptian Expeditionary Force." By Brevet-Colonel G. F. Davies, C.B., C.M.G., C.B.E., R.A.S.C. From *R.A.S.C. Quarterly*, July 1920.
5. "Maintaining Allenby's Armies." By Brevet-Lieut.-Col. W. Elliott, C.B., C.B.E., D.S.O., R.A.S.C., in collaboration with Captain Kinross (late R.A.S.C.). From *R.A.S.C. Quarterly*, January 1925.
6. "The Karm Railhead Supply Depot." By Lieut.-Colonel W. Elliott, C.B., C.B.E., D.S.O., R.A.S.C. From *R.A.S.C. Quarterly*, July 1925.
7. *Supply by Camel Transport on the Sollum Expedition 1916.* By Lieut.-Colonel W. Elliott, C.B., C.B.E., D.S.O., R.A.S.C.
8. *The Palestine Campaigns.* By Colonel A. P. Wavell, C.M.G., M.C.

* Perhaps the most striking tribute paid to the work of the Corps was the Turkish General Refet Pasha's post-war offer to Lord Allenby to fight the Palestine Campaign over again with an equal Commissariat.

CHAPTER IX

THE CAMPAIGN IN MESOPOTAMIA

WHATEVER may have been the hardships undergone and the difficulties overcome by the Egyptian Expeditionary Force, they fade into insignificance as compared with the experience of the army in Mesopotamia. Not since the days of the Crimea has a British army so suffered and endured. The enemy was stubborn and well led. Seldom since Plevna have the Turkish infantry fought more stoutly than they did in defence of the positions covering Kut-el-Amara during the operations for the relief of General Townshend's force. The Arab inhabitants of the country were unreliable and were consequently a source of continual anxiety to detachments and on the lines of communication. Roads were to all intents and purposes non-existent. In the rainy season the whole country becomes an almost impassable morass, while in the summer, dust, and lack of water away from the main rivers, suffice to render movement a matter of extreme discomfort. There were no railways, except a stretch of some seventy miles northwards from Baghdad to Samarra, while by the river route Baghdad is some five hundred miles from the Persian Gulf. These drawbacks by themselves were ample enough to make any campaign a matter of embarrassment; but they were indeed minor obstacles as compared with the general conditions prevailing.

Normal amenities of life, as judged by the meanest of occidental standards, were absent. The climate from April until well into October is one of the fiercest in the world, strong scorching winds accompanied by dust storms being among its most disagreeable features. Apart from the few palm trees which fringe the river banks, the whole of the Mesopotamian plains are treeless. The moral effect of monotonous wastes of sun-baked mud is indescribably depressing. Vast swarms of flies, sandflies and mosquitoes assist to spread malaria, sometimes of a malignant type, sandfly fever, enteric, cholera and Baghdad boils. Added to these the filth and lack of sanitation in the centres of population render dysentery, bubonic plague and various skin and eye diseases of common occurrence. Heat stroke, too, was responsible for many casualties.

Information regarding all these circumstances was no secret prior to the inauguration of the campaign, and it might therefore have been expected that every measure would have been taken to provide and equip the army with all means with which to combat and overcome such disabilities. Nor did it require any great imagination to realise that conditions affecting the *morale* of the troops would be quite different from those in other theatres. Mesopotamia was remote and posts necessarily irregular and slow. Short spells of leave, by which some change of environment might have been obtained, were impossible. Even long leave entailed an uncomfortable journey down the Persian Gulf and through the plains of India. No facilities for normal amusements and recreation existed in the theatre of operations.

Yet little consideration had been given to all these factors. The expedition, which started with one brigade landed at Fao on the 6th of November, 1914, and rose during eighteen months to a force of five divisions and one cavalry division, was equipped with a scale of transport utterly inadequate to meet the requirements of the situation, while, as regards supplies, the resources of India had not been organised and consequently proper reserves could not be accumulated in the bases in Mesopotamia. That, in spite of such drawbacks, a British force was able to give battle to the enemy at Ctesiphon only eighteen miles south of Baghdad twelve months after the original landing must be accounted a great and memorable achievement.

During this time the Army Service Corps had taken no part in the campaign. Transport and supply had been carried out by the Indian service which neither from its organisation, experience, training or *matériel* was equal to a task of such magnitude and difficulty. For these deficiencies it would be unfair to blame that Corps itself. Never having been called upon for any comprehensive or far-reaching operations, it had suffered from serious neglect as part of the body military. Its status was such that it could not attract the best *personnel*. Little money was available to be spent on it. It lacked, for instance, mechanical transport. Again the conditions obtaining widely in India under which undue importance was attached to "paper" and office work militated against practical training. Warning voices, among them notably that of Sir Douglas Haig when Chief of the Staff in India, had prior to the War been raised against this state of affairs. But they had gone unheeded, for expense on the fighting troops gave results vastly more apparent to the superficial view. Besides the Supply and Transport Corps carried out its normal peace-time functions or provided for the needs of an expedition on the North-West frontier in a sufficiently satisfactory manner.

The price to be paid for this neglect was a terrible one.

It was in February 1916 that the British Government decided that the War Office should take over from India the control and administration of the operations of which the salient points may be summarised up to that date. The 6th Indian Division, a brigade of which had, as mentioned, landed at Fao on the 6th of November, 1914, occupied Basra on the 22nd and Qurna at the junction of the Tigris and Euphrates on the 9th of December. Reinforcements in the shape of the 12th Indian Division and 6th Indian Cavalry Brigade became available by the following April when Sir J. Nixon assumed command of the force which was termed the Second Indian Army Corps. A series of successful actions were fought at Shaiba west of Basra, at Qurna and at Nasiriyeh, and a force under General Townshend consisting of the 6th Division, one brigade of the 12th Division and the 6th Cavalry Brigade advancing on the Tigris line reached Kut-el-Amara by the end of August, where the enemy was defeated, though at heavy cost. The operations were carried out in a burning north-west wind with constant sand storms and thick dust, and the troops suffered much from heat and thirst. Lack of vegetables, too, caused much scurvy. As the river was falling local pack transport had to be requisitioned to supplement it and the heterogeneous collection of camels with their calves, donkeys and cows was described by one present as "more like the outfit of 'Lord' George Sanger than the transport of a division". From the point of view of communications Kut-el-Amara had an importance even if it had been the intention to have advanced no further, because it commanded the lower reaches of the Tigris and of communication with the Euphrates by the Shatt el Hai and thus consolidated and secured the occupation of the Basra vilayet. The question of a further advance to exploit the success already gained and if possible to capture Baghdad, was debated for some two months, but General Nixon's views finally prevailed and on the 23rd of October General Townshend resumed his northward march. He fought the battle of Ctesiphon against superior numbers on the 22nd of November and was compelled to retreat to Kut, regaining that place on the 3rd of December, after undergoing great hardships, especially from the fact that no proper transport for the carriage of the wounded had been provided. Four days later Kut was invested. General Nixon was relieved by Sir Percy Lake in January and heavy reinforcements consisting of the 3rd and 7th Indian Divisions from France and 13th British Division from Gallipoli arrived the following month, when the most resolute efforts were made to relieve General Townshend. In the various attempts some 22,000 casualties were incurred. But all were useless and Kut surrendered on the 29th of April. The last hope of succour had vanished when the supply ship, the *Julnar*, ran ashore and was captured in a gallant attempt to provision the garrison four days previous to the capitulation.

The history of the administrative services during these eighteen months forms one of the most lamentable chapters of events in the whole of the Great War.

Mesopotamia was primarily a country of river communications and therefore the development of river transport was fundamental to movement. In November 1914 such transport consisted of three river steamers and seventeen lighters whose total carrying capacity was 2540 tons. In May 1915, when reinforcements had arrived from Egypt and India and operations against Qurna were in progress, this fleet was augmented to a total strength of ten steamers, four tugs and nineteen lighters, but the additional steamers then sent drew five feet of water and were plied with difficulty above Qurna, where only boats of three feet six inches draught were reliable. This last fact added to the greater numbers in the field to be provided for and the extended objectives, actually decreased the mobility of the force over that which it had previously possessed. In July additional shipping was demanded amounting to six paddle steamers, two stern-wheelers, eight tugs and forty-two barges or lighters and a grave warning added as to the consequences of delay. The Government of India did not place the order until November 1915 and the paddle steamers began to arrive in July 1916, almost a year after they had been requested. All the others arrived in sections and some were not ready until January 1917. In the course of experiments made in towing these ships from India, no less than three paddle steamers, seventeen stern-wheelers and twenty-two lighters foundered at sea. When these vessels were asked for, the total force to be supplied in the theatre of war was less than half of what it amounted to eight months later. In November 1915 the daily tonnage available for maintenance was one hundred and fifty and the daily requirements two hundred and eight. The crisis arrived in April 1916 when the daily tonnage available was less than half that was needed.

But even if shipping had been plentiful the port of Basra was incapable of dealing with it. A year after its occupation, the unloading facilities had hardly been improved. Ships were compelled to anchor in midstream and unload into native craft and were normally retained as long as thirty-nine days in the course of this process.*

As regards railways, General Barrett had suggested a light line as far as Amara early in 1915. He met with no response from the Government of India. General Nixon re-opened the question six months later and in asking for a standard-gauge line, pressed for an early decision. As the result of repeated reminders he was informed in November that his application was refused on the score of expense. It was not until the War Office took control that the construction of any railway was put in hand.

As was inevitable the failure to constitute adequate communications reacted on the question of supply. As one minor example may be cited the transport of fresh vegetables on barges attached to river steamers. These

* As giving some idea of the pressure on the port in the four months from the 1st of December, 1915, to the 31st of March, 1916, the following were disembarked:

Personnel	129,500
Animals	33,000
Vehicles	4,800
Cargo	71,500 tons

barges were also used for carriage of troops with the consequence that the vegetables on arrival were frequently unfit for consumption. Nor was there any idea of utilising the local resources of the country.

But in the major sense the supply question dominated everything and forced on the Commander-in-Chief the invidious choice of retaining troops urgently required at the front, in the base at Basra, or of sending them where strategical and tactical reasons dictated and finding himself unable to maintain them there. Both courses were equally crippling to the operations, and as might have been expected, attempts to compromise between them were disastrous. In January 1916 when the important battle of Hanna was fought as the first attempt to relieve General Townshend, some 10,000 infantry whose presence might have been decisive were immobilised at Basra. In March 12,000 men were absent from the vital point at the date of the action of Dujaila. During this very period of the culminating struggles to save the Kut garrison, the army engaged found itself fatally handicapped by the defectiveness of its transport and supply services. For all the battles of January such transport as was available was continually re-allotted in order to fit out new formations arriving. Units engaged in frontal attacks near the river were allotted only a reduced scale of first line transport, while those on the flanks, slightly better provided for, had to use their transport when emptied for the collection of wounded, since there were no other conveyances. At the Battle of Hanna grain and forage for two days were drawn but as the meagre transport could not carry it, it was thrown away on the battlefield. After each action the transport was reduced in proportion to the number of casualties and the saving allotted to fresh units, which on arriving at the point found themselves almost entirely devoid of means of conveyance. The weather added to the difficulties, for when the ground became impassable for wheels, the

THE CAMPAIGN IN MESOPOTAMIA

transport had to be converted to pack. There were no cooking or water carts, no chargers, and in many cases no pack animals either for machine guns or ammunition. The continual shifts and devices thrust an insupportable burden upon the depleted transport and supply *personnel*. At the battle of the Wadi on the 13th of January the divisions were allotted supply sections manned by *personnel* at one-third of the proper numbers. There were nine officers of the Supply and Transport Corps instead of forty with the force. By March the situation had become still worse. For the action on the 8th of that month the fighting strength of the Tigris Corps was 25,537 men and ninety-two guns. The decisive attack against Dujaila was made with 19,000 men and sixty-eight guns, the maximum number which could be furnished with transport. And even then no provision could be made for the carriage of water, nor of anything except the minimum scale of rations and ammunition. The containing attack at Hanna was completely immobilised. During the initial period of the fighting for the relief of Kut, sufficient supplies of foodstuffs were available at riverhead, though there was little fresh food, no vegetables and no fuel wood, the lack of the latter being a particular hardship for the Indian troops. But in any case there was insufficient *personnel* or transport to distribute supplies, so the men were constantly on short rations. Comforts and canteens there were none. But by the end of January even this situation no longer obtained. On the 27th of that month the rations of the troops were materially reduced. A fortnight later the army was on half rations and its total reserve was down to seven days.*

* The reserve ration situation in January is instructive:

	British	Indian	Fodder	Grain	Fuel
	\multicolumn{5}{c}{Days}
6th of Jan.	33	34	33	16	38
27th of Jan.	17	17	18	10	20

That is to say in 21 days the reserves were depleted 17 days.

Disgraceful as was this state of affairs, it was yet surpassed by the transport of the medical services. No properly equipped hospital river steamers existed and in spite of urgent representations it was not until the 31st of December, 1915, that the Viceroy asked for one from home. The necessity was apparent from the fact that a river vessel had been provided by private enterprise in February 1915, but unfortunately foundered at sea on the way out. On the date of General Aylmer's advance to the relief of Kut not one single complete field ambulance had been disembarked at Basra. The unsatisfactory state of the medical establishments was specially pointed out by General Aylmer to the Commander-in-Chief in Mesopotamia in a telegram indicating the hazardous nature of the undertaking. Headquarters of the force replied in terms surely classical. "Must leave the matter to your decision. Am confident that you and the fine troops under your command will achieve your object."

Indian war establishments provided for eight ambulance tongas for each ambulance, but the Mesopotamian Expeditionary Force was allotted extra riding mules instead, as it was considered that the country was unsuitable for wheels. In spite of this promise, army transport carts were provided for other purposes, from which they had often to be diverted in order to carry the wounded. Two motor ambulances—the only ones in the country—worked with excellent results in Ctesiphon but beyond these the medical service was to all intents and purposes unprovided with transport. It was not the only equipment with which they were unprovided, but with the rest this narrative is not concerned.

Up to the time when the campaign came under War Office control the material difficulties could hardly have been greater. There was shortage or lack of almost everything necessary to its prosecution. The situation was summed up by Sir William Robertson, then Chief of the Imperial General Staff, "In general the operations were allowed in 1915 to develop without proper regard to the vital questions of supply and maintenance". The results were so gross and so terrible that they cannot be exaggerated. No imagination unsupported by a knowledge of the country and its conditions can fathom the horrors endured. Nevertheless in other respects those eighteen months of campaigning were glorious to British and Indian arms. The more their history is studied the more astounding do the feats accomplished by the troops appear. Their performances speak for themselves. Seldom have British and never have Indian troops been required to fight under such heartbreaking conditions and in the teeth of such monstrous casualties. They did all that flesh and blood could do.

On the 28th of August, 1916, four months after General Townshend's surrender, Sir Percy Lake was relieved by General Maude who had previously commanded the Tigris Corps from the 11th of July. The force was reorganised into the First and Third Indian Army Corps, the former being commanded by General Cobbe and consisting of the 3rd and 7th (Indian) Divisions, the latter under General Marshall, and composed of the 13th (British) and 14th (Indian) Divisions. There was also a cavalry division consisting of the 6th and 7th (Indian) Cavalry Brigades and the 15th (Indian) Division at Nasiriyeh besides a mixed brigade stationed at Ahwaz in Persia. General MacMunn had been appointed Inspector-General of Communications in April. The greatest energy was pursued in setting affairs and especially administrative ones in order. The creation of wharves and the filling in of swamps to make a hinterland for the wharves at Basra were put in hand. The river steamer service was organised on scientific lines and a dockyard and workshops provided for the vessels. Steps were also taken to put the service of native craft on a proper basis. The construction of a metre-gauge railway line from Basra to Nasiriyeh, narrow-gauge lines from Qurna to Amara and from Sheikh Saad northwards along the Tigris had already begun. Land transport was provided to bring units up to their establishments and the fact that a shortage of over two thousand mules and two thousand army transport carts existed as late as November was partly compensated for by the amount of mechanical transport provided. Reserves of supplies, ammunition and stores were built up. In short the whole of the lines of communication and the administrative services were thoroughly overhauled from top to bottom.

In these measures the Army Service Corps played a large part. Its first unit to arrive in Mesopotamia had been a mechanical transport company which came from Egypt in January 1916 and was therefore in time to have the honour of taking some part in the operations for the relief of Kut.* A certain number of reconnaissances also were carried out with its vehicles with the object of discovering routes to various places and also for reporting on the suitability of different types of mechanical transport for desert work; and in connection with these pioneer activities the names of Lieutenants R. P. Dickinson and J. T. Vlasto deserve mention. A motor ambulance convoy and a base mechanical transport depot company made their appearances respectively in May and June 1916. These three companies represented the whole of the Army Service Corps in the Mesopotamian theatre when the Corps put in an appearance preliminary to taking over control of the transport and supply services from its comrades of the Indian Army. In August 1916 Brig.-General P. J. C. Scott accompanied by Colonel W. M. Parker as his deputy left England to take up the

* This unit was 596 Company Army Service Corps of about four hundred all ranks, equipped with a hundred and ten 3-ton Peerless lorries. These vehicles were, however, marked "Load not to exceed 30 cwt."

appointment of Director of Supplies and Transport. This party was the forerunner of 659 officers and some 12,200 other ranks of the Corps who eventually served in the campaign. On their way through to Basra, General Scott and Colonel Parker visited Army Headquarters at Simla in order to get in personal touch with the higher authorities and the Supply and Transport Department. Colonel Parker had prior to the war done a tour of duty with the Indian Army and therefore possessed the advantage of being fully cognisant of their methods. This experience was a factor that powerfully assisted the British and Indian administrative services in Mesopotamia.

The party arrived at Basra towards the middle of September, and found the Commander-in-Chief busily engaged with General MacMunn supervising the reorganisation at the base. General Maude was a man of strong will and of immense capacity for work; and he had a thorough understanding of administrative problems, in which few details were too small to escape his notice. While he enjoyed the benefit of the lessons which had been purchased so dearly before his own advent and also of a great deal towards the amelioration of affairs that had been accomplished by his immediate predecessor, Sir Percy Lake, his own share both in action and inspiration must be accounted the preponderant one of the success that ensued.

All through the summer of 1916 the army had been wasted by sickness, not only dysentery and scurvy due to poor rations and lack of fuel, but also from cholera which had broken out at the beginning of May. Heat stroke was common and there was much fever. The troops were in fact tired out physically, debilitated and dispirited. The turning-point came, however, at the beginning of August when the measures that were in course of being undertaken behind the front began to make themselves felt, and from the time the cold weather set in the improvement became rapid. At that period the army totalled some 150,000 men, of which 45,000 were British and the remainder Indian, and 48,000 animals. The main fighting force lay at Sheikh Saad, three hundred miles by river from the base at Basra and consisted of 25,000 British troops, 40,000 Indian troops and 30,000 animals. Opposite these lay the Turkish army covering Kut. At Amara, mid-way between Basra and Sheikh Saad and a hundred and fifty miles from the latter lay 23,000 men and 12,000 animals, including the 13th British Division which had been withdrawn from the north partly for training and partly to reduce the ration strength at riverhead. Four thousand men at Qurna completed the numbers on the Tigris line. On the Euphrates at Nasiriyeh a hundred and twenty miles from Basra were 15,000 men and 5000 animals, while near Shustar in Persia a detachment was guarding the oil-pipe line. The total daily tonnage in foodstuffs required was nine hundred, out of which six hundred were for the forces at Sheikh Saad where the sum of all daily output at riverhead reached nine hundred and fifty tons. The supply problem was firstly to maintain the army in foodstuffs and forage for their current needs and secondly to accumulate such a reserve of these commodities with the striking force at Sheikh Saad as was deemed indispensable by the Commander-in-Chief for a further advance. General Maude ordered a twenty-five days' reserve to be ready by the 15th of November, the date on which he proposed to resume the offensive in force. General Headquarters moved from Basra to "Arab Village" close behind the front at the end of October. As the new Director of Supplies and Transport arrived, as was mentioned, on the 16th of September, he was thus given exactly two months to carry out his instructions. These involved, besides feeding the force daily, the accumulation at Sheikh Saad, three hundred miles distant by river, of 12,000 tons of foodstuffs and forage. Moreover while this was being accomplished the whole of the rest of the force at Amara, Qurna, Nasiriyeh, Shustar and the base itself had to be maintained and reserves amassed for them. India, distant some sixteen hundred miles from Basra, furnished supplies and forage with the exception of one ship per month from England, which brought hospital comforts and such articles as bacon, jam, preserved meat and biscuits which India was unable to provide. At that time nothing was procurable locally except a little grain and some sheep. The minimum monthly requirements after utilising these last to the full was 20,000 tons for maintenance only, while to make up the reserve without which General Maude did not intend to commence operations 12,000 tons further were needed. The port of Basra was then undeveloped. No wharves had yet been completed and ships had still to be off loaded in the stream into lighters. It was not until the end of the year that signs of improvement in this respect became evident, but even then the "turn round" of a ship took twenty days. From the lighters the loads had to be landed, sorted and re-transferred into barges which then had to be towed the three hundred miles up the Tigris. Labour was scarce and such as was available was bad and ill organised. Consequently it was found impossible to deal with ten ships approximating to 30,000 tons per month in all. Since of this amount only 20,000 tons were allotted to supplies there was no possibility of building up the required reserve. The whole was required for maintenance.

The second difficulty was that even if more than ten ships a month could have been handled there was no properly organised Base Supply Depot to receive, check, store and cover the supplies. There was no system of any kind, no roofed accommodation and a great deal of lassitude. Furthermore when these difficulties were overcome, river transport for conveyance northwards was hopelessly insufficient.

Such was the position that had to be faced in mid-September. The determination and resource with which it was met and conquered may be claimed as one of the most solid feats accomplished by the Army Service Corps during the whole course of the War. Certainly there is no better instance of its capacity to grapple with a situation which had up to then seemed insuperable. To the energy and ability of the Inspector-General of Communications, Sir George MacMunn, a tribute must be paid, and it was a curious turn of fortune's wheel by which this distinguished officer, who had collaborated so well in the work of the Corps and with whom the Corps had so well collaborated in bearing the burden and heat of the day, should, ten years afterwards, be found prominently in the ranks of those who successfully advocated measures that were to diminish its responsibilities and in effect to lower its status.

For General Maude's projected forward movement only two months were available to create order out of this chaos. The first obvious measure was to speed up the rate at which ships could be received, off-loaded and turned round. At the same time it was necessary to remodel thoroughly the Base Supply Depot in order to hasten receipt and despatch, and to arrange for sufficient room for expansion for the future increase in the strength of the army which was in contemplation. In order to accomplish this, ships were unloaded direct into the barges which were to convey their contents up-river. This was bad from the accounting point of view, and also gave little opportunity of discriminating between the articles of supply most needed at the front. But accounting was sensibly relegated to secondary consideration. Everything went as it came out of the ships, with the result that the time taken to turn them round was greatly reduced. Simultaneously the Inspector-General of Communications speeded up the construction of wharves, hastened the supply of labour from India, Egypt and

China, and hired and organised large numbers of Arabs and Kurds. Also, while waiting for the barges, lighters and river steamers which had already been ordered from England and India, he organised a subsidiary service of "mahelas" and "bellums", the local river craft of the country.

The Base Supply Depot itself was in utter confusion. All its contents were heaped together, bacon, jam, forage, medical comforts and everything else; there was no taking of stock, no precautions against fire, no shelter against the weather, no housing for the *personnel* and no room at all for expansion. Everything had to be sorted out. Shedding to cover perishable supplies was cabled for from England. The forage was moved to an entirely new site higher up the river where date palms were cut down and cleared away to make room: this site was on the river bank, where the water was deep enough to accommodate ocean-going ships along shore without having to build wharves. The supply depot was laid out on proper lines, room being later provided for the anticipated railway sidings, while ample room was allowed for expansion by the reclamation of marsh land. Forty Army Service Corps supply officers and twenty depot units of supply, together with a number of mechanical transport units including Ford vans and the necessary supply of spare parts, were urgently demanded from England.

By the 15th of October considerable progress had been made, for the reserve at Sheikh Saad had grown to twenty-three days' supplies for troops, thirty days' grain and sixteen days' fuel. But only eight days' supply of hay was up and it was found difficult to maintain the reserve of this bulky article as, owing to the urgent need of completing the railway to Nasiriyeh, priority had to be given to the import of railway material from India. But there was an infinity of other needs with which to deal, and these were concentrated on during the latter part of October and the beginning of November.

A frozen-meat ship was obtained from England, and the troops in the trenches were getting regular issues by January in the following year. The whole of the ration for both British and Indian troops was recast, for, incredible as it may seem, up to the time when the Army Service Corps assumed control, the old Indian Army system remained in force, by which an extraordinary ration comprising no less than forty substitutes could be drawn, or at any rate demanded at will. A fixed ration of a generous nature was substituted in lieu, and provision was made for ample supplies of condensed milk and tinned fruit which had previously been lacking. Scurvy was fought by the issue of marmite, peas and lentils. Canteens were started. Experts were obtained from India for the inauguration of grass farms, two hundred and fifty acres being put under vegetable seed, while pumps and ploughs were obtained for the cultivation of barley. At the same time local purchases, especially in grain and hay, were enlarged to the amount of six thousand tons a month. Purchase officers were sent as far afield as Luristan and Shustar in Persia to obtain sheep, the requirements of which were 70,000 a month. Bakeries were everywhere established, and the troops provisioned daily with bread. Petrol was acquired from the Anglo-Persian Company at Abadan on the Persian Gulf.

During the period of these activities in October and November the situation of the Supply and Transport Directorate was not made easier by constant telegraphic requests from England for information for the Mesopotamia Commission and by the natural anxiety of the War Office to be kept fully informed of what was being done to rectify the "scandals".

When the stocktaking of the Base Supply Depot had been completed, serious discrepancies were discovered in what was supposed to have been taken over by the Army Service Corps. Since information sent to England by the Indian Government, which furnished the bulk of the supplies, was based on what they had forwarded and was alleged to be in hand in Mesopotamia, and at the same time the Directorate of Supplies and Transport in that country also had to cable home daily the number of days' supplies on each front, these two reports could not be reconciled, and therefore led to no little confusion and anxiety to those responsible at the War Office. The Army Service Corps and the Indian Supply and Transport Corps were working together in Mesopotamia, but all demands went through the directorate at Simla where the Army Service Corps had no representative. There was in fact no authority to check, co-ordinate and reconcile the two sets of information sent to the War Office. To remedy this state of affairs two senior Army Service Corps officers were sent to India, one to act as liaison officer between the War Office and General Headquarters in India and the other to keep the War Office informed of the state of supplies held at the base ports in India, the schedule of proposed shipments of supplies and what was expected to be coming forward from the sources of origin. These two appointments did much to clarify the situation and ease the strain on the directorate at Basra.

Yet the difficulties outlined above were by no means all with which the supply administration had to contend. As a complication to its efforts was the continual increase of the force. By the end of November a further 50,000 men and 10,000 animals had been added and the numbers went on continually increasing until they eventually reached high water mark at the strength of 420,000 men and 100,000 animals. However by mid-November it had been possible to inform the Commander-in-Chief that all was ready, though for various other reasons not connected with supply, the offensive was not started until the 13th of December. The succeeding three months, from the supply point of view, was a period of continual anxiety and of continual striving to increase the reserves at the front. Towards this aim the railway progress was a powerful factor. The Qurna–Amara line was completed at the end of November, the Sheikh Saad line reached Imam el Mansur some five miles east of Kut on the 20th of December, while the Basra–Nasiriyeh section was through by the 29th of the same month. The position as regards river transport was also vastly ameliorated. During the week ending the 18th of November, the amount of stores and supplies delivered at the Tigris riverhead by the flotilla reached a daily tonnage of 726, excluding what was delivered at Amara and other posts on the lines of communication. The question of the land transport was a somewhat complicated problem, for the river transport could not at all times be relied upon, and a balance had to be struck between that amount which would give sufficient at the front to meet reasonable anticipations and the presence of a number of idle animals which would consume supplies and so impair mobility. After detailed consideration it was finally decided that the force should be equipped with first and second line transport,* and with supply columns for two cavalry brigades and five infantry divisions, each carrying one day's supply; and that there should be sufficient transport in addition to allow a column of two infantry brigades and a brigade of artillery to operate three days from the Tigris. The approval of the War Office to this scale having been given, the necessary arrangements had been made for its provision and Lieut.-Colonel Leland of the Army Service Corps had arrived on the 23rd of September to take up the appointment of Assistant Director of Mechanical Transport. Nine Ford van companies were wisely applied for

* Transport for the regimental reserve and small arm ammunition was included in the first line; and the second line was calculated to carry one day's rations, one blanket and one waterproof sheet per man, cooking pots, officers' baggage (20 lb. per man) and one day's forage for animals.

in the first instance and, by the middle of November, two of these, Nos. 783 and 784 Mechanical Transport Companies, and No. 33 Motor Ambulance Convoy, had arrived. In addition, two caterpillar companies of four tractors and two lorries each, Nos. 788 and 789 Mechanical Transport Companies, for duty with the 157th Battery (four 60-pounders) and the 159th Siege Battery (four 6-inch howitzers), had also made their appearance in December.

By the end of 1916, therefore, a marked change had come over the whole of the administrative outlook. The fruits of the efforts made were soon to be garnered. The record from 1917 onwards was one of almost unbroken victory. During that phase the Army was continually expanding; it was continually moving and fighting; and continually lengthening its lines of communication. But all the time the transport and supply services kept pace with expansion and movement. Seldom have the advantages of the union of transport and supply been more clearly demonstrated. That union was indeed fundamental to the success achieved. When the means of conveying supplies consisted as they did of river barges, army transport carts, lorries, motor vans and camels, it was imperative for the supply officers to know the capabilities of each and the factors which admitted of their use or rendered them incapable. When it rained, as it did just after the operations commenced in December, mechanical transport and camels in that roadless country became ineffective, and the army transport cart was the only practicable form of land transport.

For the supply services there is no rest. The work only varies in degree according to whether the troops are static or mobile and according to whether they are near or far from the bases of supply. The intensive task of the preparatory epoch was succeeded by that in which the Army once more began to move. It was obvious that an active summer campaign was ahead. Preparations were therefore made toward perfecting the supply arrangements under the formidable climatic conditions to be encountered. The Mesopotamian climate was one subject to remarkable variations; while it has been known to snow four days in succession in Babylon in the winter with the thermometer down to 18 degrees, the summer has shown shade temperatures up to 125 degrees. Soda-water machines were ordered from England and India, and a corps of mechanics enrolled to work them up to a capacity of 15,000 dozen a day. The manufacture and distribution of ice was arranged for. Dairies and chicken farms were started. The scope of the vegetable gardens was enlarged up to 3500 acres, and further ploughs, pumps, ploughing oxen and seeds obtained from overseas. Previous demands for medical comforts were trebled. In fact every measure that careful calculation for future eventualities could suggest was taken, and taken in no half-hearted manner. Nothing was left to chance.

Once General Maude's advance started, it went from strength to strength. Kut was recaptured on the 24th of February and, after heavy fighting on the Diala river south of Baghdad, the city was entered on the 11th of March. The lines of communication then extended a distance of five hundred miles by river from the base at Basra, and the Army had reached a total strength of 300,000 men and 66,000 animals.

During this important phase the Army Service Corps Mechanical Transport bore for the first time a considerable share in the operations; and the work that it was then able to accomplish must have caused many heartburnings among those who had taken part in the attempts to relieve General Townshend a year previously. Had even a few companies of light mechanical transport been at the disposal of General Aylmer, to have endowed him with the necessary freedom of manœuvre, the relief would almost certainly have been effected.*

Apart from the tractor units employed with the heavy artillery three mechanical transport companies were then on the Tigris front. The 33rd Motor Ambulance Convoy with its Ford ambulances did good work on the whole way up during the advance, evacuating wounded from the front line. The two Ford van companies, Nos. 783 and 784, were, on their arrival, kept engaged respectively in moving Royal Engineer stores between Sheikh Saad and Sinn and supplies between Arab village and Sinn. It was the rainy season which made the "going" at times difficult or impossible; moreover neither unit possessed a workshop, and were thus entirely dependent upon spares, portable forges and such assistance as could be rendered by the floating workshops on the river. These conditions severely tested the mechanical transport, but it came through well and was able to maintain its activities right up to the time of the arrival of its workshops in June 1917. In the course of the fighting on the Shatt-al-Hai, the units were employed in taking ammunition to the front line and bringing back the wounded, during which they were constantly out all night. As the advance continued every kind of transport task fell to them. On the 23rd of February No. 783 Company took up rowers for the pontoons required for bridging the Tigris; and then both units were again turned over for the carriage of supplies, ammunition and water successively. At the beginning of March they moved to Aziziyeh carrying emergency rations and petrol, the latter being at that time so rare a commodity at the front that a number of vehicles had to be abandoned on the march owing to the lack of it. Troops and machine

* In the *Critical Study of the Mesopotamian Campaign* compiled at the Staff College, Quetta, the following passage occurs: "Had Ford Vans even been available for General Aylmer the turning of the enemy's position south of the Umm el Baran (April 17th) would have presented few difficulties".

guns were also conveyed. No. 783 Company entered Baghdad on the 11th of March, the afternoon of its occupation, being followed by No. 784 Company on the following day.*

While the mechanical transport was so thoroughly justifying its presence with the Army the supply service no less proved itself equal to each and every situation that arose, and this because it had looked ahead and was therefore not taken by surprise by an advance, the extent of which could not have been contemplated when the operations were initiated. The troops were fed by land and by water. Barges were turned into supply depots, and where the troops moved, which could never be far from the river, there also did the supply barges go. The mechanical and animal transport took up the chain where the river barges could get no further and carried the supplies to the utmost land limits attained by the troops.

The one real pause in the sweep of the movement was from the 27th of February to the 5th of March, to which the Commander-in-Chief acceded on the representations of the Inspector-General of Communications, who pointed out that he required a few days to regroup his river transport and make arrangements for a succession of temporary "riverheads" and supply dumps.

With the occupation of Baghdad the most important, and at the same time the most difficult, portion of the campaign was over, although mechanical transport activities were only now about to enter upon their most intensive phase. From the supply point of view the position was eased from the enlargement which was possible in the scope of local purchases, thereby saving

---

* In connection with the advance to Baghdad, the following extract from *Soldiers and Statesmen*, vol. II, p. 75, by Field-Marshal Sir William Robertson is of interest: "When the telegram reporting the rout of the enemy reached London, the first question which Mr Lloyd George, now Prime Minister, asked me was 'Will Maude get to Baghdad?' I replied in rather guarded terms that it depended on the condition of the transport and supply services".

the long haul from Basra. A local produce directorate was organised under Colonel E. Dickson, A.S.C. Although the summer of 1917 was an unusually fierce one, casualties from heat, cholera and other forms of disease were much below those of former years. While due credit for this must be given to the re-organised medical service, the manner in which the army was provisioned was also a powerful factor. In June 1917, for example, apples, apricots, tomatoes, cucumbers, onions and soda water and ice were all being issued, besides the generous ration previously decided upon; and the hospitals were in receipt of their full requirements of butter, milk and fowls. It was fortunate that steps had been taken towards the exploitation of these local resources, because the River Tigris was particularly low during 1917, the depth being about two and a half feet.

In the operations which followed the entry to Baghdad the mechanical transport was actively and continuously engaged. On the 18th of March Baquba, forty miles north-north-east of the capital, was occupied by the 3rd Indian Division, both companies of Ford vans co-operating in carrying both troops and supplies. On the following day Feluja, about the same distance to the east, was captured. Early in April contact was established by a Ford van convoy with a Russian force at Qasr-i-Shirin in Persia. On its outward journey this convoy came under heavy shell fire at Qizil Robat, south-west of Khaniquin. Fourteen lorries were temporarily put out of action, all but one, however, being recovered on the return journey two days later. For his gallant conduct on this occasion Captain E. G. Pelly, the Commanding Officer, was given an immediate award of the Military Cross, and Serjeants J. Ofield and D. R. Stewart were decorated with the Military Medal.

Meanwhile the army was advancing northwards astride the Baghdad–Samarra railway—the one section of the famous Constantinople–Baghdad railway which had been completed in Mesopotamia. Samarra was entered on April 23rd and the enemy driven to the hills to the north.

These various movements had, for their object, the clearance of the front and flanks of the army and to consolidate its position at Baghdad. With their successful accomplishment, except for an abortive attempt on Ramadi in July, a period of comparative quiescence followed until September, during which period opportunity was taken for re-organisation and re-distribution of the forces. A new Indian division—the 17th—was formed at Baghdad; and the 15th (Indian) Division was transferred from Nasiriyeh to Feluja on the Euphrates. To supply this force No. 596 Company—the pioneer Army Service Corps unit in Mesopotamia—was brought up with its Peerless lorries, since the river route could only handle twenty-five tons out of the one hundred and fifty required per day. They did admirable work until the railway got through on the 15th of November, during which time all the light mechanical transport was employed elsewhere. But the vehicles suffered greatly over very difficult ground, and the constant ploughing through heavy sand had a very bad effect on the engines. Meanwhile railway construction was pushed forward. By the end of July a metre-gauge line from Kut to Baghdad was through, and a similar one from Basra to Qurna under construction. The Qurna–Amara section was converted to metre gauge. On the completion of these measures there was through communication between Basra and Baghdad, except for the gap between Amara and Kut, where the river passage was comparatively easy. The light railway which had previously bridged portions of this gap from Sheikh Saad to Atab just south of Kut was taken up and laid from Baghdad to Baquba, while a light line was also laid from Sumaika to Sadiya. These developments did much to relieve the transport and supply services. In addition the rich area around Baghdad was being tapped for supplies, while large reserves were also accumulated at Balad Ruz and on the Euphrates.

The mechanical transport was now steadily increasing in amount. Nos. 729 and 730 (Ford Van) Companies reached Baghdad in June and August respectively, the former in time to take part in the first affair at Ramadi. By the end of September, in addition, ten further mechanical transport companies had arrived in the country, including five of Ford vans, one of Packards, two of caterpillar tractors for the heavy artillery and two motor ambulance convoys.* But in this direction the appetite of the Commander-in-Chief was growing and, on the 16th of September, he asked the War Office for a further ten companies of Ford vans, which he proposed to utilise to replace his muled second line transport, and thus increase the radius of action of his forces. As a further consideration mules were becoming increasingly difficult to obtain, while petrol was to be had locally. The suggestion was approved and arrangements made to send out the units during January and February 1918.

At the end of September Ramadi was again attacked, and the Turkish garrison of over 3000 men capitulated. This operation was an important one from the mechanical transport point of view, as the largest concentration of vehicles up to that time took place. Ford vans amounting to three hundred and fifty, drawn from four companies, and ten Fiats took part, the column being under the command of Major Snepp, A.S.C. After the fall of Ramadi an attempt was made on Hit a further

* By this time the following Mechanical Transport Units were in Mesopotamia:
Advanced M.T. Depot.
No. 695 (Base Depot) Company.
No. 596 Company (Peerless Lorries).
Nos. 783, 784, 729, 730, 815, 818, 953, 971 (Ford Van) Companies.
No. 976 Company (Packard Lorries).
Nos. 788, 789, 968, 969 (Caterpillar Tractor) Companies.
Nos. 23, 33, 39, 40 Motor Ambulance Convoys.
No. 322 Company (Light Armoured Motor Repair Unit).

forty miles up the Euphrates, and one hundred vans carrying infantry and Lewis guns, accompanied by ambulances and armoured cars, were detailed for this duty. After a night movement without lights in an unknown country the column reached a point five miles from Hit before dawn, when it was ordered to return. The operations on the Euphrates proved to be of the most trying nature to men and vehicles. The heat was intense and the *personnel* suffered from an indifferent supply of water. There were numerous cases of sickness among the drivers; and officers, n.c.o.'s, batmen and cooks, all had to assist in driving the cars. The vehicles were in a poor state, having done an immense amount of work day in and day out without sufficient time being allowed for even ordinary running repairs. Nevertheless the work was most effective, and earned warm commendation from the General Officer Commanding the 15th Division.

It was at this time that it was decided, owing to the numbers of companies to be handled, that it was necessary to form three companies into one column under the command of a lieutenant-colonel. Four columns were accordingly organised. Originally small concentrations had taken place for minor operations, when it was essential that a mechanical transport officer should be placed in charge because the Staff of Divisions were unused to handling mechanical transport and could not work it economically. As more companies became available the radius of action of the force increased and concentrations of mechanical transport augmented considerably, reaching as high as 1200 vans for one specific operation. It was naturally impossible to keep columns permanently intact. Companies constantly changed their columns to meet requirements, and the strength of the columns was subject to continual variation. Their commanders therefore officiated as group or area commanders, taking over control of all companies which, for the time being, happened to be working in their area. This arrangement, designed for sudden troop movements on a large scale, worked admirably.

Early in October activity was resumed on the northern front, the object being to secure the Jebel Hamrin and render the right flank more secure. After this had successfully been accomplished by the 14th Division on the left bank of the Diala river, attention was directed to the Tigris. The Daur position, some twenty miles north of Samarra, was occupied on the 3rd of November, and two days later the enemy were expelled from Tikrit after somewhat severe fighting. Among the captures in this action was the ill-fated steamer, the *Julnar*, with which a last attempt had been made to re-victual the garrison at Kut. The troops engaged returned to Samarra on the 10th of November.

During the course of both these movements the Ford van companies were kept fully occupied up to the utmost limit in the carriage of supplies, ammunition and the evacuation of minor wounded cases. For the Jebel Hamrin operation a concentration of eight complete companies, some eight hundred vehicles in all, took place. Five hundred of these worked from Baquba, where No. 784 Company was by this time fortunate enough to have its workshops, and three hundred worked from Tuwair. On the Tigris front the concentration of vans was some five hundred, which figure serves to indicate how considerable a rôle this form of transport was now playing. The mechanical transport too showed that it was capable of going anywhere, though the country over which it had to work in the Jebel Hamrin was exceptionally difficult.

These activities were the last to be undertaken by General Maude for, to the great loss of the Army, he died of cholera in Baghdad on the 18th of November.

He was succeeded by General Marshall who, up to then, had been in command of the Third (Indian) Army

Corps—his place in that formation being taken by General Egerton from the 14th (Indian) Division. General Marshall's first act was to occupy the Jebel Hamrin on the right bank of the Diala and the important town of Khaniquin, which was carried out early in December: his next to despatch the 7th (Indian) Division to Egypt. In the following March the 3rd (Indian) Division also left for the same theatre, being replaced by the newly formed 18th (Indian) Division.

The early part of 1918 was a period of preparation. The majority of the vehicles were employed in maintaining the 15th Division at Feluja and in putting reserves of stores and supplies into Sharaban and Abu Jisra on the Diala line. Here some thirty light Packard lorries of No. 976 Company were employed for the first time. Supplies for the cavalry division, engaged up the river Adhaim, had also to be provided, and these were sent up by rail to Balad and carried by four hundred vans to Atab, where the supply depot was situated, thence being conveyed twenty-five miles up the left bank of the Adhaim, where the cavalry refilled. This transport was constantly attacked by Arabs, so that convoys had to be protected by a small escort with a Lewis gun.

Of interest at this time was the departure of General Dunsterville's mission—the raising and organising of local forces in Georgia and the Caucasus. No. 730 Mechanical Transport Company was chosen to provide the necessary *personnel*, and Captain Aldham, A.S.C., was placed in charge of thirty-six vans and six cars. The transport problem was a difficult one, for the country to be traversed was, so far as anything was known about it, extremely arduous; nor were any petrol supplies obtainable until Hamadan, which was three hundred and fifty miles distant and which place was two hundred and seventy miles to the destination at Enzeli on the Caspian Sea, was reached. It eventually turned out that even at Hamadan very little petrol could be obtained, and only that at an exorbitant rate. This difficulty, however, was got over by sending a convoy with supplies in advance, and General Dunsterville, who left Baghdad on the 27th of January, reached Enzeli on the 17th of February, having been considerably delayed owing to snow *en route*. The mission spent some nine months in various parts of Persia and on the borders of the Caspian, and the larger proportion of its vehicles were, in spite of the difficulty of obtaining spare parts, kept in running order throughout.

In January and February nine of the ten Ford van companies, which had been asked for by General Maude during the previous September, arrived.* One company, No. 1023, was the first Burmese company to be formed, the officers, n.c.o.'s and men being all recruited in Burma. The remaining units came out with 60 per cent. of British drivers, and were made up to strength by Indian *personnel* trained for this duty. It was hoped that the arrival of these substantial reinforcements would have eased the situation which, despite the lull in any major operations, had been continuously one of great strain on the transport. The work had been incessant and the roads, especially in the Khaniquin area, were in the worst possible state. At the end of February two hundred and fifty-nine Ford vans were under repair out of a total of 1130 employed, and two companies suffering from smallpox had to be segregated. Yet any hopes of relief were destined to be vain. The more mechanical transport units available the greater became the radius of action of the force and they were, therefore, used to a greater extent than ever.

On the 7th of March active operations by the army were re-commenced by the capture of Hit on the Euphrates, against which a premature attempt had been made during the previous July. The enemy retired up the river some twenty-five miles to Khan Baghdadi, where

* These were Nos. 1013, 1014, 1015, 1016, 1017, 1018, 1019, 1020 and 1023 Companies.

he was surrounded and captured on the 27th of March by the 15th (Indian) Division and the 11th Indian Cavalry Brigade, over 3000 prisoners and twenty guns being taken: the remnants of the Turkish force were pursued another seventy miles as far as Anah, and subsequently a similar distance beyond. These operations ranging over two hundred miles from railhead were only made possible by a large amount of mechanical transport, and, as usual, a concentration of companies, in this instance amounting to eight hundred, was necessary. It was a good test for the Indian drivers employed for the first time in large numbers and they came through it with credit, but the chief transport interest lay in the formation of a flying column of three hundred Ford vans, which went into action outside Khan Baghdadi on the 26th of March and pursued the enemy onwards to Amah. This column commanded by Colonel Hogg—the transport being under Major Sellwood, A.S.C.—carried eight hundred fighting troops, with thirty-four machine guns and water, rations and ammunition. Practically no casualties were incurred and numerous captures were made, a large ammunition dump at Anah being blown up on the 29th of March when the force withdrew to Khan Baghdadi. These brilliant actions had the effect of clearing the Turks from the Euphrates line and permanently removed any possible menace to the left flank of the British army.

Various adjustments in distribution took place at this period, which tended to simplify the administration of the army and facilitate the problem of supply. Railway development had been pushed forward.* The collection of local resources had reached a high pitch of efficiency,

* By the end of March 1918 the following railways were in existence. *Metre gauge*: Basra–Nasiriyeh, Basra–Amara, Kut–Baghdad, Baghdad–Baquba and Baquba–Jebel Hamrin (in conversion from 2 ft. 6 in.). *Standard gauge*: Baghdad–Samarra, Baghdad–Dhibban. 2 ft. 6 in. Sumaika–Sadiya. *Decauville*: Baghdad–Mufraz. A standard gauge line from Baghdad to Hilla was completed at the end of May.

the rich Hilla area being opened up at the end of May. In February a special Directorate of Irrigation came into being. The inland water service too was further strengthened.

Then came the turn for activity on the right flank. During April and May an advance was made against the Turkish 2nd Division in the Kirkuk area; and that important town was occupied by the 6th (Indian) Cavalry Brigade and the 13th Division on the 7th of May, twelve hundred prisoners and twelve guns being taken during the operations. The supply of the force engaged presented grave difficulties, for the most advanced railhead was at Table Mountain, about twenty miles north of Baquba and some hundred and twenty miles from Kirkuk, which was the greatest range at which it was attempted to maintain a division and a cavalry brigade for any length of time. For this reason the disposition of the transport has a special interest. Some twelve hundred Ford vans in all were employed and worked practically in echelon; six hundred were at railhead covering the section to Chaman Kupri; four hundred ran from the latter place to Tuz; and two hundred went forward from Tuz with the troops during the advance. As the move was made through a hostile country it was impossible to form dumps of supplies, and, as there was insufficient transport to carry more than that required for one day, no supplies remained on hand with the fighting troops beyond those delivered daily. The stages over which the mechanical transport had to work were long, all of them being over eighty miles and the roads were in a very bad condition. On one occasion it was not found possible to run the convoys for two days on end, and the troops in the forward areas could only receive quarter rations. In a special effort made to get some supplies up a convoy of two hundred vans took thirteen hours to do thirty-six miles, every van having to be manhandled through a number of nullahs, while three rivers in flood had to be crossed. At the time of the capture of Kirkuk the troops in that area, like those in the Khaniquin area, were on half rations for some days, the former having to eat their emergency rations on the 9th of May. These difficulties, which had been foreseen by General Marshall, caused the troops to evacuate Kirkuk in the middle of May. It had been the Commander-in-Chief's original intention to have gone no further than Tuz, but the movement was extended on the representations of the War Office, which was desirous of a blow being struck against the enemy in the Kirkuk area in order to force him to summon to his assistance troops earmarked for Persian Azerbaijan and Armenia, where the situation was causing anxiety.* Nevertheless, had the advance taken place a little later in the year, when the rains were over, it is almost certain that the maintenance difficulties would have been overcome even with such transport as was available.

It is worth noting that during these operations a small mobile column armed with machine guns was formed with thirty-six Ford vans and that although some of the Indian drivers were indifferently trained in handling their vehicles, the unit proved of use. So much so that a war establishment was afterwards sanctioned for a "Lewis Gun Company in Ford Vans" though actually it was never required to come into being.

The scene was now shifted to Persia. On the 1st of June General Marshall informed General Dunsterville that a mobile motor column would be despatched for the purpose of securing the Hamadan–Enzeli road, and that it was the intention to concentrate it at the former town by about the middle of the month. This column, which consisted of one thousand infantry, a mountain battery

* General Marshall's telegram of the 2nd of May, 1918, to the War Office contained the following: "Underlying difficulty is one of maintenance.... To capture Kirkuk and maintain by this line the troops necessary to hold it entails placing the whole Corps while operations last on reduced rations."

and a field ambulance, was, with all its equipment, ammunition, baggage and rations, to be carried in five companies of Ford vans, five hundred vehicles in all.* In conception this was the most irrational transport operation conducted during the whole campaign. In the first place, to keep five Ford van companies effective and at work in and around Hamadan, two hundred and ninety miles distant from railhead at Ruz, tonnage amounting to three hundred and sixty per month was required, without including spare parts for the vehicles or rations for the *personnel*. Loaded as it was, the column could not carry sufficient petrol to get it to Hamadan, let alone to Enzeli, and a considerable maintenance service had to be organised for it. Some weeks of preparation were clearly necessary. These aspects were strongly represented by the transport authorities and fully appreciated by the Commander-in-Chief, but, since at that time the Home Government was obsessed with the idea of getting troops into Persia to counteract Turkish movements from the Caucasus and the Caspian and to endeavour to re-organise certain Russian elements which had the strongest disinclination to be re-organised, all administrative objections were overruled. In these circumstances and in spite of superhuman energy on the part of General Dunsterville and those with him, nothing material was effected except the loss of some hundreds of gallant lives, the expenditure of a great deal of money and the locking up of a mass of transport which might have been employed usefully, and even decisively, in Mesopotamia. In this instance the mobile column, which left Ruz early in June, found itself completely immobile when it reached Hamadan; and, although a supply of petrol had been put into Kermanshah, a hundred and seventy-three miles out, for its use, it only just succeeded in reaching its destination. Thus some five hundred Ford vans found

* The mechanical transport companies were Nos. 818, 1013, 1015, 1018, 1020.

themselves stationary until a line of regular communications could be organised for them; and this involved, besides a varying number of Ford companies employed on the first stage of eighty miles between Ruz and Pai Tak, the withdrawal of ten lorries from each of the eight artillery caterpillar units and the diversion of the whole of No. 596 (Peerless Lorry) Company. These lorries were employed on working the stages from Pai Tak to Kermanshah, the Napiers and Daimlers of the caterpillar companies being eventually re-allotted to the Ruz–Pai Tak portion of the route owing to road difficulties. The Peerless lorries on occasions went up to Hamadan and sometimes even as far as Enzeli. It was unfortunate that the maintenance of mechanical transport on this line had not been thought out some months ahead. For example, prior to this operation there had been available in Mesopotamia 100 per cent. spare tyres for lorries. In Persia the Daimler and Napier vehicles were averaging some six hundred miles for their rear tyres and about twelve hundred for the front ones. At that rate of consumption the stock in Mesopotamia became exhausted by the end of August, and could not be replaced until October. Yet this extravagance was the least in the whole proceeding, for the fact that no petrol was obtainable between Ruz and Hamadan meant that very little useful loads could be conveyed. To run one Ford van straight through practically nothing could be carried beyond its own supplies of petrol and oil. It was only by making stages that some useful amount of tonnage could be delivered, and calculations showed that to put twenty-five van loads or six tons into Hamadan every four days with one stage at Kermanshah, no less than a hundred and fifty vans were required, of which one hundred must be stationed at railhead and fifty at Kermanshah. For a daily delivery of the above amount no less than seven hundred and fifty vans would need to be employed on the line without any allowance being made for spare vehicles.

From the transport point of view, however, worse was to follow. In June troubles in Persia increased, and it became evident that the mobile column would be inadequate to deal with it. On the 6th of the following month, therefore, the 39th Infantry Brigade was put under orders, and the dismounted troops were conveyed in lorry convoys in three echelons from Ruz to Hamadan, each echelon taking 1100 men with reserve rations and ammunition for the journey. The mounted troops went by march route. By the 16th of July the first echelon reached Hamadan, the second on the 29th and the third four days later. The Peerless lorries of No. 596 Company, which were then allotted to this task, suffered greatly, especially with regard to tyres, and vehicles were shed at various places on the way up on this account: the petrol consumption only averaged four miles to the gallon. It was only with great difficulty that the 39th Brigade got as far as Hamadan, while the fact that other lorries had to render help reduced the maintenance tonnage that could be despatched for Ruz. The actual feeding of the posts along the line was at that time carried out by Ford van companies, the majority of which were based on Khaniquin. No. 815 Company was stationed at Chasmah Safed, Nos. 730 and 976 (Packard Lorry) Companies were at Kermanshah. Together with the Peerless lorries these were responsible for the carriage of all the troops, supplies, ammunition and stores of every nature as far as Hamadan. Three of the five Ford van companies of the mobile column were situated there also, the remaining two being forward at Resht. After the brigade had reached Hamadan the lorries gradually drifted back down the line and very few were available at the end of August. The sudden troop movement effected by transport which had a full task in maintaining the forces already on the Persian lines of communication imposed an unreasonable strain on all concerned and, as it turned out, demanded efforts and expenditure wholly incommensurate with the military results obtained: to the army in Mesopotamia fully cognisant, from experience on the spot, of the capabilities of mechanical transport it seemed so indeed. Had the campaign been drawn out as was then anticipated, General Marshall's difficulties would have been very great and, in spite of the reinforcements of mechanical transport that came to hand during a period of quiescence, would have been seriously compromised.* Nevertheless the experiences gained were most valuable. Seldom can a transport organisation have been required to carry out a more onerous task than that involved by maintaining a line of communication of five hundred and fifty miles over bad or indifferent roads, and with no facilities for obtaining petrol, oil or spares other than what it could organise for itself; and, moreover, dealing not only with feeding numerous posts and detachments but of transporting troops, wounded, and every kind of stores needed, and in addition evacuating vast numbers of refugees. The story of the Persian lines of communication can only be touched on here and its main features noted: the full tale must necessarily be left incomplete; but it was nevertheless an operation of war that merits an attention that has never yet been devoted to it.†

During the summer further progress had been made to develop the resources of Mesopotamia. A large proportion of the grain required was obtained from that year's harvest, while steps had been taken to work oil-

---

* That the War Office knew this is shown by a telegram sent on the 28th of August in which thirteen hundred additional Ford vans and five hundred Peerless lorries were promised. But, at the same time, the difficulties were never fully realised for, on the 2nd of October, General Marshall was asked to consider the feasibility of sending a cavalry force up the Euphrates towards Aleppo to assist General Allenby in the direction of Aleppo. The reply was illuminating: "In proposed operations the ruling factor is provision of transport. Practically all my transport of every description is employed on the Persian road. The maximum I can hope to make available for operations in Mesopotamia is two hundred Ford vans which would be quite inadequate".

† *With the M.T. in Mesopotamia*, by Lieut.-Colonel F. W. Leland, R.A.S.C., gives much useful information on this subject.

bearing strata at various places and to obtain coal from the Kifri mines.

In the autumn it was decided that an advance was to be made towards Mosul, for which purpose forward supply depots providing seven days' supplies for the force and ammunition were completed on the 18th of October at Jift on the Tigris.* So far as the mechanical transport for this movement was concerned its duty began early in October, when two hundred and twenty Ford vans from six companies were assembled on the 9th of October, two further companies being sent up a week later. Further additions brought the total to five hundred and fourteen. Although the operations, undertaken as they were by three divisions and two cavalry brigades, were on an extensive scale, the work of the mechanical transport engaged differed little in nature or degree from previous experiences. The main advance was made up both banks of the Tigris with a subsidiary one on Kirkuk and Altun Kupri. The strong Fat-ha position was turned on the 23rd of October, followed by fighting on the lesser Zab River. At Sharqat the enemy retreat northwards was cut off by the cavalry, the Turkish force amounting to some 13,000 prisoners and fifty guns surrendered at dawn on the 30th of October. The enemy were pursued as far as Qaiyara, where the last action of the army in Mesopotamia took place, the armistice coming into force at noon on the 31st instant.

At the close of hostilities there were forty-two Army Service Corps mechanical transport companies in Mesopotamia and Persia,† while, in addition, the Corps had to

* The railway from Samarra to Tikrit had been completed on the 1st of September.
† These were made up as follows:

Ford Van Companies	22	Workshop Unit with Light	
Peerless Lorry Company	1	Armoured Motor Battery	1
Packard Lorry Company	1	Base M.T. Depot	1
Motor Ambulance Convoys	5	L. of C. Repair Unit	1
Caterpillar Companies	8	Advanced M.T. Depot	1
		Floating workshop	1

find officers and men, vehicles, spare parts and repairs for six light armoured motor batteries and men, vehicles and repairs for six anti-aircraft sections. The base organisation for the maintenance of this vast mass of vehicles,* for which practically every item had to be obtained from England, and including as it did the training of some thousands of drivers, was perhaps the most formidable part of the whole transport task, as it was inevitably the least apparent to the superficial view. Not the least of the difficulties was the question of *personnel*. At a very early stage men, transferred from the horse transport branch, had to be trained owing to the shortage; while mechanical transport drivers from England had to be trained on Fords. Towards the end of 1917 the War Office notified that not only were they unable to obtain men for new units, but were unable to provide reinforcements for those existing; and it was therefore decided that Indians should be employed as substitutes. When these mixed companies were formed, 40 per cent. of the drivers were Indian and the remainder British, this proportion being afterwards reversed. In addition to these mixed units, Burmese companies were sent, local Arabs, Armenians, Chaldeans and Jews were also tried with varying success, while a certain number of Mauritians, who had originally come out in the Labour Corps, were employed with satisfactory results. A few Chinese were also made use of in the Base Mechanical Transport Depot, where they did good work as carpenters and masons. It will readily be imagined that, with this mixture of races and babel of tongues, patience and

* The vehicles were made up as follows:

Lorries (3 ton)[1]	560	Other motor cars	121
Lorries (30 cwt.)[1]	685	Armoured cars	97
Ford vans	3279	Motor cycles	1336
Ford cars	396	Tractors	40
Ford ambulances	405	Fowler trucks	22
Other ambulances	72	Fire engines	7
			Total 7020

[1] Including workshops and technical vehicles.

perseverance were needed to the utmost limit. But when it is remembered that the majority were either semi-skilled or altogether unskilled, it becomes a matter for wonder that the results were as effective as they were. For they were, indeed, marvellously effective. The contrast between the Army Service Corps administration and that which had preceded it is directly reflected in the tactical and strategical successes, which were gained continuously under Generals Maude and Marshall. From the time that the War Office took over control from the Indian Government the campaign was well supported and, on the whole, well "found." But such fundamental assets would not have sufficed had there not been on the spot a resourceful and skilled direction capable of adapting itself to the existing conditions, of improvisation and, above all, of foresight without which the most scientific of supply systems can little avail. In this respect the campaign in Mesopotamia was beyond all others a triumph for Army Service Corps methods and training.

In a further sense the campaign was a landmark in the history of the Corps. The old departmental conception of the services of transport and supply was utterly swept away. And not only because departmental methods as exemplified in the Indian transport and supply system had failed. They were always bound to fail when put to any serious test, just as the similar British organisations which had preceded the Army Service Corps had likewise failed. It was also because former ideas, that regarded the Army Service Corps as an organisation solely concerned with the collection and issue of foodstuffs and their distribution by convoys laboriously toiling in the wake of an army, and rarely approaching the scenes of its fighting activities, ceased to bear relation to reality. Here in a war of movement the Corps came into its own as the dominant agent in the mobility of the army. Never has this been more apparent than in Mesopotamia. On the efficiency of its fast-moving mechanical transport columns the operations depended. In this respect these columns in fact constituted a new auxiliary arm, for their scope was not confined to the subsistence of troops moving under their own power, but included the movement of the troops themselves for both strategical and tactical purposes. It was the first occasion on which an extensive and continuous use was made of mechanical transport for these ends, and it is doubtful whether up to then its full potentialities in this direction had been realised. It is a strange commentary on its presence in Mesopotamia that the very name of the Corps to which it belonged may be searched for in vain in the index of the *Official History* of the campaign.

It would be both ungracious and unjust to ignore even in a chronicle devoted to the performances of the Army Service Corps, those accomplished by its collaborators of the Indian service. Much of the executive supply work and practically all the executive animal transport work was carried out by the Indian Supply and Transport Corps. In the early stage of the campaign it had struggled with hopelessly inadequate resources. In the latter stages it had co-operated loyally with the British service; and it was only fitting that those who had so long borne the burden should have shared so largely in the final success.

The total casualties of the army give some measure of the severity of the campaign. Nearly 15,000 were killed in action or died of wounds, and some 13,000 of disease; over 51,000 were wounded and 13,000 taken prisoners or were missing. Of the dead just under 400 belonged to the Army Service Corps.

BIBLIOGRAPHY

Official History of the War. The Mesopotamia Campaign, 1914–1918. By Brig.-Gen. F. J. MOBERLY, C.B., C.S.I., D.S.O., p.s.c.

Report of Mesopotamia Commission 1917.

Critical Study of the Campaign in Mesopotamia up to April 1917. Compiled by Officers of the Staff College, Quetta, Oct.–Nov. 1923.

Life of Sir Stanley Maude. By Major-General Sir C. E. CALLWELL, K.C.B.

With the M.T. in Mesopotamia. By Lieut.-Colonel F. W. LELAND, C.B.E., D.S.O.

"Supply Services in Mesopotamia." By Colonel W. M. PARKER, C.M.G., D.S.O. From the *Royal Army Service Corps Quarterly*, April 1921.

An Outline of the Campaign in Mesopotamia. Lectures delivered at the Staff College, Camberley, 1922. By Major R. EVANS, M.C., p.s.c., Royal Horse Guards.

CHAPTER X

THE CAMPAIGN IN EAST AFRICA

THE long drawn-out struggle in East Africa presented a set of circumstances very different from those of any other theatre. In one sense it resembled what is usually termed a "small war" in that it was conducted in an uncivilised country where the chief difficulties lay in vast distances, lack of normal routes of communication and climatic conditions. Yet in other respects, such as the numbers engaged, the quality of the opposition and the duration of active operations, it was a campaign of importance, and one which would have attracted attention, had it not been overshadowed by the greater events elsewhere. As it is, East Africa is remembered by the public at large on account of the gallant fight sustained by the enemy under General Von Lettow Vorbeck, who did not lay down his arms until after the Armistice had been concluded in Europe.

The Army Service Corps did not make its appearance in this field until 1916, the transport and supply services having been previously carried out partially by the Indian Army and partially by the South African Army Service Corps supplemented by *personnel* drawn from local sources in British East Africa. These last could not be considered as other than improvisations for a special purpose, but it is well here to emphasise that the South African Army Service Corps had gained some experience in German South-West Africa in the invasion of that colony which was undertaken by Generals Botha and Smuts in 1915, and which brought about the surrender of the German forces in July of that year. The success that had been compassed in South-West Africa against 6500 German troops supported by a powerful artillery, seemed to augur well for the conquest of the richer and more prosperous colony in East Africa, where at the outbreak of war the enemy could but dispose of 5000 men in his troops and police, of which the supervisory *personnel* only were German; while at no time in the campaign were more than some 2500 Europeans available, even allowing for accretions secured from the ships that managed to evade the blockade. It would, then, have appeared that the opposition was likely to have been of no very formidable character. In actual fact it turned out that the reverse was the case, for apart from the exceptional leadership, and the efficiency with which the natives were raised, trained and organised, the natural difficulties of the country itself rendered movement of large bodies of troops at all times difficult and at certain seasons almost impossible.

The extent of the colony was about twice the size of the German Empire in Europe; the coast line north to south along the Indian Ocean was four hundred and seventy miles and from Shirati on Lake Victoria to where the southern border met Lake Nyassa seven hundred miles; the distance east to west from Dar-es-Salaam to Kigoma was seven hundred and eighty-seven miles. The country along the coast was low lying but at from twenty to thirty miles inland the level rose to a plateau of an average height of 3000–4000 feet, which constituted the hinterland. This plateau continued until it fell sharply to water-level on reaching the lakes, which were themselves a considerable height above the sea, Lake Victoria the highest being 5000 feet. Under normal peace conditions the climate is not a particularly unhealthy one, but on active service when men were subject to hardships and fatigues at all hours of the day and night, and when adequate supplies were not always procurable, malaria and dysentery were responsible for a large percentage of casualties. Certain zones are subject to the tsetse fly, which caused much depredation among the transport animals.

The rainy season varies somewhat in different parts of the country. Along the coast line the rains began in November with the heaviest fall in April, but along the northern portion of the coast there is usually a break during January and February when the rainfall is comparatively light. In the south the rains are wont to continue heavily until the end of April, during which month the heaviest fall is to be expected. At those times the rivers are flooded for miles on each side of their banks, and large areas adjoining them converted into swamps. The dry season lasts from June until October when the weather becomes cooler, though the temperature gradually rises during the latter part of this period. The soil generally consists of two varieties, "red" and "black cotton". In the wet season the red soil is capable of carrying light transport on upland roads, while the "black cotton" becomes an impassable bog. In the dry season even the red soil, after continued use by wheeled transport, is ground to sand and forms a serious obstacle to vehicles unless artificially held by wire netting or plaited plantains. At the same time vast spaces of country become waterless deserts as the smaller rivers and streams dry up, and, consequently, concentrations of men or animals, except on the main river systems, become almost impossible. As roads were non-existent outside the perimeter of the coastal ports the influence that season and soil had on movement is apparent.

As regards communications, four railway lines may be noted. The Mombasa–Nairobi line on which the British supply depended at the start of the campaign; the Tanga railway which ran from the port to Moshi at the foot of Mount Kilimanjaro; and the central railway which connected Dar-es-Salaam to Lake Tanganyika; and a line which, in the spring of 1916, was under construction between Voi (on the Mombasa–Nairobi section) and Maktau.

Such in the briefest outline were the conditions in the theatre of war, and the question at once arises as to how the enemy could, under such conditions, maintain such a superior mobility as to be able to evade the grasp of forces, which from the beginning of 1916 onwards greatly outnumbered him. Indeed that mobility by itself was the preponderating factor in his military success; for success it was to have kept engaged in Africa a large army, much of which might have been employed elsewhere. In any case such an accomplishment was the maximum that, with his limited resources, he could have been expected to do. As elsewhere in mobile warfare, problems of supply and transport dominated the situation. Nor is it obviously understandable why the British forces were unable to attain, except on certain special occasions, a mobility equal to that of the Germans by adopting like methods. The answer is simple—such methods could not be generally adopted. In the first place the enemy had an immense native population on which to draw for carrier transport, which constituted a permanent complement of the regular companies into which his troops were organised. The normal establishment of these units was a hundred and sixty-two rank and file and three hundred and twenty-two porters, and this proportion was approximately retained throughout. The enemy native troops and carriers could, to a large extent, live on the country, thus reducing the carriage of foodstuffs to a minimum, while the absence of pack, wheeled or mechanical transport enabled the fighting units to move through any country which an infantryman could traverse. Their mobility was still further added to by the portable boats which formed part of the equipment of each company, so that an unfordable stream presented no obstacle to them, while for the

British forces, on the other hand, a stream or even a deep nullah necessitated the building of a bridge of sufficient stability to withstand ordinary floods. Again the enemy had an intimate knowledge of the topography, resources and population of the country, which, as members of the civil administration were constantly with his troops, was thus at the disposal of his military leaders. Operating in hostile territory none of these advantages were possessed by the invaders. It was out of the question to recruit carriers on the scale effected by the Germans, who, when compelled to retire, did not hesitate to enlist forcibly all suitable men in the district. At the same time the local British civil authorities were against recruitment of the native population. The transport of the force as a whole was therefore organised on the basis of mules for first line, ox wagons and carts for the divisional trains and ammunition columns, and mechanical transport for the supply columns. The disadvantages of using ox transport in the divisional trains is apparent, for the contents of these formations were naturally those which were required directly the troops got into bivouac. Not only was mobility thereby hampered, but the health of the troops was prejudiced, for oxen cannot work in tropical midday heat and require a definite number of hours for resting during the day and for grazing. Nor can they keep up with troops on the move. The British could not rely to more than a limited extent on local supplies; the bulk had to be sent up from the rear, while lack of precise knowledge as to the main features of the country was a still further drawback to rapid movement.

Apart, however, from these unavoidable disabilities, there were other factors which combined to influence the situation. In comparison with that possessed by the enemy the British had a numerous artillery, a powerful contingent of mounted troops, and finally were organised to a great extent on the model of the higher formations, such as divisions and brigades, as obtained in more orthodox theatres of war. For operations in terrain such as East Africa and under the conditions of that country it was at least doubtful whether such organisation could allow of the necessary elasticity. In any case the movement of large concentrations of men and animals put a very heavy strain on services of maintenance which did not enjoy the normal facilities for their functions. In this respect more than in any other, perhaps, experiences in this theatre are fruitful in lessons, and it may well be questioned whether the conceptions of the conduct of such a campaign were wholly apt to the circumstances. It can scarcely be disputed that the Germans found a practical solution to its problems to which they had given a large measure of attention even prior to the actual outbreak of war. Had the British been organised on somewhat the same lines it would have involved the recruitment of many thousands of natives as carriers. Whether these could have been raised in the adjoining British colonies is a matter outside the scope of this narrative, though it may be observed that if such a course had been possible its consequences would certainly merit consideration. As it was the struggle was resolved into the weapon of weight against that of mobility, and in such the supply and transport services were bound to be severely tested. In fact in no part of the world affected by the Great War—with the possible exception of Mesopotamia where the climatic conditions were more trying —was the capacity of the Army Service Corps so strained. That its functions had to be carried out for one of the most heterogeneous armies ever put in the field by Great Britain did not tend to simplify the administration. British and Indian regulars, New Army troops, Imperial Service Indian troops, South Africans including large contingents of Boers, Rhodesian and East African Europeans, King's African Rifles, Nigerian and West Indian negroes and Arabs and Chinese were all included, and this involved the issue of five different types of rations—

European, Indian, East African, West African and Chinese—with all the complications inherent in such diversities.

The war which eventually resulted in the conquest of the last German colonial possession fell into three main phases. Under the first may be comprised events up to the arrival of General Smuts in February 1916, following the decision of the British Government that a serious attempt should be made to bring matters to a conclusion. The last phase involved the "clearing up" under Generals Hoskins and Van Deventer after General Smuts had driven the enemy from the Central Railway and cut him off from the coast to the east. For British arms the first period had not been a happy one. In 1914 an attempt had been made on Tanga when a fleet of British transports escorted by warships appeared off the port. The brigade which was landed, however, met with a repulse and had to be re-embarked in some haste and with comparatively heavy loss. The moral effect was far worse. From a mood of despondency the enemy began to contemplate the invasion of British East Africa and, in fact, subsequently overran a considerable area of that colony, even threatening the capital—Nairobi. In February 1916 he was in occupation of Taveta, a small settlement ten miles inside the British border, and had entrenched camps at Mbuyuni and Serengeti—the former being nearly thirty miles from the frontier. His patrols penetrated as far as Voi, from whence they carried out systematic raids on the railway running south-east, and on several occasions were able to blow up trains conveying supplies.

General Tighe commanded the British troops. The number at his disposal was inadequate to carry offensive operations into German territory and, as shown, did not even suffice to protect the border. He therefore stood on the defensive, and it may even be considered surprising that the enemy did not show greater activity.

Von Lettow's conduct at that time has come in for criticism in that he appeared to allow a favourable opportunity to slip. If, however, his transport situation is recalled it will probably be accepted that his organisation, admirable as it was for all internal purposes, would not have been equal to any sustained offensive in British territory where he could not depend on local resources and where his *personnel* would have been far from their homes and their families.

At the time of General Smuts's advent the British field forces consisted of the 1st and 2nd East African Divisions. The former under Major-General J. Stewart included the East African Infantry Brigade and a South African Mounted Brigade and divisional troops, and lay on the Longido line with headquarters at Kajiado. The 2nd East African Division under General Tighe himself was assembled at Serengeti and Mbuyuni, where Divisional Headquarters was situated on the Voi–Maktau line, the two former localities having been re-occupied without opposition towards the end of January 1916: this formation contained the 2nd East African Infantry Brigade and the 2nd and 3rd South African Infantry Brigades and divisional troops. The German forces concentrated opposite Longido and Maktau amounted to approximately 8000 men.

Prior to General Smuts's appointment, it had been the intention to have placed Sir Horace Smith-Dorrien in command. The latter fell sick and never arrived in East Africa, but his staff, which had been specially nominated in England, proceeded on their way and reached Mombasa on the 25th of January, 1916. Brig.-General P. O. Hazelton held the post of Director of Supplies and Transport, having previously seen service in France. As might have been expected the transport situation was such as to cause him some concern. In the first place it was difficult to ascertain what transport existed in the force, since depots were in the habit of retaining on their books animals which had already been issued to units. As regards the latter no record existed of what they possessed: nor was it apparent what second line transport was available. Consequently no figure could be given as to any further transport required, even supposing the regimental or first line and the second line transport were actually in being. Ignorance on these points on the part of Headquarters would have been embarrassing at any time: it was doubly so on the eve of an offensive in a practically unknown hostile country. On the supply side matters could be termed satisfactory. It was true that the Quartermaster General's Branch was vague as to the ration strength of the force; but it was ascertained that a three months' reserve had been accumulated, while the necessary machinery for replacement existed. Connection by railway to the port of Mombasa made imports easy, and many articles could be drawn from within British East Africa. At that time the provision of clothing was included with the Commissariat, and General Hazelton lost no time in handing the former over to the Army Ordnance Department in accordance with the sub-division in the Imperial Army; he also wisely inaugurated Investigation and Audit Branches before turning his attention seriously to transport affairs. Before General Smith-Dorrien's staff had started for East Africa the question of the most suitable form of mechanical transport had been examined and various residents had been consulted. On the advice of one who stated that pneumatic tyres were of little use owing to the roads being covered with mimosa thorns, thirty-hundredweight lorries with solid tyres were provided for the divisional supply and ammunition columns and arrived in June, but these vehicles proved quite unsuitable after a month's experience in the country; in dry weather they quickly ground the surface of such tracks as existed into dust which rendered them impassable where constant traffic passed over them: in the rains they sank axle deep. Previous to the arrival of these there had been three mechanical transport units with the army—two being Army Service Corps and the third the South African Army Service Corps—but, as none of these had operated on the German side of the frontier, conditions were largely unknown.

Any ideas that the Transport Directorate might have had as to a period of preparation were quickly dispelled by the new Commander-in-Chief. He made a rapid reconnaissance of the front and decided to act at once so that something might be accomplished before the rains set in. From the wider point of view this decision was correct. It was desirable to expel the enemy from British territory, while a defensive which might have been prolonged until June would have been likely to have affected the *morale* of the troops. At the same time, with the comparative state of disorder prevailing as regards the transport establishments, a natural anxiety was evinced by those responsible. General Smuts was unorthodox in his methods; but this particular kind of warfare was unorthodox. In any case he was a man of resolute determination who was not accustomed to permit doubts or hesitation to stand in the way of a course upon which he had set his mind. General Tighe's plan for the offensive had been first to occupy the Kilimanjaro area through a converging movement simultaneously carried out from Longido and Mbuyuni with Kahe on the Tanga–Moshi railway as the objective in the first instance. To this conception General Smuts decided to adhere, but he considered that some modification was necessary in the disposition of the troops in order to avoid frontal attacks against entrenched positions in the dense bush, and he accordingly brought down General Van Deventer's mounted brigade from the Longido area to Mbuyuni where it arrived on the 2nd of March. This re-distribution had the additional advantages of speed and surprise in the direction where the main blow was designed to fall. The advance started on the 8th of March, General Smuts only having landed from South Africa a fortnight previously, and at that time some of the fighting units were incomplete as regards their regimental transport. The 1st Division from Longido, with an eight-day ox convoy as a mobile magazine, had a waterless belt of desert of some thirty-five miles to traverse before reaching a bush country very difficult for movement. With a halt on the 9th to allow its slow-moving transport to catch up, it skirted the north side of Mount Kilimanjaro and reached Moshi on the 14th of March, dumping all unused supplies at that place, which thus became an advanced base; the Voi–Maktau railway line, being joined up to the German system, consolidated the lines of communication into enemy territory. The 2nd Division from Maktau, which bore the brunt of the attack in its initial stages, was more favourably situated as regards its "jumping-off" point, for the branch railway from Voi was close at hand at its back, and a mechanical transport supply column was able to work in this area: ox transport formed the ammunition column and for the rest a miscellaneous assortment was collected. The water supply was an obstacle for, east of the Lumi River, water did not exist. The troops stationed at Serengeti and Mbuyuni had been dependent on a two and a half inch pipe-line and what could be brought by rail, and for a long period the allowance had been limited to one gallon per man per day. This was the chief factor that influenced General Smuts in bringing down the mounted brigade at the last moment before the advance started.

The operations, which ensued, were highly successful. Moving into the gap between Mount Kilimanjaro and the Pare Hills against the enemy main force, Taveta was occupied on the 11th of March after brisk fighting and Moshi four days later, the enemy retreating in a south-easterly direction along the railway. His superior knowledge of the country and the fact that he was not hampered by many of the considerations which limited the rate of advance of the invading army, had given him just that margin of mobility that enabled him to slip through before the net had been too tightly drawn for escape. But if he had not been brought to decisive battle as General Smuts had intended by using the mounted troops to block his exit, he had suffered material loss. He had been completely driven from British territory, and when Aruscha was occupied by General Van Deventer on the 21st of March some 4500 square miles of German East Africa, including a rich and settled area, were in British hands. Even more important, a suitable advanced base and the railway from New Moshi as far as the Pangani River had been secured. Indeed the success had been so rapid that it had almost outrun organisation, and a halt had to be called to make provision for transport and supply before any further forward move could be undertaken, for the rains were due at any moment and it was vital to make good the rearward lines of communication.

Up to that time any gloomy supply prognostications had not been realised—the bold course had succeeded as it does more often than not. But the Army Service Corps had every reason but one to believe that the pause might, owing to the rains, be of sufficient duration to enable it to re-organise and augment its ox transport formations as they became available from South Africa, and to bring forward the necessary reserves of supplies. The exception to these anticipations lay in the will of the Commander-in-Chief. On the 8th of April, exactly one month subsequent to the original advance, General Smuts ordered Van Deventer to occupy Kondoa Irangi—a hundred and sixty miles south-west of Moshi or a fifteen days' trek for oxen over almost impassable tracks. By a re-distribution of the force General Van Deventer then had at his disposal the 2nd Division consisting of one mounted brigade, one infantry brigade and four batteries, in addition to various other divisional troops. This sudden decision threw all the carefully maturing plans of the Supply and Transport Directorate out of gear. The reserves in course of accumulation for a methodical advance when the season was more favourable were largely diverted from the Moshi area to Kondoa Irangi, as were likewise numbers of oxen, which, as might have been expected, suffered heavy losses in the course of the strenuous efforts which they were called upon to make. It may be surmised that Brig.-General Hazelton might at this stage have wished himself back in France in the well-ordered progress of the great administrative machine where such "alarums and excursions" were unknown, and indeed his position merited every sympathy. Yet to "live dangerously" is no bad training for the transport and supply service and, as on other occasions, it rose to the height of its tasks. General Hazelton exerted himself to raise and train all available trek oxen in the country. He put temptation as far as possible from the fighting units by placing all transport coming forward into the hands of the Inspector-General of Communications, under whose aegis it was dealt out by the Assistant Director of Supplies and Transport on the lines of communication, as forces lengthened their distances from their bases of supply. He established a Base Mechanical Transport Depot at Nairobi, where all spare parts were collected.

While these and other measures were in progress General Van Deventer had reached Kondoa Irangi with his mounted troops, occupying the town on the 19th of April after some fighting. It speaks volumes for the hardihood of his South Africans, mainly Boers, that this could have been accomplished. There had been no rations either for men or animals, and the former had subsisted on such meat and meal as they could find while the horses and mules had had nothing but mealie stalks and grass. As the rain had been incessant it had been rarely possible to do any cooking. The losses in animals had been heavy—nearly two hundred had succumbed. The route from Moshi to Arusha and thence onwards to Kondoa Irangi being impassable for wheeled traffic, the problem of supply was a delicate one, especially as rain had fallen heavily and was continuing to fall. Van Deventer's force had no tents, while it had even been impossible to bring up the men's kits owing to transport conditions. Clothing and boots especially were giving out. Yet there was no question of withdrawal; on the contrary, efforts were made to exploit the movement which had succeeded in threatening the Central Railway. On the 1st of May General Van Deventer received two of his infantry battalions, a battery and a machine-gun company, while he pushed out mounted patrols along the Handeni and Dodoma roads and in other directions, being fortunate enough to capture certain depots of enemy supplies, together with the posts in charge of them. These captures did something to relieve his situation, but there had never been any danger of actual starvation, for Kondoa Irangi was a very rich district in which plenty of cattle were to be found. Nor was any effort spared to alleviate the hardships which the troops were suffering. Administrative foresight had accumulated a month's supplies at Longido and these saved the situation. The question to be solved was how to convey them to Kondoa Irangi. Fortunately reconnaissances discovered a new route from Longido to Lol Kissale, not only shorter than the track via Aruscha, but one which was superior as regards physical obstacles. Within a few weeks the necessary bridging and other work on this made it possible to get wheeled transport as far as Lol Kissale, some eighty miles from Van Deventer's force. This last section could only be completed by porters, of which 15,000 were registered in the district, although owing to the fact that the enemy had impressed his own requirements, only some 7000 could be got together.

These arrangements were under way when the enemy attacked Kondoa Irangi in force on the 7th of May, only being beaten off after severe fighting which was directed by General Von Lettow Vorbeck himself.

The rains were now getting lighter and the routes consequently improving; the new road from Moschi to Lol Kissale was also working, and the railway from Voi was just about to be joined up with the German system near Kahe. The main force was then holding the line of the Ruwu River and it was possible to put in supplies at Taveta and other points along the route for its maintenance, chief use being made of carriers. On the 21st of May, therefore, General Smuts resumed his advance, having first reinforced Kondoa Irangi with two battalions and some artillery and formed an Advanced Supply Depot at Ufiome to serve General Van Deventer. The object was to clear the Tanga–Moschi railway line as far as the sea and remove all risk to the British communications by the main line from Mombasa to Nairobi and the Voi Maktau line. The advance proceeded down the Pangani River, meeting with little opposition. Supplies were sent from Mbuyuni by rail on to the German system and, as the railway was repaired, new railheads were successively opened, but the distances run over the Pare hills caused serious casualties amongst the lorries. General Smuts's plan was to occupy Handeni before the enemy had time to send reinforcements over the Pangani. The conception was bold and ambitious, for it depended primarily on the speed of its execution, Handeni being some two hundred miles from the line of the Ruwu River. It was naturally impracticable to repair the destroyed railway in any time even approximating to the speed of the advance, and again the supply problem became one of great difficulty. It became necessary to off load ammunition-carrying mechanical vehicles and turn them over to the service of supply. At Buiko a halt was made on the 31st of May, a distance of a hundred and thirty miles having been covered in eleven days and the army being over a hundred miles from railhead at Kahe. The troops were then on half rations.

To the Commander-in-Chief, however, it seemed out of the question to wait until the railway was in working order. Very extensive damage had been done by the enemy—over long stretches the sleepers had been removed, the chairs had entirely disappeared and all culverts and bridges had been destroyed. At Buiko station, the principal railway centre between New Moshi and Tanga, the workshops, water tanks and all points had been blown up. Any less resolute commander might well have hesitated before committing his troops further into the unknown, but General Smuts had no intention of sacrificing the advantages he had already gained by his rapid movements. After a week's halt, during which time supplies were rushed forward by every available means and at the cost of numerous casualties to men and vehicles, and some road-making work from Mikocheni to Makanja was undertaken, the army was transferred on the 8th of June to the right bank of the River Pangani, a bridge having been constructed for this purpose. Some fighting occurred before Mkalamo was entered two days later and Handeni was reached on the 19th. At Mombo, about thirty-five miles north of Handeni, a trolley line running to the latter place was captured and, after being equipped, was used as a hand-pushed tramway. As it was capable of conveying about thirty tons of supplies a week it was of some assistance, but the transport and supply services had by now reached what appeared to them the limit of their capacity to maintain the army, even on a reduced scale. At Buiko the position had been serious. At Handeni it seemed even desperate. Rations had been short for many days. No white flour had been issued for some time, hard biscuit eked out with mealie flour being provided in lieu. The only meat available was the fly-stricken trek ox, which had to be eaten at once as it would not keep. The Indian troops, who did not eat meat, were naturally still worse off and no ghee could be provided for them to help matters. However, the halt which was anticipated would have given time to the administrative services to overtake the troops, renovate the transport, and create reserves of supplies, ammunition, clothing and stores. But any hopes were destined to be disappointed. A resumption of movement was ordered immediately and the advance continued a further forty-five miles to Makindu, where a halt was made on the 24th of June, a total of two hundred and fifty miles having been covered in just over a month.

General Smuts had started with some 15,000 men but by the time Makindu was reached his numbers were over 20,000 and tending continually to increase. Reinforcements were constantly arriving, among which were units from South Africa and the Gold Coast, while others were drawn from the lines of communication. These accretions complicated the task of maintenance beyond that of the additional mouths to be fed as all had to be fitted out with their first line transport, while the proportionate increase required in the supply columns was a task to which the existing resources were unequal. There were, quite apart from the conditions of the country, too many troops for the transport at the disposal of the army; and all the time that the administrative services were grappling with the problem involved by the main force it was compelled to deal with General Van Deventer's division at Kondoa Irangi. That the army was enabled to keep moving testifies to the unsparing efforts of the Army Service Corps and the South and East Africans associated with it. As it was it was only dire necessity that made General Smuts call a halt at Makindu. The fighting strength had been reduced to one-half of its establishments by sickness, and the casualties among transport animals had been enormous. It was impossible further to extend the communications,

THE CAMPAIGN IN EAST AFRICA

and numbers of sick required evacuation. Towards this last purpose and of the bringing up of supplies every vehicle was brought into action and employed without ceasing.

Yet there were causes for satisfaction which, on balance, might be held to have justified so great an expenditure of energy. If the enemy had not been brought to decisive action, he had at any rate been met and defeated continually, and continually compelled to retire. Strategically the results were more considerable, for he had been hustled from some of the richest and most important areas in his colony, and found his vital artery that lay in the Central Railway and Tabora, to which his capital had been transferred, seriously threatened. In addition his troops opposite Kondoa Irangi had by the dispositions of General Smuts's main forces been effectively cut off from the northern theatre. From the maintenance point of view the operations could scarcely be deemed so satisfactory. The bulk of the mechanical transport had not arrived from England and South Africa, and their material would even under more favourable general circumstances have been insufficient to fulfil its proper functions over lines of communication so extended. Unquestionably the task of the Army Service Corps would have been simplified by a landing on the coast either at Tanga or Dar-es-Salaam. But weighty tactical and strategical reasons operated against both projects, which were carefully considered before being rejected. An appreciation of the situation which then confronted the Commander-in-Chief is both interesting and instructive, for it raises all the issues as to what extent transport and supply considerations should influence a plan of campaign. General Smuts held the view, and the experience of history supports him, that, vital as such considerations are, they should not be permitted to dominate the situation and that, therefore, imperfections and even, up to a point, deficiencies, in the maintenance services must be accepted if more important strategical results are thereby offered. Or in other words, of two projects the one easy of execution from the supply standpoint and the other difficult but yet possible from the same standpoint, the choice is for determination first and foremost by the military advantages to be gained. In this instance those advantages were overwhelming and may be contrasted with the half-hearted projects which characterised the operations dealt with in the chapter on Mesopotamia, regarding the Persian lines of communication which immobilised a vast mass of transport for no real military end. Here the execution of an attack on Tanga from the sea would have been comparatively easy but, unless the main body of the enemy was to be left on the flank of the invaders in an advance against the Central Railway, it would have been necessary to have moved northwards along the Tanga–Moshi line. Quite apart, then, from leaving Van Deventer isolated, the Moshi area and Taveta gap would have again been accessible to the enemy, who once more might have found himself in British territory; he was always, in default of opposition, able to transfer troops from a point on the central line to the northern theatre in the space of a fortnight to three weeks and one of the best roads in German East Africa was that from Handeni to Kondoa, which distance could be covered in twelve days. To obviate the enemy's advantage of interior lines it was necessary that the next blow should be delivered rapidly; and this could not be effected by a move from Tanga, which would have taken time to stage. An offensive from Dar-es-Salaam showed the same objections and additional ones even stronger, for the immediate hinterland became, after the rains, an almost impenetrable swamp through which an opposed advance would have been an operation of magnitude, quite apart from the deplorable effects that such an unhealthy district would have had on the troops. And in any case, Van Deventer might have run the risk of being overwhelmed at Kondoa Irangi before the Dar-es-Salaam expedition had got under way. Even had he been withdrawn to the Moshi area, he would not have been out of danger and would also have incurred the additional disadvantages of being separated still further from the main force.

Looked at from the broadest point of view, General Smuts's appreciation was the correct one though, as he himself admitted, "efforts like these cannot be made without inflicting the greatest hardships on all", adding that "it is equally true that the commander who shrinks from such efforts should stay at home".

When the army lay in the Makindu area the occupation of Tanga was ordered and, under arrangements made by the Inspector-General of Communications, a force was disembarked on the 7th of July, the enemy offering no opposition. This was the prelude to further landing of detachments on the coast at Pangani and Sadani on the 23rd of July and the 1st of August respectively and, confronted as they were by General Smuts's main body in the area of the Nguru mountains, the Germans were unable to undertake more than insignificant guerrilla operations in these directions.

Meanwhile Van Deventer started to move in mid-July, and by the 29th of that month his infantry were at Dodoma on the Central Railway, which, by the 9th of August, was in British hands from Kilimatinde to Kikombo; some 1500 head of cattle which were captured *en route* being of great assistance to his commissariat. This success was due primarily to the fact that the enemy had withdrawn opposite Van Deventer in order to meet the threat of General Smuts along the Nguru mountains against Morogoro, for he was unaware that maintenance difficulties would have delayed the advance of the latter even if unopposed; and he now found himself cut off from the western part of the colony and any retirement by Iringa threatened. From other directions, too, the net was closing round him. A small British force had captured Mwanza at the southern end of Lake Victoria, and were preparing to move south on Tabora. Belgian columns were marching from west and north-west in the same direction, while General Northey with a column from Northern Rhodesia had reached a point about eighty miles south-west of Iringa.

On the 5th of August General Smuts resumed his offensive against the German forces covering Morogoro. The troops moved in three columns converging on Turiani where, after some fighting, headquarters established itself on the 13th of August. On the 18th Dakawa, twenty-five miles south, was occupied, road making and bridge building having proceeded during the advance. The advanced depot was now at Handeni, while a small supply of ammunition had been brought forward to Lukigura; the problem was to get this within reach of the fighting troops, since all the vehicles of the divisional ammunition column had been taken over for supply purposes, but this was eventually solved by borrowing transport from the batteries as opportunity offered. The enemy fought stubborn delaying actions, but his position became increasingly compromised by the pressure brought on his left flank by General Van Deventer who, operating along the Central Railway, entered Kilossa on the 23rd of August. The performances of these troops were remarkable, for the minimum distance covered by any unit from the time it had left Kondoa Irangi was two hundred and twenty miles. Most of the transport was mule drawn, as the larger proportion of the mechanical vehicles had been diverted to supply services on the lines of communication as long as the force was at Kondoa Irangi, while, since reaching that place in April, few of the animals had received any grain at all. As, too, the march had been through a bad "fly" country, the wastage had been heavy.

General Smuts entered the important settlement of

Morogoro on the 27th of August, the enemy retreating south-east and escaping the enveloping movement. The lines of communication now extended to some four hundred and fifty miles from Moshi, and the force directly under General Smuts totalled 28,000 men, while almost precisely that number of oxen had been lost during the course of the three months in which the advance was taking place. The work accomplished by these patient animals, when every other means failed or were lacking, deserves to be specially remembered, for their share in the success attained was very great. The supply situation still gave cause for anxiety. Everything had to come from the Handeni depot, from whence the route was wholly dependent on the weather. The casualties in animals had caused such a shortage that the transport in possession of the artillery had still to be retained for the carriage of supplies. It was a matter of getting everything possible forward before the rain came. But at last some relief was at hand for, during the month of August, reinforcements of mechanical transport began to arrive from England and South Africa, Ford vans forming the majority of the vehicles. The heavy lorries which had proved so unsuitable were relegated to the bases and lines of communication. When the Fords and other light mechanical transport were put on the road *personnel* troubles became accentuated, since it took five drivers to work a load equivalent to that carried by a 30 cwt. lorry. The European or South African driver contracted malaria very rapidly after landing in the country so that, although vehicles might be concentrated in sufficient numbers, the proportion of sick was so high that it was found impossible to recruit enough white drivers to replace casualties, and recourse had to be made to Swahili, Uganda, Indian and Nigerian *personnel*, who were able better to withstand the exigencies of the climate. In the early stages schools had been formed in South Africa for the training of motor drivers.

When this source ran dry similar establishments for training natives were organised in East Africa itself. The provision of artificers was naturally an even greater difficulty, and ultimately recourse was had to Chinese for the heavier work.

While the Commander-in-Chief had every reason for satisfaction at having obtained a firm grip on the Central Railway and the northern portion of the coast, he was not prepared to allow his troops to rest on the laurels won at the cost of so much hardship, while the enemy still retained the bulk of his forces in the field. Van Deventer was instructed to move from Kilossa to Uleia, while on the 29th of August General Smuts's troops moved via Pugu, reaching Matombo Mission on the south of the Ruwu River on the 2nd of September. Traversing very difficult country in the Uluguru mountains and overcoming skilful resistance, he entered Kissaki on the 15th of September. All stores and supplies had been carried off or destroyed by the enemy, and the troops were completely exhausted by these operations carried out on half rations; the force about Kissaki, cut off by a sudden downpour of rain, itself actually lived for a fortnight on the meat of hippopotami shot in the Mgeta River and on millet. It was not for some weeks after the occupation that it was found practicable to run ambulances and other transport through the mountains, and consequently it was not possible to get food or medical comforts forward or evacuate the sick. The improvised hospitals were crowded with numbers down with malaria. The columns had pushed nearly a hundred miles beyond their original destination on the Central Railway, and there had been no real pause or opportunity for accumulating stores for the advance. The fighting front was then fed from a railhead at Korogwe on the Tanga–Moshi line, this step being one of the first fruits of the occupation of the port, but even then everything had to be brought up three hundred miles over winding tracks through bush and swamp. Over six hundred animal drawn vehicles had been added to the transport since the previous June, but the animals themselves were dying by thousands, and it was impossible to make good the wastage: owing to horse sickness and "fly" the life of a mule or an ox was not usually more than six weeks.* As regards mechanical transport the position was more promising, for some three hundred Ford vans which had been landed in August had reached the Central Railway towards the end of September, but, previous to their arrival, the larger proportion of the lorries were out of action and spare parts were not forthcoming to keep them on the road, apart from complete breakdowns. Although the rains were not due for some time there had been several spells of wet weather which involved holding up all traffic for several days at a time. On these occasions not only were roads impassable but bridges were washed away and had to be rebuilt, and the embankments along the hillsides sank and required bolstering up. Again for the transport and supply matters had reached a crisis. It was impossible to push the advance further.

While the 1st Division had been fighting its way through the mountains, a landing at Bagamayo, north of Dar-es-Salaam, had been effected by Brig.-General Edwards, for the Commander-in-Chief conceived that, if his communications were to be opened elsewhere, whether by active operations or not, such functions fell naturally to the Inspector-General of Communications. It was a unique rôle for such an appointment but it was a thoroughly practical one and, after defeating a hostile detachment south-west of Ruwu station, General Edwards moved on Dar-es-Salaam which surrendered on the 3rd of September. This move was followed by

* The wastage in animals for the two months 15th Sept.–15th Nov. 1916, was as follows:

Horses	... ...	10,000	Oxen	11,000
Mules	... ...	10,000	Donkeys	2,500

landings south at Kilwa Kivinge and Kilwa Kissiwani on the 7th of September, Mikindani on the 13th, Sudi Bay on the 15th and Lindi on the 16th, by which time the whole coast line except the Rufiji Delta was in British hands.

The enemy now had between four and five thousand men between the Mgeta and Rufiji Rivers and there he was, owing to the climatic conditions, most unfavourably situated as compared with the British, who were occupying higher and healthier ground. Meanwhile General Northey had entered Iringa on the 29th of August, and three weeks later the Belgians were in Tabora, General Crewe from the north being at Igalulu a few days later. These columns were much retarded by transport and supply difficulties but, seeing that the Portuguese were now in the field to the south and were holding the line of the River Rovuma, the position of the Germans appeared desperate. General Smuts indeed summoned his opponent to surrender, and to any less skilful and resolute leader than Von Lettow Vorbeck it might have seemed that enough had been done for the honour of his arms and the defence of the colony. Yet, in one element at least, the enemy still had a superiority and it was the all important one of mobility; it enabled him to continue his resistance for a further two years.

During the autumn some re-organisation took place in the British force, and 12,000 South Africans were repatriated as unfit to stand further hardships until they had regained their normal strength by a period of rest. Some additional battalions of King's African Rifles and a Nigerian brigade arrived in their place with some artillery from India. The transport situation had now become ameliorated further by the restoration of the railway line from Dar-es-Salaam as far as Dodoma. It was not until January 1917 that trains could run, but repairs were effected to the bridges which enabled them to sustain a number of Napier and Reos motor tractors of which thirty-five, dragging loaded trailers behind them, were put into use. Each tractor was capable of carrying about five tons of supplies and each trailer an additional ten tons. There was only one break of bulk at the Ngerengere River in the whole three hundred miles and by this means the depots formed at Mkesse Kilossa and Dodoma were filled.

General Smuts's plan was to establish a coastal base to the south at Kilwa and land there an adequate force, which could work north-west or north as required. He then proposed to attack from the north, and, seizing a crossing over the Rufiji above Kibambawe, move thence south-eastwards to cut the enemy's line of retreat towards Mahenge, eventually joining hands with the Kilwa force close in the enemy rear. A column based on Dar-es-Salaam was to advance to Utete while, simultaneously, Generals Northey and Van Deventer were to press in from the north and west respectively. The Kilwa force under General Hoskyns was established by the 29th of November, and there the transport difficulties were exceptional for the tracks radiating inland were of sand alternating with black cotton soil and it was barely possible to get pack mules along them. In addition Kilwa was an area subject to "tsetse" fly with the usual results in the death rate of the animals. In preparation for the forward move of the main body a supply depot with thirty days' supplies was established on the Dunthumi River, to where Headquarters moved on the 22nd of December.

On New Year's Day 1917 the operations re-commenced. By the 20th of January after some fighting the army was over the Rufiji and about Luhembero and Mkindu. Meanwhile on the 25th of December Van Deventer started from Iringa towards Lukegeta. Owing to the impossibility of getting forward the reserve of supplies which it had been designed to form at Iringa, he had been compelled to send back to the Central Railway all his troops except three battalions and one squadron. The intention was to drive the enemy south of the Ulanga River but the impossibility of supply even for so reduced a force necessitated the abandonment of the plan. During these movements there had been heavy rain which had brought all mechanical transport to a standstill, and the troops were once again on half rations. In the south the enemy had escaped from General Northey at Mfirka, and on the Mgeta River he had succeeded in avoiding the several columns which had worked round him and got across the Rufiji. In the delta area of that river he had withdrawn and British forces had occupied Kissegesse and Koge. Such was the general position on the 20th of January, the day on which General Smuts, having handed over command to General Hoskyns, left Dar-es-Salaam. The results of the last series of movements showed that, apart from supply difficulties, it was practically impossible to surround the enemy in a country of such a nature as long as his own supplies held out.

The most important and, as far as the army as a whole was concerned, the most exacting part of the campaign was over. The rains came on with intensity and no operations of importance took place until the following July. During the interim a great deal was done to put the transport and supply services on a proper footing. Mombasa as the principal base was relinquished and Dar-es-Salaam established in its place: Kilwa was likewise opened as an advanced base. The repatriation of South Africans and their replacement by other troops was still going forward during this period, which fact made it a specially complex one for the Supply Directorate, especially as rations had to be found for Belgian forces, for it was impossible to know how to stock supply depots until the nationality of the troops to be employed in the various areas was ascertained. On the other hand, the fact that a large proportion of the European and

THE CAMPAIGN IN EAST AFRICA

especially of the mounted troops were evacuated brought considerable relief to the transport services, for the amount of transport needed per head for the white soldier was, owing to the necessity of carrying additional items of medicine, food, clothing and shelter, considerably in excess of what the natives required. At this time also the prejudices of local authorities to the recruitment of native carriers were overcome, and the field forces for 1917 onwards were equipped both in first and second line with carrier transport, while light mechanical lorries took the place of the broken-down heavy lorries on the lines of communication.

General Hoskyns, who had done much to put administrative matters on a sound footing, only remained a few months in command, being ordered to Mesopotamia. He was succeeded by General Van Deventer, who at once pressed for an advance from Kilwa. At that time—July 1917—there were no motor ambulance convoys available and the full complement of box lorries had not arrived. Nevertheless the advance took place and, as an engagement ensued shortly afterwards in which there were numerous casualties, a great strain was once more thrown on the mechanical transport, who were compelled to do double and even treble journeys, while the absence of water made it necessary to form special mechanical transport convoys drawn from supply columns. The percentage of sick among the driver *personnel* became so high that once more the movement came to a standstill until reinforcements arrived.

For the purposes of this narrative it would serve no very useful purpose to follow the operations which took place during the last eighteen months of the war in East Africa. Most of the fighting was of a guerrilla nature, in which feats of gallantry and physical endurance were no less marked than in more important fields. The enemy were harried and driven from place to place in German and Portuguese East Africa, and the final surrender took place at Abercorn in Northern Rhodesia on the 25th of November, 1918.

During the war in East Africa and especially during the final period the work of the Army Service Corps did not, and could not, show the spectacular results achieved elsewhere: neither the conditions of the country nor the material available admitted of it. And certain misconceptions as to the nature and course of the operations severely handicapped the maintenance services from the beginning. Admitting that a large force would take the field and that the lines of communication would extend for hundreds of miles beyond any railheads or advanced depots, the use of mechanical transport was unquestionably the correct solution. In view of the lack of roads and the nature of the soil the original decision to use a heavy type of vehicle was an erroneous one. Certainly there were difficulties in obtaining a light type—the demands for Mesopotamia were at that time very heavy, while, in addition, the fact that the light vehicles were only capable of a useful load of 600–1000 lb., necessitated a large number and, therefore, required a greater number of *personnel*. But in practice the heavy mechanical transport had to all intents and purposes ceased to exist by the autumn of 1916: from as early as the last week in May of that year the "lift" had been insufficient to carry more than half rations, and it never came up to full requirements in spite of such renewals, replacements and additions as could be effected. While this was partly due to an insufficient number of lorries to keep pace with the ever-lengthening lines of communication, it was due in part also to the lack of sufficient workshops in the advanced sections and to lack of spare parts to replace the continual breakages caused by work across such difficult terrain. The soil, whether in wet or dry weather, could not stand heavy traffic and it reacted so that the heavy machines simply broke up. Where small timber had to be cleared it was found that, owing to the wear of

THE CAMPAIGN IN EAST AFRICA

the road or track after very little use, tree stumps projected causing heavy casualties with pneumatic-tyred vehicles. Consequently it was found necessary for road corps to follow up the original pioneer parties to ease gradients, metal or corduroy bad places, bridge rivers or cut out the large or small tree stumps. In all some four hundred and fifty miles of so-called motor roads or tracks through the bush were made during a period of six months in 1916 for light motor vehicles.

The casualties among all ranks of European *personnel* due to climatic conditions were very heavy. On the whole it was found that men of middle age were more immune from climatic sickness, and experience served to show that men under twenty-eight years of age were lacking in stamina. On one particularly unhealthy line of advance the monthly casualties exceeded the strength of the *personnel* employed, the non-effectives representing a temporary wastage of over 100 per cent. per month. On the Kilwa line vehicles were standing idle for a long time for lack of drivers and, in an endeavour to meet this situation as far as possible, every staff-car driver was transferred to the supply columns as a lorry driver, the officers affected being instructed either to act as their own drivers or hire rickshaws. On several occasions during the campaign, operations designed had to be postponed owing to sickness and casualties among drivers of supply and ammunition columns.

For the workshop *personnel* especially the extreme heat proved most trying, and where properly protected and ventilated shops were not available the expedient of working by night instead of by day was tried with success. It was found that the men could work longer hours and, given adequate artificial lighting, their output was greater per unit of time and they were more immune from sickness.

The mechanical transport native *personnel*, as in the case of Mesopotamia, was very heterogeneous in character, consisting as it did of Indians, Malays, Chinese, Seychelles islanders, Cingalese, East and West African natives. A certain amount of mixing of European and native *personnel* took place but the results were not satisfactory.

The experiment of training natives as motor drivers was inaugurated in March 1917, a small training depot being opened at Kampala in Uganda whence it was moved six months later to Dar-es-Salaam, finally being located at Dodoma in February 1918. The *personnel* enlisted were drawn from various tribes from Uganda and British East Africa and included a certain number of Swahilis. The chief difficulty was in the provision of sufficient instructors able to speak the languages, but the experiment met with a large measure of success, so much so that in addition to driving instruction a proportion of the natives were trained in repair work.

Nearly a thousand drivers were trained in all, the majority being from the Bagana tribe, as these proved most suitable.

As regards other native *personnel* employed on mechanical transport services, the most important unit was the West African Corps, of which the majority were recruited and sent out from the West Coast. This unit eventually comprised a thousand men. Indian and Chinese drivers together amounted to approximately a further thousand.

Some slight reference has been made to General Northey's force and, although space forbids any narrative of its operations, a few figures may serve to indicate its transport problem. The base of the Nyasaland field force was at Zomba in Portuguese East Africa, distant ninety miles from Fort Johnson on the southern shores of Lake Nyasa. Via the latter the expedition operated from Karonga on the northern end of the lake, through Fife and Abercorn in North-Eastern Rhodesia near the frontiers of German East Africa. The distance from Zomba to Abercorn was six hundred and ten miles, of which approximately half could be done by water. But Zomba in fact only carried out the functions of an advanced base, the real base of the force, which was mainly Rhodesian, being at Salisbury, a distance of 1200 miles from Abercorn via the Mashonaland Railway to the port of Beira and thence by sea to Chinde; by rail from Chinde to Limbe and for the final forty miles to Zomba by road. The alternative route lay from the railhead at Broken Hill, three hundred miles through North-Eastern Rhodesia to Abercorn, by which the only dependable method at any time was by carrier transport.

These spaces had to be negotiated before the vast territory of German East Africa was entered, and they were perhaps the most precarious and difficult, as they were certainly the longest communications with which any British force was involved during the course of the war.

In the early stages all transport from Limbe to Zomba and thence onwards to Fort Johnson was done by native carriers, but, in the autumn of 1915, eight three-ton Army Service Corps Packard lorries arrived and worked the former part of this route, the second stage being impracticable for heavy vehicles. Six months later, however, Fords and Hupmobiles became available, and these enabled consignments to be delivered into Fort Johnson from whence they were shipped to the north of the lake and then taken over by carriers to the posts on the enemy border.

When the advance started in 1916 twenty motor cars accompanied the column, but they could only be used where roads had actually been made by the engineers until the Bahora flats were reached, when light motor transport was able to operate during the dry season. The difficulties of maintenance were immense, but nevertheless some effective work was carried out.

Throughout the whole of the campaign in East Africa the distances over which mechanical transport had to maintain supplies were far in excess of anything on which calculations had previously been made, and could be said in many cases to have exceeded the point of economy; for naturally the limit to the employment of any form of transport is reached when its capacity to carry forward a load in addition to that required for its own maintenance ceases, and necessarily, as distances increase, the useful load carried forward decreases proportionately. The longest road route covered was that from Voi on the Uganda Railway to Morogoro on the Central Railway—about five hundred miles—and mechanical transport covered this distance up to the cessation of hostilities. A column also advancing to Dodoma from Kondoa Irangi was maintained for a considerable period from Kajiado, a point three hundred miles away, until the establishment of other railheads.

In the light of the difficulties recorded above the task of the base transport establishments was specially exacting. The Base Mechanical Transport Depot—No. 599 Company Army Service Corps—incorporated a workshop, the total strength being two hundred and one all ranks. Disembarking at Mombasa in April 1916 it was first installed at Nairobi. Advanced Mechanical Transport Depots were opened at Mbuyuni Mombo and Handeni during the summer as the advance proceeded. In September the base depot was transferred to Dar-es-Salaam, and from thence onwards various sub-depots were established as the movements of the troops dictated. These sub-depots were independent of each other and maintained their own stocks by demands on the base depot, the stock to be issued in each case being determined by the latter.

Previous to 1917 it had not been found possible to form a reserve park for mechanical transport vehicles, every vehicle available being needed for service in the field. In February, however, a park was formed under the base depot, which arrangement held good until June

1918, when it was established as a separate unit. At no time, however, was this organisation a reserve vehicle park in the accurate sense of the term, since it was mainly concerned with the reception of vehicles in transit from one area to another and those returned from the front for extensive repairs.

The base workshop at its inception had neither the *personnel*, plant nor material adequate to fulfil its proper functions, and though at a later stage, by the addition of plant obtained from the United Kingdom, South Africa and in a small measure from local sources, it was able to cope to some extent with demands it remained to the end incomplete in many respects and dependent in the main on supplies of spare parts. Shortage of certain trades, especially of moulders, pattern makers, acetylene and electric welders, were a severe handicap, and had these been available considerable financial saving would have accrued through a reduction in the numbers of non-effective vehicles, quite apart from the efficiency of the force. In addition, the general establishment of the workshop was unequal to the bulk of transport which it was required to support, as it had originally been designed for a considerably less number of units than ultimately arrived in the theatre. During 1916 and 1917 some 3000 vehicles were purchased in South Africa and two motor ambulance convoys, a light armoured motor battery and two special supply columns, Nos. 816 and 817 Companies Army Service Corps, were added. As against these disabilities, however, can be set the exceptional activity of the mobile field workshops, which, owing to the resource displayed by their *personnel* in utilising plant and tools acquired from the enemy, were able to carry out tasks more numerous and more elaborate than those with which they could normally be expected to contend.

The operation of transport and supply in East Africa is worthy of study for several reasons. Firstly, because it demonstrates the bringing into use of mechanical transport on a large scale in terrain and under conditions which would appear ill suited to its capabilities. Secondly, because it is in such terrain and under similar conditions that the British Army might expect to have to campaign in a future "small war". And lastly because for its greater part the machinery which was responsible for the maintenance of the Army was improvised.

The Army Service Corps had no supply or animal transport *personnel* engaged with the exception of the few on the Staff of the Directorate. But it was charged with the control of all the services and provided a large proportion of the mechanical transport.* As noted, the last was of a heterogeneous nature. In the early stages it was "found" by a volunteer unit formed at Nairobi, designated "The East African Mechanical Transport Corps", and the South African Army Service Corps subsequently bore a considerable share in the work. The credit for what was achieved, therefore, belongs to each and all who were harnessed in the common effort and shared the common sacrifice. Nor was that sacrifice a light one. Casualties among all European ranks involved some 50 per cent. becoming non-effective chiefly from sickness.

The Army Service Corps *personnel* at its maximum numbered just over 4000 all ranks, and it left some two hundred and seventy dead in East Africa.

At the date of the Armistice the strength of the army was 111,731.

* The following Army Service Corps transport units served in the theatre: Nos. 570, 599, 618, 626, 631, 632, 633, 634, 635, 648, 699, 816 and 817 Companies. Of the above, Nos. 631, 632 and 633 were allotted to artillery units, and Nos. 618, 626 and 699 were motor ambulance convoys.

BIBLIOGRAPHY

With Botha and Smuts in Africa. Part II. *The East African Campaign.* By Lieut.-Commander W. WHITTALL.

General Smuts' Campaign in East Africa. By Brig.-General J. H. V. CROWE, C.B.

"Supplies and Transport in East Africa." By Colonel P. O. HAZELTON, C.B., C.M.G. From the *Royal Army Service Corps Quarterly*, January 1920.

"Organisation and Administration of Supply and Transport in the East African Campaign." By Colonel P. O. HAZELTON, C.B., C.M.G. From the *Royal Army Service Corps Quarterly*, October 1920.

"Some after-thoughts of the War in East Africa." By Colonel G. M. ORR, C.B.E., D.S.O. From the *Journal of the Royal United Service Institution*, November 1924.

"Mechanised Transport in Small Wars." By Lieut.-Colonel G. C. G. BLUNT, D.S.O., O.B.E., R.A.S.C. From the *Journal of the Royal United Service Institution*, August 1928.

History of the Mechanical Transport, East Africa.

"With General Northey in East Africa." From *The Times*, August 5th, 1916.

Notes on the running of Mechanical Transport in Nyasaland with General Northey's Force. By Lieutenant E. A. SIMPSON, R.A.S.C.

CHAPTER XI

THE BRITISH ARMY IN ITALY

INTERVENTION in the Italian theatre had been foreseen by Sir W. R. Robertson, the Chief of the Imperial General Staff, as early as 1917; and a small British mission had accordingly been despatched in April of that year to explore, in collaboration with the Italian General Headquarters, various of the circumstances which would arise from such intervention. About the same time the French Government engaged itself in a similar enterprise. It was necessary to proceed with delicacy, since the war was progressing, to the superficial view at any rate, in a manner that would hardly suggest that the support of Anglo-French contingents would be needed by the Italians, but after spending some four months in Italy the British mission was able to come to certain definite arrangements and present a report thereon. It was not a wholly comprehensive document that was then drawn up—in the circumstances existing it could not have been so—but it was nevertheless in certain respects a valuable one and its initiation says much for the foresight of Sir William Robertson. Plans were drawn up, fixing the areas of concentration under various hypotheses for both British and French armies; of the railways and lines of communication allotted to each; of buses and of such administrative assistance as could be rendered within the country from Italian sources. Since the French had been first on the scene, they had naturally availed themselves of their preferences in what was offered. For both French and British an army of six divisions as a maximum was contemplated. The railway arrangements were regulated in great detail and, as will be shown later, worked with smoothness and rapidity when they came to be put into practice. The provisional selection of a base presented difficulties, which can only be appreciated by some reference to the general conception of the proposed dispositions of the Anglo-French forces. These were designed to form a strategic army of reserve to be located within the area Padova–Verona–Mantova–Montselice, the front roughly parallel with the line of railway which runs between Padova and Vicenza. For the British forces alternative areas of concentration were reconnoitred in the zones Padova–Poiana (about half way between Padova and Vicenza)–Montagnana–Rovigo and Poiana–Vicenza–Verona–Montagnana, though the latter was expected to be occupied by the French, who were expected to arrive first in Italy. In addition the possibilities of a more backward concentration were foreseen by a reconnaissance of the zone Milano–Abbiategrasso–Mortara–Pavia and Lodi. Since the British were intended to make chief use of the Southern line and in all likelihood the South-Eastern forward area of concentration, it was necessary to select some locality into which the main southern railway artery via Nice and Genoa, which formed their main lines of communication, gave direct approach. In addition it was desirable that these should be convenient of access from the sea in order to relieve a railway at all times overburdened and especially by the imports of coal required for the Italian munition factories. Savona, some twenty-five miles west of Genoa, was reconnoitred, but was found to possess no advantages sufficient to compensate for it being unduly far removed from the area in which the army might be expected. A site at Vado, some five miles west of Savona, was, however, provisionally noted in case of emergency. The port of Genoa was likewise out of the question, since it was in a hopelessly congested state and the Italian authorities were unable to allot more than a very limited amount of accommodation, amongst which was included storage for frozen meat. Search was then made on the railway lines running from Savona to Alessandria and Genoa to Tortona, for to have gone north of the River Po would have been too far forward in the event of an enemy offensive coming by Lake Garda. The most suitable places were already occupied by various Italian establishments and finally Arquata, twenty miles north of Genoa and on the main line, was chosen and reported upon as a suitable base for at least three divisions. As this selection was naturally of consequence to the supply administration, while at the same time it aroused certain ill-informed criticism when it actually came to be put into use, it may be well to give some description of it now.

Arquata itself is a small town in a valley between the hills which open out at that place to a distance of some miles. A large railway station and numerous sidings had been constructed for the receipt of overflow traffic from the port of Genoa. A British railway expert at the time estimated that up to 10,000 tons a day of stores could be handled there and, as was subsequently seen, this estimate proved not unduly optimistic. Adjoining the railway station were a number of stone cotton hangars, with further buildings under construction, most suitable for the storage of supplies and with railway sidings alongside, the surroundings being well paved and drained. There was ample room for expansion for further sheds and buildings which would be needed to apply the site to the purposes of a base. Under the charge of Lieut.-Colonel C. Rowe, A.S.C., what may be described as a model supply depot was subsequently organised at Arquata and, as no description of such has been given elsewhere, occasion will be taken to dwell upon this in some detail at a later stage.

Turning to the assistance which was promised towards the transport and supply services, there was a natural reluctance for the Italians to commit themselves definitely to the future when their own situation might have undergone alteration. But it was found possible to arrange for five hundred Fiat lorries with their drivers to be handed over on the arrival of the British Forces. It may here be recorded that this agreement was loyally carried out, as was likewise that by which rations were to be provided during the period of concentration before the British base could assume its functions. Fuel wood was always to be found from Italian sources.

Such in brief were the main results arrived at after somewhat lengthy negotiations, and they formed in some respects a thorough and in others at least a partial preparation for possibilities which, at that time, seemed to all concerned as remote. Alternative strategical dispositions were outlined. The railway movements, including detraining stations, were arranged. March routes across the Franco-Italian frontier were reconnoitred and the stages laid down. A base, corresponding to any of the strategical dispositions and conveniently situated near a large port, was decided upon, while engagements for certain assistance in kind were entered upon with the Italians, who were themselves in none too happy a position in respect of supplies in general. Comprehension of these measures is important in order to appreciate the transport and supply problems which had subsequently to be met and overcome, for in no sphere of administration is foresight more necessary for success. A tactical or strategical triumph may be attained or at least inspired by the decision of a moment, in which even previous errors can be rectified. But in that sphere which concerns the maintenance of an army are questions susceptible of no sudden solution, and omissions due to lack of prevision or preparation can rarely be made good. With all its imperfections, then, the Convention that had been concluded with the Italians was of substantial value and, in view of the circumstances existing at the time at which it was made, was remarkable for what it provided rather than for what it failed to provide.

The positive results may now be recorded. On the 24th of October, 1917, the enemy surprised the Italians at Caporetto and, during the course of the next few days, effected a complete break through. The Italian Second Army was almost wholly destroyed, over 270,000 prisoners and 1800 guns being captured. It was a disaster of the first magnitude and such as made it seem likely that Italy could no longer continue in the war. Steps were at once taken to render her assistance. The French troops moved first and were followed and overlapped in their movement by the British. It is well to consider this movement, for it was in itself a brilliant operation of war. Carried out by the two railway lines going from France to Italy by Modane and Ventimiglia, of which the latter was mainly engaged by French troop trains, the British forces commenced their entrainment in northern France on the 6th of November. By the 30th of November the headquarters of the Eleventh and Fourteenth Army Corps with Corps troops and four complete divisions, a total approximating to 80,000 men, had been detrained in Venetia. The 5th Division was held up by events in the Cambrai sector and did not complete its arrival until the 21st of December. The total distance averaged between 1100 and 1200 miles. As the French sent six divisions, the Italians found themselves in the happy position of being supported within a month from the commencement of their misfortunes by a fresh Allied army of nearly 200,000 men concentrated and ready to fight. As far as the British forces were concerned, the Italians played their part by rationing those forces up to the 4th of December, while the five hundred lorries promised were handed over with their drivers on the 23rd of November. In view of all these facts it is singular to find the opinion expressed by Brig.-General W. S. Swabey, who went to Italy as Director of Supplies, that "as far as administrative arrangements were concerned the previous convention made with the Italians might almost as well not have existed ".* Brig.-General Swabey arrived in Italy on the 20th of November and he found the army being rationed until he could get his supply system in order. Supply trains were already beginning to come to the base selected at Arquata, though some confusion existed, owing chiefly to shortage of *personnel*. It said much for the energy of the Director of Supplies that the service began to operate normally on the 4th of December and, indeed, both in that capacity and in his subsequent one of Director of Supplies and Transport, Brig.-General Swabey was conspicuously successful—so successful indeed that it is hard to understand why later he deemed it expedient to over-emphasise the difficulties of his situation. Moreover the British mechanical transport formations, which had come by march route, had begun arriving in Italy on the 15th of November. These units commenced their move from France on the 31st of October, the journey via Amiens–Meaux–Dijon–Lyons–Avignon–Nice–Savona or Genoa to Cremona and Camposampiero, averaging some 1100 miles, and they accomplished it practically without the loss of a vehicle, the daily mileage approximating to seventy. Rations, petrol, oil, grease, tyres and spares were carried and interpreters and medical officers were provided with the convoys.

On the arrival in Italy, in the early days of November, of the Headquarters of the British Fourteenth Army Corps, the situation was still obscure. It had been hoped that the Italian armies would have been able to have stood on the line of the River Tagliamento, but events made it clear that it was doubtful whether they would be able to stabilise their front even on the River Piave,

---

* "Royal Army Service Corps work in Italy." By Colonel W. S. Swabey, C.B., C.M.G., C.B.E. From the *Royal Army Service Corps Quarterly*, April 1921.

some thirty miles in rear of the former. The enemy, too, were threatening an attack from the direction of Asiago, on the Northern Front, and, had this succeeded, the bulk of the Italians would have found themselves hemmed in between the mountains and the sea, with results which scarcely bear contemplation. In this uncertainty it was obviously impossible to risk a forward concentration of the reinforcements arriving from the French theatre, and the decision was accordingly taken that the British troops would be detrained and assembled in the neighbourhood of Pavia, about twenty miles south of Milano; and at that town the Fourteenth Army Corps Headquarters established itself, making preparations for the reception of its divisions. While, however, the latter were in passage, matters took a turn for the better. It became evident that the impetus of the Austro-German thrust had spent itself, and that the enemy had, in his rapid advance, outrun his supplies and munitions. The Italians, too, were holding obstinately on their Northern Front. It was, therefore, determined to detrain the British on the line Cremona–Mantova–Montagnana for a concentration around and eastwards of the last-named town, which area in fact was largely covered in that reconnoitred by the British mission six months previously. From there the troops moved north towards the Piave, the Fourteenth Army Corps going into line on the Montello on the 4th of December. General Plumer arrived and took over command of the two British Corps on the 6th of December, establishing his headquarters at Padova.

During the period spent on the Montello the services of maintenance call for little comment. With an efficient railway system and admirable roads, no unusual difficulties presented themselves. Railheads were well forward, two and a half of the five divisions drawing their supplies thence direct by their horsed trains without interposing mechanical transport. In order that the troops should get fresh bread, the base being somewhat

THE BRITISH ARMY IN ITALY

distant, field bakeries were established near railheads, use being made of silkworm establishments which proved very adaptable for this purpose. On the lines of communication transport work was carried out by auxiliary horse transport companies assisted by small detachments of mechanical transport.

No serious fighting took place and services were generally normal throughout.

At the beginning of March General Plumer and the Eleventh Army Corps returned to France. The situation on the Italian Front had been stabilised, and this Corps and the Army Commander were required in the main theatre where the Germans were known to have an important enterprise in preparation. The British army in Italy, under the command of General Lord Cavan, then consisted of the 7th, 23rd and 48th Divisions. As far as the Army Service Corps were concerned one effect of these changes was to amalgamate the Directorates of Supplies and Transport, which had previously been separate, and Brig.-General W. S. Swabey, who had up to then held the appointment of Director of Supplies, was vested with both responsibilities.

A more active period now commenced, for, in the middle of March, the British troops were moved to the Asiago plateau on the Northern Front, where they were to gain some experience of mountain warfare. The principal reason for this move was that with the disappearance of the snows the Austrians were considered likely to undertake an offensive in this direction, where a success promised great strategical results. For the first time in its history the Army Service Corps carried out its functions in the Alps, and needed to adapt its organisation to conditions wholly new to it.

The British mountain front was divided into two divisional sectors and the supply system in each differed, inasmuch as the left sector had a rack and pinion railway and the right sector nothing but road. For the former the railhead was Chiuppano at the foot of the mountains, which locality was in view of the enemy and occasionally shelled. Owing to shortage of water on the top of the plateau, the minimum amount of transport was allowed, and this consisted only of limbered general service wagons and pack mules from the divisional train and the first line transport of the fighting units. The former worked between Campiello, a station some two-thirds up the rack and pinion railway between Rochette and Asiago, and the then existing terminus of the line. For the stage between Rochette and Chiuppano supplies were carried by the ordinary railway, but since it was only possible to work this sector by night a transfer of loads took place at Chiuppano at dusk. As it was Rochette, being under searchlight observation by night, was frequently shelled. At times it was found necessary owing to shortage of trucks on the rack and pinion railway to use what was known as the Teleferica, or wire rope carrying cradles, which was extensively employed by the Italians, but losses and frequent stoppages made this unsatisfactory for supplies, though it was continued to be used for ammunition.

For the right sector the railhead was Villaverla, a distance of six miles to Fara, where the mountains began. The divisional trains proper only worked as far as Fara and there the first line transport of units, considerably supplemented, took up the loads as far as Granezza at the top of the plateau and some fourteen miles from Fara, the rise in that distance being some 3600 feet; in a straight line it was only eight and a half miles, the bends being thus responsible for five and a half. Since the journey from railhead to Granezza was twenty miles, it was impossible for it to be accomplished by a single echelon of animal transport. To meet this situation No. 2 Auxiliary Horse Transport Company from the lines of communication was converted into a pack mule company, the mules being obtained from the divisional ammunition columns. These animals were too large for the type of work required, but eventually were adapted to it satisfactorily, Major Wheater, A.S.C., being mainly responsible. The unit was equipped with limbered general service wagons and an attempt was made to adopt the Italian method of harnessing mules with their pack saddlery straight into these vehicles, but the British type of the latter was too heavy and clumsy to make it suitable. From Fara onwards to Granezza the system was worked by placing the first line transport of units and Army Service Corps pack transport under the orders of the Officer Commanding the divisional train, who divided it into two echelons—one of which worked the stage between Fara and Schiessere, a mountain village where it was possible to obtain water for the animals, and the other from Schiessere to the destination at Granezza. The limbered general service wagons conveying the supplies were exchanged at Schiessere, the second echelon hooking in to the full wagons brought up by the first, while the latter returned with the empty wagons brought down.

The normal general service wagons were unsuitable for this service owing to their short lock, but, provided that half loads of fifteen hundredweight only were carried, they could be used in small convoys. Indeed a daily service of six such vehicles was arranged for the carriage of canteen stores and miscellaneous articles needed for the comfort of the troops.

The Italian authorities also maintained a carrier service up to the mountains from Calvene, about four miles north of Fara, and this service was placed at the disposal of the British troops. It consisted partially of pack transport (one section) and partially of carts (three sections), the latter being designed for mountain work, for which they proved most efficient. The assistance given was of great value, especially during the Austrian offensive in June when the rack and pinion railway was damaged. As illustrating the completeness with which the whole transport service was organised, mention may be made of the express parcels' delivery service which was maintained by two Fiat lorries running daily on a circular route from parcel depots formed on the plains. Throughout, the zigzag roads up the mountains—the British army had the use of two—were kept in excellent condition.

A reserve of supplies amounting to 40,000 preserved rations and 10,000 animal rations was stored at Granezza.

On the Asiago front, as elsewhere, the situation remained comparatively quiet until the middle of June. On the 15th of that month the Austrians opened an offensive which was developed from the River Astico to the sea—a distance of some seventy-five miles. Although the greatest concentration—sixteen and a half divisions were employed—was made against the Franco-British troops in the mountains, the attack was pressed vigorously along the Piave and the enemy succeeded in establishing himself on the right bank and below the Montello. From here, however, he was unable to progress and, under pressure of heavy counter-attacks by the Italians, was thrown back across the river after a week's heavy fighting.

This battle was destined to break for good and all the Austrian power of offensive. Four months later was staged the dying struggle of the Dual Monarchy. The Italian plan contemplated an attack on a grand scale on the Piave, in which the British 7th and 23rd Divisions were to take part in the Tenth Italian Army, which was placed under Lord Cavan. The 48th Division remained in the Asiago zone, where during the subsequent operations the transport work was abnormal and therefore calls for some description. On the night of the 23rd–24th of October the Austrian positions at Ave were stormed and the British troops, advancing rapidly up the Val D'Assa, occupied Levico, twenty-five miles north, on the 3rd of November, capturing over 20,000 prisoners.

Trent fell on the same day. So far as the transport and supply services were concerned this advance could scarcely have taken place at a more inopportune moment, for the 48th Division was expecting to be withdrawn from the plateau, and had therefore used up its forward dumps of supplies; while by an unfortunate mischance a supply train elected to lose itself on the railway. The troops were therefore compelled to consume one of their two days' reserves. The division was occupying the right sector, to which reference has already been made, and on the 1st of November, when it became clear that the advance was going forward, orders were issued for the second echelon of transport, which up to that time had been working between Fara and Granezza, to move up to the latter place; and for supplies to be put there direct from railhead at Villa Verla by means of three-ton lorries. Thus the horsed general service wagons of the divisional train were eliminated. It had always been anticipated that this would happen in the event of an advance across the Asiago plateau, as heavy draught horses could not be employed on the steep mountain roads; and preparations had been made accordingly. Fifty light Fiat lorries, obtained from the Italians, were concentrated at Granezza to work the next stage forward to the animal transport with the troops, but as this was continually moving further away, the task of supply became more and more exacting. After three stages of the advance these lorries were carrying supplies fifteen miles from Granezza—a total distance of thirty-five miles from railhead. From there onwards large quantities of Austrian forage were found, which served to reduce the amount required to be brought up. Twenty-seven lorries therefore sufficed for supplies forward which were taken over a further forty miles, or seventy-five miles from railhead. These lorries, with the exception of four placed at the disposal of the troops, proceeded as far as Caldonazzo, about eight miles south-east of Trent, and thus acting in place of the Divisional Train were actually delivering their loads fifty-five miles from refilling point at Granezza. It is difficult to praise too highly the work accomplished by these vehicles which did the last stage of the journey over the narrow and winding mountain road with its fifteen hairpin bends, where the least mistake spelt death; and the skill and spirit shown by the Italian drivers deserves to be put on record.

During the whole period of the advance and until all troops had been withdrawn from the plateau, there were only two days on which they had to subsist on preserved rations. On all others fresh rations, including green vegetables, were forthcoming. In this connection mention should be made of the divisional supply column which was responsible for the transport from railhead to Granezza. Owing to the gradients it was thought at first to be impossible for three-ton lorries to accomplish this, but officers and men worked night and day to keep their vehicles in order. All these operations were much facilitated by the fine weather which prevailed.

While these events were in progress in the mountain region, the battle went with equal success on the Piave front. The British divisions crossing the river occupied the northern half of the island of Grave Di Papadopoli on the night of the 23rd–24th of October. A week later the Austrian resistance was broken and the British were on the Livenza, twenty miles away; they were up to the River Tagliamento by the 3rd of November, by which time over 300,000 prisoners and 5000 guns had been taken. The Austrian debacle was complete and the Armistice came into force on the 4th of November.

In the course of these operations the troops were maintained from one railhead, successively located at Bivio, Motta and Treviso, as the advance went forward. The outstanding feature of the system was the employment of multiple echelons of horse and mechanical transport linking up the railhead with the advancing troops as far as the River Tagliamento. Owing to the possibility of the Piave rising in the rear and the comparatively long distances to be covered, large reserves of supplies were brought forward and dumped east of the river; and it was only on one day—the 26th of October—that reserve rations had to be issued. This was due to the non-arrival of a supply train owing to railway congestion. On the 31st of October a scheme, which had already been arranged, of interposing an additional link in the shape of an echelon of Fiat lorries between divisional trains and regimental first line transport was carried into effect; and divisional trains were employed in building up large dumps as reserves, in addition to their function of delivering to the Fiat lorry echelon. It was not until the 3rd of November that loaded mechanical vehicles could cross the bridges over the Piave, and directly this became possible the divisional trains were sent forward. Supplies were then drawn from railhead by the three-ton lorries of the divisional supply column to bridgeheads, where they were transferred to the Fiats which worked forwards in two echelons, delivering either to divisional trains in the normal way, or direct to the first line transport of units as circumstances allowed. There were, thus, in some instances, three echelons of mechanical and one of horse transport between railhead and the regimental vehicles, but the system worked well on the whole, although delays at times were unavoidable. After the Armistice, when the British troops were withdrawn, the normal system was gradually resumed.

Army Service Corps activities during the great battle, known to history as Vittorio Veneto, merit attention in that they furnish a profitable example of the methods adopted to meet the conditions of a general pursuit subsequent to a break through, involving as it did rapid transition from static to mobile warfare. Such test is second only to that of a prolonged war of manœuvre for the efficiency of the transport and supply services, at any rate in so far as a campaign in a civilised country is concerned. In this instance it cannot be claimed that those services were mightily tried. To the superficial view, indeed, the troops were fed with ease and regularity. Yet such appearance is in itself the highest tribute to their maintenance services; for in a sense it is no exaggeration to say that, inasmuch as these carry out their functions without semblance of strain or difficulty, they are efficient in the most comprehensive meaning of the word. Since armies can no longer be provisioned as Moses fed the children of Israel in the wilderness, chance or good fortune are not elements which can be taken into account. Preparation and foresight are the dominant factors in success, and it is just because these operate quietly and unostentatiously that they are normally apt to be overlooked. Few would have supposed that the progress of the Allied offensive would have been so rapid: that the maintenance services were able to keep pace with it was due to the fact that they had been organised not only for probabilities, but also in order to adapt themselves to contingencies as they arose.

From a bare account of the British campaign in Italy it would seem that no great rôle was played by the mechanical transport branch. And, in truth, this branch was never so prominent as it was, for instance, in Mesopotamia or even in the final phase in Palestine and Syria. Nevertheless its toil was constant and arduous. As was usual at that critical stage of the war *personnel* difficulties were experienced, and reinforcements of drivers required considerable training before they could be trusted on the mountain roads or even in some cases on any roads whatsoever. For this purpose a school of instruction was established where the driving of all types of vehicles in use was taught; nearly a thousand men passed through between its opening in April and its closing in November. The provision of artificers was also a problem, which was solved, in so far as it was capable of solution, by attaching two unskilled or semi-skilled men to one of superior attainments.

During the change of front from the Montello to Asiago in March, heavy demands were made on the mechanical transport. The Fiat lorries were fully employed in building up reserve dumps of supplies, ammunition, Royal Engineer and Ordnance stores on the plateau under the most unpleasant conditions, due to ice and snow and long hours on the steep roads. Three-ton lorries were not then allowed on those roads—though they operated, as has been shown, in the final phase as far as Granezza—and with the small capacity of the Fiat lorry and large expenditure of ammunition the supply entailed for many months a great strain on men and vehicles. As in other theatres, the Army Service Corps was responsible for the transport of the heavy artillery and also for providing a mechanical transport workshop for the anti-aircraft batteries. The Holt caterpillars for the eight-inch siege battery only arrived early in October 1918, but they did useful work in moving the howitzers into position on the Piave front. For the rest, considerable difficulty was experienced in moving guns on the narrow winding roads with their deep ditches on each side, which were found especially on the Montello front. The British four-wheel drive lorries were, in fact, unsuitable except when worked in tandem; and recourse was therefore had to the Fiat and Pavesi Tolotti tractors, which were obtained from the Italians and which did very well: six of the latter type were exchanged for nine of the British four-wheel drive lorries. Of interest also was the work of the Corps pontoon park, which was not strictly limited to its proper functions. During March, for instance, its four-wheel drive vehicles were used to convey sixty-six 18-pounder guns and twenty-four 4·5-inch howitzers from the plains to their battery positions on the Asiago plateau, these moves being carried out at night and without lights over the difficult roads already described. One gun was placed inside each lorry, the superstructure having been removed and one gun hitched on behind. Early in April twenty vehicles belonging to this unit were fitted with three hundred gallon water tanks for supplying troops on the plateau, while, in the final phase, when the pontoons had been put into bridge for the crossing of the Piave, the vehicles of the pontoon park were employed night and day under enemy shell fire in carrying footbridges, fascines, and boats to bridgeheads. Among the other mechanical transport formations the heavy repair shop may be mentioned as exemplifying some very special difficulties with which the transport administration was forced to contend. The British force arrived in Italy with a heterogeneous collection of vehicles, which had already seen so much service in France that provision for their repair was obviously beyond the capacity of the fully burdened field workshops. Accordingly the workshops with their *personnel* were in December 1917 withdrawn from two headquarter mechanical transport companies and formed into what was known as the G.H.Q. (Mobile) Heavy Repair Shop. The nucleus thus created was first accommodated in the cavalry barracks at Padova, but the enemy started to bomb this town so heavily that under pressure from the Italians the unit was ordered to leave. It moved to a spot five miles out on the road to Venice and was housed in a locomotive works, where, assisted by some thirty Italian civilian mechanics specially enrolled, it made great progress. The British forces were then ordered to the Asiago front and the repair shop packed up for removal to the new area. At this point General Headquarters stepped in. It was not considered that the military situation at that time warranted location in a forward area, so instructions were given for a site to be found south of Milano. This entailed a search over a wide stretch of country until a sufficiently suitable place was eventually found in a disused factory at Pavia.

During these wanderings this improvised unit had been attempting to deal with tasks that were far beyond its capacity and, in reply to representations to the War Office, the *personnel* of a heavy repair shop proper was sent out at the end of May, the necessary stores following shortly afterwards. From July onwards the situation assumed a different complexion and the output in repairs commenced to bear some relation to needs.*

In certain other respects the administration of the maintenance services in Italy was hampered in that the eleven months spent by the British army in that country were those of the greatest pressure and activity in the main theatre in France. The force in Italy was small and the danger there less imminent. It was, therefore, only to be expected that the principal front should have had first call on resources which, as far as man power was concerned, were beginning to become somewhat thin.

It may now be convenient to give some account of the organisation of the Base Supply Depot at Arquata. At the beginning of operations matters were somewhat embarrassed by the praiseworthy zealousness on the part of the Supply Directorate and the Transportation Staff in France, these authorities acting with such promptitude that at one time in the early stages more than five hundred trucks were at Arquata station awaiting discharge. These had, naturally, to be dealt with in a rough and ready manner, with the result that heavy losses were incurred; for, to free the congested sidings, trucks had to be off loaded anywhere and everywhere into the snow without being tallied. Further drawbacks lay in the comparative inexperience of the *personnel* hurriedly sent

*	British lorries	Italian lorries	Motor cars	Box cars	Ambulances
Average number of M.T. vehicles in Italy with British force	827	494	332	128	247
Total casualties Dec. 1917–Nov. 1918	41	55	97	23	17

from France, the necessity of night work to meet railway requirements, and very cold weather. But the task of evolving order was resolutely faced and, within a few months, the depot was notable for the smoothness and regularity of its working. The *personnel* consisted, in addition to the headquarters, of one and a half lines of communication supply companies, two field butcheries and detachments from two field bakeries, a total of seventeen officers and four hundred and two other ranks, of which one officer and a hundred and thirty-six other ranks were on detachment at various out-stations. This number was exclusive of the labour employed purely on handling the supplies, which varied from a hundred to two hundred and fifty men daily, according to the amount of work to be done. The depot was commanded by a Lieut.-Colonel with a Major as his second in command, and was divided into the four groups of Groceries A and B, Forage and Petrol, each under an officer. There were also the appointments of Outside Superintendent, Officer in Charge of Stores, Officer in Charge of Detail Issue Store and a properly qualified accounting officer. The remaining officers were assistants or understudies to the above. Besides the requirements of the field troops, provision had to be made for a number of out-stations, including the British base at Taranto, on which latter drafts in transit for the East and Royal Flying Corps at Otranto depended, the Advanced Supply Depot at Mantova, and various small subsidiary establishments at Bordighera, Cremona, Pavia, Faenza and Voghera, where hospitals and remount depots were situated.

The sources of supply were even more varied. Groceries, petrol and oils came by rail from Rouen; oats, flour and preserved meat by sea to Genoa and thence by rail: hay and straw from France, where it was obtained by the Special Purchase Department; vegetables and fruit were bought through a similar channel in Italy. Through the Italian Government were also obtained certain quantities of forage and fresh vegetables. The frozen meat was sent up from Genoa, where it was kept in cold storage after discharge from ship.

The lay-out of the depot was executed as follows. The grocery hangars were four in number, each being divided into two blocks with railway lines running both inside and outside. Each block contained supplies of every ration and had a frontage of from two to three trucks, the number required for the groceries of a division: thus any long "carry" was avoided. A small carpenters' shop was installed in one of the main hangars for the repairing of any cases that were discharged from the trucks in a damaged condition, while two aeroplane hangars were made available, in addition to the other four, for the examination and re-packing of any defective supplies and as a temporary storage for reserves of perishable commodities. All stocks were built "pillar fashion" wherever the shape of packages allowed, in order to admit of easy and correct checking and a tally board was kept on every stack on which receipts and issues were recorded. The total covered space available was some 50,000 square feet. The forage was laid out in stacks averaging a hundred and seventy-five tons of hay or three hundred and fifty tons of oats each, built alternately of oats and hay to facilitate loading, a considerable distance being left between each stack to guard against any spread of fire. Dunnage to the height of nine inches of timber was laid under all stacks, which were also covered with tarpaulins. Three baling machines for dealing with the large quantity of loose hay resulting from the handling of the bales were in continuous use. For both grocery and forage sections a complete system of hydrants, together with numerous extinguishers and fire buckets, was installed.

Petrol, together with inflammable oils, was stacked in each of the four corners of the petrol depot, a large space being left between each petrol area on which non-inflammable oils and grease were stored. Shingle or brick platforms were provided for the stacks, and also covered accommodation for carbide and solidified paraffin with a special shed for the treatment of all cans and drums that were discovered to be leaking on receipt. The petrol depot was surrounded by a barbed wire fence and patrolled by guards, while a chemical fire engine and trucks of sand were kept at hand.

Coal was received in bulk by trucks, sufficient being placed in bags to make a wall, and the interior was filled with loose coal, which was then bagged as required. Curiously enough very little coal was used during the campaign—8000 tons sent from England lasting the whole time, and even being utilised towards helping the Italian railways through a crisis.

A small department was organised to deal with returned empties coming down from railheads. Petrol cans and cases were sorted out and packed into trucks for despatch to the main petrol depot at Rouen; sacks were sorted, dried and repaired by Italian hired female labour and, with empty rum jars, likewise sent to Rouen.

The system for the loading and despatch of supplies was very complete and calculated to avert any loss or discrepancies. Reconsignment of trucks was always followed where possible in the instances of forage, petrols and oils, but in all other instances scrupulous checks of contents loaded were carried out and the trucks completely sealed on their conclusion.

Scarcely any one of the numerous details that go to make the smooth and effective working of an organisation of this kind was overlooked or ignored.

The Italian authorities—General Modena of the Ministry of War especially—were helpful throughout. There was one particular time of stress during the German attack on the British Fifth Army in March 1918 when all supply trains from France ceased. The reserves in Italy consequently fell dangerously, and Italian assistance was invoked, among the principal commodities needed being petrol and cheese. It was somewhat embarrassing when the figure nought was added by the Italians to the British demand for the latter and ten times the amount asked for produced, for the British soldier was not partial to the local article.

In comparison with the mighty campaigns that were waged by the British Army in widely separated parts of the world during the Great War, the part played in Italy was a modest one. Yet only in comparison, for the British troops which were rushed to the assistance of their Allies in November 1917 were far more numerous than those of General Bonaparte when he descended on the plains of Lombardy for his famous campaign in 1796 or than those of Napoleon III when he led the Imperial Armies to Magenta and Solferino in 1859. At any other period their operations in Alpine fighting in June 1918 and in the passage of the River Piave in October would have attracted attention from students of military affairs. Twelve years after, however, there is still no complete authoritative account. The occasion too was historical in that for the first time British troops appeared on the principal battleground of Europe which lies in the plains of northern Italy and in the Alps, and which have over the centuries witnessed the coming and going of armies. There is, indeed, little similitude between the manner in which Bonaparte maintained his armies, which had avowedly come as liberators, and that in which the British Army, likewise come to the succour of the Italians, was maintained. But the campaign of 1859 furnishes some material for comparison in the wider sense, for Napoleon III made use of precisely the same lines of communication via the coastal road, and equal use of the port of Genoa as was made in 1917-18. In certain aspects experiences in Italy had a useful and salutary effect for the Army Service Corps. Administrative officers who had in France found themselves small cogs in a vast

THE BRITISH ARMY IN ITALY

machine, which, highly organised and perfected, with unlimited resources at its disposal and near its bases of supply, operated so surely and inexorably under static conditions that many of the duties in connection with it became merely matters of routine, found themselves suddenly required to improvise and adapt for a widely differing set of circumstances. Those circumstances could not be compared in their difficulties to those obtaining in other fields, but they furnished variations from which valuable lessons were gathered. There was never any doubt as to the capacity of the transport and supply services to fulfil all that was required of them in Italy. They were scientifically organised, and the spirit of all ranks was all that could be desired throughout. Whenever special efforts had to be made the response was cheerful and immediate. Relations with the Italians, too, were excellent. At the time of the Armistice the Army Service Corps *personnel*, exclusive of officers serving on the Staff and the *personnel* at the Taranto base, numbered 275 officers and 7290 other ranks, of which the far greater proportion belonged to the New Armies.* At that time the ration strength of the army was 97,822 men and 20,482 animals.

* The distribution of *personnel* was as follows:

Mechanical transport		Horse transport		Supply	
Officers	Other ranks	Officers	Other ranks	Officers	Other ranks
140	4180	95	2120	40	990

BIBLIOGRAPHY

The Battle of the Piave (15th–23rd June, 1918). Issued by the Supreme Command of the Italian Army.

The History of the 23rd Division. By Lieut.-Colonel H. R. SANDILANDS, C.M.G., D.S.O.

"An Operation of War." By Lieut.-Colonel R. H. BEADON, C.B.E., p.s.c. From the *Army Quarterly*, January 1925.

"Supply Systems in the Alps." By Lieut.-Colonel A. H. ROBERTS, D.S.O., O.B.E. From the *Royal Army Service Corps Quarterly*, January 1920.

"Base Supply Depot. Italy." By Lieut.-Colonel C. ROWE, C.B.E., R.A.S.C. From the *Royal Army Service Corps Quarterly*, July 1920.

"Royal Army Service Corps Work in Italy." By Colonel W. S. SWABEY, C.B., C.M.G., C.B.E. From the *Royal Army Service Corps Quarterly*, April 1921.

"From Vimy Ridge to Asiago." By Major C. T. BOYD, O.B.E., R.A.S.C. From the *Royal Army Service Corps Quarterly*, April 1921.

"Working of Mechanical Transport in Italy." By Colonel W. S. SWABEY, C.B., C.M.G., C.B.E. From the *Royal Army Service Corps Quarterly*, July 1921.

General Report on the Transport Services with the British Forces in Italy, November 1917–November 1918. Compiled by the Supply and Transport Directorate, Italian Expeditionary Force.

CHAPTER XII

NORTH RUSSIA

ALTHOUGH from a military point of view the operations which were undertaken by British forces in North Russia in 1918–19 were of little importance, either as regards the numbers engaged or in their ultimate results, they nevertheless deserve attention in that they exemplified conditions which differed widely from those obtaining elsewhere, and therefore furnished experiences which were unusual and peculiar.

Two distinct forces were involved. There was firstly the Murmansk Expedition, the object of which was to prevent the Kola inlet from becoming a German submarine base after the defection of Russia. The Germans were then in possession of the Gulf of Finland, and it was therefore possible for them to send submarines by canal and rail to Kola and to operate against the northern route between the United Kingdom and America, especially since Kola is the only port in North Russia which is free from ice and therefore open to navigation the whole year round. This circumstance is due to the action of the Gulf Stream, which shortly afterwards loses its power in the waters of the Arctic. Kola is, too, practically on the Norwegian frontier and, therefore, no port further west was available. At the head of the Kola inlet and about twenty miles from the open sea lies Murmansk. Prior to 1914 it had been the intention to make this place the port of North Russia, but no steps were taken until the war, when a single-line railway was built running due south, and meeting the main system near Petrograd. This line was originally started by a firm of Canadian contractors, but they were compelled to give it up, owing to their employees declining to live in so inhospitable a climate, and the railway was completed by Austrian prisoners of war, although on the arrival of the British the line was still unballasted. About six miles from where the Kola inlet ends was the village of that name. Though only consisting of some twenty houses it was from its position a place of some importance, although before the construction of the railway the only means of communicating with it was from the sea. There was no cultivation and, therefore, no local produce: the general vegetation was in fact scrub and silver birch, and the inhabitants lived by fishing.

The British force, despatched to Murmansk in June 1918, consisted of one battalion of marines and one company of machine gunners, supported by two old battleships. The object was to hold the inlet from an attack by land. The force ultimately destined for Archangel was, a few days afterwards, also disembarked in the same desolate region, and comprised a military mission consisting of a headquarter and instructional staff from each branch of the service, some 250 officers and other ranks with a handful of marines and machine gunners and a detachment of Allied troops under the command of General Poole. The Army Service Corps included a small directorate and three depot units of supply with other details. The rôle of this nucleus organisation was to raise a new Russian army from elements still loyal to the cause of the Allies, and thus to prevent the Germans from entirely denuding their eastern front in favour of the western theatre. There was also a quantity of stores and supplies accumulated at Archangel, which it was desirable to deny to the enemy.

The Archangel force remained at Murmansk until the end of July, firstly because the ice had not cleared away from the entrance to the White Sea, and secondly because a counter-revolution, which was in process of being organised, had not come to a head; and on arrival at Archangel it was found that it had not taken place at all. The town was in possession of the Bolsheviks, and it needed a few shells from H.M.S. *Attentive* to make them withdraw. The British warship proceeded some four miles up the river and anchored off Baharitzar, where a dockyard capable of berthing twenty-eight large steamers had been constructed. This port was on the opposite side of the river from Archangel and on the same side as the railway. Archangel itself was a prosperous town of some 45,000 inhabitants, and exported large quantities of timber, flax and pitch, in addition to maintaining a considerable fishing industry. Previous to the war it was served by a narrow-gauge railway which ran due south to the main line at Vologda, but this had since been converted to standard gauge.

The general idea for the Allied forces was to secure the triangle Archangel–Viatka–Vologda, the latter on the Trans-Siberian Railway, and to use this as the recruiting area for the new Russian armies which it was intended to raise, and had this project been practicable the whole nature of the expedition, from the point of view of maintenance, would have been changed. It was originally assumed that the troops would be able to exist on local resources and would need but few supplies from home for, on arriving at Vologda, forest land is left behind and rich arable country is reached. When it became clear that this optimistic plan could not be realised, supplies had to be rushed from home before the force was frozen in for the winter. From supply aspects, too, the initial phase of the campaign was characterised by some confusion between the *Elope*, or Archangel, detachment and the *Syren*, or Murmansk, detachment, owing to uncertainty as to when the former would be able to proceed to its destination. The supply *personnel* was inadequate in numbers to deal with the work of discharge, handling, storing and despatch of the cargoes which began to arrive, especially as it was required to be scattered over a wide area, as the troops advanced and occupied new localities. The work performed was stupendous. Barges had to be loaded direct from steamers for Archangel and up river, trans-loaded for troops operating from the railway and a Base Supply Depot created. Detail issue stores were required at Archangel and Baharitzar and supply *personnel* for the forces in the field.

No transport *personnel* were sent in the first place, and the only courses open were therefore to pool all available first line transport of fighting units and place it under the control of the Army Service Corps, and to acquire such local transport as was possible. The latter was scarce and unsatisfactory, since the Russian has little idea of time or urgency, while discipline and control were difficult.

Such were the conditions under which the two expeditions were launched. We may deal firstly with the *Syren*, or Murmansk, force under General Maynard. From the transport and supply standpoint, much that will be dealt with under this portion equally applies to the conditions at Archangel and will therefore not be repeated under the heading of the latter. The object will be to outline the operations in so far as they were directly affected in the maintenance sense, and to relate such activities of the Army Service Corps as are of interest.

During the first few weeks after the landing in the Kola inlet, Kola itself, Kandalasha, and Kem, along the railway line, and Petchenga, along the coast, were occupied, thereby embracing an area of four hundred miles in length and stretching from the White Sea to the frontiers of Finland, from which dispersion it will be appreciated how difficult was the problem of maintenance.

It was fortunately possible to obtain accommodation for the Base Supply Depot adjacent to the quay at Murmansk where, although the space was limited, there were the advantages to be derived by direct railway communication with the south. Steps were immediately taken to improve this site by the construction of additional sidings and buildings and the provision of underground sheds for spirits, oils and such fresh meat as it was necessary to keep in store, the normal requirements of this latter commodity being obtained weekly from the S.S. *Nigeria*, which acted as cold storage ship for the army and navy alike.

One of the features of the expedition was the policy as regards obligations towards the civilian population, which numbered, as far as could then be ascertained, some 40,000 to 50,000 within the area originally occupied. There was little food to be obtained locally and, as the life of the force and the successful prosecution of the campaign depended upon the good will of the inhabitants, it was decided that supplies should be issued from Army stocks in such quantities as could be spared. This was handed over in bulk to the representative of the local Co-operative—the form of administration in existence—although grave doubts always remained as to whether all or indeed any considerable portion actually reached the mouths of those for whom it was intended.

On the 28th of September, 1918, a Supply and Transport Directorate was formed with Lieut.-Colonel T. C. R. Moore, A.S.C., at its head, and endeavours were made to put these services on a proper basis. Measures were taken to form transport detachments at each station, the animals being obtained locally on the agreement to feed the animals so taken over and to furnish one complete forage ration in lieu of each animal hired to enable the owner to feed his remaining animals. This system worked very well as, in addition to being cheaper than a cash payment, it enabled the local ponies to be maintained in a fit condition should more be required. Steps were also taken to equip the mobile columns with which it was proposed to operate during the winter

NORTH RUSSIA

months, and with this aim a Horse Purchasing Commission was formed, consisting of Captain Brocklehurst of the 10th Hussars in charge, an Army Service Corps transport officer and a veterinary officer. This commission proceeded south in the endeavour to acquire five hundred animals by the bartering of foodstuffs, the cost of which was assessed at local rates. On this basis, the cost of a pony worked out at ten pounds instead of fifty pounds, which would have been the price in roubles. One hundred and sixty animals were thus obtained, the balance needed being later sent from the United Kingdom, and those purchased were satisfactory in every respect, standing the winter perfectly: wastage was practically nil. The transport situation was somewhat relieved in October by the arrival of No. 1123 Army Service Corps Horse Transport Company, which unit was largely instrumental in clearing and distributing the large amount of stores which were then arriving. The question of the feeding of the civilian population had, at that time, become an increasingly serious problem, for the method adopted was not working satisfactorily. Intermittent strikes occurred on the railway and in the public departments concerned with the local administration, thereby hampering military operations and indeed placing the occupying forces in jeopardy, as with a single line and between three and four hundred miles of communications any interference with the railway led to dangerous results, no funds being then available to pay the labour employed. A scheme was evolved for provisioning the entire native population which, by this time, was ascertained to be approximately 100,000 of all kinds and, approval having been given, the Foreign Office sent out a small staff to assist the military authorities with this work, for which special food ships were despatched to Murmansk. As might have been expected from these measures, relations with the natives were thenceforth on a more amicable basis.

With the advent of the Arctic winter the necessity arose of transferring from summer to winter transport, which involved numbers of sleighs far in excess of the quantity of wheeled vehicles up to then found sufficient. To meet this situation Canadian pony sleighs were demanded from the United Kingdom and, pending their arrival, a small factory was established to turn out the local article. This, staffed by Karelian workmen under Army Service Corps supervision, was so successful that by the early part of December sufficient vehicles had been built to meet all current demands. The arrival of the Canadian sleighs and the special harness required shortly afterwards put an end to all anxiety in this direction.

During January it was decided to establish connection with the *Elope*, or Archangel, force by overland route through Soroka, Nukta and Onega, this course being considered necessary owing to the intermittent and hazardous service by ice breakers in the White Sea. The organisation of this communication was undertaken and controlled by the Army Service Corps and, during the ensuing three months, proved the safest and speediest method of contact with Archangel. Convoys of three to four hundred pony sleighs were collected from the villages and, during the course of the operations, something like fifteen hundred troops and four hundred tons of supplies and stores were conveyed by this route of three hundred miles. There was every reason to be proud of this feat, for which the tireless energy and initiative of Captain Franklin, A.S.C., were largely responsible, for difficulties were overcome which might well have daunted the most capable and experienced transport officer. Sleighs had, in the first place, to be collected from localities as far as a hundred miles apart, and then organised in sufficient detail to enable successful administration to be maintained and all costs and charges accurately computed. During the practically untried conditions of an Arctic winter there were naturally difficulties arising in connection with the storage and handling of supplies, particularly those of a perishable nature, but taking all the circumstances into account the losses through lack of proper accommodation or previous experience on the part of the Army Service Corps were very small, the only one of any consequence occurring in connection with the frozen meat supplies received from England in cold storage ships, and these occurred through the failure of the local Russian ice houses to withstand the sudden and severe thaw which came in April. According to local opinion these houses had been used with success during the previous spring and summer but, partly owing to structural defects and partly owing to the fact that green timber had been used which had been shrunk by the summer heat, they were a distinct failure, and certain quantities of meat which had been stored ashore deteriorated so as to be unfit for use. Some trouble was also experienced in connection with the provision of forage for the animals. In conformity with a practice not unknown in more sophisticated portions of the world, a ring of contractors was formed to corner all the local produce and inflate the prices. This was met by persuading the Russian Governor to publish a decree forbidding the sale of forage to anyone but the General Officer Commanding the Allied troops or on a certificate of release from the Supply Directorate. As a *quid pro quo*, the needs of the civil administration were met from Army stocks on repayment, little further trouble was subsequently experienced, prices being fixed at normal rates.

With the advent of the spring, it became evident that some expansion of the animal transport would be advisable in order to form a safeguard against the possible breakdown of the single line of railway, on which the scattered detachments of the army depended. Such a breakdown was, in the opinion of experts, likely as soon as the ice and snow melted, and damage to the bridges and the permanent way ensued, and it was accordingly decided to inaugurate a reindeer transport service which would serve the dual purpose of maintaining outposts, otherwise inaccessible, and take the place of the railway if necessary. On the 23rd of January, 1919, this organisation was duly established under the Army Service Corps, Captain Squarey being placed in command. Approximately 2000 reindeer, 500 sleighs and 1000 Laplanders—the latter being the only drivers acquainted with this form of transport—were employed, all being duly attested, armed and clothed. For three months this service operated with complete success, covering routes which extended over an area of a hundred and forty miles to the south and a hundred and sixteen miles to the west. Generally the staging system was adopted, four halts being established, each under the control of a serjeant, the trail having perforce to follow the line of the moss beds. One feat carried out in March by this new form of transport deserves to be noticed, as it was probably unprecedented in the history of the British Army. This was the transfer of a mobile column, consisting of the 11th Royal Sussex Regiment, from Petchenga to Kola, a distance of a hundred and thirteen miles in sixty-six and a half hours, without a single casualty of any description in the column.

It is worthy of record that during the operations of the reindeer transport service not one ounce of Government property was lost, stolen or deficient, and this in spite of the fact that no guards of any sort were employed. The integrity and loyalty of the Laplanders were, indeed, beyond all praise.

By March the shortage of Army Service Corps *personnel* had become very acute, owing to the arrival of fresh troops during the winter, the extension of the British line and the large proportion of evacuations which had taken place among the *personnel* after the strain of the winter period had relaxed. Establishments had been submitted to the War Office during the previous month for the Army Service Corps units considered necessary for the force, and these were approved in their entirety and gradually came into being.* In the interim, however, the burden fell heavily on the inadequate numbers at duty. There was much sickness, especially among those on the overworked clerical and supply side, and consequently much of the accounting work had to go. But the conduct of all ranks under conditions extremely disheartening and, in the physical sense, among the hardest that were endured in the course of the World War, was worthy of the best traditions of their service. The twin branches of transport and supply pulled magnificently together, exemplifying as elsewhere in wider fields the strength which lay in their union. The supply of the troops was always maintained satisfactorily in spite of every obstacle. As a further measure of precaution against the breakdown of railway communications during the period of thaw, efforts were made to build up a two months' reserve of supplies at all stations on the lines of communication and one month's reserve with all units, but these intentions were interfered with by a fire which broke out at the Base Supply Depot early in April 1919, which destroyed a large quantity of supplies at a time when stocks were low. The War Office

* These consisted of:
    Base Supply Depot.
    Advanced Base Supply Depot.
    "M" Lines of Communication Supply Company.
    Nos. 1123 and 1160 Auxiliary Horse Transport Companies.
    Two Mobile Train Companies (one with Motor Machine Gun Section).
    Investigation Department.
    Remount Depot.
At a later date the above were augmented by:
    An Agricultural Company.
    A Horse Transport and Mechanical Transport School of Instruction.
    1 Mechanical Transport Company and 1 Base Mechanical Transport Depot.

met this news by instant action, for within a few days a ship with 5000 tons arrived as replacements. With the approach of the spring it was found necessary to take in hand the provision of extra wheeled transport, and accordingly a small factory was started by the Army Service Corps for the construction of local carts, while simultaneously an officer was sent down the line to acquire all the available wheels and axles in the district. These precautions were well justified, for the thaw came suddenly on the 18th of April and for some time the roads were impassable. By the time they were normal again, sufficient wheeled transport had been built to meet all demands, while in the intervals the scattered troops were maintained by their reserve of supplies, and thus the transition from winter to summer conditions was successfully accomplished. Nevertheless the advance and prolongation of the British line at this time put a severe strain on the Supply and Transport Directorate. Some difficulty was encountered in supplying the right column during an advance on Maselskaya and subsequently to Medvyejya Gora, owing to the fact that its troops moved at a distance varying between twenty-five and thirty miles from the railway line with no connecting tracks until Medvyejya Gora was reached on the 21st of May. Recourse had to be made to the comparatively unsatisfactory method of pack transport, despite the lack of saddles or military *personnel*. The work was pushed through with improvised saddlery, and convoys manned by local peasants were despatched day after day, so that an unbroken supply was ensured during the whole of the march. The efforts of Captain Johns, A.S.C., in this connection were of great value.

The difficulties in maintaining a Russian column under Colonel Krugliakoff on the left flank during this movement also presented a certain problem, as the supplies had to be transported as the advance proceeded from a forward sub-depot at Sumski Posad over a distance of one hundred miles. Impressed local transport was utilised with success until Medvyejya Gora was reached, when the loads were transferred to railhead at Siding 11 and thence conveyed via Lumbuhzi, by cart, and Lake Onega, by boat, to Povynets: detailed distribution to units was made by local transport as the column advanced. Subsequently railhead was transferred on the repair of the Medvyejya Gora bridge to Medvyejya Gora, when the entire journey onwards was performed by boat.

The period of rest, re-organisation and re-distribution of troops, which took place during the few weeks following the completion of this operation, was utilised, in so far as the Supply and Transport Directorate was concerned, towards the initiation of schemes for training Russian administrative *personnel* in order that they might be able to conduct the maintenance services after the Allied forces were withdrawn. Accordingly, schools of instruction both for horse and mechanical transport were formed and opened on the 15th of July at Medvyejya Gora and Povynets respectively, including officers, drivers and artificers in their syllabus of training. Approximately ten Russian officers and eighty other ranks passed through the horse transport and eight officers and forty other ranks through the mechanical transport with satisfactory results, which were quickly manifest when they returned to service with their own troops. As regards instruction in supply duties the method was adopted of attaching *personnel* to the British depots on the "opposite number" principle so that they might learn the theory and carry out the practice concurrently. On this side activities were somewhat delayed, owing to the difficulty in obtaining the necessary *personnel* from the Russian army, but when they did arrive they displayed unusual energy and interest in the instruction, quickly assimilated British principles, and as a result were able shortly afterwards to staff, under Army Service

Corps supervision and advice, the depots at Maselga, Popoff, and Murmansk itself.

While this period of instruction was in progress, it was still necessary to provide for certain movements which were taking place and make arrangements for further advances which were in contemplation, the plan being that the right or westerly column which joined up with the main body of the force at Medvyejya Gora on the 21st of May should again push out to the right flank with a view to co-operating with the centre column in an advance southwards along the railway. Two columns were to move on the left flank, one on to the Shunga Peninsula and the other, consisting of irregulars, on the east side of Lake Onega, the whole to concentrate on a fixed objective further south. To meet the varying needs of these columns the following system was adopted and, in spite of varying circumstances both tactical and strategical, it was successfully carried through up to the time the troops were withdrawn from the forward areas. The right column, moving by Ostretchye and Urozosero, was supplied by means of limbered wagons from Medvyejya Gora supplemented by forward dumps, each of these latter being equipped with a small transport detachment. When the troops reached Svyat Navalok on the 6th of July and a garrison was established at Tivdia, between Lakes Lijmozero and Pulozero, it was found possible to shorten their communication which, up to then, had involved a four to five days' journey by using a route from Kapaselga as railhead to Lijmozero by boat, approximately six miles; from thence to Tivdia by sleigh two miles through marshy country; from Tivdia to Lake Pulozero five miles, also by sleigh, across Lake Pulozero by boat four miles; and finally to Svyat Navalok two miles, the total journey of nineteen miles occupying with its changes just over twenty-four hours. This route remained in operation without a hitch up to the final evacuation of the British troops.

The centre column working along the railway and by the road running alongside was a comparatively simple problem, as the road was a moderately good one.

A supply railway train was organised, consisting of a mobile supply depot, bakery truck and the necessary rolling stock to convey mules, limbered wagons and *personnel*. This train followed the advancing troops, issuing rations and fresh bread, and furnishing the transport to convey them when the troops were at any distance from the railway. The working of this system was smooth throughout.

As regards the Shunga column and the irregular or partisan column operating on the eastern side of Lake Onega, these were maintained by the extensive use of inland water transport which was conducted by mechanical transport *personnel* of the Army Service Corps. The irregular column was fed by boat from Povynets, or other suitable points on the lake side, as the advance went forward, and the Shunga column likewise by boats from Medvyejya Gora to such localities on the peninsula as were most adjacent to the scene of operations. By the date of the evacuation in September 1919 the troops were being maintained on the line of the River Nurmis and the defences were handed over to General Skobeltsin's Russians.

A serious fire occurred at the supply depot at Kem on the 26th of June, which destroyed the whole of the reserve supplies for three months, and this misfortune would have rendered maintenance in the forward areas a matter of impossibility had it not been for the strenuous efforts made at the base depot at Murmansk, the result of which was that within thirty hours two supply trains loaded with complete rations arrived and saved the situation. This incident confirmed the wisdom of the precautionary measures which had been taken to a fixed reserve of supplies and petrol on floating craft. During the winter this had been kept on the schooner *Venera* which had been borrowed from the local Government for the purpose, but on the arrival of the inland water transport barges in the spring, four were taken over and stocked with reserve supplies of all commodities, thereby guaranteeing safety against fire or other unforeseen contingencies.

During the latter months of the campaign a successful attempt was made to vary the diet of the troops by the issue of locally grown fresh vegetables, seeds being obtained from England and a farm established at Lumbuhzi early in June. Although the sowing took place rather late the results were satisfactory, and quantities of cabbage, lettuce, peas, potatoes and mustard and cress were successfully grown and issued. Endeavours were also made to establish a fishery at Podujema on the Kem River, employing Karelian peasants for the work, but this was not a success as the season was a particularly poor one for fish. Among other enterprises, which should not pass unnoted, was the salvage department organised, in the absence of the special authority usually designated for this service, by the Supply and Transport Directorate. The first occasion on which this operated was in connection with the S.S. *Ariadne Christine*—a storeship torpedoed on her way to North Russia and towed into Murmansk. On her arrival in August all available stores which could be off-loaded and which had not suffered any damage were handed over to the departments concerned, while the balance of her cargo, consisting of lard, preserved meat and other commodities which were condemned as unfit for human consumption, was disposed of in a useful manner. The lard was issued to the railways as wagon grease and charged against the Russian account, and also to supply officers as food for sleigh dogs. The preserved meat was sold to the Russians as pig food or exchanged for fish or reindeer meat or issued to the dogs. Other articles were similarly disposed of, so that practically none of the cargo was a dead loss.

No special remount or veterinary services having been provided for the *Syren* force, the responsibility for both fell on the Army Service Corps, which found the whole of the *personnel* for the remount depot, and carried out both duties.

The messing of the troops was an early difficulty owing to the scanty numbers of trained cooks available, and here again the Corps were called upon to help. Four messing instructors were obtained from home and attached to the Supply Directorate, cookery schools then being established in the different areas occupied.

In a similar manner the Welfare Department, under the control of the Supply Directorate and with the valuable help of Captain Rawson of the Canadian forces, did much to maintain the morale and well-being of the troops by the organisation of recreation, sports and entertainments and the provision of gifts and comforts which were distributed right up to the forward areas.

All these additional duties were cheerfully and willingly shouldered, and yet even in conjunction with the normal supply and transport work, of which some account has been given, they scarcely represent more than an indication of what was actually accomplished. The meeting of urgent demands at sudden and unexpected hours, the marshalling, payment, feeding and disciplining of civilian transport drivers and boatmen, the collection of the boats for the river passages, pilferages and breakdowns in transport, and all the countless minor obstructions that comprise the daily round of transport and supply *personnel* under strange and adverse circumstances need to be detailed for a real appreciation of the work. The energy, foresight and initiative of Lieut.-Colonel Moore, who was vested with the chief responsibility at Murmansk, and the work of Major H. N. G. Watson at Archangel merit high commendation. As comparatively junior officers, their regimental ranks were those of captains, they showed, as junior Army Service Corps officers showed all over the world, that they were fully capable of undertaking responsibilities usually belonging to those far senior in rank and age. Indeed many onerous and delicate tasks achieved in various fields of activity during the war by the Corps fell on the younger officers —confirmation, if confirmation is in fact needed, of the soundness of their general training.

Reference to the Archangel force stopped with recording their landing in August and the creation of a base at Baharitzar, the Army Ordnance Corps taking the northern portion of the port and the Army Service Corps the southern. It was decided that the retreating Bolsheviks were to be followed down the railway and, in fact, two hours after arrival a train was got together and every available man sent in pursuit. As a result the enemy was driven some hundred and fifty miles down the line to a point just south of Obozerskaya station. There, having destroyed a succession of three bridges which crossed streams, he took up a position on the farther side, and, as no reinforcements were available, the only course open was to keep him under observation. During this southward movement to dislodge the enemy, Major C. L. B. Fraser of the Army Service Corps was captured, and had the unpleasant experience of spending a Russian winter in a Moscow prison, being released the following April.

The British flanking force was also unfortunate, as its attack having failed, it found itself cut off from its base by an enemy column, and was compelled to attempt a detour through the forest in order to regain the railway. This was only reached after ten days' wanderings, in the course of which three unfordable rivers had to be negotiated. As rations had given out on the fourth day, the condition of the men was shocking.

Since it was desirable to follow the retiring enemy by the River Dvina in addition to the railway, a small force consisting principally of marines from the cruisers was despatched in pursuit, and this succeeded to the extent of driving him the best part of three hundred miles. No further headway was possible, as the Bolsheviks had received reinforcements. Therefore, by the end of the summer, the Allied forces were in position on the railway just south of Obozerskaya and on the Dvina, near Shenkursk and Borok. Although these positions were perfectly secure during the summer when communication was only possible down the rivers or railway, the whole of the intervening country being forest and marsh intersected by numerous streams, they were not secure for the winter months when everything became frozen and the numerous trails existing in the forests were practicable. While a few men could make their way across the snow by skis and thus carry out raids, no forces could be maintained except by the use of the principal trails which were some hundred feet wide and which were used by sleighs, being made sufficiently wide to get an even depth of snow. These considerations involved the placing of a series of posts to watch all tracks leading through the front, and thus meant dispersion. The front itself was divided into zones. A detached force at the town of Onega covered the right flank on the White Sea, some hundred and fifty miles from Archangel; the second section comprised the forty miles to Chekuevo, where the main road turned south to Petrograd; the third a farther forty miles to Obozerskaya on the railway, which point was the headquarters of the troops on the railway front. About fourteen miles from this last place to the west was the important outpost of "Bolshie-Ozerki", which was the junction of five trails through the forest. Finally, the last section farther west of the railway consisted of another detached force at Seltskoe, with advanced posts at Kodish and Sred Mekarengh covering the intervening space between the railway and the river. The whole of the above constituted a front approximately a hundred and fifty miles in length. Farther east the line was continued by the river force for another hundred and sixty miles, but here the roads followed the same line as the Rivers Dvina and Vaga to Shenkursk and Borok and, therefore, the winter dispositions of the troops differed little tactically from those of the summer. To the extreme east was another detached force at Pinega, with advanced troops at Trufnagora covering the left flank.

Towards the fulfilment of this project additional troops had been sent out before the port closed for the winter. The British contingent consisted of two battalions of infantry, two batteries of Canadian field artillery and a number of extra officers. The French sent a regiment of infantry, as did also the United States, while there were also two batteries of French artillery, and small detachments of Italians and Portuguese. In the meantime local recruiting was opened. Here the results were disappointing, for no recruits presented themselves. The loyal Russians who were supposed to be waiting to prove their zeal against the Bolsheviks were, in fact, only conspicuous by their absence. The difficulty was surmounted in the first instance by drawing on the prisons, but, even after a Bolshevik régime in Archangel, the prisoners could only provide one weak battalion. The local Government was then persuaded to introduce conscription, and by this means over 30,000 Russians were under training by British officers by Christmas 1918. Two battalions were also unwisely raised among prisoners captured from the enemy but, although these for some time promised well, they eventually proved untrustworthy and one of them murdered its officers during the following summer. None of the Russian troops were ready until the spring of 1919 so that, during the winter, the whole of this front had to be held by the Allies.

The manner in which these were maintained in their scattered posts showed a thoroughness equal to that of the Murmansk theatre. On that portion served by the railway, supplies were sent by train from Baharitzar through an advanced base at Obozerskaya. There sleigh roads were made east and west—the former to Onega feeding Chekuevo and Onega itself, and the latter to Sletskoe for the detached force base at that place. As this base could not maintain the whole of the line, additional sleigh roads had to be opened, running round the shores of the White Sea and up to the River Dvina to Yemetskoe. For the river front, supplies were railed up to Kholmorg-Orskaya, which became the railhead for the river force; thence they were transferred to sleighs which took them across country to the river, the road following which was utilised to the advanced base at Beresnik at the junction of the Dvina and the Vaga. The troops at Pinega were served direct from Baharitzar through Kholmorgori, where there was an Army Service Corps officer who was responsible for the onward journey to Pinega. On the lines of communication themselves there were certain defence troops who were fed from the main routes by special convoys under the charge of non-commissioned officers, which dropped at each post the rations required. The total length of the sleigh roads was approximately thirteen hundred miles and nine hundred sleighs were working every day on maintenance duties, conveying supplies, stores, clothing and ammunition as well as reinforcements. The organisation of this sleigh transport was carefully worked out. In the first place orders were issued that no sleighs or animals were to be withdrawn from any of the villages within a certain distance of the routes, and one-third of the total thus available was left for the domestic needs of the inhabitants. On the figures received from the district councils, time tables were prepared, and instructions were then given to each district to provide its quota of sleighs on a certain day. When this system was first adopted each sleigh was given a card, printed in Russian and English, on which were entered the weights and stores carried, together with the sum the driver was to receive for his work, based on a rate per pood per verst. For passengers there was a fixed rate of one rouble per verst. After some time an alteration was made to save clerical labour, and convoy cards were substituted for the sleigh cards, one card being given to each village providing sleighs. The head man was paid, and he in turn paid the drivers. The sleigh cards were receipted by the Army Service Corps officer at the receiving end, but the driver only obtained his pay at the base from which he worked and this ensured the men being regular in their attendance. The average time spent on each route was ten days for the journey out and return, and the time tables were so arranged that the peasant could spend one day in his own village for each journey done. The drivers were permitted to purchase full army rations for the days on which they worked, the cost of which was debited on the cards, as was also the value of any stores lost in transit. The convoys moved without escort and the losses were trifling, for the local Russians were thoroughly accustomed to this kind of work, since normally all their transport was conducted during the winter months when the land was frozen.

In addition to these purely military convoys, the ordinary civilian mail and passenger services were still running to certain points, and were efficiently maintained. The normal transport was the ordinary pony-drawn peasant sleigh. The locally bred pony was a hardy little animal of about fourteen hands, very willing and amenable to his driver. He was capable of a load of from seven to eight hundred pounds and could cover from twenty to twenty-five miles per day. The local sleighs built in the villages proved excellent. They were roughly made of split pine trees, the runners about four inches wide being inshod with metal, while the platform was about six inches from the ground. For the carriage of passengers a cradle was built above this which, when half-filled with hay, made a comfortable conveyance. The draught known as the douga was unusual. The "douga" is the crescent-shaped contrivance, familiar in Russian pictures, which goes over the horses' heads, often highly decorated and carrying bells. The shafts, which were the trunks of small trees and which were lashed by raw hide to the side of the sleigh, had their ends attached to the douga. From the pony's collar to the end of the douga were taken raw-hide lashings, but the douga, being so much larger than the collar, left some inches of twisted lashings on each side. The pony therefore worked within a rectangle made by the sleigh, the shafts and the douga, and could trot freely within this rectangle unaffected by the swaying of the vehicle on the frozen snow: the swayings were taken by the lashings between the collar and the douga and not by the animal's shoulders. The draught came straight through from sleigh to shoulders. The majority of the peasants did not use bits, merely driving on the nose bands.

In the summer the transport was for the most part carried out by four-wheeled carts drawn by one pony. Three Army Service Corps transport companies equipped with mules served on the Archangel front* and were employed in various duties. One of these, No. 1152, formed part of Brig.-General Grogan's brigade in the summer of 1919 during operations in the Dvina and Pinega sectors, when it was used for taking wounded to the hospital barges on the river and for a time acting as an ammunition column to the Royal Artillery, but, generally speaking, the activities of these units does not call for any particular comment beyond the fact that they found themselves as fully occupied as those at Murmansk.

Mechanical transport was tried but was not successful, owing to the climate and absence of proper roads. Of the latter there were a few cobbled or corduroyed with tree trunks in the larger towns, but elsewhere there

* These were Nos. 1122, 1152 and 1153 Companies.

were nothing but cart tracks over the fields which extended in the river valleys between the river and the forest. These tracks for the most part followed the rivers, only going into the forests to cut off corners, but they had an unpleasant habit at times of transferring themselves to the opposite bank of an often bridgeless river at intervals of ten or fifteen miles. As, too, the soil was alluvial and in rainy seasons quickly churned up to a liquid mud, the practical impossibility of utilising mechanical transport was apparent. Ford cars, ambulances and vans were tried, as were also three-ton and thirty-hundredweight lorries, but in winter these could only be employed where it was possible to keep the roads clear of snow, while in summer they could only be run during the dry periods, which were very brief. Consequently mechanical transport was mainly confined to the town of Archangel itself although, for a short time, a section was attached to No. 1152 Company Army Service Corps on the Pinega River in the summer of 1919.

On the Dvina front throughout, the chief means of communication with Archangel was naturally the river and *personnel* supplies; ammunition and stores were despatched by barges drawn by tugs. But this communication was by no means a sure one, for the river was liable to fall to such an extent that water-borne traffic could only with great difficulty proceed along it. Many ships ran aground and could not be refloated. It was, therefore, at all times necessary during the summer to provide an alternative means of supply, and this was done by the organisation of the local wheeled transport, to which reference has been made. An ingenious device was adopted to overcome the low water difficulty, and this consisted of two flat-bottomed barges, specially constructed by the Royal Engineers, with a Ford ambulance placed in such a position on each that the back wheels turned a pair of paddle wheels. As these vessels only drew a few inches of water they were able to go anywhere, and were even able to tow other flat-bottomed barges.

As operations of war apart from administration, the doings of the Allied Forces in North Russia do not offer any features of marked interest. In so far as they prevented the Germans making use of Murmansk and Archangel, if indeed they had ever contemplated doing so, the object was attained and, therefore, the expeditions may be said to have justified themselves up to the time of the Armistice in November 1918. Thenceforward the rôle adverted solely to that of providing a focus for loyal Russian elements with the hopes of co-operation with other anti-Bolshevik forces in the field, especially those under Admiral Koltchak, who was advancing from the east and with whom the Archangel force had even contemplated linking up via Kotlas. These hopes were all doomed to disappointment.

Admiral Koltchak was compelled to retreat, while General Denikin's successes in the south, like those of Yudenevitch from Esthonia were both ephemeral. At the same time the Allies owed to those who had remained faithful to their cause throughout a measure of protection and assistance, and on this score the occupation of North Russian territory until September 1919 was legitimate, even if it eventually proved illusory. For despite the energy and efforts put forth, in the course of which gallant men gave their lives, the Russians themselves had no lively desire to continue the struggle against the Communist Government, and, with the evacuation of the Allied troops, the military edifice, which had been laboriously and patiently created at Murmansk and Archangel, quickly fell to pieces. When it was decided to withdraw the British troops, a relief force was organised in England in June 1919 to cover the retirement from the Dvina line. This consisted of a composite brigade under Brig.-General Sadleir-Jackson, Lord Rawlinson being appointed to co-ordinate the operations.

These troops proceeded up the river to Troitsa during July and undertook an offensive on the 10th of August, which successfully prevented any serious interference with the evacuation. During these operations astride the river the supply was maintained by barges working in conjunction with wheeled transport. Rations were provided on the man for one day after zero, or the opening of the attack, and these were replenished by night convoys working both sides of the river. There was no confusion, and arrangements went well, but the task of the transport officers with their columns of droskies was not easy.

During the passage down the river after the troops had been embarked the Army Service Corps ration barge, with Major Watson, the Deputy Assistant Director of Supplies and Transport on board, was stranded for four days in the shallow channel off Khoboritza and thus formed the rearguard of the whole force. Supplies surplus on evacuation were handed over to the Russians, except the rum which was poured into the river, and one of Major Watson's final memories when supervising this measure of precaution was the sight of several of the natives in a small boat endeavouring to catch in their mouths as much as possible of the liquor as it went over the side.

If the North Russian adventure could not show the laurels garnered in other fields, it had none the less proved the adaptability of the Army Service Corps in circumstances wholly strange, and in which indeed the British Army with all its varied experiences had never encountered. Mistakes and miscalculations were made, but none of them were serious. The supreme object of feeding and maintaining the fighting troops was always fulfilled. Although the numbers involved were small, there were all the complications existing in having to deal with a heterogeneous assembly including, as it did apart from Allies, types so diverse as Russians, Finns, and Karelians scattered over many hundreds of miles of desolate country. How severe the conditions were may be gathered from the fact that winter lasted from the end of November to the middle of May, during which period the thermometer often fell at night to between 40° and 50° below zero; wind storms were prevalent and progression on foot in the thick snow was only possible with the aid of snow-shoes. In summer, which, in the absence of spring and autumn, lasted from June until October, the weather was hot and mosquitoes a torment. But knowledge was gained that may well find space in the already comprehensive transport manuals of the Corps; and in this respect some few words concerning the use of reindeer and dogs may be apposite. The reindeer proved an unqualified success, especially on bad or hilly tracks, although they cannot be considered as general transport animals, since they subsist only on reindeer moss which is akin to the white lichen found on trees in England and, therefore, they cannot move away from localities where this is found. The animals need to be turned out in the forest for at least half the day, and even then it is necessary to move daily to a fresh area. Being delicate they soon become useless if these long hours for feeding are not observed. In Russia they proved invaluable for conveying *personnel*, supplies and material to detached posts and localities which could not be reached by any other means, as they can pull easily over virgin snow and thus pass convoys of pony sleighs working on the single sleigh track. Though semi-wild they come readily to discipline when put into the sleigh and driven by their owners. Three animals normally formed a team, with one attached to the back of the sleigh to form a brake when going down hill, and a load of some 600 lb. was thus negotiated. In the draught of the three leaders the trace of the centre deer comes from its breast harness between both pairs of legs, which involves its moving astride the trace. With the two outside deer the traces come from the breast harness between the front legs only. It requires a Laplander to drive them, which he does by means of a rope attached to the antlers of the centre animal, and a long pole with which he steers them by tapping them on the head. One driver was usually in charge of three vehicles which were connected by hide through the harness of the deer to the sleigh in front.

Dog transport was to some extent employed, but its limitations were considerable, for as many as eight animals were required to draw one sleigh, and the carrying capacity per dog was therefore small. Nevertheless, for drawing stretchers with wounded over the snow or such tasks as dragging light trench mortars into position, it had its special uses, and was called upon to work in localities where, owing to the absence of moss, reindeer could not operate. The breeds of dogs provided in North Russia were of the Siwash, Husky and Malmoot tribes of Canadian origin, and were brought from Canada for the expedition together with their drivers, who directed them by word of mouth. Under these circumstances they were very amenable when in harness, but dangerous to handle otherwise. The diet to which they were accustomed and on which they throve best was fresh fish, but this was supplemented at Murmansk by corn meal and seal oil. The sleighs drawn were long and narrow, of the light "Shackleton" type, capable when properly stacked of conveying some eight hundred pounds.

BIBLIOGRAPHY

History of the Supply and Transport Services during the Campaign conducted by the Syren *Allied Forces, North Russian Expeditionary Force.* By Lieut.-Colonel T. C. R. MOORE, C.B.E., R.A.S.C.

"North Russia, 1918–19." By Major H. N. G. WATSON, D.S.O., O.B.E., R.A.S.C. From the *Royal Army Service Corps Quarterly,* April 1926.

"Transport work in North Russia." By Lieutenant F. H. E. WHITTAKER, R.A.S.C. From the *Royal Army Service Corps Quarterly,* April 1920.

The Murmansk Venture. By Major-General Sir C. MAYNARD.

CHAPTER XIII

THE WAR PERIOD IN THE UNITED KINGDOM

No account of the work of the Army Service Corps would be adequate without reference to the authority at the War Office supremely responsible for the Supply Transport and Quartering Services of the Army. Nor does such reference involve complications, for the post of Quartermaster-General to the Forces was occupied by General Sir John Cowans for the seven years 1912 until 1919, and thus covers not only the greater part of the period of preparation for war, but the whole of the Great War itself. While reputations were falling like sand castles or while men wore themselves out and were cast aside in the wrack of the storm, Cowans bore his burden from beginning to end, a fact which those who subscribe to the doctrine of the survival of the fittest will not fail to appreciate.

It is no uncommon type of mind that concerns itself with attempts to prove that eminent men often owe their success to others. A Bacon has been produced to supplant a Shakespeare, and a Berthier a Napoleon. As far as aspects of historical truth are concerned, such investigations may be deemed sound. Yet the spirit underlying them is no generous one, for it is a poor mind that is incapable of any degree of hero worship. Cowans certainly did surround himself with an able staff, among whom were those of intellect and knowledge much superior to his own. But that was to his credit, not only for the reason that he had the discernment to judge men —a much rarer quality than is usually surmised—but more perhaps as demonstrating an absence of that pettiness which too frequently shows itself among those in prominent positions, who gather round them those markedly inferior in order that their own star may shine the brighter. In truth, men of narrow intelligence do not like to have able men about them, for they do not know what to do with them. But genius is quick to see genius and knows what to do with it.

Cowans was one of the least "officious" of officials who ever entered the precincts of Whitehall. Self-importance and pomposity were totally alien to his nature. He was the very antithesis of the popular idea, sometimes fairly accurate, of the general officer. That such qualities were liable to distortion into lack of dignity was but natural. Men deficient in a sense of proportion, or what is usually termed a "sense of humour", are intolerant of those so endowed. Yet "dignity" has covered many imbecilities, and it is safe to say that the work of the world and even of the Army runs smoother on a "sense of humour". And if Cowans had not the official manner, neither had he the official mind so prone to play for safety. He was ever prepared to take risks and to launch out boldly on new and untried paths. Professionally exclusive and selfish he was not. If private interests were concerned, it was those of his subordinates or even his friends, for his heart was at times inclined to run away with his head. This was, in fact, the reason why he was so loyally served, for such recompense is for those few who do not "stand for themselves" and are able to inspire those under them with that realisation. However distinguished their labours for the State, no others can hope to receive it in full and abounding measure.

Nor, to use Prescott's words, was he "one of those great little men who aspire to do everything themselves under the conviction that nothing can be done so well by others". He could not and did not pretend to concern himself with the details of his various departments, the ramifications of which he was at times even ignorant. He had indeed no very profound knowledge of administration—he was no student; but he possessed a quick grasp of essentials, knowledge of the world and of men, and a personality which enabled him to get the best out of those with whom he came into contact. It was a curious combination of qualities in a soldier, and would seem scanty enough to have fitted him for his high position. That it sufficed is now a matter of history. His case furnishes one of those rare instances when lack of erudition was made good by a superabundance of other qualifications. When the task is considered, it is all the more remarkable.

In general there is but an imperfect realisation of the scope of the work of the Quartermaster-General. It is vaguely known that he feeds and clothes the Army, and it is remembered that during the Great War the Army was especially well fed and well clothed. But these services, ample as they are, form but a part of the responsibilities which may in a sentence be defined as provision of the troops with what they require to enable them to live and move: and in this is included all the barrack accommodation for the Army at home. The point may be emphasised that not for one single day of the war did Cowans' scope do other than grow and expand. Sometimes that growth and expansion lay in directions which could have been reasonably foreseen. More often it was the new and unexpected which he was called upon to face. As the field of the struggle widened, or the struggle itself grew in intensity and fresh operations were initiated or fresh measures were taken to meet initiation by the enemy, he was compelled at little or no notice to recast plans or estimates, seek other sources of supply, re-organise or re-equip. Demands by Allied countries were constant and continually increasing and, for the larger part, they were met. Thus he was continually called upon to improvise, reconstruct, modify or adapt. That mistakes were made was inevitable and in the nature of human things, but when the whole field of the war is surveyed it may be claimed that in no direction was success more evident and more sustained than in the department presided over by the Quartermaster-General. No single individual is indispensable, and had Cowans quitted his post it may be believed that the great machine he directed and in whose creation he had borne so large a part would still have continued to operate with all its inexorable efficiency and power. No task which must necessarily depend on a far-flung decentralisation should ever be left in any other state.

That a man should be appraised on his best form is but bare justice. Had the perfect human being ever been known it might have been possible to have judged others in the light of his standard, but since such standard has never existed, it cannot commend itself to the practical mind to regard the failings and follies of any man before regarding what he may definitely have achieved that is good and useful to his country or his fellow-men. It is given to comparatively few individuals to render services that are far-reaching in their influence. To those few, wide tolerance of deficiencies should be extended.

Such is the view of charity. But before the bar of history also it serves no worthy purpose to dilate on indiscretions and weaknesses when out-balanced by assets of far more import. It is before that bar that what has definitely been accomplished—what conquests have been won—should be thrown into major relief.

No greater contrast to General Cowans in character and method could be found than in Major-General S. S. Long, the Director of Supplies and Transport during the first eighteen months of the war. There has been occasion in an earlier chapter to set forth certain of the work done by this officer in the preparatory period while he was in charge of the Supply Reserve Depot at Woolwich, and subsequently Director of Supplies and of

Quarterings. General Long was a man who throve on work and responsibility, and in September 1914 he was called upon to undertake the combined duties of transport and supplies, relinquishing quarterings to Major-General C. E. Heath. At the same time the Movements Directorate, which had been combined with that of Transport, was likewise made a separate branch and passed outside the control of an Army Service Corps officer. Major-General F. W. B. Landon, on vacating the charge of transport and movements, was appointed Inspector of Army Service Corps and Quartermaster-General's Services. Theoretically, responsibility for both transport and supplies at the War Office might seem beyond the power of any single individual in so great a national crisis, but in practice the unification worked as it did elsewhere in a satisfactory manner. In the British Expeditionary Force, alone of all the armies in the field, were the duties under separate heads. Yet if the Army Service Corps possessed one officer, although as events subsequently turned out it was shown that it possessed at least two, who had the will and the capability to shoulder the double burden, that officer was indisputably General Long. In suppleness, finesse, patience or, indeed, in any of the finer arts of diplomacy or persuasiveness he was inferior to his chief, but in every other respect he may be judged superior. Direct, impetuous and even irascible, he nevertheless enjoyed the affectionate regard of his own entourage. Never afraid of making enemies, if he deemed that public interest demanded it, he inevitably made many friends. General Long possessed driving power of an exceptional nature, and to inefficiency or procrastination he was ruthless. Such combination is not uncommon, but when there was added to it that he knew his own mind from the beginning and was therefore able to avoid that self-deception, which is to be found so often in men otherwise talented, it will be seen that he was powerfully equipped for such situations as then arose. On the more positive and constructional side, however, his calibre was most marked. With a fertile imagination he was ever initiating, adapting, foreseeing and re-casting means to meet possibilities; and, if his methods seemed at times over-brusque, it is certain that he would never have accomplished what he did by more orthodox and official ways with their long drawn-out indecision. Sir Herbert Miles, who had preceded Sir John Cowans as Quartermaster-General, is reputed to have remarked that he owed his uniformly successful career at the War Office to the fact that during his tenure of various posts in that establishment he never gave a decision, and so avoided making any mistakes. The outlook of General Long was the antithesis of this, and it was fortunate for the Army and the country that it was so. Some instances of the enterprise and commonsense that inspired his administration will serve more effectively to demonstrate some more important aspects of the work of the Army Service Corps than any mere statistical narration.

Under the regulations then in force, whenever the War Office made any purchases, certain officers were detailed to inspect the factories to ensure that the commodities in question were up to contract, and that the various Government requirements in relation to such matters as labour conditions were duly carried out. On the outbreak of war these duties were designated to a number of retired officers, amongst whom naturally a number of ex-Army Service Corps officers had been earmarked, and for anything short of a national struggle these measures would in all probability have sufficed. But it was obvious that, in a general mobilisation, when the strength of the Army was leaping up monthly by hundreds of thousands, and purchases were going on throughout the country, that these provisions made for inspection would have been hopelessly inadequate, and that consequently the doors would be opened for every kind of malpractice in the way of inferior articles being supplied, as indeed happened during the South African war.

On the 6th of August, 1914, therefore, General Long wrote a note to Dr MacFadden, the head of the Medical Department of the Local Government Board, saying that he would be grateful if Dr MacFadden would go to the War Office and see him.

Within half an hour Dr MacFadden arrived, when General Long explained the position to him, saying: "I cannot possibly inspect all the factories throughout the country producing the hundred and one commodities required. I have neither the staff, nor if I had, are they qualified to do this work. Will you, through your Medical Officers of Health, who consist of a number, undertake to do this work? Here are some hundreds of copies of the Book of Specifications of all these commodities which we want, and I will have as many more printed as you wish. Here is a list of all the contracts which have been entered into with the various factories throughout the country. Now can you get your Medical Officers of Health and their Inspectors of Nuisances to sit on the doorsteps of these factories and see that nothing but the very best quality is allowed to be despatched for the use of our troops."

Dr MacFadden instantly agreed, and within forty-eight hours every food factory throughout the country producing anything for the Army was held in an iron grip of the very closest inspection and supervision.

At the same time, General Long got into touch with Sir James Dobbie, head of the Somerset House Analytical Department, and again on request, Sir James at once undertook to place at Newhaven a special branch of his establishment to examine and analyse where necessary every consignment of foodstuffs passing through, suppliers being informed that if the Government chemists condemned anything it would be thrown out on the rail side at the suppliers' risk, and they would have to make their own arrangement for its removal.

Here again a supply system of control was introduced, and it is particularly to be noted that this control cost the country not one penny, the work being done by public officials who were already in the pay of the country either as Government or municipal officials.

A little later, General Long succeeded in persuading the Director-General of Medical Services to agree that the inspection of all foodstuffs in barracks and camps throughout the country, canteen supplies, etc., should be handed over to the Local Public Health officers; so again the well-being of the soldier was carefully guarded at no public expense.

These measures go far to explain why the British armies in the field were provisioned in a manner superior to any in history.

But it was not only as regards quality that the public was safeguarded in the requirements of the troops. It was also as regards price. Previous to the war, whilst at the Supply Reserve Depot and as Director of Supplies at the War Office, General Long had urged as each annual review of the Army Act came up for consideration that, in the event of a general mobilisation, power should be given to the military authorities not only to billet troops and impress carriages which included motor vehicles, a power which was provided for, but also to requisition foodstuffs and other needs of the Army. To these representations the reply was invariably the same —that Parliament would never be induced to grant such powers.

The more dire the need of the community the greater is the opportunity of the few, and the outbreak of war in 1914 was no exception to this general rule. Prices at once began to soar. For instance when war was declared, the Contract Branch at the War Office which dealt with supply requirements, and which was presided over by

Mr Riley, sent out in accordance with plan all the priority telegrams already settled on, asking for immediate offers to meet the heavy demand of the various commodities required by the War Office.

The morning following Mr Riley came to General Long to say that to his enquiries for many hundred tons of sugar, urgently wanted, which he had sent to the great sugar factories and magnates of the country, he had only received offers barely sufficient to meet his wants, and that the prices demanded were—the lowest 56*s*. per cwt. and the highest as much as 75*s*. per cwt. Considering that the price two days previous to the declaration of war was only 12*s*. 3*d*. per cwt., the price was extortionate, but he could not see what he could do but accept.

General Long replied: "I am paying no such money. Wire to these people to send instantly a principal to attend in your room at an hour late this evening."

Mr Riley replied: "They may not come". General Long answered: "Make your telegram peremptory, and under the conditions they will be afraid to refuse".

On the arrival of the sugar principals, General Long went down to Mr Riley's room and said: "You were asked, gentlemen, to supply certain quantities of sugar urgently required for the troops. The total of your offers hardly comes up to our modest demands and the prices demanded are ridiculous".

A great sugar magnate replied: "You must remember, General Long, we have our commitments. We are anxious to help, but we have our civil commitments which we cannot break".

General Long replied: "I am not concerned with your civil commitments. I will tell you what the quantities of sugar are in this country, as I have had the figures from the Customs during the course of the morning; there are so many million hundredweights of refined sugar either in store or customs. There are so many million hundredweights of unrefined sugar. I have already given orders, and when you get back to your business or warehouses, you will find that troops are already put on guard to let nothing out until military requirements are met, and the Customs have been requested to release no sugar from bond pending those requirements being met".

One of the sugar trade representatives replied: "Oh, in that case, if the Government are going to arbitrarily seize our stocks, we had better make arrangements with you".

General Long replied: "The arrangements I am prepared to make are that I have no objection to paying 2d. or 3d. more than the price asked three days ago, 12s. 3d., but I won't pay more. If you do not like to take it, I shall seize the sugar. Whether you are paid or not depends upon whether we win the War. If so, doubtless you will be paid. If we lose, I do not think it matters, and no one will be paid; the country goes under".

He then turned to Mr Riley and said: "Make a contract now, not for a few hundred tons of sugar, but for an equal number of thousands of tons of sugar", and walked out of the room.

Shortly afterwards Mr Riley came to General Long's room and said: "I have made contracts, but I must point out to you that it is on your responsibility. It is entirely illegal, and you have no authority to do any such thing".

General Long replied: "I am well aware of that. Authority must be forced from the Government. As you know, there are already ominous murmurings throughout the country owing to the holding up of food. It is in the papers that no sugar can be obtained in the East End and the same will be happening to other commodities shortly. I am asking that instructions be sent by telegram to Bristol and to Liverpool to seize the cold meat stores until military requirements are met".

Having seen this all in train, General Long then went to see the Parliamentary Finance Secretary of the War Office, Mr Baker, and said: "We must pass an act at once enabling military authorities to seize foodstuffs, and for the matter of that, any other requirements which are of vital necessity".

Mr Baker told him it was utterly impossible.

General Long replied: "I do not know about it being impossible; I have already done it, and as a Government servant I have committed the country, if an Act is not passed, to a claim of millions of pounds damages. If they do not like it, they had better put someone else to carry on, but I say that if they do not do it they will have a rebellion in the country. My action is smashing the cornering of foodstuffs and forcing everyone to throw their stocks on the market owing to the fear of them being requisitioned".

At 10 o'clock that night Mr Baker rang General Long up to say that a short Act, empowering general requisitioning, had been read three times in the House of Commons, three times in the House of Lords, and had been signed by the King a few minutes previously.

It will be recollected that this resulted in the immediate release of foodstuffs all over the country, and the return to normal prices. It will too be recalled that on the outbreak of the War, the country was in a large measure seized with a food panic, with a result that numbers of people proceeded to lay in stocks of foodstuffs. Instances are on record of well-to-do people proceeding to buy large quantities, such as dozens of hams, sacks of sugar, large quantities of tinned goods, and, in fact, provisions of any kind which would keep.

This action naturally caused grave concern to the Government, as there arose a fear that in addition to causing a great inflation of prices owing to the private hoarding of foodstuffs, an actual shortage of commodities might occur. The action of the Supply Directorate at the War Office broke the commercial holding-up of supplies, and its action in forcing the Government to pass an Act empowering the military authorities to requisition anything they required was a powerful lever in keeping down prices. The Government, however, had no machinery to deal with private hoarding, and consequently to enable them to take drastic action against private hoarders the Board of Trade had to request the assistance of the War Office to use the military authorities to make an example of such hoarders by requisitioning on a number of private houses. A little later the Government were able to pass an Act giving similar powers to the Board of Trade so as to prevent private food hoarding.

It will thus be seen that not only did the supply branch of the Army do much to save the country by its measures for the supply maintenance of mobilised forces, but it did much to prevent food riots by the population generally, which might have resulted in a serious condition of affairs.

Another interesting case was the question of the meat supply, not only for the troops but for the whole country. Acting on the request of the Director of Supplies, the Admiralty requisitioned the number of frozen-meat ships, necessary to meet Army requirements. With the exception of some four Russian and some half a dozen French vessels, and that small amount which existed on the various steamship liners for carrying provisions for the maintenance of their passengers, the whole of the insulated tonnage in the world was under the British flag.

In the early stages of the War, the Admiralty had necessarily requisitioned a very large number of vessels required for the use of our fleets for the purpose of acting as colliers and store vessels. Amongst these vessels so requisitioned were a number of insulated ones, and it may be noted that it takes just as long to fit in the necessary machinery and insulating chambers into an ordinary vessel as it does to build a new insulated vessel. Again, the number of insulated vessels were little more than sufficient to meet the ordinary peace trade requirements of the world at large. When, owing to its own demands for meat ships, the Supply Directorate noticed that there seemed a likelihood of a shortage of insulated vessels, it successfully negotiated for the immediate release by the Navy of all insulated vessels which they had requisitioned, and finally succeeded in getting the complete control of all insulated tonnage removed from the control of the Admiralty and placed under the authority of a special committee formed by the Board of Trade, of which committee, owing to the fact that he represented the biggest consumer, the Director of Supplies was a prominent member.

The latter succeeded, after a considerable amount of pressure, in persuading the Admiralty that beyond some one or two refrigerated vessels required for the supply of meat to the Grand Fleet, all other Admiralty meat requirements at home and abroad should be obtained from the Army magazines, thus eliminating overlapping and waste which would have otherwise been inevitable, and centralising the distribution in the authority most competent to effect it.

Naturally on the outbreak of the War, the American meat packers and interests who controlled not only the meat in the United States, but also in South America, made a strong endeavour to increase the price of meat. Their biggest customer was, as is well known, England, and owing to the mobilised forces, the demand became greatly enhanced. The Supply Directorate, although great pressure was brought to bear from many directions, firmly declined to allow the price of meat to go up beyond a certain small increase, saying that if it was not supplied at the prices the War Office were prepared to pay, then it would requisition under the powers granted.

The packers, who were well aware that the Army would only take meat of "good average quality" thought that they could force the hands of the War Office by starting to import into England shiploads of very inferior quality meat, so that the War Office refusal to accept such meat would leave it on their hands, when they could sell it to the general public at a greatly increased price than that obtained by contract.

On the arrival of the first shipload of this inferior meat at Liverpool, General Long promptly had it refused by his local inspectors, and arranged with the Local Health Authorities to condemn it. The packers then despatched it to London, but the Director of Supplies, being warned of this, arranged with the London Health Authorities also to seize and condemn it, when it thus became a complete loss to its owners. This action naturally smashed the packers' endeavour to overcome the stranglehold which had been held on the meat supply.

In the winter of 1914 France put forward a heavy demand for her troops to be supplied with foreign meat, and at a conference which was held at the Board of Trade, where the French military representative stated his demands that they should be in a position to give the French soldier as good a meat ration as the English soldier got, General Long remarked, "But surely the Frenchman is not accustomed to eat anything like the quantity of meat that the Englishman does"; whereupon the Frenchman replied, "Pardon me, my General, we have discovered that if the French soldier gets as much meat as the English soldier, then he is as equally hard to drive back or out of his trenches as is your gallant English soldier". Ultimately the British authorities had to agree to provide France with almost as great a monthly tonnage of frozen meat as was used by the British forces at home and abroad. It was settled that the French Government were to have 15,000 tons of frozen beef a month, but in no case was the amount to exceed one-third of the world's output. Contracts were then made with the meat-exporting houses in South America and arrangements made to take practically the whole of their output. It was also agreed with the Commonwealth of Australia and the Government of New Zealand that their whole output should be at the disposal of the British Government.

When Italy entered the War, there was an immediate demand from Italy for frozen meat for her armies.

Now both France and Italy had agreed that, so far as foodstuffs coming from abroad were concerned, England should be the central purchasers for all three nations, and that neither France nor Italy would place orders on their own account. The Italians at once broke this agreement, inasmuch as an agent of the American packers had gone to Italy and induced the Italian Government to sign a contract with him for the supply of large quantities of frozen meat at 8*d*. per lb., whereas at the time England was paying 6*d*. per lb. The Italians then sent their representatives to England to ask us to provide the necessary frozen-meat tonnage, and at the same time the American packers asked permission to be allowed to send a deputation to the Board of Trade to submit a demand that the price to be paid for meat should be considerably raised. Mr Runciman, the President of the Board of Trade, was somewhat alarmed at the situation, and was consequently inclined to agree to the price going up. General Long, however, who saw Mr Runciman shortly before the meeting, maintained his position, stating that on behalf of the Army he was not disposed to agree to any increase in price. As regards the Italian contract, he proposed that that could easily become a dead letter by our peremptorily refusing to supply the tonnage.

The first meeting with the Italian representatives was easily settled, as they were told, as was also the agent for the American packers, that their contract was bound to be null and void as England would not supply tonnage, and that, instead, the necessary quantity of meat would be supplied under the already arranged British contract rates and in the necessary British ships.

When the meeting of the representatives of the American packers was held, they were disposed to be truculent, finally turning to the President of the Board of Trade and saying: "Well, as you will not pay our price, then we will send no more meat to England but will divert the whole trade to the United States or other countries".

General Long replied: "By all means do so if you think you can, gentlemen, but let me point out two facts to you. You own the refrigerators in South America and possibly can do what you please, but let me tell you that unless you put it on ships to come to this country, as every such ship is under the British flag, you will have no means of shipping it anywhere; and furthermore, as soon as that state arises, it is easy for the British Government to represent to the Argentine Government that, as the American packers have brought one of the main trades of that great country to a standstill, it is suggested that in the interests of Argentine, that Government should requisition the local freezing plants and carry on the trade for themselves".

These representations brought the American packers to a reasonable frame of mind and the price of meat was kept down to 6d. or 6½d. a pound until the middle of March 1916, when General Long left the War Office.

One of the most difficult and troublesome questions in connection with supply was the provision of hay, since it had to be collected, pressed and baled throughout the country.

Mr Chaney, of the Board of Agriculture, furnished the Supply Directorate with a mass of details and suggestions of all kinds, and Colonel G. Morgan, a retired Army Service Corps officer, was employed to go through the papers and formulate a scheme. The result was the formation of a large hay department which, as long as the stocks in Great Britain and Ireland lasted, performed admirable work; but these stocks urgently required supplementing, and immense purchases had to be made in the United States. Not only was this extremely costly, almost twice the price of that obtaining in Great Britain, but also an immense drain was occasioned in tonnage to transport the same overseas.

Early in 1916 the French authorities claimed that they were short of hay in France, and that they also must obtain hay from America and that Great Britain should supply the shipping tonnage. The Director of Supplies doubted the French claims, and therefore sent Colonel H. Maud, A.S.C., an excellent French linguist, to go across to France at once, to get a motor car from the military authorities there, and make a rapid tour through north-western and western France and to telegraph an immediate report as to whether such shortage actually did exist.

Colonel Maud telegraphed from Paris that he had found there was any quantity of hay in France, but the shortage was caused by a quarrel between the military authorities and the French Minister of Interior, so that the latter would not requisition.

General Long at once went to the Foreign Office and asked for their assistance through the British ambassador. He was told that they would certainly not interfere. It was purely a business question, and they would and could do nothing. He then wrote a personal letter to Lord Bertie, the ambassador, explaining the situation fully and asking his help. At the same time he told Colonel Maud to go and see the ambassador. Lord Bertie, unlike some diplomats, was a man of action. The result was that General Long received a wire from Colonel Maud to say: "It is agreed the French do not require any hay from America. They have plenty of their own. It is further agreed that the French Government will supply us with 5000 tons of hay at 100 frs. per ton (which was considerably less than half the price of hay in America) the only condition being that should they run short themselves within a year, Great Britain will replace".

The Director of Supplies replied: "Ratify at once and get ambassador to counter-sign the Agreement".

Of a somewhat different nature to the instances recounted above was the question of the provision of cooks, which may be noticed in that it furnished a typical example of the manner in which the Army Service Corps set itself to assist when called upon for duties outside its real field.

Quite early in the War, when the New Armies came and were coming rapidly into existence, complaints arose on all sides that, although there was any quantity of food for the troops, they had neither the means to cook it nor knives and forks, nor men capable of cooking. This was a matter for the Adjutant-General's department which was responsible for interior economy, but that branch invoked the assistance of the Supply Directorate, which arranged for large numbers of cooks to be supplied from numerous organisations, both men and women; for instructions to be sent out for men coming up to enrol to bring their own knives and forks and spoons; and for regimental authorities to do the best they could by local purchases. By these means the difficulty of cooking and serving of food was quickly overcome.

It was early in August 1914 that labour troubles started which threatened to compromise the whole task of the Supply and Transport Directorate. The first to occur was at Bristol, where a number of dockers were employed loading mechanical transport. At that period, the Government rate of wages, and even that of dockers, was extremely low. With even the slight rise in the price of foodstuffs these labourers found it hard to live, and threatened to strike unless they received increased pay.

General Long at once sent a minute to the Finance Branch of the War Office suggesting that the matter was urgent, should be settled at once, and proposed that as the Board of Trade had a special branch to deal with labour conditions and its payments, that Government department should be asked to settle the question on the best terms possible.

Sir Charles Harris, the head of the War Office Finance Branch, replied that under no circumstances would he agree to any Government department interfering in a War Office labour question, and that they would go into it themselves.

General Long replied: "The matter brooks no delay. If you won't allow the Board of Trade to settle it at once, then settle it yourself, but failing any immediate settlement being arrived at I will take the responsibility for authorising the local Military Authorities to make the best arrangements and terms they can".

Almost immediately afterwards, similar trouble took place at Woolwich Arsenal and other places, and, owing to the Finance Branch of the War Office being unable to to deal with such questions, all kinds and conditions of employment had to be settled locally by the various authorities concerned and, as a consequence, the wages condition throughout the country became one of hopeless confusion, which might well have been avoided had the suggestion been acted upon that the Board of Trade should have taken the matter into its hands from the beginning.

At Liverpool large quantities of supplies urgently required were being loaded on a vessel. The local labour union authorities refused to allow their men to work beyond a certain hour in the evening and declined to make arrangements for the dockers to carry on the work continuously. The Liverpool Supply Embarkation Officer telephoned the information to the Director of Supplies at the War Office. It was two o'clock. Everyone was away at lunch. General Long could not find the Quartermaster-General nor the Secretary of State, Lord Kitchener. It was necessary to act and to act at once. He therefore telephoned back: "Tell the union authorities that the instant the dockers knock off work, I will at once have soldiers drafted in to carry on".

When the Quartermaster-General and the Secretary of State returned, the Director of Supplies reported his action to the Quartermaster-General, who went at once to see the Secretary of State, and on his return said: "Lord Kitchener says he won't take the responsibility of possible troubles, but he won't try and cancel your orders, although now almost too late. If it goes through, well and good". The dockers remained at their work.

Among the chief difficulties which the spending departments at the War Office had to face was the fact that no scheme had been worked out by the Finance Branch as to what it would have to do in the event of a great National War. The result was that with the best intentions in the world, the attitude of that branch could not always be helpful to the military authorities.* It claimed and very rightly claimed in so far as peace regulations were concerned that before any expenditure was incurred it must be consulted and its concurrence obtained—indeed, such functions under normal conditions were necessary and inevitable. But under the abnormal conditions that prevailed from 1914 onwards modifications in this system were essential, and had they been made in the early stages before the squandermania

* As an instance may be quoted a paper written by Sir Charles Harris of the Finance Department in which, after the situation had become stabilised in France, he advocated the withdrawal of large masses of transport and their suitable employment at home until required overseas for a forward movement. This paper reached the hands of the Prime Minister. Without doubt the proposal would have effected great economy as would also the withdrawal of the cavalry corps on the same premise. But it would naturally have been a still greater economy not to have entered the war at all as certain opponents of British intervention pointed out in 1914.

of Mr Lloyd George and his entourage of "business men" obtained control, an immense economy would probably have been achieved. It will be remembered that on occasions there were grave complaints of shortage of uniforms, underclothing, equipment, in addition to the well-worn question of shell shortage. Now these shortages were not due to the want of prescience on the part of the directors of the departments concerned. The latter made out their demands as to what they considered necessary, but, according to regulations, they had to submit the same for financial approval. The finance authorities were in the very nature of things bound to query the amounts and, anticipating like many other people that the war might be over before the demands were required, often only agreed to an order for some lesser quantity. The result was that the departments concerned found themselves short of requirements.

It is easy to be wise in the light of after-events, and had the war come to a sudden termination in 1915 or 1916, the system of financial control in force would have effected large savings to the public purse. But it was apparent from the very early stages of the war that there was undue rigidity and centralisation for the unprecedented circumstances which had arisen. Had wider powers been delegated to the military heads of the War Office spending departments, the happy mean might have been achieved and the transition from parsimony to the prodigality which subsequently ensued, might have been avoided.

As will have been gathered from the above, General Long was anything but complaisant to the dicta of financial authority, and invariably took upon himself the responsibility of ordering what he considered necessary. The result was that whatever shortage and deficiencies existed elsewhere, none existed in the articles with which the Supply Directorate was charged. And this condition obtained in spite of the fact that the bulk of its commodities could not be produced in the United Kingdom, but had to be imported from abroad.

No outline of the more important work of the Supply Directorate would be complete without mention of the Army canteens whose activities play so important a part in the life and comfort of the soldier. The organisation of this service does not properly belong to the Army Service Corps but, as in many other instances of "no man's children", it fell to the Corps in the person of the Director of Supplies to launch them on their war-time career.

Owing to grave irregularities which took place in 1912 and which culminated in a trial at the Old Bailey, it was realised that the time had come to put matters on a more satisfactory basis than the contract system then obtaining. Accordingly a special committee was appointed under the chairmanship of Lord Rotherham to investigate the question. On this committee, besides certain Members of Parliament and prominent business men, was General Long in his capacity as Director of Supplies. This body had, however, only held a few meetings when the outbreak of war occurred. Troops were then being moved at the shortest of notice and with the utmost frequency, while new units were coming hourly into existence. Consequently the canteen situation grew chaotic. Commanding officers who, a few hours previously had been Territorial officers with limited military experience or even civilians, were appointing their own contractors, in some instances the first applicant who presented himself, regardless as to his suitability. Matters reached such a stage that it was found that salesmen from Covent Garden had been appointed, while in other instances those of even less qualifications were given the business. The canteens would be stocked and opened and then possibly the unit ordered to some other part of the country. The relieving Commanding Officer would then as often as not order the contractor out and instal his own. Meanwhile the sums paid by the contractors for the privilege of conducting the canteens were in most cases totally inadequate and in many instances nothing. Affairs reached such a stage that some form of immediate control being necessary in the interests of the troops and of the country, the Director of Supplies took upon himself the responsibility of sending orders forbidding any Commanding Officer to turn out a contractor without having previously obtained War Office permission. At the same time Lord Rotherham's Committee was reassembled under the presidency of Sir Charles Nicholson, M.P. This committee recommended the immediate formation of a Board of Control with powers to draw up an approved list of contractors, regulate prices, maintain continuity of approved contractors, appoint inspectors, and make the necessary provisions for a rebate to be paid by the contract holders. At that time the canteen trade at home amounted to some ten millions sterling per year and was steadily rising, so the necessity of a firm centralised control, quite apart from other aspects, was eminently desirable. The Board of Control duly came into being and lasted for a year, during which period it did valuable work, and not only paid all its working expenses including the wages of inspectors but amassed some £180,000 credit as an Army Fund.

It was then decided to introduce a national canteen system and the Board of Control was requested to make recommendations. The report submitted to the Army Council advocated a national scheme in which it was calculated that the gain to the Army would be some two millions sterling per year and possibly more. Meanwhile the case for such an institution was being reinforced by insistent appeals from France and Flanders for field force canteens, and these demands became too strong to be ignored. The Army Council therefore accepted the proposals of the committee and General Long was instructed to take steps to put them into execution. He sent for Mr A. Prince, Managing Director of Messrs Richard Dickeson and Co., and Mr F. Benson of the Canteen and Mess Co-operative Society, secured their services in an honorary capacity and began operations. Considerable modifications were made as regards the original recommendations of the Nicholson Committee, one result of which was that Messrs Prince and Benson became salaried officials as General and Assistant General Manager. The modifications were made after General Long left the War Office and certain of them may be held as open to considerable criticism. But the "Expeditionary Force Canteens" were launched in their career of usefulness. General Long requested that, in the first place, use might be made of money which was still left from profits made by the South African Field Force Canteen fifteen years before and, overcoming the opposition of the Finance Branch at the War Office, obtained some £27,000 to be returned out of the profits. Later the Treasury was induced to loan at interest sums which reached a total of £720,000 on condition that it was paid back as early as possible, and this was done. Throughout its wonderful development the Expeditionary Force Canteens paid for everything and everybody connected with its business.

On the transport side, even before he was called upon to undertake the additional duty of Director of Transport a few weeks after the outbreak of war, General Long's activities were equally evident. Well equipped in all transport respects as was the original Expeditionary Force, it became at once obvious that the question of the provision of vehicles to replace casualties and to meet the immense expansion of the forces was a matter of urgency. Owing to circumstances beyond their control the Territorial Force had to requisition large numbers of horse transport vehicles of which many, such as heavy delivery vans, were quite unsuitable for service in the field.

The reserve of military vehicles was quickly used up, and, with the exception of the Royal Arsenal, Woolwich, and some two or three comparatively small wagon works in the country, there did not appear to be any other source of supply. Meanwhile demands from France became insistent to replace those which had been lost through accident or had fallen into the hands of the enemy during the retreat to the Marne. The Director of Artillery, who was responsible for producing the necessary military vehicles, stated that it was impossible to obtain any more than those which could be produced by the Royal Arsenal and the two or three private wagon companies, which numbers were quite inadequate. Although General Long as Director of Supplies had no responsibility in the matter, at this time his assistance was invoked as a transport expert. He at once replied: "I will produce them by thousands", and at once got into communication with the heads of all the great railways, arranging with them that he would send to each of their large wagon construction centres patterns of the Army vehicles required, getting them to turn on the whole of their resources for the instant production of wagons, with the result that within a week vehicles were forthcoming by the thousand.

The mobilisation of the Territorial Force and raising of the New Armies demonstrated a further important transport weakness due to the system prevailing, by which different departments were responsible for various provisions.

The unit, for example, an infantry battalion, in order to obtain its first line transport, drew from the Army Ordnance Department the necessary vehicles, saddlery, harness and other transport equipment, and then drew from the Remount Department the necessary animals. It can readily be understood that in practically all cases the unit had neither saddlers nor other men accustomed to fit saddlery and harness, and in some instances it could not even put its harness together. Similar situations had arisen during the South African war, but the lessons had unfortunately been forgotten. In 1914 it was due entirely to the initiative of General Long that a common-sense solution was reached. He arranged with the Army Ordnance and Remount Departments that no transport equipment would be issued by the former, or animals by the latter, to units requiring transport, but that application in bulk was to be made to the nearest Army Service Corps Transport Depot which would be responsible for the provision of the complete "turn outs", that is, animals with the harness fitted and vehicles required. This method worked with complete smoothness, as might have been expected from the concentration of detail issues in the hands of one department.

As further emphasising certain similar defects in the peace time organisation may be cited the question of the recruitment of wheeler artificers which arose about this time, when an urgent demand for such *personnel* was received from the British Expeditionary Force in France.

The Director of Transport passed the demand on to the Adjutant-General's Branch for recruiting, asking that endeavours be made to recruit at once the several hundred asked for. The Director of Recruiting passed the minute on to the Director of Artillery saying: "If I recruit these men, will it not interfere with the building of vehicles which I understand are urgently wanted". The Director of Artillery replied: "It certainly will. Under no circumstances will I consent to the enlistment of wheelwrights, their retention in this country being much more important". The Director of Transport then intervened by pointing out that in the Royal Arsenal at Woolwich there was only one wheelwright who passed the vehicles as constructed and that, indeed, no further skilled artificers were required, for the vehicles were built on mass production, the spokes, felloes and naves being cut out and the tyres shrunk on by machinery. The requirements for France were general wheelwrights, one of whom was to be found in most villages throughout the country and who was trained to carry out repairs to vehicles.

During the winter of 1914 complaints arose in France over the large amount of unauthorised transport, particularly motor vehicles of all kinds, which not only were obstructing the roads, but also without authority consuming large quantities of Government petrol, oils, grease, tyres and other stores. The Transport Directorate took this matter up with the Quartermaster-General in France, with the result that stringent orders were issued that no unauthorised transport of any kind was to be permitted. Any found in possession of officers or others was confiscated. At the same time it was arranged that, except in the case of transport moving with a military unit, the lists and particulars of which were known to the Embarkation Staff Officers, no motor vehicle was allowed to leave Great Britain except accompanied by a pass signed with the signature of the Director of Transport himself; so that by no possibility could any unauthorised vehicle get into France from Great Britain. The endeavours which were made to circumvent these orders were amusing but, generally speaking, it can be claimed that the evasion of the orders were singularly few, and the clearance of the roads in France materially helped the efficiency of the lines of communication.

Shortly after the formation of the Ministry of Munitions, Mr Eric Geddes, as he then was, was sent to the War Office by Mr Lloyd George to say that the Minister of Munitions proposed at an early date to take over the control of all motor factories in this country, and the provision of all motor vehicles required by the Army.

A meeting was held at the War Office to discuss the

question. After Mr Geddes had stated his proposals, the Director of Transport declined to allow responsibility for the major part of the transport of the Army, which was carrying out its functions in a perfectly efficient manner, to be handed over to civilian control. General Long won his point for the time being but, as is usual in the long run when powerful political interests supported by unlimited newspaper propaganda lay behind it, the civilian point of view ultimately prevailed, and in 1916 the Ministry of Munitions took over direction of production. How expensive this was for the country may be judged from the fact that while the Transport Directorate met every call made upon it from all Government departments with a sub-division of its staff consisting of Brig.-General Sir Capel Holden, twenty-five officers and less than a hundred clerks, the Ministry of Munitions within a few months of its formation found it necessary to take over the whole of the Grand Hotel, London, where no less than five hundred officials and an immense number of clerks were employed to do the work. With great ingenuity the department was then split up into numerous sub-departments, each presided over by a director. There was a director of tyres, a director of carburettors, a director of wheels, of ball bearings, of bodies and so on *ad infinitum*, with the result that it took weeks for papers to pass round these various functionaries to obtain their sanction.

In this, as in many other matters, extravagance occurred which would have been avoided if the conduct of their own affairs had been left in the hands of the soldiers. The Supply and Transport Directorate was naturally not the only sufferer in this respect. Other branches concerned with provision were affected, and the country is to-day in course of paying the bill for much of this prodigality—a quality to which, from their very training in organised economy, soldiers are not prone. But soldiers are not usually persuasive talkers, and indeed it is unnecessary that they should be, since their profession is one of action rather than words, and therefore, as far as the judgment of public opinion is concerned, are at the mercy of those who possess the means and the will to draw attention to their actions. One day, however, it may be believed that the full truth will emerge, and when it does the nation will have reason to revise its opinions as to where the credit of its organisation for war is justly due.

In March 1916 General Long resigned his appointment for reasons upon which there is no necessity to dilate, but which were entirely creditable to himself. He did not, however, retire to a leisured ease, but accepted a high appointment in the business world in which he was as successful as he had been in the Army.

The Quartermaster-General did not hesitate long over nominating his successor, and it says much for the acumen of Sir John Cowans that he chose so junior an officer as a regimental lieutenant-colonel in Alban Crofton Atkins. The latter, with the temporary rank of brigadier-general, had for some time been acting as deputy to General Long at the War Office, so was, therefore, on the spot. Nevertheless the appointment was an unusual one, for it involved passing by the claims of a number of senior officers, including several major-generals, who could have been made available and therefore gave rise to criticism. Seldom was any such similar selection more brilliantly justified by results. General Crofton Atkins certainly enjoyed the benefit of his predecessor's work, much of which it is doubtful that he would have been able to have carried through by himself, for he lacked the exceptional driving power of General Long. But he was at the same time equally firm when necessity arose, and his brain was equally quick and alert; while he was adept at handling men and getting the best out of them. Outstanding among his assets were his facility for grasping the essentials of a situation and taking an instant decision thereon. His comprehension of transport and supply problems was, too, masterly, for in these respects his education had been thorough and, although of a highly strung temperament, he brought to every problem a refreshing sense of humour which powerfully assisted in lubricating friction or disunion. His chief weakness, if indeed weakness it can be called, lay in his exaggerated sense of loyalty especially to his subordinates, which led him at times to overlook mistakes or deficiencies which might better have been met with a ruthless dismissal, and would almost certainly have been so met by General Long. As might have been expected, however, his unselfish and upright character endeared him to all with whom he came in contact.

General Crofton Atkins remained at the post of Director of Supplies and Transport until the end of the war, and survived long enough to receive special promotion to the rank of Major-General and a Knight Commandership of the Bath; he was employed for some time after on the Disposals Board which was charged with the sale of surplus stores and supplies. He died while yet a comparatively young man in 1925, having worn himself out in the public service.

The scope of the office of Director of Supplies and Transport would from its nomenclature seem wide and to tax the powers of any one authority, but, in fact, that nomenclature is not wholly comprehensive, for the responsibility includes the administration of all the *personnel* administering those services. Unlike the Cavalry, Artillery, Royal Engineers, Infantry and Royal Army Medical Corps, the administration of which are vested in the Adjutant-General, the administration of the Army Service Corps *personnel* was carried out under the Quartermaster-General by the Supply and Transport Directorate. In this connection the name of Lieut.-Colonel F. W. Stringer, one of the Assistant Directors of Transport for the first twenty months of the war, deserves to be remembered not only for his ability but for the sobriety and impartiality of his judgments in the delicate questions arising over decisions regarding *personnel*. Like General Crofton Atkins he spent himself in his duty and literally died in harness in 1916. How great was the task may be gauged from the numbers involved. By May 1915 the strength of the Corps had reached 4500 officers and 125,000 other ranks, some nineteen times that of nine months previously, and actually exceeding the figure for the whole of the Regular Army with the colours in the United Kingdom prior to the outbreak of war. By the date of the Armistice the Corps had on its muster rolls no less than 10,547 officers and 325,881 other ranks, of which 3535 officers and 81,851 other ranks were serving in the United Kingdom. The raw material in the way of candidates for commissions and recruits for the ranks were forthcoming at the beginning in almost unlimited numbers. Business and professional men of all descriptions, and those following country pursuits with a good knowledge of horses, came forward as officers in the supply, mechanical and horse transport branches. Every candidate for a commission was personally interviewed in the Directorate at the War Office, which process, although it involved an immense amount of work, was so successful that the failures were less than 1 per cent. It may be recorded that for every commission given some ten candidates were interviewed, the balance being urged to join the fighting arms as more suitable to their age and qualifications. In this respect a just sense of proportion was observed throughout. For the rank and file thousands of efficient clerks, chauffeurs, mechanics of every description, butchers, bakers, grooms and coachmen were enlisted.

In the matter of the expansion of its pre-war units at the time of the Armistice no less than three hundred and forty-six supply units of various kinds, six hundred and forty-eight mechanical and five hundred and fifty-nine

horsed or muled transport companies were in existence.*
In the early stages of this expansion the chief difficulty
lay in the absence of regular Army Service Corps officers
and non-commissioned officers to leaven the mass. This
was surmounted by arrangements being made in the
early winter of 1914 for a large proportion of the regulars
in France being returned for service with the New
Armies, their places being taken by territorials and newly
commissioned officers from home and non-commissioned officers promoted from the units serving in the
Expeditionary Force.

The third great responsibility with which the Army
Service Corps was charged was that of quartering the
Army at home. As already noted, Major-General C. E.
Heath occupied the post of Director of Quarterings, and
he held it throughout the War, and was also Deputy
Quartermaster-General from 1916 onwards.

The influx of recruits during the latter part of 1914—
for August the numbers were 168,249 and for September
383,329—threw an overwhelming strain upon the resources in accommodation, since that available in the
whole of the United Kingdom was only sufficient for
174,800. For the first weeks matters had to be left to
local arrangements, while the policy was being formulated at the War Office. It was then decided to clear the
barracks of married families and to make use of as many
accessory buildings as possible; and by this means pro-

---

* These were made up as follows:

Supply units		Mechanical transport		Horse or mule transport	
Field bakeries	45	M.T. companies	605	H.T. companies	552
Bakery sections	58	Mobile repair units	22	H.T. Depots	7
Field butcheries	29	M.T. depots	21		
Railhead supply detachments	73				
Depot units of Supply	84				
Lines of communication supply companies	38				
Supply depots	19				

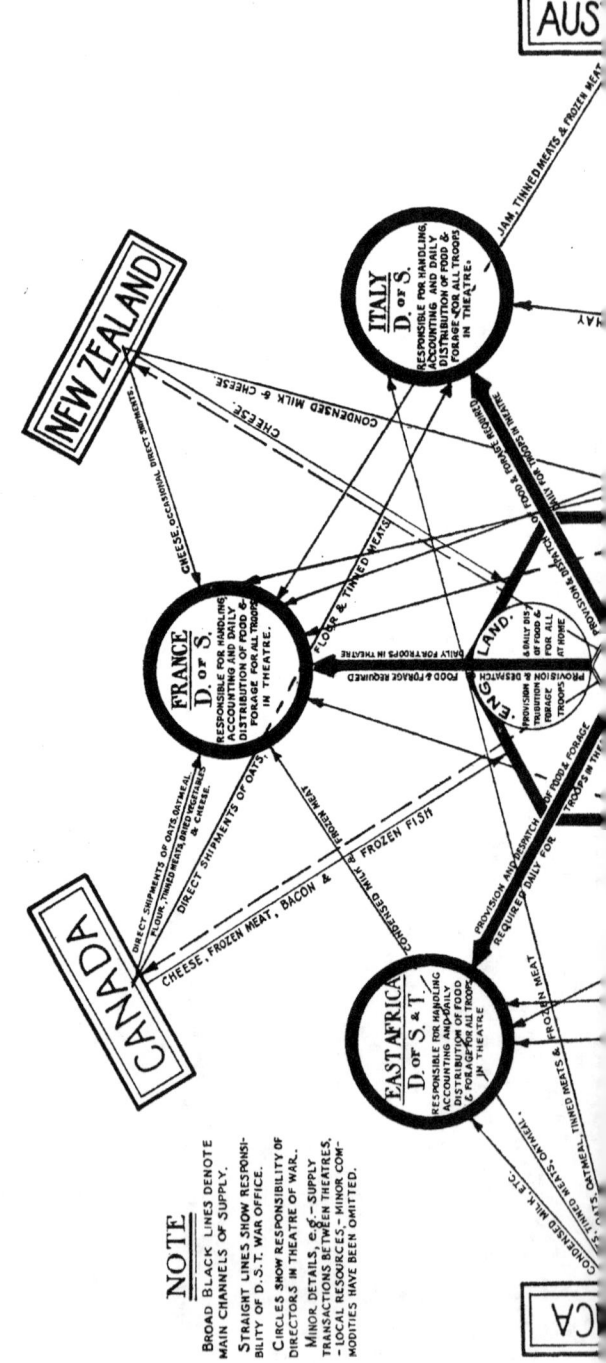

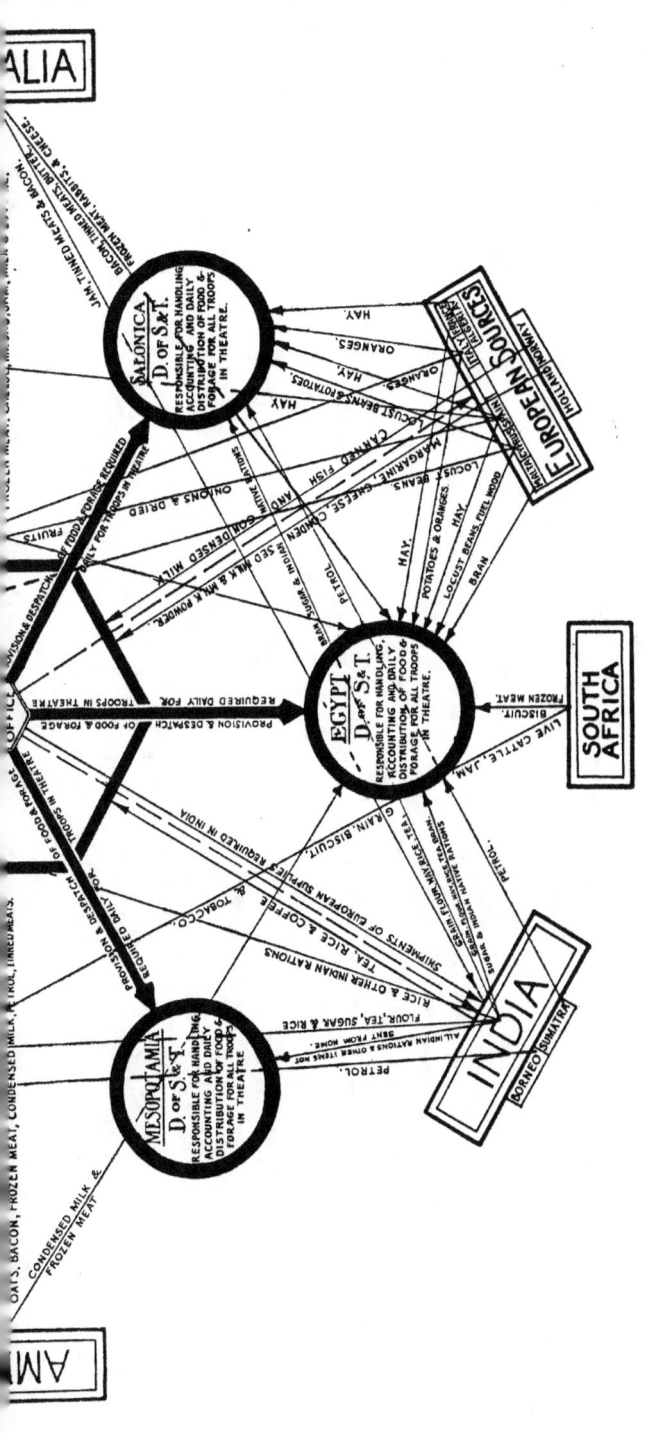

vision was made for 262,000 men. This, however, was only a portion of the numbers as, apart from the New Armies, accommodation had to be provided for largely increased numbers of the Special Reserve and the Territorial Force. Many of the troops had to be placed under canvas, while others were housed in specially hired buildings, but the bulk were billeted on the population, as many as 800,000 being provided for in this way at one time.

Premises had also to be acquired for hospitals, prisoners of war and for the storage of munitions, equipment, clothing, supplies and mechanical transport, and the work on this account, particularly in connection with the acquisition of schools, poor law institutions and asylums was very heavy.

Meanwhile the provision of large hutted camps was proceeded with up to accommodation for 850,000 men, which was the largest housing scheme ever attempted in Great Britain. The bad weather occurring in the autumn of 1914 aggravated by difficulties of shortage of labour and congestion of traffic, did much to delay the completion, but by May 1915 sufficient had been done to accommodate some 580,000 men therein, while the total number of troops for which quarters were then found in the United Kingdom reached the huge number of 1,407,000.*

* These were accommodated as follows:
  In barracks 262,000
  In huts 580,000
  Under canvas 264,000
  Billets and hired buildings 301,000

CHAPTER XIV

THE WAR PERIOD IN THE UNITED KINGDOM (*continued*)

IN an early chapter some outline was given of the steps which had been taken to organise the Mechanical Transport Branch of the Corps prior to the War. That narrative may now be continued into the realms of expansion and maintenance to meet the needs of the large army which was in the United Kingdom and ultimately the six major Expeditionary Forces which were on the continent of Europe, in Asia and in Africa.

Very early during the course of hostilities it became clear that the system by which mechanical transport affairs were dealt with in the same branch of the War Office as was charged with Animal Transport and Army Service Corps *personnel* would be inadequate, and accordingly a special sub-division of the Directorate of Supplies and Transport was formed. This was known as Q.M.G. 5. B,* and its nucleus was provided from the *personnel* of the establishment of the Chief Inspector of Mechanical Transport.

But a mere sub-division on these lines could not suffice to handle the ever growing responsibilities, and a second development occurred in November 1914, when, on the 27th of that month, a separate branch known as Q.M.G. 3 came into existence. As head of this was appointed Lieut.-Colonel H. N. Foster who had, it will be recalled, previously held the appointment of Chief Inspector of

---

* Up till then:
Q.M.G. 5 dealt with transport and A.S.C. *personnel*.
Q.M.G. 6 dealt with supplies.
Q.M.G. 1 dealt with quarterings.

Subsidised Transport, while Colonel H. C. L. Holden, an artillery officer who had rendered conspicuous services on the War Office Mechanical Transport Committee, was posted as Technical Adviser.

The plans which had been drawn up to meet the eventuality of mobilisation went smoothly in practice. The Inspector of Subsidised Transport, with a somewhat enhanced staff, undertook the impressment of vehicles needed to complete the Expeditionary Force, which work was put into operation on telegrams being sent out by the Director of Transport on the 4th of August, 1914. The intention to complete mobilisation by the fifth day was successfully accomplished, and arrangements were made to continue the impressment of vehicles against future needs when the Field Army had been equipped according to its establishment. A reserve of 25 per cent. was provided by this means, but no sooner was this completed than it was decided to increase the Expeditionary Force by two divisions from home and one from India, and at the same time to call the first of the New Armies into being. In the meantime, the existing regular mechanical transport units had proceeded to their mobilisation stations and thence to their mobilisation store depots to pick up their complement of stores. They then moved to their pre-arranged ports of embarkation,* where the vehicles, which had been called up were collected with their drivers, and where also men of the Special Reserve had been despatched.

There were two minor exceptions to this system, and these lay in the transport required for the Royal Flying Corps which was assembled at various stations throughout the country, and in the formation of an intermediate depot in Kensington Gardens to deal with the vehicles

---

* These ports were as follows:
For Headquarter units—Southampton.
For Army Troops and 1st, 2nd, 3rd and 4th Divisions—Avonmouth.
For the Cavalry Division and 5th and 6th Divisions—Liverpool.

from the London area. By the end of August this last establishment and also the port of Liverpool were closed down for mechanical transport, Aldershot being opened in lieu. This depot subsequently moved to Grove Park and later on to Camberwell, ending up at Kempton.

At the ports of embarkation the officers in charge of the vehicle depots were furnished with lists showing the numbers required to complete units embarking, the impressing officers being informed daily of the needs of each port and at the same time obtaining enlistment of the drivers who had not already joined the reserve.

Among the number of impressed vehicles, it was found that some three hundred arrived at Liverpool mechanically unfit from various causes, the principal of which were due to the over-anxiety of the civilian drivers to reach their destinations in the shortest possible time. These casualties were sent to the Army Service Corps at Bulford for repair and subsequent despatch overseas, and, since the mobilisation of the 7th Division was put in hand early in September, the mechanical transport units required for it came to be mobilised at the above station, which fact inaugurated Bulford as the mobilisation depot. Early in September Major F. L. Lloyd, R.E., who had been the first secretary to the Mechanical Transport Committee, assumed command.

There were two reasons which made "impressment" necessary at a very early stage. The smallness of the subsidy in the case of the main scheme had not encouraged civilian purchasers to make it an outstanding advantage to acquire the subsidy type, while the scheme had not been long enough in operation to provide the numbers needed at once.*

For the purposes of impressment the country had been divided into areas, to which were allotted the travelling inspectors—regular Army Service Corps officers, who had been similarly employed under the

* About seven hundred vehicles had been subsidised by August 1914.

subsidy schemes. These were supplemented by newly commissioned officers who, prior to the war, had been connected with the motor trade. In the case of new vehicles the War Office instructed as to the price to be paid, while for others the assessment was done by the impressing officer, who made out a note in quadruplicate, giving all details of the vehicle, and then passed copies to the vendor, the regimental paymaster of the Command concerned, and to the officer in charge of the reception depot, retaining the fourth in his own hands. The paymaster, being authorised to meet on sight the charge shown on the note, no delay occurred in settling claims, and store credit was given in due course by the reception depot by certifying on its copy that the vehicle in question had been taken on charge, and then passing that copy to the paymaster. This system was not wholly satisfactory owing to the possibility of impressment notes being given by two or even more impressment officers in succession for the same vehicle, which had, unknown to them, been delayed in delivery or had been moved to another area after its initial impressment. This was subsequently remedied by the centralisation of issue of notes through the Finance Department of the War Office, to whom their rendition was covered on the part of the payees by a copy of the letter sent from the Mechanical Transport Branch in which was contained the necessary order and the price assessed.

Eventually the arrangements of definite contracts were entered into with the manufacturers by the Contract Branch of the War Office, but this could not be undertaken until the production of vehicles had settled down to a normal steady output, since the time element prevented its adoption in the early stages. But the exercise of the power to impress vehicles remained confined to Q.M.G. 3, and it was, in fact, required to be exercised from time to time for any abnormal or urgent needs.

THE WAR PERIOD IN THE UNITED KINGDOM

The ramifications of the Inspecting Staff on which fell the responsibility for producing the vehicles were so far reaching that it is of interest to explore them somewhat further.

Maintenance in quality was, naturally, considered of equal importance to volume of output, and a high standard of inspection was fixed from the beginning with the result that, although rejections were heavy in the early days, when demands were extremely pressing, there was a continual improvement in quality, and consequently a continual reduction in the number of rejections. The inspecting Army Service Corps officers not only tested vehicles manufactured in their respective areas, but assisted the makers in obtaining material by applying the necessary pressure on the firms concerned with the production of that material, and in some cases invoking the aid of the War Office towards that end. The provision of spare parts was handled in the same manner, and delivery often maintained and accelerated by personal interviews with indispensable workmen who were recommended for exemption badges.

How effectively these methods operated is indicated from the fact that the output was increased from ninety lorries per week in 1914 to two hundred and fifty a week by July 1915, and by October 1915 it had been sufficiently augmented to allow the release of seventeen hundred vehicles to firms employed on the production of other munitions requiring transport.

A further duty which devolved upon the impressing officers was the notification to manufacturers of defects brought to light by service conditions, while suggestions for general improvement from a military point of view were continually being put forward and, if found practicable, embodied in the design.

As the war progressed and new expeditions were launched, the resources of the United Kingdom were inadequate to meet them. Trials of American types of vehicles were therefore arranged when their manufacturers had agents on the spot, and also for American vehicles brought over with the early Canadian divisions, and, as a result, contracts were made which produced some 8500 lorries and 5500 motor cars by the end of 1916.* Bodies for the American chassis including the four-wheel drive lorries were, however, fitted in England.

With regard to Ford vehicles, it had always been recognised that their design and construction rendered them eminently suitable for certain conditions, but for some time they could not be made available owing to the pacificist views of Mr Ford himself, and he was able to prevent their sale to the War Office except in the form of ambulances. Fortunately, at a later date, Mr Ford modified his opinions and his products were then introduced in large numbers, a considerable proportion being shipped direct from the United States to the eastern theatres of war, thus saving shipping.

Although mechanical transport policy aimed at restricting the various types in use in order to simplify maintenance and the supply of spare parts, that policy was always traversed by the prior need for quantity; and indeed other and unusual factors intervened to complicate the question. Of these, two instances may be cited. Foreign Office representation made it imperative to take over the entire output of the Berna Company's factory in Switzerland in order to prevent the enemy from obtaining it. The delivery was made direct to the British Commission in Paris. Again, when the army went to Italy in the winter of 1917 a number of Fiat lorries were necessarily acquired.

As it stood, the list of types manufactured in the United Kingdom was comprehensive enough, including as it did eleven varieties of three-ton, four of thirty-

* The types of lorries were: Packard, Peerless, Pierce-Arrow, Locomobile, Saurer, four-wheel drive, and Holt caterpillar tractors. The cars were chiefly Studebaker, Maxwells and Overlands.

hundredweight lorries and seven of motor cars, fixed as standard for military service, not counting those of the Royal Flying Corps.*

As regards the latter, by a curious anomaly the provision of its mechanical transport was originally in the hands of the "Inspector of Iron Structures", but this arrangement did not last, and Q.M.G. 3 soon assumed the duties. The Leyland lorry and the Crossley car were adopted as standard, but there were a number of Maudsley and A.E.C. lorries allotted to make good the deficiencies in Leyland production.

Certain vehicles, chiefly ambulances, were presented to the War Office from time to time during the first three years of the war. These presentations were most acceptable when they took the form of actual cash, as it was then possible to place this against orders for standard types—the vehicles being inscribed with the names of the donors; but when the vehicle itself was presented it was seldom of a standard type and for that reason led to complications.

In concluding this brief survey of the machinery by which the mechanical transport service was equipped, reference may be made to the question of reserves. Never for one moment was vigilance allowed to relax in this respect. Shipping considerations alone dictated a careful watch on the reserves in each particular theatre, while the number of obsolete vehicles in use and their disposal and replacement demanded constant attention.

Let us turn now from problems of material to those of men.

Following the despatch of the Expeditionary Force

---

* The three-ton lorries were as follows: Albion, Maudsley, Dennis, Pagefield, Daimler, Thornycroft, Karrier, British Berna, Wolseley, Hallford and Napier, of which the last four were reserved for Home Service only. The thirty-hundredweight lorries were: Daimler, Straker Squire, Napier, Belsize, of which the last two were reserved for Home Service. Motor cars comprised Sunbeams, Vauxhalls, Wolseleys, Austins, Daimlers, Singers and Siddeley Deasys.

and the absorption of the reservists, a reception depot for recruits was opened to deal with the expansion of the army. This was located at Grove Park, Lee, in South-East London, where the workhouse buildings of Greenwich and adjoining boroughs were taken over. Officers, who had been commissioned for the Mechanical Transport Branch of the Corps reported there for duty and, after being put through a driving test, were given instructions on the military side of their work before being sent overseas. Other ranks, both drivers and artificers, were dealt with in a similar manner, after being classified according to their trade in civil life. Under the system of voluntary enlistment which obtained until 1916 these recruits were originally paid at the high rate of six shillings a day to bring them into line with those who had been entered for the Special Reserve prior to mobilisation, and in order to attract men with the necessary skill. Experience soon showed this system to be unsatisfactory, as a number of unskilled men, drawn by the high rates, contrived to slip in, while, not unnaturally, discontent was caused among those serving on lower rates in the Mechanical Transport Branch quite apart from the invidious comparison created *vis-à-vis* other arms of the service. However, the first step required was to check the influx of unskilled men, which the ordinary recruiting officer was not qualified to do, and to this end a test centre was set up at Grove Park, through which candidates were required to pass before being finally approved. This failed to meet the case, as it became so unduly congested that it was impossible to cope with the volume of work. Accordingly qualified officers were sent out to assist the recruiting officers by a verbal technical examination. This plan proved successful and was extended to the point of establishing seventeen officers with staffs as permanent affiliations to recruiting districts.

With the introduction of conscription many of these difficulties disappeared. On receipt of their calling-up papers the men reported to the recruiting offices, where representatives of the Mechanical Transport Branch picked out those skilled for enlistment into the various technical services, including the Royal Flying Corps, Tank Corps and Army Ordnance Corps. At a later stage these last Corps sent out their own recruiting officers but, by that time, competition had become so keen that artificers were distributed on a definite War Office allotment, all tradesmen other than drivers being sent to a Trade Test Centre at Woolwich from whence they were despatched direct under instructions from the Adjutant-General's Department. The interests of each Corps were watched at Woolwich by officers who picked the men best suited to the work of each particular Corps. This resulted in the Army Service Corps mechanical transport officers in the various recruiting centres having only to deal with the drivers and learner-drivers whom they forwarded direct to Grove Park, and this arrangement was maintained up to the end of the war.

In connection with the provision of skilled drivers and artificers it is of interest to recall that the first Tank unit was entirely an Army Service Corps establishment, since the whole of the *personnel* was formed by that Corps.

As in the case of all the administrative services and departments, the decision made in 1916 that men of high physical category would be required to transfer to the infantry bore hardly on the efficiency of the mechanical transport. There were then serving some 80,000 skilled men who came under the terms of this edict, and these could only be replaced by men less skilled and of a comparatively low medical category. Such circumstances inevitably had a marked effect on the efficient operation of the mechanical transport, and this was reflected by a heavy multiplication of accidents and the abuse of the mechanism of the vehicles. Serious financial loss was also involved and made itself almost at once apparent by the increased demand for spare parts for replacements, increased strain on the repairing facilities, and a rise in the number of evacuations of *personnel* through sickness. The complexities of an equable and effective adjustment of the man-power resources of the nation need no emphasis here, but it may be accepted that under the conditions then prevailing the infantry had the prior claim to those most physically fit. Yet few would maintain that that thesis should in practice be carried to its logical conclusion for, by the absorption of those of a high degree of technical skill, which skill used extraneously might be essential to assist the fighting men in their task, the infantry might ultimately stand to lose rather than to gain. And even above the interests of the infantry upon whom the heaviest sacrifice fell there were the interests of the army and finally of the country. The question is only susceptible of solution by balancing the degree of technical skill, and its value to the whole machine, against the more direct and obvious call for numbers in the ranks of those who are actually to do the fighting, a process very difficult to carry out where hundreds of thousands of individuals were involved within the army and millions within the nation.

While recognising, then, the necessities for sacrifice it may yet be doubted whether the full extent of the mental and physical strain to which the drivers of the mechanical transport were normally subjected in the field was fully appreciated. In fact, some modifications in the original instructions were found necessary. In the Egyptian Expeditionary Force, for instance, it was found impracticable to replace the high-category men, for no others could have effectively performed the work upon which the operations so largely depended. The transfer of artificers everywhere had to be stopped at an early stage to avoid disaster. For the rest the situation was met by a form of dilution, so that skilled men who were at the same time of high medical category were reserved for units working in the forward areas, and under specially onerous conditions. Skilled men of lower medical categories were drafted to bases, lines of communications, or were retained in the great depots in the United Kingdom, where the work was of a more regular nature and the conditions easier.

As the supply of trained men became practically negligible, it was necessary to devise a scheme for the instruction of drivers. The first arrangement made was in February 1915 in conjunction with the London General Omnibus Company, who had for some time maintained a school of their own. Recruits were there given a six weeks' course for a fee of five pounds.

Subsequently the Army Service Corps established its own training school at Osterley Park, and further reference will be made to this institution in noting the various organisations.

Reverting to the history of the Directorate at the War Office which, as has been indicated in a reference made in the preceding chapter, was destined to undergo certain vicissitudes of fortune.

By pre-war intentions, when the Expeditionary Force was once launched and its vehicles provided, further requirements both for vehicles and spare parts were assigned to the Department of the Chief Inspector of Mechanical Transport. These arrangements, which might have responded to the needs of a comparatively small force, were at once recognised as inadequate for the great armies which were being called into being, and therefore, in so far as vehicles were concerned, the War Office retained control of supply. This system held good for two years, after which it was decided that the War Office should place its orders through the newly formed Ministry of Munitions instead of direct on the firms manufacturing, and since the Ministry of Munitions was in no position to do this through its own resources, a portion of the staff at the War Office and from the Home Mechanical Transport Depot, which under Lieut.-

Colonel Brander* dealt with spare parts, was in October 1916 transferred to the establishment presided over by Mr Lloyd George. The Supply and Inspection Sections from Q.M.G. 3 were both so removed.

As the war progressed the Army Council decided, as a result of representations addressed to the Secretary of State for War by the Quartermaster-General and the Surveyor-General of Supply, that the latter should include in his functions an advisory capacity in regard to the supply of mechanical transport. The outcome of this resolution was the setting up of the "Mechanical Transport Board" which, formed in September 1917, consisted of the Quartermaster-General as chairman, the Surveyor-General of Supply, the Director of Supplies and Transport, the head of Q.M.G. 3, with three civilian members of the Surveyor-General's staff. The terms of reference were that the Board "should deal with questions of policy and principle arising in connection with the administration provision and maintenance of mechanical transport". As invariably happens in such circumstances one of the first steps was towards an increase of establishment and an enhancement of grades, though in this particular instance there was a good case for re-organising the branch of Q.M.G. 3, which up till then had been decidedly over-burdened. The augmented staff consisted of seventeen officers with two additional for the purpose of liaison with the Ministry of Munitions, and five sub-divisions were organised, dealing respectively with the *Personnel*, Mobilisation, Home Service, Provision and Technical, Statistics and Accounts.

A glance may be cast at the work under the above sections, in so far as it has not already been described.

* Lieut.-Colonel M. S. Brander, a very able organiser, succeeded Lieut.-Colonel Donohue in September 1916, when the latter's services were required for inspection work in the field. Colonel Brander had previously been in command of the base depot at Calais, of which some account has already been given. In January 1918 Colonel Brander was succeeded by Lieut.-Colonel T. R. P. Warren, A.S.C.

THE WAR PERIOD IN THE UNITED KINGDOM

As concerned *personnel* there may be added the instance of the recruitment of women drivers. From the points of view of tradition, prestige and even convention, it might have been supposed that the engagement of women would have provoked weighty opposition. And certainly there were to be found those who adduced reasons strong enough against so drastic an innovation. But neither the Quartermaster-General nor the Director of Supplies and Transport possessed types of mind that leaned unduly on the past. The opportunity to harness new sources to the national effort was, therefore, eagerly seized, and in December 1916 Lady Londonderry, who was President of the Women's Legion, was authorised to form a section of female motor drivers, with Miss Christobel Hills in charge. These drivers were first attached to the Mechanical Transport Companies of the Army Service Corps in London, but in the following year were taken over for direct control by the War Office, with a Headquarters situated in London with a Commandant, a Deputy and four Assistant Commandants. A school was started at Twickenham, where a six weeks' course was given to a hundred and fifty pupils at a time, and women drivers were subsequently employed on cars, ambulances, box vans, and motor cycles and side-cars at home. They signed on for one year at a time, and received twenty-five shillings for the first month on probation, afterwards being paid at the rate of thirty-eight shillings a week with uniform found.

The experiment was fully justified and enabled an equivalent number of men to be replaced for service overseas. Yet the precedent really went above and beyond the substantial material benefits that accrued, for it powerfully assisted to exemplify in deed the unity of the whole nation, and in addition pointed a way of service which up to that time had been considered the prerogative of men and men alone.

It is, therefore, in no qualified or patronising spirit

that tribute is paid to the contribution made to the women mechanical transport drivers.*

The work of the *Personnel* Section of Q.M.G. 3 ranged from the enlistment of recruits through every phase of the movement of individuals down to the final discharge, including provisions for new units, reinforcement, the training of officers, of male and female drivers, and of coloured labour and the dilution of white labour with the latter. Probable requirements in man-power were estimated for from month to month, a difficult question at all times, but especially so when man-power resources became increasingly acute, and when full reasons were required for every demand by the harassed department of the Adjutant-General, while at the same time the needs of the various theatres overseas varied from week to week.

In the Mobilisation Section of Q.M.G. 3 the work of the other sections was co-ordinated. *Personnel*, vehicles, spare parts, and equipment were all gathered into one cohesive whole and fitted in to organised units according to the authorised war establishments. Final movements for shipment were also arranged in conjunction with the Movements Branch. The scope of this particular task may be gauged from the fact that for all other arms and branches of the service that task was carried out by a Special Mobilisation Branch under the Adjutant-General, which communicated the necessary instructions in detail to all concerned. Mechanical transport companies were,

---

* Many amusing and legitimate stories are extant concerning the women motor drivers, and it may not be out of place to quote one as exemplifying the spirit of that organisation.

A well-known political peer and member of the Cabinet being deposited at his destination instructed his driver to call for him an hour later.

"Very good", she replied.

"Perhaps I should say", rejoined the Minister, "that I am normally accustomed to be addressed as 'My Lord'".

"Very good, my Lord", answered the chauffeuse, "but perhaps I ought to add that I am normally accustomed to be addressed as 'My Lady'"—which was perfectly true.

however, invariably dealt with by Q.M.G. 3 direct, while, in the case of those units which possessed a quota of mechanical transport, it was the custom of the Adjutant-General's Department to refer units in question to Q.M.G. 3 for action.

The Home Service Section dealt, as its name implied, with all mechanical transport work in the United Kingdom, which included emergency provisions in the event of civil disturbances, invasion, or breakdown of the existing civilian transport services. All voluntary work, whether individual or collective, was in its hands. Special units such as those employed on Canadian forestry activities throughout the country, and others dealing with Army postal work peculiar to the London district, and also one to deal with mechanical vehicles of the infant Signal Corps likewise fell to the charge of this section.

Technical questions, raised from at home or abroad, were dealt with by the fourth section, that is Q.M.G. 3 D. Its main rôle naturally was liaison with the Ministry of Munitions, which, as shown, had become primarily responsible for the supply of vehicles and spare parts. But there remained the important duty of distribution, the release of vehicles by makers to civilian owners and also for export to various countries, as well as the technical administration of the Home Repair Depot and Home Mechanical Transport Depot. In addition, in order to make good any deficiencies in supplies from the Ministry of Munitions, the administration of the Army Act dealing with the impressment of vehicles also came within the purview of Q.M.G. 3 D. Finally may be mentioned also what was termed the "rationing" of spare parts and accessories as between the various theatres of war, and their control and issue to Dominion or Allied Forces.

The Statistics and Accounting Section was responsible for furnishing to all the others figures required by them on given data, and it also performed the secretarial duties for the Mechanical Transport Board such as preparing agenda, collecting information and circulating the proceedings.

Among the more general aspects of the work of Q.M.G. 3 that which concerned liaison with the Artillery Directorate was the most important, for the artillery programme exercised a profound influence on mechanical transport preparations. As an example a six-inch howitzer battery intended for France required four-wheel drive lorries for towing purposes. But if the destination of any particular battery was, for instance, altered to Egypt, possibly at short notice, Holt caterpillar tractors took the place of the four-wheel drive lorries and caterpillar track trailers were, in addition, needed for ammunition and stores. At the same time the medical category of the *personnel* suitable for France was not the same as that of men suitable for Egypt.

Existing establishments were continually under review and modification with the object of increased economy in money, man-power and material, apart from alterations made possible by changes in terrain and other local conditions. As a result, the various Commanders-in-Chief in the field were from time to time given instructions to carry out reforms tending to greater saving and efficiency. Occasions, too, arose in which Allied Governments requested information on mechanical transport subjects, and sent delegations of their experts to examine and report on the British system. The extent to which many of its principles were adopted abroad was flattering to British military organisation—not always or even often liable to foreign approbation.

But perhaps the most momentous collaboration was that involved by the contact with the General Staff Branch, which was effected by daily conferences under the chairmanship of the Director of Staff Duties. At these conferences were considered the innumerable demands from all theatres for mechanical transport, and their priority in relation to the proportionate significance of the operations in each. Thus complete harmony was established between the combatant and maintenance points of view prior to engaging on or pursuing strategical, or in certain instances even grand tactical, enterprises. The value of this commonsense method may be particularly stressed as in contrast to the "water-tight" departmental ways of former times.

Details of the interior working of the Headquarters' control and its resultant functions have been somewhat laboured, but they have been laboured designedly, and for two reasons. In the first place they furnish an example of the administration of a great new auxiliary service called upon in the very early days of its life to undertake burdens for which there was no precedent and which, therefore, demanded unusual qualities of initiative, imagination and prescience.

Secondly, while all portions of the Corps touched directly upon the activities of their brethren in the fighting arms in that food and ammunition were required to be delivered punctually at all times and in all places, which delivery was for the larger part effected, at the last, by animal transport, yet none except certain horse transport *personnel* attached bore quite the same position *vis-à-vis* the fighting arms as the mechanical transport units. For, as shown in the course of the narrative, those units were often integral parts of a fighting arm. They were, to recall some instances, required to provide vehicles and drivers by thousands for the heavy and medium batteries; to man armed motor boats, to drive armoured cars, and to furnish field workshops for them, to find the fighting transport for anti-aircraft, artillery and pontoon parks, and finally to supply a nucleus for the infant Tank Corps. It was a rôle calculated to satisfy the most adventurous of organisations.

It now remains to give some short account of the principal great base establishments in the United Kingdom, through whose agency the executive part of the work was performed. To certain of these reference has already been made in the course of the narrative dealing with the general aspects of administration, but a few details may be added.

The task of the Home Mechanical Transport Depot was to supply from the outbreak of war all stores for the equipment and maintenance of vehicles coming under the control of the War Office, and later also to carry out the same functions for Admiralty and Royal Air Force vehicles. In addition, spares and accessories were also provided from time to time to Dominion and foreign Governments, which included those of the United States, Italy, Belgium, Serbia, Greece and Portugal. And the scope was even extended further than military fields, for all departments of the British Government employing mechanical transport made demands on the organisation which had been set up in the first instance for the needs of the British Army alone.*

The nomenclature "Inspection Branch Mechanical Transport" had been retained, on the move from a building adjoining the workshops of No. 52 Company, A.S.C., at Aldershot in February 1915 to Shorts Gardens, London, until Lieut.-Colonel Brander took command in September 1916. An Army Council Instruction was then issued, altering the title to denote the real purpose of the organisation. In the interim the original depot in Shorts Gardens had been augmented by a number of sub-depots opened in various parts of London, with one

* Among the more important of the departments may be mentioned:
Food Production Department.
Ministry of Food.
Foreign Office.
General Post Office.
Timber Supplies Department.
Navy and Army Canteen Board.
Contractors to War Department.
Y.M.C.A.
British Red Cross.
Office of Works.

at Liverpool.* At the close of 1918 the total area occupied was 456,680 square feet, and even the store accommodation was inadequate for a wholly economic and efficient administration.

In August 1914 the staff had comprised only a dozen men and it rose two months later to seventy-five. From then onwards the increase was rapid, the maximum being reached in December 1918 at 2431;† and in this connection the most noteworthy fact was: the increase in the output of stores was greatly in excess of the proportionate increase in the amount of labour employed, in spite of the continual depreciation in the physical quality of the *personnel* available, the substitution of much female for male labour, and the disadvantages inherent in the dispersion due to outlying stores and offices becoming necessary instead of expansion on the site of a central depot.

The initial difficulties naturally lay in the lack of data on which to estimate for provision, and there the technical knowledge of that portion of the staff previously connected with the motor trade was valuable. But records of experiences of vehicles under war conditions were essential for a full answer to the question, and *these* were carefully compiled from records coming to hand. There

* These were, with dates of opening:

Sub-depot

No. 2 Camden Town, May 1915	Tyres. American vehicle spares "except Studebaker"
No. 3 Carlow Street, N.W., January 1916	
No. 4 Gray's Inn Road, W.C., April 1915	
No. 6 Seaforth Barracks, Liverpool, August 1915	Studebaker spares. Mobile workshop equipment. Stores in transit awaiting shipment. Temporary storage of American spares and tyres

In addition a No. 5 sub-depot was subsequently opened in Cressy Road, N.W., in June 1918. This dealt with oil and paints.

† These were divided as under:

Officers	 60	Civilians: males	 321
Other ranks	 1400	females	 650

were, as might have been supposed, many complications in the study of such experiences, for results in France differed materially from those in Salonika, while neither were of little value for Mesopotamia nor East Africa. As an instance, a schedule of spare parts for a given type of vehicle if destined for Salonika would show four times the number of springs as would appear on a schedule for the same vehicle if destined for France. It was found also that, whereas in England the pre-war average mileage of a lorry solid tyre might reasonably be put at a minimum of 10,000 miles, this varied materially in the different theatres, and in Palestine reached as low a basis as a few hundred miles per tyre.

Again the weak points of different types of vehicles showed marked variation. Thus, if 1000 vehicles of a given contractor's make required a certain supply of repair parts for upkeep, it was found that 1000 vehicles of another make required a totally different proportion to maintain convoys on the road.

Any detailed examination of the internal working of the depot is uncalled for here, but one aspect is so significant that it should be set down. A continuous process of stocktaking was in operation from April 1917 onwards, involving a count and check of the actual stocks against their respective store ledger balance. This work was carried out at all the sub-depots and among the stores purchased and held with the makers. The total deficiencies brought to light for the whole period up to the end of 1918 as a result of this stocktaking amounted to £1057, and in practically all cases the origin of deficiencies could be traced to an early period of the war when great urgency was demanded. Since the value of the stores received and issued from 1915 to 1918 inclusive was approximately sixty million pounds, the loss amounted to a ratio of 0·0017 per cent. on the turnover, and even then, had it been permissible to employ stocktaking surpluses in reduction, those deficiencies would have been almost obliterated. Finally, the volume of work may be summed up most appropriately by the figures for the vehicles in service and, therefore, requiring maintenance in December 1918. They were 164,319, divided as follows: lorries 66,742, cars and ambulances 42,584, motor cycles 48,308, tractors 5400, and steam wagons 1285.

The second of the great installations to which attention must now be directed is that which was established at Grove Park, Lee, for the purpose of receiving and training *personnel*.

After the British Expeditionary Force had been provided for in August 1914 by the incorporation of the reservists, special reservists, and supplementary enlistments, the machinery was evolved to meet reinforcements and expansion and, in addition, the needs of depots in the United Kingdom.

The inauguration of the scheme which had been prepared against the eventuality of war was the formation of No. 1 Reserve Mechanical Transport Depot, for the accommodation and training of recruits, in which a start was made with eight hundred on the 23rd of September. From thence onwards recruits poured in, on several occasions reaching as many as four hundred a day, while the numbers clothed in a single week exceeded at times 4000. The pressure became so great that the accommodation became unequal to dealing with it however it was stretched, and consequently various measures of decentralisation were taken. By the end of 1915 there were sub-depots at Eltham, Lee and Catford, while a technical school of instruction had been opened at Osterley Park, with a driving school at Hounslow. For the time being these measures sufficed, but activities tended to increase continually as new units were formed at a rapid pace, while the transfer of skilled men to the fighting arms and the necessity of training their replacements, besides the normal flow of unskilled or comparatively unskilled recruits made the task very burdensome. In June 1917, therefore, a further re-organisation took place, when what was known as the Mechanical Transport Reception and Training Centre came into being, and this included the depot at Grove Park with sub-depots at Eltham, Kelsey Manor and Mottingham Camp, and further depots at Lee, Shortlands and Norwood, a mobilisation centre at Sydenham and a mechanical transport repair depot at Camberwell. They were placed under Colonel R. O. Burne, who held the appointment of Assistant Director of Transport. Later the vehicle reception depot which was formed at Kempton Park and the training depot at Isleworth, which included the schools at Osterley Park and Hounslow, also came under the same control, although the Camberwell repair depot was removed from it. These changes resulted in a marked improvement, and the volume of work may to some extent be gauged from the fact that the area normally contained over 20,000 men at a time, the highest figure being 24,135. From the date of opening the Grove Park depot until the Armistice no less than 284,564 men arrived, an average of 1327 a week.

A glance may now be cast on certain of the more important activities.

A cadet company was started towards the end of 1915 to train as Army Service Corps mechanical transport officers, n.c.o.'s and men who had applied and been recommended for commissions. A short, but intensive course of five weeks' duration was given at first, but this was subsequently extended to eight weeks. The total number commissioned through this agency was 2510, while only a hundred and five who went through the course failed to pass out.

Reference has already been made to the provision for testing recruits, when dealing with the question of *personnel* generally, and it therefore remains to be added that a special company was formed for this purpose in July

1915, and that this company dealt with an average of 50,000 men a year during the course of its existence. For eighteen months the work was carried out under great difficulties owing to shortage of appliances with which to conduct the tests, but in the late autumn of 1916 shops were erected which enabled all classes of artificers to be examined, and lecture-rooms were also built for the purpose of giving trade instruction and "brushing up" courses to men who, though incapable of passing a test at the first attempt, needed only a little tuition to become useful mechanics. Those who were clearly useless as artificers were, unless of the physical category A 1, sent to learn driving. Drivers who passed their tests were posted to the depot at Shortlands, where their documents were completed before they were posted either to the Bulford mobilisation centre or to a home service company: those who were recommended for instruction were sent via the Sydenham depot or Eltham sub-depot to the training centre at Osterley Park.

From the Sydenham depot drafts for overseas, *personnel* for conducting convoys for embarkation, and for home service duties were provided, while Eltham was used to accommodate men unavailable for various reasons for mobilisation until May 1917, when it merely dealt with those awaiting instruction and posting. The depot at Norwood was started in November 1916 for instructing drivers, but it only carried out these functions for some three months and subsequently took the place of Eltham for "unavailables".

The Isleworth Mechanical Transport Depot embodying the Osterley Park and Hounslow centres has an important rôle. There was accommodation for 2200 men and intensive twenty-eight day courses in driving and technical instruction were given to recruits, a large proportion of whom were category "B" men who, having been wounded, had been transferred from the infantry. Those who failed to pass were sent as packers and loaders to the Army Service Corps Supply Branch, the successful being despatched to the mobilisation centre at Bulford. The technical instruction was given at the school at Osterley Park itself, while the driving was taught at the London General Omnibus Company's premises at Hounslow, which had been taken over for that purpose. The work of these establishments is of high interest, as it represented the earliest attempt made by the British Army to grapple with the problem of what may be termed "mass production" of technical *personnel*. As it eventually turned out some 45,000 semi-skilled men, it may be said to have been successful.

Towards the opening of this chapter there has been noted the inception of the Bulford Mobilisation and Embarkation Area under the command of Major (afterwards Colonel) Lindsay Lloyd, and from September 1914 its functions were steadily built up with these main objectives, which lay in the mobilisation of mechanical transport units, the repair of vehicles and the despatch overseas of reinforcements of men and vehicles. Four mobilisation companies were formed, and these were charged with the preparation of new units. The various ranks required by the war establishment had to be grouped together and equipped according to the scale laid down in the mobilisation store tables. Officers were selected by the Headquarters of the Centre and vehicles were issued by the Vehicle Department. All the multitudinous details required to turn a mass of men and vehicles into a unit definitely allocated for some special purpose were undertaken—or, in other words, the material provided from other establishments in the form of men and vehicles was shaped into field formations.

As the accommodation at Bulford itself was inadequate to deal with more than a fraction of the *personnel* undergoing mobilisation, units, as soon as their mobilisation commenced, were billeted or camped at various points in the Southern Command, where there were at the same time facilities for training, easy access from Headquarters of the Area, and reasonable propinquity to the port of embarkation. To these ports arrangements were made for the journey, selected officers being appointed to conduct the convoys: no point, however small, was overlooked.

One particularly noteworthy side of this work was the furnishing of the Mechanical Transport Sections for the heavy artillery batteries which was there undertaken from the spring of 1916 onwards. For this purpose a Heavy Artillery Mechanical Transport Headquarters Company with two sub-depots were formed in June 1916, and this machinery was instrumental in preparing and despatching overseas no less than two hundred and ninety-three Army Service Corps units, including 14,362 all ranks, for service with the Royal Artillery. For the rest two hundred and eighty-one mechanical transport companies containing 54,026 all ranks were launched and sent into the field; while detachments amounting to 3357 were likewise provided as drafts and reinforcements. To realise the import of these figures it should be remembered that this work involved the selection, instruction, and appointing to acting-rank of the vast bulk of the warrant and non-commissioned officers and artificers.*

The Workshops and Stores Department divided into seven sub-sections was sufficiently large to justify a Lieut.-Colonel to command it. In so far as repairs were concerned, it dealt with eighty to a hundred vehicles at a time, these being received via the Vehicle Department from evacuation from overseas, and from units mobilising which required defects to be put right. The Vehicle Department was responsible for the receipt, testing and issue

---

* The numbers are not without interest:

Mechanist Serjt.-Majors: Warrant Officers, Class I	204
Company Serjt.-Majors: Warrant Officers, Class II	242
Company Quartermaster Serjeants	218
Mechanist Staff Serjeants	315
Other n.c.o.'s	8288

of vehicles both to units mobilising and to Expeditionary Forces direct, and, while it provided covered accommodation for some seven hundred vehicles, the numbers on hand at times greatly exceeded that number.

Subsidiary to the Headquarters at Bulford were the embarkation depots at Avonmouth and Portsmouth, the establishment of the first being officially approved in April 1915 and of the second in January 1917, when the necessity arose for a larger output. The titles of these organisations explain themselves, but it may be added that "inward" mechanical transport vehicles and stores had to be handled as well as those "outwards", while a good deal of minor repair work had to be carried out.*

To complete the review of the responsibilities of the Bulford area, may be mentioned the tractor depot at Avonmouth. This, the only one of its kind in the country, was originally started at Aldershot in December 1914 when it was called the "Caterpillar Section" and first attached to No. 52 Company, Army Service Corps. Seven months later its increasing importance caused it to be constituted as a separate unit, and in April 1916 it was moved to Avonmouth.

Its story has a certain historical interest, for it was the parent unit of all the roadless transport which was in future to effect so profoundly the science and practice of war.† None of the *personnel* joining this unit except one, who was an American, had ever enjoyed any previous experience of caterpillar work, and Mr Rose, who was Messrs Holt's representative in Great Britain, instructed the first detachment of six men for some time, subsequently paying occasional visits of inspection. On the

* During the year 1917 Avonmouth embarked 30,000 officers and men and 21,929 vehicles. For the first five months of its existence, *i.e.* from January to May 1917, Portsmouth embarked 13,246 officers and men and 7841 vehicles.

† It will be recalled that the Hornsby-Ackroyd tractor purchased in 1903 and subsequently converted to a caterpillar was the first vehicle of this type in the Army, but it was purely experimental and even aroused ridicule in certain quarters outside the Army Service Corps.

4th of February, 1915, the first overseas draft, consisting of fourteen men and three caterpillars, went out to join the 10th Siege Battery, Royal Garrison Artillery, but no officer was available, and the departure of the draft reduced the home section to three men and one caterpillar. From thence onwards, however, progress was comparatively rapid. Caterpillars began to arrive, commencing at the rate of two or three a week and, by the end of February, the *personnel* had attained a strength of one officer and sixty men. By July these numbers had increased to eight officers and two hundred and thirty-five n.c.o.'s and men, and the output rose accordingly. The nomenclature Tractor Depot, A.S.C., was given in February 1916.

Such were the modest beginnings of an organisation whose activities played a far-reaching part in the operations of the war. The heavy howitzers, for instance, depended almost entirely on its services. There is no occasion to pursue its history in any detail. Like other new creations brought about by the needs of the time, that history was one of continuous growth and development; the permanent staff ultimately comprising nineteen officers and five hundred and thirty-two other ranks, and fifteen hundred caterpillar tractors and two hundred trucks were through their agency despatched overseas.

Such were the chief parts of the machinery responsible for the creation and maintenance of a great service operating for the first time in history with the British armies in the field and, in many instances, under conditions which its most enthusiastic exponents could never have contemplated a few years before. And the thought inevitably arises as to how immense were the resources of Great Britain towards the production and the manipulation of mechanical forms of road transport. They were indeed immense, and the Army and the nation owes much to the highly organised motor industries and the able engineers which they gave to its service. Super-

THE WAR PERIOD IN THE UNITED KINGDOM

ficially it might seem that much of the work carried out within the Army Service Corps establishments in the United Kingdom barely appertained to the profession of arms, and might have almost been effected within civilian factories and workshops. But it needs little thought to refute such a view. In the first place the genesis of the organisation lay on carefully matured plans to meet specific military needs, which plans could expand and develop as the military situation dictated, and in so doing embody and assimilate all the necessary supplementary or reinforcing elements required from outside. Secondly, it was essential that those in whose hands the direction of the mechanical transport service lay should be in practical touch with its operations in many fields of war; and this practical touch could only be obtained by a constant interchange of *personnel*. The most brilliant engineer would lose much of his value if unacquainted in fact with the actual conditions he was required to combat or provide against. And lastly the question of discipline and uniformity of methods even in home depots needs no emphasis, especially since by far the larger proportion of the rank and file were in process of transit to and from the armies.

It was fortunate, therefore, that there existed a trained nucleus of soldiers, for only by and through such nucleus could so great a task have been consummated.*

Before turning to the provision of Army Service Corps supply and horse transport *personnel*, to which comparatively brief reference only is required, it will be

* For those interested in financial statistics the following figures of expenditure on mechanical transport material are given:

1914–1915	£7,362,000
1915–1916	£20,217,249
1916–1917	£25,000,000
1917–1918	£49,000,000,

of which a total of £45,264,850 was spent on purchase of vehicles.

convenient to deal with one article of supply regarding which as yet nothing has been said—the more so, because that supply as an army demand lacked precedent, while it will in the future have an importance second to none.

The provision and the distribution of petrol was by no means the simplest duty which fell to the Army Service Corps during the war. In the early stages there were few difficulties, but as the enemy submarine campaign developed and the naval and military requirements of Great Britain and her Allies increased, a critical shortage began to be felt. Oil tank vessels, never too numerous, were, owing to their slow speed, about eight knots, peculiarly liable to submarine attack, while the submarines affected consumption by the increased activities of destroyers in combating them.*

In consequence, towards the end of 1915, the Government assumed control of petroleum supplies through the medium of the Petrol Control Committee, which concerned itself mainly in the restriction of private consumption and economy propaganda. These half-measures proving ineffective, the Petrol Executive was created to take over the entire purchase and control of imports. "Tanker" construction was accelerated, and tonnage saved in collaboration with the United States Government by re-routing tank steamers in such a manner that demands were met by supplies from the nearest source; moreover, continuous day and night loading speeded up discharge.

In the earliest part of the war, the War Office had been drawing its supplies for France entirely from the Far East, Persia and Egypt through the "Shell" group, by

* In this connection it is interesting to note that a destroyer under full steam consumed about two hundred tons of petroleum fuel every twenty-four hours. Consequently, as a 6000-ton "tanker" under war conditions averaged sixty days for an "out and home" journey from Mexican ports, it required theoretically the services of one "tanker" to maintain one destroyer under full steam.

which the contract was held, but later under the action of the Petrol Executive the Asiatic Petroleum Company ("Shell") ceased, so far as Western Europe was concerned, to act as contractor, and became, in a sense, the War Office agent for the storage and distribution at overseas ports of the bulk supplies purchased and shipped for the armies. Similarly the Petrol Executive stored the War Department cargoes delivered at ports in the United Kingdom and set them off against supplies delivered in detail throughout the country under contract with the inland distributing firms. The Asiatic Petroleum Company continued to supply under contract in Egypt for the forces operating in Palestine, Salonika, and also East Africa. Requirements in Mesopotamia were obtained locally.

In sum, therefore, the re-routing resulted in Western Europe, including Italy, drawing on Transatlantic ports, the Middle East or Egypt, and all theatres east of Suez other than Mesopotamia on the Far East—that is, the Dutch East Indies and, to a small extent, Burmah.

The success of these measures was reflected between the summer of 1917, when stocks were dangerously low, and the position at the date of the Armistice when the position was well in hand to serve the naval, military and aerial programme projected for the summer of 1919.

To meet the initial necessities in 1914 the Supply Directorate had a contract with the Asiatic Petroleum Company for delivery at Portishead, Bristol, whence shipments were made to French ports in cans and cases. Including aviation petrol, consumption during the earlier months did not exceed 250,000 gallons a month, supply being taken mainly in two-gallon cans, four cans to the case, but also to some extent in four-gallon cans of two cans to the case. The latter was a flimsy contrivance, and the only reason for using it was the fact that the contractors happened to have a four-gallon-can manufacturing plant ready for export to the East and they diverted it to Portishead in order to increase the output of that installation. By the end of 1915 the War Office was required to make provision for 1,600,000 gallons a month, and the amount was rising rapidly. Portishead was, therefore, producing over 50,000 gallons a day and it was not long before still more was demanded of it. Supplemented by stocks filled at Fulham and railed to Portishead or Avonmouth for shipment, it attained what was considered to be its maximum capacity of 85,000 gallons, and even this amount could not keep pace with expenditure. The Supply Directorate aimed at keeping in France at all times a reserve stock equal to thirty days' consumption at the current rate, and it therefore followed that, whenever the official average figure was raised, a corresponding increase had to be made in the reserve in order to bring stocks to the required level. Difficulties were further enhanced by the limited facilities at the French ports, only one petrol berth at each being usually available. By the adoption of "heroic" measures, which included special exhortations from the Quartermaster-General urging the employees at Portishead to greater efforts, a production of 100,000 gallons a day for some weeks was effected, and this served to tide over a very critical period. It was obvious, however, that resort would have to be made to other means and, as subsequent events proved, recognition of this was only made just in time to avoid serious consequences. The Directorate of Supplies having obtained the consent of the Finance Board at the War Office, the sanction of the French Government and the local Port Authorities, the Shell Company leased the necessary tank storage from the French Refining Companies on behalf of the War Department and undertook the purchase, delivery and setting up of the plant for the manufacture of the cans and cases and for their filling. The Shell Company also engaged the necessary expert *personnel*—all of whom had

THE WAR PERIOD IN THE UNITED KINGDOM

to be turned into a quasi-military body before being embarked.

It was not until the end of 1917 that these two installations which were set up at Calais and Rouen and employed some 3000 hands, of which 2400 were women, were able to carry out the whole of the filling for the British armies in France and Italy. A few months later they did even more, for the War Office then undertook to supply the French and Belgian troops in the Calais area.

By the beginning of 1918 the monthly consumption of petrol in France had risen to eight million gallons for transport and three-quarters of a million gallons for aircraft. Between the commencement of the British advance in August and the Armistice it jumped once more, and eventually reached a monthly average of ten and a half million gallons for transport and one and a half million gallons for aircraft. Taking the two grades of spirit together, it will be seen, therefore, that between 1914 and 1918 the consumption in France multiplied itself forty-eight times, and that aviation petrol taken alone multiplied itself a hundred and fifty times. The 12,000,000 gallons consumed monthly represented 40,000 tons of shipping, and required approximately twelve "tanker" vessels to maintain it. Against these formidable figures the Supply Directorate aimed at holding a reserve of 50,000 tons of transport petrol in France and 36,000 in the United Kingdom; also 50,000 tons of aviation petrol between France and the United Kingdom.

In connection with the distribution of the immense quantities of aircraft petrol, it was only after the large bombing planes of the Handley-Page type had been constructed that it was realised how obsolete had become the system of supplying petrol in two-gallon cans. The tank capacity of the machines in question was 1400 gallons, and the seven hundred cans required to fill up occupied twenty men no less than eight hours. To ameliorate this state of affairs, inland filling installations were erected at each aerodrome. These consisted of sunk tanks at the nearest point on the railway connected to overhead and storage tanks situated in the aerodromes by means of pipe-lines running through one or more pumping stations according to the distance and intervening gradient. Trains of railway tank cars were despatched from Rouen as required and decanted by gravity feed into the sunk tanks alongside the railway. Aeroplanes were then able to draw their petrol through flexible leads from the overhead tanks under the supervision of one man, the operation taking less than one hour.

In order to replenish the aircraft installations a hundred and fifty rail tank cars, carrying 3000 gallons (ten tons) each, and a hundred and eighty road tank lorries, carrying 600 gallons each, were requisitioned and sent to France, where they eventually distributed in bulk some 15 per cent. of the total daily deliveries. There were, however, certain objections to their use as they were liable to block the roads in the act of filling, while the time occupied in replenishing a mechanical transport column rendered them unworkable in the forward areas. As a compromise, therefore, mechanical transport formations were furnished with a number of specially reinforced two-gallon cans and allowed to set up their own filling installation at the formation's headquarters, where the petrol could be decanted from the road tank lorry into these cans. While wasteful of petrol this method saved the ordinary petrol cans from going backwards and forwards between the front and the base port, though it would naturally have been quite impossible in mobile warfare.

The pre-occupations of the War Office had been much relieved by the system of direct supply of petrol to secondary theatres, but it will not be out of place to record certain anxious periods through which the supply authorities passed. As previously noted, for the Middle

East the contractors obtained their stocks from the Egyptian oilfields, supplemented as required from the Persian Gulf and the Far East, and four-gallon non-returnable cans were issued from the refinery at Suez, the output of which was 100,000 gallons a day. From this source, in addition to the Egyptian Expeditionary Force, the whole of the Allied armies in Salonika had to be maintained.

To convey such an inflammable cargo as petrol packed in the flimsy four-gallon can in commercial use required ships fitted with a suitable coffer-dam, and this frequently led to difficulties. In December 1917, for instance, two vessels caught fire when loaded at Port Said and became a total loss. The incident, coming as it did during a severe stringency of shipping, so aggravated the situation at Salonika that, in spite of the despatch measures taken to get a further cargo loaded and convoyed through the submarine-infested Aegean sea, the telegraphic return of supplies in hand from Salonika showed "NIL" on the day prior to the arrival of the relief steamer. A week before this the Chief of the Imperial General Staff had received a personal cable from the G.O.C. Salonika pointing out that, owing to the shortage of petrol, any idea of active operations was out of the question, and that it is doubtful whether the troops could be maintained in their existing positions.

The troubles in this respect at Salonika were enhanced by the fact that it was impossible to supply it in bulk because no tank storage suitable for petrol existed there, while the erection of such storage was not attempted because the Admiralty would not allow any tank vessel, except such as were needed for refilling the fleet, to enter the Mediterranean owing to the risk of submarine attack. This decision clinched a long argument which the War Office had with local "experts", chiefly French, on the subject of using some oil tanks, which did exist at Salonika, in the course of which it was found that the installations in question were only designed for storing kerosene and were not safe for petrol.

In East Africa the difficulties were mainly connected with shipping, the petrol coming from Sumatra in cofferdam vessels. No sooner was a consignment landed at one port than the zone of operations necessitated a new base, possibly several hundred miles away. Consequently crises became endemic, and one was met by using up a stock of aviation petrol which, by chance, happened to be at the right port.

In this theatre the War Office aimed at a ninety days' reserve but were never able to attain it and, as in Egypt, reliance had to be placed on the commercial four-gallon can, a peculiarity of which was that it never retained anything approaching four gallons when on service.

In the United Kingdom, the military consumption of petrol grew to 1,500,000 gallons a month, this rate being maintained fairly consistently until the Armistice. About one-quarter of the total was used by vehicles employed on work directly relating to the Army, while, apart from this, was aviation petrol, which varied between 1,200,000 and 1,400,000 gallons a month.

The system of issuing petrol under licences threw considerable work on the War Department in connection with issuing on repayment to a great number of individuals and firms who would, under other circumstances, have obtained their supplies from civilian stocks. These conditions applied particularly to the owners of motor vehicles voluntarily placed at the disposal of the War Department for ambulances and other services.

In recording the manner in which provision was made for the *personnel*, comprising divers trades and occupations, of the two great branches of the Army Service Corps other than the mechanical transport, it is not proposed to weary the reader with any such detail of

THE WAR PERIOD IN THE UNITED KINGDOM

figures as was deemed necessary in the case of the latter. Nor is it meet to enlarge upon the difficulties which were met and overcome in forming hundreds of new units, for such difficulties were similar to those encountered by all other arms of the service, and therefore present few features of unusual interest. The text will therefore confine itself to indicating in general terms the machinery which was put in motion.

Prior to the war there were two Supply Companies stationed at Aldershot, the *personnel* of which included butchers, bakers, clerks and issuers. Of these "A" Company was the depot where all recruits were received and trained, while "C" Company received the trained men, holding them for service in the Aldershot Command or drafting them elsewhere as required. On mobilisation, this last unit, to all intents and purposes, disappeared, as its *personnel* was required for the Expeditionary Force and "A" Company had to take over draft-finding in addition to the duties of reception and training. The rush of recruits was so great, butchers and bakers especially coming forward, that for some weeks confusion reigned. But Britons are at their best when they are "muddling", and that is why they are so often at their best. By various shifts and devices, such as sending men on leave until they could be dealt with, and making no attempt to compete with much of the documentary part of the work, "A" Company normally accustomed to handle some two to three hundred recruits a year managed to grapple with six thousand men by the end of 1914. To assist in relieving the pressure a new company was formed, lettered "K", and this took over the *personnel* from the depot company as soon as they were equipped, and assisted in finding drafts for new army units.

The work threw an almost intolerable strain on the permanent staff, for it was not of that straightforward nature which would have obtained had all the men been required for the same purpose. As it was the excellent raw material which presented itself needed to be sorted out, tested in the various trades, and classified according to degrees of skill in those trades. It could not be accepted that a man was a competent butcher or baker merely because he said so: the same applied to clerks, and in this direction the difficulties were perhaps the greatest. However efficient a recruit might be in typewriting, shorthand, accountancy, book-keeping, and other clerical arts and crafts, it was indispensable that he should have some knowledge of Army Regulations and procedure, channels of communication, and methods of correspondence before he could be of much practical use. For clerical staffs had not only to be found for regimental offices, supply depots, and organisations of a like nature where a business training was a valuable asset, but for the headquarters of the brigades and divisions of the New Armies where orders and training memoranda had to be prepared and where the majority of the staff officers themselves were untrained. Both in "A" and "K" Companies no efforts were spared to give intensive teaching in these directions, and it meant for long periods at a time from sixteen to twenty hours' work a day for the permanent staff.

During the first half of 1915, 10,000 men passed through "A" Company, and in addition new burdens were placed on its organisation by the responsibility for the Labour Companies which, as Army Service Corps units, were recruited to work at the docks in France. There was, indeed, no training concerned, but the administration of numbers of undisciplined men and their mustering in companies for despatch overseas could not be coped with in other than a rough and ready manner. Many of the labourers should never have been enlisted: there was an unduly high proportion of undesirables, while some 2000 were discharged on medical grounds out of nearly 21,000 who joined up to the end of 1915.

THE WAR PERIOD IN THE UNITED KINGDOM

No less than a hundred and eighty-two deserted during this period, although in justice it must be recorded that the majority of these were subsequently discovered in other branches of the Corps.

As the strength of the Army grew and the necessity for drafts of supply *personnel* as reinforcements and for the formation of new supply units grew likewise, some re-organisation of the arrangements for their provision became imperative. In fact it had been too long delayed. The defunct "C" Company was resuscitated, and took on its strength all supply *personnel* employed on duties in the Aldershot Command, while "K" Company took the place of "A" as the Reserve Supply *Personnel* Depot. Consequent on these measures "A" Company was, in February 1916, moved to Catterick in Yorkshire, where its future duties were to receive all men invalided from the Expeditionary Forces, and to sort them out by means of Medical Boards. Those fit were re-posted to "K" Company, while those likely to become fit were taken through a graduated course of physical instruction. Permanent unfits were discharged. In December 1916 "A" Company was moved from Catterick to Southport, where it continued these functions.

As in other branches of the Army Service Corps the work of those charged with supply *personnel* was traversed by the constant calls for high-category men for the infantry. Consequently, just as a new unit was built up and all the various ranks and trades adjusted in accordance with its authorised war establishment, it was liable to be upset completely by a demand for all category "A" men, irrespective of rank or trade, to be transferred to such and such an infantry regimental depot or reserve brigade in the United Kingdom. This procedure was heartbreaking to those who had struggled to evolve an efficient unit, but it could not be avoided, and at times was not even without a certain humour. On one occasion, for instance, 1000 men were required for a certain regiment in the north of England and there being a large surplus of butchers at the time at Aldershot, the whole 1000 men were found from them. The battalion which was subsequently composed largely of such tradesmen must have been unique in the British Army or indeed any other army, but it may be recorded that it did extremely well. In this case the men had been voluntarily enlisted and had joined the Army Service Corps in order to be employed at their trade. When they discovered that their services were requisitioned for a higher form of killing than which they had contemplated, they received the news with cheers, and went rejoicing.

Exclusive of any labour *personnel* the numbers of other ranks in the various trades of the Supply Branch was, at the date of the Armistice, 51,585, of which 30,388 were serving overseas in the Expeditionary Forces—figures which give some comprehension of the volume of work dealt with by a very limited machinery.

In respect to expansion, the Horse Transport Branch was more favourably placed, for there were in existence in peace time three depots, situated at Aldershot, Woolwich and Bradford. Again, there were not quite the same complications as concerned trades, for saddlers, wheelers and farriers in civil life were easily adapted to service methods, while in 1914 there were still a good number of men in the country who were acquainted with horses. The permanent depots had between them to deal with between six and seven thousand reservists on mobilisation and, after despatching these to the Expeditionary Forces, proceeded to handle the influx of recruits.* At Aldershot there were formed, among other horse transport units, up to the end of 1915 no less than thirty-one divisional trains, thirty reserve parks, and five Army Troops trains for the new armies.

Bradford dealt with nearly 25,000 recruits alone during

* In February 1916 No. 1 Company from Aldershot went to Catterick as a Horse Transport Discharge Depot, and ceased to receive recruits.

the course of the war and Woolwich with a very similar number, although these formed only a portion of the men that passed through. But this output was far from satisfying the requirements in *personnel*, quite apart from the question of animals and vehicles. Shortly following mobilisation a Reserve Horse Transport Depot was formed at Deptford, from which place it was afterwards removed to Park Royal, Willesden, and in February 1915 a similar organisation came into existence at Blackheath. In addition to training recruits, finding drafts and forming new transport units for overseas, these depots had to fit out numerous individual fighting units with first line transport complete, and to maintain the reserves in animals, vehicles and transport equipment for the armies in the field, besides giving courses of instruction not only to Army Service Corps but also to infantry officers. Their scope was, in fact, far greater than that of the permanent establishments, except Aldershot, since they corresponded to what on the mechanical transport side was represented by the Bulford mobilisation area.

At this stage may be noted also a further training activity, which, though not strictly speaking within the legitimate field of the Corps, yet furnished a typical example of the burdens that were shouldered unostentatiously to assist the general cause.

In 1915, when the Machine Gun Corps was created, the question arose as to the training of its men in riding, driving and horsemastership. Neither cavalry nor artillery were willing to undertake this work, which involved dealing with numbers running into thousands, and the Adjutant-General's Branch, which was responsible for organisation, approached the Army Service Corps. With all its other pre-occupations the Directorate of Transport hesitated before embarking on this new commitment, especially as it was at that time menaced with a "comb out" of its fittest *personnel*. But the task was accepted, and a centre having a permanent establishment of over eight hundred, including some of the most expert instructors in the Corps, was set up at Grantham where it did admirable work.

Passing now to certain general aspects of the administration, attention may be directed to the important step which was taken by the merging of the Territorial Force Army Service Corps into that of the Regular Army. In the early stages there was no necessity for this, but directly the Territorial divisions began to take the field, throwing off their second line formations, complications began to arise. The question of reinforcements could not be kept in water-tight compartments, while in instances of divisions going to the Dardanelles the larger portion of their trains were left behind and, therefore, became available for re-allotment. That re-allotment might be more conveniently made by the posting of a Territorial train to a New Army division. Again, in the Territorial Army Service Corps were a number of ex-regulars and, in any case, a *personnel* of some experience in transport and supply duties, whereas such experience was scarce in the New Army units. Some dilution was desirable.

These and other factors made it apparent that organisation would be vastly simplified by bringing all the *personnel* on to one list, and this was accordingly done in September 1916. The introduction of the measure was delayed to that date through the national reluctance to interfere with a service which had done very well standing on its own feet, and to avoid as long as possible any appearance of destroying its entity. The union only anticipated what had to be done in other quarters in the Army at a later date, although when it was initiated by the Corps it was received as somewhat dangerous. In practice the posting and distribution of all ranks was much facilitated, and the work of the Corps went more smoothly at a time when its difficulties were markedly enhanced by the bulk transfers to other arms which took place from 1916 onwards. The situation then arising furnishes a useful study in the science of distributing national man-power in war, calling into question as it did the whole balance of the structure of the Army. The numbers borne on the strength of the Army Service Corps were subjected to the most drastic scrutiny, and every man was required to be justified.

Serving in the United Kingdom at that time—July 1916—were just over 1,500,000 all ranks, this including formations awaiting embarkation, permanent staffs, recruits, sick and wounded, and non-effectives of every description. Of this number the Corps consisted of some 73,000 officers and men or approximately 5 per cent. exclusive of the Remount Department and the Dominion Army Service Corps, numbering nearly 5000, which were concerned with looking after their own troops.* To carry out the transport and supply services in the United Kingdom even with such assistance as was obtained from extraneous sources, a proportion of 5 per cent. could not be considered high. But, in fact, in no way did that proportion represent the number available for such duties. In the first place there were included over 12,000 in units awaiting embarkation, and, secondly, all the non-effectives, a number showing considerable variations from week to week. Including the latter and recruits under training a round figure of 60,000 existed to carry out Army Service Corps duties (less Remounts) and of this total 13,000 were unfit for service overseas. How comprehensive those duties on the training side alone will have been gathered from what has been already set out. But training, the preparation of new units and the maintenance and repair of mechanical and horse transport vehicles, or, in other words, tasks involved mainly by the presence of great

* The detail of the British Army Service Corps was as follows: Horse transport: 357 officers; 17,219 ranks. Mechanical transport: 620 officers; 34,501 other ranks. Supply: 123 officers; 8578 other ranks. Recruits: 180 officers; 8657 other ranks. Territorial Army: 12,000 all ranks.

armies abroad, was only half of what was demanded of the Corps. Unlike the purely fighting arms it had its essential functions to carry out in feeding and in finding transport for the masses of troops stationed in the United Kingdom, and even these functions were abnormally stretched by the necessity of having to find mechanical transport companies for such duties as railway, Post Office services and munitions. The actual numbers thus employed varied between some thirty and thirty-five thousand which were only barely adequate, and they were in process of rapid turn-over to low-category men often of an equally low degree of trade skill.

The conceptions that were held in certain uninformed quarters at the time that there was in the Army Service Corps in the United Kingdom an almost unlimited reserve of man-power for the fighting arms was erroneous even before any serious measures of "combing out" took place. In this respect the Corps was not always treated generously or even justly. Yet this very treatment manifested an attitude which was in effect flattering. It was never disputed that the transport and supply services reached a high standard, and this standard was so normally and universally taken for granted that the difficulties overcome in attaining it were either ignored or unrecognised. The troops were fed and moved so surely and so regularly that these processes were made to look simple and the enterprise and foresight devoted to them was unrealised. It was thus assumed that, in spite of all demands made on the Corps—tending to dislocate its machinery—the previous happy state of affairs would always persist. And this was a doctrine fraught, as the history of war shows, with elements of danger.

But the extent to which the Corps adapted itself to circumstances almost justified such faith. Partial failures there were especially in the early months of the war with regard to the satisfactory feeding of the new armies, but these were not due to any shortage of foodstuffs but to a temporary insufficiency of equipment and to a want of experience in interior economy on the part of regimental officers and men. In certain other respects, too, matters were not always conducted as economically as possible, for like every other branch of the Army the Corps had much to learn.

Nevertheless, surveying the whole field of its labours and the heavy responsibilities which fell to its lot both at home and abroad, and bearing in mind also the improvisations inevitable in so great a crisis, criticism may well be silenced, and in this connection testimony from an authoritative outside source may bear quotation here.

Writing in a well-known service periodical on the *Life of Sir John Cowans*, published in 1925, the reviewer made his peroration as follows:

Another point to which we wish to draw attention is this: in their admiration for their subject, the biographers seem to us to fail to recognise the sterling qualities, brilliant abilities and invaluable assistance of that arm of the Service with which Sir John Cowans' work was largely concerned. We refer to the Royal Army Service Corps. It is doing no injustice to the other branches of the Land Forces to say that, at the outbreak of war, the Army Service Corps was the most efficient branch of the Army and it is a matter of history that, alone of all branches, it had emerged from the South African War with an enhanced reputation. Sir John Cowans had, therefore, a splendid instrument with which to work.

Reference has been made in the preceding chapter to certain senior officers who bore the chief responsibility for the transport, supply and barrack services at the Headquarters of the Army. To these names may fitly be added in conclusion three others, which were for two generations familiar and respected throughout the Army Service Corps, not only from their long association with the administration at the War Office and Record Office, but for the constructive and solid work for which they had been responsible, and the counsel and guidance they had given to young staff officers.

Lieut.-Colonel A. G. Gleeson, as a young military clerk, originally joined the office of the Commissary-General at Headquarters as far back as 1880, and with a short break between 1886 and 1888 served continuously in the War Office until his retirement at the age of sixty in 1920. He had previously seen active service in the Kaffir and Zulu Wars of 1877-9, and in 1895 he received his commission. His work in the Transport Directorate began with the creation of the Corps in 1888 and thus lasted thirty-two years.

Lieut.-Colonel G. Dixon's career was on similar lines, except that as Colonel Gleeson's name was ever associated with "transport" that of the former has been identified with "supply". As a military staff clerk he participated in the Zulu War and subsequently in the Egyptian Campaign of 1882, arriving at the War Office in 1888. Commissioned in 1892 he retired at the age of sixty-three in January 1914. He rejoined on mobilisation, taking up his work where he had laid it down eight months before, but work far more strenuous and far more exacting. He died worn out in April 1917, to the great loss of the Directorate.

Equally meritorious was the record of Major T. Grapes, who spent the last twenty of forty-seven years' service in the Army in the capacity of Assistant Officer-in-Charge of Records—a post always onerous, but during the war almost overwhelming. Major Grapes died in 1925 having, like Colonel Dixon, spent his health in his devotion to duty.

BIBLIOGRAPHY

The History and Development of Mechanical Transport, R.A.S.C. Prepared from various sources by the Directorate of Supplies and Transport, War Office.

"Petrol Supply in the Field." By Lieut.-Colonel J.C.M. DORAN, C.B.E., D.S.O. From the *Royal Army Service Corps Quarterly*, July 1924.

Historical Records of Nos. 1, 2 and 3 Depots and Nos. 1 and 2 Reserve Horse Transport Depots, Royal Army Service Corps.

CHAPTER XV

THE CORPS IN INDIA

IF any proof were needed outside the events of the War to justify the organisation of the transport and supply services of the British Army, that proof will be found in the record of the Army Service Corps in India, for it was there that the old and new conceptions of those services have been most visibly contrasted in times of peace.

Previous to May 1916 the Army Service Corps did not serve in India, its responsibilities being carried out by the Supply and Transport Corps of the Indian Army. It was, however, the custom for a limited number of captains and subalterns of the British service to be seconded for duty with that organisation for a period of five years, and it was, as events subsequently turned out, fortunate that even this limited provision existed, for the experiences thus gained were to prove of value when the time came for the sister services to co-operate in the field.

In constitution and in scope, and even to some extent in its duties, the Supply and Transport Corps differed from the Army Service Corps. It was in the first place a departmental branch, and therefore suffered from the lack of prestige inherent in a non-combatant status. Its officers were drawn from Indian units or from British units serving in India, and were posted to the Corps on a period of five years' probation. This system of probation was unsatisfactory, because the main inducement lay in the enhanced rates of pay, and so long an interval of seconding before permanent transfer enabled many to put their financial affairs in order before returning to their regiments. Thus the Corps was naturally enough made a convenience of by a certain proportion of officers, who had no intention of making it their permanent career, and who could, therefore, never fully identify themselves with its fortunes. In the non-commissioned ranks, too, the establishment was even lower in proportion to the strength of the Army than it was in the British service. There were a certain number of British warrant and non-commissioned officers who came on one year's probation, of which half was spent on supply and half on transport duties and, at the conclusion of which, an examination was held before final transfer was approved. It will thus be observed that in contradistinction to the Army Service Corps the warrant and non-commissioned ranks were unspecialised. The rank and file were Indian *personnel* specially enlisted and paid, a point about them being that they were generally looked upon as much inferior to fighting men and, indeed, usually classed as followers, although their behaviour on many occasions on service had been admirable, and their duties were invariably well carried out. As compared to the British service, however, the amount of clerical work was enormous, necessitating a large staff of clerks and long office hours. One reason for this was that the Supply and Transport Corps was called upon to do work such as the auditing of accounts which properly belonged to the Accounts Department, and this occupied so much of the time of the officers that it not only prevented them studying the larger and military aspects of their profession, but also engendered sedentary habits which necessarily re-acted on the practical work in the field. The well-ordered routine of an office furnishes but scanty training for the "rough and tumble" of active operations.

As might normally be expected under such conditions, opinions were divided as to whether the Corps was adequately equipped and trained for its rôle. It was felt by a number—and they were, if a minority, at any rate a powerful one—that the system prevailing was fully equal to any strain to which it might reasonably be put; and that therefore any further degree of militarisation was unnecessary. Departmental they were and departmental they were content to remain. After all the organisation had generally met demands made upon it for expeditions on the North-West Frontier of India, the customary battle-ground of the Indian Army. On the other hand, there were those who saw further and who realised that since all transport and supply problems were indissolubly bound up with strategy and a sound knowledge of military history, the higher the military spirit of the transport and supply organisation the better is it not only for itself, but also for the troops which it serves. It is probable that the views of these would have ultimately prevailed even had the Great War not intervened.

In certain respects, and especially in regard to its identification with the divisions of the Field Army, the Supply and Transport Corps enjoyed definite advantages. For each division except that of Burmah there was an Assistant Director of Supplies and an Assistant Director of Transport. Each transport unit was usually commanded by a major who was available to assist in transport matters generally. At the various out-stations there existed a Brigade Supply and Transport Officer who was responsible to the Divisional Supply and Transport Officer for all administrative and executive work. The duties of this individual included receipt and issue of all stores within his brigade, and the maintenance of his transport in such state that it was at all times ready for active service. While not directly the accountant, he was also responsible for taking all necessary measures to ensure correct accounting and to prevent fraud. In respect of stores, too, his work went considerably beyond that carried out in the British Army; for he not only had to maintain reserves of food, forage and fuel, but also of mobilisation clothing for both British and native units, and mobilisation equipment such as harness, saddlery, waterproof sheets, ambulances, vehicles, blankets, sheets and hospital stores. Minor contracts were, too, sometimes handled, while the numerous trifling articles of foodstuffs which the Indian soldier required for existence at times taxed the mathematical genius of even the stolid and not easily exasperated baboo.

With so wide a scope comprehending many duties which properly fall to the Army Ordnance Department, little time was left for the outdoor duties involved by the care and management of transport units. Any detachments of these latter which might be under brigades were commanded by British warrant or non-commissioned officers—a practice which, except in the case of very small groupings, could not commend itself to those brought up in British Army doctrine and methods. The transport formations themselves were of varied natures, consisting of Camel Corps, Pack Mule Corps, Mule Vehicle Corps and Elephant Corps according to the nature of the terrain to be negotiated. Like those of the Army Service Corps certain of these units were merely cadres capable of considerable expansion on mobilisation, but on the frontiers and in certain up country stations they were kept at war strength. Obvious weaknesses are revealed when it is stated that many of them were split into small detachments as a more or less permanent measure, and sometimes to save expense even hired out to contractors. In addition, Government transport could always be requisitioned through the Cantonment Magistrate or Resident Commissioner at a fixed rate. Under the somewhat extraordinary arrangements for hiring the Government took a percentage of the money obtained, while a further percentage was shared among the *personnel* at rates laid down according to rank.

THE CORPS IN INDIA

Facilities existed for training apart from the numerous punitive expeditions since the great distances which units had to move on change of station were often carried out by march route, but as an offset to this supplies were nearly always done by contract which prevented officers from obtaining any practice in the important art of requisitioning as required in war, and this circumstance was in fact one of the weakest spots in the training of the Corps and may be emphasised also on account of the fact that in the Army Service Corps the aim was at all times and especially in war to eliminate the contractor and middleman on the score of both efficiency and economy. Indeed, such elimination is among the fundamental justifications for a militarised transport and supply organisation, for the system of allowing contractors to accompany an army has never proved equal to the stress and strain of operations in the field.

The Supply and Transport Corps of the Indian Army had, however, one further deficiency which calls for notice, not only on account of its gravity, but also because it was the reason for the intervention of the Army Service Corps in India. And that lay in the lack of mechanical transport. In this direction any hasty conclusions as to want of foresight are not entirely warranted. Consideration had been given to the matter even as far back as 1905. But conditions in India differed so widely from those in the United Kingdom, quite apart from unlikelihood of the Indian Army becoming involved in a major war, that to all intents and purposes little progress had been made by 1914. In Great Britain mechanical transport was, during the decade preceding, coming more and more into commercial employment. In India its development was in very early stages. If the Indian Army had introduced mechanical transport it would have needed to have provided all it required on mobilisation and to have employed it in peace as best it could. Financially such an undertaking would have been formidable, if not impossible, and it could only have been done at the expense of savings in other military respects. That obstacle alone might have appeared insuperable. But there were in fact others. *Personnel* difficulties were great, while the question of roads and bridges, especially on the frontiers, was even more serious. Nevertheless certain tentative efforts were made, and that they failed may be imputed to the fact that a type suited to Indian needs and conditions had not been evolved, or at any rate if it had been evolved, it had not been tried out, which amounted to much the same thing.

As far back as 1902 four Thorneycroft steam lorries with experts to drive them had been sent out for the Delhi Durbar. These vehicles had been designed to carry a load of five tons on macadamised roads, and as such were highly efficient, but at Delhi stores had to be conveyed from the central depot to the various camps over what amounted to ploughed fields, and this shook the entrails out of the engines. They were likewise condemned on every side for other reasons. Complaints poured in that they frightened mules, horses and camels. Landlords objected that their houses were being shaken, while tenants complained that the smoke ruined their gardens. As a consequence the vehicles were denied the use of certain roads, which had the effect of confining them to inferior routes. A further handicap under which they laboured was the need of first class coal, the quality at Delhi being so inferior that it was found impossible to keep up steam. Three of the lorries were eventually sent to Quetta where efforts were made to work them at a profit, but there was too much mule transport for the vehicles to be continually employed.

In 1905 four large traction engines were ordered from England, but they were of an obsolete type and were quickly found to be useless. This, however, did not deter further experiments, and shortly afterwards four "Ursula" traction engines of fourteen tons and two "Dolls" of ten tons were imported under the charge of a specially engaged engineer, who was remunerated at what then seemed the handsome salary of six hundred rupees per month. A Captain Nugent of the Royal Engineers and a Lieut. Hewitt of the Supply and Transport Corps took two of these vehicles fully loaded from Peshawar over the Kohat Pass to Bannu, a distance of a hundred and twenty miles, and this trial run proved that the "Doll" was a success, but that the "Ursula" was too heavy for the roads. A water tank containing five hundred gallons formed part of the load, but even then more water was required every ten miles, an obvious handicap on active service. An experiment was then conducted with a "Doll" for the purpose of pulling a heavy gun on manœuvres at Quetta, and here satisfactory results were obtained.

Pursuing the matter further a journey was made from Quetta to Chaman over the Khojak Pass, but this was disastrous and involved a heavy bill for road repair. It was this incident that decided the Government of India that all mechanical transport vehicles, which had been under trial in India, were to be sold as being unsuitable for active service, while their employment in peace was not remunerative. The tractors in question were therefore put up for sale, but no purchaser could be found and one was eventually handed over free to the Mint.

These unhappy experiences may perhaps be imputed to the fact that mechanical transport was tried too early in India before any design suitable to the country had been evolved, for it was clearly an error of judgment to have sent out heavy engines. It was especially unfortunate that a letter issued by the Mechanical Transport Committee in 1907 which was sent to the Governors of all colonies asking a series of questions embodying advice as to suitable types for certain conditions was not sent to India, for had it been so sent and been answered by an expert the natural prejudices of the Indian Government as a result of the road and bridge destroying forms of transport might well have been overcome. In 1910, however, a questionnaire was submitted by the Government to resident officials with a knowledge of engineering in eighty districts throughout the country as to the practicability of mechanical transport in civil employment. The replies were fifty-seven in favour, ten doubtful and thirteen against, among the latter being Quetta where, no doubt, the bill for repairs in the Khojak Pass was fresh in the memory of the authorities.

In so far as the Army was concerned, then, comparatively little progress was made, although interest in the subject was kept alive by discussion and argument among the more progressive.

By 1915 the transport situation was giving rise to considerable anxiety, as it was tardily realised that India had drained herself of mules and camels by equipping units for the forces in the various theatres. With this realisation the purse was opened wide, and the Military Works Services at Army Headquarters were deputed to organise mechanical transport. The immediate officers concerned were Colonel Nugent and Major Burgess of the Royal Engineers, and the initial step taken was to purchase secondhand vehicles in Bombay and Calcutta, mainly Fiats, and these were sent to Peshawar. Colonel Hodgkinson, an Indian cavalry officer, obtained *personnel* by recruiting in his regimental area, and by this means two Indian mechanical transport companies were formed.

The late Lord Montagu of Beaulieu was, in his capacity as Mechanical Adviser to the Government of India, one of the pioneers of progress. He arranged for a number of Indian Standard Leyland and Thorneycroft lorries to be despatched from England direct from the makers, and also for 5000 Ford chassis direct from America, for which he incurred the displeasure of the

Ministry of Munitions. Lord Montagu of Beaulieu was also responsible for the workshops built at Rawal Pindi.

The war in Mesopotamia quickly proved the shortcomings of the organisation of the Supply and Transport Corps for a campaign of magnitude where the conditions differed from the accustomed ones. It was just after the fall of Kut el Amara that it was decided to send some Army Service Corps units to India. A motor ambulance convoy and three supply columns were accordingly despatched in May 1916. Subsequently a further company was formed as a depot unit for all Army Service Corps *personnel* serving in India, and embarked in March 1917.*

An inauspicious incident followed the landing of the three companies, which arrived at Karachi on the 4th of June, when the *personnel* together with some British infantry drafts entrained for Rawal Pindi, Nowshera and Peshawar, for the train conveying them was that ill-fated one about which much was subsequently heard both in England and India. Among those who died *en route*, owing to heat combined with the inadequate arrangements made for the journey while crossing the Sind desert, were ten men of the Army Service Corps.

No. 693 Company with its three-ton Albion lorries was, in the first instance, posted to Nowshera, from where it worked until October, when it was sent to Rawal Pindi. The duties while at Nowshera comprised convoys to the Malakand, Chakdara, Cherat and Murree, and long journeys with climbs of over twenty miles and gradients of one in twelve were successfully carried out daily. As one record of this unit showed that over 60,000 miles were travelled by a daily average of twenty-five working lorries in one month, it may be said to have been kept fully employed. During October and

---

* These were Nos. 630, 692, 693 and 694 Companies A.S.C. and No. 871 Depot Company. No. 630 was a motor ambulance convoy and Nos. 692, 693 and 694 were supply columns.

November the work consisted of the prosaic task of bringing the stores and baggage of the troops from Murree to the plains, the run from Rawal Pindi being seventeen miles on the flat and twenty miles uphill with a gradient for the most part of one in seventeen and in some places one in twelve. Although it was an arduous run to undertake and to do the return journey in one day the convoys were maintained with satisfactory results. The men on the whole kept fit, and the vehicles stood up to their work in spite of adverse road conditions. Nor were many accidents recorded, although the route was often congested badly with bullock carts, camels and mule transport.

Until February the company remained active between Rawal Pindi and brigade camps which had been established at Burhan and Hassanabdal—thirty-four and twenty-nine miles distant respectively—and at the same time carried out the station duties at its Headquarters. In April a detachment was detailed for the Northern Army Staff Tour at Kohat whence it proceeded via Peshawar, a distance of about a hundred and fifty miles, and subsequently had to traverse a good deal of rough ground. Here again the vehicles proved fully equal to everything they were asked to do.

In May 1917 the Waziristan Field Force operated against the Mahsuds, and the small detachment of No. 693 Company, which took part, had their first experience of active service in India on the very indifferent road between Dera Ismail Khan and Tank, during a period when the heat was terrific. Up to the end of that month the thirty-eight supply lorries had, during their year in the country, covered 327,471 miles.

No. 694 Company had a somewhat less normal start to its career in India. When it arrived at Rawal Pindi it was found that no one expected it, and that the vehicles which had been designed to equip it had been handed over to a lately raised Indian mechanical transport unit—

No. 2 Indian Company. By various shifts, however, such as withdrawing ten three-ton Fiats from No. 1 Indian Mechanical Transport Company and twenty Albions from No. 692 Company Army Service Corps a nucleus of lorries was provided, while during the course of the ensuing ten months fifty-nine one-ton Star vehicles were added. It was not until December 1917 that a proper establishment was laid down and the unit gradually brought up to it; it then consisted of six officers and three hundred and twenty-six other ranks with ninety-nine supply vehicles of a hundred and thirty-seven and a half tons gross capacity. Included were sixty-five one-ton Star vehicles and thirteen Thorneycrofts, the basis of the organisation resting on the idea that on the frontier the forces were broken up into small detachments operating in separate valleys, so that a section of the company could be set to work complete and independent of Headquarters. With its light lorries the company proved extremely useful on the thinly metalled roads on the frontier and for crossing boat bridges after its subsequent move to Peshawar, where opportunities were vouchsafed for active service.

Early in 1917 when punitive measures were put into force against the Mohmands a great deal of transport work was carried out between Peshawar and Shabkadar and thence along the blockade lines, in the course of which four boat bridges not negotiable for other than light vehicles had to be passed. During the Waziristan operations in the summer, one section of Stars worked from Bannu up the Tochi valley, under the most trying conditions. The road surface was bad and the heat was described by those who were acquainted with Mesopotamia as worse than any experienced in that country; the vehicles had to proceed to Miranshah and back daily—a distance of eighty miles, and the return journey had to be completed by noon when the picquets were withdrawn; on the outward journey the road rose 2000 feet in the forty miles and four rivers had to be crossed. In these circumstances the *personnel* were subjected to great discomfort and, although here again the lorries stood up well, it was subsequently discovered that the salt in the rivers damaged bearings in the wheels and back axles, while pneumatic tyres only averaged 2500 miles. Some mule lines at Bannu were adapted for use as a workshop, and the men lived in quarters vacated by a native battery. Water was only obtainable from a well in the fort and even that had to be boiled. Ice for hospital purposes had to be fetched from Kohat, eighty miles distant.

A second section worked for a short time between Dera Ismail Khan and Tank and on the unmetalled tracks beyond the latter place, but there again the conditions were such that the rate of sickness rose rapidly towards the end of the operations.

In the spring of the following year the company's services were required by what was known as the Marri Punitive Force, which involved an average daily trip of eighty miles to Sakhisarwar and back on a road over which grass matting had been laid.

On its arrival No. 692 Company was sent straight to Peshawar, and from there employed in carrying stores, ammunition supplies and forage to the extreme outposts of the Indian Empire. Frequent convoys went to Landi-Kotal through the Khyber Pass and also to Chakdara, Kohat and Dargai. There were also weekly convoys to Cherat, a hill station, thirty-nine miles from Peshawar, and intermittent ones to Shabkadar, Subhan, Khwar, Michnee and Abasai for various regiments holding the frontier posts. In July 1917 a great number of the Albion lorries were detailed to take stores and electric plant to the Waziristan Field Force at Tank. The continuous work through the passes was specially exacting, for the roads, which were narrow, steep and winding and which often traversed river beds, were at times washed away

THE CORPS IN INDIA

in parts by the severe storms experienced in the late summer. Lorries frequently became stuck and were only with great difficulty released, while in one instance a three-ton vehicle was carried eighty yards down a river by a wall of water, four feet high, catching it broadside while in a nullah. During the period 1916 to 1918 some 25 per cent. of the *personnel* became casualties from heat stroke and fever, but the unit maintained its working efficiency throughout.

The No. 630 (Motor Ambulance Convoy) Company made its appearance two weeks after the supply columns, and spent its first few months between Rawal Pindi and Murree. After a short period at Peshawar it was sent to Dera Ismail Khan for the Waziristan operations, and kept busy the whole of the summer of 1917 over very bad roads which necessitated an overhaul of all cars on return to Rawal Pindi.

In March 1918 portions of the unit were again in the field participating in the activities of the Marri Field Force and at Dera Ghazi Khan, carrying sick and wounded. The Daimler ambulances, which formed the largest part of the equipment, proved very reliable.

The bald recital of what were, for a large part, merely routine duties, does not lend itself to the making of any exhilarating story—sound and solid work unmarked by abnormal incident rarely does, but some detailed account of the introduction of the Army Service Corps to Indian conditions is justified on two grounds. Firstly, it is due to those who there served to say that they bore as useful a part in the war as their comrades in other fields where the physical risks were greater, but where there was more distinction and recognition to be gained. In some respects the sense of isolation from the arena of conflict on dull, monotonous, but yet essential duties was, quite apart from the severity of the climate, more exacting than service on which the eyes of the whole world were fixed. Yet the security of the north-west frontier of India was vital to the stability of the British Empire.

Secondly, the details given show that the potentialities of mechanical transport in India were fully exploited from the outset and indeed brought no small measure of relief to the transport services of the Indian Army always hard pressed when frontier work was on hand. The manner in which the task was grappled with from the outset shows that the employment of mechanical transport in those regions was in fact overdue.

Under conditions which were wholly strange to all the conduct of the men was beyond praise. A serious drain on the establishments of units was caused by the call for volunteers for North-West Persia, but in the case of artificers the loss was made good by the training of drivers in the company workshops.

We may now turn to the Army Service Corps *Personnel* Depot which was established at Bangalore just a year following the advent of the service companies.

Prior to that date there were some four hundred and fifty details of all three branches of the Corps included in the British Details Depot appropriated to the army in Mesopotamia, and where any men delayed *en route* or invalided from that country were received. When No. 871 Depot Company arrived under Lieut.-Colonel Peyton, endeavours were made to collect and absorb these details, and after some difficulty a provisional establishment was sanctioned for a depot for all Army Service Corps *personnel* in India, and four hundred and eighty-five all ranks were taken on the strength.* Three companies corresponding to the three branches of the Corps and one for all those who were on leave from Mesopotamia were formed, and work was commenced on the

* These consisted of:

Officers	...	...	...	21	Mechanical transport	...	81
Supply	...	...	...	87	Furlough details	...	...	173
Horse transport	...		...	123			

site allotted as a camping ground. In contrast to the more convenient practice at home by which the work of constructing and equipping the lines would be carried out by the Royal Engineers, everything except the laying on of water and the erection of such buildings as cookhouses fell to the unit concerned, and occupied a considerable time. By 1917, however, the Army Service Corps was accustomed to turn itself to any or every kind of duty and, possessing as it did a number of tradesmen, was usually able to overcome all difficulties with credit.

But as a British Administrative Corps, with no tradition in India, it found itself much less adaptable to Indian administrative methods. It was found that hundreds of men were scattered throughout India, a great proportion being employed without any authority after having been passed out of the convalescent sections. Within a few months over seven hundred were so traced. A further source of waste was stopped by preventing men being held at convalescent depots for various unauthorised reasons. Every sort of delay and procrastination were experienced in getting the establishment of the unit fixed and training put on a proper basis.

In April 1917 the full administration of mechanical transport was transferred from the Department of Military Works to that of the Director of Supplies and Transport at Army Headquarters.

Following the close of the war further Army Service Corps units made their appearance in India, and, it must be admitted, in somewhat fortuitous fashion. No. 622 Company was intercepted on its way from East Africa; two motor ambulance convoys, Nos. 656 and 1091 Companies, and two heavy artillery units, Nos. 789 and 1028 Companies, were annexed from the army in Mesopotamia.

Sufficient has been recorded to indicate the nature of

the Army Service Corps work and the strange conditions in India, and there is no useful purpose to be served by elaborating details of various frontier operations. The Third Afghan War in which six Army Service Corps companies participated in May 1919, although chiefly confined to the lines of communication, only lasted a month and presented no features of any special interest. But the operations of 1919–20 deserve some notice in that it was then for the first time that mechanical transport on a considerable scale took its place in the scheme of things in the forward area.

Waziristan was, too, a part of the world where subsequent developments owed much to the work of the Corps.

For long this turbulent country had been a running sore on the North-West Frontier, and, although the policy of the Indian Government had been one of noninterference, an obstacle standing in the way of its fulfilment was the pretension of the Amir of Afghanistan to some legal form of sovereignty over a great part of the territory. In 1893 an agreement was reached with the Amir that Waziristan was wholly subject to Indian suzerainty, and the subsequent delimitation of the boundary involved in the agreement established what was known as the Durand line or the Western Frontier, and consequently of India with Afghanistan. Trade routes along the River Gumal to the south and along the Tochi valley to the north were protected by a system of Government subsidies by which the tribes in return for an annual fixed payment pledged themselves to noninterference and also promised to abstain from raiding British territory. These undertakings were not observed, and from time to time punitive expeditions had to be launched. The effect of these measures was not, however, sufficiently lasting, and they were gradually replaced by preventive ones. Fortified posts and blockhouses were built which, garrisoned by local levies or local militia raised for this duty, were originally placed at points where the raiders might sally forth from their hills into the plains or harry the caravans proceeding along the trade routes, and by 1899 this practice had so far grown that two long, narrow strips of territory lying to the North and South of Central Waziristan along the trade routes were garrisoned on that principle. By 1919 there were two forces—the Northern and Southern Waziristan Militia, together some 3000 strong, employed in these garrisons, and they were supported by regular troops based on Bannu and Dera Ismail Khan.

The events of the Afghan War proved too much for the loyalty of the rank and file of a portion of the militia who deserted and turned against their British officers. Following on this misfortune Wazir and Mahsud raiding parties went so far as to invade the border districts and even to penetrate into the Punjab.

Such was the state of affairs which prevailed at the beginning of the operations of 1919.

Waziristan itself is a mountainous country with ill-defined irregular boundaries, lying roughly between the Indus plain on its Eastern or Indian side and the watershed of the Suleiman mountains on its Western or Afghan side. In shape it approximates roughly to an irregular lozenge-shaped parallelogram, a hundred and sixty miles in length and sixty miles in breadth, and the greater part of it can best be described as a tangle of rocky mountain ridges terminating abruptly to the East and South-East in a long face of steep hill which skirts the plain of the Indus or the Derajat.

Of the climate it is sufficient to say that it can prove unpleasant at all seasons, the foothills and lower valleys being especially torrid in summer. Tank, for example, is well known for its temperature of a hundred and twenty degrees and over.

The main routes leading from the Derajat or from the plains of the Indus into Waziristan are none other than the watercourses. Two principal highways follow the channels of the River Tochi and Gumal respectively, but even these cannot be described as constituting main lines of communication from India into Afghanistan or Baluchistan, while all the lesser lines of access into Waziristan itself end in the difficult passes of the Suleiman mountains which are blocked by snow for some part of the year.

Passing over preliminary events, the story may be taken up in November 1919 when the Waziristan Field Force under Major-General S. H. Climo consisted of some 30,000 combatants and 35,000 non-combatants, and included six brigades of Indian infantry and four regiments of cavalry.* Out of these a Striking Force of two brigades with a battalion of pioneers, artillery, engineers, signals, with supply and medical units was organised under Major-General Skeen, for, with lines of communications extending between three and four hundred miles, a considerable number of troops were absorbed in its protection. Thus 8500 fighting men with 6500 non-combatants and some 9000 animals only were available for the mobile operations. The communications merit attention as showing the difficulties of an expedition of this nature, and at the same time show the rôle of the mechanical transport.

The ultimate base was situated at Lahore, whence the normal broad-gauge railway extended to the Indus, a main line running parallel to the left bank of that river, keeping generally between ten and twenty miles distant from its normal channel. Railhead for the expedition was at Darya Khan, situated opposite to Dera Ismail Khan. Eighty miles north of Darya Khan another branch of the railway ran to Mari Indus opposite Kalabagh on the right bank of the river.

* The eventual daily average strength was increased to:
    Combatants ... ... 41,800.
    Non-combatants ... ... 37,900.

Neither at Darya Khan nor Mari had the Indus been bridged, and there was thus a break in communications, but between Mari and Kalabagh a ferry had been established by which stores were conveyed to the terminus of the Trans-Indus narrow-gauge railway at the latter town. From Kalabagh the Trans-Indus railway runs south-west for fifty miles to Lakki, where it bifurcates, the north branch going thirty miles to Bannu, and the southern going to Tank and Kaur Bridge, a distance of fifty miles.

From Darya Khan stores were conveyed the fifteen miles to Dera Ismail Khan by wheeled transport, the road across the sandy river bed being laid with grass, while pontoon bridges traversed the channels. From Dera Ismail Khan radiated the various routes on the right bank of the Indus, including the direct main road to Tank, along which was laid a 60 cm. Decauville railway. A serious drawback was the absence of lateral communications, and especially of a direct way between Tank and Bannu. Vehicles were compelled to go round by Dera Ismail Khan, a detour of eighty miles.

Animal transport with draught and pack thus came to play an important part. Forward of Tank pack animals only could be employed, and as many as 4000 constituted at times a single convoy. A good deal of work was done on the routes in order to marshal the animals on as broad a front as possible, but roads were not the only source of difficulty, for rinderpest and foot and mouth disease caused serious losses. The presence of light mechanical transport was, then, of great value. Six companies of Fords were employed, first working above Bannu where the track was improved to admit of their use and subsequently on a motor road which was constructed from Manzai above Tank to Khirgi and eventually extended to Jandola. The percentage of vans continually under repair was high, the daily number in the workshops amounting to 12, 14, 15, 29, 40 and 65 per cent. of the strength of each of the six companies, but the work performed proved beyond doubt the potentialities of mechanical transport in those regions and may well have caused some searchings of heart that so many frontier affairs in the past had lacked such assistance.

It will have been observed that in advance of the broad-gauge railway there existed no method of forwarding stores and supplies to the front without change of means of transport even after the passage of the Indus. Forward of Tank the Ford vans operated the section of twenty miles from Kaur Bridge and Khirgi, while from Tank to Khirgi and Khirgi to Piazha Ragzha mule and camel pack transport were utilised.

In the Bannu District it was possible to employ draught animal-wheeled transport from the latter place as far as Idak some twenty-five miles west, while from Idak to Dardoni, a further twenty miles, Ford vans again worked on the road and pack animals on the track. Forward of Datta Khel and Piazha Ragzha the Striking Force had to rely on pack transport alone, and even then the going was so bad that it was necessary to work the camels on a three-quarter instead of a sixth-sevenths basis.

The daily average tonnage with which these communications were capable of dealing was as follows: the Trans-Indus railway to Bannu and Tank together, six hundred tons; the Decauville line from Dera Ismail Khan to Tank, a hundred and sixty tons: and these lines were used for conveying supplies, stores, and reinforcements throughout the campaign.

These communications cannot be said to have erred on the side either of completeness or simplicity; but there was no alternative, and it can be definitely stated that had it not been for the Decauville line laid from Dera Ismail Khan to Tank and the presence of six light mechanical transport companies it would have been impossible to have maintained a concentration, as numerous as was the Striking Force, in front of Tank.

As the course of operations showed that the number of troops was none too great for what turned out to be a serious task, the introduction of mechanical transport may be deemed to have shed fresh light on the solution of frontier problems.

As a transport and supply study the expedition of 1919–20 is of interest, as are also subsequent operations in those parts of the world, for indeed the Army Service Corps had by no means finished with Waziristan.

In 1922 a "roads" policy in Wazir and Mahsud territory was sanctioned by the Viceroy, and this led to the construction of what is known as the Waziristan circular road, a terrain all too familiar to many members of the Army Service Corps for a period of some five years—and an even more unpleasant route on which to put in time than the famous Seres road on the Balkan Front.

Northwards from Dera Ismail Khan the new road runs to Bannu via Yarik, Pezu and the Pezu Pass, Shah Baz Khel Serai Gambila and Serai Naurang, and, with the exception of the passage through the Pezu Pass, it is without any gradient. Two lines of mechanical transport could be worked successfully throughout its length, and the passage of small spates and irrigation canals across the road are provided for. The surface is water bound, no tar or asphalt being used, while stone for re-making the surface abounds.

From Bannu the road proceeds up the Tochi Valley by way of Mirzail, Saidgi and Idak to Miranshah, whence it is possible to march to Datta Khel. Continuing over the Tochi River the road, passing across the Khaisora Valley, reaches Razani and from there the ascent of the Razmak Narai and Alexandra Ridge is made via Greenwood's Corner, a hairpin bend built out on a bastion. One of the most striking features of the road is the skill with which it has been sited, graded and constructed. The gradient hardly ever varies and every corner has been banked with such care that it is not, as is elsewhere often the case, destroyed by repair.

From Razmak camp, which is the largest enclosed camp in the world, the route goes past Makin and Piazha, along the Takki Zam to Jandola, which latter place is the headquarters of the South Waziristan Scouts. Here a branch proceeds to Sarwekai, from whence it is possible to proceed to Wana, while the main artery passes along the Takki Zam to Khirgi and then across a wide valley to Manzai, subsequently following the railway to Kaur Bridge. From Kaur Bridge via Tank to Dera Ismail Khan the ground is comparatively flat, and over this section several water stations are available for mechanical transport.

Such, without certain subsidiary roads, is the great highway for which the advent of mechanical transport was responsible. Three hundred miles long and requiring the construction of many bridges and causeways for the crossing of rivers liable to the most violent spates, this great feat of engineering was completed in the space of a few years, and may fairly be claimed as a most potent instrument in the pacification and civilisation of those lawless parts.

No apology is offered for a somewhat detailed reference to road building in a chronicle devoted to the Army Service Corps, for the Corps played as large a part in its construction as it did in its subsequent early use. From the end of 1921 onwards vast quantities of mechanical transport were stationed in Waziristan, and a considerable portion remained there right up to the period when the Indian Army Service Corps took over. An ever-increasing line of communication stretching westwards from Dera Ismail Khan and Bannu necessitated great daily convoys of supplies and stores.

By 1926 the Headquarters of a Mechanical Transport

Group, containing five companies, was located permanently at Bannu, detachments being stationed at different posts and garrisons.* Razmak including Razani was fed weekly by ten supply convoys of twenty-one lorries each, additional vehicles being provided for other stores. The convoys ran in accordance with "open" and "closed" hours, during which protection by regular troops and armoured cars was provided.

In September 1921 an Army Service Corps officer in the person of Major-General F. M. Wilson was appointed Director of Supplies and Transport in India, where he remained four years. The department was further strengthened by the nomination as Deputy-Director in March 1923 of Colonel W. M. Parker, whose distinguished services during the Mesopotamia Campaign there has been occasion to notice elsewhere. Colonel Parker was at Simla until July 1928.

Prior to the advent of General Wilson, a certain reorganisation of the mechanical transport units had taken place. By this the Army Service Corps companies lost their original identity, and were merged into what were known as Mechanical Transport Units India, the officers, warrant officers and a proportion of other ranks being provided from the Royal Army Service Corps *personnel* available, the balance being formed from Indians specially trained, a nucleus being available from the Indian mechanical transport companies which were in the early stages of their existence when their British colleagues first made their appearance in 1916. There were thus created thirty field units exclusive of the Khyber Ropeway Company and the Central Stores Depot, Base Motor

* No. 5 Indian M.T. (Motor Ambulance Convoy) Company was at Dera Ismail Khan with detachments at Manzai.
No. 13 Indian M.T. (Karrier lorries) Company was at Bannu.
No. 17 Indian M.T. (Albions, Crossleys, Fords) Company was at Razani.
No. 18 Indian M.T. (Light Albions) Company was at Idak.
No. 22 Indian M.T. (Motor Repair Unit) Company was at Dera Ismail Khan.

THE CORPS IN INDIA

Transport Workshops and Reserve Vehicle Park at Chaklala Training School at Sitapur, Advanced Technical Inspection Branches at Peshawar, Rawal Pindi and Poona.

Mechanical transport for the Army in India may therefore be said to have been placed on a comprehensive basis and, in order to obtain the necessary liaison, an Army Service Corps officer was appointed to the India Office under the High Commissioner.

By the end of the Great War, the *personnel* of the Royal Army Service Corps may be said to have had a vast experience of all kinds of transport. In the Khyber Pass, however, a further method was introduced and organised under the administration of the Corps into a successful and economical means of transport. This consisted of the Khyber ropeway. Originally projected as a war measure during the Third Afghan War, the line was surveyed and work begun during 1919, but it was by no means an easy task, especially as such a long monocable had never before been constructed and, therefore, there was very little precedent upon which to work.

The Italians had a ropeways or what was known as a "telerifice" at Asiago and elsewhere, and the Germans also operated one in Serbia, but in neither of these instances was the system a monocable. A fixed tightrope, carriers hanging from small wheels that ran thereon and a light tow-rope and winding apparatus were the elements of the system. Since the rope was fixed and had no wheels off which to jump neither the alignment or grading needed absolute accuracy.

Obviously there are few parts of the world where ropeways could be usefully employed in war, since a light railway is more effective besides being quicker and more economical to build and requiring less labour to operate and maintain. But, until the coming of the railway to the Khyber, the ropeway was responsible for some effective work.

Major K. J. Macmullen, of the Royal Engineers, was sent out by the War Office in September 1919 and tests showed that the line as it had then been constructed could never work satisfactorily. Addressing himself to the rectification of these defects Major Macmullen carried out successful experiments in January 1920. The ropeway ran from the Peshawar Valley over the Khyber Pass, through tribal territory to the Afghan border—a distance on the rope of twenty-two and a half miles. It was built in six sections with stations at Jamrud (on the N.W. railway), Mile 3 (Bagiari), Shahgai, Ali Masjid, Zintara Landi Kotal and Landi Khana. Of these Jamrud, Ali Masjid, Landi Kotal, and Landi Khana were military camps, and the stations were inside the wire perimeter, while for the others stone forts were erected to contain the stores.

Each section of the line, that is, the space between two main stations, had its own moving monocable or endless rope, and it was from this wire rope that carriers each with three hundredweight of freight hung suspended by clips and were carried up the line. The latter was supported on standards varying in height between ten and a hundred and fifty feet. On level ground they were about twenty-five feet high, which enabled the carriers to clear a loaded camel or anything else passing underneath. The actual power was provided by 40 H.P. stationary Crossley engines, which had originally been manufactured for searchlight work during the war. Started on petrol but run on kerosene one or two engines were required to work each section of the line according to the average steepness of the gradient. The pace of a rope was four and a half miles per hour, and the journey of a carrier from Jamrud to Landi Kotal occupied rather over four hours and to Landi Khana half an hour longer, but this last section was not much used. Jamrud was the headquarters of the company.

Deliberate damage to the ropeway was uncommon,

but one night the wily tribesmen cut the cable about three-quarter way through near Bagiari. The following morning work started at daylight, and the cable stood until there were seventy carriers on the line: it then snapped and all the carriers fell to the ground. The loose end of the cable went whipping up the valley until it fouled the last standard but one before it reached Shahgai. This standard was seventy feet high and it bent down and touched its toes as if it was engaged in Swedish exercises. Meanwhile the strain being removed from the tension trolley at Shahgai station this trolley rushed down its little line, which happened to be on a very steep hill, and broke itself, the wheel upon it and the winch at the bottom. The huge vertical power wheel was also crumpled. All this damage was put right in forty-eight hours.

One experience, for many years rare to British troops, came the way of the Royal Army Service Corps in February 1922 in the convoy to Kabul to escort the British Minister on his taking up the appointment. For this duty twelve Albion three-ton lorries and seven motor cars were detailed under Captain Breadmore. Very little information about the route was available and undoubtedly thirty-hundredweight lorries or more preferably still "six wheelers" would have been more suitable vehicles. On parts of the road between Peshawar and Jellalabad tarpaulins laid on sand were found necessary, and the whole journey of two hundred and four miles occupied between 12.30 p.m. on the 27th of February and 6 p.m. on the 7th of March, snow being encountered at 5000 feet and the road rising to 8200 feet. It was anticipated that the outward trip would have occupied five days and in fact the return one only took four days.

By October 1923 mechanical transport was firmly established in India and included three main groups located respectively at Peshawar, Quetta and Chaklala. There were a total of thirty-six units besides the Inspection Branches.* All were classed as Royal Army Service Corps units, and the necessary reliefs of British *personnel* provided from home.

As early as 1922 the Government of India put forward proposals for the re-organisation of the Supply and Transport Corps, which included amalgamation with the Royal Army Service Corps. In pursuance of these proposals the constitution of the former was to be changed from that of a department to that of a combatant organisation, and the whole of the British officers and other ranks of the new Corps were to be furnished by the Royal Army Service Corps, to which were to be transferred all British officers and other ranks of the Supply and Transport Corps should they so desire. The Indian *personnel* were to be transferred without change of status to the newly formed Indian Army Service Corps. This approach by the Government of India was in effect an offer to place in the hands of the Royal Army Service Corps the responsibility for the transport and supply services of the army in India, and it requires little imagination to envisage the scope which would have been thus afforded.

Unfortunately, after lengthy negotiations lasting until 1927, these approaches were rejected, and it is difficult to consider that rejection as other than a grave error on the part of those responsible both from the point of view of the Royal Army Service Corps and the future efficiency and welfare of the Army as a whole.

* These were divided as follows:

Heavy Motor Transport Companies	10
Ford Van Companies	2
Light Motor Transport Company	1
Motor Ambulance Convoys	8
Medium Artillery Companies	4
Mobile Repair Units	4
Heavy Repair Shops	4
Mechanical Transport Training Centre	
Central Stores Depot	
Khyber Ropeway Company	

It was true that the effects of any subsequent "Indianisation" of the Indian Army was a matter requiring the most careful consideration, but such policy was one touching all arms of the service and not peculiar to any one. The negotiations really broke down on the relative seniority of the *personnel* to be amalgamated—an important consideration, but by no means a vital one. No good purpose is to be served by disguising the fact that individual interests of the existing generation were allowed to prevail over the corporate future of a great ancillary service. But for the Royal Army Service Corps the matter was not to end in the mere rejection of fresh fields of effort and enterprise. For when the decision was once taken the Government of India proceeded with re-organisation on its own account by the formation of the Indian Army Service Corps and, in order to include mechanical transport, was compelled to call upon the Royal Army Service Corps to provide the necessary *personnel*. This involved the transfer of a hundred and thirteen officers, a hundred and two warrant officers and nearly seven hundred n.c.o.'s and men as a permanent measure, numbers approximating to one-fifth of the strength of the British Corps, and therefore that Corps, having declined the invitation to absorb the Indian transport and supply organisation found itself instead partially absorbed by the latter, and was thus compelled to make sacrifices without any compensating factor whatever, unless the avoidance of service in India could be deemed such factor.

That the Royal Army Service Corps as a body would have welcomed amalgamation there is hardly room to doubt. Indeed it would have been extraordinary had professional soldiers not desired to enlarge their professional scope. But unfortunately the negotiations lay with those who were wholly out of touch with the feeling of the Corps, and who were, it would seem, unduly influenced by the prospect of the Royal Army Service

Corps having to share in future posts and appointments which had up to then been its peculiar appanage. The facts that, even if such reason had been good and sufficient, the period of transition would have been a comparatively short one, a couple of decades at most, and also that there would have been equivalent compensation by the share of the appointments in India, seemed to have been ignored.

It must be admitted that the conditions under which the Royal Army Service Corps served in India were not popular with that Corps, but those conditions were, it may be claimed, those which amalgamation would have of itself provided the real remedy. Attachment to a different organisation for long periods is never popular, while the fact that such attachment involved a high proportion of the Royal Army Service Corps *personnel* being located in the most unpleasant stations in India intensified the feeling of "pulling the chestnuts from the fire" for others, although such a situation was, of course, unavoidable. It may further be added that the Corps as a whole was dissatisfied with the manner in which *personnel* were allotted to the Indian roster, and indeed with some of the postings by which officers with little or no mechanical transport experience or knowledge were despatched to employment for which they were quite unsuited.

In 1928, however, the die was cast and the Royal Army Service Corps bade farewell to the army in India. Recognition of its work was given in an Indian Army Order dated the 30th of May, in the course of which the Commander-in-Chief, Sir William Birdwood, wrote: "The members of the Royal Army Service Corps, who came to India, have worked with such loyalty that they have brought into being a service which the Indian Army Service Corps will be proud to maintain".

BIBLIOGRAPHY

"The Indian Supply and Transport Corps." By Captain R. J. SLAUGHTER, A.S.C. From the *Army Service Corps Quarterly*, January 1912.

"Supply and Transport Work in India." By Captain C. E. H. WINTLE, A.S.C. From the *Army Service Corps Quarterly*, April 1907.

"Mechanical Transport in India." By Captain G. AYLMER, A.S.C. From the *Army Service Corps Quarterly*, January 1911.

Report on the working of the Army Service Corps Mechanical Transport in India since the outbreak of War. Dated July 1918. By Lieut.-Colonel J. H. B. PEYTON, A.S.C.

Waziristan 1919–20. By Lieut.-Colonel H. De WATTEVILLE, C.B.E., p.s.c.

"The Waziristan Circular Road." By Captain H. J. COOPER, R.A.S.C. From the *Journal of the Royal United Service Institution*, August 1926.

"The Khyber Ropeway Company." By Lieut.-Colonel R. P. CRAWLEY, D.S.O., O.B.E., M.V.O. From the *Royal Army Service Corps Quarterly*, April 1924.

"From Peshawar to Kabul." By Captain R. G. BREADMORE, O.B.E., R.A.S.C. From the *Royal Army Service Corps Quarterly*, January 1927.

CHAPTER XVI

IN DIVERS FIELDS

THERE have now been set out, within restricted space, the chief activities of the Army Service Corps in the more familiar theatres of war. But no survey of the work of the transport and supply services should omit some mention of certain other operations, which, though of minor import, were equally fruitful in lessons and equally creditable to those concerned.

The Corps cannot claim to have played any prominent rôle in the campaign which took place in the Cameroons between August 1914 and April 1916, but it did bring some contribution to the success that was there obtained. For other reasons, too, General Dobell's operations are of interest. In the first place they furnish a unique example of a "small war" in that the fighting troops on both sides were, except their officers and a few n.c.o.'s, wholly native; secondly, until the arrival of No. 706 (Ford Van) Company Army Service Corps in September 1915, the maintenance services were mere improvisations; and lastly, because of the abnormal difficulties which lay in great distances, paucity of communications and lack of supplies from local sources.

The German colony comprised an area of some 300,000 square miles—the extreme length from north to south being eight hundred miles and from east to west six hundred miles. The topography varies considerably, but the main features are the Cameroon Mountains rising to 13,000 feet in the south-west corner in the neighbourhood of Buea, and the central plateau of Ngaundere. The southern or coastal belt, for a width of seventy to eighty miles from the sea, is covered with a heavy forest in which the trees often rise to a height of two hundred feet. The intervals between trees are filled in with undergrowth so dense that it is often impossible to see five yards through it. North of this forest is a belt of grass country which grows thinner as it reaches north.

Roads are practically non-existent with the exception of one motor road from Kribi to Jaunde: other routes consisted of paths ten to twelve feet wide.

Two railways existed—a stretch of a hundred and twenty miles running from Duala to Eseka, and a northern line of a hundred miles between Duala and Nkongsamba. Rivers and creeks were only navigable for a few miles inland from the coast.

The expedition was an Anglo-French one, the main British contingent consisting in the early stages of 4300 West African native troops, which number was increased by September 1915 to nearly 10,000 with fourteen guns: and there was also a detached northern force of 2500 with seven guns, to which were united seven hundred and fifty French troops. The latter also organised an Eastern column. Administrative and departmental services were conspicuous by their absence, and therefore had to be improvised. Transport and supply was organised by Captain Waldback, late of the Royal Irish Regiment, who officiated as Director with conspicuous success. Under him was a body of officers (chiefly drawn from the Political Department of the West African colonies) who had come out in charge of the native carriers who, until the making of roads fit for mechanical vehicles, represented the only possible form of transport. The French authorities had contemplated the use of mules and actually landed some two hundred after the occupation of Duala. Beyond drawing a few old railway trucks that were put together they proved useless, and were soon evacuated, for the prevalence of tsetse fly made the country impossible for animals.

The first objective was Duala, which was captured after a bombardment from the sea on the 27th of September, 1914, and which formed a safe and suitable base for the movements to follow. By the beginning of 1915 the British troops were holding Duala, the northern railway, Bare, Victoria and Dibombe. During January, February and March there was constant fighting about Bare and in April the control of the expedition was transferred from the Colonial Office to the War Office. The summer conditions brought a lull in activities and opportunity was taken to effect some re-organisation. Reinforcements arrived and arrangements were made for a Ford van mechanical transport company to be sent from England, in anticipation of which a motor road was put in hand from Edea and completed as far as the covering troops at Ngwe. There had been much sickness among the carrier transport, and it was found necessary to provide 1500 a month from the British West African colonies to replace casualties.*

The use of motor transport on the Cameroons Expedition had been initiated in May 1915 with three Ford lorries which ran between Edea and Ngwe, a distance of thirty miles on the Edea-Jaunde road. These operated from the 18th of May to the 23rd of June, making about fifty complete journeys. The rainy season prohibited further use of the road, but the experience gained justified extension of this means of transport during the autumn,

* The following is an extract from some notes written by Lieut.-Colonel R. H. Rowe, of General Dobell's Staff: "The chief difficulty met with was the carrier capacity on long lines of communication. A 'carrier' or 'porter' carries a load of about 60 lbs. or twenty to twenty-five rations. Long lines were divided into stages of a few days' march each. The country operated in was stripped bare and practically all food had to be brought up. Thus the carriers on the first stage had not only to bring up the rations for the troops at the front but enough for themselves and also for the carriers employed on the further stages beyond. A few simple sums in arithmetic will soon show that as the line of communications increases, the number of carriers required very soon grows to an impossible figure out of all proportion to the troops engaged or the resources in men available".

and an Army Service Corps Mechanical Transport Company, No. 591, for use in the Cameroons, was directed to be formed by the Army Council in September 1915.* Captain J. E. Davies was placed in command; this officer had had previous experience on the West Coast of Africa which proved very useful. The unit was mobilised in the Mechanical Transport Depot at Grove Park and embarked at Liverpool on the 29th of September, landing at Duala on the 19th of October. A week later the company arrived at the railhead at Edea, fifty-five miles distant, and was there inspected by General Dobell.

The offensive had been resumed by the Expeditionary Force on the 22nd of September, the British column being directed on Jaunde by a narrow bush track about a hundred miles in length via Ngwe–Wumbiagas–Ndog, while the French moved by the line of the midland railway, and consequently to the south of the British. From the first, the most strenuous fighting took place. Every foot of the road was contested. The British were obliged to convert their track into a motor road, while the French had several important bridges to repair in order to supply themselves by rail. In front of the completed motor road and railhead 7000 carriers were employed in bringing up supplies.

The first task of the Army Service Corps was to operate the thirty-mile route between Edea and Ngwe by transporting as rapidly as possible the considerable accumulation of stores at railhead forward. The "lift"

---

* The establishment was:

Personnel: 2 officers.
1 warrant officer.
6 n.c.o.'s.
60 rank and file, with native labour to be added as required.

Vehicles: 27 Ford delivery vans.
4 ambulances.
2 cars.
1 armoured car.
4 motor cycles.

was then extended to Wumbiagas, a further twenty-two miles, which place the British force was timed to leave on the 1st of December. The carrying capacity of the vans had been officially estimated at ten hundredweights, but this over such roads was impossible. Sir Charles Dobell therefore wired to Nigeria and the Gold Coast for additional vans, and on it being represented to him that the service could be carried out with much greater success if the establishment were increased to allow of native drivers and fitters, these were applied for also. Five additional vans were received from the Gold Coast during December, and six from England in January 1916, while the native *personnel* of the company gradually increased to a hundred and twenty, of whom sixty were skilled or semi-skilled drivers and fitters. To this increase in *personnel* may be largely attributed the success of the operations, and the very highest praise must be given to the *esprit de corps* which these natives displayed. No work was too arduous, and no hours too long for them, and it is a matter for regret that, following a similar precedent of a hundred years previously, they were not held as qualified for the medal given to those participating in the war.

By the 6th of November the British main forces were on the line Eseka–Wumbiagas, and, a week ahead of the projected programme, the final advance on Jaunde started on the 23rd of November. It was in this locality that the German main concentration of some 2400 rifles with forty machine guns lay, and severe fighting took place at first, but by mid-December this began to slacken; and the fact that many prepared positions were abandoned to the Allies without a blow being struck made it clear that retreat with a view to disengaging himself was the main pre-occupation of the enemy. On the 1st of December Jaunde was entered, and the enemy retired south and south-east. In the northern part of the colony his detachments were being harried by a column under

General Cunliffe, who, early in November, had reached Banjo Mountain, where he delivered an action which has been described as "one of the most arduous ever fought by Native African troops". Early in January it became clear that the back of the enemy resistance was broken. On the 1st of January, 1916, the day on which the main British force entered Jaunde, General Cunliffe's advanced troops were on the Sanaga river some fifty miles north, and movement in that direction being effectively stopped, there was little left to the Germans but to retreat into Spanish Guinea to the south-west. Although the pursuit was taken up with vigour by the Allies and the enemy rearguard engaged on several occasions, the main body succeeded in reaching neutral territory, where 1000 Europeans and 6000 African troops reached Spanish Muni and laid down their arms.

The Cameroons were then entirely cleared, with the exception of a small group which held out gallantly at Mora, and did not capitulate until the 18th of February, 1916.

The part which the mechanical transport played in these highly successful operations may now be recounted.

The section of the road over which the company worked continued from Wumbiagas on to Ngung, nineteen miles forwards, this stage being opened on the 18th of December. Thence it proceeded to Dschangmangas, twenty-two miles, and to Jaunde, a further twenty-seven. Thus from railhead at Edea a route of a hundred and twenty miles had to be operated eastwards. When the enemy turned south and the British gave chase the line of communications ran from Jaunde, a hundred and seven miles south-west, to Lolodorf via Olama, the section Jaunde–Olama being opened on the 25th of January and the Olama–Lolodorf one on the 4th of February. The route further proceeded eighty miles to Kribi on the coast via Bikoko, this stage commencing to be worked on the 15th of February. The circuit Duala–

Jaunde, Jaunde–Kribi, over which the mechanical transport operated, was thus some three hundred and sixty miles, and it may be remarked that practically up to the time of the company embarking for England running detachments were maintained along this route. From Kribi to Duala the circuit was completed by a sea voyage of sixty miles.

While the activities of a single unit hardly call for any elaborate description, some few details are not without interest, since there was no precedent for any considerable use of mechanical transport on service in West Africa, where its introduction was definitely a success.

On the advance to Jaunde the use of the vans had, with one exception (their passage over the Sogsunge Hills), been restricted by the progress in repair of the roads. From Jaunde to Kribi the original German motor road was used and found to be generally in excellent condition. The bridge at Lolodorf had been broken during the retreat of the Germans, and ten days were occupied in its repair, while the last nine miles into Kribi were, owing to the German abandonment of this port a year before, in bad condition and completely overgrown. The very numerous concrete and iron bridges, particularly that at Bipindi, forty-six miles east of Kribi, had not however been damaged, the line of the German retreat into Muni having left the main road shortly after crossing the Ngyong at Olama and having passed through Ebolowa.

At Olama vehicles crossed the river on a bridge built on canoes. From the time of the arrival of the vans at Jaunde two services were maintained. Firstly, there was the transport from Edea of mails, *personnel* and rations, which ceased when a month later Kribi became a base and when the German Government stores seized at Jaunde had been evacuated. Secondly, there was the rationing of the Kribi and Jaunde garrisons. In February and March 20,000 lb. of rubber alone, besides many valuable medical stores, botanical specimens, and a large quantity of ivory were transported, while the balance of rations was so carefully adjusted that, on the final evacuation, nothing remained. Jaunde was completely evacuated on the 18th of March, as were Olama and Lolodorf two days later. From that time until the shipment of the cars to Duala between the 3rd and 10th of April the company was engaged in generally overhauling cars with a view to sale.

A peculiar and unforeseen difficulty cropped up after the cars had been running some three weeks. The leaves of nearly the whole of the front springs which, in Ford cars, are placed transversely, broke almost simultaneously. This was not due to overloading. It appeared to be due to excessive lateral motion set up in the van body, and with some misgiving as to the effect on the drivers of taking away the awnings, the upper portion of the sides and the tops of the van bodies were removed. This immediately put a stop to the wholesale breakage, and it was found possible to repair to a great extent the broken springs pending the arrival from England of a fresh consignment. This, however, took considerable time, as neither blacksmiths, forges nor flux were available on a large scale. At no time, however, did this prevent the transport of the required daily tonnage. The only other serious difficulty, but one which for a period of a fortnight nearly suspended work, was due to the omission of spare tyres from the table of stores which had been made out in West Africa and sent to England before the company arrived. When this was discovered a cable was sent but, by an unlucky mischance, the telegraphists left out the request from the message in which it should have been included, and this was not discovered until two boats on which the tyres should have arrived had come in. Another cable was immediately sent, and it is worthy of record that the Army Service Corps officer in charge of the Camden Town Tyre Depot had

IN DIVERS FIELDS

those tyres on board the boat at Liverpool within twelve hours after receipt of the cable. For a week the vans ran on covers placed one inside the other and well packed, on covers filled with grass and on old ropes. The frequent passage of the vans over the Sogsunge Hills caused one of the most difficult periods of the campaign. In two places vans had to be lowered by ropes and pulled up by the same means, taking nearly fifty native labourers to cope with this.

Some comparison between the capacity of the Ford vans and the alternative transport of native carriers is not out of place. For the period the 25th of October (when the company started work forward from railhead at Edea) to the 30th of November, after which date the second stage was entered upon, the equivalent numbers of carriers required for the lift of two hundred and sixty-nine tons of supplies, the total distance to be run with loads being over 30,000 miles, would have been 1454. For the month of December, when the "lift" was two hundred and twenty-six tons of supplies, the total distance to be run with loads being 34,000 miles, the carriers would have been 1941. In each case no allowance is made for the proportion of carriers who would normally fall sick or for the number of medical, Royal Engineer and miscellaneous loads which were conveyed, a hundred and ninety-five during the first of the above periods and two hundred and forty-six during the latter. It is on the conservative side to say that 2500 carriers would have been required during the month of December 1915 to perform the work done by the mechanical vehicles, and a comparison of the cost shows how great a financial saving was effected by the use of the latter* once the capital cost was met. Yet even these calculations

---

*
	£	s.	d.
Pay and maintenance of 2500 carriers at £2. 5s. per head for one month	5625	0	0
Cost of mechanical transport	2774	18	9

IN DIVERS FIELDS

take no count of the cost of the European supervision required for the carriers or of the number of the latter necessary for conveying their own rations.

The *personnel* of No. 591 Company had almost all recently joined the Army before embarkation for the Cameroons, but their health in that trying climate was splendidly maintained throughout. Although work was frequently continued day and night, and was at all times most arduous, and that owing to sickness and accidents among the officers and the very numerous detachments into which the unit became split supervision rested largely on junior n.c.o.'s, the conduct of the men was exemplary. In spite of the fact that it was not usually possible to place restrictions upon the consumption of alcohol and that native women, as a legacy of German habits, were easily procurable, the Army Service Corps as the sole unit representing the Imperial Army in the Cameroons worthily upheld its high standard of discipline and honour. Sir Charles Dobell did not omit to acknowledge its services: "The Ford Van Company", he said, "was invaluable during the advance—each car had to do over 100 miles a day and to do this native drivers had to be trained to take their turn with Europeans. Each Ford Van was worth about 150 carriers and at a pinch it could always do a bit more".

One noteworthy aspect of the campaign by which a vast area fell into the hands of the Allies was its cheapness to the British Exchequer—the total cost being less than £2,700,000. Although material and supplies had to be obtained for the greater part from England, the strictest economy was exercised and demands were, therefore, comparatively light. The fact that the troops were nearly all native Africans was mainly responsible for this happy and unusual state of affairs. With a specially prepared ration those brave and hardy troops could on certain occasions go for six days with only what they carried on the man, and their marching powers

were wonderful. A column was once known to do eighty-seven miles in forty-seven hours in full-service order carrying a hundred rounds of ammunition per man with cape and blanket.
Happy the lot of the Supply and Transport Corps under such circumstances!

Although the campaign undertaken by Generals Botha and Smuts, which successfully accomplished the subjugation of the German colony of South-West Africa, culminated in July 1915, some seven months before the Cameroons were cleared of the enemy, the latter operations have been given priority in the telling, since they were initiated some few weeks before the Union forces moved into hostile territory.

With the exception of some artillery and armoured cars and a few individual officers, Imperial troops took no part in German South-West Africa, but some short account of events is justified not only because they have never attracted the attention which they deserve, but also because the military enterprise was far more a problem of "supply" than it was of overcoming any resistance of the enemy. And the manner in which the improvised South African transport and supply services grappled with their task is one of high professional interest.

The German colony comprised an area of over 320,000 square miles, the greatest length from north to south being approximately nine hundred miles. Access from the sea was available through the ports of Luderitzbucht in the south and Swakopmund near Walfisch Bay, three hundred miles further north, both these places being served by railways. The line from Luderitzbucht ran eastwards about a hundred and seventy miles to Seeheim, where it bifurcated, the southern branch going to Nababis on the frontier of Cape Colony and the northern via Keetmanshoop to the capital, Windhoek, three hundred and fifty miles away. From Windhoek the railway proceeded via Okahandya and Karibib westwards to Swakopmund, linking up just before reaching the latter place with a line which ran north-east to Grootfontein and Tsumeb, about three hundred and seventy miles distant. This system, which joined up effectively the principal centres in the country, gave the Germans the immense advantage of easy communication on interior lines and, had they been fully exploited, might have enabled them to have sustained a long resistance. To the invaders the advantages were not so obvious, as the enemy consistently destroyed the permanent way and bridges behind him, and these had to be rebuilt as the advance proceeded. The speed and efficiency with which these repairs were carried out under great difficulties was one of the most remarkable features of the campaign.

Few countries in the world lend themselves less to military movement, for from some eighty miles inland from the coast there is a belt of dry waterless desert with heavy sand dunes which made progress slow at all times and on occasions almost impossible.* Beyond this certain areas are fairly fertile, but water was almost always scarce, while any supplies other than such cattle which had not been driven off by the Germans were unobtainable. A secure line of communications would have needed to

---

* A well-known war correspondent has described the country inland from the coast as follows: "North and south sand to the very horizon and beyond; east sand also to the ridges that fringe the great interior plateau; a parched and under the searching South African sun, a blinding desolation as far as the eye can reach with sand dunes and lava kopjes here and there to break the demoniacal monotony of the plains. The railway was destroyed by the Germans as they retired. It was rebuilt by the Union forces as they advanced. It is laid on a permanent way raised about a foot, sometimes more, above the surrounding waste and along one section it has constantly to be watched by gangs of natives lest it disappear in a night. The dunes are eternally shifting and we saw at one point several hundred yards of track, which actually had been lost under a drift, 20 ft. or 30 ft. high, rendering necessary a deviation of the line".

have been consolidated had only a small force been engaged.

With their trained reservists the Germans mustered some 7000 field troops and they were particularly strong in artillery and machine guns; they had also, for a short time, the assistance of 1000 South African rebels. These numbers were not known at the time—the estimate was in fact put at some figure between 9000 and 10,000 but the Union Government wisely took no risks. Their plan of campaign envisaged a series of converging movements by which the enemy would be driven from his railways and principal centres and forced into an inhospitable wilderness where he could not maintain himself. It was a thoroughly sound conception and, depending as it did on superior powers of mobility, was admirably adapted to the qualities of the South African troops. Three main columns took part. From Cape Colony there were what were known as the Southern and Eastern forces, under Colonels Van Deventer and Berrangé respectively, and these having disposed of the Germans and rebels under Maritz, who had crossed the Union frontier, invaded the hostile territory and entered Keetmanshoop on the 20th of April 1915. Meanwhile the Central column under General Mackenzie had been advancing from Luderitzbucht leaving Aus about seventy miles east on the 15th of April, their progress having been dependent on the rate of railway reconstruction, but Gibeon, two hundred and ten miles away to the north-east from Aus, was entered by the mounted troops on the 27th of April. The southern portion of the country with its railway system was then cleared of the enemy. During the concluding stages the operations of these columns were directed by General Smuts, who came up to Kalkfontein on the 11th of April for that purpose.

The Northern or main force, some 30,000 strong, was under the command of General Botha, who arrived at Walfisch Bay in February, bringing with him three mounted brigades as reinforcements, which latter, if disclosing the Commander-in-Chief's intentions to push the matter to a rapid conclusion, made the water situation one of great difficulty, which had to be relieved by supplies sent from Cape Town. On the 22nd of February General Botha directed his first effort against the enemy with the intention of clearing his front and covering railway reconstruction before launching the movement against the capital. The operations with their limited objective were successful, but there was not sufficient transport in hand to carry the advance up the dry bed of the Swakop River, and it was evident that major events would have to wait on railway progress on the Otavi line which, by this time, had, under infantry protection, covered seventy miles. The main body moved at the end of April, Karibib being entered on the 2nd of May and Windhoek on the 12th of May without opposition. Over two hundred miles had been covered in sixteen days across a terrain which was of itself a serious obstacle. The troops went right away from their supply "trains" and subsisted mainly on such fresh meat as could be obtained *en route*, the animals faring especially badly in the dried-up country. After the fall of their capital the Germans retired northwards, and it was not until the middle of June that sufficient supplies could be collected to allow of a pursuit. This was undertaken by four mounted brigades and one infantry brigade, when the railway had been put in order between Karibib and Windhoek and gave through communications to Swakopmund. The main body advanced along the line of the railway via Omaruru up to which place little damage had been done, but men and animals again suffered severely from the shortage of water. But the forward march, which once more outran supplies and, consequently, depended almost entirely on a fresh meat ration alone, was pressed with the greatest vigour. On the 1st of July, thirteen days after leaving Karibib, the 1st Mounted

Brigade entered Otaviefontein having covered three hundred and fifty miles in thirteen marching days. It was a remarkable "trek" but the 1st Infantry Brigade did even better, for on its arrival on the 4th of July it had in sixteen days covered two hundred and forty-five miles practically without a break, the last forty-five being covered in thirty-six hours, a feat which under ordinary circumstances would have been exceptional, but which, under the conditions of that country where water was hard to find, heavy dust the rule, and when transport difficulties never permitted more than half, and for six days quarter rations only, may be considered among the great marches of history.

The enemy was then fully concentrated at Tsumbeh, ten miles north, and completely surprised by the rapidity of the advance and the size of the concentration against him, he surrendered without a fight on the 9th of July. As it transpired later he had other plans for continuing the struggle which, had they matured, would certainly, in view of the ample material and transport resources still remaining to him, have involved a prolonged and costly guerilla war such as eventuated in East Africa. That he was effectively prevented from carrying out this design was due to the amazing mobility of the South African troops, which enabled him to be gripped in the pincers of a converging movement most ably directed and executed.

Such in bare outline was the course of the operations, and it has been desirable in the first place to recall it in order that the task of the transport and supply may be appreciated. Certainly those services were powerfully assisted by the endurance of the troops, but even the hardiest troops cannot exist indefinitely on fractions of the normal ration, and it is unnecessary to delve deeply into the history of the campaign to observe that "supply" generally materialised at the critical moment and, in any case, at all times strove to keep up with the pace set by the South African generals. It was not through any lack of foresight or effort when it failed to do so.

The circumstances obtaining in Damaraland throw a certain light on General Smuts's subsequent campaign in East Africa in that they serve to explain to some extent his mind and methods in that theatre which are not always comprehended by the more orthodox.

Reference was made in an earlier chapter to the stage which the South African Army Service Corps had reached by 1914, and it now remains to continue this by some reference to its performances in the field. It is not proposed to enter into any detail as to the work of individual units, but to indicate in general terms the manner in which the troops were maintained.

It should be appreciated in the first instance that the Union had a formidable force in South-West Africa, in all 50,000 men, and the occasion was noteworthy in that for the first time in the history of the British Empire a dominion conducted a campaign of magnitude against a European enemy beyond her own borders with practically no extraneous assistance.

We may turn first to the southern front. Colonel Berrangé's Eastern force, consisting of four regiments of mounted rifles, some artillery and certain ancillary troops, marched during February 1915 from Kimberley a hundred and fifty miles north-west to Kuruman in Bechuanaland, and from there commenced their long "trek" across the Kalahari Desert on the 6th of March. The troops were in heavy sand almost before camp was out of sight and they ploughed through similar terrain for the greater part of the six hundred miles which they subsequently negotiated. There was, of course, no railway which could be utilised, and water holes were few and far between and at most irregular distances. From one place, Bushman Pits, it was no fewer than a hundred and ten miles to the next water hole, and the natives who inhabited this area relied for liquids on a species of desert melon. The water problem was surmounted by mechanical transport ably organised by Major Rose. A series of portable tanks were used to set up water bases, and these were replenished by lorries travelling to and fro carrying drums of water from the last water hole. The magnitude of this task will be appreciated from the number of animals—some 2000—for which provision had to be made.

For supply, mule transport was impossible in the heavy sand, and even the ox-wagons which were utilised to supplement the mechanical transport had their severe limitations. In order to prevent animals from being overtaxed and to minimise the wear and tear on the vehicles, convoys were worked in easy stages throughout. When the column, as frequently happened, got out of touch with the wagons, supplies were brought up by motor. Thus the troops were never without rations and, although only half-scale was issued on several occasions, game was fairly plentiful.

There were times when the lorries and motor cars were beaten by the sand and the gradients combined, and animals had then to be brought to the rescue,* but on the whole the mechanical transport performed miracles, especially when the paucity of spare parts, which were practically unobtainable from the United Kingdom or France, is considered. The energy and ingenuity of the *personnel* responsible could hardly be surpassed. Mobile workshop sections were organised in the desert and travelled up and down the routes to effect repairs.

The Eastern force effected a junction with Colonel Van Deventer at Kiriis West sixty miles east of Keetmanshoop on the 14th of April. Van Deventer's troops had, likewise, arduous experience for, as in the case of

* One particular stretch of seven miles contained many gradients of one in three and lorries and motor cars were helpless. To get over the difficulty donkeys were stationed along the route and when necessary pulled the cars, but even so it took three hours to get seventeen motor vehicles over a patch of a hundred and fifty yards.

those under Colonel Berrangé, they were far from any railway and had a broad tract of desert to cross. They were also involved in considerable fighting. But here again mechanical transport proved its worth, and within the borders of German South-West Africa the situation was ameliorated by substantial captures made from the enemy.

As far as the Central force operating from Luderitzbucht was concerned, the supply problem was chiefly solved by railway communications as the advance was conducted eastwards. The enemy had been confident that the eighty-mile stretch of Namib Desert, separating Luderitzbucht from the inland and comparatively fertile plateau which begins at Aus, would prove a serious obstacle and, owing to the shortage of transport, so indeed it proved. It took six months to reconstruct the line to Aus, the task of re-bridging being particularly arduous, but the delay was largely due to the fact that it was undesirable to push out the necessary detachments to cover the work while there was a possibility of their being overwhelmed, while the organisation of the necessary railway *personnel* was very imperfect. Consequently activities had to wait upon events in north and south. When these had developed a railway regiment, which was formed, quickly put matters right and the two hundred and ten miles from Aus to Gibeon, including over thirty bridges and culverts, was completed in sixty days, on some occasions as much as five miles being done in the twenty-four hours, shifts being worked at night.

The situation became one which subsequently found some parallel in the movements of Generals Murray and Allenby across the Sinai Desert and in Palestine, and with his railhead continually moving forwards, Sir Duncan Mackenzie felt justified in launching his mounted troops in pursuit. Leaving Aus on the 16th of April he entered Gibeon eleven days later after having inflicted a severe defeat on the enemy. There was practically no mechanical transport available, and the slow-moving ox and mule wagons could not be expected to deal with so rapid an advance. Consequently the troops were often on half or even quarter rations, while the animals lived entirely on the country. But the district was not an unfertile one and captures of cattle from the enemy helped to eke out supplies. Nevertheless, after entering Gibeon, men and horses were completely exhausted and a halt would have needed to have been called even if there had been any great object in following the enemy north where he joined the main force opposing General Botha. The latter had ample means for dealing with the combined strength of the Germans and indeed it was even to the advantage of the Union army that a general "round up" could be effected by one stroke.

At Gibeon the supply situation improved daily as the railway crept forward, and the gap to be bridged by the animal transport narrowed.

Shortly after the occupation of Gibeon, General Mackenzie's force suffered a grievous loss in the death from an accident on the railway of a gallant officer in Sir George Farrar who had been acting as Deputy Assistant Quartermaster-General and who, in that capacity, had been responsible for the supply arrangements. The value of the work of this very able and energetic officer can hardly be over-estimated and his reputation was such that the enemy were wont to estimate the progress of the Union troops by the spot in which Sir George Farrar happened to be. He met his death when returning in a railway trolley in a driving rainstorm, having gone forward to supervise personally the opening of a new base from which to despatch convoys to Gibeon. In the rain-mist the trolley collided with a construction train, and Sir George was thrown over the embankment, sustaining internal injuries.

It was pathetically significant that in his delirium he

talked of little else but of the new transport which was arriving, and about feeding the men at the front and, although he showed a certain despondency at the slow progress made, almost the last words he spoke showed that he was not unmindful of what had been done. "When we consider the conditions", he said, "we find that a great deal has been accomplished." Of that, indeed, much was his own work.

The operations of General Botha in the north have been sufficiently described to indicate what could be done towards maintenance in his final march north from Windhoek and Karibib. It was only due to the presence of a well-organised mechanical transport column that the army, after having surrounded the enemy at Otaviefontein, could be provisioned.

Under Major Hope a convoy consisting of forty-three lorries each carrying two tons of supplies reached Otaviefontein in six days from Usakos west of Karibib, a distance of two hundred and seventy miles over very difficult country, and brought relief at the critical moment to the famishing troops.

Yet it was not only the work of the mechanical transport that made possible such brilliant results as were achieved in South-West Africa from the maintenance point of view. Mule and ox transport, which the South Africans were admirably adapted to handle efficiently, played a striking part and, considering the conditions obtaining, the wastage in animals was surprisingly small. The use of motor vehicles was, however, a wholly new departure, for the Union Defence Force and its organisation had to be improvised from the beginning. It was first used in August 1914 on a small scale to meet the needs of the troops thrown forward from the Prieska base to deal with German detachments threatening the border near Upington, and experiences encouraged the organisation of a fleet of cars shortly afterwards to conduct the pursuit of de Wet and other rebels. The successful results established its utility and the miscellaneous collection of vehicles which had been assembled were retained for service in South-West Africa, although the possibilities of their employment in that country were unknown. Its use with the force which crossed the Kalahari Desert alone made that undertaking possible, and much the same observation applies to the operations of General Van Deventer in the south and General Botha in the north, where it grew to considerable dimensions, being used not only for the conveyance of supplies and stores but also for movement of troops, ambulance work and other miscellaneous services. At first very many different types of vehicles were pressed into service but as the organisation expanded the necessity for standardisation was appreciated and steps taken to that end.

The Supply Branch rose bravely to the crisis. From having to deal in peace with the modest numbers of the permanent force and police and to provide for the training camps of the citizen force it was called upon to feed what almost amounted to the nation in arms. There were but few officers who had previous experience of supply work in the field although a small number of ex-British Army Service Corps n.c.o.'s who had transferred to the Union Government were available. A large number of officers and subordinate *personnel* were hastily recruited, the more responsible posts being filled by permanent officials. In view of the heavy financial responsibility these measures of improvisation caused some misapprehension to the higher authorities at the time, but for the most part such fears proved to be groundless.

Heavy purchases of flour in the Australian and Canadian markets were made at the outbreak of war at a time when the stocks in the Union were small, and this proved an advantage to the civil population by preventing an inflation of prices. Otherwise most commodities—pre-

IN DIVERS FIELDS

served meat and cheese were the principal exceptions—were obtained within South Africa itself. There was never any failure to replenish either Base or Field Supply Depots and, on the whole, the service was most efficiently administered.

Not only from the operations' point of view, then, the conception and execution of the campaign in South-West Africa, in which a force of 50,000 men were employed under circumstances of great hardship and difficulty, were those of which the Union of South Africa might well be proud. From start to finish there was no real "hitch" and coming immediately after grave internal difficulties the results were almost miraculous. But when genius is at the helm, as it was in the powers of the leadership of General Botha and the driving power and organising ability of General Smuts, nothing is impossible.

It remains to recall but one more series of operations. It is a far cry from the sandy deserts of South-West Africa to the alternately muddy and dusty plains of Mesopotamia, which were left in a previous chapter of this volume at the period when the last organised Turkish forces surrendered in November 1918. The interim up to 1920 had been, including, as it did, the Persian lines of communications, one of continuous activity.

When Sir Aylmer Haldane arrived to take over command on the 20th of March 1920, the situation from a military point of view was far from satisfactory. Two Indian divisions—the 17th and 18th—with a cavalry brigade and a proportion of lines of communication troops were scattered throughout the country, while a mixed brigade with a number of additional battalions were in Persia. For various reasons there was a strong current of unrest among the Arab population, a current which was stimulated from outside by Sharifian agitation from Syria and the newspaper clamour for evacuation which had, for some time, been raging in irresponsible portions of the English press. The first explosion occurred early in June when the Political Officer and his Staff at Tel Afar, forty miles west of Mosul, were murdered, and three weeks later trouble broke out some three hundred miles south on the Middle Euphrates where a disaster to a British column near Hilla in July so far encouraged the rebels that, by the end of August, over 130,000 armed men had joined the insurrectionary forces. The position was one of real gravity, and heavy reinforcements were obtained from India in the shape of the 6th Division and eleven additional battalions of infantry. Even then the task of restoring order was serious. The problem differed entirely from that which the overcoming of the Turkish armies had offered two years before, for the Arab tribesmen commanded a power of mobility which, while making them a constant danger to weak detachments, enabled them to avoid being brought to battle and dealt with *en masse*. Fortunately it was found possible to localise the disturbances to two main areas, north-east of Baghdad and on the Middle Euphrates, for had the powerful Muntafiq tribes on the Upper Euphrates and the Bani Ram and Bani Rabia bordering on the Tigris risen, Baghdad might easily have become a besieged city. As it was the main operations lasted until the middle of October and were followed by the process of disarming the tribes, which involved the movement of columns throughout the country.

Colonel H. G. Burrard, of the Royal Army Service Corps, only arrived in August to take over control of the Supply and Transport Directorate. He found his department in a far from satisfactory state. With demobilisation still in progress the *personnel* situation could hardly have been easy, but in Mesopotamia it was aggravated by the facts that the senior officers of the directorate were absent on leave in England and a number of the temporary officers who had been definitely promised release were chiefly, and perhaps very naturally, concerned as to when this undertaking was to be carried out. In all branches of the Corps there was a shortage of *personnel* as compared with establishments, and the number of sick was high. For the executive duties in animal transport and in supply the Indian Supply and Transport Corps was mainly responsible and it was also understaffed. In the Royal Army Service Corps mechanical transport matters were unsatisfactory chiefly owing to lack of *personnel* possessing the necessary technical skill, and there was in certain units a sad falling off from the high standard of administration maintained up to the close of the war against the Turks.

The troops were in fact for the most part exhausted and war-weary. In the aftermath of a long struggle with its inevitable reaction such circumstances are at least understandable, especially in such an exacting climate as that of Mesopotamia, but they certainly presented the responsible authorities with an unusually onerous task. Fortunately there had been appointed in Colonel Burrard an officer who had both the ability and energy to make bricks with the minimum of good straw.

On the supply side reserves were much depleted and as regards certain items almost non-existent—a position made more serious by the comparative rapid increase of strengths as reinforcements arrived and the fact that the rebels had cut the main artery of communication which lay in the Basra–Baghdad railway. This last misfortune could only be countered by sending men and material from Basra to Kut by river, and then on by the line which was still open from there on to the capital. The volume of traffic, made necessary by the necessity of provisioning out stations before communications between them and Baghdad could be further interrupted, the Tigris route found difficulty in meeting, as the river portion to Kut was uncertain, while the output of the railways onwards from Kut was limited by scarcity of rolling stock. A further adverse factor was the scarcity of local supplies drawn largely from the disaffected areas. Of transport there was as far as quantity went a good deal available—in respect to animals, horses, mules, camels, oxen and even donkeys were present in organised formations. Indeed there was more than was required for normal purposes since, in the aftermath of the Great War, the process of liquidating the equipage of the large army which had disposed of the Turks had not been completed. But much of this was administered in an extravagant fashion and as in the case of everything uneconomical was inefficient. The Director of Supplies and Transport did not lose time in reorganising many of these, and in some cases returning them to India. Of the Royal Army Service Corps there were at one time as many as twenty mechanical transport companies, but for the reasons already indicated the efficiency of these varied greatly, and it redounded much to the credit of certain commanding officers that under the difficult conditions prevailing a high standard was still maintained. Some five of these units were employed up the Persian lines of communication to Kasvin—the expense of which was enormous; it cost for instance 1000 rupees to convey a ton of stores from the Mesopotamia railhead near Khanaquin to Kasvin. By a most unhappy occurrence the Advanced Mechanical Transport Depot in Baghdad was burnt down with the best part of its contents early in August—the outbreak being imputed to the work of native incendiaries, and this loss threatened to paralyse all movement except by animal transport, rail or river. Fortunately some small consignments of stores had arrived in Basra and a portion of these had reached Kut, so that by the exercise of the most rigid economy the service companies were kept going until replacements could be obtained from England. Similar attempts were made by rebel agents against the various supply depots but these were frustrated, and the golden rule of not "keeping all the eggs in one basket" was thenceforth observed. But an increased number of guards was thus inevitably involved—at a time when there were none too many men available for the punitive columns.

In relation to the working of transport and supply the operations required for pacification of the country call for little comment here. The difficulties which were apparent in 1914 to 1918 again manifested themselves and, indeed, from the scattered nature of the garrisons were even accentuated. General Haldane disposed of some 50,000 British and Indian troops and 120,000 followers, and he never at any time had one man too many until the tribes had been completely disarmed. Nevertheless in spite of all adverse circumstances the situation was met in the fashion in which a crisis is wont to be met by British troops. Throughout the terrible heat of the late summer with treachery everywhere abroad, movement was constant, and in the service of the columns the bulk of the work fell on the Mechanical Transport Branch of the Royal Army Service Corps. Without its aid it is certain that the operations would have been prolonged well into the winter and possibly even longer. It is, too, worthy of record that in no instance was any beleaguered garrison compelled to surrender for want of provisions.

With the short outline of the three campaigns—for all are worthy to be so termed—may be concluded the activities of the transport and supply services in fields, which, with the sole exception of Gallipoli, were fields of victory. Nor were those activities limited to successful operations in face of the enemy, and to the comprehensive tasks involved by the administration within the United Kingdom itself. The permanent overseas garrisons of the British Army, such as the important stations at the Cape, at Gibraltar, Malta and their like had all to be provided for; and the fluctuation of strengths, and coming and going of troops often made those tasks heavy ones, although in the light of the great events elsewhere they appear insignificant enough. Yet with very depleted staffs and with *personnel* of a low physical standard and but little experience the duties were carried out without any breakdown, and their performance contrasted strongly with what happened under similar conditions in the past.

The close of the Great War found the Royal Army Service Corps at the height of its prestige and, in conclusion, it is apposite to summarise its record under the supreme test.

Sound organisation is not comprehended by the fitness of the machine under given conditions, but by its adaptability to any conditions. Towards this end simplicity and capacity for expansion are the determining elements. Both were present. The structure, as has already been shown, had been designed in conformity with the rôle of the Expeditionary Force to meet the needs of a campaign in Western Europe. And in all its essential features that structure remained unchanged until the end of the war. The solution of the major transport and supply problems of 1914–19 had been sought and found in that period which had succeeded the campaign in South Africa.

Yet the organisation would have fallen short of its purpose had it failed to provide a *personnel* capable of meeting situations which had not been envisaged as normal and capable also of absorbing and assimilating an accession of strength over thirty-fold of its original numbers. It did not so fail. Whether in the amphibious operations in the Dardanelles, the mountains of Macedonia, the bush of East Africa, the deserts of Mesopotamia and Palestine, or the snow-bound wastes of North Russia, it proved equal to every reasonable call made upon it.

IN DIVERS FIELDS

In East Africa, as in Mesopotamia, the Corps was set to remedy the mistakes or make good the shortcomings of others. In India its assistance was invoked towards the deficiencies of the Supply and Transport Corps of the Indian Army. All these accomplishments proved the adaptability which had been inculcated by the methods of training just as the heavily burdened system in France proved the soundness of the organisation.

But the ramifications of the Corps extended above and beyond the strict exercise of the duties of supply allied to transport. With the mechanically drawn heavy artillery its *personnel* became an integral part of fighting units. Towards the formation of the Tank Corps in 1916 large drafts were made upon it. When the Machine Gun Corps came into existence in the same year the additional task was imposed of providing a school for the instruction of its thousands of recruits in riding and driving. And all these and many other activities outside the real field of the Corps were from 1916 onwards carried out under the handicap of a *personnel* continuously in a state of flux, and continuously lower in bodily efficiency by the transfer of the most able-bodied categories to the fighting arms. During the war some 1200 officers and over 82,000 of the other ranks were so transferred. The necessity for such a step could not be disputed and no attempt was made to dispute it, but it was none the less a severe obstacle to the performance of technical duties, especially as the *personnel* withdrawn had for the larger part to be replaced by that only semi-skilled or altogether unskilled. As a further drawback from the technical point of view, a high proportion of the most capable of regular officers were employed away from Corps duties on the staff of the Army.

As far as casualties within its own ranks were concerned the losses of the Corps were considerable. Two hundred and eighty officers and 8187 of the other ranks gave their lives, figures which should dispel any idea that the administrative services did not share to a material extent the sacrifices of their brethren in the fighting arms.

BIBLIOGRAPHY

"The Campaign in the Cameroons." By Major-General Sir CHARLES DOBELL, K.C.B., C.M.G., D.S.O. From the *Journal of the Royal United Services Institution*, November 1922.

"Brief Note on Strategy and Tactics of the Campaign in the Cameroons." By Lieut.-Col. A. H .W. HAYWOOD, C.M.G., D.S.O. From the *Journal of the Royal United Service Institution*, May 1920.

Report on the Mechanical Transport in the Cameroons Campaign. By Captain J. E. DAVIES, R.A.S.C.

How Botha and Smuts conquered German South-West Africa. By W. S. RAYNER and W. W. O'SHAUGHNESSY.

Louis Botha, or Through the Great Thirst Land. By KEITH MORRIS.

Information supplied by the South African Ministry of Defence.

The Insurrection in Mesopotamia 1920. By Lieut.-General Sir AYLMER HALDANE, G.C.M.G., K.C.B., D.S.O.

INDEX

Abbeville, advanced depots at, 91, 93

Abercorn, Germans surrender at, 320

Achi Baba, 166

Admiralty, and frozen meat ships, 390

Advanced Base M.T. Depot, location and moves of, 91; size and task, 108; in East Africa, 324; at Baghdad, 511

Advanced Supply Depot, at Mancourt, 91; at Abbeville, 91; their capacities, 93; in Italy, location of, 346

Ahwaz, mixed brigade at, 259

Ain Musa, 223

Aldham, Captain, 278

Aleppo, fall of, 242

Alexandretta, supply depot at, 242

Alexandria, main base, 166

Allenby, Gen. Sir E. H. H. (afterwards Viscount, Field-Marshal), 233; offensive of, 1918, 240

Ambulances, motor, 122

Amiens, advanced base at, 119; dispossession of, 119; concentration of bus companies at, 141

Ammunition columns, 54; R.A. not A.S.C. unit, reasons for, 56

Ammunition parks, 54; cadres of, 58; reduction of, 127

Anderson, Captain (afterwards Major-General) N. G., in Somaliland, 18

Animals, losses of, in East Africa, 305

Anzac, 158, 161, 167, 174, 175

Arab rising in Mesopotamia, inception of, 508; strength of rebels, 509; R.A.S.C. in, 510; extravagance of transport administration, 511

Archangel force, at Murmansk, 353

Ari Burnu, 158, 171

Armistice, position of troops in France at, 146

Army Corps, France, I, II; Gallipoli, Australian, 165; New Zealand, 165; Ninth, 169; Eleventh, 332, 335; Fourteenth, 332, 334

Army Council and A.S.C. officers, 9

Army Ordnance Department, xix, 27; repair shops of, 36; repairs to M.T. in base workshops of, 90; overburdening of, 91; impracticability of M.T. repair system of, 109; in Russia, 368

Army Service Corps, xix; scale and scope of, xxix; struggle for existence, xliii; breach of faith to, xliv; bearing of Haldane reforms on, 17; of Territorial Force, 18; *personnel* with Indian Army, 18; responsibility for A.S.C. services in Somaliland 1909, 21; taking over M.T. 1902, 26; principles of its organisation,

INDEX

46; Paul's memorandum on supply system, 52-4; reforms in principal field formations, 61; of Dominions, 74-77; stations on eve of Great War, 77; size in 1914, 78; dispersion of, 79; advance beyond departmental conceptions, 80; advantage of superior status, 80; simplicity of system of, 85; takes over repairs to M.T., 110; method of record of achievements, 117; in Expeditionary Force, 118; effect of liberal establishments, 123; work in *Official History*, 124; strength of, in France, 126; *personnel* in infantry, 128; attitude to changing circumstances, 129; duties of divisional, 129; horsemastership in, 129; records of units of, 130; transport corps of the Army, 137; elasticity of, in 1918, 145; of dominions, 154; casualties in France, 155; conception of task at Gallipoli, 165; supplies at Gallipoli, 175; strength at Gallipoli, 176; units at Salonika, 181; in Serbia, 183; during withdrawal at Salonika, 186; units for reinforcement of Balkan force, 190; motor boat section of, in Balkans, 203; prefix of Royal to, 209; Milne's despatch commendation of, 209; M.T. units with Serbian Army, 210; strength and casualties of, in Balkans, 215; supplies to refugees in Balkans, 219; unique experience of, in Balkans, 220; in Egypt and Palestine, 221; motor boat coy. on Suez canal, 222; strength of, in Egypt, 227; and water supply, 233; driving armoured cars with Hedjaz Army, 245; strength of, in Egypt, 245; absence of, in Mesopotamia, 252; strength of, in Mesopotamia, 261; its achievements in Mesopotamia, 264; Mesopotamian campaign a landmark for, 289; absence of, in *Official History* index, 290; appearance of, in East Africa, 292; East African *résumé*, 320; activities in Alps, 335; lessons learnt in Italy by, 349; strength of, in Italy, 350; shortage of *personnel* in Russia, 360; abilities of officers of, 368; responsible for canteens, 400; strength of, 409; in India, 457 *et seq.*; in Waziristan, 466; convoy to Kabul, 482; projected amalgamation of, with S. and T. Corps, 483; transfer of officers from, to R.A.S.C., 184; departure of, from India, 485; task of, in Cameroons, 490; in Arab rising, 509; R.A.S.C., summary of its record, 513-515

Arquata, base of, 330
Aruscha, 303
Asiago, 334; situation on, in June, 1918, 338
Atkins, Major-General Sir A., K.C.B., xxviii, 407; his term as D.S.T., 407-409
Attichy, railhead, 119
Auld, Colonel, A.Q.M.G. for A.S.C., 2
Austrian offensive, at Caporetto, 332; at Asiago, 334, 338
Auxiliary Omnibus Park, 141; location of companies of, 141

INDEX

Aylmer, Captain G., 486
Aziziyeh, 271

Badcock, Lieut.-Colonel G.E., 249
Bagamayo, landing at, 315
Baghdad, 250
Bagnall-Wild, Captain R. H., secretary M.T. Committee, 32
Baharitzar, base at, 368
Bailleul, advanced G.H.Q. at, 122
Balkans, primitive difficulties in, 84; nature of operations in, 126; operations in, their origin, 179; sphere of action in, 184; railway serving British force in, 184; political aspect of operations in, 191; effects of force in, 191; defensive rôle in, 194; leave arrangements from, 205; final attacks in, 206; armistice in, 207; distribution of army in, after armistice, 217; supply commitments in, after armistice, 218; withdrawal of troops from, 219
Baluchis, the 127th, their despatch to Burao, 21
Bangalore, depot at, 470
Bannu, 467
Baquba, 273, 274
Baring-Gould, Major E. S., 249
Barter, system of, at Damascus, 245
Barrack Department, the executive functions of, 14; its *personnel*, 14; the administration of work of, 15; unpopularity of duties of, 15
Barrett, Major B. H. H., viii
Base H.T. Depot, at Salonika, 184
Base M.T. Depot, at Bisley, 35; lay-out of, 40; locations of, 91; staff of, 104; size of and tasks of, 104–5; *personnel* branch, 106; tonnage of stores of, 107; addition of Portuguese section, 107; air raid on, 107; comparison of depots, 107; at Kalamaria, 202; Chinese in, in Mesopotamia, 288; at Nairobi, 304
Base Supply Depots, home, 66–7; in France, 91; in Salonika, 182; at Qantara, 227; at Basra, its remodelling, 264; at Arquata, 345; at Murmansk, 355
Basra, 252, 253; state of port of, 263; remodelling of depot at, 264; chaos at port of, 265
Beadon, Lieut.-Colonel (afterwards Colonel) R. H., xix, 151, 351
Bearne, Lieut.-Colonel L. C., 210
Beaulieu, Lord Montagu of, 464
Beersheba, water at, 233; capture of, 234
Belashitza mountains, 197
Bernard, Colonel Sir E., 244
Berrangé, Colonel, 499; composition of his force, 502; his difficulties, 503; his junction with van Deventer, 503
Birch, Sir Noël, Director of Remounts, 13
"Birdcage", in Balkans, 194, 199
Birkbeck, Major-General, Director of Remounts, 12
Blunt, Lieut.-Colonel G. C. G., 327
Botha, General, 292, 499
Boulogne, base bakery at, 89; safety of, 119
Bourcicault, Brig.-General, Director of Supplies, 65
Boyce, Brig.-General (afterwards Major-General Sir) W. G. B., 86
Boyd, Major C. T., 351
Brander, Lieut.-Colonel M. S., 424

INDEX

Bread, continuous provision of fresh, 52; field bakeries for fresh, 53; question of supply of, in war, 63
Breadmore, Captain R. G., 486
Bruce, Captain C. A., death of, 229
Buiko, 306
Bulgaria, intentions of, 179
Buller, Sir Redvers, and reorganisation of A.S.C., xviii, xli, 1
Bunbury, Colonel H. N., his promotion, 9
Burma, men from, in M.T., 279
Burne, Colonel R. O., 433
Burnett, Colonel, R.I. Rifles, A.Q.M.G. for A.S.C., 1
Burrard, Colonel H. G., viii; during Arab rising, 509
"Business men", 399

Cairo, base for operations to Siwa oasis, 226
Calais, base bakery at, 89; petrol depot at, 89; base M.T. depot at, 91; advanced base M.T. depot at, 91; driving schools at, 93
Camel, Somali, 22
Camel transport corps, xxxv; its formation, 177; replaces First Australian Divisional Train, 224; scepticism regarding, 224; organisation of, 228; effect of mud and rain on, 237, 249
Camels, vi, xxxiv; casualties among, 228
Cameroons, A.S.C. in, 487–496; description of, 487; railways in, 488; composition of expedition to, 488; first objective, 489; mechanical transport in, 492–496; cheapness of expedition to, 496
Campbell, Sir W., 242
Campiello, 236

Canteens, 400–402
Caporetto, Italians surprised at, 332
Carrier Transport, 295; prejudices against recruitment of, 319
Carter, Brig.-General (afterwards Major-General Sir) E. E., 86
Caterpillar, Hornsby-Ackroyd, 30
Cavan, General the Earl of, 335
Census Branch, organisation of, 92
Ceylon, a support for Mesopotamia, 177
Chakdara, 465
Chaman Kupri, 281
Cherat, 465
Chiuppano, railhead, 336
Clayton, Colonel (afterwards Lieut.-General Sir) F. T., viii; A.Q.M.G. for A.S.C., 1; his service, 2; his memorandum on staff employ, 8; his promotion to Major-General, 9; his character, 10; his suggestions for training, 49; his opposition to Haig when D.S.D., 52; Director of Supplies, 86; I.G.C., 86
Clerks section of A.S.C., their training and work, 16
Climo, Major-General S. H., 474
Cœurdercy, Captain, 210
Collard, Colonel A. W., at Reserve Supply Depot, 72
Commissariat and Transport Staff, abolition of, 3
Commissaries, xvii
Compiègne, railhead, 119
Connaught, H.R.H. Duke of, Colonel A.S.C., 1
Constantinople, A.H.Q. at, 217
Contractors, Indian (bunniah), rapacity of, 22
Contracts, elimination of contractors, 63; local, 65–6; cessation of peace, on mobilisation, 66

INDEX

Cooper, Captain H. J., viii, 486
Cowans, Sir J., 151, 379
Crawley, Lieut.-Colonel R. P., 130, 486
Crewe, Brig.-General, 316
Crowe, Brig.-General J. H. V., 327
Crompton, Colonel R. E. B., his fuel researches, 32
Ctesiphon, 252; retreat from, 253
Cumont, Lieut.-Colonel, 151

Dabaa, 223
Dakawa, 312
Damascus, occupation of, 245; system of barter at, 245
Danube, invasion project via, 208
Dardanelles, expedition to, xxx–xxxi, 156; formation of Levant Base, 176
Dar-es-Salaam, 293; surrender of, 315; restoration of railway at, 316
Davies, Brig.-General (afterwards Major-General) G. F., 247, 249
Davies, Captain J. E., 490, 515
Dawes, Colonel (afterwards Brig.-General) C. G., 151; his characteristics, 152–3
Dead Sea, motor boats on, 222
Dedeagatch, transport of 22nd Division to, 209
Dedeli Pass, 184–5
Deir El Belah, railway at, 232
Delest, Captain, 210
Dera Ismail Khan, 466
Desert Mounted Corps, 239, 241
Despatches, mention in, of Omnibus Park, 142
Diala, 278
Dickinson, Lieutenant R. P., 260
Dickson, Colonel E., 273
Director of Supplies and Transport, in Aldershot Command, 4; S. S. Long at War Office, 61; Major-General E. Gibb, 93

Directorate of Irrigation, 281
District Barrack Officer, the inception of, 15
Division, 5th Cavalry, xxxv, 241
7th, 335, 338
9th, 130
10th, 168, 183, 185, 197, 200, 234, 240
11th, 168
13th, 168, 254, 259, 281
22nd, 190, 197, 208
23rd, 335, 338
26th, 194, 197, 207
27th, 190, 206, 207
28th, 190, 197, 206
29th, xxx, 157, 158, 161, 165, 172
42nd, 162
48th, 335, 338
52nd, 162, 230
53rd, 169, 230
54th, 169, 230
60th, 200, 232
Anzac Mounted, 230
a French, at Gallipoli, 162
Royal Naval, 165
Greek, 207
3rd Indian, 239, 254, 259, 278
6th Indian, 252
7th Indian, 239, 240, 254, 259, 278
12th Indian, 252
14th Indian, 259, 277, 278
15th Indian, 259, 274, 276, 278, 280
17th Indian, 274
18th Indian, 278
1st East African, 299; locations of, 299, 302, 315
2nd East African, 299; locations of, 299, 303
Divisional train, inception of, 56; lack of mechanical vehicles for, 56; cavalry, abolition of, 60; history of 9th, 130–133
Dixon, Lieut.-Colonel G., 456
Dobbie, Sir J., 385

INDEX

Dobell, General Sir C., 490, 515
Dodoma, 305, 311
Dog transport, 378
Doiran, 184, 186–187; operations in region of, 200–201
Dominions, A.S.C. of, 74–77
Donkey transport, 231
Donohue, Major (afterwards Colonel) W. E., C.I.M.T., 27; his increased responsibilities due to the subsidy schemes, 38–39
Doran, Lieut.-Colonel P. C. M., 456
Douzies, supply rendezvous at, 119
Dujaila, action of, 256
Dunne, Colonel W., at Reserve Supply Depot, 71
Dunsterville, General, his mission, 278

East Africa, primitive difficulties in, 84; campaign in, 292 *et seq.*; extent of colony, 293; four railway lines in, 294; climate of, 294; lack of elasticity of forces in, 297; phases of operations in, 298; re-organisation of forces in, 316; *résumé* of A.S.C. activities in, 323; casualties in, 326
Edwards, Brig.-General, 315
Egerton, Gen., 278
Egypt (*see also* Palestine), campaigns in, 221
Egyptian Expeditionary Force, use of camels in, 22
Egyptian Labour Corps, work of, 223
El Arish, 222; water supply to, 227
Elliott, Colonel W., viii, xxxvi, 243, 247–248, 249
Emergency rations, loss of, at Gallipoli, 160
Emerson, his aphorism about London, 83

Enzeli, 279
Esher Committee, xx; its report, 6
Expeditionary Force, 1914, M.T. for, 37, 39; mechanical transport in, 56; A.S.C. activities in, 83; size in 1918, 85; A.S.C. in, 118; size in 1914, 124

Fao, landing at, 251
Fanatis, 227
Farrar, Sir G., his work and death, 505
Field bakeries, their proposed capacity, 53; divisional strength of, 61
Field butcheries, their proposed establishment, 53; divisional strength of, 61
Fifth Army, retreat of, 142; M.T. in retreat of, 142–143
Fitzwilliam, Colonel The Earl, gun-towing with Sheffield Simplex cars, 34
Foch, Marshal, allied armies under, 143; counter-offensive of, 143; his ability to advance after the armistice, 146
Forage, compressed, held at S.R.D., 62; at S.R.D., 72
Ford, Major-General (afterwards Sir) R., 151
Ford cars and ambulances, 170
Fortescue, the Hon. Sir J., viii
Fort Rupel, 197
Foster, Captain (afterwards Colonel) H. N., appointed Inspector of Subsidised Transport, 38, 412
France, manœuvres in, 34; bases in, 83; war in, 117
Franklin, Captain, 358
Fraser, Major C. L. B., taken prisoner, 368

INDEX

Fuel, petrol supply, 89; coal supply, 89

Gaba Tepe, 158
Gallipoli, primitive difficulties in, 84; operations on peninsula of, 156; French contingent, 158; in comparison of operations in, to Crimea, 173; evacuation of, 174–176; animals left at, 175; supplies left at, 175
Gaza, first battle of, 202; fall of, 236; advance after fall of, 236
Geddes, Mr (afterwards Sir) E., effect of his activities on M.T., 405; his numerous directors, 406
General Staff, foundations Esher Committee, 6; Clayton's suggestions to, 49; drafting of F.S.R., 50; Test-Staff Tour of C.G.S., 50; proposals for reorganisation of T. and S. services, 51
Genoa, congestion of, 329
German South-West Africa, enemy strength in, 293, 497 et seq.; description of colony, 497; difficulties of movement in, 498; strength of German forces in, 499; C.-in-C.'s intentions, 500; fall of capital, 500; ensuing pursuit, 500; a great march, 501; surrender of enemy, 501; strength of force in, 502
Gibb, Brig.- (afterwards Major-) General E., Director of Labour, 93; Director of Supplies and Transport, 93
Gilpin, Brig.-General F. C., 86
Givenchy, 122
Gleeson, Lieut.-Colonel A. G., 456
Gough, General Sir H., 239
Granezza, 336

Grapes, Major T., 456
Greece, doubtful neutral, 179; ban on supplies by Government of, 181; mobilisation of, 182; objects to move to Doïran, 183
Greeks, obstruction by, 188; prohibit sale of petrol, 189
Grogan, Brig.-General, 373
Groushkonsky, Private, award of D.C.M. to, 162

Hadfield, Colonel, his promotion, 9
Haifa, motor boats at, 222
Haig, Sir D. (afterwards Field-Marshal The Earl), his tribute to Haldane reforms, 16; Director of Staff Duties, 52; troops of, on eve of 1918 offensive, 145; his warnings concerning Indian Army, 252
Haldane, Mr (afterwards Viscount, O.M.), Secretary of State for War, 16; principles of his reforms, 16; his references to military M.T., 33; effect of his reforms, 80
Haldane, General Sir A., 508; his task in the Arab rising, 508 et seq.; strength of his force, 512, 515
Hamadan, 278, 283
Hamilton, Sir Ian, Military Secretary, 5; C.-in-C. at Gallipoli, 162, 168
Handeni, 305, 312
Hanna, battle of, 256; immobilisation of action at, 257
Harris, Sir C., 397
Hasanli, 184, 186
Havre, see Le Havre
Haywood, Lt.-Colonel A. H. W., 515
Hazelton, Brig.-General P. O., 299, 304, 327

INDEX

Heath, Colonel (afterwards Major-General Sir) C. E., his record, 9; appointment as Director of Remounts, 12, 383
Helles, 158, 160–161
Hindenberg line, smashing of, 145
Hippopotamus meat, 314
Hit, capture of, 279
Hobbs, Colonel (afterwards Major-General) P. E. F., 23
Holden, Brig.-General Sir C., 406, 413
Horse (horses) transport, *personnel* for Remount Department, 12; draught and pack animals, 46; disadvantages of, 49; reserve convoys, 54; reduction of, on mobilisation, 57; in 1913 manœuvres, 59; absence of, in certain trains, 60; short term of colour service, 79; main depots, 93; advanced depot, 113; advanced depot at Madras, 163; at Salonika, 184; trials of, in Palestine, its organisation, 231
Horse Transport Branch, organisation and administration of, 450–451
Hoskins, General, 298, 317, 319
Howell, Lieut.-Colonel G. L. H., 141
Hutchinson, Captain (afterwards Colonel) T. M., instructor in M.T., 31

Igalulu, 316
Imbros, 163
India, A.S.C. in, 457 *et seq.*; transport formations in, 460; local purchase of M.T. in India, 464
Indian Supply and Transport Corps, 252; lack of officers of, in Mesopotamia, 257

Indian troops, maintenance of, 121
Inland Water Transport, in Palestine, 233
Inland Water Transport Committee, in Egypt, 177
Inspectorate of M.T., inception of, 27; staff of, 28; progress with regard to, 31; Inspectorate of Subsidised Transport, 38
Inspector-General of A.S.C., the appointment at the War Office, 4
Inspector-General of Communications, in East Africa, 304
Intelligence branch, non-co-operation of, in Gallipoli, 158
Investigation department, scope of, 90; task of, 101–102
Iringa, 312; fall of, 316
Ismailia, 222
Italy, campaign in, 328 *et seq.*; mission to, 328; location of strategic army of reserve, 329; base in, 330; detraining British forces in, 334; mountain warfare experienced in, 335; supply system in, 336; progress of offensive in, 338 *et seq.*; transport arrangements up the River Tagliamento, 346; model supply depot in, 346 *et seq.*; comparison of campaign in, to Napoleonic Wars, 349

Jaffa, capture of, 237; supply depot at, 237
Jebel Hamrin, 277
Jericho, fall of, 237
Jerusalem, fall of, 236
Jews, Russian, in Zion Mule Corps, 161
Johns, Captain, 362

INDEX

Kabul, A.S.C. convoy to, 482
Kahe, 307
Kaimakchalan, capture of, 200
Kajiado, 299
Kampala, M.T. training depot at, 322
Kandalascha, 355
Karelians, 366, 376
Karm, railway extended to, 234
Kelly, Lieutenant F. J., A.S.C. in the Balkans, 220
Kem, supply depot at, 365
Kermanshah, 285
Khan Baghdadi, 280
Khaniquin, 273, 279, 282
Kibambawe, 317
Kigoma, 293
Kikombo, 311
Kilimatinde, 311
Kilossa, capture of, 312, 314
Kilwa Kissiwani, 316
Kilwa Kivinge, 316
King, Brig.-General C. W., Director of Supplies, 86; invalided, 120
Kirkuk, 281, 282; advance on, 287
Kissaki, plight of troops at, 314
Kitchener, F.M. Earl, xix, xxx, xlii; ignorance of transport, 157; conception of Gallipoli operations, 170; sent to Gallipoli, 174
Koe, Brig.-General, D. S. T. at Gallipoli, 164; I.G.C. in Balkans, 193
Kohat, 466
Kola inlet, 352
Kondoa-Irangi, 303; occupation of, 304, 305, 312
Korogwe, 314
Kosturino, 183
Krithia, first battle of, 160; Russian Jews in, 161; second battle of, 165
Krivolak, 183
Krugliakoff, Colonel, 362

Kut-el-Amara, 250, 253; fall of, 254; relief of, lack of supplies, 257

La Bassée, 122
Labour, A.S.C. responsible for, 93; Labour Corps, 93; Brig.-General Gibb director of labour, 93; scarcity of, in Mesopotamia, 263
Lahore, base at, 474
Lake, Sir P., 196, 253; supercession of, 259
Lake Beshik, 194, 197
Lake Doiran, 183, 197, 200
Lake Langaza, 194, 197
Lake Tahinos, motor boats on, 204; destruction of native craft on, 204
Lake Tanganyika, 294
Lake Victoria, 293
Lamotte Breuil, railhead, 119
Landon, Major-General (afterwards Sir) F. W. B., 383
Landrecies, 119
Land Transport Corps, xviii
Laplanders, 360
Law, Captain (afterwards Colonel) W. H. P., 61
Le Cateau, concentration at, 118
Le Havre, base bakery at, 89; repair shop at, 91; base H.T. depot at, 93; hangars at, 98; safety of, 119; evacuation of, 120
Leland, Colonel F. W., 268, 291
Lemnos, Zion Mule Corps in, 161
Levant Base, formation of, 176; its dispersal, 177
Lindi, 316
Lines of communication, functions of, 58; modification of, 58; A.S.C. work on, 83; railway, in August 1914, 120; supply company, 128; in Mesopotamia, 270; their

INDEX

extent in East Africa, 313; longest in East Africa, 323
Llama, xxxix
Lloyd, Captain F. L., R.E., in South Africa, 24; secretary to Mechanical Transport Committee, 25; vacation of secretaryship of M.T. Committee, 32, 414, 435
Local Produce Directorate, in Mesopotamia, 273; its activities, 287
Local resources, 177; operations of board of, in Egypt, 243; operations of board of, in Mesopotamia and environs, 266; scantiness of, in East Africa, 296
Lol Kissale, 305
London General Omnibus Company, and 1908 exercises, 33; their repair scheme, 40
Long, Brig.-General A., xxxii; in Balkans, 194; in despatches, 209
Long, Colonel (afterwards Major-General) A. S., viii, xxi, xxvi, xxx; in charge of Supply Reserve Depot, 61; Director of Supplies and Transport, 61; Director of Supplies, 65; personal explanations of, to certain officers, 68; perturbed at lack of transport for Gallipoli, 157; his character, 383; his achievements, 383–406; his resignation, 407
Longido, 299, 301; reserve supplies at, 305
Loos, offensive, 123
Lorries, early types of, 26; availability on mobilisation, 55; infantry moves by, 135
Ludd, Base depot at, 231
Luhembero, 317
Lukegeta, 317
Lukigura, 312
Lumbuhzi, 363
Lumi River, 302

MacFadden, Dr, 385
Mackenzie, General, 499; his Central Force, 504
MacMunn, General, I.G.C. in Mesopotamia, 259; his energy, 264
McNalty, Bt.-Major (afterwards Brig.-General) C. E. I., in command of No. 77 Coy A.S.C., 28
Mahemidiya, railway to, 227
Mahenge, 317
Mahon, General Sir B., 196
Makanja, 307
Makindu, advance to, 308, 311
Maktau, 295, 302
Malakand, 465
Malaria, havoc by, xxxix; ravages of, in Balkans, 205; in Mesopotamia, 251; in East Africa, 314
Maltese cart, for medical stores, 46
Man power, anxiety for, 125
Mansfield-Clarke, Sir Charles, Q.M.G., 2, 4
Maps, traffic, 141
Marshall, General, 259, 278
Maselskaya, 362
Massalas, Colonel, 197
Masters, Private G., award of V.C. to, 144
Matruh, objective of, 223; poor water at, 224; base for Siwa operations, 226
Maud, Colonel, and supply of hay in France, 394
Maude, General Sir Stanley, 259; his characteristics, 261; advance of, 270; death of, 277
Maxwell, General, xxx, 158

INDEX

Maynard, Brig.-General Sir C. C. M., 355, 378
Mbuyuni, 298, 299, 301, 302
Meat, provision of, 52–53; special vehicles for, 53; field butcheries for fresh, 53; Base Meat Depot, 63
Mechanical Transport, vi, xxi; in Franco-Prussian War, 24; first use of, in war, 24; instruction in, at Chatham, 24; branch of A.S.C., 26; first company of, 28; strength of, in Great War, 29; recruitment of *personnel* in 1905, 29; rapid increase of, 30; the assurance of future of, 32; success in 1914, 33; responsibility for peace time repair of, 35; control of, 41; comparison with French system, 42; with German system, 43; with Austro-Hungarian system, 44; with Italian system, 45; Paul's proposals regarding, 52–54; appearance in W.E.'s, 56; limitations of, 54; in Expeditionary Force, 56; certain mistrust of, 56–57; cadres of, for Expeditionary Force, 59; administration and operations of, 102 *et seq.*; in third battle of Ypres, 157; pooling of, 138; general reserve of, 139; organisation of French, 139; operation of mass movement of, 140; in Fifth Army retreat, 142–143; strain on, on 11 November 1918, 146; in M.E.F., 164; in Balkans, 192; lent to Serbian Government, 192; sickness in Balkans in, 199; with Serbian Army, 210–215; disposal of, in Balkans, 219; difficulties of, in Palestine, 239; vehicle census of, in Palestine, 240; advent of, in Mesopotamia 261; expansion of, in Mesopotamia, 268; justification of, in Mesopotamia, 272; increase of, in Mesopotamia, 275; Burmese company of, 279; difficulties of, in Mesopotamia, 281; strength of, in Mesopotamia, 287; *personnel* of, in Mesopotamia, 288; unsuitability of, provided for East Africa, 300–301; reinforcements for, in East Africa, 313; *personnel* in, in East Africa, 313; immobilisation due to sickness, 321; *résumé* of, 323 *et seq.*; route of, of British army in Italy, 333, 340; in a pursuit, 341; mountain road driving school for, 342; work of, on Italian front, 343; heterogeneity of, in Italy, 344; uselessness of, in Russia, 373; organisation and administration of, in England, 412–439; expenditure on, 439; absence of, on S. and T. Corps, 461; in India, 464; in Waziristan, 466 *et seq.*; in Marri force, 468; reorganisation of, in India, 479; in Cameroons, 490; improvisation of, in South Africa, 506; unsatisfactoriness of, in Arab rising, 510
Mechanical Transport Committee, 1900, composition of, and activities of, 25, 26; expenditure on experiment, 82; liaison with motor world, 33; strength of, 126
Mediterranean Expeditionary Force, strength of, 164; General Monro in command of, 172

INDEX

Medvyejya Gora, 362, 363
Merrone, General, 151
Mesopotamia, xxxvii, 250; primitive difficulties in, 84; geographical features of, 250; climatic conditions in, 250, 270; size of expedition to, 251; administrative chaos in, 252, 254; wastage by sickness in, 261; distribution of forces in, 262
Mgeta River, 314, 316
Mikidani, 316
Mikocheni, 307
Mikra Bay, concentration of Serbian Army at, 198
Miles, Sir Herbert, Q.M.G., his opposition to Haig when D.S.D., 52, 384
Military train, xviii
Millet, a diet, 314
Milne, General (afterwards F.M.) Sir G., xxxiii, 196
Milner, Lord, and Allied Supply Board, 149; his ability, 154
Mitchell, Captain G. O., 194
Mkalamo, 307
Mkindu, 317
Mobilisation, arrangements for foodstuffs on, 65
Mobility, A.S.C. contribution to, 58
Modena, General, 348
Mombasa, Port of, 300
Mombo, capture of, 307
Monastir, Serbian Army at, 200
Monro, General Sir C. C., 173, 190
Mons, 119
Montello, 334
Moore, Lieut.-Colonel T. C. R., 356, 378
Morgan, Colonel G., 394
Morogoro, 311; Smuts at, 313
Morris, Keith, 515
Morto Bay, 160

Moses, 342
Moshi, 294, 302
Motor boats, 204, 222
Mount Kilimanjaro, 294, 302
Mudros, 158, 163
Mule cart train, Indian, at Gallipoli, 164
Mules, in Russia, 373; in South-West Africa, 506
Muleteers, enlistment of Greek, 196, enlistment of Cypriot, 198
Murmansk, 352; size of force despatched to, 353; base supply depot at, 355, 365
Murray, General Sir A., 226; misapprehension of, regarding supply, 232; supersession of, 233
Murree, 465
Mwanza, 312

Nairobi, 294
Napoleon, a dangerous model, xlvii
Nasiriyeh, 253, 259
Naval Division, Royal, 158
Naval Mission, British, conveyance of, 193
Nehamas barn episode, 188
Neuve Chapelle, 123
Ngerengere River, 317
Nguru mountains, 311
Nixon, General Sir J., 253; relief of, 253
North Russia, operations in, 352 et seq.; object of, 354; routes of columns in, 364–365; failure of flanking force, 368; situation at end of summer in, 369; allied forces in, 370; withdrawal of forces from, 375; climatic conditions in, 376
Northey, General, 312, 317
Nowshera, 465
Nutka, 358

528

INDEX

Octroi, 121
Offensive, German, 1918, 143
Official History, trench stores, 123; A.S.C. work, 124
Officers, A.S.C., their share in the higher commands, 6; their habits of economy, 6; their source, 10; their responsibilities, 11; their dislike of barrack duties, 15; courses in M.T., 31; duties as inspectors of supplies, 50; shortage of, 68; first to land in France, 68; "bugbear" of, 101; on directorate staffs, 103; reduction of requisitioning, 127
Ofield, Serjeant J., 273
O'Hara, Major (afterwards Colonel) E. R., 161
Onega, 358; covering force at, 369
Ordnance Department, xix
Orr, Colonel G. M., 327
Ostretchye, 364
Otavi line, railway progress on, 500
Outreau, Advanced depot at, 94
Ovens, various types of, 88; use of, in Salonika, 182
Owen, H. C., 220
Ox transport, disadvantages of, in East Africa, 296; losses in, 313; "life" of an ox, 315

Pack transport, vi; necessity for, in Gallipoli, 158; in Balkans, 195
Paget, Lady, 192; rescue of her hospital, 192
Paget, Lieut.-General Sir A., 33
Palestine (*see also* Egypt), augmentation of forces by foreign contingents, 238; administrative problems in, 242
Pangani River, 303; advance down, 306

Paris, repair shop at, 91
Parker, Colonel W. M., viii, 260, 291
Pare Hills, 302
Patterson, Lieut.-Colonel J. H., 161
Paul, Colonel (afterwards Brig.-General) G. R. C., xxi; A.D.T. at War Office, 34; at the French manœuvres, 34; his memorandum on M.T., 34; his study of continental methods, 51; his opposition to Haig, 52; his memorandum on Supply System, 52–53; his death, 79
Pay, A.S.C., higher rate of, 10
Payot, Colonel C., 151
Pelley, Captain E., 273
Percival, Captain (afterwards Sir, K.C.M.G.) H. F. P., viii; at Test Staff Tour, 51; his attainments, 78
Pershing, General, and allied supply board, 149
Persia, operations in, 282–286
Peshawar, 465, 467
Petrol, the control committee, 440; provision and distribution of, 440–446
Peyton, Lieut.-Colonel J. H. B., 486
Piave, 338, 340, 341
Pigott, Major G. E., D.S.T. in Somaliland, 18; his organisation of camel transport, 22
Plumer, Lieut.-General Sir H. (afterwards Field-Marshal Viscount), and gun towing by M.T., 35, 334
Poole, General, 353
Port Said, cold storage plant at, 177; economy of plant, 177
Portuguese, on River Rovuma, 316

INDEX

Povynets, 363
Prescott, an aphorism, 380
Provost, xvii
Pugu, 314
Pursuit, battle of Vittorio Veneto an example of, 341

Qantara, 222; filtering plant at, 227; base supply depot at, 227; water installation at, 227; doubling of railway at, 234, 238; fish curing at, 244
Qasr-i-Shirin, 273
Qatiya, loss at, 229
Qizil Robat, 273
Queen Mary's Army Auxiliary Corps, employment of, 89
Qurna, 252, 274

Rafa, water supply junction at, 227; railway at, 230; reorganisation of yeomanry at, 231
Railhead, 59
supply, 100; at the battle of Ypres, 123
Railways, immobilisation of light, 139; heavy demands on, 144; destruction of, in Balkans, 208; repairs to, in Balkans, 214; across Sinai desert, 227; progress of, in Mesopotamia, 268; in East Africa, 294; Voi-Maktau, 302; in Italian theatre, 329
Directorate of, 177
Rain, interference by, at Gallipoli, 172; effect of, on Palestine theatre, 236, 237; fall of, in East Africa, 294; incessant, in East Africa, 304–305; immobilises M.T. in East Africa, 318
Ramadi, 274; attack at, 275
Raper, Colonel, 2

Ration, active service, scale of, 69; complaints concerning, 69; institution of two rations, 95; higher scale, 95; forage, 96; Fijian, 96; prisoner of war, 96; allied rations, 96; reduction of, in Mesopotamia, 257
peace, scale of, 72
Rawal Pindi, 464, 466
Rawson, Captain, in Russia, 367
Rearward services, co-ordination of, 149
Reeves, Colonel, original A.Q.M.G. for A.S.C., 1
Refet Pasha, General, 249
Refilling points, inception of, 54
Regulating station, position in Supply System, 53
Reid, Colonel H. G., viii
Reindeer transport, xxxix
Reindeer, transport by, 360; "mastership" of, 377
Remount Department, its success in the Great War, 12; suppression of military *personnel*, 13; claim of A.S.C. to, 13, 453
Remount Service, its history, 11
"Rendezvous", 59; definition of, 81
Repair shops, heavy, location of, 91; their systems and output, 91; in Italy, 344
Requisitioning, reduction of officers for, 127
Reserve parks, reason for, and inception of, 57; reduction of, 127
Reserve Supply Depot, Major-General in charge of, 4; Colonel Long in charge of, 61; inadequacy of arrangements of, 62; organisation of, 69; genesis and *personnel* of, 69–70; in 1835, 70; in South

INDEX

African War, 71; size of, 72; later site of, 73; "Admiralty" system at, 72; numbers of, fed by Qantara in Egypt, 234
Resht, 285
Rhodesia, Northern, 312
Riley, Mr, of Contract Branch, 387
Road Transport, organisation into three echelons, 46; test of British system 1899–1902, 47; unsuitability of British system for war, 48; transformation of, 49; elasticity of, 138
Roberts, Lieut.-Colonel A. H., 351
Roberts, Field-Marshal Lord, V.C., Commander-in-Chief, xlii, 5; inspection of Motor Volunteers 1903, 27
Robertson, General (afterwards Field-Marshal) Sir W. R., 259, 328
Robrovo, 184
Romani, railway to, 227; battle at, 229
Ropeways, in Italy, 336; in Khyber pass, 480–482
Rouen, bakery at, 89; petrol depot at, 89; repair shops at, 91, 111; driving schools at, 93
Rowe, Lieut.-Colonel C., 330, 351
Royal Edward, loss of, 172
Rufiji Delta and River, 316, 317
Ruwu River, 306

Sadani, 311
St Julien, 122
St Nazaire, base at, 120
St Omer, school at, 106; repair shop at, 111; G.H.Q. at, 122
Salisbury, 323
Salvage, 90
Sandilands, Lieut.-Colonel H. R., 351

Selwood, Major, 280
Salonika, strength of forces from Gallipoli, 179; "Q" arrangements at, 180; maintenance of troops at, 184; base activities at, 187; destruction of, by fire, 202
Samarra, 250
Sarrail, General, 183, 196
School of Instruction, 93
Scott, Colonel P. C. J., 193, 260
Sea of Galilee, motor boats on, 222
Searchlights, mobile, in South Africa, 27
Sedd el Bahr, 158, 166
Serbia, allies' hopes regarding, 179; move of allied troops into, 183; concentration of army of, at Mikra Bay, 198; advance of army to Belgrade, 215
Serengeti, 298, 302
Seres road, remaking of, 201
Shabkadar, 467
Shatt-al-Hai, 271
Shargat, surrender of Turks at, 287
Sheikh Saad, 260; reserve supplies at, 265, 274
Shirati, 293
Shunga Peninsula, 364
Simpson, Lieutenant E. A., 327
Simpson, Captain H., in 9th Divisional Train, 133
Sinai, occupation of, 229
Sinai Desert, 226
Sisman, Major, 198
Siwa oasis, capture of, 226
Skeen, General, 474
Skobeltsin, General, 365
Slaughter, Captain R. J., 486
Sleighs, vi; system of use of, 372–373
Smith-Dorrien, General Sir H., 299

INDEX

Smuts, General, 196, 292, 302; his bold action, 303; his appreciation, 311; hands over to General Hoskyns, 318
Snepp, Major, 275
Sollum, 223; establishment of bakery at, 225; raid from, 225
Somaliland campaign 1909, troops engaged in, 18; description of, 18-22
Sorel, Lieut.-Colonel W. L., 212-213
Soroka, 358
South African Army Service Corps, 292, 326, 502
Squarey, Captain, 360
Staff College, A.S.C. officers and, 7; A.S.C. quota being produced, 79
Status of A.S.C., advantage of, 80
Steam lorries, in India, 462; their limitations, 462
Stewart, Serjeant D. R., 273
Stewart, Major-General J., 299
Strategy, absence of, on Western front, 116
Striedinger, Lieut.-Colonel (afterwards Colonel) O., viii, xxxi, 180; his task at Salonika, 180; his purchase of local supplies at Salonika, 181
Stringer, Lieut.-Colonel F.W., 408
Struma River, 197; valley of, 198
Strumitza, 184; German-Bulgarian concentration in valley of, 185
Subsidisation of vehicles, "earmarking", 31; two schemes for 1911, 37; Inspector of Subsidised Transport, 38; Paul's scheme for, 53
Sudi Bay, 316
Suez Canal, operations for defence of, 221
Sugar, General Long and supply of, 387
Sukerieh, 236
Supplies, Director of, 6; instructions for, of Expeditionary force, 64; Brig.-General Long, 65; and ration scale, 68; Brig.-General King, 86; Major-General Clayton, 86; Brig.-General Carter, 86
Supply board, allied, 149-153
Supply branch, organisation and administration of, 447
Supply columns, inception of, 54; cadres of, 59; reduction of, 127; 29th divisional, 184-185
Supply Directorate, support of D.M.O., 65; watches its schemes operate, 68; transfer of control of S.R.D. to, 73; complications of, 87; base depots of, 87; investigation department, 90; task of, 94, 100; anxieties of, 166; the problem in Egypt, 230; difficulties of, in Mesopotamia, 266-267
Supply Parks, 54
Supply *personnel*, replacement of fit, 127
Supply Reserve Depot, *see* Reserve Supply Depot
Supply system, its uselessness, 52; "demands" on, 54; margin of safety in, 57; basic desideratum, 57; advantages of reorganisation of, 57; transport in, 81; reorganisation of, at Gallipoli, 159, 164, 166; situation of, in Egypt, Oct. 1915, 181; in Balkans, after armistice, 218; in Mesopotamia, 262; in East Africa, 292 *et seq.*; in Italy, 336-337; in Archangel theatre, 370-371; in South-West Africa, 570

INDEX

Supply and Transport Services, reorganisation of, advantages of, 54; test of their systems, 59
Surrey yeomanry, and motor boats on Struma, 204
Suvla, operations at, 168–171
Svyat Navalok, 364
Swabey, Brig.-General W. S., xxix, 332, 333, 351
Swann, Lieutenant, in motor boat section in Balkans, 205

Tabora, threat to, 309; movement on, 312; Belgians at, 316
Tactics, modifications of, 116; superiority of German, 135; of transport, 136
Tanga, 311
Tank, 466
Tank ships, water, 167
Tarver, Major (afterwards Major-General) W. K., 61
Taveta Gap, 310
Taylor, Lieut.-Colonel F. G., viii
Territorial Force, organisation of, 16; composition of, 18
Terry, Captain C. E., first soldier to land in France, 68
Thomas, Lieutenant H., 192
Tighe, General, 298, 299; his plan for the offensive, 301
Townshend, General Sir C. V., 250
Tractors, in Egypt, 235; in Mesopotamia, 271; in East Africa, 316; Italian, 343; "caterpillar" section, 437–438; in India, 462; their difficulties at Quetta, 463
Training Establishment, A.S.C., Colonel Long commandant of, 61, 78
Transport, reduction of scale of, 126; extension of success lay in, 135; tactics of, 136; second line, 136; tactical use of, in Mesopotamia, 137; pooling of, 138; lack of, in Mesopotamia, 256; disgrace of, for medical services, 258
Transport, Director of, Brig.-General Gilpin, 86; Brig.-General Boyce, 86, 102; his staff officers, 102–103; and transport for Gallipoli, 157
Transport Directorate, scales of baggage made by, 50; officers of, 102–103
Transport and Remounts, Director of, 6
Transport and Supply Park, organisation of, 56
Tripoli, motor boats at, 222
Tsetse fly, havoc by, xxxix
Tudor, Lieut.-Colonel C. L. St J., 213
Turks, surprise of, 168
"Turn-outs", 113
Turtle, story of, 154
Tuz, 281

Ufiome, advanced supply depot at, 306
Uleia, 314
Urozosero, 364

Van Deventer, 298, 301; occupies Aruscha, 303, 317; succeeds Hoskyns, 319, 499
Vardar River, 197
Vehicles, internal combustion, mobile searchlight, 26; at Malta 1903, 28; in 1904, use of paraffin in, 32; gun-towing 1914, 34; types of workshop vehicles, 37; 1400 for Expeditionary Force 1914, 37; special, for meat conveyance, 53; steam, 58; analysis of, 90
Veles, 183

533

INDEX

Venizelos, M., efforts of, 179; organisation of National Army by, 206
Verdun, defence of, 125
Versailles, Supreme War Council, 154
Villaverla, 336
Vittorio Veneto, battle of, 341; A.S.C. activities in, 341
Vlasto, Lieutenant J. T., 260
Voi, 294
Volo, 181
Vologda, 354
Vorbeck, General Von L., 292; driven from British territory, 303; skill and resolution of, 317

Wadsworth, Corporal A. R., award of D.C.M., 137
Wagon Master, xvii
Wagon Train, Royal, xviii
Waldback, Captain, 488
Ward, Sir Edward W. D., Permanent Under-Secretary of State for War, 5; an A.S.C. officer, 5
Warfare, trench, in Balkans, 200
Warren, Sir Charles, and Bechuanaland Expedition, 1
Warren, Lieut.-Colonel T. R. P., 423
Water supply, on Gallipoli, 159, 167; across Sinai desert, 227; at Wadi Ghazze, 232; at Beersheba, importance of, 233; lack of, at Dujaila, 257; indifferent, on Euphrates, 277; in German South-West Africa, 503
Watson, Major H. N. G., 367, 376, 378
de Watteville, Lieut.-Colonel H., 486
Wavell, Colonel A. S., 249
Waziristan, operations in, 466; description of, 473-478; railway system in, 474-475
Wellesley, Sir A. (afterwards Duke of Wellington), xvii
Western desert operations, 222
Wheater, Major, 337
Whittaker, Lieutenant F. H. E., 378
Whittall, Lieut.-Commander, W., 327
Whittingham, Colonel C. W., and Camel Transport Corps, 229
Wiette, wounded from, 122
Wilson, Major-General F. M., 479
Winter, Colonel S. H., at Reserve Supply Depot, 71
Wintle, Captain C. E. H., 486
Women's Legion, 424
Wytschaete, 122

Ypres, fighting round, 121; battle of, 122; medical activity at, 122

Zion Mule Corps, 161, 164, 166
Zomba, base of Nyasaland force, 322

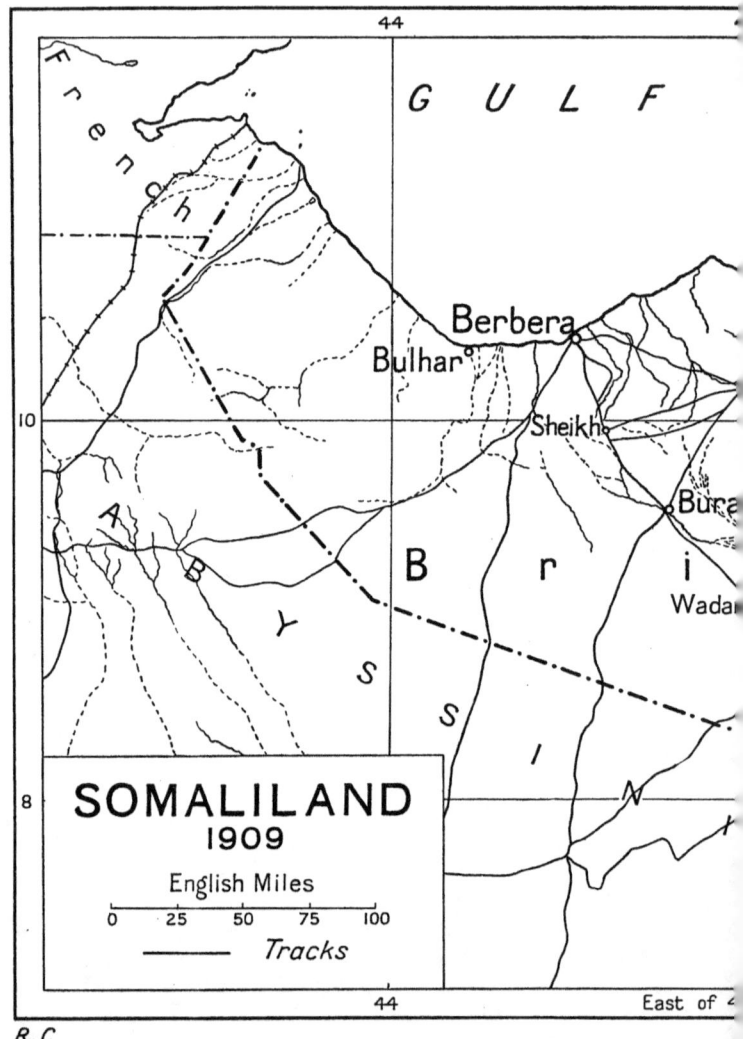

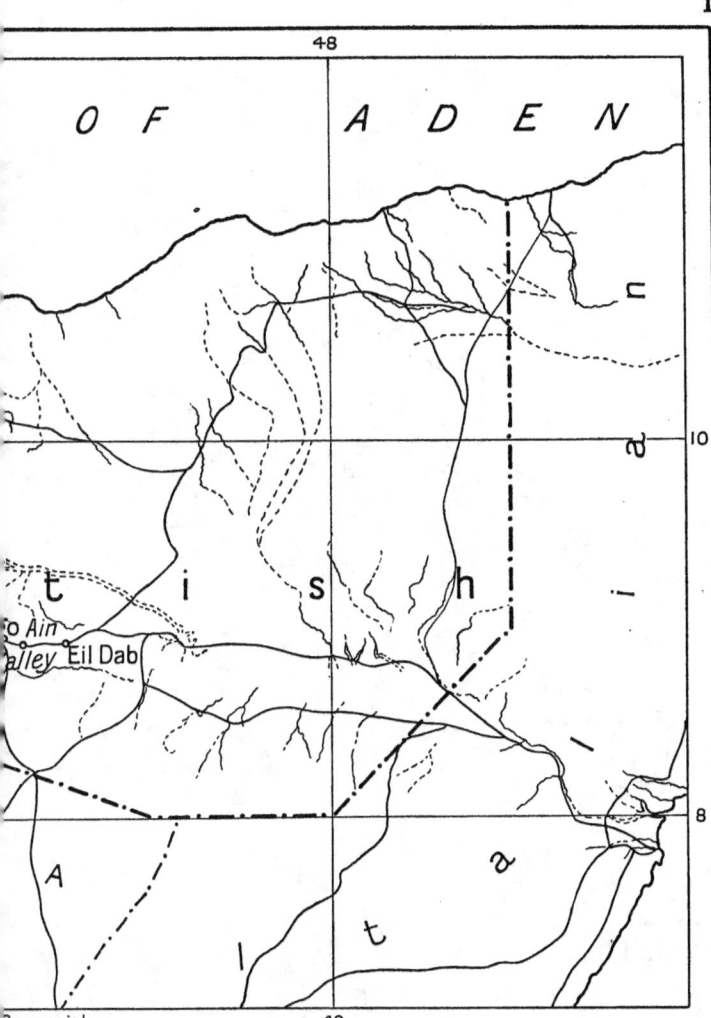

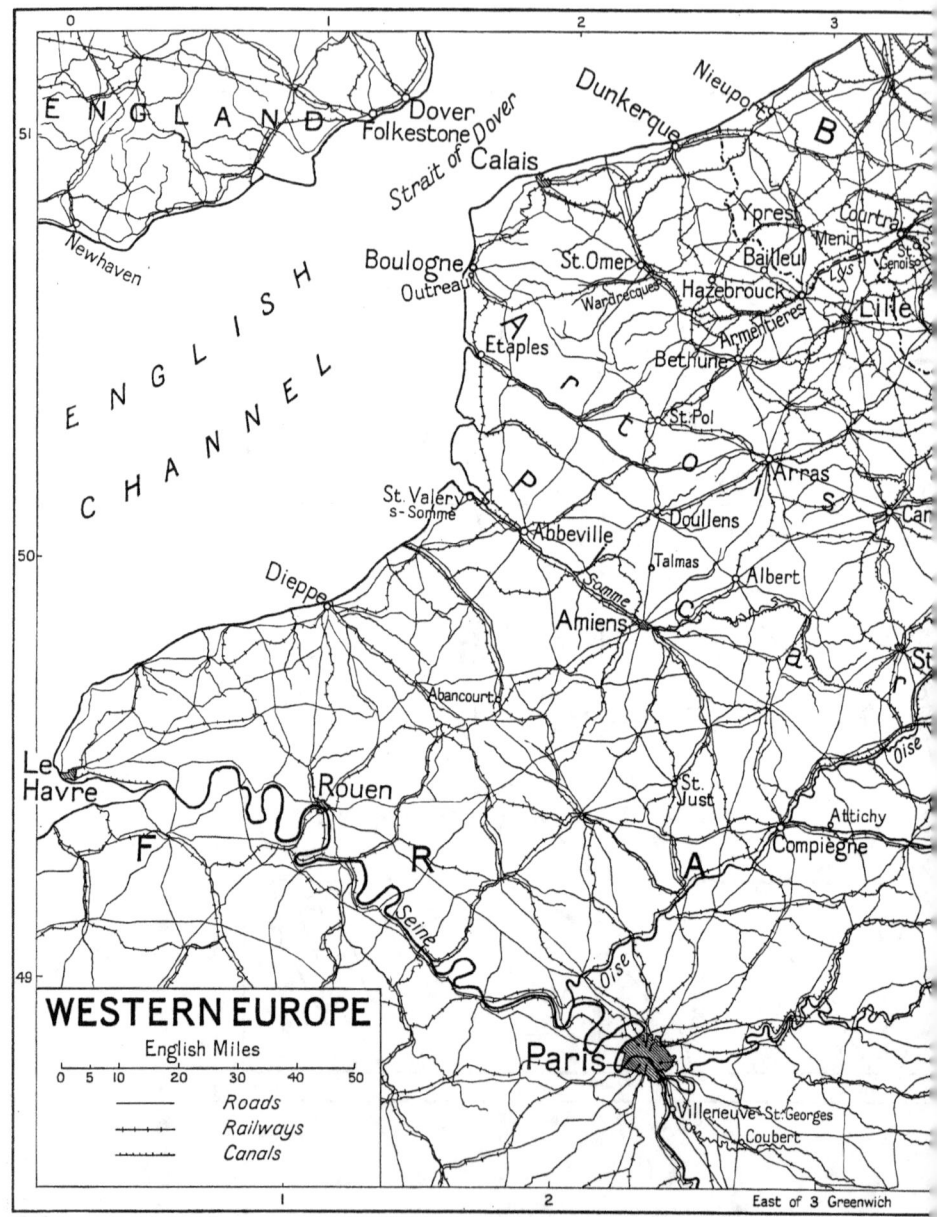

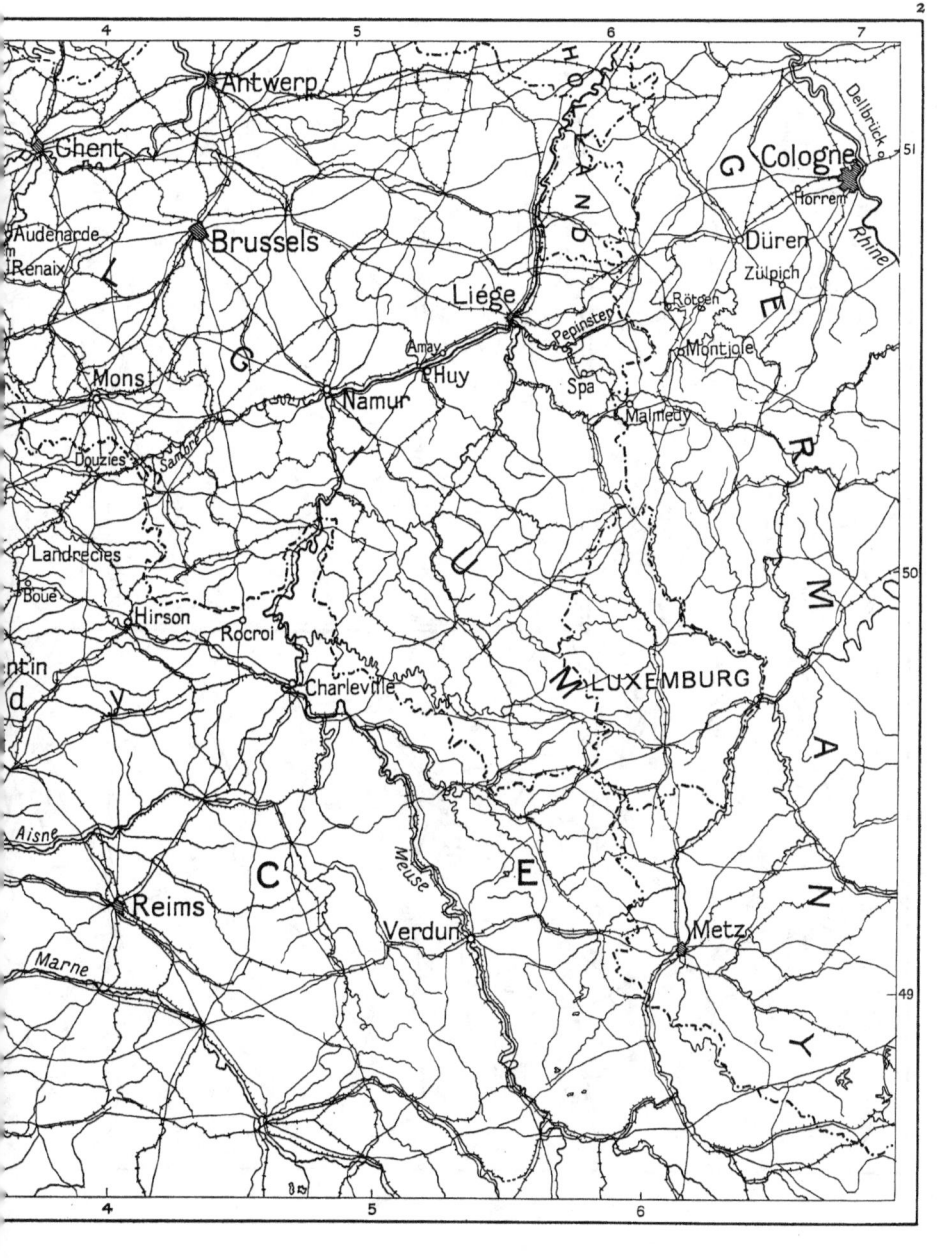

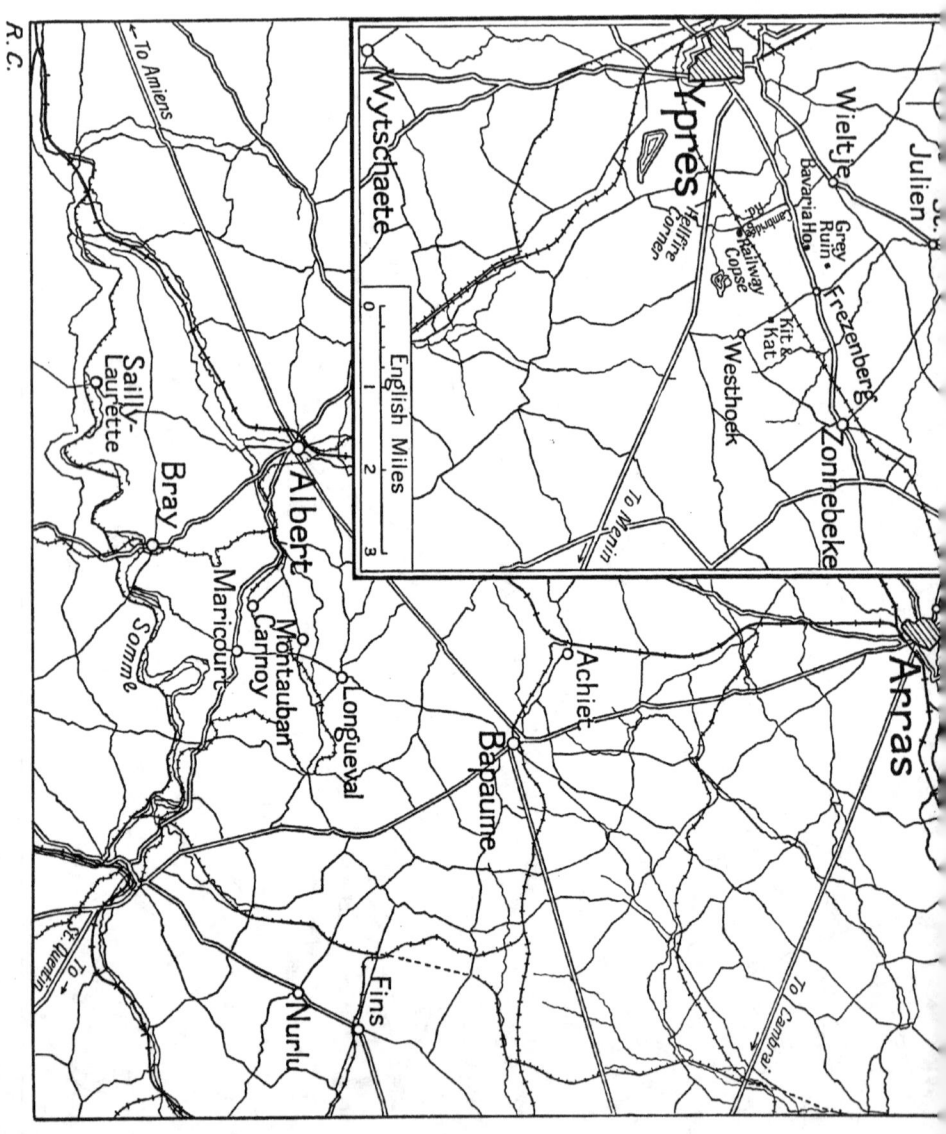

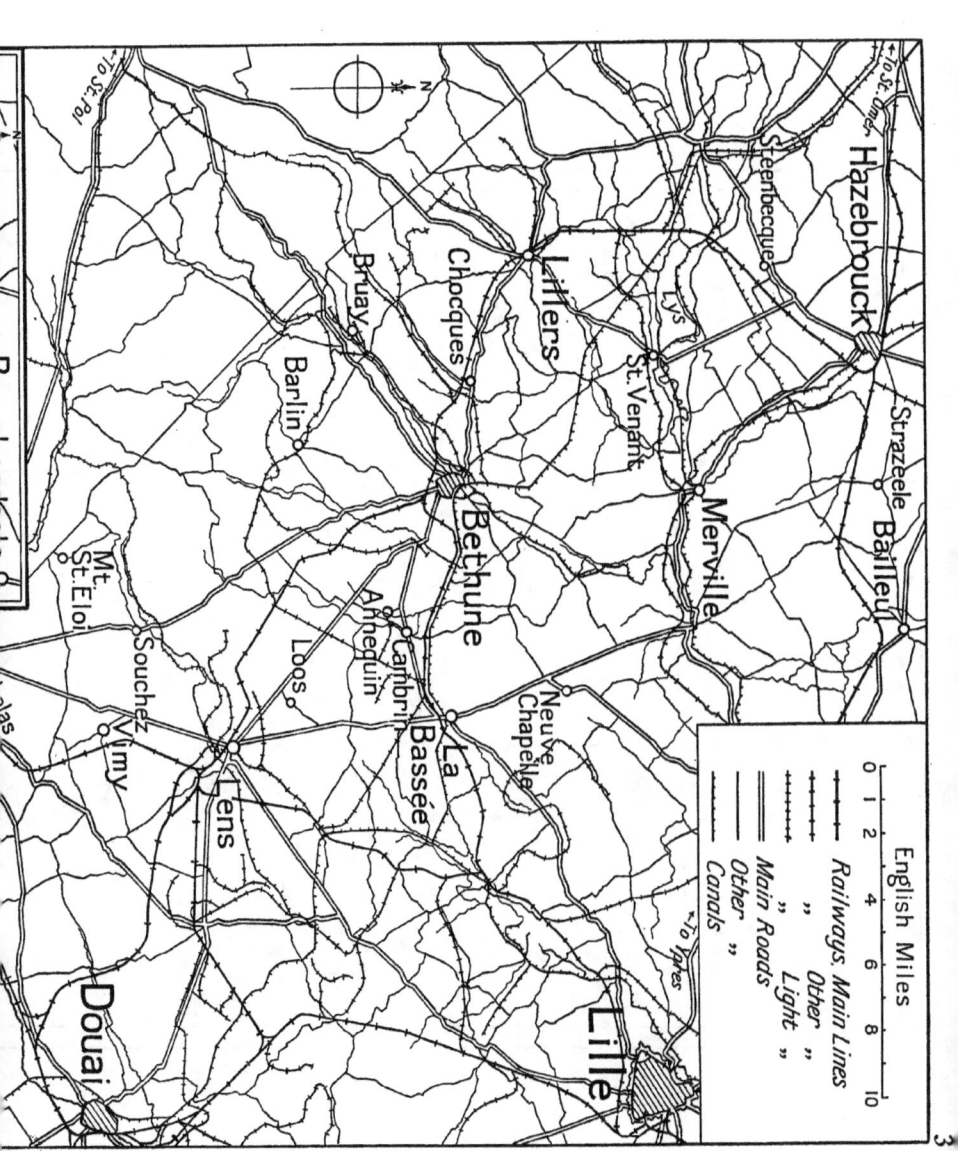

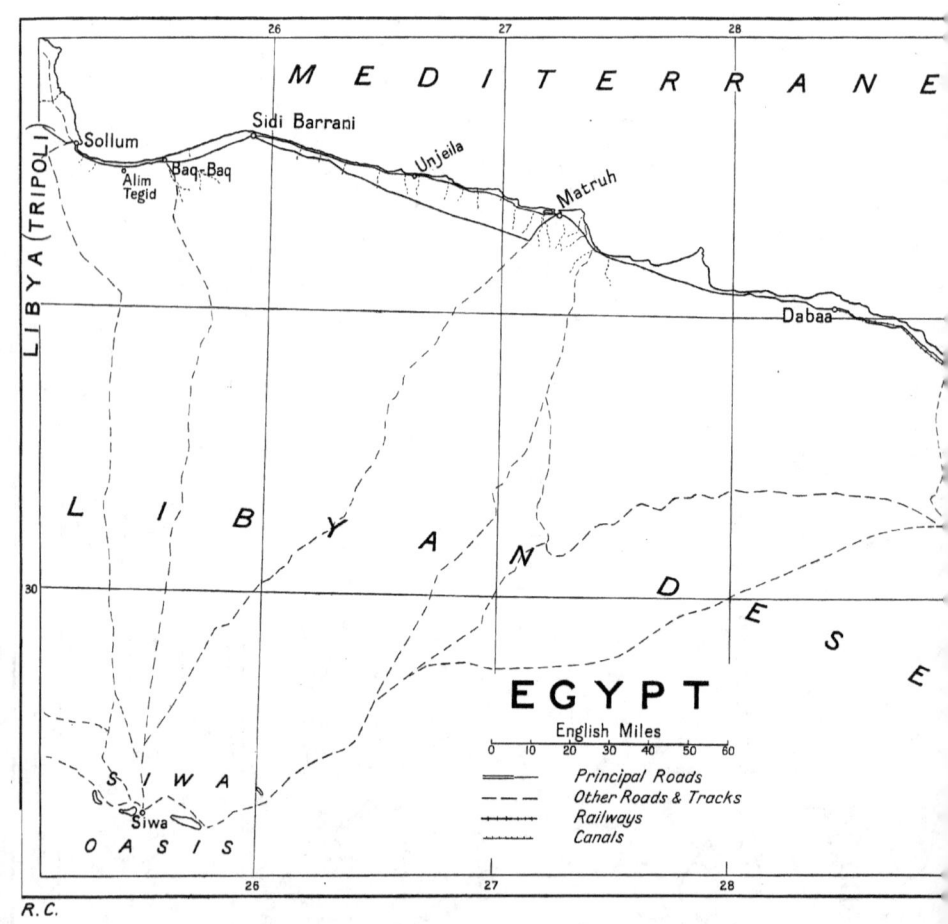

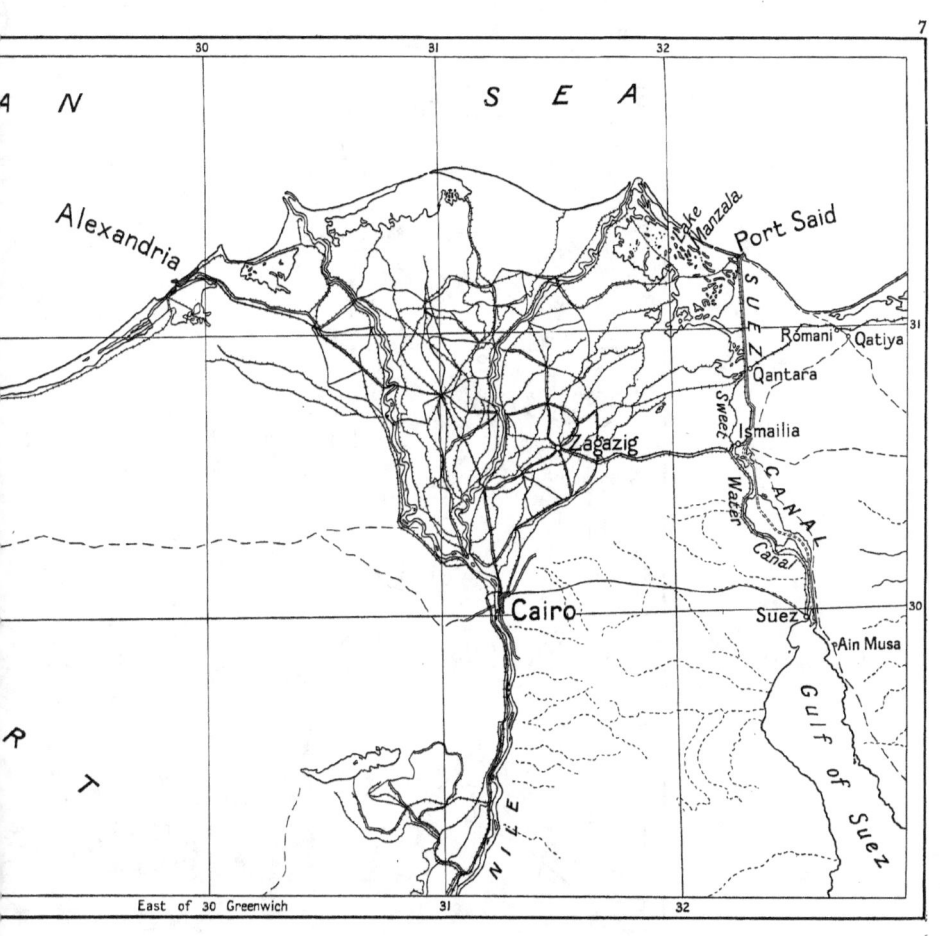

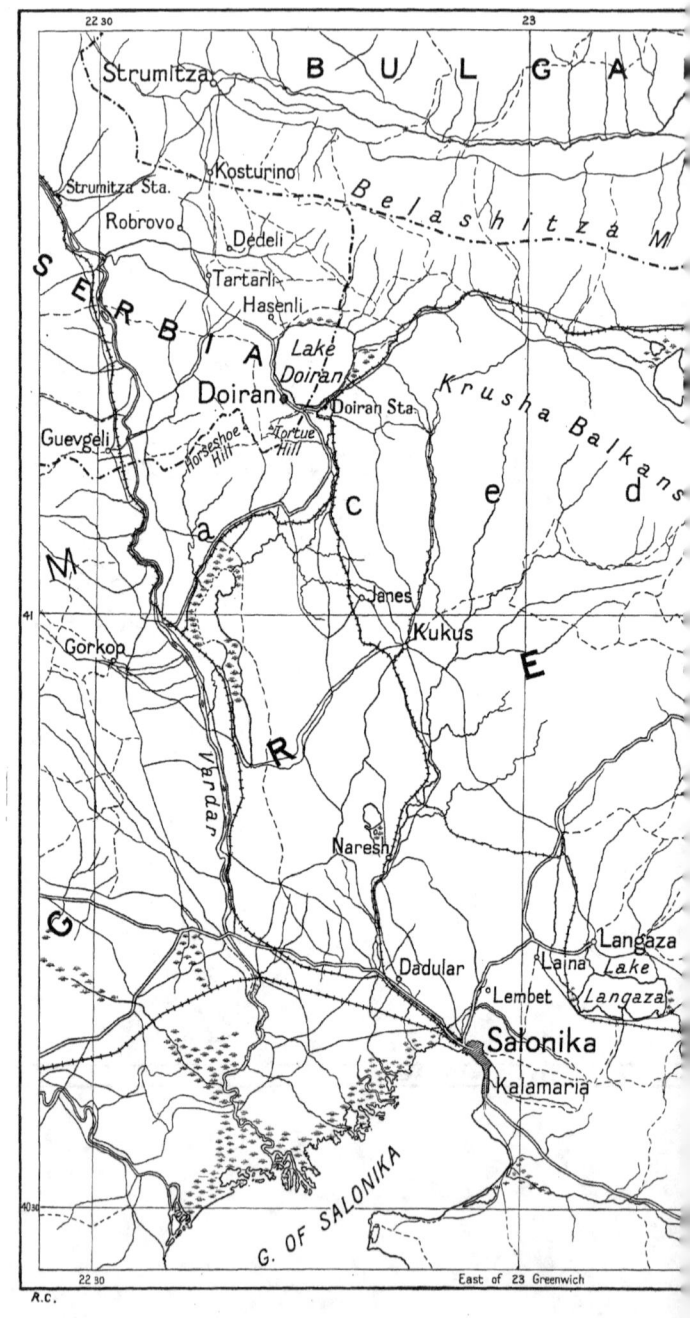

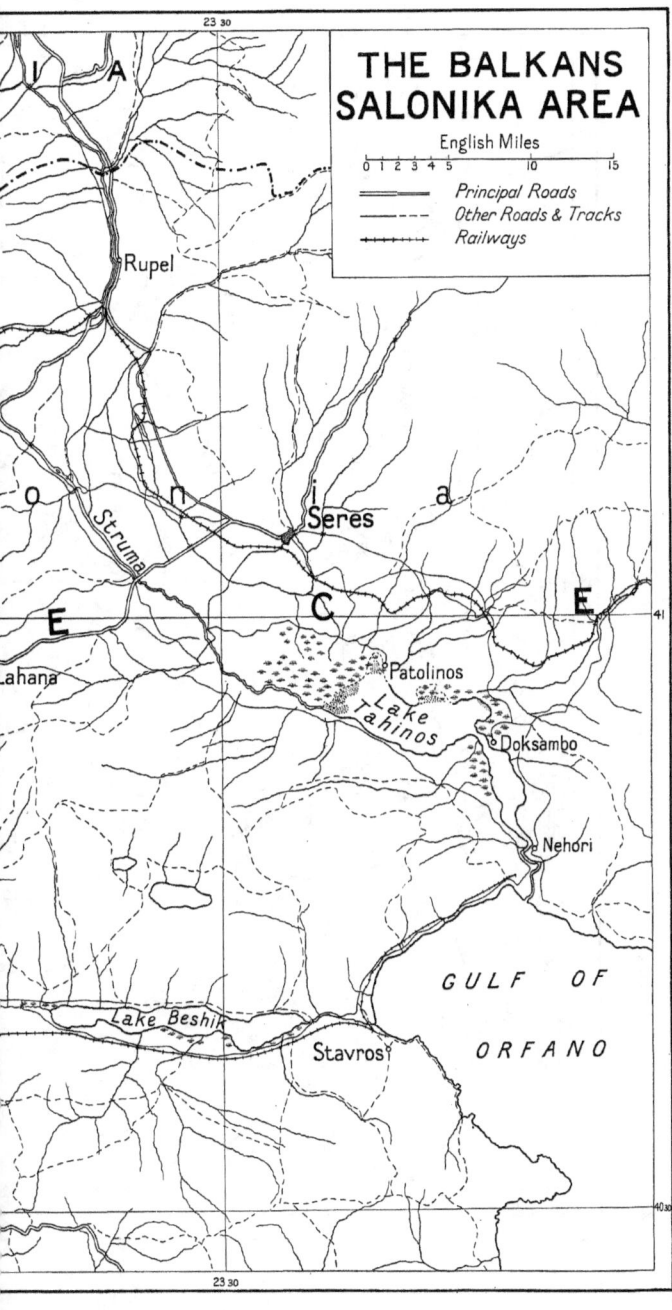

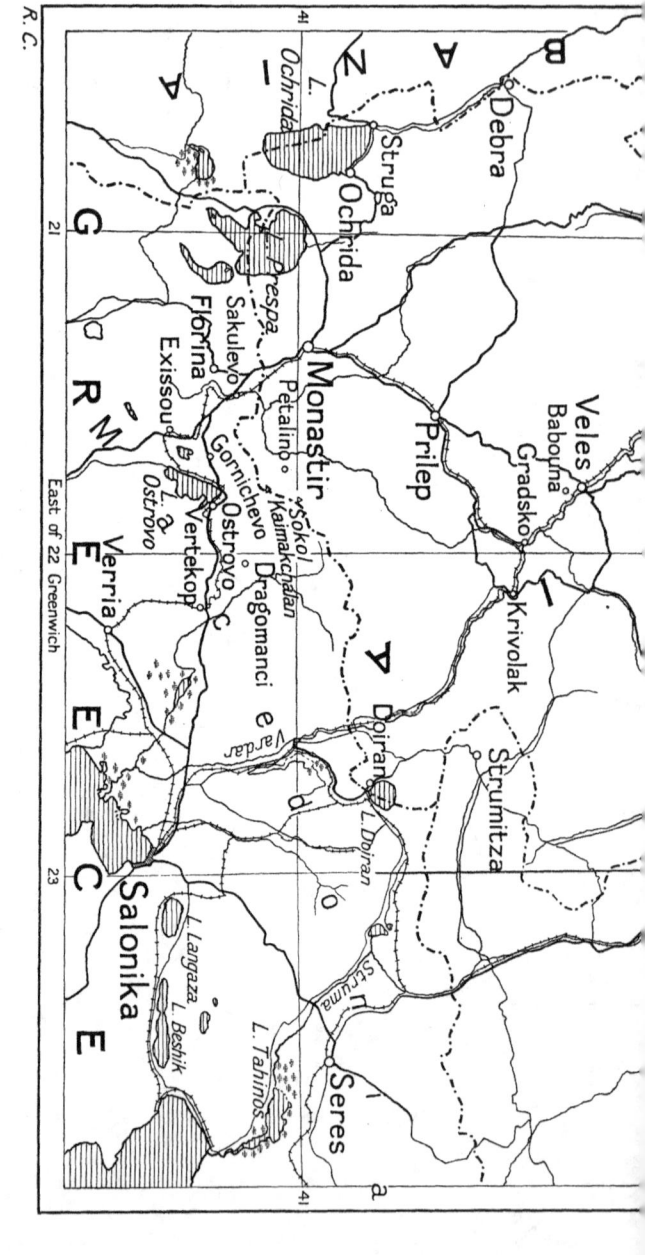

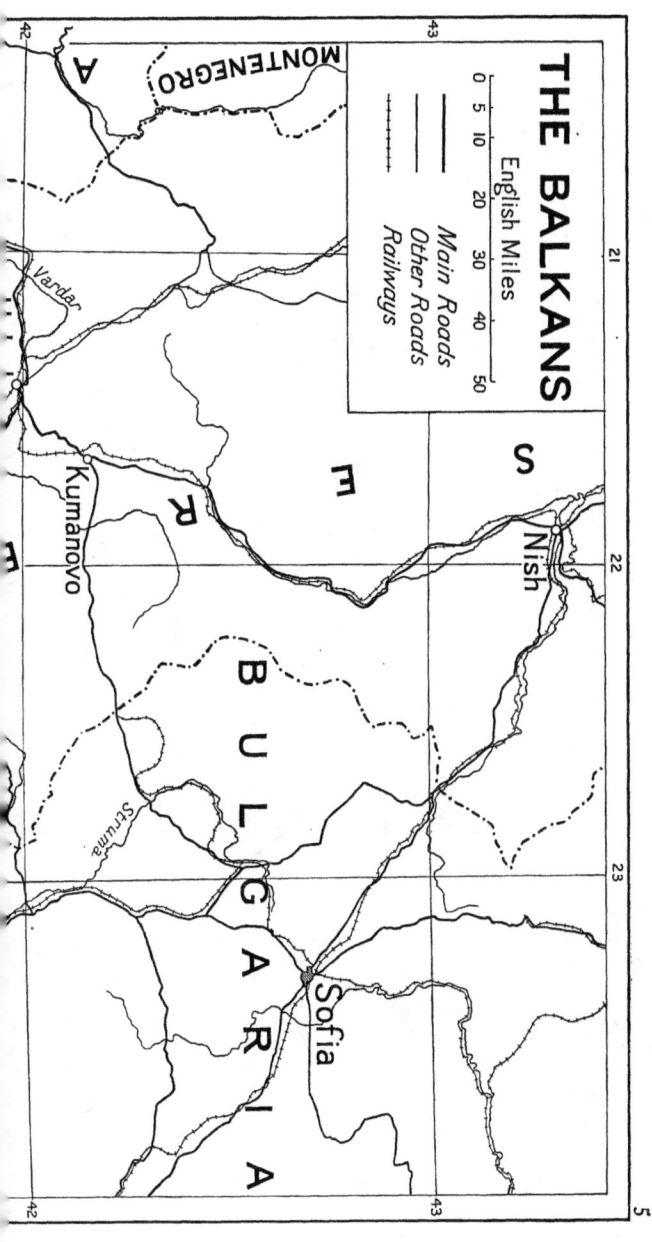

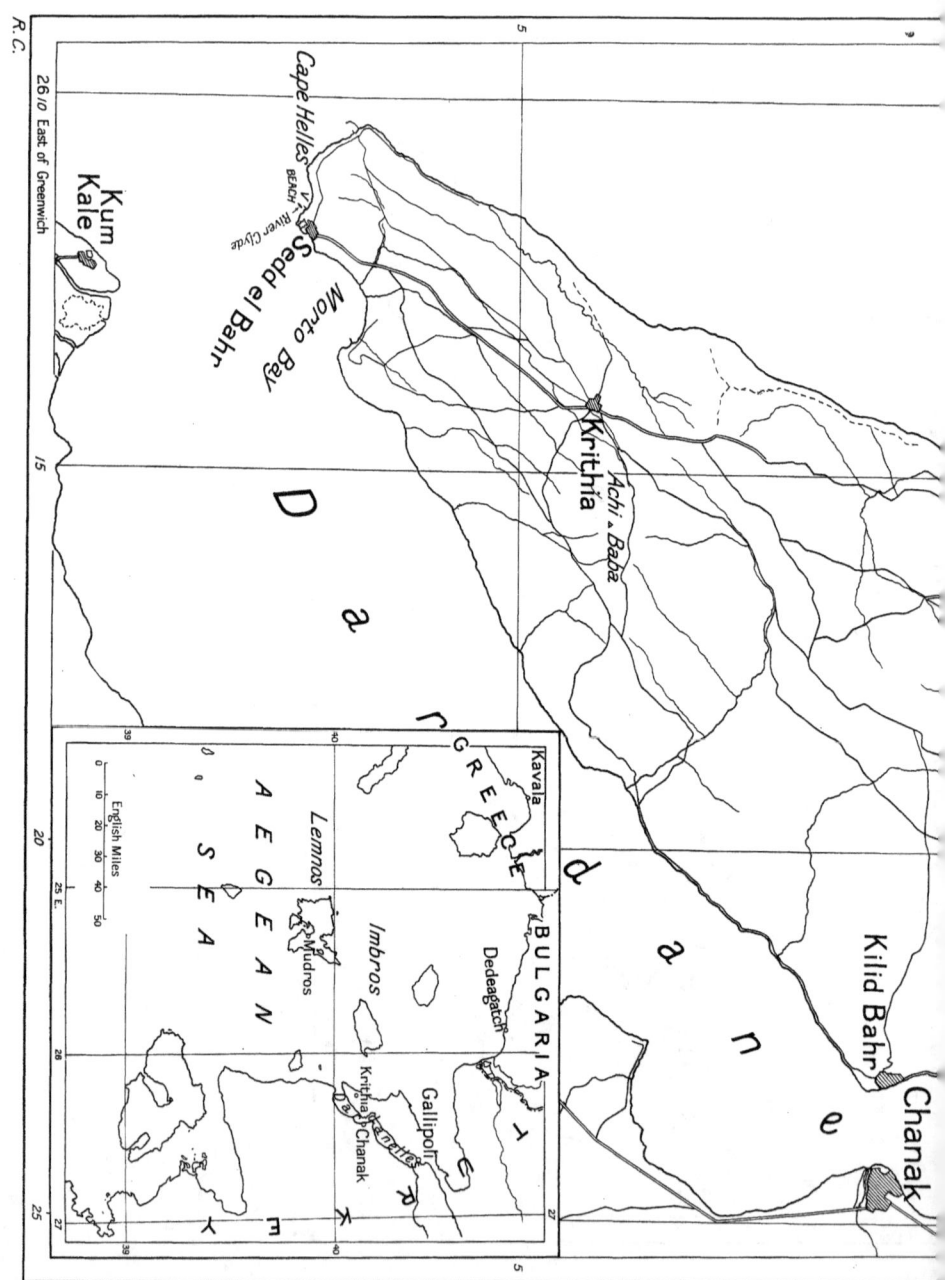

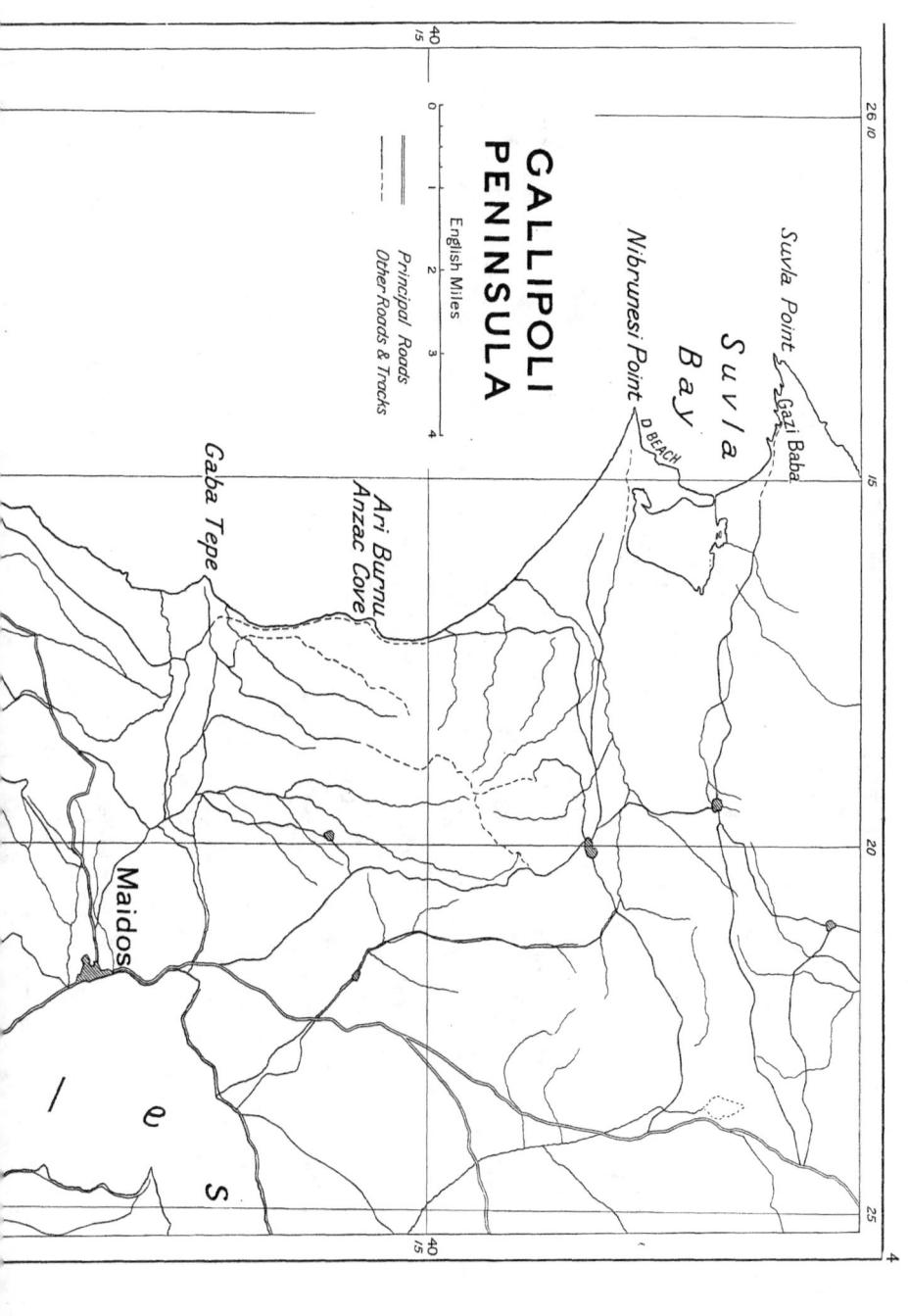

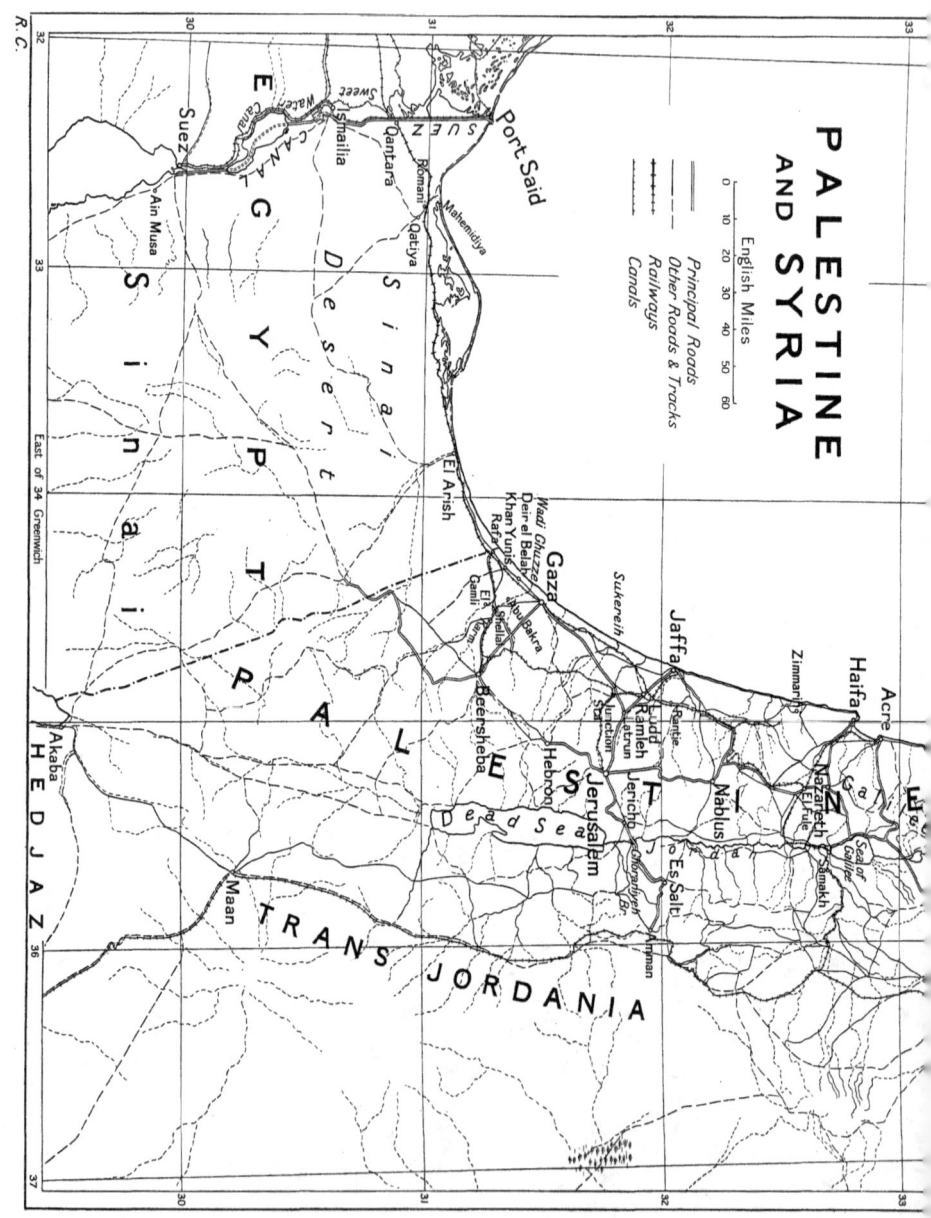

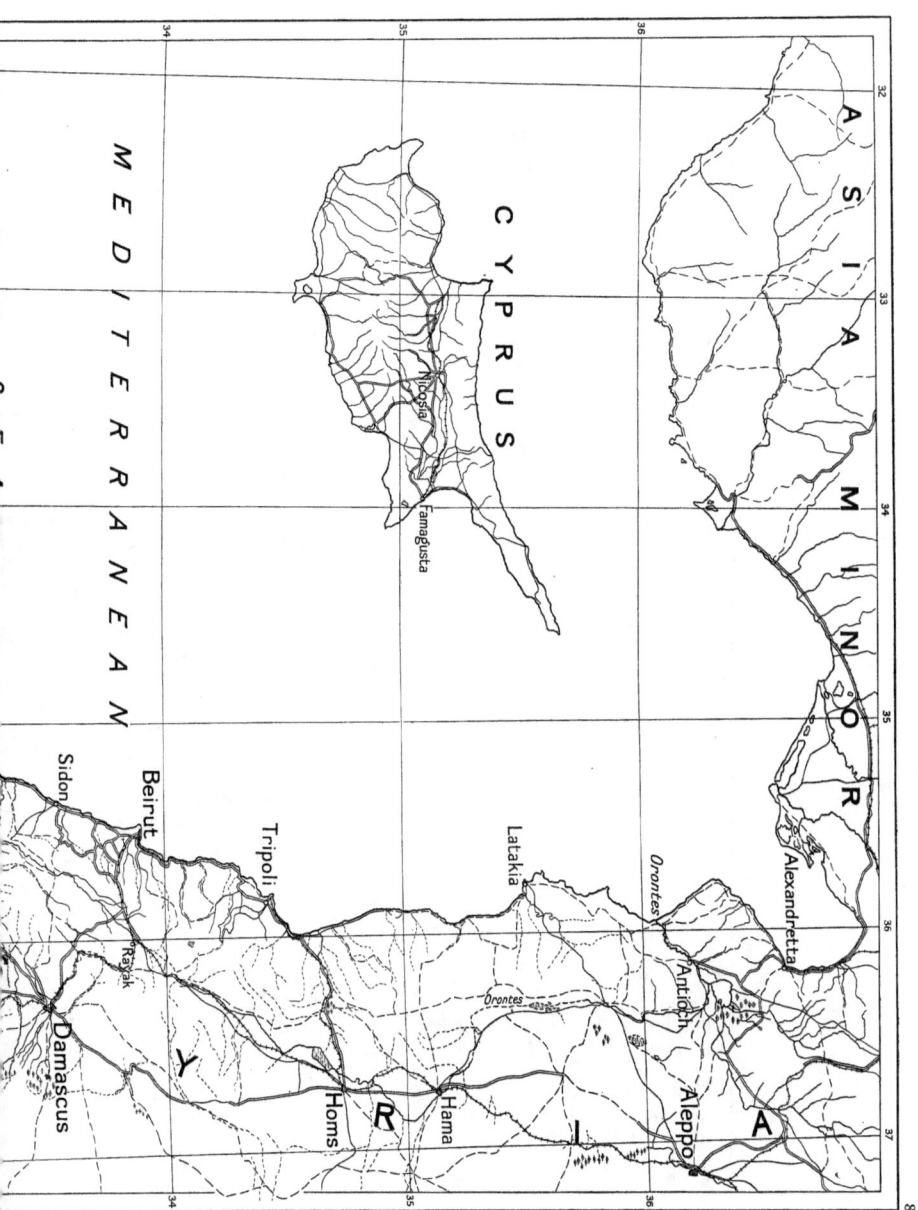

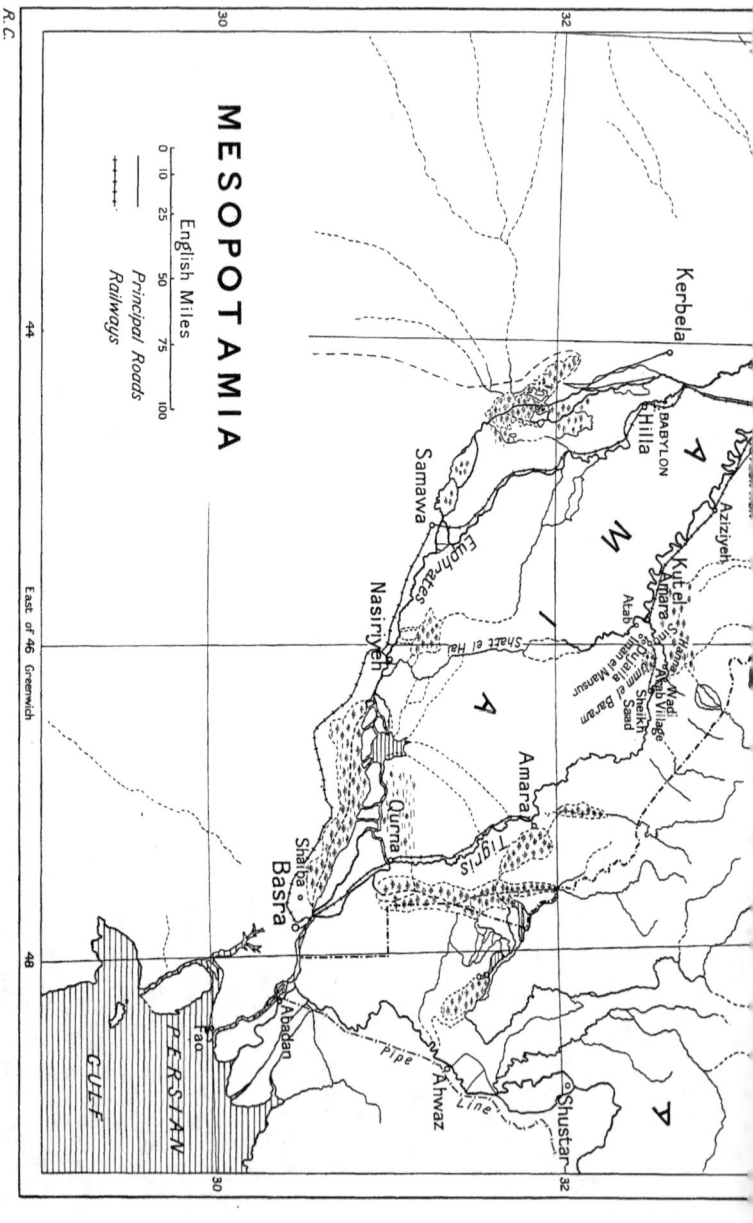

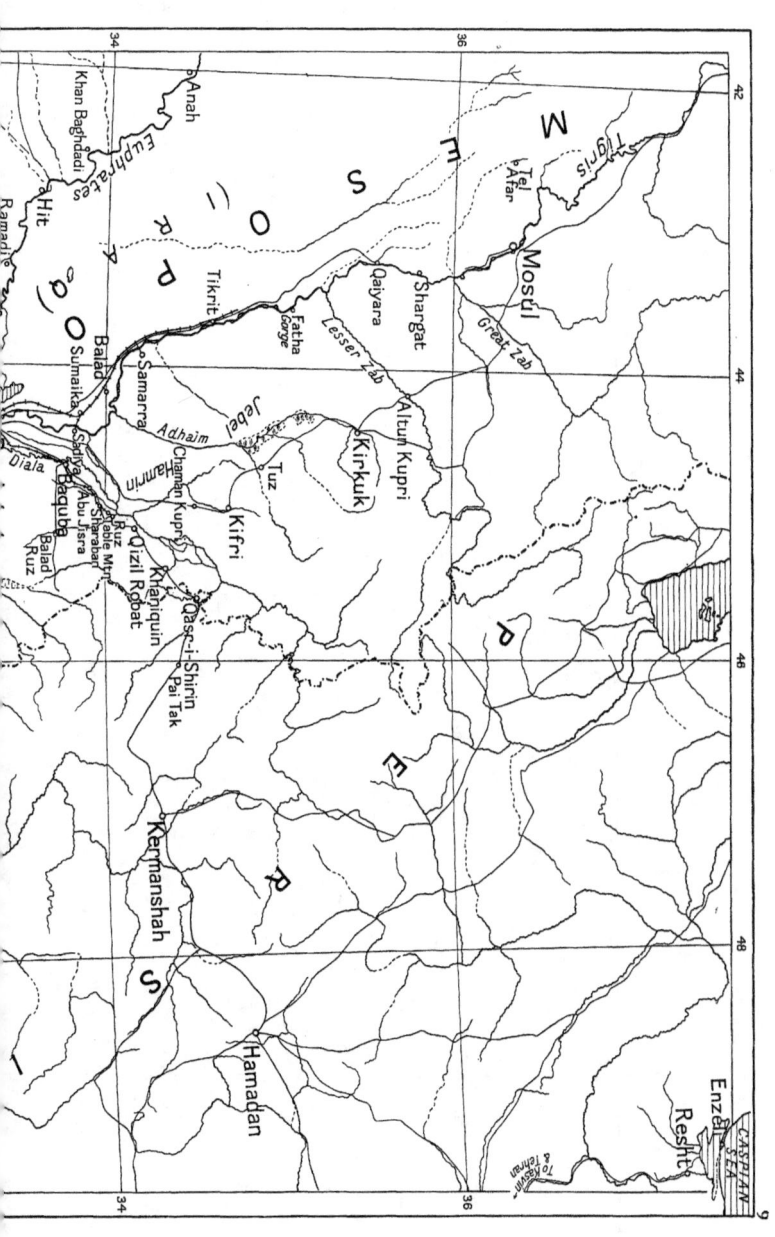

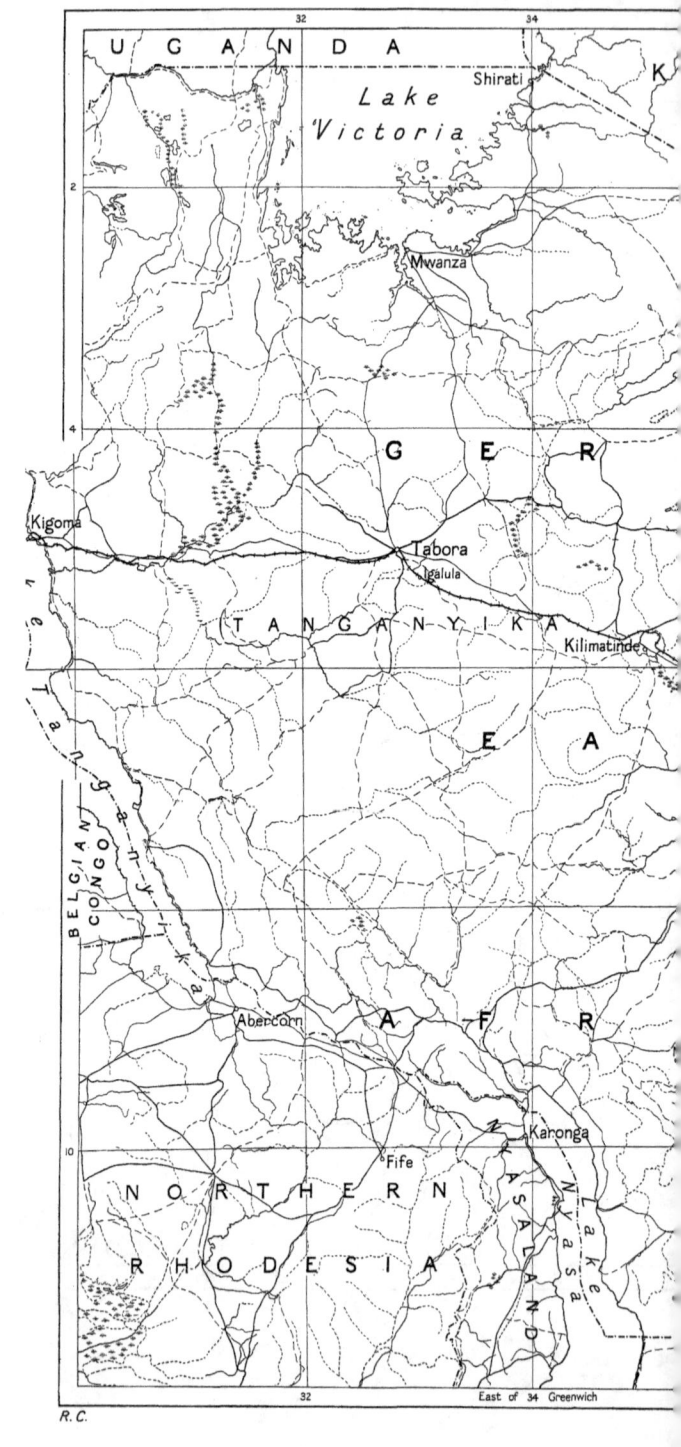

EAST AFRICA

English Miles

Principal Roads
Other Roads & Tracks
Railways

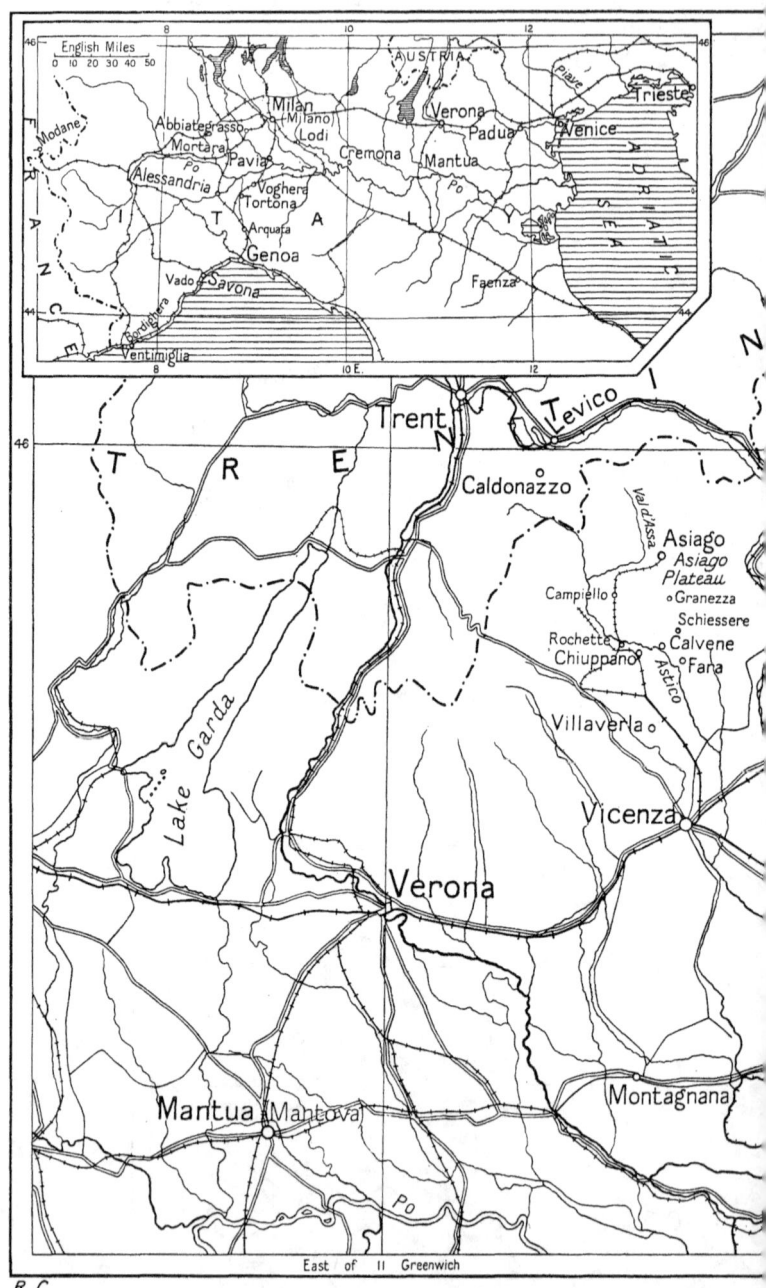

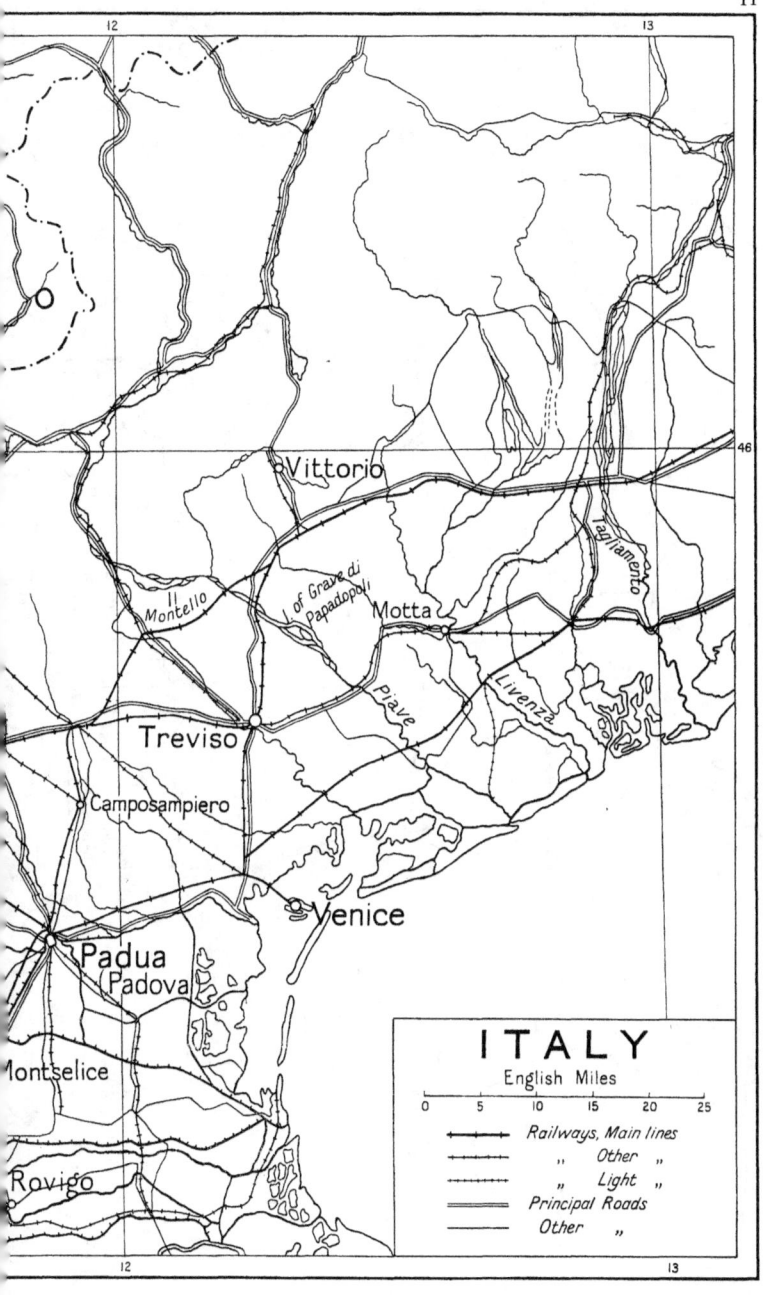

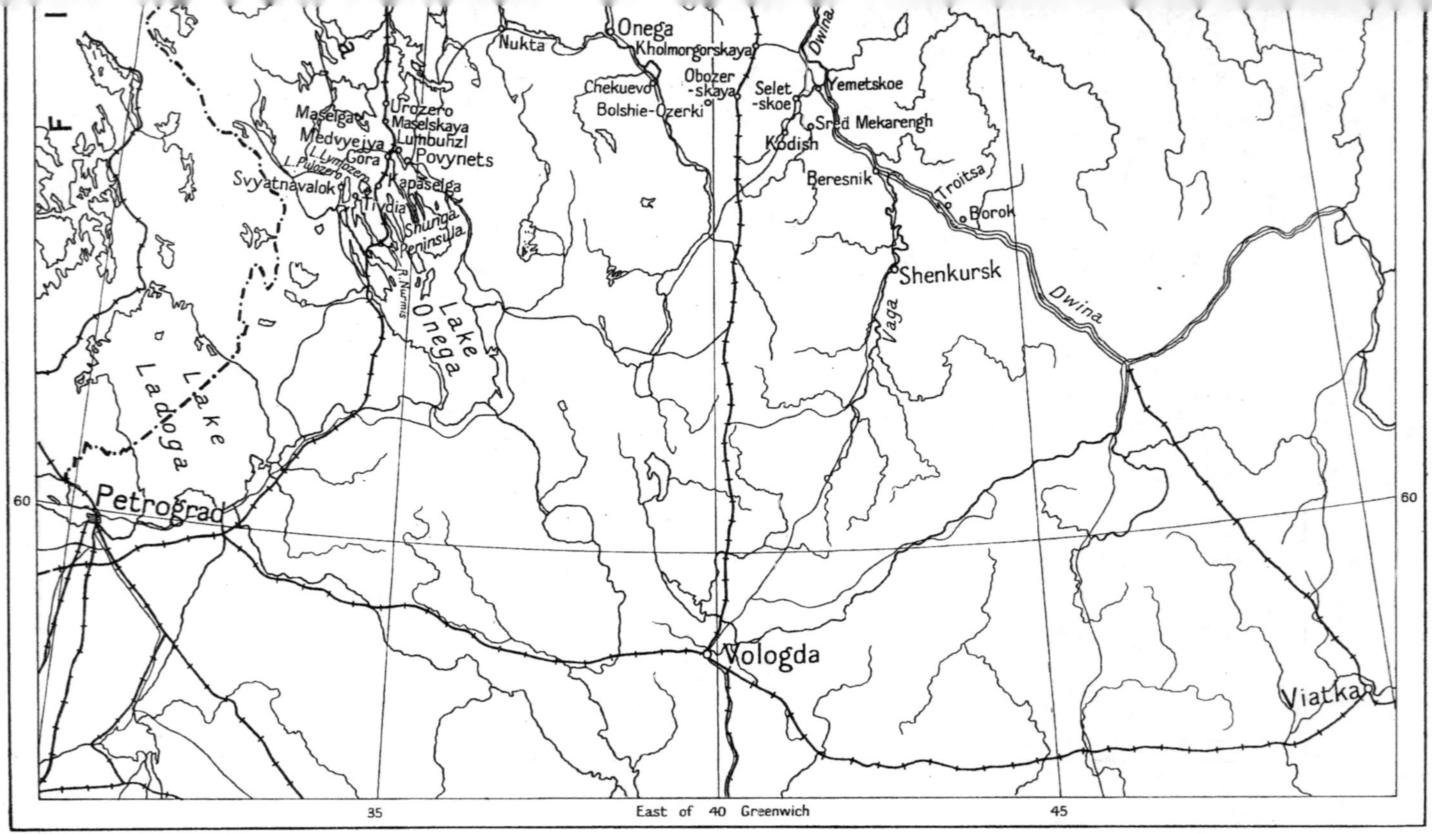
F
I
Lake Ladoga
Petrograd
Lake Onega
Onega
Nukta
Kholmorgorskaya
Chekuevo
Obozer -skaya
Bolshie-Ozerki
Selet -skoe
Dwina
Yemetskoe
Sred Mekarengh
Kodish
Beresnik
Troitsa
Borok
Shenkursk
Vaga
Maselga
Urozero
Maselskaya
Medvyejya Gora
Lumbuhzl
Povynets
L. Lymozero
L. Pulozero
Svyatnavalok
Kapaselga
Tivdia
Shunga Peninsula
R. Nurmis
Vologda
Viatka
60
35
East of 40 Greenwich
45
R. C.

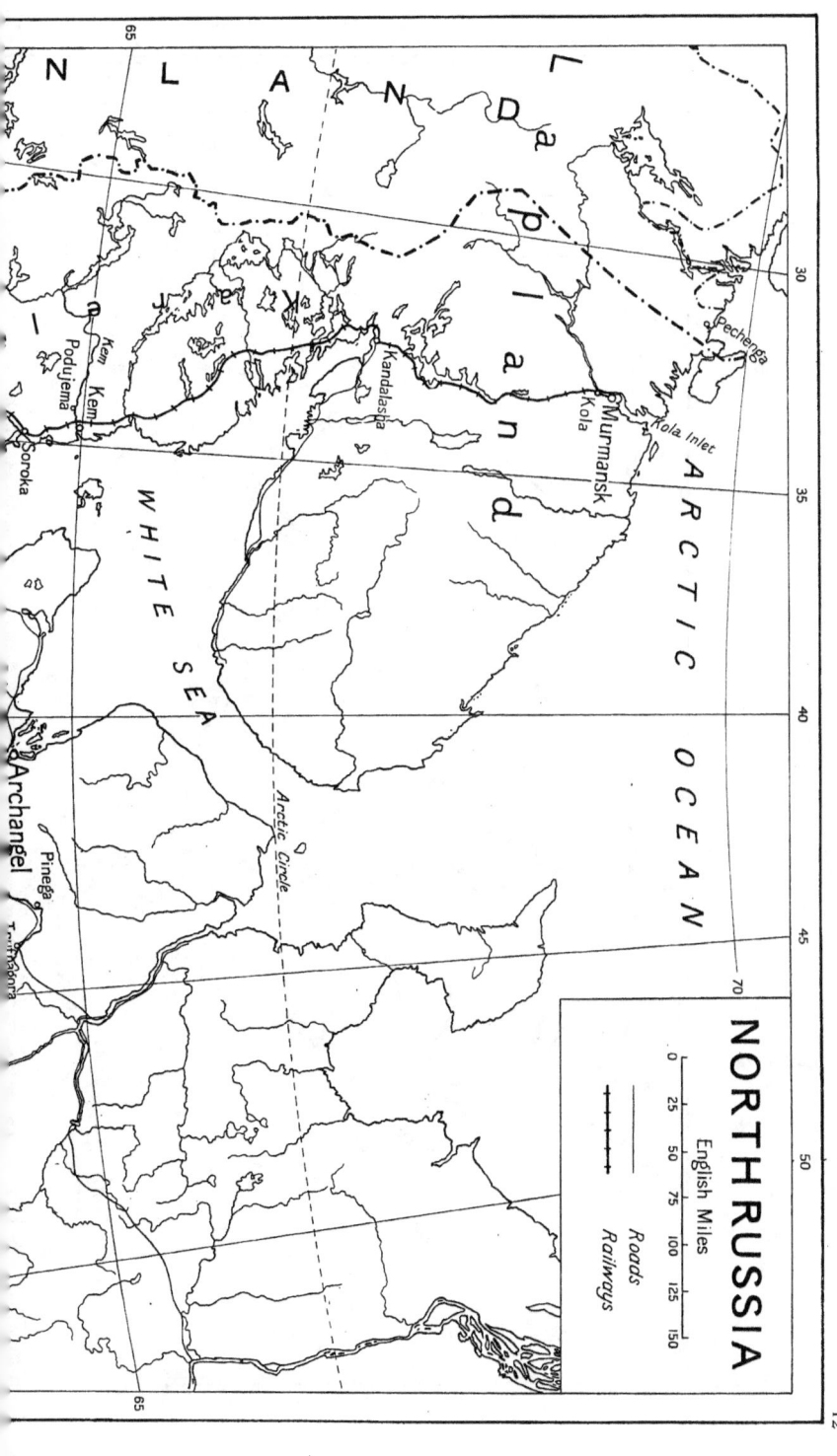

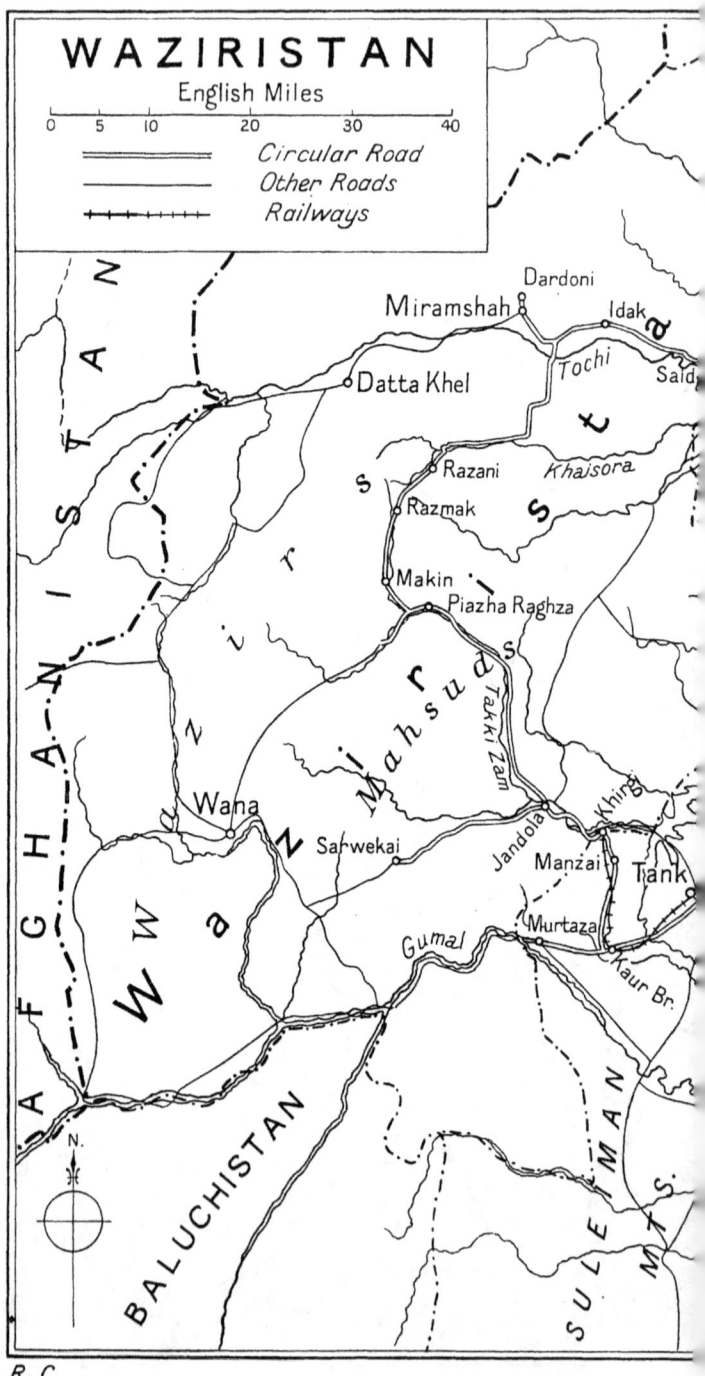

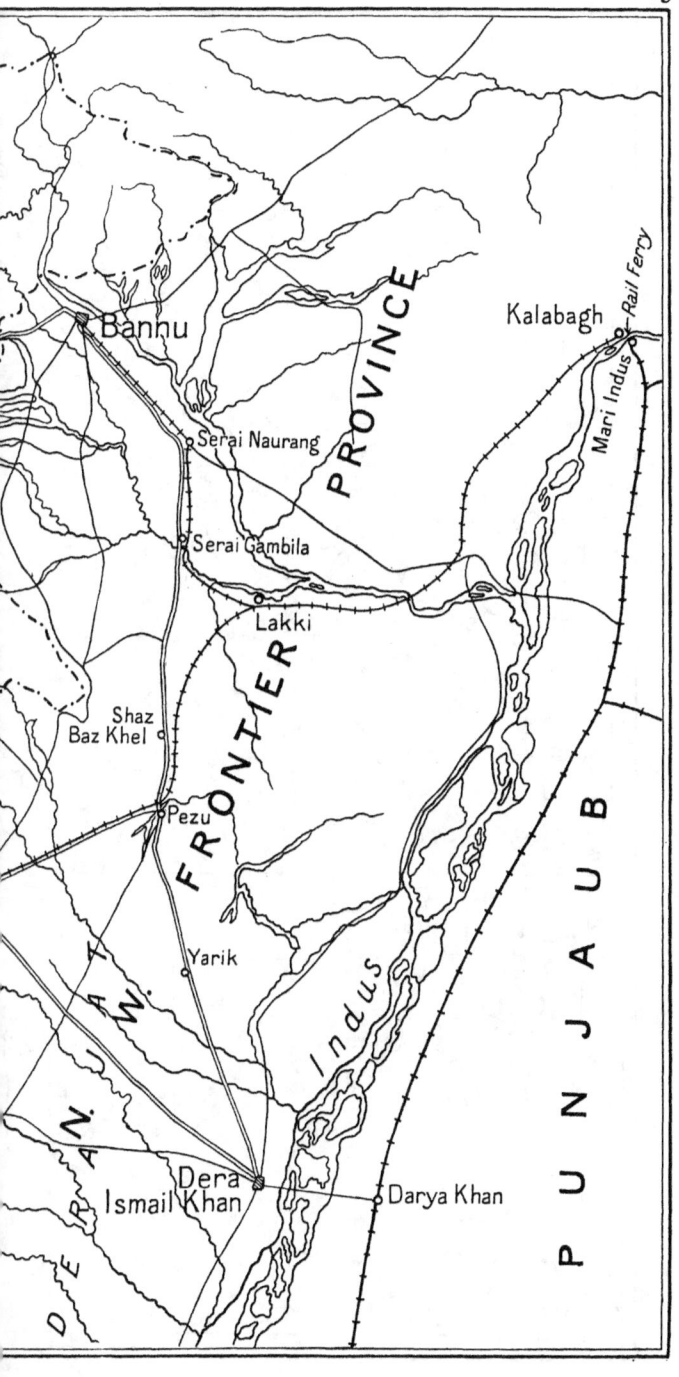

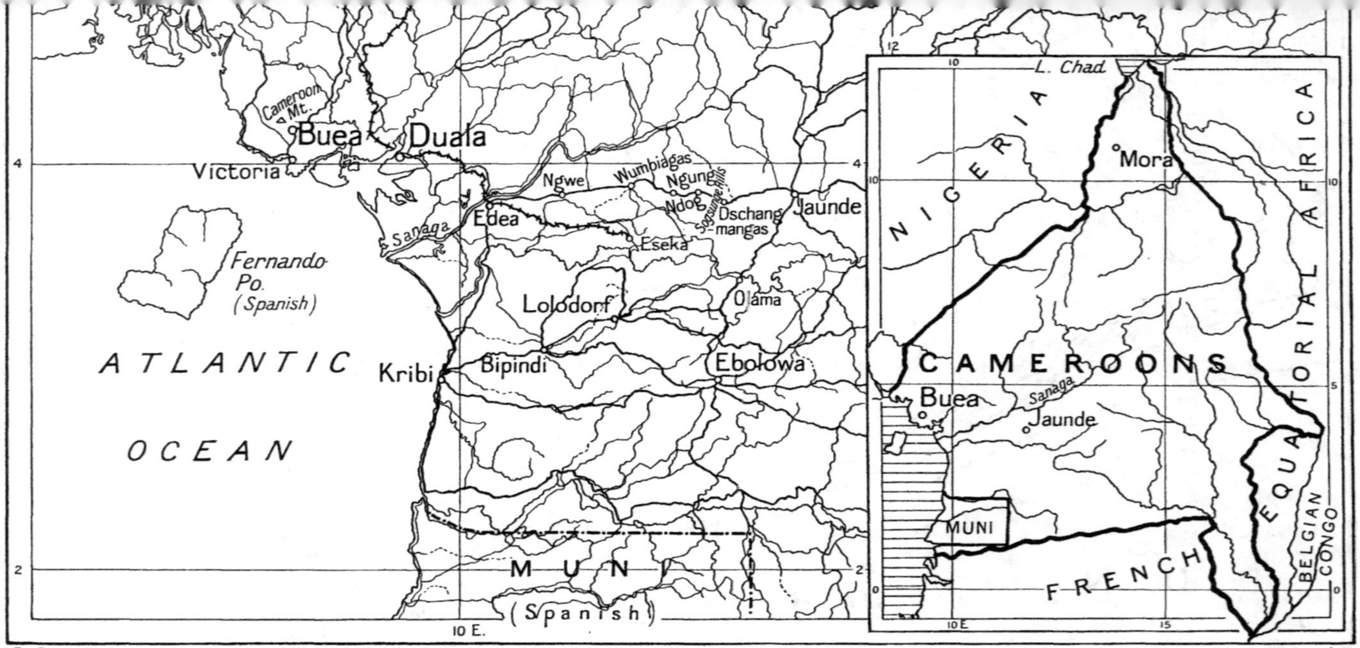
Cameroon Mt.
Buea
Duala
Victoria
Ngwe
Wumbiagas
Ngung
Ndog
Sogsunge Hills
Dschang
mangas
Jaunde
Edea
Sanaga
Eseka
Fernando Po. (Spanish)
Lolodorf
Olama
ATLANTIC
OCEAN
Kribi
Bipindi
Ebolowa
MUNI
(Spanish)
10 E.
L. Chad
NIGERIA
Mora
CAMEROONS
Buea
Sanaga
Jaunde
MUNI
FRENCH
EQUATORIAL AFRICA
BELGIAN CONGO
10E.
15
R C.

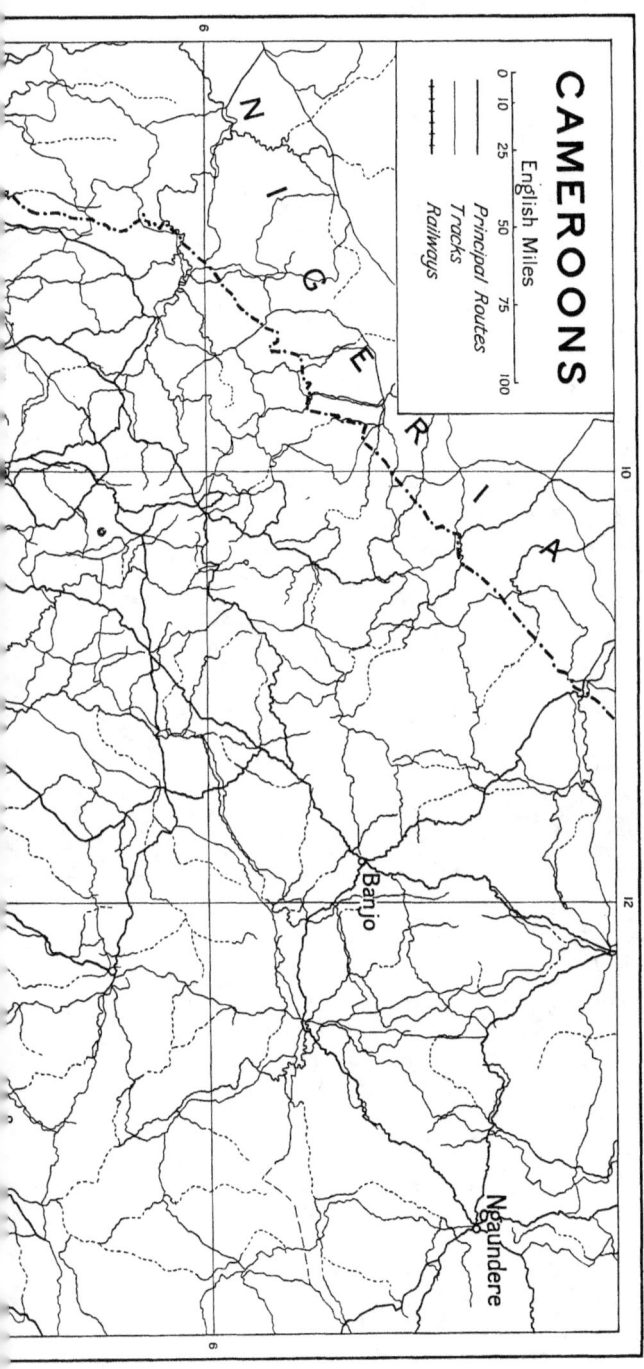

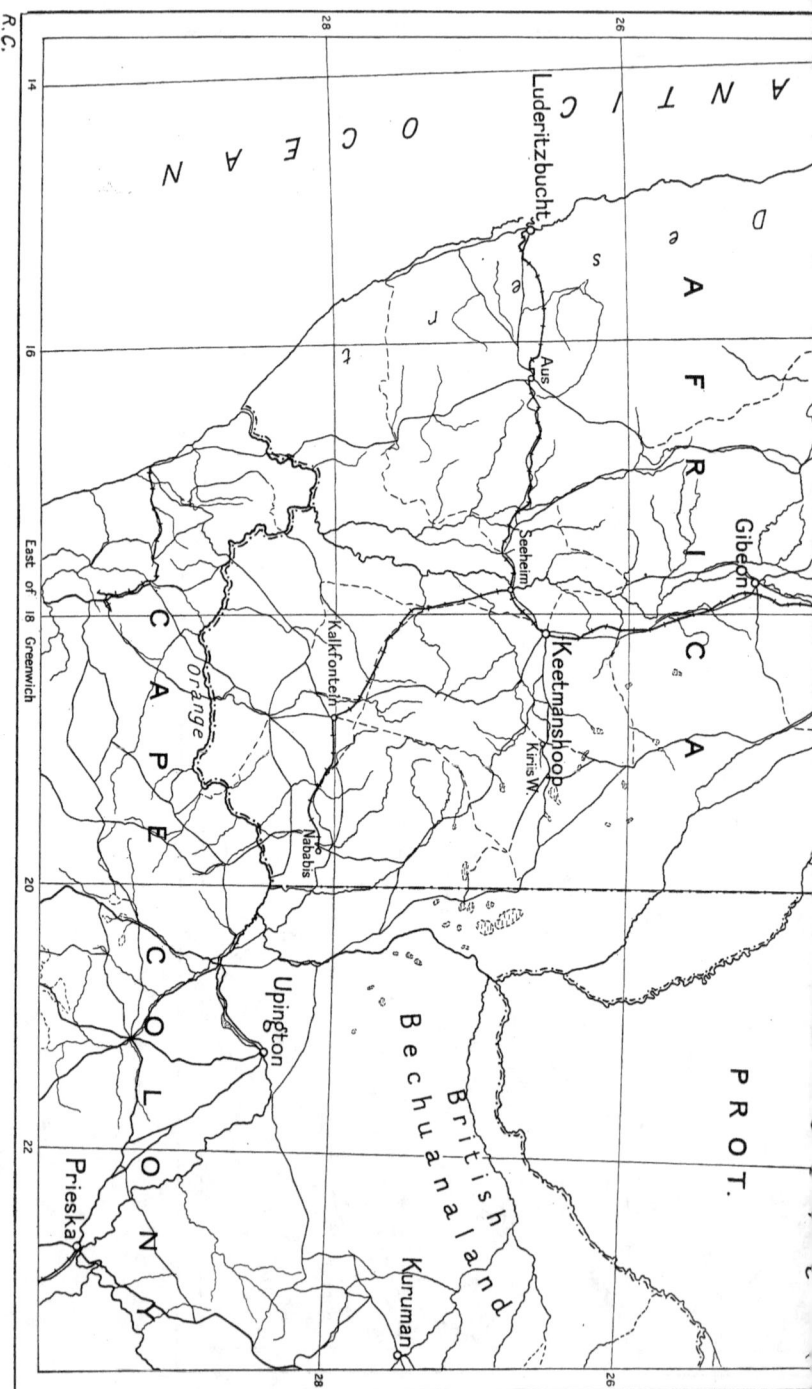

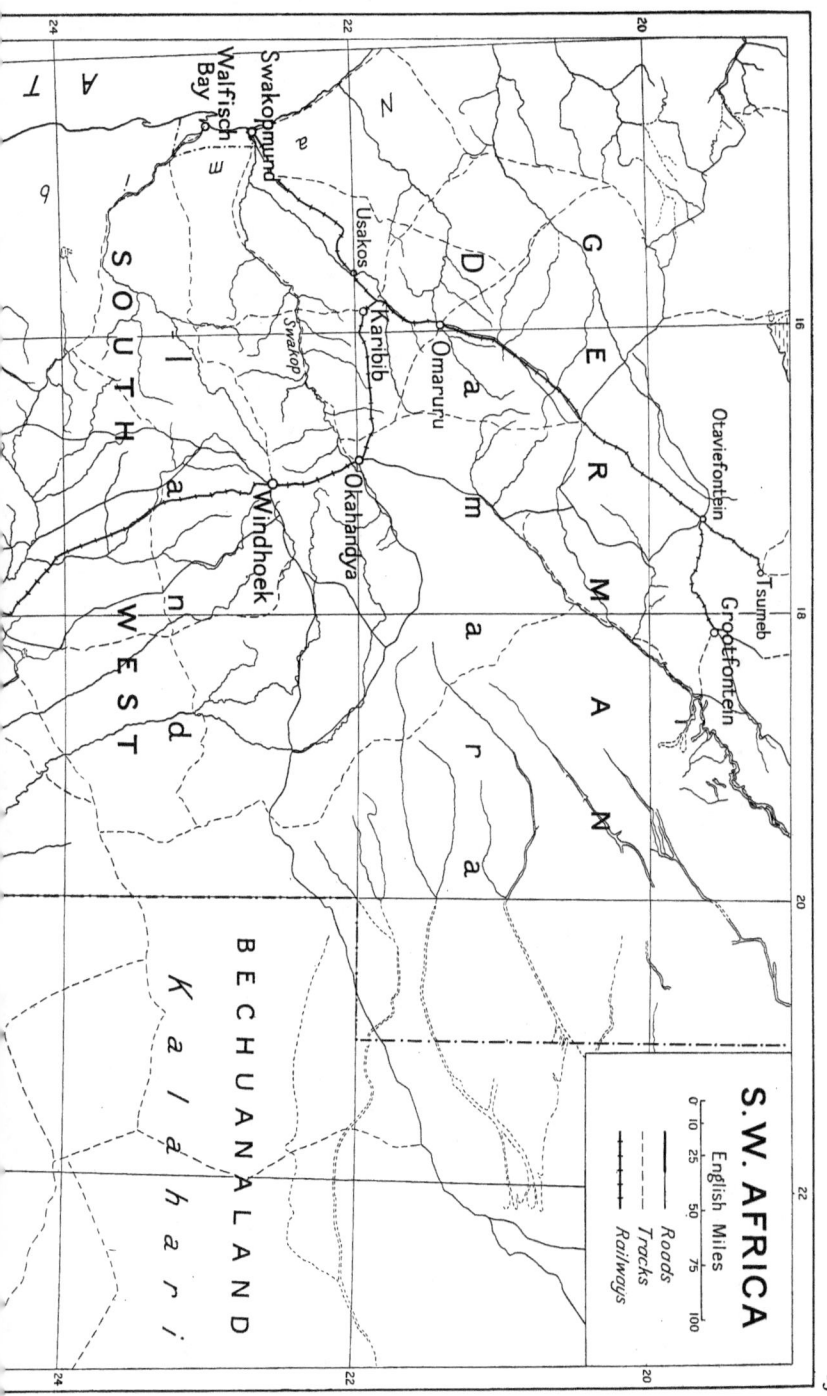

www.ingramcontent.com/pod-product-compliance
Lightning Source LLC
Chambersburg PA
CBHW052342230426
43664CB00042B/2641